Monetary Policy in Times of Crisis

Monetary Policy in Times of Crisis

A Tale of Two Decades of the European Central Bank

Massimo Rostagno
Carlo Altavilla
Giacomo Carboni
Wolfgang Lemke
Roberto Motto
Arthur Saint Guilhem
Jonathan Yiangou

OXFORD
UNIVERSITY PRESS

OXFORD
UNIVERSITY PRESS

Great Clarendon Street, Oxford, OX2 6DP,
United Kingdom

Oxford University Press is a department of the University of Oxford.
It furthers the University's objective of excellence in research, scholarship,
and education by publishing worldwide. Oxford is a registered trade mark of
Oxford University Press in the UK and in certain other countries

First Edition published in 2021

Impression: 1

Published in the United States of America by Oxford University Press
198 Madison Avenue, New York, NY 10016, United States of America

British Library Cataloguing in Publication Data

Data available

Library of Congress Control Number: 2021931190

ISBN 978–0–19–289591–2

DOI: 10.1093/oso/9780192895912.001.0001

Printed and bound by
CPI Group (UK) Ltd, Croydon, CR0 4YY

Preface

The first 20 years of the ECB's lifetime offer a clear demonstration of how a central bank can navigate macroeconomic insecurity and crisis.[1] The ECB spent its first ten years—those of the 'Great Moderation'—wrestling with a severe dearth of data on the newly formed monetary union and underdeveloped data-processing capacity, seeking to steer the economy through a fog of uncertainty and gain greater insight into how the euro area was functioning. After Lehman's demise, macroeconomic insecurity became a worldwide condition afflicting all central banks, and the ECB—operating in an incomplete currency union—suffered more than its fair share of it. As the global economy in 2020 moves into a new phase of unheralded uncertainty, we believe that a retelling of the ECB's first 20 years holds multiple lessons of wider significance for the central banking community and researchers of monetary policy. We condense the facts and lessons of those first 20 years in this volume of monetary policy in crises.

The volume ends in December 2018 on the eve of a decisive turn in the trajectory of the economy. The year 2019 saw the euro area economy slowly crawling to a halt, caught in the middle of international trade disputes, fears of a hard Brexit and the growing influence of its entrenched structural frailties. The year 2020 will go down in the history books as the year in which the euro area, ravaged by the Covid-19 pandemic, lost in a couple of quarters probably as much output and income as it had gained over the previous 15 years—and monetary policy was jolted into yet another phase of extraordinary innovation and expansion. Do these events—based on what we have observed so far in the first half of 2020—upend or reverse the conclusions we have distilled out of the prior 20 years of ECB history? We believe not: there is, in our view, full continuity and affinity among pre- and post-virus lessons along at least three axes.

First, we believe that the slow and circumspect pace at which the ECB ventured into policy normalization in 2018 has been vindicated ex post. Certainly, with a more assertive type of forward guidance that signalled—already in 2018—higher policy rates and a shrinking balance sheet in the near future, market rates would have been pushed higher, creating some more space for bringing them back down during the 2020 crisis. At the same time, the economy would have been in a worse place than it was at the outbreak of the disease owing to the ensuing tightening of financing conditions. It takes around 18–24 months for higher rates to translate into

[1] The authors are from the European Central Bank. The views expressed in this volume are those of the authors and do not necessarily reflect those of the ECB, its Executive Board or Governing Council, or the European System of Central Banks.

weaker spending, incomes and inflation, and Germany and Italy ended 2019 without positive growth as it was. In a higher-interest-rate world, they would have suffered a deeper contraction, and pulled the whole euro area into a recession.

Second, it is our reading of the events that the monetary policy boldness we have witnessed in the face of the 2020 crisis can only be understood in the context of the decade that preceded it. The decisions taken to dislodge the too-low inflation environment that beset the euro area economy in the 2010s—and the institutional Rubicons crossed—created a disposition towards pre-emptive action, a playbook for implementing unconventional policy in short order, and an understanding of transmission in crisis that was instrumental in facilitating the ECB's reaction to the Covid-19 shock. The 2016 version of TLTRO provided a tested infrastructure that the ECB could simply re-programme in coronavirus times, and utilize as a vehicle to funnel the stimulus associated with negative rates straight to those firms struggling for survival. The new Pandemic Emergency Purchase Programme (PEPP), unveiled on the night of 18 March 2020, embodies and perfects the philosophy—elaborated through the learning process that we describe in the volume—of *combining* rather than *separating* instruments and intermediate policy objectives. Reflecting that philosophy, PEPP conflates two elements: a market functioning, backstop-type intervention mode, on one hand, and a stance-supporting mission founded on duration extraction, on the other. These two engines were activated with varying intensity over the two phases of the post-pandemic emergency. The backstop engine was the first to be ignited, when the top priority (in March and April) was to ensure financial stability and lean against fragmentation amidst a market panic of unseen virulence. The second engine took over when markets eventually calmed, and the clouds shrouding the macroeconomic outlook—which were impenetrable to begin with—started to dissipate, exposing the economic ruins that the shock might leave behind. The PEPP's double key facilitated a necessary pivot in monetary policy, from the earlier interventions typical of a crisis-relief programme and justified by market functioning considerations, towards a steadier and more predictable configuration geared toward re-anchoring medium-term inflation. The 'inflation-gap' approach to calibrating the overall envelope of a purchase programme, inaugurated in 2015, was redeployed as the ECB upscaled PEPP in June 2020.

Last, we quote verbatim a passage from an earlier draft of this volume which, with hindsight, has become more relevant:

> one cannot rule out more extreme scenarios than those faced by the ECB in the years following the financial crisis, in which the economy sinks into an even deeper and more lasting contraction, and ingrained disinflation takes hold. Should the economy ever find itself in such a predicament, a more policy-enabling environment—including a comprehensive set of non-monetary policies—would

be helpful for monetary instruments to exert the favourable effects that we document in this book.

The sudden depression that wracked the economy in early 2020 has indeed evoked the spectre of those extreme scenarios. We draw attention to Chapter 2 in particular where monetary-fiscal policy interactions in the face of such shocks are studied and translated into policy options. We also invite readers to review Chapter 6, where we discuss the 'missing role' of fiscal policy in the euro area's institutional architecture, and how monetary and fiscal policies can best partner when deflation risks loom. What has happened on those fronts since the pandemic escalated in early March? A fact is worth some reflection: Europe has risen to the occasion. Yet again, as in Mark Twain's famous quip, 'reports of the euro's death have been greatly exaggerated'. We note that, unlike in the aftermath of the 2008 crisis, the policy initiatives taken outside the monetary policy domain have been as forceful as those decided within it. This time around, the ECB has not been left alone. The Commission's plan for a Next Generation EU Fund, in particular, comes about as close as one could have imagined to the new and more intimate forms of interaction between monetary and fiscal policy that our draft imagines. Faced with shocks as dramatic as those that threatened the stability of the euro area and the global economy between March and June 2020, Europe has 'come of age' alongside the ECB.

*　*　*

The list of colleagues and friends to whom we are indebted for the realization of this volume is too long to be reported exhaustively. First, we want to thank Fédéric Holm-Hadulla for actively contributing to Chapter 5. We are also especially grateful to Fabian Schupp and Andreea Vladu for their great support in implementing several of the counterfactual yield curve scenarios that we document in Chapter 6, as well as to Maarten Dossche, Jacob Hartwig, and Beatrice Pierluigi for contributing with their analysis on savers and borrowers in Chapter 6. We owe a number of commentators a large debt of gratitude. We are particularly indebted to Klaus Adam, Nuno Alves, Ulrich Bindseil, Lorenzo Bini-Smaghi, Tobias Blattner, Benoit Coeuré, Miguel Boucinha, Vítor Constâncio, Mario Draghi, Eugenio Gaiotti, Felix Geiger, Philipp Hartmann, Federic Holm-Hadulla, Otmar Issing, Christophe Kamps, Stephan Kohns, Luc Laeven, Philip Lane, Michele Lenza, Silvia Margiocco, Klaus Masuch, Stefano Neri, Peter Praet, Wolfgang Schill, Torsti Silvonen, Stefano Siviero, Frank Smets, Lars Svensson, Guido Tabellini, Carlos Thomas, Jean-Claude Trichet, Oreste Tristani, Jens Ulbrich, Ignazio Visco, Thomas Vlassopoulos, Bernhard Winkler, Andreas Worms, and Charles Wyplosz for their comments on an earlier draft of this volume. We bear full responsibility for any remaining errors or omissions. We thank Julian Schumacher for his empirical analysis of the 'well past' phrase used at times by the ECB in its forward guidance, as reported in Chapter 6; Giovanni Trebbi for his contribution to the analysis of Taylor rules; and Lennart Brandt, Andrea Cubells Enguidanos, Maria Dimou, Maria Eskelinen, Christopher Greiner, Michele Marcaletti, Cornelius Nicolay, Ala Olaru, Christian Osterhold, and Jonathan Öztunc for their outstanding research assistance. We are also very grateful to Anita Gibb and Paul Williams for their precious editing suggestions.

July 2020

Contents

List of Figures

List of Boxes

List of Tables

Introduction

Two Decades, Two Regimes

Institutions dedicated to serving the public good must look to the past to learn from experience; and look to the future to prepare, as best they can, for the trials that might lie ahead. The 20th anniversary of Economic and Monetary Union (EMU) offers an opportunity to apply such a perspective to the monetary policy of the European Central Bank (ECB): to evaluate its accomplishments and to learn the lessons that can improve the conduct of its policy in the future.

Our 'Tale of Two Decades' is intended to contribute to this endeavour. It is largely a tale of 'two regimes': one—stretching slightly beyond the ECB's mid-point— marked by decent growth in real incomes and a distribution of shocks to inflation almost universally to the upside; and the second—starting well into the post-Lehman period—characterized by endemic instability and crisis, with the distribution of shocks eventually switching from inflationary to continuously disinflationary. Throughout these 20 years, the challenges facing monetary policy have been immense.

At the start, the ECB had to establish its credibility from scratch as a new and untested central bank, in a field of policymaking which places a premium on track records. It had to do so while contending with a large coalition of euro-sceptics, as the creation and endurance of the euro appeared to upend the entrenched conviction in the international academic community and among pundits that the euro 'can't happen, it's a bad idea, it won't last'—as Lars Jonung and Eoin Drea (2009) summarized the thinking, looking back on the euro's first ten years. And, it had to prove itself in an uncooperative environment of persistent inflationary shocks, and in conditions of profound uncertainty.

The uncertainty surrounding the disturbances driving the business cycle is a perpetual challenge for central bankers. But, when applying an area-wide perspective to a diverse group of sovereign states, whose economies had grown apart for decades, such difficulties were necessarily amplified. For the first generation of ECB policymakers, guided by the intellectual influence of its first Chief Economist, Otmar Issing, the weight of uncertainty was felt acutely. Not only did they face an exceptionally 'data poor' environment—in 1999, area-wide time series were patchy, many statistical indicators were still under construction, and reliable measures of inflation expectations were lacking. More importantly, the creation of the euro area *itself* implied a major regime shift. It could not be known with any degree of

Monetary Policy in Times of Crisis: A Tale of Two Decades of the European Central Bank. Massimo Rostagno, Carlo Altavilla, Giacomo Carboni, Wolfgang Lemke, Roberto Motto, Arthur Saint Guilhem, and Jonathan Yiangou, Oxford University Press (2021).
© Massimo Rostagno, Carlo Altavilla, Giacomo Carboni, Wolfgang Lemke, Roberto Motto, Arthur Saint Guilhem, and Jonathan Yiangou.
DOI: 10.1093/oso/9780192895912.003.0001

confidence whether the statistical regularities emerging from past data, once it was available, would be informative of the structure of the new monetary union, or whether past parameters and the model coefficients they yielded would in fact prove misleading. Even some years after the establishment of EMU, extracting accurate signals from the economy remained more challenging for the ECB than for time-tested central banks. As Otmar Issing observed in 2002, 'we were studying the evolution of a moving object, which was changing for the very reason that it was being observed, as in the famous Heisenberg paradox' (Issing, 2002c). The situation facing policymakers was one best described as Knightian uncertainty.

In this context, there was a material risk that the transition to the new monetary union could prove disorderly, disappointing the high hopes that had been placed on the euro by the public and confirming the dire warnings of a number of academic economists that the euro was a project doomed to fail. The early policymakers therefore placed a premium on providing a firm compass for the economy and, above all, avoiding policy mistakes. At the heart of their approach was the plan to establish a robust monetary policy framework—a *strategy*, in the ECB's parlance—that could navigate the fog of uncertainty and pin down inflation expectations, an endeavour which occupied the bulk of the ECB's intellectual resources in its first years. Three features of the policy framework that emerged reflected these imperatives. The first was the ECB's characteristic quantitative definition of price stability, which operationalized its Treaty-given objective and provided an anchor for keeping inflation expectations in check. The second feature was the two-pillar policy strategy, with its unique focus on monetary phenomena, which afforded the dual benefit of anchoring the new institution in the best monetary tradition available in Europe— the Bundesbank's inheritance—and offering timely proxy indicators to measure the actual state and direction of the macro-economy and trends in prices, in the absence of reliable data. Third was the medium-term orientation of policy, which was designed, in a highly noisy economic environment, to ensure that the central bank did not generate unnecessary volatility by overreacting to short-term, and possibly inaccurate, information. It is to the credit of the ECB's first leaders that the birth of the euro proceeded as smoothly as anyone could have hoped for; and that price stability was unperturbed by a series of early shocks including repeated energy price spikes, a long trend of foreign exchange depreciation and the bursting of the dotcom bubble.

When credibility was eventually secured, the challenges took a new form: the ECB had to contend with a deep and protracted crisis that called for courage and creativity in its policy responses. All the while, the ECB had to stand in for missing institutions in EMU's economic governance framework, institutions which in other major economies proved crucial for managing the global financial crisis and its aftermath. For this reason, over the two decades of EMU, ECB policymakers have invested considerable energy in fostering and actively contributing to the process of institutional reform, to an extent unprecedented for a central bank in modern history. There are two such institutional advances that are central to our monetary-policy story: the creation of the European Stability Mechanism (ESM) during the leadership of President Trichet, and the birth of the Single Supervisory Mechanism (SSM) under President Draghi. The ECB's investment in institution-building proved to be far-sighted: with the creation of these new institutions, the key enabling conditions were put in place for new monetary policy initiatives by the ECB at critical junctures during the crisis.

However, some of the idiosyncratic features of the ECB's policy framework, and its vocal insistence of the importance of complementary institutions, did not always sit easily with the prevailing intellectual paradigm of the early 2000s. This book goes to some lengths to explain the criticisms of the ECB in that period, not in order to re-litigate the past, but because they exemplify the spirit of the Great Moderation and ideational currents that the young central bank had to navigate. Key tenets of that intellectual framework were that inflation was a sufficient summary statistic for the state of the economy, and that a committed central bank could always master the economy perfectly at all nominal scales, regardless of the steady-state level of inflation and abstracting from the stance and strategy of other policies. In this context, the ECB's conviction that studying money and credit was essential to form a holistic picture of macroeconomic developments was naturally prone to criticism. But it was largely born out by the ensuing events, as excessive leveraging set the stage for the Global Financial Crisis, and then as prolonged deleveraging paved the way for the sluggish euro area recovery thereafter. Likewise, the ECB's support for institution-building—beginning already with President Trichet's tireless advocacy for the Macroeconomic Imbalances Procedure to reinforce the EU multilateral surveillance system—was motivated by the intuition that the 'monetary policy hubris' inspired by superficial interpretations of the dominant macroeconomic paradigm was misplaced. As critical as a stability-oriented central bank was to furthering economic prosperity, the degree of success of an economy—and a currency union in particular—was a function of a broader set of institutions and policies than monetary policy alone (Constâncio, 2018).

*   *   *

It is primarily around the ECB's characteristic definition of price stability that we focus our two-decade/two-regime story. While the EU Treaty establishes the ECB's primary objective as maintaining price stability, the drafters of the Treaty were unspecific about what rates of inflation would be consistent with the statutory objective and by what methods the mandate should be executed in the month-to-month conduct of policy. Therefore, the Governing Council (GC) was called upon to establish its own quantification of the objective. It did so as early as October 1998, by formulating an objective norm that was consciously made to differ from the standard inflation targeting framework practised by some prominent central banks at the time. Rather than expressing a preference for a particular rate of inflation, a 'target' that could be changed if circumstances changed, the GC opted for announcing a description of a state of affairs that, in its assessment, would qualify price stability unconditionally, almost *always and everywhere*: year-on-year positive inflation rates *below 2%*. Unlike a target, a price stability definition establishes a set of conditions that serves as a timeless constraint on policy conduct. Essentially, it represents an environmental factor that disqualifies inflation rates that fall outside the admissible zone.

Why did euro area monetary policymakers elect to define the ECB's primary objective in this way? While various reasons can be mentioned, two are worth highlighting. First, in light of the fundamental uncertainty facing policymakers about the structure of the new euro area economy, there were grounds for pursuing a more open, timeless definition of price stability that would remain relevant even if the underlying parameters of the economy were to shift. Formally committing to an inflation target—as other, more established central banks had recently done—may have unduly tied the ECB's hand at a time when the euro area was newly formed and data scarce. Gradually refining the objective as the parameters of the economy crystallized was a prudent tactic. Second, the decision may have reflected the external circumstances prevailing at the time, inducing a degree of path-dependence. The euro area began monetary union with an average inflation rate well below 2%, driven both by low levels of inflation in 'core' countries—for example, the Banque de France since 1994 had defined price stability explicitly as an inflation rate *below 2%* in the medium term—and by the monetary restriction that formerly high-inflation countries were applying in order to meet the criteria for joining the single currency (see Figure 2.1). In this context, the area of admissible inflation rates in the new monetary policy regime had to be made sufficiently ample to include the recent history of very contained inflation outturns.

The initial macroeconomic conditions that defined the time around the launch of the euro proved to be largely accidental, however. Soon after monetary union began in 1999, the low-inflation environment evaporated and inflation rates decompressed virtually everywhere except Germany, leading euro area inflation to repeatedly test the 2% ceiling. While, at the outset, the lack of precision about the effective floor of the price stability zone had made it hard to provide grounds for rate reductions, the mounting price pressures of the early 2000s pushed inflation expectations towards the upper edge of the price stability definition, thus increasing the likelihood of inflation overruns. For this and other reasons, building on past experience, less than five years after the 1998 announcement, the ECB began a wide-ranging strategy review, which led to a landmark clarification of the strategy in May 2003. The 1998 price stability definition was confirmed: having established a timeless definition of what defines stable prices, it was difficult to later amend it without creating what President Duisenberg termed 'a big credibility problem'. But, crucially, the GC put forward the new concept of a 'policy aim', specifying that not all positive inflation rates below 2% were equally desirable, but rather that policy would seek to deliver an inflation rate 'close to 2%' over the medium term. The rationale was the need to provide a buffer against deflation risks, both at euro area and country level. Indeed, in a heterogeneous monetary union, the union-wide inflation rate sets the bar around which cross-country relative price adjustments need to take place. Having that bar too close to zero would have meant some countries undertaking these adjustments in a deflationary environment. While the level of the focal point within the definition—the 'policy aim'—was not defined precisely, statements from ECB policymakers at the time implied that inflation expectations within a narrow interval between 1.7% and 1.9% were consistent with the GC's policy inclinations. This alignment with established facts that had solidified over the past few years of monetary union allowed the GC to refer to the 'below but close to 2%' as a clarification—not an innovation—of the strategy.

This decision provided a neat compass to calibrate policy, which in fact turned out to be critical amidst the macroeconomic dislocations and deflationary pressures that followed the financial crisis. But, when overlaid on the pre-existing price stability space, the *close to 2%* concept had a side implication, too. If one assumes a bell-shaped distribution of inflation pressures, pushing the policy aim—and thus the mode of the distribution—towards the top 2% edge of the price stability norm implies, mechanically, that almost half of the time inflation will lie *above 2%* (see Figure 3.21). In other words, given the salience of the 2% ceiling in defining stable prices in this framework, such a configuration may be thought of as creating an inherent tendency for policymakers to focus attention on inflation *overshoots* rather than *undershoots*, since the more frequent deviations on the upside violate conditions of price stability, while those on the downside—if moderate—remain within the norm. Should agents catch on to this tendency—real or putative—and coordinate their actions according to expectations of a more vigorous monetary policy response to upside deviations, over sufficiently long spells of time the inflation rate that agents expect to prevail in the medium term would edge down and pull realized inflation— both headline and core—in the same direction.

In any event, the framework, including its potential asymmetry, was well calibrated to the conditions facing policymakers at the dawn of the new century. In fact, it functioned satisfactorily for more than a decade. Using a large-scale empirical dynamic stochastic general equilibrium (DSGE) model, we show that in the decade before the crisis the euro area experienced a series of persistent, inflationary, pro-cyclical supply shocks (see Figure 3.2). This finding is robust across alternative modelling approaches. In these circumstances, a policy framework with a perceived ceiling of 2% was particularly effective in keeping inflation expectations and realized inflation in check. Inflation frequently broke through the 2% line, but it invariably snapped back quickly—and faster than in other advanced economies experiencing a similar upset of shocks, including the United States. One explanation for this is that the upper ceiling may indeed have promoted expectations that the ECB would penalize inflation above 2% more vigorously in order to minimize the probability of inflation too frequently exceeding levels compatible with the objective. Inflation expectations would then internalize the ECB's assumed propensity to treat 2% as a 'pain threshold' and, as a consequence, fluctuations in realized inflation would be mitigated. We demonstrate how this mechanism might have worked using a threshold Bayesian vector autoregression (BVAR) with two regimes: pre- and post-crisis. Prior to the crisis, inflationary cost-push shocks triggered a sharp revision to interest-rate expectations, as agents might have internalized the likely stabilizing response of the

ECB, but a very muted reaction in inflation expectations and in realized inflation (see Figure 3.13).

Crucially, this self-stabilizing mechanism ensured that *actual* policy changes could be relatively moderate, and therefore the effect of supply shocks on inflation could be contained without large sacrifices in terms of growth. We show how, throughout the first ten years of monetary union, pointed communication expressing the GC's concerns about outbursts of inflation caused the forward curve to adjust in directions that delivered much of the restriction needed to counter those price pressures, even as the reaction in the policy rate was muted. Consistent with this, macroeconomic volatility—captured by the trade-off between the variability of the level of activity and the variability of inflation—fell considerably in the euro area's first decade and was comparable with that of the United States (see Figure 3.19). Per capita GDP growth rates were also similar between the two jurisdictions prior to the crisis and remained so in its immediate aftermath, only diverging in the wake of the euro area's second recession (see Figure 3.15). In short, in the pre-crisis era, it seems that the ECB's price stability framework functioned in precisely the way that the ECB's first generation of policymakers intended, and that theory predicts an ideal inflation-stabilizing framework *should* work when tested by unfavourable disturbances: automatic adjustments in underlying conditions, including expectations, did a large part of the stabilization job. A credible monetary regime with a clear nominal anchor improved the ability of the economy to absorb shocks, allowing monetary policy itself to be more patient. The upshot was better outcomes not only for inflation but for real activity as well, because a less activist central bank, in these conditions, injects less volatility into the economy.

The stubbornness of upward inflation pressures nonetheless set limits to how patient policymakers could be. Persistent above-2% realizations, and a seemingly inertial policy path, led to insistent criticisms of an 'inattentive policy' in the mid-2000s. Thus policymakers were confronted with the classic dilemma created by conditions of supply-side disturbances: while the central bank can most of the time maintain composure in the face of such disturbances, so long as they are judged to be transient, it needs to demonstrate anti-inflationary action if inflation ultimately challenges its credibility. The dilemma became most evident in two controversial episodes in the ECB's history: the rate hikes of 2008 and 2011. In both cases, staff were projecting inflation falling to levels below 2% over the medium term. But the GC, faced by realized contemporaneous inflation well above 2% and signs that measured inflation expectations were drifting in the same direction, felt compelled to act nimbly and with greater urgency. We attempt to assess the merits of those decisions by running stochastic simulations, that is, simulating macroeconomic outcomes on the basis of our workhorse DSGE model, given a mix of shocks to the economy similar to those seen historically, and measuring the probability of inflation falling below the 2% ceiling within a medium-term horizon.

The analysis suggests that, in 2008, risks to price stability were skewed to the upside, with higher-than-2% realizations more likely than inflation undershoots.

This inference holds even if one assumes that policymakers had completely ignored ('looked through') risks coming from the supply side (see Figure 4.15), an approach that might anyway have not been justifiable given the concrete possibility that the past extended period of relatively high inflation could, in and of itself, contribute to amplifying the degree and persistence of inflation overshoots. Given the concerns at the time that a 'credibility gap' might be emerging, the case for acting was therefore sound. Moreover, with the euro area expanding from 12 to 15 members around this time, consolidating price stability expectations—which could become de-anchored during currency transitions—may have been a non-trivial secondary consideration counselling a precautionary move. The case for action in 2011 appears weaker. To be sure, in the first half of 2011, backward-looking data pointed to a rapid reabsorption of slack and building price pressures. Real-time indicators of business activity remained comfortably robust up until the time when debt runs on major countries deflagrated in June. Inflation-adjusted short-term interest rates had not been so low for so long since the 1970s. But set against this, credit and money growth had been very subdued since 2009, reinforcing the message of the staff projections that inflation—after an oil-induced flare-up—would gradually reconverge downwards over the medium term. Our stochastic simulations tend to confirm these predictions. Unlike for 2008, we fail to detect a positive tilt to the distribution of shocks, even abstracting from supply shocks (see Figure 4.34).

So why did the ECB hike rates in 2011? We note that, under conditions of persistent one-sided supply shocks, a regime centred on a *price stability definition* can eventually shift from mimicking the effects of an ideal *inflation targeting* framework to displaying some similarities with a *price level targeting* strategy. Contrary to an inflation targeting framework, which would have instructed the ECB to simply guide projected inflation back to target, a regime identifying a price stability ceiling, when put under stress for a sufficiently long period of time, de facto requires the central bank to eventually reverse the shocks in an effort to demonstrate its commitment to delivering an inflation rate that falls within the norm over the long haul—just as a price level targeter would do. There are of course key differences between the two approaches, notably in the degree to which they can steer expectations of future policy. We nevertheless believe that the way in which the ECB's price stability regime functioned in 2011, demanding a tightening into a negative supply shock, simulates how a price level targeting strategy might work in practice.

A key part of our narrative is the effect of the *below 2%* regime on the *inflation process*. As a matter of accounting, a strategy that is successful at systematically stabilizing headline and expected inflation in the face of persistent upward pressures from its volatile components can only mean that core inflation has to make space and adjust downward. We perform rolling cross-correlations between energy inflation and core inflation and, indeed, we find that an episode of high energy inflation in the euro area between 1999 and 2007 was invariably followed by a period of softening core inflation, which was not the case in the United States (see Figure 3.12). The path of the price level tells a similar story. Faced with a similar array of shocks, headline consumer price index (CPI) inflation and the CPI level moved broadly in lockstep with energy and food prices in the United States, while in the euro area headline inflation was largely immunized from swings in energy and food prices (see Figure 3.1). The corollary was that core CPI inflation in the United States broadly maintained a 2% trend, whereas in the euro area core inflation measured by Eurostat's Harmonized Index of Consumer Prices (HICP) excluding food and energy departed early from a path consistent with a 'below but close to 2%' annual average.

Core inflation is not the ECB's objective, in no small part because it fails to capture the welfare costs of price increases that impact heavily on citizens' budgets. But core and other measures of underlying inflation are important metrics to unearth the slow-moving trend driving price formation. Their level today is a good guess about the level around which headline inflation is likely to settle tomorrow. So, suppression of core inflation comes at a cost if it weakens the capacity of the economy to generate price pressure domestically. Indeed, the self-stabilizing mechanism described above admits two regimes, rather than just one. In the first regime where shocks are mainly to the upside and are supply-led, a price stability ceiling promotes a muted reaction of inflation expectations. But if the economy enters a second regime where the shock configuration reverses and negative demand shocks dominate, the ceiling ceases to bind and act as a stabilizing factor. Instead, as the central bank responds to the negative demand shocks and interest rates descend toward their lower bound, expectation formation changes: agents start expecting a smaller monetary policy response—as the room for conventional rate adjustments is eroded—and revise down their inflation expectations accordingly. As a consequence, core inflation starts to follow realized inflation downward. The key correlation between core and headline inflation, which in the face of persistent inflationary shocks was negative, becomes positive; and given the 'gravitational pull' of core inflation on headline inflation over the medium term, the inflation process might become anchored at a lower level. The switch is illustrated in our threshold BVAR exercise, which identifies a second, crisis regime in which interest rate expectations do not move in response to an adverse shock, while inflation expectations and core inflation respond to negative headline inflation in the same direction (see Figure 3.13). This shift to the second regime undermines the capacity of the monetary policy framework to act as an automatic stabilizer. While a negative correlation between core and realized inflation acts as a circuit breaker to prevent adverse inflation shocks from destabilizing the objective, a positive correlation has the reverse effect: adjustments in inflation expectations and core inflation become *accelerants*, rather than dampeners, of adverse disturbances. The presence of a lower bound on the conventional instrument of monetary policy has long been shown to introduce a non-linearity which can alter the law of motion of inflation and degrade macroeconomic outcomes. Our finding is that the likelihood of such a non-linearity coming into play is larger when inflation expectations have been forced to bounce against a hard upper ceiling, and are expected to encounter no seemingly hard floor on their way down.

Did the euro area enter such a regime after the financial crisis? Although not a definitive test, our analysis provides some support for this conclusion. Estimates using our DSGE model show that negative demand shocks weighed on euro area inflation by more than 1 percentage point on average after 2008, while in the previous ten years their effect was neutral overall, with periods of both upward and downward pressure (see Figure 3.2). In parallel, we find that after 2008 the dynamic relationship between core and headline inflation changed, with the correlation between energy fluctuations and core inflation moving from negative to strongly positive (see Figure 3.12).

The switch to the 'second regime' was not immediately apparent, however. Headline inflation recovered quickly after the Lehman crash and stayed elevated for four years thereafter. Despite stubborn inflation pressures, the ECB was nevertheless courageous in its response to the meltdown and, in fact, led the international trend of responding to the crisis with its exemplary early reaction in August 2007. The ECB's pledge to exercise the central bank's traditional role of lender of last resort without restrictions enhanced the stability of the financial system, defused the threat that financial institutions might respond to the funding crunch by curtailing credit to the broader economy and, ultimately, forestalled a ruinous implosion of the banking system. The effect of the decision to guarantee an elastic supply of liquidity to the banking system by moving to 'fixed rate with full allotment' lending in regular and longer-term operations can be quantified using our DSGE model. We simulate the extreme case in which the Eurosystem would have maintained its pre-crisis operational framework based on actively adjusting liquidity supply in order to set the marginal cost of reserves for banks equal to the policy rate target in conditions of reserve scarcity. We find that this would not have prevented a severe deleveraging process in which banks would have sought to align their liquidity needs with the size of their balance sheets by shrinking the latter (see Figure 4.19). The process would have resulted in material downside risks to price stability and a deeper contraction than was observed.

The potency of the response was nonetheless partially constrained by two principles that governed the conduct of monetary policy at the time: a 'passive' approach to liquidity provision—a consequence of the ECB's tradition—whereby the central bank's balance sheet would expand and contract endogenously based on autonomous liquidity demand from banks; and the 'separation principle', under which the GC emphasized that stance considerations and liquidity management should be seen as distinct and pursued with different tools. To be sure, the separation principle played an important communication role in deflecting insistent public criticism that the ECB's non-standard measures would soon lead to runaway inflation. It also played a tactical role in mollifying resistance within the GC against a long sequence of extraordinary liquidity operations. By separating rate policy from liquidity management, the message implicit in the 'separation' doctrine was that rates could always be raised to tame inflation, while extraordinary liquidity conditions could be maintained—at *any* level of the policy rate—to safeguard financial stability. With the privilege of hindsight, however, we conjecture that the separation principle may have had the collateral effect, at least in mature stages of the financial crisis, of weakening potential synergies between policy instruments. To test this conjecture, we perform a counterfactual exercise in which we assess how the economy might have developed if the ECB had instead deliberately and explicitly used its longer-term refinancing operations (LTROs) as a signalling tool to convey an intention to maintain policy rates at the stipulated low levels for the entire life of the facilities. We find that this complementarity between instruments—provision of long-term liquidity and rate forward guidance—may indeed have provided extra support to activity and inflation (see Figure 4.19).

The emergence of disinflationary forces following the onset of the sovereign debt crisis marked the starting point of an evolution towards a different monetary policy approach: one that moved from 'separation' to 'combination' and from 'passively' providing liquidity to seeking to ease the stance by 'actively' deploying the central bank's balance sheet. It nevertheless entailed a series of policy iterations before the template for a holistic policy strategy was reached and deliberately applied. The Securities Market Programme (SMP) represented the first venture into an active and material balance sheet policy and proved decisive in containing the most insidious phase of the euro area's existential crisis in 2010–2011. The leading idea behind SMP was that sovereign borrowing yields were instrumental in the even transmission of monetary policy across the euro area. Therefore, undue exaggerations in market pricing of sovereign risk could shake the basis for the pyramid of credit in individual nations and in the whole euro area. This notion was not undisputed at the time, with many in academic and policy circles embracing the proposition that the sole admissible response to a debt run in a currency union was a unilateral sovereign default. But, as two ECB Executive Board members observed, it made no sense for the euro area to embrace a doctrine of automatic sovereign default that was considered alien everywhere else in the world, and would only be seen by investors as a self-imposed handicap and one more reason for them to shun exposures to the euro area (Trichet (2011a) and Bini Smaghi (2011b)). Despite its originality, however, the governance of the SMP was still shaped by the separation concept, leading to a policy of sterilizing the liquidity injected so as to avoid affecting the stance. Likewise, the two 3-year LTROs launched in late 2011 most likely averted the complete meltdown of the euro area financial system which was unfolding at the time, as the contagion was rapidly moving from periphery to core countries. However, the borrowing rate was indexed to that of the main refinancing operations, a vestigial reflex of the pre-crisis convention to make decisions meeting by meeting, in a highly data-dependent manner, with no pre-set direction.

It was only with the announcement of the Outright Monetary Transactions (OMTs) that the ECB pro-actively committed its balance sheet capacity for the purpose of eradicating, once and for all, the market pessimism that, at the time, was being expressed in bets on a euro break-up (so-called 'redenomination risk'). Three developments made the OMTs possible. The first was the widespread realization that the debt crisis had mutated into a radical loss of faith in the foundations and prospects of the currency union: the source of infection in the euro area was no longer localized fiscal distress (Constâncio (2011), González-Páramo (2011b), and Bini-Smaghi (2011c)). The second development was a strengthening conviction in the GC, encouraged by President Draghi and Chief Economist Peter Praet, that—whatever the causes of the infection—the ECB bore full responsibility for inflation determination in the euro area, and that inflation would be indeterminate, or irrevocably destabilized, in a macroeconomic system under constant threat of dissolution.

The OMTs could not have happened, however, without a third development: the possibility, created by the prior efforts of President Trichet, to foster the birth of the ESM and develop it into an institution that could partner the central bank in an extreme emergency. The ECB's efforts in actively promoting its vision for that institution, which included endowing it with paid-in capital and a rich array of instruments, such as precautionary interventions, bank recapitalization instruments, and primary and secondary market securities purchases, eventually bore fruit. An ESM conditional assistance programme was defined as a necessary condition for OMT activation.

Why did the two traditional mainstays of the ECB's operating framework—a sharp separation between the stance and liquidity considerations, and the habit of making monetary policy by passive liquidity operations only—ultimately come to be superseded? Two factors conspired to produce that outcome. The first was the realization that the overnight rate was to be maintained at a level as low as feasible, if monetary policy was to exercise the degree of control over the whole of the short-to-medium term portion of the term structure that persistent disinflation demanded. This required an ample supply of liquidity in order to squeeze the front end of the curve towards the deposit facility rate—the administered rate that represents the floor of the ECB's rate corridor. Indeed, in various phases throughout the crisis period, the ECB witnessed spikes in the volatility of overnight and longer-term money market rates due to scarcity of liquidity. In these instances, the euro area yield curve became more vulnerable to the trans-Atlantic spillovers, with forward rates moving in sympathy with similar adjustments in the US yield curve, despite diverging economic cycles. This observation led to the conclusion that liquidity conditions were not separable from, but were in fact a precondition for, setting the stance at the level most appropriate for the euro area. The stance had to be extraordinarily accommodative, and expected to remain so for a considerable period of time to come. Ample liquidity conditions were thus to be seen as a concrete demonstration that the GC was disinclined to press ahead on rate normalization before the economy and inflation had themselves durably normalized.

The second factor was the dire state of the banking sector. The phase in 2013 during which banks began to rapidly reimburse the central bank liquidity borrowed under the 3-year LTROs revealed the widening fracture between banks' individual business strategies in a stagnant economic environment, and the strategy that was desirable collectively. The 'passive' liquidity provision paradigm had been predicated on the presumption that banks' demand for liquidity would be representative of the economy's liquidity needs. But this presumption was being shattered in 2013–2014 as the economy needed more accommodation and credit, yet banks in vast regions of the euro area were in fact contracting credit and withdrawing accommodation. In other words, there was an externality associated with banks' capital structure choices that led to a socially deficient level of credit and liquidity. This externality was particularly strong in the euro area 'periphery'. Reeling from the shock of the sovereign debt crisis, banks in the 'periphery' were being forced to reduce riskier assets and cut back on credit to domestic borrowers much more than banks in the 'core' (see Figure 5.17), and the mirror images of this phenomenon were, on one side, the extraordinary sluggishness with which bank lending rates in the 'periphery' declined in response to the ECB's easing adjustments between late 2011 and 2014 and, on the other side, an accelerated drain of cash from the system. We employ a multi-country BVAR to show that, by mid-2014, total lending to euro area firms was lower than one would have expected in similar cyclical and financial conditions—in other words, the 'credit gap' was negative. Furthermore, a counterfactual exercise with the same BVAR points to a negative contribution of the credit gap to the output gap, which was particularly large for Italy and Spain, but borderline statistically significant for Germany, too (see Figure 5.21).

The situation could have been mitigated if banks in vulnerable countries had received immediate and robust injections of fresh capital, including from public sources. But, before the launch of the Single Supervisory Mechanism (SSM) and European banking supervision in 2013–2014, no euro area agency possessed the authority to spearhead the kind of system-wide stress tests that had, in the United States, proven decisive in reassuring shareholders and restoring confidence in the banking system. A central resolution authority able to credibly restructure and inject funds into struggling banks was also absent. Indeed, while bank bailouts had taken place on a staggering scale in 'core' countries in the first phase of the crisis, lack of fiscal space had prevented other governments from rescuing their national banking systems with the same vigour. In Spain, a systemic stress test and recapitalization occurred only in the second half of 2012 in the context of the European Financial Stability Facility (EFSF)/ESM financial assistance programme targeted to that end. In Italy, recapitalization never happened on a scale that could have cushioned loan origination. In such conditions, deleveraging the loan book was the most effective way for banks to improve their capital base. As a result, the period of deficient demand in the 'periphery' was longer and more painful than would otherwise have been the case.

Once more, the ECB's efforts to promote and actively design new euro area institutions—this time, the SSM under the purview of President Draghi and Vice-President Constâncio—proved instrumental. In 2013, the ECB seized on the opportunity of the start of the SSM to insist on a comprehensive assessment of bank balance sheets, including an in-depth asset quality review, as a precondition for banks to enter the new supervisory regime. The assessment had the effect of frontloading the ongoing deleveraging process and tilting it towards a macroeconomically beneficial result, with banks strengthening their balance sheets in advance of the outcome. This put the sector on a stronger footing to transmit the ECB's monetary impulses, especially when the credit-easing measures were later scaled up. More generally, the SSM helped increase transparency and reduce financial fragmentation. This represented a second occasion on which the advocacy of ECB policymakers for EU institutional reform paid dividends for monetary policy.

But monetary policy also had to take its own responsibility. Whereas the OMTs had dispelled the paralysing sense of dejection inspired by the talk of a euro area break-up, the pledge to deliver a rate of inflation in line with the 2003 policy aim set in place the necessary coordinates to guide a renewed offensive against entrenched disinflation. An early forerunner of the new approach was the decision in July 2013 to emphasize, for the first time in public communication, the connection between the objectives of policy and the path of interest rates most consistent with those objectives. Such forward guidance was intended to raise the transparency of monetary policy at a time of heightened uncertainty, and to solidify—in the public's perception—the ECB's commitment to exercise control over the short end of the curve as an indispensable precondition for steering the stance of policy. The effect on short-term market rates was substantial: we show that they became significantly less sensitive to macroeconomic news and decoupled from developments across the Atlantic (see Figure 5.11). Longer-term yields were less affected by forward guidance, however, reflecting the perception that overnight rates—which were now close to zero—were nearing their effective lower bound. A perceived non-negativity restriction binding current and future policy rates skews their predictive distribution upward, since it truncates the distribution of conceivable future rates from below. This in turn reduces the sensitivity of long-term rates to movements at the short end and, in already disinflationary conditions, can induce an unwarranted tightening bias.

Thus the strategy to combat entrenched disinflation was further developed in late 2013 and early 2014. In April 2014, President Draghi used a speech in Amsterdam to articulate what additional measures the ECB would take to respond to the prolonged period of low inflation, charting out three contingencies and the reaction function in each case (Draghi, 2014a). The first contingency was an unjustified tightening of the policy stance emanating from receding excess liquidity and/or external spillovers, which would warrant additional measures to strengthen control over the short end of the yield curve. The second was a persistent impairment of the transmission of the policy stance through the banking sector, which would call for more targeted credit-easing measures. The third contingency was a worsening of the medium-term outlook for inflation caused by a broad-based weakening of aggregate demand, and/or a loosening in the anchoring of inflation expectations. This would necessitate engaging in a large-scale asset purchase programme that could directly influence longer-term yields.

For all practical purposes, around the time the President spoke in Amsterdam, the ECB was already convinced that the first and second contingencies were facts. In the latter part of 2014, it became evident that the third contingency was materializing, as weak macroeconomic data combined with the sharp fall-off in oil prices in late summer to drive headline inflation into negative territory. Of pressing concern for policy—and consistent with a switch to the second regime—was the fact that both inflation expectations and core inflation had begun to correlate in a downward direction, raising the spectre of an outright deflationary spiral. Inflation expectations were becoming, at all horizons, less well anchored and more sensitive to low realized inflation. Measures of core inflation were on a downward trend too, implying a higher risk that low realized and expected inflation would become entrenched in wage-setting behaviour and persistently drag down inflation dynamics (see Figure 5.28). While there were many structural causes—some of which had global reach and pre-dated the birth of the ECB (Constâncio, 2015, Coeuré, 2019a)—that were likely to have co-determined the downward trend in headline and core inflation, we view these developments as key facts supporting the central prediction of our two-regime BVAR exercise.

With the three contingencies triggered, the GC unveiled, from mid-2014 onwards, a radical first-of-its-kind policy package comprising three main elements: the introduction of a negative interest rate policy (NIRP), a step that no major central bank had taken in central banking history; a new series of targeted long-term refinancing operations (TLTROs) establishing tight incentives for banks to pass on lower funding costs through lending rates; and a large-scale asset purchase programme (APP) encompassing public and private sector securities. In due time, forward guidance (FG) on the size and duration of the APP and, subsequently, on the likely outlook for policy rates was added to the package—in its characteristic combination of a date-based and a state-contingent element—to facilitate coordination of investor expectations in the market.

In June 2014, when negative rates were introduced as a technical adjustment to the Eurosystem rate corridor, there was no policy playbook or consolidated body of facts that could inform ECB policymakers about the efficacy of the NIRP as an instrument of monetary accommodation. Those central banks that had brought their policy rates to negative levels before were very few, and had used the instrument as a protection against undesired currency appreciation and monetary spillovers from abroad, not as a deliberate stimulating measure. So, it took some time for NIRP to reveal its potential. Before long, however, and already in the course of 2015, the NIRP developed into a self-standing active tool to ease credit conditions, as the ECB observed its powerful interactions with FG and the APP.

Monetary policy easing, even when enacted through conventional rate reductions, always drives down both the expectations component of long-term rates—because a significant portion of the news contained in rate cut announcements is about the expected path of the policy rates over the next several quarters (Gürkaynak et al., 2005)—*and* the inflation-adjusted term premium—because they influence the investment habits of important market participants (Hanson and Stein, 2015). But the NIRP affords a higher horsepower version of these two conventional engines of monetary easing. On the one hand, it is a demonstration that monetary policy is not constrained by a zero lower bound. Because the NIRP shatters the notion that zero is the lower bound on policy rates—so much so that the qualifier 'zero' has now disappeared from the economic debate on the lower bound constraint—the probability distribution of the expected future short-term rates becomes immune to the upward tilt and tightening bias at low levels of interest rates that we describe above. On the other hand, to enforce negative rates, central banks charge a fee on the reserve holdings of commercial banks. That fee operates as a *Gesell tax* on banks' excess liquidity holdings and, as such, promotes tax avoidance practices among banks. Prominent among these are strategies to shed liquidity and seek longer-dated investments in an attempt to escape the charge. To push the analogy with a tax further, one can say that a Gesell tax is in effect a *Pigovian tax* which, when applied on polluting activities, forces agents to internalize the uncharged disservice that they impose on the rest of the system while pursuing their own best interest. In the case at hand, the disservice is created when banks decide to hoard excess liquidity instead of lending it on, which may be the most attractive course of action from their individual cost-minimization perspective but leads to an inefficient collective outcome. While the banking system as a whole cannot dispose of excess reserves, a Pigovian tax, or Gesell tax, on free reserves adds extra downward pressure on long-term rates through term premium compression by incentivizing each individual bank to shift its portfolio from short-dated to long-dated exposures. As such, NIRP is a key complement to APP, as it has empowered the portfolio rebalancing process through which large-scale asset purchases are expected to work.

FG, the APP and TLTROs have been critical in cementing and amplifying the stimulus introduced by the NIRP. If used in conjunction with a FG formulation that explicitly allows for the contingency of a future rate cut to even more negative levels, the NIRP produces an inversion of the yield curve in its short to medium-maturity segments. As those segments of the curve that are subject to inversion provide the pricing kernel for loan rate fixation in the euro area, the NIRP in conjunction with FG give a secure handle on bank-based transmission. The APP, for its part, is at the centre of a web of interlocking influences that spread widely across instruments. The APP saturates the money market with the surplus of liquidity that is necessary to keep the overnight rate close to and controllable by the rate on the Eurosystem deposit facility. This is a pre-condition for arbitrage to ensure that the negative return to reserves under the NIRP translates into negative returns to other short-term liquid assets. And it is a necessary condition for FG on the future path of the deposit facility rate to be able to influence expectations of the future path of the market overnight rate.

Furthermore, the APP and FG provide key safeguards to contain the rate volatility side effects that the NIRP may otherwise bring about. At the zero lower bound, in a no-NIRP world where expectations of a rate cut are entirely priced out and the central bank inspires expectations of a zero-rate for long, the volatility of future rates hits a minimum. To the extent that the term premium compensates investors in long-dated securities for short-rate volatility, the reduced rate volatility in a no-NIRP scenario suppresses the term premium, too. But, as the NIRP re-establishes the possibility for a two-way variation in short-term interest rates, it has the potential for increasing rate volatility, and the term premium as a result. As we note below, FG and purchases of long-dated securities are a straight way to cap the term premium, and thus can stem the perverse volatility effect. At the same time, FG can also help anchor the rate expectations in conditions in which they may be destabilized to the upside while the central bank purchases bonds under an APP. If the bond purchases have the desired effect of accelerating economic recovery and reflation, investors may react to the brightening outlook by bringing forward the date by which they expect the central bank to raise its policy rates. Failing to push back on those expectations through a better anchoring of the front end of the forward curve may inadvertently produce a tightening in financial conditions at a time when bond purchases are meant to be easing them. FG, again, is an effective complement to APP in this respect.

Certainly, the four measures were initially developed in a modular way with specific tools assigned to specific contingencies. That was the mould that shaped the Amsterdam speech. Over time, however, as the ECB gathered evidence that each instrument had the positive cross-externalities that we categorize above, the measures were combined into a holistic frame, with each of the constituent tools intended to reinforce the others. The 'combined arms' approach of using the four tools in concert shaped up into a deliberate policy course. Initiated in 2014 as a quantitative means to restore the size of the Eurosystem's balance sheet towards its 2012 level in the face of accelerated LTRO repayments, APP evolved rapidly into an instrument to secure supply scarcity in the market for long-dated bonds. This was firmly guided by the 'stock view' of central bank purchases, namely that it was the size of the central bank portfolio weighted by its maturity relative to the total stock of maturity-weighted outstanding bonds, not the act of adding to the portfolio, which mattered for long-term yields and, ultimately, for the economy. The size and duration of APP were therefore repeatedly redefined, as the ECB saw a need, first, to upscale the stimulus, then to re-normalize it, and finally to phase out the monthly pace of bond acquisitions.

This began in January 2015, when the APP was designated the primary instrument of monetary policy for two main reasons: because the ECB judged that policy rates were already close to their lower bound, and because, in the highly fragmented financial landscape of the time, the APP was indeed the instrument that could achieve the maximum benefit in the largest number of member economies. Based on these considerations, between January 2015 and June 2018, FG mainly referred to APP. In this period, the formal policy statement governing the FG on purchases was based on a dual-key approach: it gave time-contingent guidance, referring to a calendar date to indicate the time for which the public could expect the monthly purchases to run; and it gave state-contingent guidance by indicating that, in any case, purchases would continue even beyond that calendar date, until the GC was sufficiently confident that projected inflation was on a path toward the policy aim—a 'sustained adjustment' over a medium-term horizon. In line with this FG architecture, at each recalibration, the GC updated the date-based element of the APP forward guidance, extending the minimum horizon for the monthly purchases (corresponding to a minimum size of the programme), while always keeping their intentional horizon linked to the inflation objective (through its *sustained adjustment* threshold).

In March 2016, FG bifurcated, as the outlook for the policy rate had to be coordinated with the FG on the duration of the asset purchases in order to communicate an optimal sequencing for policy normalization (Praet, 2017b). Finally, in June 2018, FG reverted from referring to the duration of the APP back to a statement of intent on the future path of the policy rates. The main difference with the pre-June 2018 formulation is that the policy rate path communicated as part of the post-June 2018 FG was made more explicit and was elevated to the primary tool for conveying information about the likely evolution of the overall stance. Otherwise, the post-June 2018 FG maintained the characteristic dual-key contingency that had been applied when signalling the APP's duration: a calendar time to indicate the nearest date for a lift-off, and a 'sustained adjustment' condition invoking an inflation outcome to justify the start of rate normalization.

As for the TLTROs, the intermediate objective of the first-generation was to promote competition among banks for good credit to the economy. Competition would squeeze lending rates and margins on bank loans; lower lending rates and bank mark-ups would stimulate stronger demand for borrowing in the broader economy and promote growth-friendly capital formation as a result. Ultimately, the expansion in loan volumes and the fall in expected losses on new and outstanding loans—the latter due to a stronger economy—would validate lower margins and lending rates ex post, and restore banks' profits. While TLTRO-I successfully set in train the virtuous loop described above, the second generation of TLTROs (TLTRO-II), launched in March 2016, was designed to leverage the NIRP in an effort to further boost participating banks' incentives to lend while giving banks an effective shield against excessive margin pressure. The best performers among participants in terms of loan creation could borrow TLTRO funds at negative rates. Both vintages of TLTROs—I and II—debunked the presumption that any long-term refinancing facility offered to banks on attractive terms would inevitably find its way into funding governments, as banks would use the funds to bid at sovereign bond auctions. Banks' public bond portfolios tapered off measurably following TLTRO-I and II.

Throughout, in order to help anchor the decision process and calibrate these measures, the textbook impact analysis used by generations of economists to trace the macroeconomic propagation of a monetary policy impulse was reverse-engineered. Whereas the canonical exercise ran from a standardized adjustment to the instrument of monetary policy onto the response which that action would induce in real and nominal variables, the problem at hand implied running the exercise in reverse order: from an 'inflation gap'—the shortfall of projected medium-term inflation with respect to the 'inflation aim'—back to the requisite instrument adjustments that would help offset it (see Figure 5.29). The very notion of a negative 'inflation gap' would have been unthinkable had the 2003 strategy exercise not pinpointed a medium term 'inflation aim' at the upper edge of the numerical definition of price stability; and had those negative deviations—large and persistent as they were—not come to be seen as equally undesirable as deviations on the upside.

Still, the extent to which such innovative instruments might have accelerated the economic recovery and helped close the 'inflation gap' remains a subject of active discussion among researchers and policymakers. This book contributes to the debate with novel quantitative results. Notoriously, efforts to measure the effects of monetary instruments, particularly when they are combined in complex packages, are bedevilled by identification issues. We adopt a general identification scheme which assigns sets of instruments to observed adjustments in the yield curve that financial intermediaries use as the basis for pricing credit and in credit spreads, respectively. In this general taxonomy, the NIRP, the public sector purchase programme (PSPP—the sovereign bond component of the APP) and FG are seen as primarily influencing the yield curve, while TLTROs and the private bond components of the APP are important determinants of the 'intermediation wedge'—the difference between the final cost of loans for households and firms and the risk-free interest rate that banks and other intermediaries take as reference for rate fixation in pricing those loans. Our main contribution is in trying to tease apart the effects of the NIRP, the PSPP, and FG in particular on financial conditions, growth and inflation. Here, again, the general identification assumption is that the NIRP and FG enhance the central bank's traction on the short to medium-maturity segment of the term structure of money market interest rates, while the PSPP operates principally on the long end of the sovereign cash curve.

According to our taxonomy, *signalling* is a major avenue through which the NIRP propagates. This fact makes it a natural companion to and complement of FG, which however complicates the econometrician's task of separating its marginal contribution from that of FG. To isolate the impact of the NIRP and FG, in combination and as separate instruments, we use an innovative methodology that requires minimal priors on the underlying macroeconomic structure and on the power of central bank pronouncements to influence agents' expectations in general. We start from the risk-neutral densities of rate paths that are embedded in the rate option contracts observed over the entire period between 2014 and 2018. Incidentally, the forward curves implied by the overnight spot swap curves can be thought of as the mean of those densities. Then we manipulate those densities to make them minimally consistent with the alternative policy scenario that we want to simulate: a world without the NIRP, with or without FG. By 'minimally consistent' we mean that we alter those rate paths making up each density to the extent, and only to the extent, that they might embody expectations that would patently be inconsistent with the counterfactual policy regime that we entertain. For example, a world in which the central bank makes a formal commitment not to bring rates to levels below zero should be one in which no rate path in the bundle that makes up the predictive density extracted from rate options should contemplate a rate cut once the overnight has been brought to its zero lower bound.

As for the quantification of the pure APP effect, we concentrate on its *duration channel* (Praet (2018b) and Coeuré (2019b)). Investors with an aversion to interest rate risk, or duration risk, will require higher expected returns (a 'term premium') on long-term bonds, relative to what they could earn from investing in short-term securities. By purchasing long-dated assets, a central bank thus reduces the amount of duration risk that is borne in aggregate, while simultaneously increasing the amount of short-term risk-free bank reserves in the system. If assets with different maturities are imperfect substitutes, in order for investors to be willing to make those portfolio adjustments, the expected excess returns on securities—the 'term premium'—have to fall, which means that the long-term interest rates paid by these securities also have to adjust downward. To note, according to the duration view, purchases of a given security or in a certain maturity bucket do not only affect bond yields locally. Rather, by extracting aggregate duration risk the central bank decreases the current and future market price of risk, which influences the pricing of term premia across longer-dated assets and across maturities. Therefore, asset purchases are a means to put downside pressure on long-term interest rates and introduce monetary easing in conditions in which the space for conventional policy action is restricted.

Our fundamental identification choice views TLTROs as acting principally on the banks' 'intermediation wedge'. In particular, TLTROs compress all the funding cost components of the wedge by offering euro area banks a way to replace more expensive sources of funding with more affordable long-term borrowing from the ECB. This funding cost relief has a direct and an indirect element. For each participating bank, it comes principally through the direct substitution effect and is a function of the bank's take-up in the operations. For non-bidders, it is the product of a positive externality: as bidders withdraw from the markets for alternative funding instruments, and thus contribute in those markets to a negative demand shift, the attendant drop in borrowing costs benefits all banks.

We run the estimated yield curve and lending rate impacts of the NIRP, FG, the APP and TLTROs respectively through a large Bayesian VAR where they can be interacted with the macroeconomic state. We find that, in the absence of the package, GDP would have been roughly 2.7% lower by end-2018, and annual inflation one third of a percentage point weaker on average over 2015–2018. Around a fifth of the overall impact on the 2017 (i.e. the peak-year) growth rate is attributable to the NIRP as a standalone instrument, a surprisingly sizeable contribution given the limited scale of the cumulated rate adjustments in negative territory (only a 40-basis point cut spread over an interval of two years). Our estimates show that the APP explains the lion's share of the overall effect on output growth in 2017. TLTROs, for their part, led to a persistent compression in lending rates and enduring support to the economy, accounting for another fifth of the overall impact on output growth in 2017.

We suspect that our approach delivers only an absolute lower bound to a realistic quantification of impacts. First, as we explain in the last chapter, our manipulation of the rate-options-derived predictive densities—the basis of our impact analysis for the NIRP and FG—might well underrate the speed at which investors would have expected the policy interest rates to rise looking into the future in a counterfactual no-policy world. Secondly, our narrow concentration on the duration channel likely understates the efficacy of the APP. To the extent that the purchases are a concrete demonstration of a desire to provide additional stimulus, they may reinforce the signal—conveyed primarily by FG—about the likely trajectory of future policy rates, even over far-distant horizons. Third, in quantifying the degree to which the financial stimulus spurred growth in the euro area, we consciously avoid placing too sharp restrictions on the channels connecting policy and the macroeconomy, and on the data generating process of the macroeconomy in general. By feeding counterfactual forward and sovereign yield curves into a vector autoregression, we likely capture the way *contemporary* financial easing supports consumption and capital formation. We nevertheless shut down any further direct impacts on consumption and business investment working through confidence. If the announcement of a bold policy initiative were to boost consumers' income prospects and the expected 'marginal efficiency of investment', for example, such optimistic expectations would encourage more borrowing and more income creation for a given quantum of financial easing than our methodology is able to detect.

Despite these caveats, the evidence suggests that the 'combined arms strategy' has done a solid job of revitalizing the economy and thereby laying down the conditions for inflation to return to its medium-term norm. But the evidence still raises three questions. First, were these measures compatible with the legal framework in which the ECB operates, as laid down in the EU Treaties? Might these policies have inadvertently contributed to adverse side effects that can obstruct their transmission and diminish their favourable effects in future? And what about the general policy environment in which this strategy had to work its way to the economy? To be sure, the overarching premise on which the strategy was predicated was that the costs of allowing inflation to deviate from its medium-term norm—and the economy to consistently fall short of capacity for an extended period of time—were unacceptably large compared with any future economic benefits that might have accrued from using monetary policy to lean against the potential negative side effects, say in the form of financial imbalances, that a low-interest-rate world can generate. But in deploying its policy package, did the ECB remain strictly within its mandate, and was this balance between benefits and costs always positive?

We address these questions by, first, examining the constitutional complaints that have been brought against the PSPP. In the general architecture of our narrative, this short detour into seemingly unfamiliar legal grounds provides an opportunity to appraise the 'law and economics' of the ECB's unconventional policies, an introspective self-appraisal exercise which no central bank—as a key agent of public policy—can or should try to eschew. The starting point is the ruling of the Court of Justice of the European Union (CJEU) in December 2018, which confirms that, in order to enable the pursuit of price stability, central banks need to be equipped with a high degree of statutory instrument independence, allowing them to decide the appropriate settings of their policy measures so as to address the specific challenges at hand. As we describe, however, statutory instrument independence puts the onus on central banks to deploy their measures in a manner and on a scale that is effective, efficient and cost-conscious, namely alert to any measurable unintended side effects that might be associated with protracted applications of such measures.

The impact analysis that we describe above demonstrates that the time-varying combination of tools deployed since 2014 was indeed *effective* in the ECB's legitimate battle against pernicious disinflation. But, were they *efficient* as well? Could the ECB have made use of alternative means with potentially less unintended effects? And would compensating for the PSPP with more intensive use of other tools have secured the same outcomes? We conduct an exercise that seeks to work out the implications for NIRP had the ECB never activated PSPP but still aimed to achieve the same historical impact on inflation that we ascribe to PSPP in our empirical analysis. We find that the additional DFR cuts necessary to generate the same path for inflation would have required reducing the DFR to unprecedented and possibly unviably low levels from 2015 onward (Figure 6.27)—and such cuts would have been accompanied by more severe side effects than we saw in actuality.

We delve into the question of the unintended side effects of monetary policy by concentrating on two areas of cost valuation: the banking sector and the income/loss accounting of private savers. Though the list of supposed collateral effects of monetary policy is longer—for example, effects on real estate prices or household inequality—these two areas are more directly linked to monetary policy transmission, insofar as they might, in theory, so impede the transmission mechanism as to cause the additional policy stimulus to 'backfire' and become contractionary.

On the banking front, we measure the costs in terms of banks' ability to generate income and capital buffers organically and, on that score, we confirm that, throughout the period covered by our chronicle, the all-in general equilibrium advantages of the policy strategy have consistently outstripped any adverse effect that banks might have had to endure because of the extraordinarily challenging low-rate environment which they had to navigate. In fact, we seek confirmation that monetary policy was not *in and of itself* a decisively negative factor sapping banks' earnings by using a model counterfactual. We find that, in a no-NIRP, no-PSPP world, euro area banks' net interest income would indeed have been higher, but their *overall* return on assets would have been weaker, as the negative contribution to the banks' earnings from other income sources—in a world in which the yield curve would have been higher and steeper—would have more than offset the positive impact of higher rates on the interest margin.

To sharpen our focus on the banking system, we entertain the notion that monetary policy could at some negative level of interest rates hit the 'reversal rate': a configuration of interest rates so low that banks lose an economic incentive to lend, and so there ceases to be any follow-through on monetary policy easing via the wider expansion of lending, but rather the reverse. We do not find evidence that the 'reversal rate' might have been anywhere in sight in the euro area at the end of 2018. However, the 'reversal rate' is state-contingent, or—said differently—is not independent of the 'neutral rate'. One can certainly imagine scenarios in which macroeconomic prospects are downgraded—the 'neutral rate' falls—to the point where risk-adjusted returns from lending fail to keep up, even as the central bank eases policy further, and thus financial stability vulnerabilities emerge. How the 'neutral rate' interacts with the 'reversal rate' deserves constant reconsideration, and—in our view—should figure highly among research priorities in the coming years.

In terms of the effects on private savers—who gained and who lost out as a result of the ECB's unconventional policies—we explore whether negative income effects produced by falling market rates might eclipse positive intertemporal substitution effects and thus thwart the central bank's plans to reflate the economy. Here, we extend existing research that traces the impact of monetary policy to the net-wealth position of households. We find that, first, positive cash flows to net savers, which have fallen since 2014, would have declined even in the absence of the ECB's policies, since the fall in market interest rates has an underlying trend that transcends monetary policy action. By contrast, interest payments of net borrowers, which have become less onerous since 2014, would have remained broadly unchanged, suggesting an important role for monetary policy in easing the financial burden of those households that are likely to spend more. Second, if the ECB had compensated for lower stimulus via the PSPP by cutting policy rates more deeply into negative territory, the income benefits to the net borrowers and the income losses to the net savers would have been twice as large. Our conclusion is that, all else equal, the ECB's policies since 2014 have shored up aggregate household spending through a robust consumption channel. By and large, this channel has worked via redistribution to the benefit of those household income/wealth groups that have a substantially higher marginal propensity to consume.

As for the policy mix, a key lesson we distil from our story is that the policy consensus that formed around inflation targeting had failed to internalize an essential fact: that monetary policy is an intimate part of public demand management, and *not only* when extraordinary circumstances force the central bank to move away from conventional instruments, but *always* and at *all* times. Seen in this light, it is highly pertinent that, in its fight against disinflation and economic dislocations, the ECB had to contend with adverse forces in contexts in which the economy was facing persistent inertia in, or even cross-currents from, other public demand management policies. Fiscal policies, for example, turned sharply restrictive as early as 2010 and remained contractionary until 2014. What is remarkable is that this odd combination of an expansive monetary policy and a restrictive fiscal stance in years marked by economic contraction and looming risks of deflation did not impede the robust expansion that started in late 2016 and reached a climax in 2017. We view this fact as testimony to the potency of monetary policy instruments, when a central bank is determined to deploy them with the necessary conviction and vigour.

However, building on the model analysis expounded in Chapter 1, one cannot rule out more extreme scenarios than those faced by the ECB in the years following the financial crisis, in which the economy sinks into an even deeper and more lasting contraction, and ingrained disinflation takes hold. We show that, should the economy ever find itself in such a predicament, a more policy-enabling environment—including a comprehensive set of non-monetary policies and growth-enhancing fiscal interventions—would be helpful for monetary instruments to exert the favourable effects that we document in this book.

The ECB's two-pillar strategy—with its unique monetary pillar—occupies a large part of the early chapters of this book. Our interpretation is that, after the strategy review of May 2003 which addressed some of the weaknesses in the initial configuration of the monetary analysis, the monetary pillar has performed essentially two functions. First, it has been a reminder of the fundamental fragility of macroeconomic equilibria and the role that money, as an indicator and instrument of policy, can usefully play should the economy ever lose its anchor. We show that indeed, if one allows for a wide spectrum of possible scenarios—including extremes featuring high inflation or deflation—money demonstrates a more robust association with prices and the economic state than the conventional interest rate instrument of monetary policy. The latter's capacity to control the economy is constrained by the effective lower bound; the quantity of money is not. Faced by those extreme conditions, the central bank has only one choice: to switch from a focus on interest rates to a focus on money and credit creation in order to regain control over inflation and the economy. In fact, it is not too far-fetched to view the global shift to quantitative easing policies and heightened attention to credit, once interest rates approached their lower bound, as a manifestation of this principle.

The second useful function the monetary pillar performed over the years was to offer timely proxy indicators to measure the actual state of the macroeconomy in the exceptionally data-poor environment in which the ECB's Governing Council had to make decisions. Credit in particular was studied for its good cyclical properties, especially in an economy so reliant on banks, and its ability to provide some advance signals about economic slack—which is notoriously hard to measure in real time—and asset price developments that could influence price dynamics further down the road. The benefits of such a holistic approach to policymaking were confirmed in relatively short order. The monetary analysis was conceived, naturally, with upside risks in mind and proved useful to that end. In particular, in late 2005, buoyancy in monetary data carried dispositive information about an accelerating recovery, which was otherwise slow to show through in real-time conjunctural analysis, as well signalling emerging financial imbalances. This informed the decision to hike policy rates in December 2005, which proved timely in hindsight, but was taken against the publicly-stated advice of a large number of euro area governments and the mainstream academic community at the time. However, with the shift in focus and broadening of scope which occurred in the aftermath of the sovereign debt crisis, the monetary analysis proved equally valuable in disinflationary conditions, providing an essential input into the ECB's diagnosis of the emerging risks from sustained bank deleveraging and emerging credit rationing.

In search of evidence that this second function was indeed active and helpful, we review the period before the crisis. We find that credit growth clearly informed the ECB's reaction function and, using our DSGE model, we conduct a counterfactual exercise in which we test how the economy would have developed if the ECB had *not* given credit the same weight. We find that fluctuations in euro area inflation and economic activity would have been much more ample both in upswings and downswings (see Figure 3.11). At the same time, we do not find evidence that a stricter 'leaning against the wind' strategy would have led to superior outcomes. We model a world in which the ECB pursued a monetary policy sufficiently tight to halt the sustained decline in credit spreads between 2005 and 2007, and find that GDP growth would have been a full percentage point lower in each of the years 2005–2007, and inflation more than half a percentage point lower at the onset of the 2008 crisis (see Figure 3.26). These sustained inflation undershoots would probably have weakened the underlying inflation process to an even greater extent at the onset of the crisis, while probably being insufficient to meaningfully dampen the financial cycle.

Based on these theoretical considerations and empirical analysis, we believe that the twofold role that the monetary analysis appears to have played in the policy framework has added value. It is a subject of future reflection whether these functions could be preserved even in the absence of a codified role for money in the ECB's monetary policy framework.

On a methodological note, throughout the book we support our narrative to the extent possible with evidence coming from quantitative models. Employing state-of-the-art quantitative methods provides a disciplining device and helps ensure consistency in the reasoning. To this end, we make use of the two main quantitative approaches for macroeconomic modelling employed in the profession: the dynamic stochastic general equilibrium (DSGE) approach and the Bayesian Vector Autoregressive (BVARs) approach. Each of them has advantages and disadvantages. The strength of DSGE models over BVARs resides in their reliance on microfoundations and optimizing behaviour of economic agents, thereby ensuring a high degree of internal coherence. At the same time, by being fully structural, DSGE models have two main drawbacks. First, they need to take a stand on the exact transmission channels through which monetary policy operates. This becomes a challenge, for example, for the analysis of unconventional monetary policy measures: the discussion about their most relevant transmission channels is still unsettled in the profession. The strength of BVARs, on the other hand, plays out especially in such situations, since they can capture in a flexible manner empirical interrelationships among variables by relying on minimal identifying restrictions. Second, DSGE models—unless they are very small and therefore run the risk of being empirically implausible—have to be used in their linearized form. Whereas linear models may be sufficient to analyse some questions, they cannot provide (by definition) any insight on issues such as the potential asymmetric dynamics triggered by inflation being above or below its 2% ceiling. Here, again, the flexibility of BVARs comes in handy.

Although it would be ideal to carry out our analysis with one consistent framework across our whole chronicle, this would come at the cost of providing partial or likely even incorrect answers. Thus we take an eclectic view and make use of both DSGE and BVAR approaches. However, to ensure consistency and continuity to the maximum extent possible, within the DSGE approach we choose a (linearized) large DSGE model that features a detailed financial sector and has proven to have good empirical fit; within the BVAR approach, we choose a large model encompassing real, nominal and financial variables with minimal identifying restrictions, and for some of our analyses we restrict attention to a smaller version of the model and allow for regime switching. All model-based inference that we present should be regarded as illustrative of some aspects of the broader discussion we enter into, without an ambition to be all-encompassing.

*   *   *

This book intersects at least three currents of prior research. A large literature, very active in the early years of the ECB, has examined the ECB's policy framework and its style of monetary policy management. In Chapters 3 and 4, we make a careful attempt to review the proposals and assess the criticism advanced by a series of thoughtful reports authored by groups of prominent economists for the CEPR between 1998 and 2008 (particularly Begg et al., 1998, Alesina et al., 2001, and Galí et al., 2004). Relative to these reports, we enjoy the privilege of hindsight, as well as access to a more complete set of information about the thought processes and analyses that inspired the ECB's monetary framework and policy choices over the first ten years of its history. More recently, Micossi (2015) and Hartmann and Smets (2018) have revived the tradition of those reports, the latter covering the same twenty years of ECB policies that are the subject of this book. Our undertaking complements and adds to this paper by offering a broader range of analytical tools and novel analysis to evaluate the key monetary policy decisions taken over the period, as well as delving into the internal discussions and considerations that underpinned those decisions.

Other contributions reviewing the ECB's first two decades—such as Papadia and Välimäki (2018)—explore wider questions concerning the mandates and institutional arrangements governing central banks and their appropriateness for the post-crisis age. Our focus however remains firmly on the effectiveness of the ECB's monetary policy strategy in delivering its Treaty-given objective. More generally, our book adds to the broader literature charting the historical evolution of the ECB, such as Padoa-Schioppa (2004), Scheller (2006), James (2012) and Mooslechner (2019), as well as the literature taking stock of the euro's achievements and challenges at various points in its history, such as OECD (1999), Issing et al. (2001), Issing (2008), Buti et al. (2010), Pisani-Ferry (2014), Sandbu (2015), Bénassy-Quéré et al. (2018) and, more critically, Stiglitz (2016) and Mody (2018). Unlike some of these contributions, however, we do not attempt to chronicle the evolution of European monetary integration over earlier decades, or rehearse the reasons for monetary cooperation in Europe. We take Monetary Union as a fact, and seek to describe the ways in which the monetary policy of its central bank, the ECB, has made it work and last. We only note in *passim* that a fundamental quest for currency stability has motivated legions of countries in history to conceive arrangements or accede to international agreements that, while limiting their scope for domestic monetary discretion, could inoculate them against macroeconomic mismanagement. The euro is probably the most inclusive and successful among those projects. It is the most inclusive, because—unlike unilateral pegs whereby satellite economies lose their monetary sovereignty—the creation of a supranational central bank gives all members a seat at the table. It is the most successful, because—in spite of the turbulence of the years that we try to document—the euro has survived unscathed with its approval rating among citizens in euro area countries climbing to an all-time high of 75% by end-2018, according to Eurobarometer, up from a low 62% in Spring 2013. We believe many euro-critics under-report on these few simple facts, and underrate their meaning.

In our chronicle, we devote considerable space to the crisis years. And here our way crosses that of many authors who have explored the European debt crisis in detail, and its fallout on the financial system. Like Visco (2018), for example, we highlight how missing EMU institutions did at times perpetuate the euro area crisis, especially as regards banking sector repair. In line with Véron (2015), we emphasize the importance of banking union as one essential part of the institutional construction of the euro area. Similar to Popov and Van Horen (2014), Acharya et al. (2018), De Marco (2019), and Baldwin and Giavazzi (2015)—and the 18 contributions included in that book—we identify the negative feedback loop between sovereigns, banks, and firms as one of the key transmission channels of the sovereign debt crisis. However, unlike Lane (2012, 2013, and 2015a) and Lane and Milesi-Ferretti (2012 and 2015), we do not study the euro area's pre-2008 risk factors, notably the cross-border credit boom, which led up to the twin sovereign-banking crises.

The second stream of literature to which we connect is a nascent line of analysis—at the border between economics, history and political science—that has stressed a sort of 'clash of cultures' permeating the European institutional debate and policy practice. Brunnermeier et al. (2016) is the clearest reference in this literature. We try to find a trail of clues of such a fundamental cultural dichotomy in the narrow domain of the ECB's monetary policy, and indeed we find some. We mentioned above the accelerated process by which banks began to shed excess liquidity along with other core assets at a critical macroeconomic crossroads, in 2013 and 2014. That was an instance in which two opposing views challenged each other. One view—of Keynesian *and* monetarist lineage—saw it as a central bank's responsibility to forestall such a process, noting the adverse externalities that individual banks' decisions, however rational independently, were having on collective outcomes. The other view—which we see as a direct descendant of the once-prominent 'real bills doctrine'—was faithful to the gardeners' old saying: *harsh pruning leads to buds in May*. Adherents to this second view saw deleveraging as a symptom, and unescapable stage, of a process by which banks were restoring themselves to good health in the wake of the post-crisis hangover. Obstructing that process would have meant suppressing self-reform incentives in the private sector.

Finally, we contribute to the expanding literature on the effects of unconventional policies. Not surprisingly, given the innovative features of many of these policies and the limited stretch of time over which researchers have been able to observe their effects, empirical results on their efficacy span a broad spectrum between considerable impacts (Swanson (2017), Eberly et al. (2019), Sims and Wu (2019), and, on the euro area, Szczerbowicz (2015), Podlich, Schnabel, and Tischer (2017), Mouabbi and Sahuc (2019), Gibson et al. (2016), and Neri and Siviero (2019)), to heterogeneous impacts (Burriel and Galesi (2018) and Deutsche Bundesbank (2016)), to rather moderate impacts (Pattipeilohy et al. (2013), Greenlaw et al. (2018), and Belke and Gros (2019)). Despite relying on a time-series methodology which, in backing out the macroeconomic propagation of the ECB's measures, does not give too much credit to any direct expectation channel of monetary policy, we find very sizeable effects. This applies to the NIRP as well, the target of vigorous criticism from among market analysts and academics alike (Brunnermeier and Koby (2018) and Eggertsson et al. (2019) are important academic contributions which express scepticism about negative rates). In line with Altavilla et al. (2018), Altavilla et al. (2019) and Demiralp et al. (2019), we contend that many of the channels through which the NIRP exerts its impact are overlooked or downplayed in the existing literature. Notably, the over-emphasis that much of the literature places on deposits as *the* source of funding for banks has led to an under-estimation of the space left for banks to offset the NIRP-induced rate pressure on their asset side with substantial cuts in a wide spectrum of funding costs on their liability side. In other words, banks are *payers* as much as they are *receivers* of low (and negative) rates. We show that this rate-resetting mechanism has shielded euro area banks' bottom lines at least until the time of writing.

The remainder of the book is organized as follows. Chapter 1 recalls the intellectual backdrop against which the ECB and the euro were instituted, highlighting the dominant ideational and practical influences on the drafters of the EU Treaty and on the economists at the national central banks who set up the new central bank. We also explore the role of the New Keynesian model in shaping the intellectual climate of those years and informing the thrust of the 2003 monetary policy strategy review. Chapter 2 details how those foundational principles were operationalized in the design of the ECB's monetary policy strategy, laying out the rationale for the ECB's adoption of a strategy centered on a 'price stability definition' in 1998, the 'strategic headaches' the strategy created in the ECB's early years, and the internal debates that prefaced the strategy review in 2003. It outlines the considerations that led to the introduction of the new 'policy aim' and the reassignment of the role of money in the two-pillar strategy.

Chapter 3 focuses on the ECB's 'strategy in action' and assesses its adequacy over the pre-crisis era. This chapter elaborates on the trade-off created by moving the policy aim toward the price stability ceiling in 2003, and introduces the regime-switching analysis which underpins our main narrative about the two decades of monetary union. In doing so, it revisits a number of key policy decisions and, using insights from a variety of analytical tools, reviews the merits of the various criticisms levelled at the ECB by observers at the time. Chapter 4 focuses on the ECB's performance during the Great Financial Crisis and the ensuing sovereign debt crisis. It recounts the various phases of the crisis with the aim of highlighting the real-time dilemmas facing ECB policymakers at critical junctures and the debates that surrounded key ECB interventions, and also with the aim of quantifying the effects of those policies—such as the guaranteeing of an elastic supply of liquidity through the fixed rate full allotment procedure, the sovereign bond purchases under the SMP and the announcement effect of the OMTs. This chapter also provides a detailed history of the ECB's role in the institutional reform debates that marked this phase of the crisis, especially in the context of the setting-up of the ESM. Chapter 5 documents the long slide into disinflation that began in late 2012 and provides a window into the internal analysis that underpinned the launch of the policy package between 2014 and early 2015. It explains how ECB policymakers approached the challenge of increasing accommodation once interest rates drew close to zero, and lays out the legal framework in which unconventional monetary policies had to be made.

Finally, Chapter 6 describes the various recalibrations of the package up until 2018, expounds on the methodology and documents the results of our analysis of the macroeconomic impact of the package of measures launched since 2014. We conclude the book with an analysis of the efficiency and the costs and benefits of the strategy—from the lens of an evaluation of its potential to undermine financial intermediaries' capital position and lending capacity and its effect on private savers and borrowers—along with some considerations on the policy mix.

1
The Foundations

The design of the ECB was the confluence and product of a decades-long evolution of ideas and an accumulation of real-world experience.[1] In this chapter, we try to unwrap the ideal and practical ingredients of European monetary reform and discuss them separately. We first concentrate on the ideas that were widely available and influential at the turn of the last century, when the drafters of the EU Treaty and many economists at work in the national central banks set out to design the ECB. We illustrate them in three principles of healthy monetary governance, in the inflation targeting (IT) framework that was dominant at the time and in large measure embodies those principles, and in the model of reference that demonstrates the optimality of IT. We dwell on the model of reference, the New Keynesian model (NKM), to identify as carefully as we can what the model says and what the model does not say about the stability of the macroeconomy and the stabilizing capacity of monetary policy. The insights we derive from this analysis will be important for placing in context what we have to say in Chapters 2, 5, and 6.

As for the real-world experience, the Deutsche Bundesbank and its foundational 'stability culture' were the role model and major source of inspiration for the ECB. We therefore look over some key details of the Bundesbank institutional set-up before moving to the Treaty provisions about the ECB.

1.1 Three High-Level Principles

Since the inception of central banking, economists and policymakers have been debating the wisdom of competing frameworks for articulating central banks'

---

[1] For an in-depth introduction to the history, role, and functions of the ECB within the framework of Economic and Monetary Union (EMU), see Scheller (2006). Specifically, the historical account is framed around the three stages of EMU. Stage One started in July 1990, with the abolition of restrictions on the movement of capital. Stage Two was marked by the creation of the European Monetary Institute (EMI) in January 1994 to strengthen central bank cooperation and monetary policy coordination as well as to make the necessary preparations for establishing the European System of Central Banks (ESCB), for the conduct of the single monetary policy, and for creating a single currency in Stage Three. The third and final stage of EMU began on 1 January 1999: the conversion rates of the currencies of the 11 Member States were irrevocably fixed and the ECB took over responsibility for conducting the single monetary policy in the euro area. For a review of how the framework for the ECB took shape also in relation to various influences from pre-EMU experiences of individual national central banks, see James (2012), in particular chapter 8, 'Designing a Central Bank'.

Monetary Policy in Times of Crisis: A Tale of Two Decades of the European Central Bank. Massimo Rostagno, Carlo Altavilla, Giacomo Carboni, Wolfgang Lemke, Roberto Motto, Arthur Saint Guilhem, and Jonathan Yiangou, Oxford University Press (2021).
© Massimo Rostagno, Carlo Altavilla, Giacomo Carboni, Wolfgang Lemke, Roberto Motto, Arthur Saint Guilhem, and Jonathan Yiangou.
DOI: 10.1093/oso/9780192895912.003.0002

institutional missions. These debates and the frameworks that they produced have always reflected the economics profession's evolving understanding of monetary economics—the *reference model* of the day—and, obviously, recognition that earlier frameworks had failed. At the start of monetary union, the profession had reached an exceptionally deep and shared conviction that a monetary policy framework would not be sufficiently robust to cope with the wear and tear of time and history, or successful in contributing to social welfare, unless it encapsulated a few key principles. These principles can be cast as follows.

1.1.1 Independence, Delegation, Accountability

The first principle can be expressed in three words: *independence, delegation, accountability*.[2] By the start of the 1990s it had become widely accepted that it was preferable to outsource monetary policy to a de-politicized agency rather than keep it within the influence of short-term political considerations and directions. See Box 1.1 for a partial survey of the arguments in favour of central bank independence.

Delegation to a central bank run by professional economists is one way of ensuring that the monopoly power to create money is not abused to the point where the socially attractive functions of money as a reliable metric and store of value are degraded or lost entirely. It also corresponds to the basic fact that one needs specialized competencies in this highly technical domain. To name just a few of these competencies, a central bank has to have the capacity and authority to interpret economic data, amalgamate them into a general diagnosis of the state of the business cycle, project the most likely path for the economy in the future, detect and quantify risks that the economy might derail in unfavourable directions, and apply appropriate instruments to ward off such risks. A central bank should therefore be made statutorily *instrument independent* of the administration and the Treasury.[3] Instrument independence implies that a central bank should be free to decide the appropriate settings of its policy instruments, and thus discharged from any obligation to finance government budget deficits, directly or indirectly.

But an independent agency cannot be irresponsible. Delegation of trust cannot be unconstrained. The very notion of a 'derailing economy' which central bank experts should seek to prevent and correct by appropriate settings of monetary policy instruments can only be defined in respect to trajectories that are considered socially desirable. The unelected agency should therefore receive an explicit institutional mission—a set of goals or *objectives*—from elected legislatures which make the collective preferences regarding the direction of the economy explicit. Combining

---

[2] See Tucker (2018) for a detailed account of these principles.
[3] Further dimensions include institutional, personal, and financial independence. Debelle and Fischer (1994) propose a distinction between 'instrument independence' (the central bank's authority to choose the instrument most appropriate and efficacious to achieve a given goal) and 'goal independence' (the central bank being able to set or quantify its policy goal(s)).

Box 1.1 Central bank independence

The modern case for central bank independence begins from the 'inflationary bias' that would otherwise be present in monetary policy if the central banks were not protected from short-term political influences. The time inconsistency hypothesis is at the root of such bias: governments with a high rate of time discount, particularly as elections approach, and a natural concern about unemployment, are likely to have a tendency to surprise the economy with bouts of easing measures in an attempt to lift activity above what structural factors may sustain in the longer haul. Politically subservient central banks will thus be pushed to pursue systematically easier monetary policies than would be commensurate with low and stable inflation. But, with an expectational Phillips curve model of output determination—which, as expectations catch on with past surprises, becomes vertical in the long run—the only result of their repeated efforts to stimulate the economy by surprise is that inflation will be higher on average. Following the seminal contributions of Kydland and Prescott (1977) and Barro and Gordon (1983), which formalized this logic, the 'inflation bias' was the subject of a vast literature that flourished in the 1980s and 1990s and added precision to the analytic argument for central bank independence. Rogoff (1985), in a classic article, shows that appointing a central banker who is more conservative than society improves the credibility-flexibility trade-off. Persson and Tabellini (1993) and Walsh (1995) suggest that the inflationary bias can be eliminated by designing contracts through which the government makes the central banker's salary contingent on the inflation outcomes. And, closer to the subject of this section, Svensson (1997) argues in favour of giving the central bank a formal inflation target as a means to achieve an optimal contract. Summarizing roughly 25 years of research, Cukierman (2008) observes that 'the evidence is consistent with the conclusion that inflation and actual [independence] are negatively related in both developed and developing countries'.

However, as inflation was conquered in the second half of the 1990s, the 'inflation bias' motivation for central bank independence drew increasing criticism, for example in McCallum (1995), Blinder (1998), Vickers (1998), and Posen (1993, 1995). First, it was argued that in practice central bankers do not attempt to target a level of output exceeding the natural rate, so there is no inflation bias to start with. Second, as in Posen (1993, 1995), the observed relationship between inflation and central bank independence might not reflect a causal link, but simply the fact that varying preferences for low inflation may inspire different legislations to promote these preferences. Eggertsson and Le Borgne (2010) develop an alternative theory of delegation based on the complexity of the monetary policy task ('more art than science!' in their words) and the higher rents that politicians can extract from the fiscal policy lever relative to the rents that can be generated by monetary policy. The

(Continued)

Box 1.1 Continued

paper models the decision to delegate as a balance between the costs (inability to remove incompetent central bank officeholders via the electoral process) and the benefits (the independent central banker can focus on a longer time horizon). Tucker (2018) has recently articulated a purely constitutional rationale for central bank independence as follows: 'Under fiat money, independence for the monetary authority is a corollary of the higher-level separation of powers between the fiscal authority of the legislature and the elected executive government: if the elected executive were to control the monetary levers, it would have the power to tax (through unexpected bursts of inflation). Central bank independence is therefore grounded in the values of constitutional government.'

The relevance of central banks' independence and the means to safeguard it have continued to be a subject of academic and policy discussion up to the present day. In fact, the role of central banks during and after the financial crisis appears to have revived the debate. On the one hand, a central bank may not have been able to resort to the unprecedented tools employed to address the new challenges without its independence in achieving its objective, see Fischer (2015) and Draghi (2018c). On the other hand, the recourse to extraordinary measures may have increased the 'risks to its reputation, perceived legitimacy and independence', see Caruana (2013). Moreover, given central banks' increased involvement and institutional role in safeguarding financial stability, 'there is a possibility that the blurring of independence in the field of financial stability may also raise questions for central banks' independence more broadly', see Goodhart and Lastra (2018a). However, in a recent survey of both central bank decision-makers and academic economists, Blinder et al. (2017) report that central bankers and academics were not overly concerned about threats to central bank independence. Specifically, about 90% of governors and 80% of academics replied that central bank independence was not or only slightly affected due to the crisis. In a similar vein, indices of legal central bank independence have remained broadly stable in a pre- vs post-crisis level comparison. Looking forward, about one-third of academics saw some threat to central bank independence in the future while very few (below 10%) central bankers showed such signs of worry.

delegation and independence conforms to the basic economic dictum that principals (in this case, parliaments and the public) are better off monitoring their agents' (central banks') outputs rather than their inputs (the specific settings of policy instruments).[4] Indeed, the monitoring of outcomes completes the logic of the first principle, and calls for the central bank to be held accountable to the people's

---

[4] See, e.g., Fratianni, von Hagen and Waller (1997) for a representation of central banking as a political principal agent problem.

representatives. Accountability, in turn, presupposes transparency about the hierarchy of the central bank's institutional goals. Only when armed with such transparency, can the public judge whether the central bank is successfully delivering on its mandate. The costs of opacity can be high: disorientation about the ultimate goals of monetary policy can lead to a less predictable and efficient transmission of policy actions and as a consequence to poor macroeconomic performance. In summary, a clear hierarchy of objectives enhances the potency and legitimacy of monetary policy. This is true in all circumstances, but especially in the face of significant economic disturbances. In general, times of economic uncertainty put a premium on the clarity and predictability of central banks' objectives and policies.

1.1.2 Prominence of Price Stability

The second principle prescribes that *price stability, possibly expressed in measurable terms, be assigned a prominent status* in the specification of the central bank's statutory mission. Why such a prominent role for price stability? Four considerations are salient here.[5] Controllability is one: a central bank has reasonably tight control over medium-term inflation because, as the sole provider of cash in the economy, it can determine the scale on which the money value of all goods and services is measured. As the scale of money values—the economic system's *numeraire*—is embedded in the cash issued by the central bank, and varies over time depending on the amount of cash issued, it is entirely natural that inflation—the drift in the *numeraire*—should be considered the province of central banks. The costs of inflation offer another perspective from which to look at central banks' inflation-stabilization mission. High inflation is very costly for society. It is a regressive tax that falls disproportionately on people who have limited availability of substitutes to cash when deciding in which form to set aside their savings. More often than not, these people belong to underprivileged groups, so high inflation—eating away at the purchasing power of cash or cash-like instruments such as overnight bank deposits—aggravates economic disparities.[6] This probably explains why inflation is so unpopular with the public. A further reason for giving price stability privileged status in a central bank's founding charter is that in the medium to long run, stable inflation and sustained growth are not substitutes but they are complements. In other words, there is no long-run trade-off between the level of inflation and the level of real income. In fact, high and variable inflation go together.[7] And an inflation rate that is variable and unpredictable not only complicates long-term economic planning but also creates

---

[5] These issues were discussed in detail at the First ECB Central Banking Conference in November 2000 entitled 'Why Price Stability?'. See García Herrero et al. (2001).

[6] See, e.g., Albanesi (2007) who discusses the vulnerability of low-income households to inflation and provides cross-country evidence of a positive relation between inflation and income equality.

[7] See Ball (1992) as a seminal reference rationalizing the positive relation between high inflation and high inflation uncertainty via the public's uncertainty about the central bank's reaction to high inflation, and more recently Dmitriev and Kersting (2016) invoking a seigniorage argument.

incentives for households and firms to spend resources on managing inflation risk rather than focusing on the most productive activities. By contrast, stable prices allow people to rely on money as a measure of value when concluding long-term contracts, engaging in long-term planning, or borrowing and lending for long periods. This all favours investment in productive capital, which typically has long gestation times and is the primary source of long-term growth. The clarity afforded by a numerical objective of price stability keeps longer-term inflation expectations firmly anchored and enables accountability.[8] An accessible and transparent norm for price stability means the public can plan and act accordingly, and the job of the central bank is made easier because economic and financial uncertainty is reduced. Finally, a numerical objective is *monitorable*. If it is time-bound, the goal is also *enforceable*, meaning that a horizon for delivery makes it possible to fault the central bank if it does not deliver. If the price stability goal is superimposed hierarchically upon other lower-ranked objectives, i.e. if the central bank's priorities are ordered lexicographically with price stability on top, the goal becomes highly *verifiable*, in the sense that it deprives the agency leadership of the ability to assert success on the basis of whatever objective variable happens to be closer to target.

1.1.3 A Strategy

Third, an articulation of goals is not sufficient. The discipline and clarity of a mandate provide too tenuous an anchor for the economy, unless they are embedded in a *broader strategy* describing how the central bank intends to go about enforcing its mandated objective(s), including its approach for disclosing judgements about the economic outlook and resulting monetary policy stance to the public. There are two reasons for this. First, shocks hit the economy all the time. If left unattended, they have the potential to push the economy onto trajectories that are inconsistent with the goal(s) assigned to the central bank. A strategy embodies the high-level operating modalities which the central bank commits to follow in order to offset the destabilizing shocks and bring the economy back to the desired path. Knowledge of the strategy and in particular of the resolve with which the central bank is prepared to defend and enforce its objective in the face of adverse shocks is as important as the objective itself in anchoring the public's expectations. In addition, shocks may present central banks with complicated alternatives in the day-to-day conduct of policy. While there is no such thing as a long-run trade-off between inflation and growth or unemployment—in fact, as argued before, there may even be a *trade-in* in the long run—shocks occasionally drive inflation and real growth or unemployment in opposite directions. At these cross-roads, for example when the economy is hit by a commodity price shock that raises consumer price inflation but depresses aggregate

---

[8] See, e.g., Gürkaynak, Levin and Swanson (2010) providing empirical evidence (based on US, UK, and Swedish monetary policy) for that point.

demand, the central bank has to make tough choices. Countering the burst in inflation may mean deepening the economic slump. If the central bank has received a
plurality of objectives such as price stability and maximum sustainable employment,
each with equal weighting, the strategy has to instruct the central bank on how to
balance these against each other precisely at those times when they might demand
conflicting monetary policy actions. If the central bank has received a primary
objective such as price stability, with priority over any further normative consideration, the strategy should aid the central bank in calibrating the *horizon* over which
it wants to attain it.[9] Generally, it is never desirable to compromise too much on any
single objective, even when this is subordinated in the hierarchy of the central bank's
statutory priorities. As explained below, the speed with which inflation is brought
back to target will have to vary depending on the state of the real economy.
Accordingly, the vigour of the policy response to a shock that drives inflation away
from target needs to be tailored optimally to the source of the shock that causes the
deviation.[10]

1.2 The Model of Reference

All of these principles are hard-coded in the model that, by the second half of the
1990s, had emerged to prominence—and, by the eve of the financial crisis, to
dominance—as the macroeconomic paradigm of choice: the NKM. Each of them
has a stylized counterpart in the model.[11] The principle of delegation and central

---

[9] See, e.g., Fahr et al. (2013) and the references given therein.
[10] The notion that no long-run trade-off exists between inflation and output—the concept of a vertical
long-run Phillips curve—was first suggested at the end of the 1960s by Milton Friedman and Edmund
Phelps, and their insights were gradually accepted by most economists over the following 20 years. By the
early 1990s, as a new generation of monetary models was being tested and used for policy analysis, the
question was: is there any such short-term trade-off that may be reliably exploited by monetary policy? If
not, then monetary policy should focus exclusively on inflation (or the price level) and ignore the consequences, if any, for the real economy. John Taylor (1994)—using a new-generation macroeconomic model
in which output depends on real interest rates, inflation responds to deviations of GDP from potential,
and monetary policy sets the short-term nominal interest rate in response to deviations of inflation from
target and deviations of output from potential—argued against such an exclusive focus on inflation on the
grounds that there is indeed an inflation/output *variability* trade-off in the short run. As the economy is
hit by shocks that have opposite implications for prices and output, keeping the inflation rate extremely
stable about a target in the face of such shocks may entail accepting much greater fluctuations of GDP
about potential (or unemployment about the natural rate), even in the long run. If so, monetary policy
may wish to balance its effects on inflation and output variability: price stability should not be pursued to
the exclusion of aggregate demand management. Taylor (1994) shows that an appropriate calibration of
Taylor's preferred monetary policy rule, one with an approximately balanced response to inflation and
output deviations, would yield roughly equal variance of inflation and output. We will return to the infla-
tion/output variability frontier in Chapter 3.
[11] See Clarida, Gali and Gertler (1999) as well as Woodford (2003) and Walsh (2017) for textbook treat-
ments. Christiano, Motto and Rostagno (2003) and Smets and Wouters (2003, 2007) have greatly expanded
the model and demonstrated its empirical properties. The bare-bone version of NKM combines the techniques of dynamic general equilibrium theory pioneered in real business cycle analysis with nominal frictions and a monetary policy rule. The real business cycle component of NKM is evident in that private sector
behaviour depends on the expected future course of the economy. Temporary nominal price rigidities provide the key friction (hence, the 'Keynesian' denomination) that gives rise to non-neutral effects of monetary

bank autonomy in policy management is implicit in the fact that in NKM the agent responsible for monetary policy is described as a self-standing and in fact *the single* macroeconomic policy authority presiding over demand management. That entity's numerical target for inflation is what—under certain conditions—pins down inflation in steady state in the model. Furthermore, positive (or negative) inflation distorts consumption. So, in keeping with the thought process supporting the second principle, inflation acts as a wasteful tax and its suppression should therefore figure prominently among the central bank's tasks.[12] Finally, a 'policy rule' linking the short-term interest rate instrument of monetary policy to deviations of inflation from target and of aggregate income from its trend is the model's compact representation of the central bank's strategy. Some specification of the Taylor rule is often used for this purpose, and consistent with the third principle its calibration is such that the response of the nominal short-term interest rate to inflation innovations is always larger than one-for-one, so that the *real* rate always increases if inflation or inflation expectations rise. Incidentally, the restriction that the policy rate responds to inflation by more than one-for-one is called the Taylor principle (Taylor, 1993 and 1999) and is a fundamental stability requirement of the model.[13] But the policy rule leans against output fluctuations too, and the model environment also offers a compelling rationale for this aspect of optimal monetary policy. Risk-averse consumers prefer smooth consumption paths. Reducing the amplitude of output fluctuations around its natural rate is therefore a way for the central bank to achieve consumption smoothness over time. This is welfare-enhancing in the model.[14] In the long

---

policy and therefore makes the framework particularly attractive for evaluating monetary policy. Clarida et al. (1999) describe the difference between NKM and the traditional IS/LM model as follows: 'Within the model, monetary policy affects the real economy in the short run, much as in the traditional Keynesian IS/LM framework. A key difference, however, is that the aggregate behavioural equations evolve explicitly from optimization by households and firms. One important implication is that current economic behaviour depends critically on expectations of the future course of monetary policy, as well as on current policy.'

[12] In NKM, prices are 'sticky', as they can only be adjusted at discrete random intervals, see Calvo (1983), or firms face a convex cost function of price adjustment, see Rotemberg (1982). As a consequence, at each point in time the consumption bundle is made up of goods whose price has just been updated to reflect current marginal cost conditions, and goods whose price has remained at a sub-optimal (constant) level for possibly a long while. Therefore, non-zero inflation—making some goods cheaper or more expensive than others just because of the price-setting inertia embedded in the sticky-price mechanism—causes consumption patterns to deviate from the allocations of income to the various goods included in the bundle that consumers would otherwise have chosen. Because goods consumption is distorted, so is production: a discrepancy between actual prices and the prices that reflect cost minimization leads to a discrepancy between output and its 'natural level'. In summary, in NKM inflation is a distortive tax, although the 'tax base' in the model is not cash—the model is cashless—but rather manifests itself in sub-optimal consumption and production patterns.

[13] If the policy interest rate responds to increases in inflation by less than one-for-one (so that the real policy rate does not rise in the face of higher inflation), inflation expectations and the economy become unstable in NKM. The problem arises from the fact that, if policymakers do not react sufficiently aggressively to increases in inflation, spontaneous upsurges of inflation expectations can ultimately be self-reinforcing: they lead to a widening output gap on impact, which in turn creates more inflation that the central bank accommodates, which again feeds back on the economy, feeding the boom and so on.

[14] The NKM allows one to meaningfully discuss and formally treat welfare considerations, as it is centred around a representative utility maximizing agent. The common quadratic objective function of monetary policy that penalizes deviations of inflation from target and deviations of the output gap from zero can be derived by deploying a second order approximation of the welfare function, see Woodford (2003).

run, if there are shocks hitting the supply side of the economy, the volatility of infla-tion can be reduced only by allowing greater volatility in output growth, and vice versa. Again, in support of the third principle, if monetary policies are chosen opti-mally, then neither side of that long-run volatility trade-off should be totally suppressed.

Dynamically, it is the tight combination of the central bank's numerical inflation target and the 'policy rule' that keeps the NKM economy on an even keel in the face of stochastic disturbances. But this conclusion requires quite a few further assump-tions or modelling choices. We list three of them here, because they are not unim-portant for understanding the foundations of the consensus—both on the workings of the macroeconomy and on the monetary policy strategies that can stabilize it—that had formed at the inception of monetary union.

The first critical assumption is that shocks are bounded and stationary processes. They can temporarily drive the model away—not too far—from its steady state, or rather its balanced growth path.[15] But they fade over time, and so does their impact on the economy. Hence, while the model is non-linear and in fact may admit more than one steady state (see Box 1.2), the modeller can conveniently 'linearize' the equations describing the economy around that steady state which reflects the object-ives of the central bank—with inflation at target and output at its trend level—on the safe working hypothesis that only the vicinity of this steady state will ever be explored. The 'mild shocks' hypothesis means that no exogenous disturbance is powerful enough to jolt the economy from the neighbourhood of the 'virtuous' steady state, around which it tends to circle, to any other, less familiar place. So, the dynamics of the system around the stationary values of the state variables that repre-sent an equilibrium in the absence of disturbances give a good approximation of all of the system's possible paths.

The second modelling choice relates to observability. While not directly observ-able, at each point in time the *state* of the model economy can be inferred rather precisely from two observable quantities: inflation and output. In fact, in many cases inflation alone is a sufficient statistic for the state. What is the state? In a dynamic system, the *state* is made up of a set of underlying variables that evolve over time in response to exogenous disturbances and, through their motion, determine the jour-ney of the system as a whole. In NKM, the state includes productivity and preference factors as a minimum. There is an important aside to note here: in the canonical form of NKM the state does not include financial variables, such as determinants of risk taking and drivers of optimism or pessimism in portfolio allocation. Even in expanded variants of NKM, where observables do include productive capital and its price, credit and even money, the financial block of the state is typically an amplifier rather than a source of volatility.[16] And even when the financial block of the expanded NKM model becomes a non-trivial source of volatility, the shocks that originate there share the same boundedness and mean-reversion properties as all other shocks. They may be persistent, but they are not explosive. Furthermore, even when the model is augmented with a financial sector, two observables—inflation and output—can still stand in to a reasonably accurate degree for the prevailing state, and the details of the structure of the financial system are not quite necessary for the purposes of controlling the system and steering it in the desired direction.

The third, and fundamental, assumption underpinning the NKM structure does indeed relate to the system's controls. Borrowing from control theory jargon, one can say that a NKM economy is *completely controllable* by one single instrument: the short-term interest rate manoeuvred by the central bank.[17] This means that monetary policy can always transfer the system from any initial state x to any desired final state y in finite time, *all by itself.* The short-term interest rate instrument that controls the economy is certainly not unconstrained: it occasionally hits a lower bound at which its room for manoeuvre is truncated on the downside. At that point, if the economy demands further stimulus—i.e. a lower interest rate—because inflation is below target and output below trend, the lower bound can indeed blunt the capacity of monetary policy to achieve its goals. In NKM, however, what matters for output and, indirectly, inflation is not a single rate action but the whole expected future stream of interest rate actions: in other words a direct outcome of the strategy, i.e. the central bank's (well-understood) state-contingent plan to set rates at current and future times. Once the interest rate is stuck at zero and cannot be reduced, the central bank can resort to managing expectations about the future rate policy by committing to a strategy.[18] In practice, at the lower bound the central bank should pledge to maintain the short-term interest rate at that level for an extended future period that stretches well beyond the time when the negative shocks currently depressing the economy will have ebbed away and the economy will have resumed its upcycle back towards the steady state. A promise that the zero-rate policy will endure well into the future economic recovery—in other words a promise to be more supportive than needed in the future—will lift today's income expectations and boost present spending. Ultimately, the interest rate path—actual or expected—is the key control of NKM dynamics.

1.3   The Policy Framework of Reference

NKM—combining rigorous micro-foundations, a superb (if parsimonious) architecture, and surprisingly good empirical properties—has exerted, and continues to exert, a great deal of appeal over researchers and practitioners alike. But how did its

---

[17] See Anderson and Moore (1979) as a classic control theory reference and Hansen and Sargent (2013) for the application of this principle to economic models.

[18] See, e.g., Williams (2014), Mertens and Williams (2019), and the references given therein discussing strategies for monetary policy confronted with an occasionally binding lower-bound constraint.

ascent to intellectual dominance influence the debate over monetary policy regimes at the turn of the century? Here, a certain—at least superficial—affinity between the Taylor-style policy rule embodied in the model and the 'flexible inflation targeting' regime springs to mind. While flexible IT was codified and indeed applied when NKM was still in its infancy, it is legitimate to say that the model and the policy framework have developed an intimate symbiosis through the years.[19]

The give-and-take between the model and the real-world IT framework has gone in both directions. Essentially, real-world IT offered the new-born NKM one fundamental insight: to be effective in delivering on its mandate, a central bank does *not* need an 'operational' or 'intermediate' target—such as, a target value for the growth rate of a monetary aggregate, or an exchange rate peg—distinct from its *ultimate* objective. If the ultimate objective is minimizing and stabilizing inflation and inflation expectations, then that precise objective should be elevated to operational target in the framework. As had become the norm in at least three advanced economies that adopted IT arrangements in the course of the 1990s, to make the identification between the 'operational' and 'ultimate' objectives practical and actionable, the central bank could be assigned to keeping *forecast* inflation around a certain numerical value over the projection period.[20] Indeed, by the end of the 1990s, when King and Wolman (1996), Kimball (1995), Yun (1996), Goodfriend and King (1997) and many others laid down the main building blocks of NKM, and Woodford (1996) and Clarida et al. (1999) assembled the various parts, with the latter also coining its name, IT was for all practical purposes already widely interpreted as 'flexible inflation forecast targeting' (Svensson, 1997).

In exchange, NKM supplied central bankers and law-makers—who in those years were revisiting the charters of central banks around the world—with a general conceptual framework through which they could look at the economy. We have summarized the main elements of such a conceptual framework above. Implicitly, the framework entailed a very optimistic message for monetary reformers. The message,

---

[19] For an overview of the history and track record of inflation targeting, see Adrian, Laxton and Obstfeld (2018). The affinity between a Taylor-rule based policy framework and flexible IT is only superficial. In fact, a Taylor rule is not optimal under flexible IT in any realistic model of the economy. Even the type of strict IT operated in the simple model studied in Svensson (1997) would prescribe that the central bank responds to inflation, output *and* other exogenous variables to the extent that these affect inflation. In general, optimal policy requires the response to all the determinants of the forecasts of the target variables, not just a response to the target variables. More generally, the concept and basic articulation of flexible IT pre-dated NKM and in fact was proved to be an attractive framework for conducting monetary policy in backward-looking models that resemble NKM only for their shared emphasis on real variables. The case for 'inflation forecast targeting' resides in selecting a policy rate and policy-rate path that deliver targeting variables which are sufficiently close to the policymakers' desiderata, and this approach does not presuppose backward- or forward-looking models with model-consistent expectations or otherwise, to be operated. See Svensson (1999) for an exhaustive discussion of alternative monetary policy frameworks in a backward-looking model.

[20] New Zealand, with the Reserve Bank of New Zealand Act of 1989, was the first country in recent times to adopt an inflation-targeting 'contract', becoming an international norm-setter for the design of modern monetary institutions. According to this 'principal-agent contract', the Governor of the Reserve Bank agreed on a target inflation path with the government, with his job on the line if he failed to achieve the targets. Other countries followed the example in the early 1990s, with Canada and the United Kingdom spelling out clearly defined inflation contracts with the central bank.

despite the 'K' part of the NKM acronym, was uncompromisingly *monetarist*. It can be summarized in three points:

- For a central bank, earning a reputation as a guardian of price stability is of paramount importance. Typically, building reputation requires an extended period of trials and learning. In monetary affairs, however, commitment to a policy rule or adoption of a binding institutional arrangement can quicken the credibility-earning cycle.
- An optimal institutional arrangement embeds IT, and IT encapsulates the essence of optimal policy. Optimal policy posits that a central bank should adjust the nominal rate sufficiently to offset any movement in future inflation. As for output disturbances, the central bank should offset demand shocks but accommodate supply shocks. Adherence to the IT prescriptions makes the transmission channel more efficient: it improves the output/inflation volatility trade-off, as it reduces the effective cost in terms of output loss that is required to lower inflation.
- Insofar as IT is in place, the possibility of abnormally large tail risks leading to radical disequilibrium is minimal. Price and macroeconomic stability are ensured regardless of the course of fiscal policy, or structural policy, or financial regulation. Monetary policy can *'just do it'* alone.[21]

The last point is of central importance for what we will argue below, and needs qualification. On the face of it, the point says that a monetary policy rule incorporating IT is sufficient to safeguard stability and does not need to be augmented by any further policy responses—by the central bank itself or by another policy authority—that can be mobilized to assist in anchoring the economy when exogenous disturbances threaten to precipitate it onto an off-equilibrium trajectory. In fact, as we show in Box 1.2, things are more complicated. NKM builds its monetarist stability proposition on the assumption that two pre-conditions are met. One is that there is, in the background of NKM, a *passive* fiscal authority which is always committed to adjusting the future stream of taxes and expenditures as needed to maintain the public debt on a sustainable path. If this precondition is met, and the effects of any shock to the price level or to the central bank's interest rate on the level of public debt are always neutralized ex post by an offsetting fiscal decision that keeps the debt stable in expectation, then an IT central bank becomes the sole authority responsible for macroeconomic stability. Indeed, in this case, monetary policy *can do it* alone: *monetary dominance* is guaranteed. However, if that condition cannot be counted on to apply in all conceivable states of the world, then exogenous variations in the government's budget deficits can easily become a source of disturbances to the rate of inflation and to real activity. In extreme conditions, when fiscal decisions become entirely

---

[21] See McCallum (1995 and 1997).

unresponsive to the evolution of public debt, the institutional configuration turns into outright *fiscal dominance*.[22] Besides manifestly violating the first principle of healthy monetary governance in mature democratic societies—'independence, delegation, accountability'—history loudly demonstrates that such an arrangement fails to deliver price stability most of the time.[23] In any event, although not so visible in the model, the fiscal foundations of IT are critical for proving its value in NKM. Only fiscal institutions that force debt sustainability restrictions on day-to-day tax and spending decisions can eliminate non-monetary sources of macroeconomic instability and truly make inflation—as in the popularized NKM doctrine—'always and everywhere a monetary phenomenon' (Friedman, 1970).

The second precondition on which the NKM monetarist proposition is founded rules out the possibility of insufficiently anchored inflation expectations becoming an autonomous source of radical instability. But 'inflation scares' or 'deflation scares' are a possibility in NKM. These are types of vortex that can develop in the expectations formation mechanism in the model and destroy its equilibrium stability. Deflation scares are especially troubling. As we noted *in passim* above, and show analytically in Box 1.2, the model admits at least two steady states. One has positive inflation close to the central bank's target and the interest rate positive at the value dictated by the Taylor rule. This 'virtuous' equilibrium is the steady state of choice for analysts for a number of reasons. First, because—under the 'nominal anchor' of a Taylor rule that feeds back aggressively enough on inflation—it fulfils the desired state of affairs, where, on average, inflation is at the central bank's intended target and output is at potential. Second, because, by adopting a particular model selection hypothesis around it, one can make inflation and macroeconomic dynamics determinate, in other words unique. And, finally, because those economic dynamics are

---

[22] In synthesis, *monetary dominance* assumes that the valuation equation for government debt (the no-Ponzi-game condition in Box 2.2), which states that the real value of nominal debt equals the present value of real primary surpluses, holds by ex post lump-sum taxation. Any shock—such as to the interest rate that is used for the discounting of the real primary surpluses in that equation—that may upset that equality ex post is offset by an adjustment to the stream of surpluses just sufficient to reinstate the equality. Therefore, the debt sustainability equation plays no role in price level determination which is entirely devolved to the central bank. *Fiscal dominance* makes the opposite assumption: the stream of the government primary deficits is not adjusted ex post by lump sum taxation to compensate for shocks. Consequently, the price level has to jump in order for the unchanged stream of future nominal primary surpluses to equal the nominal value of current debt, which is pre-determined. So, assuming the central bank behaves passively, it is fiscal policy that is in control of inflation. This is the essence of the so-called fiscal theory of the price level. See Cochrane (2019) for a recent overview of that literature.

[23] The 'most of the time' qualification essentially refers to the fact that in NKM it is possible to define fiscal dominance regimes—where the government has full discretion on the deficit and the central bank, for its part, commits to an *interest rate peg*, i.e. it makes the settings of the policy rate unreactive to economic conditions—in which inflation does remain low and stable. Leeper (1991), Woodford (2003) and Sims (2016) describe this theoretical case. Historically, however, episodes in which a passive central bank is confronted by a dominant, but prudent government which takes the task of stabilizing inflation upon itself by adjusting its deficit plans appropriately are extremely rare. Much more frequently, the active fiscal authority/passive central bank combination ends in tears (hyperinflation). There is more on this in Box 2.2.

Box 1.2 The fragility of economic equilibria in NKM

Here we draw on Christiano and Rostagno (2001, henceforth CR) to sketch a stripped-down version of the flexible-price optimising model that lies at the core of NKM. We use yet another variety of the range of cash-in-advance environments explored in CR, one which displays global equilibrium properties that are similar to those of more canonical specifications of NKM. Studying the global behaviour of this model, we document three key results that are expounded in more colloquial terms in the text. First, if the central bank operates an inflation targeting-style Taylor rule which responds aggressively to inflation, the model admits two stationary equilibria: one in which inflation is at the central bank's target and the Taylor rule is active, and one with perennial deflation, with the policy interest rate stuck at its lower bound, and the Taylor rule deactivated. Second, perturbations of sufficient magnitude can easily set the economy off on trajectories that push it farther and farther away from the desired stationary equilibrium. Non-fundamental shocks to inflation expectations—self-fulfilling 'inflation scares' or 'deflation scares'—can be a source of such perturbations. If they develop for any reason, the economy can leave the desired stationary equilibrium and spiral off to hyper-inflation or deflation. Disinflation paths are particularly worrisome, because permanent deflation is an absorbing state in NKM. Third, and most importantly, the fiscal regime is fundamental for selecting equilibrium outcomes. The economy cannot durably settle around the 'virtuous' equilibrium, even with a central bank devoted to a particularly aggressive inflation stabilisation strategy, unless the fiscal authority cooperates. In normal times, when the economy gravitates around the 'virtuous' equilibrium, stability can only be maintained if the fiscal authority delegates first-mover status to the central bank and commits to fiscal plans that always stabilise total debt ex post, whatever the level and path of the interest rate decided by the central bank. In abnormal times, when the economy—for whatever reason—is already drifting away from the desired equilibrium, the role of fiscal policy becomes even more essential. We defer to Box 2.2 for a study of constructive strategies for exiting deflation.

We adopt a Lucas-Stokey (1983, 1987) variant of the cash-goods credit-goods model environment explored in CR, in which the economy is populated by a continuum of identical households, a central bank and a fiscal authority. Households have a log utility over goods consumption:

$$E_0 \left\{ \sum_{t=0}^{\infty} \beta^t \left[\log c_{1t} + \log c_{2t} - \left(y_{1t} + y_{2t} \right) \right] \right\} \tag{B.1.2.1}$$

In (B.1.2.1), c_{1t} is consumption of cash goods, c_{2t} is consumption of credit goods, and y_{1t} and y_{2t} denote output of cash and credit goods, respectively β is a discount factor. Cash goods can only be purchased using currency. Households convene in the morning of each day t in the asset trading market where they allocate their financial assets, carried over from the previous period *t-1* between currency and interest-bearing one-period bonds:

$$A_t \geq M_t + \frac{B_{t+1}}{1+R_t}.$$
(B.1.2.2)

In (B.1.2.2), M_t is the amount of cash at hand available for transactions at time t, B_{t+1} is the nominal value of one-period bonds payable at time *t+1*, and R_t is the one-period nominal interest rate. In the morning all information is revealed. Currency holdings are costly (as they imply foregoing interest) but are the only means of payment satisfying the cash-in-advance constraints for cash goods:

$$P_t c_{1t} \leq M_t,$$
(B.1.2.3)

where P_t denotes the price of goods (cash or credit). Note that since all information is revealed at the start of the period (before asset trading starts), households set aside exactly enough currency to finance their anticipated cash goods purchases. After the asset market closes, the household enters the goods market. As in Lucas-Stokey, we can imagine that the household consists of a worker-shopper pair. During the goods market, the pair splits, with the shopper making purchases of cash goods and credit goods, and the worker producing y_1 and y_2 and selling output. The cash and IOUs accumulated by the worker cannot be spent on consumption goods or assets within the period but have to be carried over to the asset trading part of the following period when they are finally cleared. After the goods market closes at the end of day t, the household reconvenes and consumes. In summary, the household's wealth evolves as follows:

$$A_t = M_{t-1} + B_t + P_{t-1}y_{1t-1} + P_{t-1}y_{2t-1} - P_{t-1}c_{1t-1} - P_{t-1}c_{2t-1} - P_{t-1}\tau_{t-1} \geq M_t + \frac{B_{t+1}}{1+R_t}$$
(B.1.2.4)

where τ_{t-1} denotes net taxes paid during the goods trading phase of the previous period. The aggregate resource constraint is equal to:

$$c_{1t} + c_{2t} + \bar{g} = y_{1t} + y_{2t} = \bar{Y},$$
(B.1.2.5)

where $\bar{g} \geq 0$ denotes a constant flow of government spending, and $\bar{Y}$ is a constant endowment which at the end of the trading day needs to be allocated to the household for consumption.

Throughout, we have imposed the condition that the stochastic discount factor for pricing arbitrary non-monetary financial claims $Q_{t,t+1}$ must equal the nominal interest rate on one-period riskless bonds:

$$\frac{1}{1+R_t} = E_t\left[Q_{t,t+1}\right]$$
(B.1.2.6)

(*Continued*)

Box 1.2 Continued

We also place restrictions on the prices faced by the household:

$$P_t > 0 \text{ and } R_t \geq 0 \tag{B.1.2.6a}$$

And on the expected stream of income, present and future:

$$E_t \sum_{j=0}^{\infty} \left[\left(\frac{1}{1+R_{t+j}} \right)^j \left(P_{t+j} \left(y_{1t+j} + y_{2t+j} - \tau_{t+j} \right) \right) \right] < \infty, \ \forall t \tag{B.1.2.7}$$

If these restrictions did not hold, the household's consumption opportunity set would be unbounded, which (given non-satiation in preferences (B.1.2.1)) would give rise to infinite consumption demand. This would be incompatible with equilibrium in an economy with bounded resources. Condition (B.1.2.7) can be equivalently expressed in the form of a transversality condition:

$$\lim_{T \to \infty} E_t Q_{t,T} A_T = \lim_{T \to \infty} E_t \prod_{j=0}^{T-1} \left(\frac{1}{1+R_{t+j}} \right) A_T = 0 \tag{B.1.2.8}$$

Optimization requires that households maximize (B.1.2.1) subject to (B.1.2.2), (B.1.2.3), (B.1.2.4) and (B.1.2.5) by selecting a sequence made of $\{M_t, B_{t+1}, c_{1t}, c_{2t}, y_{1t}, y_{2t}; t \geq 0\}$, taking $\{A_t, R_t, P_t, \tau_t; t \geq 0\}$ as given. This problem has a solution if and only if (B.1.2.8) holds. The necessary and sufficient conditions for optimization imply that $c_{2t} = 1$ at all times which, combined with (B.1.2.5), implies that c_{1t} is also a constant, $c_{1t} = \bar{Y} - 1 - \bar{g}$ (B.1.2.11). Intertemporal optimality requires that:

$$E_t \left[\frac{c_{1t+1}}{c_{1t}} \right] = E_t \left[\frac{\beta(1+R_t)}{\pi_{t+1}} \right],$$

which, with c_{1t} constant, gives a simple Fisher equation of the following form:

$$E_t \pi_{t+1} = \beta(1+R_t) \tag{B.1.2.9}$$

The Central Bank

We assume monetary policy is governed by a non-linear Taylor rule of the type:

$$R_t = \max \left[0, \tilde{R} + \alpha(\pi_t - \tilde{\pi}) + \frac{\chi_t}{\beta} \right], \tag{B.1.2.10}$$

where χ_t is the monetary policy disturbance term. Substituting (B.1.2.10) into (B.1.2.9), we obtain a difference equation describing the equilibrium evolution of inflation in this economy. As the interest rate process governed by the Taylor rule is truncated at $R_t = 0$, the inflation process is bounded from below as the nominal interest rate reaches its zero lower bound:

$$E_t \pi_{t+1} = \beta(1+\tilde{R}) + \alpha\beta(\pi_t - \tilde{\pi}) + \chi_t \text{ for } R_t > 0$$

$$\text{and } E_t \pi_{t+1} = \beta \text{ for } R_t \leq 0 \tag{B.1.2.11}$$

Determinacy and Multiplicity

If the central bank satisfies a version of the Taylor principle, $\alpha\beta > 1$, and under the fiscal requirements specified below, the difference equation in (B.1.2.11), representing the dynamic process for inflation, explodes unless one disallows all the explosive paths and only concentrates on one single solution. Indeed, the dynamic properties of (B.1.2.11) depend on the size of the coefficient on π_t. If $\alpha\beta > 1$, which is equivalent to $\alpha > \dfrac{1}{\beta}$, then all but one solutions explode. That single non explosive (locally bounded) solution is for any χ_t process:

$$\pi_t = -\sum_{j=0}^{\infty} \frac{1}{(\alpha\beta)^{j+1}} E_t[\beta(1+\tilde{R}) + \chi_{t+j} - \alpha\beta\tilde{\pi}]. \tag{B.1.2.12}$$

In other words, under the Taylor principle, the stable inflation rate path is determinate and bounded.

However, existence of a unique bounded solution for inflation of the sort that we describe in (B.1.2.12), which never leaves a neighbourhood of $\tilde{\pi}$ for any arbitrary bounded forcing processes like that governing χ_t, hinges critically on a particular equilibrium selection hypothesis which assumes inflation jumps to the singular value given by the discounted stream of shocks and fundamentals that is reported in (B.1.2.12) on the right-hand side of the equal sign.

But this instant adjustment cannot be taken for granted in all states of the world. In fact, the economy admits two stationary states: one where π_t is positive and consistent with the central bank's target:

$$\pi^* = \beta(1+\tilde{R}) = \tilde{\pi} > 1 \Rightarrow \tilde{R} = \frac{\tilde{\pi}}{\beta} - 1 \tag{B.1.2.13}$$

and another equilibrium where there is deflation and monetary policy is passive. To see this, go back to the Fisher equation and plug $R_t = 0$ into it, which yields:

$$\pi^L = \beta < 1 \tag{B.1.2.14}$$

The equilibrium dynamics can be represented graphically in the phase diagram below.

The troubling feature of the phase diagram is that trajectories that start close enough to π can be gradually absorbed by lower-inflation state π^L. An interest rate rule that responds to off-equilibrium inflation more than one-for-one—like under the active IT-style Taylor rule assumed in this box—destabilizes an otherwise stable

(Continued)

Box 1.2 Continued

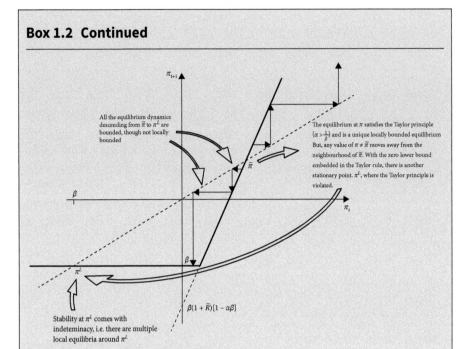

All the equilibrium dynamics descending from $\tilde{\pi}$ to π^L are bounded, though not locally bounded

The equilibrium at π satisfies the Taylor principle $(\alpha > \frac{1}{\beta})$ and is a unique locally bounded equilibrium But, any value of $\pi \neq \tilde{\pi}$ moves away from the neighbourhood of $\tilde{\pi}$. With the zero lower bound embedded in the Taylor rule, there is another stationary point. π^L, where the Taylor principle is violated.

Stability at π^L comes with indeteminacy, i.e. there are multiple local equilibria around π^L

$\beta(1 + \bar{R})[1 - \alpha\beta]$

Figure B 1.2.1 Equilibrium dynamics

economy. Furthermore, when interest rates reach a proximity of the lower bound, NKM predicts that inflation becomes indeterminate. In other words, in a neighbourhood of π^L, the deflation state is indeterminate as well as stable, with multiple self-confirming equilibria around it. These equilibria are generated by 'sunspots' or 'self-confirming expectations' and imply fluctuations of arbitrarily large size. When the 'active' Taylor rule cannot operate, sunspot volatility breaks out.

As shown in CR, using (B.1.2.4) and (B.1.2.9), the transversality condition (B.1.2.8) can equivalently be expressed in terms of an infinite-time intertemporal budget constraint of the household:

$$\frac{A_t}{P_t} = \sum_{j=1}^{\infty} \left(\frac{\beta^j}{\pi_{t+j}} \right) \left[R_{t+j-1} \frac{M_{t+j-1}}{P_{t+j-1}} + s_{t+j-1} \right], \qquad (B.1.2.15)$$

where we define the government's real primary surplus as $s_t = \tau_t - \bar{g}$ Note that, as in this economy $\pi_t \geq \beta \ \forall t$, the right-hand side term in (B.1.2.15) is finite, unless the evolution of the real primary surplus s_t makes it explode. Given the fact that, in this simple economy, private wealth A_t has to be equal to total public liabilities, condition (B.1.2.15) can also be interpreted as the government's debt-valuation equation, stating that the real value of total net government liabilities must equal the present value of the expected future primary budget surpluses, corrected to take account of the government's interest saved on that part of its liabilities that the public is willing to hold in monetary form. Importantly, this is not a constraint imposed on the government, but follows from private sector optimization together with market clearing.

The Monetarist Equilibrium

Let us concentrate on the single determinate solution described in (B.1.2.12), where inflation never leaves a small neighbourhood around $\tilde{\pi} = \beta(1+\tilde{R}) > 1$. Can this 'virtuous' solution to the difference equation (B.1.2.11) in this economy be characterized as a 'monetarist equilibrium', in the sense that the law of motion governing inflation can be seen as being pinned down by monetary policy alone? The answer is a qualified 'yes'. The qualification is important and concerns the law of motion of government liabilities given the rule that the fiscal authority is assumed to follow in response to the events. A monetarist equilibrium, i.e. the set of solutions described by (B.1.2.11) and (B.1.2.12), can be supported in this economy *if and only if* one assumes a 'passive' or 'Ricardian' fiscal regime.

Along the lines proposed by Woodford (1996, 2003), we define a Ricardian fiscal authority as one which always stands ready to validate the debt valuation formula (B.1.2.15) by adjusting the stream of its primary surpluses as necessary to satisfy (B.1.2.15) ex post, whatever the sequences of R_t and P_t might turn out to be as a result of the central bank's periodic decisions, so that the household's transversality condition is always satisfied.

There are multiple fiscal regimes that can be defined as Ricardian in this sense. One of these simply features a fiscal policy rule by which, in each period, the primary surplus is chosen to pay off a certain positive fraction of the outstanding total liabilities, taking into account the interest savings on the monetary base. Such a fiscal policy rule can be described as follows:

$$P_t s_t^* = \gamma(1+R_t)\left(M_t + \frac{B_{t+1}}{1+R_t} \right) - R_t M_t, \text{ with } 0 < \gamma \le 1 \qquad \text{(B.1.2.16)}$$

Insofar as the government follows a fiscal rule like in (B.1.2.16), the transversality condition (B.1.2.8) is satisfied under any path for P_t and R_t that the central bank might choose. To see this, start from (B.1.2.4) and use the definition of primary surplus, the fiscal rule in (B.1.2.16) and the flow budget constraint $B_{t+1} = (1+R_t)(A_t - M_t)$ to obtain:

$$\frac{A_{t+1}}{1+R_t} = (1-\gamma)A_t$$

By sequential forward iteration, the above expression implies:

$$E_t\left\{ \frac{A_{t+T}}{\prod_{j=0}^{T-1}(1+R_{t+j})} \right\} = (1-\gamma)^{T-t}A_t, \ \forall T > t \qquad \text{(B.1.2.8a)}$$

(*Continued*)

Box 1.2 Continued

But this condition guarantees that the transversality condition indeed always holds, i.e.:

$$\lim_{T \to \infty} E_t \left\{ \frac{A_{t+T}}{\prod_{j=0}^{T-1}\left(1+R_{t+j}\right)} \right\} = 0, \qquad (B.1.2.8b)$$

regardless of the path of R_t. In other words, neither (B.1.2.8) nor (B.1.2.15) place any additional restriction on possible equilibrium paths for goods prices or asset prices. The equilibrium looks 'monetarist', as control by the central bank over R_t (and by implication, over the money base) is sufficient to pin down the equilibrium path for inflation and, given some initial condition, the price level too. If monetary policy uniquely determines equilibrium, then a change in fiscal policy (provided it remains 'Ricardian', i.e. faithful to (B.1.2.16)) does not change the equilibrium path of prices.

Non-Ricardian Fiscal Policy

Can a 'monetarist' equilibrium survive if fiscal policy becomes 'active', or 'non-Ricardian' (again, in the sense of Woodford (1996, 2003))? The short answer is no. Imagine you are at t=0, with a pre-determined value of A_0 and the government commits to a stream of future real primary surpluses (adjusted to take into account the budget interest savings on the monetary base) which is unresponsive to the evolution of its total liabilities. As an example, such a fiscal rule could take the following form:

$$s_t = A_0 K \pi_{t+1} - R_t \frac{M_t}{P_t} \qquad (B.1.2.17)$$

We start from a pre-determined price level $P_{-1} = 1$, and study only perfect foresight equilibria with no uncertainty regarding the behaviour of the central bank or the fiscal agent. From (B.1.2.15), we have:

$$\frac{A_0}{P_0} = \sum_{j=1}^{\infty} \left(\frac{\beta^j}{\pi_j} \right) \left[R_{j-1} \frac{M_{j-1}}{P_{j-1}} + s_{j-1} \right] \qquad (B.1.2.18)$$

Using the fiscal rule (B.1.2.17) to eliminate the terms indicating the primary surpluses, we obtain:

$$\frac{A_0}{P_0} = \beta \sum_{j=0}^{\infty} \beta^j A_0 K,$$

which implies that:

$$P_0 = \frac{(1-\beta)}{\beta} \frac{1}{K}$$

Note that $P_0 = \tilde{\pi}$, if and only if $K = \bar{K} = \dfrac{(1-\beta)}{\beta}\dfrac{1}{\tilde{\pi}}$. If fiscal policy is more expansionary, even by a tiny amount, with $K < \bar{K}$, then $P_0 = \pi_0 > \tilde{\pi}$ and conversely, if fiscal policy is more restrictive, even by a tiny amount, with $K > \bar{K}$, then $P_0 = \pi_0 < \tilde{\pi}$. So, unless $K = \bar{K}$, a fiscal rule that does not react passively to the endogenous evolution of public debt, as in (B.1.2.16), but rather sets its fiscal plans according to some exogenous value of K, will likely throw the economy off into one of the explosive trajectories to the right or the left of $\tilde{\pi}$. Under a fiscal rule of the type described in (B.1.2.17) with $K \neq \bar{K}$, the system cannot satisfy both (B.1.2.17) and the monetarist law of motion (B.1.2.11) where $P_0 = \tilde{\pi}P_{-1}$, so the price level will have to jump outside its monetarist path in order for (B.1.2.18) to be satisfied at all times. A coefficient $K < \bar{K}$ will generate inflation in excess of the central bank's target. A coefficient $K > \bar{K}$ will generate sustained disinflation and will eventually get the economy trapped in permanent deflation.

We conclude by highlighting two results. First, for the monetarist regime (where the central bank is tough on inflation) to deliver an inflation process bounded around $\tilde{\pi}$, fiscal policy has to cooperate, i.e. be 'passive' or 'Ricardian'. This argues for the implementation of fiscal safeguards that force debt sustainability considerations on everyday tax and spending decisions. Citing Sims (2016): 'an increase in the interest expense component of the budget [should call] forth, at least eventually, an increased primary surplus—revenues minus non-interest expenditures. This is the most easily understood restraint on fiscal policy required for central bank independence, and one most economists find quite plausible. The European Monetary Union puts limits on debt-to-GDP ratios and deficits, probably with this sort of mechanism in mind.' Second, the macroeconomic policy authorities do indeed need to worry about entrenched instability in this economy: $\pi^L = \beta < 1$ is a global attractor and non-fundamental shocks to expectations can drive the economy there. Once $\pi^L = \beta < 1$ is reached, monetary policy becomes passive ($R_t = 0$) and the economy is trapped in a deflationary equilibrium. Box 2.2 studies strategies for monetary policy to regain potency in these conditions.

locally bounded, and thus justify the convenient, standard practice of restricting analysis to the local neighbourhood around that specific stationary point, as if the economy could never possibly leave that region.[24] In fact, however, south-west of the

---

[24] Certainly, the 'virtuous' equilibrium in NKM is dynamically explosive: when an inflation surprise (positive or negative) hits, the central bank reacts by raising or lowering its interest rate more than one for one with inflation, and this reaction tends to raise or lower subsequent inflation even further. Inflation then spirals off to ever-higher or lower values and eventually leaves the local region around the 'virtuous' steady state. For only one value of inflation today will inflation fail to explode. This is where the model selection hypothesis comes in: the New Keynesian modellers assume that inflation today jumps to that precise unique inflation value leading to a locally bounded equilibrium path that keeps the economy revolving around the 'virtuous' point over time. This is indeed the assumption we make in Box 2.2, where inflation is supposed to jump to the unique value defined in equation (B.1.2.15) in response to a shock. But this method of inducing determinacy is certainly not uncontroversial. Cochrane (2011), for example, has challenged the economic rationale behind ruling out non-local nominal paths.

desired steady state, the model defines another, 'liquidity trap' steady state where inflation is negative and the central bank's interest rate is perennially stuck at its lower bound. The reason for this multiplicity is simple: if the interest rate is constrained to be non-negative (or not 'too negative'), then there must be a point where the interest rate is at its lower bound, the Taylor rule is de-activated (monetary policy is 'passive') and the economy is in deflation (because otherwise the nominal interest rate would not be so low). In a seminal paper published at the end of the 1990s, Benhabib, Schmitt-Grohé and Uribe (2001) established two results concerning the nature of this equilibrium: that it is a global attractor—many paths of the macroeconomy that start far from it end in this region—and that there are multiple local equilibria near this point. In other words, the 'liquidity trap' is globally stable and locally indeterminate. Why is this disturbing and what does it have to do with unanchored inflation expectations? It is disturbing because inflation trajectories starting arbitrarily near the 'virtuous' steady state can unravel and eventually be absorbed by the 'liquidity trap' steady state, where inflation and the economy start behaving erratically. And this unravelling and erratic behaviour is due to 'sunspots', non-fundamental shocks to agents' expectations.

1.4 Wrapping Up: Lessons from Theory for Institutional Design

While somewhat buried inside its deep structure, and wrapped beneath its monetarist appearance, NKM had a multifaceted and somewhat more humbling message for the architects of monetary reform than was evident in the three main points listed above. On the face of it, and rather superficially, those three main points could inspire a sort of 'monetary policy hubris', whereby monetary policy could *just do it* all by itself. In reality, as critical as a stability-oriented central bank is to furthering economic prosperity, the degree of success of an economy—and a currency union in particular—is a function of a broader set of institutions and policies than monetary policy alone (Constâncio, 2018). Furthermore, the deeper message coming from NKM entailed the following proposition: instability can develop in economies even under healthy monetary institutions. Box 1.2 utilizes a particularly simple and transparent version of the optimizing model that underpins any NKM to substantiate this proposition. It documents a few results. First, despite solid institutions, delusional beliefs may occasionally develop in the economy, and lead it astray into panics and protracted periods of dismal performance. 'Inflation scares' and 'deflation scares' are rare events if institutions are really sound, but they are not impossible. And, as one should have learned from history if not from NKM itself, financial markets provide a hospitable ground where such adverse expectational trends can start and explode.

In these conditions, IT cannot be the only defence: it needs reinforcements and contingency plans or a 'regime-shift' device that can be activated when the IT boundaries are reached and its stabilizing powers exhausted. Box 1.2 provides two examples of circumstances where IT runs out of road: a fiscal crisis that leads to sustained runaway inflation, and sustained disinflation fuelled by a 'deflation scare'. It shows that, in normal times, macroeconomic stability is not sustainable unless the fiscal agent abstains from systematically destabilizing its own debt. Box 2.2 offers two examples of approaches that a central bank can deploy in deflationary conditions. One prescribes that the central bank—when things precipitate—switch to a constant-money-growth rule supported by public bond buys. Another example applies when the central bank has the technology to implement negative interest rates. The constant money growth example is noteworthy and very consequential for what we will say about the 2003 ECB strategy review. In a nutshell, as Box 1.2 and Box 2.2 together show, if one allows for all possible macroeconomic scenarios that are consistent with NKM, spanning the whole gamut from 'good' to 'nasty', with hyperinflations and deflations standing at the 'nasty' limits of the range, then the connection between money and inflation proves to be more robust than that between interest rates and inflation. From this perspective, therefore, it would not be difficult to conclude that money should be given some non-secondary status in the central bank's armoury of monitoring variables and instruments.

1.5 Designing the ECB: The ECB's Real-World Model

By the time the negotiations over the Maastricht Treaty laying the foundations of EMU started, the German central bank was widely recognized to have done a better job of containing inflation in the face of adverse shocks than any other OECD central bank. It was also clear that this superior performance was attributable to a great extent to the institutions of German monetary policy. First, the Deutsche Bundesbank Act of 1957 had explicitly mandated the German central bank with a mission: to regulate the amount of currency and credit in circulation with the aim of 'safeguarding the currency'. In practice, in pursuit of that mission, the Bundesbank—at least since the collapse of the Bretton Woods system in 1971—had consistently been following the simultaneous tradition of articulating a medium-term inflation goal—variously referred to in Bundesbank communications as the 'unavoidable level of inflation', 'price norm', or 'medium-term price assumption'—and then, based on this goal, establishing a target for the growth of a key monetary aggregate. Second, Article 12 of the Act had forbidden the federal government from formally participating in monetary policy decisions, thereby restricting political influence. Third, Article 20 of the Act had prohibited the central bank from financing government deficits.

These few tenets of the Bundesbank statute bear obvious resemblance to the three principles of good monetary policy governance—in fact, one could argue that they largely inspired the three principles, as the Bundesbank was already held in high regard because of its standard-setting performance before the consensus around the three principles crystallized in academic and policymaking circles. One omission—relative to the second principle—is noteworthy: a concrete, actionable definition of the objective. The absence of a clearly articulated objective meant that, in German formal law, the principal (parliament, the government, the people) delegated to the agent (the central bank) full policymaking powers, including the authority to decide the appropriate operating policy target. The model of delegation was one in which the founding legislation identified a high-level purpose for the central bank—specifically, that of preserving the value of the currency—and devolved the task of translating that general purpose into an operational goal to the central bank itself. In other words, the German central bank enjoyed some degree of *goal independence*, something that central banks with an explicit IT mandate typically do not possess.

This observation merits a pause. What militates in favour of leaving the central bank goal undefined in a monetary constitution and delegating it to the central bank itself? At least two sorts of rationalization come to mind. The first has a political economy character (Bernhard and Leblang (2002) and Crowe (2008) can be interpreted in this way). Monetary policy is particularly contentious, so it may make sense for the founding fathers of a constitution to avoid descending into the particulars of monetary policy design—such as a numerical target for the central bank—and delegate them to expert technocrats to figure out. Taking these particulars off the constitution-setting agenda paves the way for a broader agreement on the constitution, which is arguably the higher-order objective of the constitutional legislators. Since high-level central bank bureaucrats are selected from within a supposedly conservative-minded group of experts, and are most concerned with maintaining a reputation for competence and institutional loyalty among their professional peers (Wilson, 1989; Alesina and Tabellini, 2007), they can be trusted to fulfil the goals of their organization and of the public at large, and to pursue prudent policies in that endeavour. So, granting some degree of delegated goal discretion to an inflation-averse central banker—such as the paradigmatic Rogoff-style 'conservative' central bank governor—might help society achieve a second-best outcome.[25]

A second motivation for goal delegation has to do with the desirability and workability of aggregating social preferences on such specialized matters as the formulation of monetary policy. Elected politicians should decide whether and where a bridge or a new motorway should be built, but it would be undesirable for society if elected politicians were to become involved in the detailed engineering of the structure. In the field of public policy, citizens are surely extremely averse to a high, sustained pace of price increases, because they intuitively appreciate that such a process can ultimately only debauch their hard-earned savings and grip the economy. In other words, citizens can tell qualitatively when price stability holds, and one can quote Alan Greenspan's famous definition of price stability here as particularly fitting.[26] But it is

---

[25] See Box 1.1 for a selective summary of the central bank independence literature, also quoting Rogoff's seminal 1985 paper.

[26] 'Price stability is best thought of as an environment in which inflation is so low and stable over time that it does not materially enter into the decisions of households and firms' (Greenspan, 2001).

questionable whether the general public would be able to express preferences for CPI over PCE as a metric of price stability, or for a 2% annual rate of inflation over 1% or 3%. The optimal choice depends on detailed information which may not be available to them, or which, even if available, may not be easy to process. Processing that information requires fine analysis of the properties and statistical biases of the multiple price indices that exist, on the link between the inflation average and the inflation variance, the risks of deflation incurred at various levels of average inflation, and so on. Only technicians can elaborate and summarize this information.[27] Partial goal delegation can minimize the informational and analytical requirements demanded of political decision-makers and the public, and thus—while sub-optimal in other respects—may dominate more prescriptive approaches.[28]

1.6 The Treaty

The Bundesbank, arguably embodying a happy coincidence of ideals and experience, was adopted as the model for the newly-founded ECB and for the entire refurbished system of national central banks (ESCB). Shadowing the three articles of the Bundesbank Act mentioned previously, the Treaty on the Functioning of the European Union (TFEU), first, identified a hierarchy of statutory objectives, with price stability given primacy: 'The primary objective of the ESCB shall be to maintain price stability. Without prejudice to the objective of price stability, the ESCB shall support the general economic policies in the Union with a view to contributing to the achievement of the objectives of the Union as laid down in Article 3 of the Treaty on European Union' (Article 127). The unspecific terms in which the 'primary objective' was cast were borrowed from the model of delegated goal discretion that had been applied—and had performed rather well—in Germany since 1957. But there were two innovations compared with the Bundesbank model. *Price stability* replaced 'safeguarding the currency' as the key code-phrase for expressing the high-level goal to be assigned to the new monetary institution. The new language

---

[27] The debate over the optimal level of trend or target inflation is currently in full swing once again among those 'technicians', see, e.g., Adam and Weber (2019) and the discussion in the Deutsche Bundesbank (2018).

[28] Based on a survey of firms' macroeconomic beliefs in New Zealand, Coibion, Gorodnichenko and Kumar (2018) document how firms have exhibited both a significant upward bias in inflation forecasts and widespread disagreement relative to professional forecasters. While most managers do not appear to view inflation as a major consideration in their decisions and, hence generally devote few resources to tracking it, short-run swings in inflation expectations coincide closely with large changes in gasoline prices. In a similar vein, Mankiw, Reis and Wolfers (2003) document that the dispersion in US households' inflation forecasts is much larger than that of professional forecasters; Coibion and Gorodnichenko (2015) find that more than half of the historical differences in US inflation forecasts between households and professionals can be accounted for by the level of oil prices, and they suggest as a natural explanation the fact that households might pay particular attention to oil price changes when forming their expectations of other prices, because gasoline prices are among the most visible prices to consumers. Overall, Coibion et al. (2018) conclude by arguing that monetary policymakers' success in achieving low and stable inflation may therefore have inadvertently made their work more difficult, by inducing firms and households to pay less attention to inflation and other aggregate risks.

was an act of deference to the previous 20 years of debate on the best way in which monetary policy could contribute to societal welfare (the first principle). By the standards of the 1990s, domestic price stability was simply a much more precise criterion for measuring the soundness of the currency. The *hierarchy of objectives—* with a clear identification of what comes first—rather than the *singularity of one objective* was also new and again a veiled reflection of years of scholarly debate over macroeconomic trade-offs in the short term and in the long term. It encapsulated the notion that it was desirable to single out one criterion against which central bank performance could be appraised and thus the mandate could be enforced, and this single criterion should be given the status of primary objective. For all the reasons provided above under the second principle of good monetary governance, price stability is the most satisfactory approximation of this ideal yardstick. The trade-offs encountered in the management of monetary policy should not be disregarded, however, as they have repercussions on society's collective well-being along wider dimensions than the welfare costs of too high or too low inflation. This motivated reference to the subsidiary objectives enumerated in Article 3 of the Treaty, among which, and most relevant for a central bank, are: 'the sustainable development of Europe based on balanced economic growth and price stability, a highly competitive social market economy, aiming at full employment and social progress, and a high level of protection and improvement of the quality of the environment'. The primary objective should take precedence over any other subsidiary consideration, in the lexicographic sense that only when the overriding objective is achieved can the central bank turn to its secondary objectives.

Second, the Treaty made sure that the ECB and the NCBs, which would collectively sit on the Governing Council of the ECB, had full independence. To this end, the TFEU stipulates that: 'neither the European Central Bank, nor a national central bank, nor any member of their decision-making bodies shall seek or take instructions from Union institutions, bodies, offices or agencies, from any government of a Member State or from any other body' (Article 130). In addition, Article 283 prescribes security of tenure and length of appointment of the members of the ECB's Executive Board and GC.[29]

Third, the TFEU prohibits monetary financing:

> Overdraft facilities or any other type of credit facility with the ECB or with the NCBs in favour of Union institutions, bodies, offices or agencies, central governments, regional, local or other public authorities, other bodies governed by public law, or public undertakings of Member States shall be prohibited, as shall the

---

[29] Specifically, Article 283 prescribes that the Executive Board of the ECB, comprising the President, the Vice-President and four other members, shall be 'appointed by the European Council, acting by a qualified majority, from among persons of recognised standing and professional experience in monetary or banking matters, on a recommendation from the Council, after it has consulted the European Parliament and the Governing Council of the European Central Bank. Their term of office shall be eight years and shall not be renewable. Only nationals of Member States may be members of the Executive Board.'

purchase directly from them by the European Central Bank or national central banks of debt instruments.   **(Article 123)**

This prohibition of direct funding of public bodies was reinforced by two further provisions. The first was meant to exclude circumventions of Article 123 by outlawing legal acts that might force private credit institutions to grant public bodies *'privileged access to credit'* (Article 124). The second provision—contained in Article 18 of Protocol (No 4) on the Statute of the ESCB and of the ECB—clarified that the prohibition of direct central bank financing of public bodies was not meant to obstruct the implementation of monetary policy. Specifically:

> In order to achieve the objectives of the ESCB and to carry out its tasks, the ECB and the national central banks may: operate in the financial markets by buying and selling outright (spot and forward) or under repurchase agreement and by lending or borrowing claims and marketable instruments, whether in euro or other currencies, as well as precious metals; conduct credit operations with credit institutions and other market participants, with lending being based on adequate collateral.

In synthesis, combining Article 123 and Article 18 of the Statute of the ESCB, it is easy to see the purpose of this piece of legislation: to *enable* instrument independence, which would otherwise be nullified if the ECB or any NCB were to be held liable for guaranteeing a cap on the borrowing cost faced by any public entity. Setting caps on the level of interest rates that the central bank can apply would simply mean depriving the central bank of the capacity to work towards meeting its mandate in all states of the world. This being said, provided there is no such coercion coming from the fiscal side, or any surreptitious intention, on the side of the central banks, to provide cheap finance to one or more sovereigns, there is no limitation on the nature and scope of monetary policy operations. In particular, the ESCB is not restricted as to the type of securities that it might decide to 'buy and sell outright' in the open market. Once more, instrument independence (and tool availability) was the dominant consideration.

The Bundesbank model was notably extended in two directions, both intended to make the newborn institution the child of its time, a time of high theory for monetary policy design. Article 284 established the bedrock foundations of the new institution's accountability regime. It states that:

> The ECB shall address an annual report on the activities of the ESCB and on the monetary policy of both the previous and current year to the European Parliament, the Council and the Commission, and also to the European Council. The President of the ECB shall present this report to the Council and to the European Parliament, which may hold a general debate on that basis. The President of the ECB and the other members of the Executive Board may, at the

request of the European Parliament or on their own initiative, be heard by the competent committees of the European Parliament.

Influenced by the contemporary debate on the two-way connection between accountability and legitimacy (the first principle), the drafters of the Treaty wanted the new central bank bound by the obligation to explain and justify the actions or decisions taken, and take responsibility for any fault or damage. The additional disclosure requirements and parliamentary oversight of Article 284 were meant to secure and preserve public support for the new institution. Although the formal independence of the ECB was enshrined in the Treaty, its effectiveness and authority depended on the continuing acquiescence of European voters, what Goodhart and Lastra (2018b) refer to as 'societal legitimacy'.

The other major addendum to the Bundesbank regime was the Treaty's general framework laying out the fiscal requirements for price stability. The framework is complex and has become more complicated through the years.[30] We shall restrain ourselves to the primary Treaty provisions included in Article 126, which are simple and transparent, and from which we quote selectively:

> Member States shall avoid excessive government deficits. The Commission shall monitor the development of the budgetary situation and of the stock of government debt in the Member States with a view to identifying gross errors. In particular it shall examine compliance with budgetary discipline on the basis of the following two criteria: (a) whether the ratio of the planned or actual government deficit to gross domestic product exceeds a reference value, unless either the ratio has declined substantially and continuously and reached a level that comes close to the reference value, or, alternatively, the excess over the reference value is only exceptional and temporary and the ratio remains close to the reference value; (b) whether the ratio of government debt to gross domestic product exceeds a reference value, unless the ratio is sufficiently diminishing and approaching the reference value at a satisfactory pace. The reference values are specified in the Protocol on the excessive deficit procedure annexed to the Treaties.

Monetary constitutions rarely seek to discipline the high-level decision space open to the fiscal authority. But, as we saw in Section 1.4 and Box 1.2, it makes eminent economic sense to do so, as the interconnections of fiscal and monetary policy institutions are intimate. Box 1.2 in particular expounds the basic ideas asserted by contemporary macroeconomic theory: fiscal standards that promote debt sustainability are key enabling conditions for a central bank to be in full control of its

---

[30] A central role is assigned to the Stability and Growth Pact, which is secondary legislation based on Articles 121 and 126 of the Treaty. See Buti and Giudice (2002) for an interim and Leiner-Killinger and Nerlich (2019) for a recent summary of the effectiveness of the fiscal rules framework.

target variable. Conversely, a fiscal regime that cannot be assumed to enforce debt sustainability in all scenarios is one that places an additional restriction on inflation determination, over and above those imposed by the monetary regime. It is clear that, in a multi-country monetary union, this proposition can only grow in salience. For, in a multi-country setting, all it takes for the law of motion of the system-wide rate of inflation to be perturbed and possibly permanently destabilized is for a single country to issue extra debt without any intention to increase primary surpluses in the future to back it with new revenues. In other words, there is an inherent issue of free riding in a single currency union, as the perceived inflationary effect of national fiscal decisions is diluted—in the eyes of the fiscal authority that makes them—by the fact that each country's debt is only a small part of the total.

It is therefore unsurprising that the designers of the embryonic ECB discussed and finally wrote into Treaty law an arrangement designed to insulate monetary policy from fiscal policy, with the intention of guaranteeing systemic safety in the face of potential instability in national budgetary policies. As Otmar Issing observed at the time,

> monetary union may reduce a government's incentive to conduct a prudent fiscal policy, as under a single currency there is no (national) exchange rate risk and upward pressure on interest rates caused by higher national budget deficits is reduced in the single capital market. The partner countries will have to share the adverse consequences of an undesirable fiscal policy stance of a member-state in the form of higher interest rates. Without appropriate safeguards the capital market of a single currency thus creates an incentive to build up deficits.
>
> **(Issing, 1996)**

In fact, it is remarkable that these fiscal requirements for price stability became constitutional law in Europe before the economics profession could even prove their value.[31]

---

[31] Of course, while the basic results of the theory of monetary/fiscal policy interactions were still being worked out when the Treaty was signed in Maastricht in early 1992, forerunners of the fiscal theory had already drawn attention to the intimate connection between monetary and fiscal institutions. Thomas Sargent's work, with and without Neil Wallace, had long provided a framework for thinking about the channels by which the fiscal regime could influence price level determination. See Sargent and Wallace (1981), Aiyagari and Gertler (1985) and Sims (1988) for early glimpses into what would later be known as the fiscal theory. Probably inspired by the Treaty provisions, Woodford developed the basic free-rider intuition in an influential paper on the fiscal requirements for price stability. He observed: 'a reason for a country that cares about price stability to be concerned about the prospect of sharing a common currency with a country that is unable to control its public debt, in the precise sense of following a Ricardian fiscal policy rule. Adherence to a Ricardian fiscal policy by one country, or even maintenance of a balanced budget at all times, will not protect it from price level instability generated by variations in the budget of the other government, even if the monetary policy rule adopted by the common central bank ignores the paths of both countries' public debts' (Woodford (1996), p. 3).

2
The ECB Strategy and Its Critics

As we saw in the previous chapter, while using the formulaic convention of the time, *price stability*, to signify the ultimate objective that was to be assigned to the ECB, the Treaty devolved the full specification and operationalization of the objective to the new institution. Accordingly, the technical staff at the European Monetary Institute (EMI)—the precursor of the ECB—started to struggle with specification and operationalization issues at an early stage. As early as February 1997, the EMI published a report entitled 'The single monetary policy in Stage Three: Elements of the monetary policy strategy of the ESCB' in which the strategy was described as 'the set of procedures according to which the central bank decides how to achieve its final objective, price stability' and was said to involve five key elements. These were: (a) the public announcement of a *quantitative definition* of the final objective of 'price stability'; (b) the announcement of *specific targets* against which the European System of Central Banks' (ESCB) performance could be assessed; (c) the monitoring of a *broad range of indicators*; (d) a *prominent role for money* within this set of indicators, including the public setting of targets or monitoring ranges if money demand was sufficiently stable in the long run; and (e) the ability of the ESCB to make its *own forecasts for inflation*, potential growth and other economic indicators (italics added). The report did not make recommendations either for the quantification of the objective or for the operating principles that should guide policy in pursuit of the objective.[1] It did three things instead. First, it cleared the table of possible strategic approaches that, in the view of the EMI, would not be appropriate for a major continental economy (exchange rate targeting) with largely unknown structural characteristics (targeting an elusive natural rate of interest). Second, it identified some guiding principles that any selection process over a strategy would have to follow. These principles included, most notably, a *medium-term orientation*—to secure some flexibility and discretion in response to short-term deviations from the objective—and *continuity*—with the best experience gained by participating national central banks (NCBs) before the start of Stage Three. Finally, the report provided

---

[1] The report cited the uncertainty over the composition of the group of countries that would adopt the euro from the outset in January 1999 as one reason for not advancing a precise recommendation. To quote the report: 'The decision on a strategy for the ESCB will have to take into account the economic environment and the financial market structure prevailing in the single currency area in Stage Three. For legal reasons and on economic grounds, this decision can only be taken after the establishment of the ESCB, when the initial composition of the Monetary Union is known.'

Monetary Policy in Times of Crisis: A Tale of Two Decades of the European Central Bank. Massimo Rostagno, Carlo Altavilla, Giacomo Carboni, Wolfgang Lemke, Roberto Motto, Arthur Saint Guilhem, and Jonathan Yiangou, Oxford University Press (2021). © Massimo Rostagno, Carlo Altavilla, Giacomo Carboni, Wolfgang Lemke, Roberto Motto, Arthur Saint Guilhem, and Jonathan Yiangou.
DOI: 10.1093/oso/9780192895912.003.0003

arguments to weigh the two surviving competing strategies, monetary targeting and inflation targeting (always listed in this order) against each other.

2.1 The Idea of a Range

Despite appearances, the preparatory work of the EMI at its Monetary Policy Sub-Committee was progressing rapidly towards substantive results too. An internal EMI proposal for a quantitative definition of price stability, while potentially very contentious, actually received an early blessing from the NCBs sitting on the Sub-Committee, with almost no opposition. In its proposal, the EMI contemplated basing the quantitative definition on a headline consumer price index (Eurostat's Harmonized Index of Consumer Prices, HICP), rather than an underlying measure of inflation.[2] Most importantly, the EMI proposal envisioned an inflation objective expressed as a range of values below 2% rather than as a point target. This latter outcome—surprising as it may appear today—was partly deliberate and partly historical accident.

A positive range for inflation below 2%, possibly comprising very low rates, was even more appealing politically than it was from an economic welfare point of view. It was seen as a prize crowning decades of inflation-fighting policies and regime trials around Europe. The new currency could not have introduced itself with stronger credentials to the peoples of Europe: the seemingly intractable problem of high inflation that had plagued the continent for 30 years had been conquered at last.

But the *below 2%* concept was path dependent and thus partly fortuitous too. Of note, the Banque de France had selected a similar regime to define its objective already in 1994, when—following a constitutional reform—the French central bank announced that: *'L'objectif final de la politique monétaire de la Banque de France demeure la stabilité des prix, qui ne devront pas augmenter globalement de plus de 2% en 1994, comme dans une perspective de moyen terme.'*[3] This precedent was certainly influential in nudging the decision toward the notion of 'below 2%'. But path-dependency asserted itself in another way as well. Since at least 1996, HICP inflation

---

[2] The HICP was first published in March 1997. Raw price data are collected by the national statistical institutes, aggregated into national HICPs and forwarded to Eurostat which then publishes the overall HICP for the euro area. Eurostat (2001) states that 'the HICP [is] a Laspeyres-type price index that is based on the prices of goods and services available for purchase in the economic territory of the Member State for the purpose of directly satisfying consumer needs' (p. 19). The HICP covers household final monetary consumption expenditure as defined by the European System of Accounts (ESA 95). Household final monetary consumption is defined as the component of consumption expenditure incurred by households regardless of nationality of residence status, in monetary transactions, on the economic territory of the member state, on goods and services that are used for direct satisfaction of individual needs or wants, and in one or both of the two time periods being compared. The HICP is intended as a pure price index, meaning that 'it is only changes in prices that are reflected in the measure between the current and base or reference period. The HICP is not a cost-of-living index' (p. 19).

[3] 'The ultimate goal of the Banque de France's monetary policy is to ensure the stability of prices, which should not increase overall by more than 2% in 1994, as in a medium-term perspective'. See Banque de France, 'La définition de la politique monétaire pour la France', press release of 27 January 1994.

had been falling sharply in all the countries that would adopt the euro (see Figure 2.1). Between 1996 and 1999, the euro area annual inflation rate declined by as much as 1.3 percentage points, with core inflation dropping by more than headline. There were two dominating drivers behind this trend: a sustained drop in the price of commodities, and monetary restriction in formerly high-inflation countries—which had to restrain domestic credit conditions in order to meet the inflation criterion for joining the single currency.[4] Indeed, more than half the decline in euro area core inflation was accounted for by Italy and Spain, where the inflation-adjusted policy interest rate had either increased or been kept constant at restrictive levels over the period.

Neither of the two late-1990s disinflationary forces could be expected to last after monetary union. Oil price shocks are typically erratic, and the tightening pressure applied in the periphery was due to be relieved anyway, as the ECB would take over and implement uniform monetary conditions across the area. In fact, as one can see in Figure 2.1, the inflation slump started to reverse soon in 1999, aided by the economic recovery from the aftermath of the growth scare following the East Asian-Russian crisis, the rise in oil prices and the euro depreciation. But the prolonged period of historically low inflation had arguably become entrenched in the collective

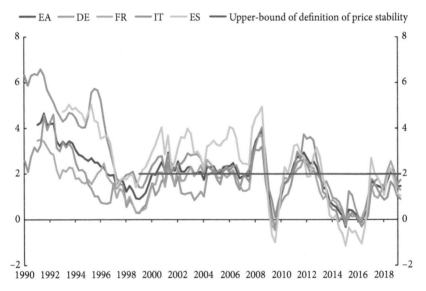

Figure 2.1 HICP inflation in the euro area and four largest euro area countries (year-on-year % change)

Source: Eurostat.
Latest observation: 2018Q4.

---

[4] The price stability convergence criterion stipulates that the consumer price inflation rate in the candidate country should not exceed the rate of the three best-performing Member States by more than 1.5 percentage points.

imagination of the European people. Therefore, the range of admissible inflation rates in the new regime had to be made sufficiently ample to include the recent history of very contained inflation realizations. With inflation falling toward 1% in Germany and France in 1997 and heading toward 0% in 1998, excluding low values from the objective range would have been seen as an act of betrayal of the people's aspirations and acquisitions, and would probably have destabilized inflation expectations.

2.2 The Targeting Function

While the idea of a range to quantify the ultimate objective did not quite encounter opposition in the EMI preparatory processes, the question whether the central bank should also have subsidiary targets for intermediate variables—anything pertaining to points (b), (c) and (d) of the five key elements of a strategy according to the EMI report—required more debate. Did the ECB really need an intermediate target or a targeting function, given that the final objective was to receive a quantitative definition? Some participants in the discussions—who had a distinct preference for inflation targeting—held the view that a numerical definition of price stability would naturally map into transparent and cogent guidelines for the decision-makers in the management of everyday policy. After all, New Zealand, Sweden and the UK were recent examples of central banks targeting final objectives *directly*, without the inter-position of an intermediate target to steer policy. In their opinion, the policy rule would be sufficiently clear: 'Change rates if the objective is at risk by as much as needed to minimize the risk.' As a strategy for conducting monetary policy, inflation targeting had appealing features, including avoidance of the 'velocity instability' problem that could arise when policy relies heavily on a single intermediate target, and greater ease in explaining policy objectives to the public. An intermediate target would only bring noise and confusion. As for continuity with the Bundesbank tradition, these participants in the internal debate contended that it was debatable whether the success of the Bundesbank in keeping inflation low and stable was due to its practice of targeting money. Whereas the money targets had been missed most of the time in Germany since their adoption in 1974, the Bundesbank had earned an inflexible anti-inflation credibility through its de facto aggressive reactions to realized and expected inflation.[5]

---

[5] A nascent literature in those years had set out to estimate the 'true' reaction function of the Bundesbank. Bernanke and Mihov (1997), in an early contribution, found that, holding constant the current forecast of inflation, German monetary policy responded very little to changes in forecasted money growth. They concluded that the Bundesbank was much better described as an inflation targeter than as a money targeter. Clarida and Gertler (1997) and Clarida et al. (1998) reached the similar conclusion that since 1973 the Bundesbank's behaviour could be characterized by a Taylor rule reasonably close to that implicitly describing the behaviour of the Fed over the same period. Gerberding et al. (2005), however, reach different conclusions. Using a real-time data set for Germany including the Bundesbank's own estimates of potential output, they re-estimate the Bundesbank's reaction function and find that deviations of money growth from target are highly significant.

Others held the opposite view. They argued that an ultimate objective expressed in numerical terms was not inconsistent with the identification of an 'intermediate target'. In fact, they pointed to evidence that the majority of central banks at the time operated under regimes that, in one way or another, were based on a central bank pledge to keep a selected variable—an exchange rate or a monetary aggregate—close to a numerical norm. And this practice was justified not on grounds that the intermediate variable mattered per se, but because it was more controllable by the central bank instruments, and was reliably linked to the final objective. In fact, even the recognized pioneer of inflation targeting, the Reserve Bank of New Zealand (RBNZ), found it useful to establish—in parallel with the formal target—an informal operational target for the exchange rate, with appropriately defined bands or trigger points which, if reached, could prompt a deviation from the interest rate path most consistent with tracking the bank's regular inflation targeting strategy. Other hybrid solutions were also not unusual. Central banks with an official intermediate monetary target, such as the Bundesbank and the Swiss National Bank, were adjusting the target interval and their response to it according to the observed and projected course of inflation. In any event, given the transmission lags, it was even disputable whether directly targeting the final objective was a viable option at all: any inflation targeting regime was ultimately operated by trying to hit its own definition of an intermediate target, with an inflation *forecast* taking the place of money or the external value of the currency as the go-between connecting the settings of the instrument today and the future realization of inflation. Ultimately, the nagging concern in the camp of the inflation targeting sceptics was the connection between inflation and the instruments of policy. As Poole (1994) had put it some years previously:

> The instrumental issue would be irrelevant or uninteresting if the relationship between instruments and goals were so precise that errors in achieving goals were economically irrelevant. At the present state of knowledge, such errors are far from irrelevant. We simply do not know with much precision what the outcome will be of adjusting policy instruments in particular ways. Thus, no possibility exists that a 'price rule' or 'direct targeting' will make the instrumental question irrelevant in the foreseeable future. Arguing for such an approach ducks the key issue of how to achieve the goals of policy.

By early 1998 it had become clear that, first, it was advisable to announce a strategy alongside a numerical objective; second, the choice could be narrowed down to only two alternatives: monetary targeting and inflation targeting;[6] and third, hybrids

---

[6] The EMI report gave the reasons for narrowing the choice to the two alternatives of monetary and inflation targeting as follows: 'First, an exchange rate objective is not considered appropriate since, for an area potentially as large as the euro area, such an approach might be inconsistent with the internal goal of price stability. Second, the use of an interest rate as an intermediate target is not considered appropriate given difficulties in identifying the equilibrium real interest rate which would be consistent with price stability. Third, employing the growth rate of nominal GDP which can be viewed as consistent with price stability as an intermediate target would provide a clear nominal framework and would have the

combining elements of both regimes would be preferable to any of the two extremes. An intermediate target making reference to some monetary aggregate could be monitored continuously and had proved to be controllable over short horizons and to a satisfactory degree in the Bundesbank's past experience. Insofar as the connection between money and prices could be expected to remain stable and dependable in the union environment, then monetary targeting presented the advantage of a shorter time for transmission from instruments to measurable outcomes, and thus could enhance transparency and accountability. The contemporary literature, while generally unsupportive of monetary targeting, had recognized this as one of its potential advantages. According to Persson and Tabellini (1993):

> The effect of policy actions on asset prices or the money supply is readily observable. The effect on prices is observable only with substantial delay. It may thus be harder for society to commit to 'punishing' a central bank for actions undertaken six months or a year ago. If the central bank deviates from a financial target the penalty is more immediately related to the policy actions. It may therefore be easier to sustain such penalties than in the case of inflation targets.

But the 'ifs' on which the optimality of monetary targeting was predicated were critical, and controllability and stability could not be taken for granted in the euro area. The stability of broad money demand—a stable econometric relationship linking the money stock to the price level, real income, and nominal interest rates—was ascertained for countries in isolation. But transition to Stage Three could affect money demand in single countries and in the whole area. Potential future instability would make it difficult to identify one single broad measure of the money stock that could be targeted.[7]

Inflation targeting could short-circuit transmission in a different, possibly even more powerful way. It would communicate that monetary policy was intent on attaining the numerical inflation norm over relatively short horizons—shorter,

advantage of not being sensitive to shocks in the income velocity of money. However, nominal income would be difficult to control by the ESCB, could lead to misinterpretation of the ultimate goal of the ESCB, could be subject to substantial data revisions and might lead to an indeterminate price/volume division in the short run, thus creating uncertainty about the inflation performance of the economy. Furthermore, the fact that nominal income targeting is not used at present in any EU Member State makes it inadvisable for the ESCB to adopt this strategy. For these reasons, special attention is paid in this report to only two strategies, monetary and direct inflation targeting' (EMI, 1997).

[7] The preparatory technical debate had led to the conclusion that a broad monetary aggregate—one including not only cash and overnight bank deposits, but also longer-maturity bank deposits and some short-term marketable securities—could perform better in terms of a triad of criteria: stability, controllability, and leading indicator properties. While a narrow money aggregate (M1, for example) was more controllable by the policy instruments, a broad aggregate (M3, for example) consistently outperformed narrow aggregates in terms of stability of money demand and leading indicator properties for inflation. However, econometricians within the staff had warned that, with the transition to Stage Three, a new system of money and banking statistical information would become available, and therefore some of the data series on which existing empirical research had been based would be discontinued. These statistical breaks in the time series might undermine the relevance for Stage Three of studies using the 'old' monetary aggregates produced prior to the introduction of the statistical system.

anyway, than those afforded, under monetary targeting, by the co-integration between money and prices in the long run. In so doing, and quite apart from the quality of the inflation forecasts that would support the regime, the demonstrative effect of an inflation targeting central bank reacting to forecasts in a predictable manner would serve to anchor expectations more solidly and help the new institution quickly earn an anti-inflationary reputation. Of course, inflation targeting had its own list of 'ifs'. At the very least, it required a fully functioning forecasting machinery made up of the following elements: a model of a still non-existing economy; new series of backdata; a team of experts on countries (easy, given the ample repository of country expertise at the NCBs) and on economic sectors cutting across country boundaries (less trivial); a straightforward mechanism to aggregate and cross-check the forecasts of the national economies; and a clear ownership scheme for the overall forecasting exercise either at the staff level or at the level of the policymakers.

It is interesting to note, in the light of what we write above on the fragility of economic equilibria, that in the internal debate on the strategy there was a constant preoccupation with flexibility and robustness. In an attempt to burnish its anti-inflation credentials, the ECB might be tempted to over-react to shocks, and this was to be avoided. An unequivocal rule would prevent recourse to such wasteful signalling. But it could be too constraining as well. In addition, if one had reason to believe that inflation and macroeconomic forecasts would be exceptionally imprecise at the start of monetary union, the *attenuation* theory mitigated against pursuing strategies that focused heavily on stabilising inflation and measures of slack, and in favour of looking for alternative sources of information to robustify inference. To be sure, Brainard's (1967) attenuation principle is not general. Depending on the nature of the uncertainty, optimal policy should be less or even more aggressive than prescribed by certainty-equivalent policy (Söderström, 2002). But the principle was interpreted as dictating caution in the conditions of heightened uncertainty that the ECB had to navigate at the beginning of its life.

A hybrid strategy would offer a more robust solution: the ECB would follow a principal rule centred on its quantitative objective, but would retain 'rules of exemption' to depart from the principal rule if extraordinary circumstances and/or dissonant evidence produced by certain information variables suggested a deviation. The idea of switching points around an overarching strategy—similar to that of the RBNZ—had a lot of appeal.

2.3 The October 1998 Announcement

The Governing Council (GC) of the newly created ECB discussed a proposal for the main elements of the ESCB strategy at an informal meeting on 10 September 1998. The strategy was finally adopted at the 13 October 1998 meeting of the GC and announced immediately with an elaborate press release posted on the ECB's website.

The strategy had three main elements: (1) a quantitative definition of price stability; (2) a prominent role for money with a reference value for the growth of a monetary aggregate; and (3) a broadly-based assessment of the outlook for future price developments.

2.3.1 The Quantitative Definition

'Price stability shall be defined as a year-on-year increase in the Harmonized Index of Consumer Prices (HICP) for the euro area of below 2%. Price stability is to be maintained over the medium term.' Aside from the selection of the index, this statement has two notable aspects. First, in line with the prior general agreement reached at the staff level, the objective was indeed expressed as a price stability comfort zone with a clearly identified ceiling—*below 2%*—and a fuzzier floor, which one could infer from reference to only year-on-year *increases* in the HICP being consistent with price stability. Second, and critically, this was more a statement on a state of nature than a statement on policy intentions. Saying that 'price stability is a range of values below 2%' is different from saying, for instance: 'in pursuit of its price stability mandate, the ESCB shall strive to stabilize inflation around levels below 2%'. The latter would have been in the spirit of inflation targeting, in which the principal (the government), or the delegated trustee itself (the central bank, if under goal independence) identify a *target pro tempore*, with the understanding that the target can be changed—as many inflation targeting central banks have indeed decided to do since the 1990s—if conditions evolve and policy priorities are adjusted. By contrast, the formulation chosen by the GC had a scientific quality, almost implying that 'price stability is always and everywhere a positive rate of inflation below 2%'.

Was the decision to go this way, rather than the target way, dictated by an intention to signal that the GC was using goal independence with parsimony? A target arbitrarily decided by a supranational agency might have looked like a preposterous infringement in the sphere of public choice. Instead, implying that a below-2% set of values was a sort of timeless environmental factor pre-set by nature that the ECB was merely ratifying in its official objective was a far less controversial starting point for the new institution. We do not know whether these considerations carried any weight in the deliberations that led to the final 'price stability' formulation. But in Chapter 3 we argue that this final formulation was of great significance for shaping the 20 years of monetary policy history that followed.

2.3.2 The Medium Term

'Price stability is to be maintained over the medium term.... [T]he statement that "price stability is to be maintained over the medium term" reflects the need for monetary policy to have a forward-looking, medium-term orientation. It also acknowledges the existence of short-term volatility in prices which cannot be controlled by monetary policy.' This indication was meant to communicate that the ECB policymakers, being forward-looking in the exercise of their constrained discretion, would be trying to bring inflation under control while minimising disruption to output and employment. As we saw in Chapter 1, the central bank may want to absorb rather than reverse the first-round effects of changes in the price of certain volatile items, and more generally those caused by supply-side shocks of uncertain duration. The medium-term qualification was all the more necessary here, because of the particular composition of the price level index to be monitored by the ECB. Indeed, unlike in the cases of other central banks that had announced a target for inflation, HICP did not, by construction, disregard shocks to oil/energy/food/indirect taxes, or terms-of-trade shocks, or the direct effects on the price index of interest changes themselves.[8] Therefore, the requisite flexibility was made part of a 'gradualist policy rule' rather than achieved through the small print of the statistical properties of the price index.

2.3.3 The Prominent Role of Money

The text described the 'policy rule', i.e. the operating strategy narrowly defined, as comprising two key elements. One was the status of money in the new framework:

> Money will be assigned a prominent role. This role will be signalled by the announcement of a quantitative reference value for the growth of a broad monetary aggregate. The reference value will be derived in a manner which is consistent with—and will serve to achieve—price stability. Deviations of current monetary growth from the reference value would, under normal circumstances, signal risks to price stability. The concept of a reference value does not imply a commitment to mechanistically correct deviations over the short term. The relationship between actual monetary growth and the pre-announced reference value will be regularly and thoroughly analysed by the Governing Council of the ECB; the result of this analysis and its impact on monetary policy decisions will be explained to the public.

As we saw, the technical debate prior to the strategy announcement had highlighted two ways of regarding money: as a potential policy target and, to a lesser extent, as an important information variable. The econometricians had expressed a preference

---

[8] In the UK, for example, a variety of price indices had been developed, such as RPIX and RPIY, and more would be developed in the 2000s, which by construction excluded those items most subject to supply shocks.

for a broad money aggregate, such as M3, but had warned that, in view of the uncertainties surrounding its controllability, adopting an explicit monetary target would be problematic.[9] At the same time, evidence in favour of M3's leading information properties with respect to inflation was seen as robust. The GC had to position the new central bank within the spectrum defined by these two polar options, a *target* and an *indicator*, keeping in mind *continuity*—with the best practice of policymaking demonstrated by the Bundesbank's monetary targeting—and the appeal of retaining an *escape clause* to handle baffling and risky situations—the idea of switching points around an overarching strategy centred on price stability, as we put it above. The concept of a *quantitative reference value for the growth of a broad monetary aggregate* stands at the point where a target and an indicator intersect. Like an information variable, it would help detect risks to price stability that would be difficult to identify elsewhere. Like a target, it would suggest the opportunity to correct deviations, though not in a mechanical fashion. Again, the need to secure flexibility and robustness in policymaking was an all-embracing perspective.

2.3.4 The Broadly-Based Assessment

'[I]n parallel with the analysis of monetary growth in relation to the reference value, a broadly-based assessment of the outlook for price developments and the risks to price stability in the euro area will play a major role in the ESCB's strategy. This assessment will be made using a wide range of economic and financial variables as indicators for future price developments.' This seemingly obvious statement in the October 1998 press release was dictated by the singling out of money as a privileged information variable and was meant to clarify the role of inflation forecasts in the framework. Once more, the quest for flexibility and robustness was a potent motive behind the proposal, with staff noting that, in practice, a forecast could not constitute a complete summary of all the information relevant for monetary policy decisions. A well-designed monetary policy would not solely react to deviations of a plausible inflation forecast from the announced definition of price stability in a mechanistic fashion, but rather there would be simply no alternative to undertaking a transparent, systematic and coherent assessment of a broad range of indicators, including money, before making monetary policy decisions. Furthermore, staff observed that changes in the financial system associated with the move to Stage Three, such as enhanced competition in the euro area banking industry, the deepening of securities markets, the introduction of the new operational framework of the

---

[9] Staff noted that using money as a target would imply that monetary policy would have to react to eliminate deviations from target, i.e. to keep the aggregate within the announced target band by changing short-term interest rates. Attempts to target an aggregate that could not be easily controlled by the ESCB in the short term would bring the risk of a loss of credibility as soon as pre-announced commitments were missed.

ESCB and the higher credibility of monetary policy in some countries, were likely to result in changes to economic structure, institutions and behaviour that were difficult to predict. The behaviour of both the public and private sectors in the euro area was also likely to be affected by other changes resulting from the transition to Stage Three, such as the introduction of the Stability and Growth Pact or the greater price transparency between previously segmented national markets. To address the uncertainties raised by these issues, a large element of judgement would therefore have to be introduced into the forecasting process, in order to allow for the regime shifts and structural changes that were a seemingly inevitable consequence of EMU. Simply relying on historic relationships for forecasting purposes, it was argued, was unlikely to produce accurate or effective forecasts, and while introducing judgemental adjustments into forecasts in these circumstances was both appropriate and necessary, such adjustments were likely to compromise the transparency of the forecasts for any potential user.[10] While left out of the final statement, these considerations were the intellectual backdrop to replacing *inflation forecasts* with a 'broadly-based assessment of the outlook for price developments and the risks to price stability'.

2.4 The Critics

The disclosure of the main elements of the ECB's strategy did not draw much praise from within the Anglo-Saxon circles of academics who took an interest in scrutinizing the fledgling central bank. Certainly, communication by the ECB was less than fully effectual in promoting a deeper appreciation of the serious problem that it was trying to solve: combining principles of transparency and predictability, and its unwavering commitment to deliver on price stability, with the imperatives of flexibility and robustness in the particularly challenging environment of the start of Stage Three. The international academic community, for its part, was prescient (though admittedly not very quick) in pointing out the perils of the range that the ECB had chosen to quantify its primary objective. But it was less attuned to the advantages of a mixed strategy with built-in 'checks and balances' and appropriate exemption clauses. At times, a certain measure of inflation-targeting fundamentalism—advertising an over-simplified form of inflation targeting, which had been purged of its original complexity—played a role in commentary.

---

[10] Staff also encountered a further problem with according forecasts a central role in the overall strategy, which was the timeliness of the forecasts themselves. Under the arrangements prevailing at the time, the Eurosystem's 'broad' forecasting exercise was conducted at bi-annual frequency, thus considerably less frequently than the fortnightly GC meetings scheduled for Stage Three. Moreover, the ESCB forecasts were produced—for good reasons—under the assumption that short-term interest rates were unchanged. In this sense, the outlook produced was a conditional projection rather than a true unbiased forecast (i.e. the best possible forecast of actual out-turns for future inflation). The conditional projection approach implied an inconsistency with the inclusion of variables in the forecast (such as long-term interest rates) that embodied expectations of the actual future short-term interest rate path.

2.4.1 Communication on Price Stability and the Two Pillars

As the ECB took off on its maiden flight in early 1999, its communication started to be intensely parsed for more exegesis on the strategy and for hints on how the strategy would orient policy decisions concretely.[11]

In a speech delivered in New York in November 1998, Wim Duisenberg, the first President of the ECB, sought to clarify the position and significance of the boundaries of the price stability zone:

> The phrase 'below 2%' clearly delineates the maximum rate of inflation deemed to be consistent with price stability. The wording 'year-on-year increases' implies that persistent price decreases—that is to say deflation in the measured price index—would not be considered to be consistent with price stability either. We did not announce a floor for inflation, because we know that the price index may include a measurement bias, but we do not know its magnitude.
>
> **(Duisenberg, 1998a)**

The statement helped dispel the suspicion that the ECB was inclined to countenance deflation. However, it did little to soften the perception that the ceiling was a harder line to transgress than the floor, and that the only reason for conceiving of a floor in the definition of the price stability objective was measurement bias in inflation statistics.[12] Otmar Issing, the new institution's Chief Economist and dominant intellectual figure in the ECB's first Executive Board, in a later intervention, alluded to the fact that the floor might better be understood as a thick buffer starting well above zero, rather than the dividing line between positive and negative inflation. According to Issing (2000): 'In practice, a "grey zone" exists—as expected inflation falls towards zero, the Eurosystem becomes increasingly concerned about the development.' But the idea that a 2% inflation rate was a kind of watershed between outcomes that were consistent with the mandate and outcomes that were outside the mandate lingered on.

In another early pronouncement meant to promote public understanding of the strategy, President Duisenberg famously referred (in the press conference of 13 October 1998) to the *prominent role of money* and the *broadly-based assessment* as: 'the two pillars, one pillar [being] thicker than the other is, or stronger than the other, but

---

[11] Hartmann and Smets (2018), making use of a machine learning approach to text and topic recognition, show that the bulk of speeches by ECB Executive Board members in the first years since the inception of the euro was indeed focused on explaining the monetary policy strategy of the new central bank and the particular role assigned to monetary analysis in it.

[12] At the April 1999 press conference, President Duisenberg was asked 'Can we draw the conclusion that from now we have some kind of informal bottom on your inflation target?' His reply (quoted from the transcripts of 8 April 1999) was as follows: 'No, you cannot draw this conclusion. We are sticking to our definition of price stability which says that we regard price stability as being an increase in the rate of inflation of below 2%. And what I said today is that the present situation [an annual HICP inflation rate that had remained at 0.8% for the last four months] and the prospects for the increase in the rate of inflation are such that they seem, for as far as we can look forward, also to remain well below that ceiling of 2%.'

how much I couldn't tell you'. The 'two pillars' image—offered almost casually, with no intention to forge a monument in the ECB's communication about its framework—soon took a life of its own. As we saw before, in essence, the prominent role of money was meant to be rooted in Brainard's attenuation principle in conditions of structural uncertainty. But a somewhat different story started to develop around the two-pillar concept. The story was—or at least it was perceived to be—a representation of the policy control problem as one in which the policymakers faced a duality of information variables, with 'money' and 'real' quantities co-existing side-by-side. Furthermore, in the two-pillar story, the partition of indicators justified a dichotomy of views about the functioning of the macroeconomy: one giving money and monetary phenomena an active role in price determination, and one downweighting money in transmission to a veil or a *recursive quantity*—essentially, an afterthought.[13] It is true that, as argued above, the quest for robustness was obviously the leading preoccupation behind the design of the strategy. But the 'two-pillar' concept was interpreted by many commentators as implying that the ECB policymakers were trying to have policy fare acceptably in a context in which they did not know which of two paradigms of transmission might be true. And, building the case for robustness on paradigm competition was somewhat awkward for two reasons. First, the relative standing of the two models of reference was disproportionately unbalanced. On one side, as a champion of the family of models that featured no explicit reference to monetary aggregates, was the NKM which was a fully-specified macroeconomic framework giving a complete—if stylized—representation of the main economic relationships. On the other side were mostly reduced-form or partial-equilibrium conditions linking money and prices with no clear underpinnings other than the quantity theoretic connection between money growth and inflation in the very long term. Also, the two-model interpretation of the strategy was untimely, as it came at a juncture when the two paradigms (if they had ever stood separately) were actually unifying. And, paradoxically, even the most prominent defenders of the 'money' view—Ben McCallum, for example—were actively promoting the notion that the NKM was not incompatible with either the long-term link between money growth and inflation, or with the quantity theory, for that matter.[14] For one, the model in the

---

[13] The ECB's Monthly Bulletin (ECB, 2000) described this dichotomy as follows: 'The distinction between the two pillars of the strategy is mainly a distinction between economic models or approaches to the analysis of the inflation process. The first pillar can be seen as representing approaches which assign a prominent role to money in explaining the future evolution of price developments. The second pillar comprises analyses of a broad range of factors and captures models of inflation which focus mainly on real economic variables, such as the interplay of supply and demand in the goods and labour markets. Against this background, in practice, the strategy implies focusing on monetary indicators under the first pillar, while concentrating on conjunctural and mainly non-monetary indicators under the second pillar.'

[14] As noted by McCallum (2001), in the NKM (or 'new synthesis paradigm', to use the term preferred by McCallum) inflation in the medium term was entirely pinned down by the steady state nominal money growth rate, which was implied by the interest rate operating algorithm used by the central bank to guide policy decisions. The leading indicator properties of money growth with respect to inflation were obviously fully reproducible in the NKM environment, and the seemingly causal relationship between money to prices was in fact the reflection of a 'general equilibrium' chain reaction tying together by amalgamation all structural relationships in the system. Karl Brunner's forgotten adage that 'of course, it is not money as such which drives up prices' comes to mind.

NKM tradition described in Box 1.2 does incorporate money, does satisfy the quantity-theoretic condition linking money and prices over long periods and, in certain states of the world, does even support an active role of money in price determination (see Box 2.2). But it does all this within a unified framework, with no segmentation of variables or transmission channels. Eventually, the two-pillar concept twisted the rationalization of the strategy in directions that would grow more difficult to defend as time passed.

2.4.2 Academic Critiques

Even before the strategy announcement, the Centre for Economic Research (CEPR) launched a series of annual reports by distinguished ECB watchers called 'Monitoring the European Central Bank'. A first thoughtful and provocative paper entitled 'Safe at Any Speed?' published few days before the announcement, inaugurated the series (Begg et al., 1998). The authors lamented the ECB's apparent lack of inclination to adopt a formal rule, a theme that would become recurrent in subsequent reports:

> What should the rule look like? Since one purpose of the rule is to facilitate communication, it should be simple. Interest rates should reflect deviations of inflation and output from their target ranges. Since monetary policy takes time to work, it is forecast levels of these gaps that should influence policy. The ECB should announce its forecast for the Euro-11 inflation and output, and thus the expected deviations of these variables from target. Based on these forecasts, it should explain what its normal rule would then imply for interest rates and whether or not the ECB considers that any deviation from this normal reaction is required.

Aside from its emphasis on the 'rule', the document carried useful advice—whose relevance unfortunately was revealed in years closer to the date of writing—on issues ranging from the balance of power within the Eurosystem between the centre (the Board) and the rest (the NCBs), to whether the ECB was prepared to fight a major financial crisis.[15] In the event of a global meltdown, the authors contended, 'it is

---

[15] Begg et al. (1998): 'One lesson [from the early history of the Fed] is that problems are created when the central Executive Committee is weak in relation to the chairmen of its constituent banks. Based in Frankfurt, the Executive Board and its staff, however excellent in quality, will remain small in scale and operational experience in relation to national central banks…A weak centre and strong national interests contain three dangers: inertia in policy formulation, slow transition to a truly European mentality and conflict between constituent interests organized along national lines. How quickly the ECB achieves effective centralization may be one of the keys to its eventual success.' In the authors' view, these design flaws could be exposed in the event of a major global financial crisis. In particular, the ECB would face two stern tests: '[T]he requirement that all ECB credit be collateralized may hamper the ability of the ECB to respond swiftly enough to a sudden demand for liquidity….In order to avoid the risk of difficult discussions at the time of a crisis, it should be understood and clearly spelled out that the rules for collateral

almost inevitable that [an ECB concerned about signalling its inflation-averse stance] will hesitate longer in reducing interest rates than the Bundesbank would have done in the same situation'.

The 2001 CEPR report (Alesina et al., 2001) turned up the temperature on the inflation targeting rule controversy:

> Inflation targeting is, in essence, a way of setting monetary policy in order to keep output close to potential, wherever potential output happens to be, while keeping inflation close to target. The Bank, therefore, need not worry about the output gap, which is always very hard to measure. The change in inflation is a sufficient indicator for deciding when interest rates should be changed. In sum, inflation targeting is simply a very good idea! The ECB should therefore abandon its 'two pillars' strategy and adopt a simple inflation targeting rule.

The authors' insistence that inflation alone might carry virtually all the information needed to measure the state of the cycle—a sort of 'divine coincidence' between inflation deviations from target and output gaps—appeared naïve, but was based on the view that, most of the time, shocks that are seen as causing a trade-off in fact 'influence potential output, rather than the relation between the output gap and inflation. In short, the relationship between the change in inflation and the output gap is likely to be quite close.'[16] Of course, the unresolved question in this line of thinking was that of measurement. Indeed, as we shall document in Chapter 3, the ensuing 15 years of macroeconomic history in the euro area was one plagued by persistent trade-offs of obscure nature, duration and consequences, and bouts of financial turbulence with undefined implications for medium-term inflation.

A notable complaint among external experts was that the publication of a reference value was complicating the pursuit and communication of the true overriding objective of policy, namely price stability. The 2001 CEPR report, for example, included an unequivocal statement to this effect:

> The ECB should closely monitor developments of monetary aggregates. Its mission, however, is to maintain price stability in the medium term. The growth rate of M3 can only be a servant in this quest and not a target in itself. [...] As for providing a nominal anchor, obviously there should be one. Money growth rates will do, but inflation targeting or inflation forecast targeting provides an even

---

could be suspended in case of a crisis. And: 'As the consolidation of the European banking industry advances, the ECB will find itself without an adequate supervisory system. The European Union should start thinking now about setting up a EU bank supervisor. This authority could rest with the ECB itself, or be delegated to an independent institution.'

[16] An increase in the bargaining power of unions might be a case in point: 'If this produces a wage push, inflation will increase, but higher real wages (assuming unchanged productivity) would also lower potential output. It is then the opening up of an output gap, induced by the fall in potential output, that raises inflation, not the shock in itself. When the central bank responds to the increase in inflation by raising interest rates, output falls, keeping close to potential.'

better nominal anchor. What is there to fear by replacing something good with something even better?

In a written briefing prepared ahead of the regular testimony of the ECB President before the Committee of Economic and Monetary affairs (ECON committee) of the European Parliament, Lars Svensson expressed the same view in even more uncharitable terms: 'Under successful inflation targeting, inflation would be stable and in a sense exogenous to money growth. Then one could argue that endogenous money growth is caused by exogenous inflation' (Svensson, 2002). In sum, of the three main elements of the announced strategy, the second and third—the two pillars—were those that most intensely caught the eyes of the international academic commentators.

It took more time, instead, for the quantification of the objective to rise to prominence in the ECB-and-its-watchers debate, almost as if the 'rule' could be operated irrespective of whether the *target* within the rule was sufficiently or insufficiently defined, or was pitched at the right or wrong level. And, when the issue started being debated in earnest, it was more about the precision and symmetry of the ECB's objective than about its ambition.[17] In any event, Lars Svensson ('the definition is asymmetric') and Charles Wyplosz ('the 0–2% inflation target range is far too narrow to allow for shocks') deserve credit for launching the debate in the European Parliament in briefings prepared ahead of the regular testimony of the ECB President before the ECON committee of the European Parliament in May 2001 (Svensson, 2001b and Wyplosz, 2001a).[18] Likewise, the German Council of Economic Experts

---

[17] To our knowledge, Peter Bofinger, a German professor of economics at the University of Würzburg— and successor of Otmar Issing in that chair—was the first to express concerns about the lack of a firm floor in the ECB's price stability range. He did so as early as April 1999 in a briefing paper prepared for the ECON committee of the European Parliament (Bofinger, 1999): '[T]he present HICP inflation rate of 0.8 % would be close to deflation for all central banks except the Reserve Bank of New Zealand. Thus, for most central banks it would indicate a need for an expansionary policy stance, while the ECB seems to regard this as "price stability"... [What is required is] a more transparent definition of the ECB's inflation target, preferably in the form of a band with a precise upper and lower bound.' Lars Svensson, in a comprehensive paper written in May 1999 (Svensson, 1999), was also quick to draw attention to the ambiguity of the range: 'A lower bound might be inferred from the reference value for money growth. When the reference value was announced on December 1, it appeared that a point inflation target of 1.5 percent had been used. If that point inflation target is interpreted to be in the middle of the interval, the lower bound is 1 percent. Hence, it seems to me that the definition could also be interpreted as the interval 1–2 percent, equivalent to an inflation target of 1.5 percent.' In a briefing prepared for the ECON committee in June 2000 (Svensson, 2000), Lars Svensson reiterated that: 'In practice, the Eurosystem seems to use 1.5 percent as an inflation target, and a better, unambiguous and symmetric specification of its operational goal would be an inflation target of 1.5 percent, possibly with a tolerance interval of plus/minus 1 percent.'

[18] Lars Svensson elaborated on a number of aspects that will become relevant for what we will have to say in Chapter 3: '[A] range is inferior to a point inflation target, since a range may be interpreted as a "zone of indifference" and the edges of the range may be interpreted as "hard-edged", that is, thresholds for policy adjustments. A range provides a less precise anchor for inflation expectations. There is a big difference between inflation expectations of 2% and 0%. A symmetric point target provides the best anchor for inflation expectations. Symmetry, in the sense of being equally concerned about over- and under-shooting the target, is necessary for avoiding a bias in inflation expectations relative to the target... If a range is announced around the point target, it is important that the edges are interpreted as "soft-edged" and not as thresholds for policy adjustment, thus allowing for a gradual and medium-term approach to monetary policy as we address the empirical question.'

sought to bring a similar discussion into the limelight of the German domestic debate (Sachverständigenrat zur Begutachtung der gesamtwirtschaftlichen Entwicklung, 2002). The European Parliament was alerted to the matter and, in September 2001, the chair of the ECON committee, Christa Randzio-Plath, quizzed the ECB President with the following challenging question: 'Why is the ECB the only central bank in the world which has such a strict, narrow definition of price stability?' The President replied with a letter, in which he said the following (Duisenberg, 2001c):

> In setting the numerical value for our definition of price stability, three considerations also had to be taken into account. First, the Treaty mandate of maintaining price stability, for sound economic reasons, does not allow us to exclude, in an arbitrary manner, low positive numbers for increases in the price level from the definition of price stability. In this sense, it would not have been appropriate to exclude inflation rates below a certain value, say 1.5%, from the definition of price stability. At the same time, in view of the potential existence of a measurement bias in the HICP inflation, we did not deem it appropriate to specify explicitly 0% as the lower boundary for the definition of price stability. Taking this into account, we have decided not to exclude low positive inflation rates from the definition, but deliberately to leave the lower (positive) boundary of the definition of price stability open. Secondly, there are strong arguments for setting a relatively narrow range of price increases admissible over the medium term. Only then is the definition effective in anchoring inflation expectations—thus fully reaping the benefits of price stability. Thirdly, setting an upper boundary of 2%, the definition should allow for a sufficiently large safety margin to ensure that the potential risks associated with deflation are avoided. As I have emphasized at previous meetings with your committee, the ECB's definition of price stability precludes inflation as well as deflation.

But was the objective too ambitious? Jean-Paul Fitoussi and Jérôme Creel, of the Centre for European Reform, had no doubts:

> The current target of 2 per cent or lower is clearly too restrictive, probably because of the unusually low inflation that prevailed in 1998 when the ECB first set its policy goals. This not only implies the risk that the Bank could strangle a potential upturn in the eurozone economy. It also undermines the ECB's credibility and standing directly, because by the end of 2002 it will most probably have missed its target for the third year out of the four it has been in operation. If the ECB is reluctant to increase its target for now, it should at least add a margin of error of plus or minus 1 per cent.
>
> **(Fitoussi and Creel, 2002)**

Paul De Grauwe, in a book on the European Monetary Union, argued along the same lines, noting that 'the optimal inflation rate may be of the order of 2.5% to 3.5% per year' in the euro area (De Grauwe, 2002).

2.5 Pragmatism and Strategic Headaches

Despite the harsh critiques it levelled at the ECB's strategy, overall the 2001 CEPR report found that, 'regardless of the rhetoric' in the first two years of existence, the ECB had 'shown good judgement, in its actions [... and] a certain amount of flexibility in interpreting its mandate of price stability', rightly resisting the temptation to prove its value as an uncompromising inflation fighter at all costs. It is difficult to disagree. Panel A of Figure 2.2 shows the co-movement of the interest rate on the ECB's main refinancing operations (MRO rate) and money growth over those years, while Panel B of the same figure decomposes money by its counterparts.[19] As is apparent from the two panels of the figure, the euro area economy entered monetary union with buoyant money growth, fuelled by very dynamic loan creation (see the contribution of the yellow bars to money growth in Panel B). Notwithstanding the signals that the ECB was receiving from its money pillar, over the first months of operations the GC became increasingly worried about the underlying health of the real economy. As shown by the red dotted lines departing from the thick blue lines in Panel C and D of Figure 2.2, the internal projections available for the April GC meeting were indicating downside risks to growth for both 1999 and 2000, and were pointing to the slowdown in growth as a potential further drag on an inflation rate already hovering below 1%. In those conditions—with the two pillars sending contrasting messages—the GC concluded that the second pillar was more informative after all. So, at its 8 April 1999 meeting, the GC decided to 'buy some insurance' against worse macroeconomic outcomes with a hefty 50 basis point reduction in the leading ECB interest rate.[20] Internal thinking included an explicit recognition that such significant move would not bring the risk of a breach in the upper boundary of the ECB's definition of price stability. The introductory statement read out by the President at the press conference mirrored this conviction in the following words: 'In our current assessment of the situation, it appears unlikely that HICP increases will be out of line with the Eurosystem's definition of price stability.' The formulation used to justify the rate reduction would set a standard for future communication. Whereas rate hikes—because of a sharply defined inflation ceiling—ordinarily would invoke 'upward risks to price stability', rate cuts would invariably eschew any

---

[19] Here, the premise is that any change in the broad monetary aggregate M3 is mirrored in the developments of its counterparts, and notaby credit to the private sector, credit to general government, and net external assets. The decomposition of money by counterparts has been a relevant source of information underpinning the ECB's monetary analysis, contributing to a better understanding of the underlying factors driving monetary developments and providing a signal of risks to price stability. For an early introduction to the ECB's monetary analysis, including an analysis of the counterparts of monetary aggregates, see Papademos and Stark (2010).

[20] At the press conference that day, President Duisenberg downplayed an M3 growth rate higher than the reference value as 'presumably reflecting the unwinding of the influence of some special factors related to the start of Stage Three and the introduction of the euro...Monetary growth is, at the current juncture, not a risk for future price stability.' In answering a question, he added: 'Inflation is not a danger, which enabled us to, let me say, to pay more attention to the second area of objectives of the ECB—that is, to support the general economic policies of the European Community.'

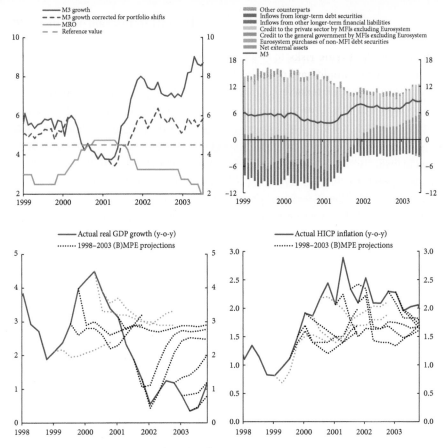

Figure 2.2 ECB policy rates and M3 developments

Panel A: M3 growth, M3 growth corrected for portfolio shifts, and ECB MRO rate
(year-on-year % change and percentages per annum)
Source: ECB BSI.
Notes: Corrected for the combination of level shift/temporary change in January 1999 and for portfolio shifts with a linear increasing intervention effect derived from a univariate time series model.
Latest observation: June 2003.

Panel B: M3 growth and counterparts (year-on-year % change, contributions in percentage points)
Source: ECB BSI.
Latest observation: June 2003.

Panel C: Actual and projected real GDP growth (year-on-year % change)
Sources: Eurostat and ECB projections.
Notes: ECB staff real GDP growth projections as available to the GC at the time of ECB's interest rate decisions between 1999 and 2003. The red dotted line is winter 1999 MPE, the latest projection available to the GC at the time of the April 1999 rate cut; the green dotted lines are spring 2000 BMPE and summer 2000 MPE corresponding to the rate hikes of June and September 2000; the black dotted lines are the other projection vintages corresponding to rate decisions during the 1999–2000 tightening cycle and 2001–2003 easing cycle.
Latest observation: 2003Q4 for realized real GDP growth.

Panel D: Actual and projected HICP inflation (year-on-year % change)
Sources: Eurostat and ECB projections.
Notes: ECB staff HICP inflation projections as available to the GC at the time of ECB's interest rate decisions between 1999 and 2003. The red dotted line is winter 1999 MPE, the latest projection available to the GC at the time of the April 1999 rate cut; the green dotted lines are spring 2000 BMPE and summer 2000 MPE corresponding to the rate hikes of June and September 2000; the black dotted lines are the other projection vintages corresponding to rate decisions during the 1999–2000 tightening cycle and 2001–2003 easing cycle.
Latest observation: 2003Q4 for realized HICP inflation.

reference to 'downside risks to price stability', as the latter phrase—in the price stability regime—would have indicated risks of outright deflation.

The April 1999 rate reduction was completely reversed as early as November, as the downside risks to growth and inflation dissipated in the course of the summer. The ECB continued to tighten the stance for much of 2000 (see Panel A), as rising oil prices and the falling external value of the euro were seen as posing risks of second-round effects in wage and price-setting in the euro area. As shown in Panel D by the green dotted lines, in the forecasting exercises of spring and summer 2000, for the first time in the short history of monetary union, the two-year-ahead inflation rate was predicted to reach 2%, a level seen by some members of staff as inconsistent with the definition of price stability, with growth keeping sustainably above 3%—far in excess of potential.

Brisk money growth was invoked as a reason for restricting credit conditions throughout this period. But, in fact, the indicator properties of headline money growth were increasingly being called into question in internal analysis. By late 2000, ECB monetary experts (and policymakers) began to entertain the view that past M3 data had likely been distorted upwards by expanding non-euro-area residents' holdings of short-term marketable instruments. The deflating stock market dotcom bubble in the United States had encouraged a shift in international financial portfolios towards euro-denominated liquid assets, and this inflow of funds was, in the view of some experts, artificially distorting the price signal coming from money. Indeed, shortly before the GC meeting of 10 May 2001, staff confirmed the hypothesis that money was being distorted by ongoing portfolio re-allocations, and that a gradual release of the statistical revisions was in order. We show the M3 growth series corrected for statistical distortions due to the financial inflows in Panel A along with the headline figures. In Panel B, the influence of the financial inflows on yearly money growth is visible in the increasingly positive contribution of the banks' net external asset position vis-à-vis the rest of the world (the red bars). Net external asset acquisitions are the banks' accounting footprint of those inflows, as non-residents' purchases of euro area securities are settled through the banks. While the surprise announcement of a downward revision to money growth was used to motivate the rate cut at the May meeting, a new wave of sustained money growth that started as early as the late spring of 2001 did not prevent the two aggressive rate reductions that the GC decided on later in the year, in September and November 2001. Once more, the underlying concern inspiring those decisions was about the growth outlook, which had darkened dramatically in the wake of the sharp deceleration in the United States, with the mark-down in the two-year-ahead inflation projections to levels well below the 2% threshold acting as an enabling condition (see Panel D).

Clearly, the first few years of actual monetary policymaking exposed some loose ends in the general framework. First, the range of price stability was probably too wide to steer policy with any precision: there is no clear relationship between point forecasts for HICP inflation and the direction of monetary policy action between 1999 and 2002. Both tightening and easing decisions were taken with medium-term forecasts at—or, much more frequently, comfortably below—2%. 'Upside risks to price stability' or 'lower inflationary pressures' were the formulas used to rationalize rate hikes and rate cuts, respectively, in the absence of a firmer focal point within the range. Second, growth projections and, notably, the balance of risk to growth were the indicators most tightly correlated with monetary policy decisions in this period. While this fact earned the institution high marks for pragmatism and 'good judgement' in a dicey macroeconomic environment, the letter of the strategy did not quite support an anchoring role for growth in decision-making.

As a consequence, in more than one instance, the public was left wondering about the compass that the GC was following in practice to chart its way through the data. Finally, the money pillar was pivotal only when it was judged to be in agreement with the second pillar; otherwise it played a subordinate role. Again, this was probably a wise attitude on the side of the GC in view of the noisy signals that M3 was releasing, but did not accord well with the 'prominent role' that money commanded in the strategy.

All in all, the autumn of 2002 was a defining moment in shaping the ECB's internal views about the viability of the strategy as it had been communicated since 1998. The terrorist attacks in the United States on 11 September 2001 and their global aftermath the following year had manifestly suppressed growth, forecast inflation and credit, but had given a huge boost to money growth. Except in the very early months of 1999, loans had mostly co-moved with the cycle, while money growth had been out of sync with almost anything else. At the same time, looking back at the past four years of monetary union from the vantage point of late 2002, enough evidence had already accrued to suggest that *actual* inflation had a seemingly inherent tendency to remain above 2%. Some countries in a catch-up process, notably Spain, were pulling euro area inflation upward vigorously, while mature economies like Germany were slow to disinflate sufficiently on the other side, because of domestic rigidities and various inertial forces (see Figure 2.1 above). The conventional trade-offs brought about by the shocks to oil and food prices of the early 2000s were being compounded—it appeared—by the systematic discordance of money, and enduring cross-country divergences in a heterogeneous monetary union. All of this made communication about monetary policy decisions very challenging.

2.6 The Strategy Review

Against this uneasy backdrop, in October 2002 Otmar Issing launched a major ECB internal exercise of reflections on, and potential review of, the ECB's monetary policy strategy. The project was aimed at promoting public understanding of the ECB's policy goals, strategy, and actions. It advanced on two parallel tracks: one work stream concentrated on the definition of price stability and a second work stream focused on the role of money. As it happened, the process lasted seven months and occupied almost full-time a small contingent of ECB economists, who produced an extensive body of quantitative and conceptual work (surveyed in Box 2.1) to help identify options and inform the final decisions. After the ECB had shared the options identified with the broader circle of Eurosystem stakeholders in early 2003, it prepared the GC's final decisions, which were taken on 8 May 2003. A press release outlining 'the outcome of the ECB's evaluation of its monetary policy strategy' was posted on the ECB's website on the same day.

2.6.1 The Definition of Price Stability

Conceptual work on the definition of the objective concentrated on the desired properties of the price index, and on the ambitiousness of the objective, along with its symmetry, and its format—range versus point. Aside from the statistical considerations around the HICP, which played a secondary role overall in the discussions, early staff analysis focused on an evaluation of the balance between the costs and benefits of inflation, and took its cue from two real-world observations.

The costs of inflation were judged to be high, and probably higher than previously thought, as a flurry of new research using simulations of NKM for welfare analysis was demonstrating in those years.[21] But the costs of deflation, or excessively low inflation, were seen as substantial as well, and the case for a positive inflation buffer in steady state could not be based—it was argued—solely on the premise of measurement error distorting inflation statistics upward. Downward nominal wage rigidities were a source of friction that added to the reasons in favour of a positive inflation rate. The difficulty for firms to operate nominal cuts to salaries stood in the way of relative wage adjustments across firms and sectors facing differential productivity conditions if inflation was too close to zero, as the least productive firms and industries would face constraints in lowering their salaries—relative to their competitors—not only in money terms but in real terms too. In a heterogeneous currency union, where real convergence across member countries had further room to run, this mechanism would have a disproportionate adverse impact on the more mature economies. In a currency union, the union-wide inflation rate sets the bar around which cross-country relative price adjustments need to take place. With non-zero dispersion in average inflation rates across members, having that bar too close to zero would mean some countries having to undertake the adjustment in conditions not too far from deflation. This would make the adjustment unnecessarily painful and difficult to achieve, and would cripple the capacity of low-inflation, mature economies to adjust to shocks. A final cost of low inflation was related to the

---

[21] For instance, in an early investigation of welfare-maximising monetary policy conduct, Khan et al. (2003) find that 'the average level of nominal interest rate should be sufficiently low, as suggested by Milton Friedman, that there should be deflation on average.' They also note that 'as shocks occur to the real and monetary sectors, the price level should be largely stabilized, as suggested by Irving Fisher, albeit around a deflationary trend'. In a similar vein, Schmitt-Grohé and Uribe (2004a, 2004b) summarize the literature on optimal monetary policy in environments with nominal rigidities and imperfect competitions by noting that optimal monetary policy features an inflation rate that is zero or close to zero at all dates and all states.

probability of hitting the lower bound on the nominal interest rate put in place by the central bank, a problem that had attracted attention in the wake of the 2001–2002 global slowdown. Low steady-state inflation generated low nominal interest rates on average, which reduced the room for the central bank to ease policy in severe downturns. The shortfall in policy support that a frequently binding lower bound would create over long spells of time would be felt in poor macroeconomic performance and sustained below-trend growth.

There were two facts that influenced the starting point of the internal discussions on the strategy review: the level of long-term market-based inflation expectations, which had hovered stably within a small interval between 1.7% and 1.9%; and recent statements by Otmar Issing hinting at the fact that the ECB would become vigilant if it saw inflation descending below 1%.[22] These observations set important coordinates for the strategy exercise and, in effect, reduced the selection space to two broad options. One was, not surprisingly, the option of moving all the way to an 'inflation target'—with or without a tolerance band around it. This would essentially buy symmetry and win applause among virtually all professional observers.[23] At the same time, it would be seen as an about-turn from the price stability concept that the ECB had embraced in 1998. The original 1998 statement that price stability was defined 'as a year-on-year increase in the Harmonized Index of Consumer Prices (HICP) for the euro area of below 2%', as mentioned already, had for five years conveyed the implicit message that the ECB's definition of its own objective was not the result of an arbitrary choice, but reflected a law of nature, a timeless environmental factor. In Wim Duisenberg's words addressed to the European Parliament:

> The difference between a quantitative definition of price stability and an inflation target is that the latter does not necessarily define 'price stability', but quantifies the objective with respect to price developments that monetary policy is aiming for. In fact, historically, there have been many instances when inflation targets were set at levels significantly away from 'price stability', often in cases where countries starting from high levels of inflation set a path of inflation targets over time in order to bring inflation down to lower levels. Therefore, there is a

---

[22] In a speech in Milan (Issing, 2002a), delivered a few months before launching the strategy review, Issing remarked: 'Reviewing the various arguments in favour of a small positive inflation rate and their application to the euro area, it is clear that there is still a lot of uncertainty about what may happen when HICP inflation moves down towards zero percent. In view of these uncertainties, the central bank should be vigilant when inflation falls towards an excessively low level, say below 1%.' Svensson, in his briefing paper later that year (Svensson, 2002) prepared for the ECON committee of the European Parliament and referring to the speech delivered by Issing, welcomed the progress in ECB communication on its objective, but regretted that 'external observers [had] to resort to word-for-word analysis of this kind in order to find the true objectives of the Eurosystem'.

[23] The group of advanced countries that had embraced formal inflation targeting, arguably successfully, had grown since the times of the first EMI debates on the strategy. The Bank of England had a target of 2.5% (for the RPIX index), Sweden's Riksbank had a target of 2% with a ±1% band (for CPI), Bank of Norway 2.5% ±1% (for CPI), while the Bank of Canada, Reserve Bank of Australia, and Reserve Bank of New Zealand had a range of 1% to 3% (all for CPI).

conceptual difference between the ECB's definition of price stability and an inflation target. Similarities exist only when such inflation targets are aimed explicitly
at achieving 'price stability'.

(Duisenberg, 2001b)

A target would have been arbitrary and possibly out of line with the fixed measure
of 'price stability'.

The alternative to a target was to have a price stability range, 1998-style, and a
policy focus within it. Expressing the objective as a wide set of admissible inflation
values was not inconsistent with identifying, within those values, a 'focal point' or a
'thick point' that could guide the monthly policy deliberations more cogently. After
all, the GC's modus operandi—according to Otmar Issing—and the public's views
about the ECB's de facto inflation goal—as embodied in inflation expectations—
seemed to have spontaneously come close already to the common understanding
that such a point (or thick line) existed and was closer to 2% than to 0%. The 'range-
cum-focus' option would thus offer a number of advantages: it would ratify the
understanding shared by the GC and the public, ensure continuity with the 1998
announcement, build a more recognizable buffer away from deflation, and, not least,
glean the advantages of a point target—a better anchor for policy decisions and
expectations—without necessarily paying its costs: commitment to 'stronger activ-
ism' and 'fine-tuning of inflation'.[24]

Whether a focal (thick) point located somewhere close to the 2% frontier was
compatible with minimizing the costs of excessively low inflation was really an
empirical question. As Box 2.1 reports, the empirical analysis that was produced in
the course of the subsequent few months to shed light on this issue was reassuring
overall. First, the measurement bias distorting upward HICP inflation was judged to
be contained thanks to the continuous improvement in the quality of index, and
'likely to further decline in the future'; second, while there was evidence of concentration of pay changes at zero in low-inflation conditions, the incidence of nominal
wage cuts was also substantial; third, a steady state rate of inflation as low as 1%
would generate very infrequent encounters with the lower bound.[25]

The 8 May 2003 statement on the price stability objective mirrored the range-
cum-focus option. At the start, it reiterated the 1998 language literally, it reassured
that nothing about that language had changed, but clarified that, within the set of
admissible inflation values compatible with the 1998 stipulations, the GC had
definite policy preferences:

---

[24] Aversion to inflation fine-tuning was entrenched in ECB communication, and often mentioned as
one of the reasons supporting the ECB's avoidance of formal inflation targeting. For instance, Otmar
Issing (2002b) notes how 'the medium-term orientation of our monetary policy strategy and our aversion to
fine-tuning of short-term developments in prices and real variables has helped to provide a firm compass.'

[25] With a steady state rate of inflation of 1%, the frequency of hitting the lower bound was found to be
once every 14 to 50 years, while raising steady state inflation to 2% would reduce the frequency to once every
50 to 100 years. Box 2.1 elaborates on the model simulations underlying these findings in more detail.

'Price stability is defined as a year-on-year increase in the Harmonized Index of Consumer Prices (HICP) for the euro area of below 2%. Price stability is to be maintained over the medium term.' Today, the Governing Council confirmed this definition (which it announced in 1998). At the same time, the Governing Council agreed that in the pursuit of price stability it will aim to maintain inflation rates close to 2% over the medium term. This clarification underlines the ECB's commitment to provide a sufficient safety margin to guard against the risks of deflation. It also addresses the issue of the possible presence of a measurement bias in the HICP and the implications of inflation differentials within the euro area.

In his intervention at a press conference following the publication of the decision on 8 May, President Duisenberg describes the part of the decision reconfirming the below 2% range as motivated by credibility considerations. Indeed not being seen as reneging on the 'below 2%' formulation—in which the ECB had invested a large amount of communication capital—proved to be a hugely important sticking point in the discussions. But, the policy 'aim' was indeed a significant innovation. It created a buffer to guard against deflation at the euro area level and in single countries. It removed much of the room for manoeuvre—and potential scope for policy licence—that the broad and slack *below 2%* definition had granted the GC over the past five years of operations. In doing so, it had the potential for improving communication enormously. It brought the ECB one step closer to the wider community of central banks that had been explicit about their targets. So much so that, when asked about the level of the 'below but close to 2%' policy 'aim' during the press briefing following the announcement of the results of the strategy evaluation, Otmar Issing could say: 'This "close to 2%" is not a change, it is a clarification of what we have done so far, what we have achieved—namely inflation expectations remaining in a narrow range of between roughly 1.7% and 1.9%.'[26]

The 'close to 2%' clarification of the inflation aim was overall well received and proved effective at anchoring inflation expectations in the subsequent period. Evidence from the ECB Survey of Professional Forecasters (SPF), in particular, illustrates that following the 2003 strategy review the distribution of long-term inflation expectations moved from being tri-modal—with a significant share of respondents expecting inflation to be as low as 1.5% in the long term—to a bi-modal and then uni-modal distribution, with the bulk of the distribution being concentrated between 1.8% and 2.0%—in line with the 'below but close to 2%' formulation (see Figure 2.3).

---

[26] Jean-Claude Trichet, upon becoming President, confirmed this quantification of the policy 'aim': 'Since January 1999, medium and long-term inflation expectations, as measured by survey data, have remained stable most of the time within the range of 1.7 to 1.9%, thus at a level compatible with the definition of price stability' (Trichet, 2003b).

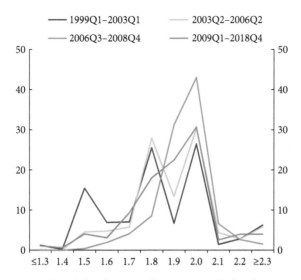

Figure 2.3 SPF respondents' distribution of long-term inflation forecast over selected sub-periods (% of respondents)

Source: ECB Survey of Professional Forecasters (SPF).
Latest observation: 2018Q4.

The symmetry question had not been answered thoroughly, however. It remained to be seen to what extent inflation levels truly close to 2% could become the authentic focus of monetary policy, even if that meant running the risk of seeing inflation almost half of the time out of the 'price stability' zone. Only history could tell if shooting for something 'close to the edge' was a viable approach. In Chapter 3 we will seek to recount that history, concentrating principally on the issue of symmetry and ambitiousness. In fact, as we shall argue at the end of Chapter 3, the 8 May 2003 decision traded safety—away from zero and deflation—for symmetry, making the definition of the objective possibly more asymmetric in public perceptions than it had been in the few years that preceded the review.

Box 2.1 Empirical inputs into the strategy review

This box provides a survey of the technical analyses that informed the Governing Council's evaluation of the ECB's monetary policy strategy in 2003. This survey draws heavily on 'Background Studies for the ECB's Evaluation of its Monetary Policy Strategy', edited by Otmar Issing and posted on the ECB's website on 8 May 2003, the day of the strategy announcement. Reflecting the two work streams of the strategy review exercise, the box is divided in two sections, starting with a survey of the studies

(Continued)

Box 2.1 Continued

on the ECB's price stability definition (Section 1) before turning to the two pillars and the role of money (Section 2).

The ECB's Price Stability Definition

The work carried out by ECB staff concentrated on the following four aspects of the ECB's price stability definition: (i) the measurement bias in the HICP index; (ii) downward nominal price and wage rigidities; (iii) sustained inflation differentials in EMU; and (iv) the zero lower bound of nominal interest rates.

The Measurement Bias in the HICP Index

On (i), the analysis started from the observation that inflation may be subject to a positive measurement error ('substitution bias'), which would imply that strict price stability (zero inflation) as measured by the price index would de facto imply a declining price level. ECB staff analysis conducted on this occasion (Camba-Mendez, Gaspar and Wynne, 2002; Camba-Mendez, 2003) concluded that in general, while the estimation of the measurement bias in the HICP was surrounded by uncertainty, the bias was probably small and likely to further decline in the future, taking into account the continuous improvements implemented by Eurostat. On the other hand, as stressed by Wynne and Rodríguez Palenzuela (2004), the paucity of basic research on the accuracy of the components of the HICP impeded a meaningful estimate of the bias.[27] Wynne (2005) sought to fill the knowledge gap on the bias by comparing the HICP with survey responses on the cost of living from the European Commission's Consumer Survey. It found that the euro area HICP may have overstated the true rate of inflation by about 1 to 1.5 percentage points over 1996–2004, a number somewhat higher than the estimate used by Cecchetti and Wynne (2003) in their discussion of the ECB's definition of price stability.

Downward Nominal Price and Wage Rigidities

As regards (ii), the ECB staff review of empirical findings in the literature (Rodríguez Palenzuela, Camba-Mendez and García, 2003; Coenen, 2003; Yates, 1998) suggested that, in practice, the importance of downward nominal rigidities was highly uncertain, while the empirical evidence was inconclusive, particularly for the euro area. This reflected, notably, the scarcity of observations due to the rarity of prolonged periods of very low inflation in any country. That said, on the price-setting side, available evidence based on the distribution of changes in euro area price indices

---

[27] The only comprehensive survey available at the time (Hoffman (1998), on Germany) concluded that the overall bias in the German CPI was of the order of 0.75 percentage points a year. Hoffman later revised his estimate of bias down to 0.5 percentage points based on improvements in the German Federal Statistical Office's methods.

indicated that nominal price cuts were not as uncommon as often believed. In particular, there was little evidence that low inflation in the euro area affected the skewness of the distribution of those changes, as would be expected in presence of downward rigidities. As far as wage-setting behaviour is concerned, evidence based on both micro surveys and aggregate data generally pointed to some concentration of wage changes around the zero mark but also a substantial proportion of wage earners having experienced wage cuts.[28] At the macro level, the presence of downward nominal rigidities was found to be usually associated with non-linearities in the Phillips curve relationship at low inflation, implying that shifts in unemployment produce a smaller change in the rate of inflation.[29] Here too, however, the empirical evidence was found to be quite mixed.[30]

Sustained Inflation Differentials across Euro Area Countries

As regards (iii), the analysis by ECB staff was motivated by the recurrent claim that inflation differentials between euro area countries—if persistent—had the potential to exacerbate the cost of downward nominal rigidities and push some countries into periods of protracted deflation. While inflation differentials are and should be considered a normal feature of any currency area, the ECB staff review did not find any evidence that the dispersion of inflation rates across euro area countries was larger than that observed across regions of equivalent size in the United States. In addition, the possibility that an individual country in the euro area could fall into a 'deflationary spiral', while the euro area would on average remain at price stability, was seen as an unlikely event, as significant gains in competitiveness would push up demand for their products, thereby counteracting deflationary pressures. As regards the role of the Balassa-Samuelson effect, which was often mentioned as the main factor underlying sustained inflation differentials across euro area countries, the ECB staff assessment found that the size of this effect was plausibly limited in the euro area,[31] and that it was likely to diminish further in the future given the substantial convergence among countries in terms of per capita GDP. Going beyond this assessment, however, was challenging at the time of the review given the lack of a reliable breakdown of the persistent component in inflation differentials according to the underlying causes.

(*Continued*)

---

[28] See Card and Hyslop (1997), for the United States and Nickell and Quintini (2003), for the United Kingdom. Altonji and Devereux (2000) claim that the large proportion of wage cuts reported in the survey data can be attributed to measurement error and misreporting.

[29] Ball, Mankiw and Romer (1988) is a classic reference work dealing with this argument.

[30] For example Wyplosz (2001b) finds evidence for a non-linear relationship between inflation and unemployment in the euro area but Svensson (2001a) points out that the findings do not seem to be robust.

[31] See Rodríguez Palenzuela, Camba-Mendez and García (2003), and references therein. The range of empirical estimates of the Balassa-Samuelson effect reviewed by the authors showed that an average inflation rate of, say, 1.5% for the euro area as a whole would imply an average inflation rate of close to 1% in lower-inflation countries.

Box 2.1 Continued

The Zero Lower Bound of Nominal Interest Rates

Finally, as regards (iv), maintaining a small positive inflation rate rather than zero inflation might be desirable to the extent that it reduces the probability that nominal interest rates will approach the zero lower bound, which risks constraining the central bank in its ability to respond to deflationary shocks. Against this background, the ECB staff analysis conducted for the strategy review was aimed at assessing the likelihood of euro area nominal interest rates hitting the zero lower bound and/or a deflationary spiral being triggered for various levels of inflation objectives. Using a small macro model, Coenen (2003) finds that under Taylor-type wage contracts—which imply a low degree of inflation persistence—and with an inflation target of 1% the zero lower bound constraint becomes binding with less than 7% frequency, or equivalently, once every 14 years. With a target of 2% this frequency falls to 2%, while quickly approaching zero for inflation targets exceeding 2%.[32] Working with an alternative model also featuring modest inflation persistence, Klaeffling and López Pérez (2003) find that, when the equilibrium real interest rate is assumed to be relatively low (at 2%), the probability of hitting the zero lower bound becomes negligible only under inflation targets above or equal to 1%, implying a frequency of around 2% at the lower bound or, equivalently, once every 50 years. With respect to estimating the frequency of hitting the lower bound, however, it was important to stress the high degree of uncertainty and the dependence on a number of specific assumptions.[33] That being said, the overall conclusion from this model-based analysis pointed to the need to limit the likelihood of the zero lower bound as one of the key considerations in the determination of a small positive margin in the definition of price stability.

The Two Pillars

The prominence given to money and the publication of a reference value for money growth, within the money pillar, was justified on three distinct though related

---

[32] By contrast, under Fuhrer-Moore-type wage contracts—which imply higher degree of inflation persistence—Coenen (2003) finds that the likelihood of hitting the zero lower bound is quantitatively much more important, with a frequency of about 24%. This type of contract, however, was seen as less plausible in the case of the euro area. Coenen and Wieland (2005), in particular, show that only Taylor-type contracts fit inflation dynamics for a country like Germany that already enjoyed a credible and predictable monetary policy before joining EMU, while some member countries that experienced a long-lasting disinflation with possibly imperfectly credible monetary policy were better described by Fuhrer-Moore-type contracts. Thus, as it was perceived that the ECB would probably face a similar environment in the future to that faced by the Bundesbank in Germany, the use of Fuhrer-Moore-type contracts was considered misleading.

[33] In particular, both model exercises may have possibly underestimated the true risks arising from the zero lower bound, because of fiscal policy being assumed to occasionally boost aggregate demand during sustained periods of deflation to prevent the economy from falling into a deflationary spiral. On the more general issue that, prior to the global financial crisis, most economic models probably tended to underappreciate the risk of hitting the lower bound on nominal interest rates, see Chung et al. (2012).

grounds: (a) money's predictive properties with respect to price pressures at medium-term horizons; (b) money's 'natural, firm and reliable' anchoring function; and (c) the close link between money and prices in the long run. This second section of the box first reviews the methodology that was employed for the derivation of the reference value for M3 growth. Second, the section reviews the indicator properties of money and tests of money demand stability in internal analysis at the time of the evaluation of the ECB's monetary policy strategy, as the findings of both streams of analysis were key sources of information on which the final outcome of the review was based. Third, it summarizes the ECB's view on the role of money and monetary analysis upon finalization of the strategy review in 2003.

The Reference Value

The ECB introduced a reference value (RV) for money growth on 1 December 1998. It was clarified that the RV would refer to the broad money aggregate M3 and that it would 'be consistent with—and serve the achievement of—price stability'. The derivation started from the quantity equation (identity), $Mv = PY$, equating the nominal money stock times velocity to the price level times real income. Converting to growth terms and choosing 'trend' levels for the respective components would provide the RV. For trend growth, the ECB Governing Council (GC) estimated a range of 2% to 2.5%, while velocity was assumed to follow a trend decline with a rate of about 0.5% to 1% per annum. Taking these assumptions together with a quantification of the price stability objective, the GC set the reference value at 4.5%.[34]

The GC envisaged monitoring monetary developments against this reference value using a three-month moving average of the monthly 12-month growth rates of M3. This use of an average was aimed at preventing erratic monthly changes from distorting the overall picture. Importantly, from the outset, the monitoring that was envisaged—comparing actual money growth with its RV—was understood to be neither narrow nor mechanical. Indeed, the ECB's first Monthly Bulletin of 1999 clarified that 'the deviation of money growth from the reference value will prompt further analysis to identify and interpret the economic disturbance that caused the deviation'. This 'further analysis' with the ensuing economic interpretation was at the heart of the monetary analysis conducted by ECB staff and proved to be dynamic in terms of scope and with respect to its role in the overall policy assessment.

The choice and use of a reference value in internal policy deliberations and official communication were based on the general idea that 'money constitutes a

(Continued)

---

[34] One combination to end up with that point estimate is to combine an output growth rate of 2.25%, a velocity trend decline of 0.75% and an inflation rate of 1.5%.

Box 2.1 Continued

natural, firm and reliable "nominal anchor" for monetary policy aiming at the maintenance of price stability'.[35] Specifically, the introduction of a reference value essentially rested on two preconditions: (i) a stable relationship between money and the price level over the medium term—typically analysed by exploring the stability of money demand relations—and (ii) money growth having leading indicator properties for future inflation.[36]

In the period from the 1998 announcement of the strategy, and—at an intensified pace—in the immediate run-up to the strategy review of May 2003, ECB staff embarked on an ambitious agenda of empirical analysis to extract signals from money growth as regards risk to price stability. In the light of the two conditions for the reference value, a considerable part of this analysis was devoted to the monitoring of money demand stability and to studying the leading indicator property of money for inflation.

Money Demand

Traditional money demand analysis connects the level of a broad monetary aggregate, the price level, real income and an interest rate. The econometric framework is usually a vector error correction model (VECM), in which those variables constitute (one of) the cointegration relationships. Money is typically the log of M3 divided by the price level, income enters as log GDP, and the interest rate variable is either a short-term market interest rate, proxying for the opportunity cost of holding money, or it may show up as the own rate of return of holding money (possibly relative to a market rate). The Coenen and Vega (2001), Brand and Cassola (2004) and Calza, Gerdesmeier and Levy (2001) models (that latter referred to as CGL), are typical examples of such models that have featured prominently in ECB staff's money demand analysis from 1999 onwards.[37] The initial specification and estimation of these models needed to rely on pre-EMU data (synthetic euro area aggregates of the respective variables), but the models were gradually updated as genuine euro area data came in.

With a given model at hand, stability of money demand can essentially be examined at three levels: first, the very existence of a cointegration between the variables mentioned (and the number of cointegrating vectors in the VECM); second, parameter stability of the long-run (i.e. cointegration) relationship between real money, GDP and the interest rate variable; and, third, parameter stability of the VECM

---

[35] See ECB (1999), Monthly Bulletin article of January 1999 entitled 'The stability-oriented monetary policy strategy of the Eurosystem'.

[36] Ibid.

[37] See also the synopsis in Masuch et al. (2003) detailing the difference in specification especially as regards the measure of the interest rate variable.

short-run dynamics. From a monetary policy perspective, the long-run stability of money demand was essential, while the stability of short-run dynamics was somewhat less of a concern: if the analysis confirmed a stable cointegration relation, but short-run dynamics were less stable, the important long-run link between money and prices would still prevail, but the system might show a changing degree of swiftness in moving back to equilibrium.

The cointegration residual, i.e. the difference between observed (log) real balances, and their equilibrium counterpart given by GDP and interest rates is referred to as a monetary overhang (*oh*):

$$oh = m3 - c - b_y\, y - b_i\, i$$

where m3 denotes the log of real M3, *y* the log of real GDP and *i* is the interest rate.

While from 1999 to mid-2001 M3 exhibited annual growth rates between 4% and 6%, M3 dynamics subsequently accelerated, exhibiting growth rates of almost 8% by the end of 2001 and almost 9% in early 2003; see Figure 2.2 in the main text. ECB staff analysis singled out portfolio shifts from other asset classes into money as one of the main drivers of the observed high M3 growth. Those shifts were probably brought about by the rising uncertainty of financial market participants after the stock market downswing led by the information technology sector (bursting of the dot com bubble) and the terrorist attacks in the United States on 11 September 2001. In order to gauge the size of the impact of portfolio shifts, ECB economists relied on money, banking, flow-of-funds and payment statistics as well as on model-based tools.[38] In May 2003, this estimate signalled a growth contribution of 2.5 to 3 percentage points of annual M3 growth in the first quarter of 2003. The influence of portfolio shifts on M3 growth was to remain a prominent topic for the years to come, and the ECB regularly reported estimates of M3 adjusted for those portfolio shifts; see Figure 2.2, Panel A, in the main text.[39]

Standard money demand models that did not foresee a role for those special factors could not easily capture the buoyant money growth, which manifested itself in a sizeable and rising monetary overhang; see Figure B.2.1.1 for the example of the CGL model.

A rising overhang could in principle signal excessive money growth (relative to the money demand benchmark) with possible upside risks for future inflation, but it could also reflect instability in the long-run money demand relationship. With hindsight, the model did in fact start to show signs of instability as reflected by the strongly trending model residual after 2001. However, identifying potential parameter

(Continued)

---

[38] See ECB (2003b).
[39] See, e.g., ECB (2005a, 2005c, 2009): January 2005, October 2005 and January 2009 Monthly Bulletin boxes.

Box 2.1 Continued

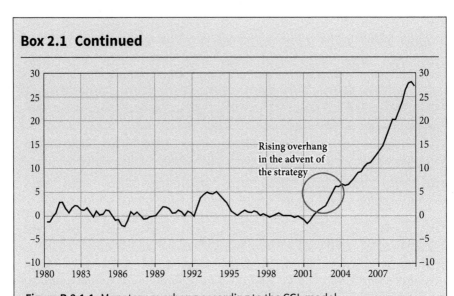

Figure B.2.1.1 Monetary overhang according to the CGL model

Source: Reproduced from Papademos and Stark (ed.) (2010). Annotation added.
Notes: The figure shows the percentage of the money stock (i.e. actual money exceeding equilibrium level by x%), corrected for the estimation sample mean; parameters estimated over sample 1980–2001.

instability in real time was evidently a much greater challenge.[40] The bottom line of internal ECB analysis using state-of-the art econometric methods to test for long-run stability of money demand[41] was that existing specifications of money demand models were giving rise to sizeable deviations from long-run equilibrium, but the hypothesis of stable long-run money demand specifications was not to be rejected. The Monetary Policy Committee (MPC) also discussed this issue in depth at the time and concluded in March 2003 that members 'seem to agree that long-run stability is a feature of money demand in the euro area'. At the same time, the MPC expressed 'doubt that factors that have contributed to the money-demand stability in the past would continue to do so in the future'.

One of the factors that the MPC identified as becoming potentially more prominent and challenging in the future was indeed the impact of portfolio shifts on money demand. To the extent that those factors or their drivers (like higher risk aversion and uncertainty) would co-determine the long-run relationship between money and

---

[40] A key issue was that the rise in the overhang took place at the end of the sample and did not revert. The results of stability tests could depend on whether one more year of observations was included or not or on using specific tests. See e.g. the discussion in Kontolemis (2002) and Carstensen (2004).

[41] See in particular Bruggemann et al. (2003), who conducted a battery of tests including on the constancy of the cointegration space and, conditional on the cointegration relation, the constancy of parameters. Importantly, using data up to the fourth quarter of 2001, they do not find evidence for stock market variables entering the cointegration space, while Carstensen (2004), using one more year of data, finds 'conventional money demand specifications to become unstable in 2001'. Augmenting these data with stock market variables restores a stable cointegration relationship.

prices, omitting these drivers from traditional money demand specifications would lead to large residuals or unstable parameters in those relationships.

To sum up, at the outset of the strategy review, ECB staff analysis confirmed long-run money demand to be stable, but deviations from long-run equilibrium values had become more sizeable. However, it was uncertain whether stability (based on traditional money demand models) would continue to prevail and—if it did not—whether more refined models of money demand would be able to come to the rescue.

The Leading Indicator Property of Money

Turning to the second condition discussed in the context of establishing a reference value and—more generally—a prominent role for money, ECB staff analysed the leading indicator property of money for future inflation over the medium-term horizon. The econometric framework for such exercises was mostly reduced-form predictive equations, in which future inflation is projected on the basis of contemporaneous and lagged monetary variables as well as other non-money predictors.[42] The monetary predictors were typically chosen based on (i) monetary aggregates as such, possibly 'treated' by excluding certain components or adjusting them beforehand, or (ii) measures of real money gaps.

As for the monetary aggregates as such, ECB staff tested various specifications, and it turned out that overall M3 growth is the preferred measure for improving upon single univariate time series forecasts of inflation. However, it also became evident that cleaning for outliers is important and—during the 2001–2003 period— the correction for portfolio-shift effects was considered as well. Moreover, ECB staff examined several variants of money aggregates which subtracted those elements from standard measures that were deemed to give too noisy a signal for future inflation. This included, for instance, M3 adjusted for non-euro area resident holdings of marketable instruments or M3 excluding the holdings of money market funds. ECB economists found that among those 'exclusion measures' there was none that uniformly dominated across forecast performance criteria.[43]

(Continued)

---

[42] See Nicoletti-Altimari (2001) as a typical exercise of that time concluding that 'the results support the idea that monetary and credit aggregates provide significant and independent information for future price developments in the euro area, especially at medium term horizons'.

[43] To give a flavour of such analysis, in an internal note of November 2001, ECB staff reported a thorough analysis of various such 'exclusion measures' regarding their implied velocity trend (relevant for the quantification of the reference value, see above), their leading indicator property, and their performance in money demand equations. ECB economists considered M3, M3 excluding the holdings of money market funds ('M3_adj'), M3 less holdings of money market paper and short-term debt securities ('M3_mmpds'), M3 less holdings of money market fund shares ('M3_mmf'), M3_mmf less repurchase agreements ('M3_mmfrepo'), and M3 less foreign currency components ('M3_fcc'). Most measures shared the same trend decline in velocity and the same statistical short-term dynamics. Money demand models with M3 and M3_adj performed well and were stable, whereas the results for the other exclusion measures were model dependent. In terms of forecast performance for future inflation, M3 and most exclusion measures were found to be useful, with the ranking of results turning out to be a bit horizon-dependent to a small extent. M3_mmf and M3_mmfrepo were found to clearly perform worse than the other measures.

Box 2.1 Continued

The other class of predictors was real money gap (RMG) measures. An RMG captures the difference between the actual level of a monetary aggregate (deflated by the price index) and a benchmark level. That yardstick is either derived by accumulating the reference value of money (from a given starting point) or by resorting to money demand models, in which the long-run relationship was evaluated at long-run levels of output and interest rates to obtain the benchmark of the money stock. A positive RMG is expected to predict elevated levels of future inflation. Conceptually, RMGs based on the reference value have the advantage that they are readily computable in real time, even at high frequency, and do not depend on further parameters; at the same time, they are somewhat rigid as they do not respond to possible changes in velocity. RMG measures based on money demand models can be re-written as the sum of the money overhang (as defined above), the output gap (i.e. the difference between actual output and potential), and the interest rate gap (i.e. the difference between the actual interest rate and a measure of the natural rate). Thus, RMG measures based on money demand take into account possible time variation in equilibrium levels of the underlying variables and their decomposition lends itself to a more granular economic interpretation of their dynamics, but they are by construction subject to model and parameter uncertainty.

ECB staff found that money indicators improve the forecasting of inflation over and above other macroeconomic information (such as past inflation, oil prices or economic slack measures). It also found that the improvement in forecasting became more marked for longer prediction horizons. In particular, real money gaps (and, for those based on money demand, especially the monetary overhang component),[44] but 'pure' indicators of money growth were likewise informative, with M3 turning out to be superior to its more narrow counterparts for longer horizons (of around three years).[45] Having a battery of such inflation prediction models at hand, ECB staff used those tools to report a range of money-enriched inflation projections and also explored forecast gains from model averaging. Overall, the ECB confirmed the leading indicator properties of money for inflation.

[44] In an internal analysis of September 2002, ECB economists scrutinised the leading indicator performance of various RMG measures, concluding that (i) overall they contain useful information for future price developments over and above what is contained in real activity measures such as the output gap, (ii) while RMGs based on the reference value and those based on money demand models differed until the early 1990s they have provided very similar signals since the inception of the euro.

[45] However, over time evidence accrued that the narrow aggregate M1 has shorter-term predictive power for real activity, see, e.g., Brand, Reimers and Seitz (2003).

Revisiting the Role of Money in the Review of the Strategy

At the outset of the strategy review, ECB staff summarized their overall take on the role of money, relying on the analytical results obtained over the first four years since the birth of the euro (partly as described above).[46]

Regarding the two conditions of money demand stability and the leading indicator property of money, ECB economists Masuch et al. (2003) concluded: 'First, a stable long-run relationship between money, prices and a small number of other key macroeconomic variables exists; second, monetary developments are leading indicators of future price developments at longer horizons.'

At the same time, an internal ECB assessment at the end of 2002 stressed several intricacies that have emerged in analysing and interpreting the signals from monetary aggregates over the euro's first four years. In particular, staff noted that as of late 2001 the distortion of M3 signals stemming from portfolio shifts had led to a gradual de-emphasizing of deviations of M3 growth from the reference value in both internal analysis and externally communicated reasoning. The staff review proposed broadening the analysis under the first pillar, including a better integrated analysis of money and credit aggregates and their constituting sub-component, a synoptic approach to the analysis of money/credit on the one hand and financial markets/ asset prices on the other hand, as well as a widened scope and more intensive use of models, especially of those allowing for more structural analysis.

The view of outside observers was mixed: some confirmed their assessment of the need to have a prominent role for money in the ECB's policy deliberations, while others contested that view, doubting the long-run stability of money demand and pointing to the declining strength of the leading indicator property of monetary aggregates for inflation. At the more conceptual level, as expounded further in the main text, a debate re-emerged as what extent money deserves special attention within a separate pillar, or whether it should be subsumed under a broader framework of analysis geared to understanding and quantifying risks to price stability.[47]

Based on the result of its staff's own analysis, the prevailing academic results at that time and the experience with money in informing policy decisions and shaping official communication, the GC decided in its review of the strategy to maintain a prominent role for money. However, it modified some elements in the framework of how money entered policy deliberations and official communication.

As regards the reference value, the GC acknowledged its prominent role in pointing to risks to price stability and thus informing policy decisions. It emphasized that deviations in money growth from the reference value, such as the strong upward deviation of M3 growth in 1999 and early 2000, 'were important factors in dispelling

(Continued)

[46] See Issing (2003).
[47] See in particular Begg et al. (2002), noting their mention of the 'poison pillar', as well as the references given in Issing (2003), p. 20.

Box 2.1 Continued

the uncertainty about possible deflationary risks and, subsequently, in formulating an assessment of the need to increase interest rates in order to contain inflationary pressures'.[48] At the same time, the GC acknowledged the increased complexity in deciphering the signals from monetary developments, in particular in the light of the significant portfolio shifts after mid-2001, and it highlighted the risk of a (perceived) 'mechanistic' and misleading monetary analysis based on a too rigid and short-term interpretation of the reference value. Against this backdrop, the ECB decided to stop the regular annual review of the reference value—also with a view to dispelling the possible misconception that the reference value could be used as a form of implicit monetary targeting. Abandoning the annual review would stress the medium-term nature of the reference value. Moreover, the ECB let go of the 'official' focus on the three-month moving average of annual M3 growth, acknowledging that a more comprehensive assessment—based on a wide set of indicators measuring the trend in money growth as part of a broad-based monetary analysis—would be a more adequate set of tools for identifying and communicating risks to price stability.

As regards its explanation of policy decisions in official communication, the ECB decided to change the way in which insights from monetary analysis were reported in the introductory statement, which until April 2003 had started with an assessment of the 'first pillar' (money) followed by an analysis of the 'second pillar'. The new structure (still maintained today) would start with an 'economic analysis' focusing on the short- to medium-term risks to price stability, followed by a 'monetary analysis' assessing the 'medium to long-term trends in inflation in view of the close relationship between money and prices over extended horizons'.[49] The intention of this new structure was to better clarify that the 'monetary analysis mainly serves as a means of cross-checking, from a medium to long-term perspective, the short to medium-term indications coming from economic analysis'.[50] At the same time, as early as 2003, ECB staff foresaw the conceptual difficulty of operationalizing this cross-checking within its quantitative monetary analysis, highlighting that there 'may be scope to better clarify the existence of "a bridge" between the two pillars which ensures the use of all the information provided by the monetary and non-monetary analysis'.[51]

These adjustments regarding the reference value and the role of money in the introductory statement notwithstanding, the ECB emphasized the continued and increasing need for monetary analysis. In 2003, ECB economists pointed out several

---

[48] See Issing (2003), p. 23.
[49] See ECB press release of 8 May 2003 'The ECB's monetary policy strategy'.
[50] Ibid.
[51] Issing (ed.) (2003), p. 26.

dimensions across which money will (continue to) play a role for a price stability-oriented monetary policy.[52]

First, money can serve as a readily available proxy variable, which—unlike several other economic entities—is available in real time and is not subject to revisions. One variant of this role of money as an 'informative real-time statistic' is that money may—given its close link to real activity—work as a proxy for current GDP, which by itself may only be observed with a lag. Another variant is that money can serve as a proxy for genuinely unobservable economic entities. A case in point is the 'overall financing conditions' that may play a role in affecting aggregate demand. Those financing conditions—especially the variety of discount rates relevant for assets of different maturity and riskiness—may only be imperfectly correlated with the short-term interest rate instrument of the central bank, so that a comparison of that rate with a benchmark may only constitute an imperfect measure of the prevailing monetary conditions.[53] Looking (also) at monetary aggregates can—owing primarily to their nexus with credit—help the policymaker achieve a more holistic perspective of the monetary policy stance.

Second—and this is a point closely related to money's ability to proxy for a broader set of financing conditions—assigning a prominent role to money can constitute a safeguard against myopia and short-termism in monetary policy making. Issing (2002b) singles out examples where a narrow focus on interest rate benchmark may have led monetary policy astray and where money provided additional useful information. As a case in point, if the Federal Reserve System had paid more attention to measuring excess money growth in the 1920s, it may have realized that its policy was too lax—contrary to the signal offered by a pure Taylor rule-type benchmark.

Third, money and credit may have a distinct role to play in monetary policy transmission in the presence of financial frictions and imperfect substitutability between marketable assets.[54] A change in the money supply may lead to a rebalancing of portfolio holdings and hence relative prices and returns, eventually impacting on consumption decisions and aggregate demand.

Finally, monitoring and reacting to money growth may provide a 'nominal anchor' to the economy and give protection against the occurrence of undesirable equilibria. Christiano and Rostagno (2001), for instance, study a model in which an active Taylor rule allows for two possible steady states, only one of them corresponding to the desired level of low inflation. Using instead a rule that switches from a Taylor rule to

(Continued)

---

[52] See Masuch et al. (2003).

[53] See, e.g., Nelson (2002) which was referenced at that time. See also Andres, Lopez-Salido and Nelson (2009) as a later study in a similar vein (money as proxy) discussing a model, in which the forward-looking character of money demand implies that current real balances constitute a proxy for expected future variation in the natural real rate of interest.

[54] See, e.g., King (2002).

Box 2.1 Continued

---

constant money growth whenever money growth leaks outside a certain interval is shown to pin down the inflation target as the only possible steady state.

These conceptual considerations were not of a merely academic nature but shaped the research agenda and day-to-day monetary analysis carried out by ECB staff. The ECB developed its monetary analysis further after the review of the strategy, expanding both the scope of indicators being monitored and the econometric and model-theoretic toolkit.

This enhanced monetary analysis[55] included the following elements: accentuating the relevance of credit and loan dynamics in addition to traditional monetary aggregates; improving models of money demand by adding variables to the long-run equilibrium relation, such as financial market uncertainty (relevant for capturing the drivers of portfolio shifts) or (housing) wealth; refining the reduced-form models incorporating the leading indicator properties of money for inflation; exploring the (shorter-term) predictive power of monetary aggregates for future economic activity; implementing probabilistic early warning models of risks to price stability; fleshing out trend measures of 'underlying money growth'; integrating money into dynamic stochastic equilibrium models of the economy; using money and credit to identify asset price misalignments; and analysing the role played by banks and other financial intermediaries in shaping the dynamics of money and credit.

2.6.2 The Two Pillars

The role of money was the other major assignment for the strategy exercise. As we saw before, the informative content of money for purposes of quantifying risks to price stability at cyclical frequencies had already degraded measurably in the early years. Staff monitoring money at the ECB were bogged down by the constant activity of statistical filtering to extract signal from noise. But it soon became clear that even the underlying money trend that was constructed to distil the signal (see Figure 2.2 Panel A) was only weakly related to price developments at leads and lags that mattered for policy decisions. By the time of the strategy review, this statistical quandary was already showing through in money demand instability.

Formal stability of the money demand function is neither necessary nor sufficient for granting money a prominent role in a policy framework. As Lucas (1980) notes, numerical stability of money demand does not necessarily imply a quantity theoretic relationship between money growth and inflation in the long run, which is what the

---

[55] See Papademos and Stark (2010) as an interim summary of that work.

data tend to bear out. Conversely, the quantity theoretic condition continues to apply even as empirical money demand functions fail formal stability tests during periods of lasting shifts in the opportunity cost of holding money—resulting from changes in the own rate on money, and as real balances increase driven by the adjustment to a new low inflation, lower nominal interest rate regime. But it is true that the lack of a stable and reliable connection between money growth and inflation over the cycle is a sufficient reason for dropping money growth from a central bank policy reaction function, *unless* there are reasons to believe that money growth is a good stand-in for other variables that are worth monitoring and acting upon. This last qualification became very important in the strategy exercise.

ECB staff approached the money-role discussions in broad agreement over some key principles. First, nobody doubted the truth of the twin propositions that periods of sustained inflation could not occur without monetary accommodation and, symmetrically, that sustained reductions in money growth would eventually lead to lower inflation and deflation. They also unanimously acknowledged that chronic noise in M3 and incipient money demand instability should prompt a radical rethinking of the way the role of money in policymaking had been represented in official communication. Departures of observed M3 growth from the reference value could not in the future receive the prominence they had been given in the review period. At the same time, they also agreed, crucially, on the qualification which we report above: that, even if money velocity shocks were obfuscating the link between money growth and inflation, money could still retain a meaningful role in policymaking as a 'proxy' reaction variable.[56] But views started to polarize when it came to identifying those reaction variables for which money growth could usefully proxy in the central bank policy rule.

One camp argued that those variables were broad financial conditions. Accordingly, they advocated broadening the first pillar and turning it into something similar to a 'financial pillar'. They envisaged that monetary developments, credit developments, sectoral balance sheets and financial developments should be

---

[56] The quantity theoretic identity, $Mv = Py$, states that nominal output $(P\,Y)$ is proportional to the stock of nominal money, M, *given* a certain value of velocity v. For an expansion of the way $Mv = Py$ was utilized in the derivation of the ECB's reference value for M3 growth, see Box B.2.1. The quantity theory asserts that v tends to be determined by a set of slow-moving factors (demographics, innovations in the financial system) which bear no necessary relationship to forces, such as union wage-push or oil price inflation, that are important determinants of inflation in the short term. So, v is likely to move only slowly and predictably in the short term and those short-term non-monetary determinants of inflation—such as cost-push shocks etc—must affect M to have a systematic effect on inflation. In other words, the equation acquires more than an identity status for adherents to the quantity theory of money. All of this having been said, v might be subject to short-term shifts as well, of the kind we mention in the text, namely changes in the own rate on money (if M is a broad measure of money including interest-bearing instruments) and adjustments in households' and firms' money-holding preferences, as the perceived rate of steady state inflation changes and the expected level of nominal interest rates changes in tandem. When nominal interest rates are low, for example, the opportunity cost of holding money is low, and people hold larger real balances. Moreover, the penalty for holding balances that are temporarily larger than they need to be is small. Thus, fluctuations in the amount of money (either created by the central bank or as a consequence of financial developments) are largely absorbed by fluctuations in the amount of real balances held rather than in the rate of inflation. These shifts in v can blur the connection between M and P, possibly for extended periods of time.

jointly analysed with a view to drawing implications for medium-term price stability, with asset prices and financial flows complementing one another to form a natural part of this comprehensive analysis. For example, the inclusion of asset prices in the analysis would help exploit in full the information provided by monetary variables for the emergence of asset price booms and busts, while a broader first pillar would provide insurance against a possible structural break in the demand for M3. Such an enhanced analysis of monetary and financial indicators with a view to detecting at an early stage the build-up of financial imbalances and the associated risk of asset price booms and busts would contribute to the medium-term orientation of monetary policy. The strategic upshot of this position was that the two-pillar structure should be maintained as an expository device used to organize the information for, and the discussion in, the GC in a systematic way and to communicate to the public along the same lines; and the reference value for M3 growth should be abandoned.[57]

The other camp thought that financial conditions were measurable in their own right, and didn't need to be approximated by money. This group was convinced that the interpretation of the two pillars as reflecting two different families of models/indicators—analyses using money on the one hand, and all the remaining analyses on the other—was partly the outcome of an ex post rationalization and had created more controversy and communication challenges than necessary. According to this view, it would be easier for the ECB to take into account monetary and financial variables in the assessment of the short-term economic situation and in forecasts, thereby countering what had been criticized as an artificial and inefficient partitioning of the information set. At the same time, along the lines of thought developed in Box 1.2, they took seriously the fundamental fragility of macroeconomic equilibria, even those enforced by stability-oriented monetary policy regimes. They maintained that, if radical instability were ever to emerge, the connection between money and prices was more robust and dependable than that between prices and interest rates. Therefore, money had a useful role to play in warning the central bank about the risk that the economy might be heading toward undesirable equilibria—excessive inflation or sustained disinflation. If those equilibria ever became a concrete possibility, money growth had the attractive dual property of a warning indicator—a stand-in for the unobservable de-anchoring risk—and an instrument, or an operating target, to which the central bank could switch to halt the perverse dynamics (see Box 2.2 for an analytical proof). The strategic implication was that money should not be used as a high-frequency input into policy decisions; rather, the medium- to long-term compass that indicators of monetary imbalances offer could help the central bank to look beyond the transitory impact of the various shocks and maintain policy on a steady course. The role of monetary analysis thus would be of a more medium-term nature, providing a cross-check to the policy implications emanating from conjunctural analysis. In

---

[57] The idea of converting the money pillar into a 'financial pillar' was not unprecedented. The Second Report of the Centre for European Policy Studies (CEPS) Macroeconomic Policy Group, for example, had advocated that the ECB 'monitor M3 developments primarily with an eye to asset price inflation, given that the first pillar has thus become redundant in its present form.' Even the reference value could be salvaged, according to the CEPS report, as its 'principal utility at present is to signal the potential for asset price inflation' (CEPS, 2000).

particular, this line of thinking held, the similarity in how money growth policies and interest rate policies react to shocks suggested that *both* should have a role as a consistency check on the other when deciding how monetary policies should respond to shocks. The two pillars gave two reinforcing recommendations for policy, and if interest rate policies were to become unreliable—perhaps because inflation moved very high or very low—then money supply policies could be brought into play.

Eventually, the 8 May 2003 announcement of the results of the strategy review on the role of money took elements of both positions. Once more, the statement began by asserting continuity with the past: 'The Governing Council confirmed that its monetary policy decisions will continue to be based on a comprehensive analysis of the risks to price stability. Over time, analysis under both pillars of the monetary policy strategy has been deepened and extended. This practice will be continued'. The two-pillar notion was preserved, but the pillars were 'deepened and extended'. The following paragraph clarified the role of money, introducing the concept of 'cross-checking', and modified the hierarchy of the pillars:

> However, the Governing Council wishes to clarify communication on the cross-checking of information in coming to its unified overall judgement on the risks to price stability. To this end, the introductory statement of the President will henceforth follow a new structure. It will start with the economic analysis to identify short to medium-term risks to price stability. As in the past, this will include an analysis of shocks hitting the euro area economy and projections of key macroeconomic variables. The monetary analysis will then follow to assess medium to long-term trends in inflation in view of the close relationship between money and prices over extended horizons. As in the past, monetary analysis will take into account developments in a wide range of monetary indicators including M3, its components and counterparts, notably credit, and various measures of excess liquidity. This new structure of the introductory statement will better illustrate that these two perspectives offer complementary analytical frameworks to support the Governing Council's overall assessment of risks to price stability. In this respect, the monetary analysis mainly serves as a means of cross-checking, from a medium to long-term perspective, the short to medium-term indications coming from economic analysis.

The pillars were assigned to different time perspectives, to highlight the temporal trade-offs that policymakers regularly face. From its long-term perspective, monetary analysis—as the money pillar was to be referred to—was, to quote from the 2004 CEPR report,

> a sort of escape clause, which should override the recommendations that are produced by the model-based 'economic analysis' under certain circumstances—in particular, when the 'monetary analysis' indicates that policy has got quite far off-track. This 'cross-check' is not required to give finely calibrated advice about what should be done at each point in time to respond as well as possible to

constantly changing conditions; instead, it is intended simply to ensure that policy cannot go too far off track over the long run.

(Galí et al., 2004)

In line with this re-interpretation, the reference value lost its short-term indicator function: 'To underscore the longer-term nature of the reference value for monetary growth as a benchmark for the assessment of monetary developments, the GC also decided to no longer conduct a review of the reference value on an annual basis. However, it will continue to assess the underlying conditions and assumptions.'[58]

Box 2.2   How to escape from sustained deflation

This box is a companion to Box 1.2 and is meant to answer the question left open at the end of that box. The question is: given the fragility of the 'good' equilibrium in NKM, and the fact that the deflationary steady state is an attractive, globally stable equilibrium, does the gravitational pull around that state make escape impossible? What can monetary policy do to jolt the economy out of that trap or prevent that it falls in it in the first place? The box is divided in two parts. In the first part, to seek an answer to our questions, we use the same cash-in-advance model as the one developed in Box 1.2. We assume the economy has sunk into the permanent deflation equilibrium that lies to the south-west of the stationary 'virtuous' equilibrium targeted by the central bank. Wouldn't the continuous fall in the price level result in an increase in aggregate private wealth, given a constant or even rising nominal stock of money, and wouldn't this wealth effect support aggregate demand by enough to lift the economy off the trap eventually (the so-called Pigou-effect)? As proposed in Christiano and Rostagno (CR, 2001), the following strategy can work. The central bank follows its typical inflation targeting rule but keeps monitoring money growth and 'cross-checking' the inflation targeting prescriptions with the signals extracted from monetary developments. If money growth moves beyond some pre-defined thresholds around the rate of growth that is consistent with the 'virtuous' equilibrium, the central bank abandons inflation

---

[58] In his reply to a question regarding the fate of the reference value at the press briefing after the publication of the strategy decision on 8 May, Otmar Issing said: 'We did not say that we will no longer publish a reference value. But we will discontinue the practice we have adopted so far, namely that of the Governing Council reviewing the reference value in December each year. What is behind that? It is mainly that there was a misconception that the yearly review would lead to a yearly reference value indicator, a kind of normative indicator for the development of money. This was never intended. It was a "timeless" concept right from the beginning. A yearly review in this context has perhaps led to some confusion. So what we will do is not skip the reference value; we are keeping it. But this will be monitored and if there are changes, for example in the trend of potential growth – hopefully in the upward direction – in the euro area, which is badly needed, then this will have consequences for the reference value. But this might or might not happen. And when the time comes, then we will do it in a more technical way and not in this preannounced procedure that gave rise to expectations which were never intended from our side.'

targeting and switches to a different operating regime where it targets a constant rate of money growth and implements this new policy by means of bond purchases. The fiscal backdrop required for this switch to be effective is also spelled out in the remainder of this box.

In the second part of the box, we seek to generalize the idea of a monetary switch as an effective instrument to address deflationary contingencies. To this end, we study a cashless economy in which the central bank can implement unboundedly negative nominal interest rates. This economy belongs to the same family of general-equilibrium optimizing frameworks consistent with NKM, except that there is no lower bound on the central bank's policy interest rate. For this reason, we call it a 'Gesell economy', after the German economist—much admired by Keynes—who advocated taxing money as a way to implement negative interest rates and thereby defeat the deflation of the 1930s. Not unlike the cash-in-advance economy of the previous section, a Gesell-economy is also fragile to 'inflation' and 'deflation' scares. But, unlike the cash-in-advance model environment used in Box 1.2 and in the first part of this box, once a Gesell economy—for any reason—is caught in a deflationary spiral, prices carry on falling at an accelerating pace without limit. We show that if the central bank pledges to switch to a negative interest rate policy of a kind that is congruent with an appropriately supportive fiscal policy—in the sense made more precise in this box—in the event that prices are ever seen to start falling, the pledge itself will suffice to rule out all those negative trajectories, and the economy may never leave the desired equilibrium in the first place.

Returning to the cash-in-advance economy studies in Box 1.2, imagine the economy is in fact in the deflationary equilibrium, and fiscal policy is described by a 'Ricardian' reaction rule such as equation (B.1.2.16) in Box 1.2. As shown before, a Ricardian fiscal policy does not place any restriction on inflation or any other endogenous variables in the economy, so under such a fiscal regime the deflationary equilibrium (which is stable) will perpetuate itself indefinitely, with P_t falling at a rate β and $R_t = 0$ at all times. In other words, under such a scenario, deflation occurs simply because it has come to be expected to occur—and given these expectations, deflationary pressures cannot be offset by a reduction in interest rates.

What happens to money in this economy? We know that when $R_t > 0$:

$$M_t^s = M_t^D = M_t = P_t c_{1t} = P_t \left(\bar{Y} - 1 - \bar{g} \right) \quad \forall t \tag{B.2.2.1}$$

This implies that, in the 'virtuous' monetary equilibrium under an active Taylor rule, money has to grow at the same rate as prices, for the cash-in-advance constraint to be satisfied:

$$\frac{M_{t+1}^s - M_t}{M_t} = \tilde{\pi} \quad \forall t \tag{B.2.2.2}$$

(Continued)

Box 2.2 Continued

But in a deflationary, liquidity-trap equilibrium with-trap equilibrium with $R_t = 0$, money demand is undefined, so equation (B.1.2.19) in Box 1.2 does not necessarily hold. In other words, with the interest rate at its zero lower bound, $M_t^D \geq P_t c_{1t}$, the economy seems to be in a bind: the conventional interest rate instrument is out of order, and the money stock does not even seem to be defined.

How can one extract the economy from this perpetual deflationary equilibrium? Having the central bank jettison the interest-rate based Taylor rule and switch to a money-growth rule in the spirit of (B.2.2.2) above is a necessary part of a successful strategy to reflate the economy. Indeed, sticking to the old interest rate rule, instead, would not require money balances to be supplied beyond the quantities that are demanded at a zero nominal interest rate, and that amount, as we saw, is undefined in those conditions. But for such a monetary policy switch to be effective, the fiscal authority needs to cooperate, i.e. to become 'non-Ricardian'. Otherwise, the new constant money growth rule would be ineffectual.

To see why a constant-money-growth rule married to a 'Ricardian' fiscal policy would not be capable of jolting the economy off the trap, conduct the following experiment. Imagine that, in line with its new rule, the monetary authority keeps creating money at a rate $\tilde{\mu} = \tilde{\pi}$, so that $M_{t+1}^s = \tilde{\mu} M_t$, that the fiscal authority remains wedded to a Ricardian policy rule like (B.1.2.16) and, despite money balances growing in nominal terms indefinitely at a positive rate $\tilde{\mu}$, prices continue falling at a rate β. Would this be an equilibrium configuration consistent with optimizing behaviour and with meeting all the constraints? Note first that, if such equilibrium exists, the central bank would accumulate an increasing amount of seignorage revenues. To see this, manipulate the consolidated flow budget constraint

$$A_{t+1} = M_t + B_{t+1} - P_t s_t = M_{t+1} + \frac{B_{t+2}}{1+R_{t+1}}$$

to obtain:

$$\frac{M_{t+1} - M_t}{P_t} + \frac{B_{t+2}}{1+R_{t+1}} - B_{t+1} + P_t \tilde{s}_t = 0,$$

which, in the deflationary equilibrium, becomes:

$$\frac{M_{t+1} - M_t}{P_t^L} + \frac{B_{t+2}}{1+R_{t+1}} - B_{t+1} + P_t^L \tilde{s}_t = 0,$$

with $P_t^L = \beta^t P_0 \; \forall t$.

Here the seignorage revenue, given the constant money growth $\tilde{\mu}$, satisfies the following condition:

$$\frac{M_{t+1}-M_t}{P_t^L}=\left(\frac{\tilde{\mu}}{\beta}\right)^t\frac{M_o}{P_o}(\tilde{\mu}-1)\to\infty \text{ as } t\to\infty,$$

which indeed means that seignorage increases without bound in real terms in this equilibrium.

But this situation does not lead to any violation of equilibrium conditions, including the transversality condition that we report in equation (B.1.2.8) of Box 1.2. This seemingly odd conclusion is due to the fact that, under the 'Ricardian' rule—represented in equation (B.1.2.16) of Box 1.2—that in this candidate equilibrium describes the behaviour of the fiscal authority, the government uses the seignorage revenue initially to run down its bonded liabilities B_t, and, eventually, when B_t is reduced to zero, to accumulate unbounded claims against the households, i.e. by driving B_t to $-\infty$. This policy is implicit in (B.1.2.16), by which at each time the fiscal authority retires a fraction γ of its *total* liabilities. Therefore, despite unbounded growth in seignorage revenues and money holdings, the transversality condition always applies even as prices keep falling. In conclusion, with a 'Ricardian' fiscal policy, a monetary policy which, after bringing its interest rate instrument to the effective lower bound, should resort to money growth in an attempt to lift the economy off the deflationary trap would fail. The increase in the real value of the government obligations that people hold in this economy due to falling prices would not be enough to convince them to spend more, simply because the *nominal* value of these obligations is expected to continue falling at an even higher pace. If total nominal debt is expected to fall, this is because taxes are expected to remain high in the future, which is why people are reluctant to spend, and in fact are encouraged to save the current real capital gains on their wealth, in the first place.

Escaping the Liquidity Trap

Coupling the new money-based monetary regime with a 'non-Ricardian' fiscal policy would work, however. To see this, go back to the definition of A_{t+1} and redefine it in the deflationary equilibrium as follows:

$$A_{t+1}=M_t+B_{t+1}-P_t s_t=A_t-P_t s_t.$$

Now, imagine a fiscal regime in which the fiscal authority commits to retire a fraction of its *bonded* liabilities only, and rebate all seignorage revenues to the households. A rule that embodies this pledge is the following:

$$P_t s_t^* = \gamma^* B_{t+1} - (M_t - M_{t-1}) \tag{B.2.2.3}$$

Replacing (B.2.2.3) into the definition of A_{t+1}, after some manipulation we find:

$$A_{t+T}=(1-\gamma^*)^{T-t}B_{t+1}+M_{t-1}(2\tilde{\mu}-1)^{T-t} \tag{B.2.2.4}$$

(Continued)

Box 2.2 Continued

Inspecting (B.2.2.4), it is obvious that, thanks to the periodic rebates of seignorage, A_t grows unboundedly in this regime, even as B_t is brought to zero. Accordingly, under a monetary-fiscal policy combination given by (B.2.2.2) and (B.2.2.3), the transversality condition $\lim_{T \to \infty} A_{t+T}$ is violated. This means that this candidate deflationary equilibrium with $R_t = 0$ and $\pi_t = \beta \ \forall t$ is not compatible with household optimality. Optimizing households would not be willing to accumulate as much wealth as they would receive from the fiscal rebates of seignorage revenues. They would rather reduce the amount of assets held and use them to purchase goods. In fact, already at time t, the anticipation of an infinite stream of tax rebates would make households feel wealthier, i.e. able to afford larger consumption, and this would encourage higher demand for goods in excess of the amounts that the economy can supply (recall that in this endowment economy $\overline{Y}$ is constant). Only a sufficient rise in prices can restore equilibrium by reducing the real value of the nominal assets held by households.

In conclusion, if coupled with a suitably 'non-Ricardian' policy regime, a central bank resorting to a money growth rule would indeed be able to extricate the economy from the deflationary equilibrium. Real money balances growing asymptotically large would not be consistent with optimal saving behaviour and thus would not support deflation indefinitely.

A Cashless Gesell Economy

The equilibria studied above make the fundamental assumption that nominal interest rates cannot be reduced to negative levels because, as they tend to fall below zero, bond holders (the households) can avoid the negative nominal returns by massively shifting to currency. Now imagine an economy in which the central bank has easy access to technology that allows the nominal rate of return on currency and bonds to be equalized. We call it a 'Gesell economy', after Silvio Gesell's early proposal to eliminate the 'zero lower bound' (and the associated possibility for the public to store paper currency massively when the interest rate paid on bonds falls below zero), by issuing 'stamped currency', i.e. a type of paper money which only retains its nominal value by being stamped every month. In the remainder of this box, we assume that, either through a 'stamped currency' technology or (more conveniently) by establishing a crawling peg exchange rate between paper currency/electronic money and bonds (as originally suggested by Robert Eisler or, more recently, by Miles Kimball and others) the distinction between money and bonds becomes meaningless. It is easy to see that a cash goods/credit goods economy in which money and bonds become perfect substitutes (both when $R_t > 0$ and when $R_t = 0$) is completely isomorphic to the type of cashless economy studied by Woodford (2003). So we revert to an endowment economy version of Woodford's model where the purchase of any good or service can be done using interest-bearing bonds.

In this endowment economy, households maximize:

$$E_0 \left\{ \sum_{t=0}^{\infty} \beta^t \left[\log c_t \right] \right\}, \tag{B.2.2.5}$$

subject to:

$$E_t Q_{t,t+1} B_{t+1} = B_t - P_t c_t + P_t y_t^s - P_t \tau_t$$

$$c_t = \overline{Y} - \overline{g} = y_t^s$$

$$E_t Q_{t,t+1} = \frac{1}{1+R_t}$$

$$P_t > 0$$

$$\lim_{T \to \infty} E_t Q_{t,T} B_{t+T} = \prod_{j=0}^{T-1} \left(\frac{1}{1+R_{t+j}} \right) B_T = 0$$

This problem has a solution if and only if condition (B.1.2.7) in Box 1.2, appropriately redefined, holds. It is easy to show that the chief equilibrium condition in this cashless endowment economy can be cast in the same Fisher equation terms applying in the cash-credit goods environment studied in Box 1.2 and in the first section of this box, where inflation, as in condition (B.1.2.9) of Box 1.2, evolves according to $E_t \pi_{t+1} = \beta(1+R_t)$. In what follows, we study only perfect-foresight equilibria for this economy.

The Central Bank
As there is no possibility for arbitrage between paper currency and bonds at any level of R_t, in this Gesell economy the central bank can follow a *globally linear* Taylor rule with no kink:

$$R_t = \overline{R} + \alpha(\pi_t - \overline{\pi}).$$

Replacing this globally linear Taylor rule into the Fisher equation, we obtain the equivalent of condition (B.1.2.11) in Box 1.2:

$$\pi_{t+1} = \beta(1+\tilde{R}) + \alpha\beta(\pi_t - \overline{\pi}) \quad \forall t \text{ and } \forall R_t \tag{B.2.2.6}$$

Note that this equilibrium difference equation describing the deterministic inflation dynamics in a Gesell-economy, unlike in the zero-lower bound variant of the cash-credit goods economy, is not truncated downward at any value $\pi^L = \beta$. In other words, when monetary policy is 'active', namely $\alpha\beta > 1$, and when fiscal policy is 'Ricardian', or $P_t \tilde{s}_t = \gamma B_t$, this economy admits *only one* stationary locally bounded equilibrium $\tilde{\pi} = \beta(1+\tilde{R})$. Otherwise, the result that we discussed in Box 1.2 remains valid: insofar as the fiscal agent stands ready to offset any impact of interest rate or

(Continued)

Box 2.2 Continued

price dynamics for the level of its debt, the law of motion for inflation in (B.2.2.6) describes a monetarist equilibrium in which the central bank is in full control of inflation determination.

To see this, start from the household's flow budget constraint:

$$\frac{B_{t+1}}{1+R_t} = B_t - P_t \tilde{s}_t = (1-\gamma)B_t.$$

By forward iteration of this expression, and using the Fisher equation, we obtain:

$$\frac{B_t}{P_t} = \tilde{s}_t + \beta \tilde{s}_{t+1} + \beta^2 \tilde{s}_{t+2} + \cdots,$$

which, using the Ricardian fiscal rule, becomes:

$$\frac{B_t}{P_t} = \gamma \frac{B_t}{P_t} + \beta \gamma \frac{B_{t+1}}{P_{t+1}} + \beta^2 \gamma \frac{B_{t+2}}{P_{t+2}} + \cdots \qquad (B.2.2.7)$$

But recall that $\dfrac{B_{t+1}}{P_{t+1}} = (1+R_t)(1-\gamma)B_t = (1+R_t)(1-\gamma)\dfrac{B_t}{P_t}\dfrac{1}{\pi_{t+1}}$,

$\dfrac{B_{t+2}}{P_{t+2}} = (1+R_t)(1+R_{t+1})(1-\gamma)^2 \dfrac{B_t}{P_t}\dfrac{1}{\pi_{t+1}\pi_{t+2}}$, etc. Replacing these expressions into (B.2.2.7), and dividing by $\dfrac{B_t}{P_t}$ one gets:

$$1 = \gamma \left[1 + (1-\gamma) + (1-\gamma)^2 + \cdots \right].$$

As the right-hand side of the above equation converges to 1, the intertemporal budget constraint is satisfied for any value of P_t, which in turn proves that (B.2.2.7) does not place any additional restriction on the determination of inflation in the Gesell economy case over and above those consistent with (B.2.2.6). This means that, if the economy ever enters a trajectory that departs from $\tilde{\pi}$ and, say, sinks into ever more negative rates of inflation, an active monetary policy coupled with a Ricardian fiscal policy cannot arrest the implosion (see diagram below).

How to Arrest Accelerating Deflations in a Gesell Economy

A negative rate policy coupled with a certain type of fiscal policy can stop the implosion, and in fact prevent it for ever starting. To see this, imagine that the fiscal policy rule governing the primary surpluses is of the following sort:

$$P_t s_t^* = \gamma B_t + D_t R_t B_t,$$

where $D_t = 0$ if $\pi_t \geq 1$ and $D_t = 1$ if $\pi_t < 1$. Imagine the economy sinks into ever-accelerating deflation. The flow budget constraint in such a putative deflationary equilibrium looks as follows:

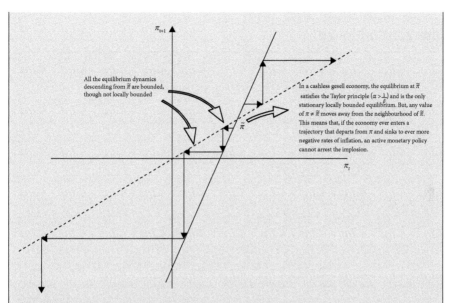

All the equilibrium dynamics descending from $\bar{\pi}$ are bounded, though not locally bounded

In a cashless gesell economy, the equilibrium at $\tilde{\pi}$ satisfies the Taylor principle $(\alpha > \frac{1}{\beta})$ and is the only stationary locally bounded equilibrium. But, any value of $\pi \neq \tilde{\pi}$ moves away from the neighbourhood of $\tilde{\pi}$. This means that, if the economy ever enters a trajectory that departs from π and sinks to ever more negative rates of inflation, an active monetary policy cannot arrest the implosion.

Figure B.2.2.1 Equilibrium dynamics

$$\frac{B_{t+1}}{1+R_t} = B_t - P_t s_t^* = (1-\gamma - R_t) B_t$$

Or:

$$B_t = P_t s_t^* + \frac{1}{1+R_t}\left[P_{t+1} s_{t+1}^* + \frac{1}{1+R_{t+1}}[P_{t+2} s_{t+2}^* + \ldots] \right]$$

Using the fact that, with deflation, $P_t s_t^* = (\gamma + R_t) B_t$, the above condition can be simplified into:

$$\frac{B_t}{P_t} = (\gamma + R_t)\frac{B_t}{P_t} + (\gamma + R_{t+1})(1-\gamma - R_t)\frac{B_t}{P_t} + (\gamma + R_{t+2})(1-\gamma - R_{t+1}) \qquad \text{(B.2.2.8)}$$

$$(1-\gamma - R_t)\frac{B_t}{P_t}\ldots$$

Or, equivalently:

$$1 = (\gamma + R_t) + (\gamma + R_{t+1})(1-\gamma - R_t) + (\gamma + R_{t+2})(1-\gamma - R_t)(1-\gamma - R_{t+1})\ldots, \qquad \text{(B.2.2.8a)}$$

which, again, must hold alongside any equilibrium deflation dynamics. What can the central bank do to arrest deflation in this economy? Imagine that monetary policy is described by our canonical Taylor rule, except when the nominal interest rate falls to zero, in which case the central bank commits to set the interest rate to a negative level, low enough to generate interest *revenue* for the government that

(Continued)

Box 2.2 Continued

systematically outpace the speed γ at which the government retires its own outstanding debt. A contingent policy rule satisfying these conditions is:

$$R_t = \tilde{R} + \alpha(\pi_t - \tilde{\pi}) + \frac{\chi_t}{\beta} \quad \text{for } R_t > 0,$$

$$\text{and } R_t = -\delta \ \text{ for } R_t \le 0 \ \text{ with } |\delta| > \gamma \qquad (\text{B.2.2.9})$$

Would continuous deflation be an equilibrium in a Gesell economy where the central bank ordinarily follows a Taylor rule but commits to abandon it and revert to a permanent negative interest rate policy if the economy ever enters deflation, and the fiscal authority, similarly, behaves in a Ricardian fashion in normal times, but threatens to deviate from such a rule and start rebating its interest revenue to the households if the economy ever falls into deflation? The answer is: no, such a policy configuration would not be consistent with a dynamic equilibrium with permanent deflation. To see this, we check whether condition (B.2.2.8a) or, equivalently, the transversality condition would be satisfied. Imposing the contingent negative interest rate policy (B.2.2.9) in (B.2.2.8a) we obtain:

$$1 = (\gamma - \delta)\Big(1 + (1 - \gamma + \delta) + (1 - \gamma + \delta)^2 \ldots\Big).$$

Note that, as $1 - \gamma + \delta > 1$, the second term on the right of the above expression does not converge and therefore the equality cannot be satisfied. Equivalently, going back to the flow budget constraint:

$$\frac{B_{t+1}}{1 + R_t} = (1 - \gamma + \delta)B_t,$$

and iterating it forward, we obtain:

$$\frac{B_{t+T}}{\prod_{j=0}^{T-1}(1 + R_{t+j})} = (1 - \gamma + \delta)^{T-t}B_t$$

As $\delta > \gamma$, this means that the transversality condition is obviously violated:

$$\lim_{T \to \infty} \frac{B_{t+T}}{\prod_{j=0}^{T-1}(1 + R_{t+j})} = \infty$$

In conclusion, a threat by the central bank to resort to a negative rate policy coupled with a similar and coordinated threat by the fiscal authority to become non-Ricardian if inflation were ever to become negative would rule out negative inflation equilibria and thus keep the economy anchored at $\pi_t = \tilde{\pi}$.

3
Strategy in Action

The year 2003 was a momentous one for the European Central Bank (ECB). It started with the evaluation of the ECB's strategy, and ended with the handover from the Duisenberg to the Trichet presidency. Generally speaking, Duisenberg's record at the helm of the ECB was not uncontroversial. As the fifth Centre for Economic Policy Research (CEPR) report noted when President Trichet took office, inflation had been higher than 2% most of the time since the launch of the euro, and yet—as remarked by the previous CEPR report published a year earlier—the euro area had not been immune to the global slowdown of 2001–2002. In fact, the authors of this latter report were of the opinion that the ECB had been ostensibly less active than the US Federal Reserve (Fed) through that phase in trying to cushion the economy against the negative effects of the international cycle.[1] The question was whether the ECB's interest rate decisions—and the strategy guiding them—were adequate for it to be able to deliver on its Treaty mandate over the long haul.

In this chapter we want to take up this question and test the underlying soundness of the ECB's framework when it comes to the practical conduct of policy. In so doing, we extend the 'strategy in action' observation period beyond the record that was available at the time of the two reports to cover the years between the start of monetary union and 2008, when the euro area entered a new and dramatic phase of its short existence. We take this longer-term perspective for two reasons. First, as Figure 3.1 shows, slight inflation overshoots became a constant feature of the pre-crisis times in the euro area: they are not a phenomenon confined to the Duisenberg presidency. Second, the conviction expressed in the 2004 CEPR report, that the ECB was not making 'particularly strong efforts of bringing inflation down again, when it should have been regarded as too high' endured throughout the first ten years since the euro area central bank was established, to the point that the last CEPR watchers report, written at the end of 2007, echoed much the same critique: '[a]nnual euro area-wide HICP inflation has been close, *but above* [original emphasis], 2% since 2000. This means that for most of its existence the ECB has failed to meet its primary

---

[1] One should note that, despite converging on the same severe indictment of the two-pillar strategy, the two reports came to strikingly divergent evaluations of the ECB's real-world policy choices. Whereas the fourth CEPR report absolved the ECB and concluded that 'having successfully negotiated a difficult period of adverse supply shocks until 2001, the ECB has already demonstrated its commitment to price stability' (Begg et al., 2002), the fifth report emitted the opposite verdict, namely: 'the ECB has failed to achieve its stated key objective of avoiding inflation in excess to 2%, even if one is willing to concede that it has missed this objective by only a small amount' (Galí et al., 2004).

Monetary Policy in Times of Crisis: A Tale of Two Decades of the European Central Bank. Massimo Rostagno, Carlo Altavilla, Giacomo Carboni, Wolfgang Lemke, Roberto Motto, Arthur Saint Guilhem, and Jonathan Yiangou, Oxford University Press (2021).
© Massimo Rostagno, Carlo Altavilla, Giacomo Carboni, Wolfgang Lemke, Roberto Motto, Arthur Saint Guilhem, and Jonathan Yiangou.
DOI: 10.1093/oso/9780192895912.003.0004

objective of price stability, at least according to its own quantitative definition'
(Geraats et al., 2008).[2]

We consider the fifth CEPR report published in 2004 (Galí et al., 2004) as paradigmatic in at least two respects: for its outspoken criticism of the overall architecture of the ECB's strategy, which it shared with previous as well as later expert
assessments and for the undisputed authority of its authors. We therefore organize
our discussion here around that report, taking our cue from an important statement
made by President Duisenberg before the EU Parliament.

First, Duisenberg's statement. In reply to a question by a member of the EU
Parliament during his regular hearing before the ECON committee in November
2000, Wim Duisenberg said: '[A]t what point would I say that we can talk about a
failure? That would be if, over the medium term future, we were to have domestic
inflation of our own making, not caused by external factors, but of our own making,
which would over time, continue to exceed the definition of, at maximum, 2% inflation.' In his prepared remarks, a few minutes before, he had clarified that, notwithstanding current oil-related inflationary pressures, 'when forming their expectations,
economic agents should count on the commitment of the Governing Council (GC)
of the ECB to maintaining price stability, defined as HICP inflation below 2%, in the
medium term. Monetary policy will not accommodate inflationary tendencies in
the euro area.' One can recognize several elemental principles of modern central
banking in these words: first, a central bank cannot be held responsible for each and
every twist and turn in short-term inflation figures, as there are always special
('external') factors that inch inflation up or down at a high frequency of measurement, which monetary policy simply cannot control; second, and as an implication,
a central bank will have to see through those factors and seek to back out those
underlying forces driving inflation that can be traced to the stance of monetary policy
(to its 'own making') in the medium term; third, 'medium term' is a forward-looking
concept ('medium term future'). Finally, there is faith in one fundamental tenet
of contemporary monetary theory: an overall strategy, even more than contingent
actions, can anchor agents' expectations.

The 2004 CEPR report adopted Duisenberg's definition of a performance standard, but found the notions of medium term and underlying inflation ambiguous, the
insistence on special factors to justify high inflation unpersuasive, and that tough
price stability rhetoric unsupported by demonstrative action would ultimately lead

---

[2] The analyses and conclusions of the 2004 and 2008 CEPR reports share clear commonalities. Both
reports, for example, note with alarm the shift in the distribution of the SPF inflation expectations to the
right: 'We see that the probability mass gradually shifts towards higher inflation levels as the horizon
increases. This is reflected in the implied distribution mean [...] which becomes as high as 1.84% for the
five-year-ahead forecast [...]. While a mean of 1.8% certainly qualifies as "below but close to 2%", a look at
the distribution should raise serious concern: forecasters attach an increasing probability of violating the
upper bound of 2% as the horizon increases' (Galí et al., 2004) and '[A]ccording to the collective judgement of SPF respondents, there is only an even chance of the ECB delivering price stability in the euro
area in two years' time. For a horizon of five years, this probability has also steadily shrunk from around
60% to close to 50%. This suggests that the ECB's failure to deliver an inflation rate below 2% may now
start affecting its credibility' (Geraats et al., 2008).

to a loss of credibility and de-anchoring of expectations. Outside Duisenberg's quote, the report argued that the monetary pillar—although de-emphasized after the strategy review—was nevertheless confusing and distracting for the public and for the ECB itself. The ECB, in its assessment, had not given much attention to it anyway and had used it as a rhetorical means of borrowing reputation. It should have been dropped altogether. The report drew two main conclusions: that the ECB's self-selected performance test had been failed due to 'inattentive policy', and that the ECB would have done better to revise its target lower—to build some safety headroom away from the 2% ceiling—or, equivalently, revise it higher by declaring an official range centred at 2% with a clearly defined lower bound.

In the next few sections we try to uncover the extent to which inflation and output over the ten years spanning 1999 to 2008 were driven by special factors outside the ECB's control and whether the ECB's policy can be judged to have been *inattentive* to the direction of underlying inflation as the ECB could see it looking into the medium term future. We also assess whether the ECB disregarded information from the monetary sector and, if not, whether paying attention to that information was detrimental to performance. With that evidence to hand, we then move to assessing the relative merits of the report's main normative proposals: a lower inflation target within the price stability range, or a higher symmetric target range around 2%. To anticipate, we find little empirical support for the *inattentive policy* assertion, or for the conclusion that the monetary pillar was ignored or uninformative, and we identify many drawbacks to the lower-target advice. Both reduced-form regime-switching analysis and a structural counterfactual exercise favour a higher target range with a hard lower threshold.

3.1 Special Factors

The report was sceptical that special factors could be persistently unidirectional: 'There were many months in which special factors were appealed to in order to explain why inflation rates were too high. The random distribution of these special factors appears to be oddly one-sided, though: none ever seems to have led to inflation rates which are too low' (Galí et al., 2004). Before moving to the identification of these factors, we therefore take a look at the observables. Figure 3.1 shows the evolution of inflation and the price level since the inception of monetary union, in the euro area (HICP) and in the US (CPI), together with core and non-core components of the two indices.

For the time being, we take the non-core components as a proxy for the special (or *external*) factors. It is apparent from the figure that the non-core elements of the price indices of these two large economies went through wild synchronized swings over the entire period—unsurprising, given that 'non-core' items by and large reflect the prices of commodities that are traded in organized markets with a global reach. It is also clear that, at least until the global financial crisis, these outside shocks to

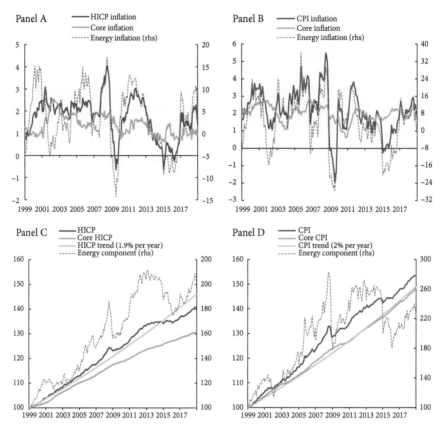

Figure 3.1 Inflation developments in the euro area and the US

Panel A: EA headline, core and energy inflation (year-on-year % change)
Source: Eurostat.
Notes: Core inflation is HICP inflation excluding food and energy.
Latest observation: December 2018.

Panel B: US headline, core and energy inflation (year-on-year % change)
Source: Bureau of Labor Statistics.
Notes: Core inflation is CPI inflation excluding food and energy.
Latest observation: December 2018.

Panel C: EA price indexes (Index, January 1999=100)
Source: Eurostat.
Notes: Core HICP is HICP excluding food and energy.
Latest observation: December 2018.

Panel D: US price indexes (Index, January 1999=100)
Source: Bureau of Labor Statistics.
Notes: Core CPI is CPI excluding food and energy.
Latest observation: December 2018.

prices look predominantly one-sided, i.e. inflationary. Finally, the degree to which these fluctuations have filtered through to headline inflation and the general level of prices has been comparatively very moderate in the euro area: in spite of these disturbances, the dark blue line has kept reasonably close to the 2% threshold in Panel A and has quite tightly shadowed the yellow trend line in Panel C, which we construct assuming that the 'below but close to 2%' inflation norm was 1.9% since the beginning of the euro.[3] Obviously other factors must have been at work to absorb the inflationary impulses that the one-sided *external* influences were exerting through the years.

The narrative-approach-based identification of the 'special factors' and of other factors possibly pulling goods price inflation in the opposite direction can be complemented with more rigorous model-based analysis. We generate structural inference using historical shock decomposition analysis, a natural by-product obtained when estimating a dynamic stochastic general equilibrium macroeconomic model. Specifically, we use a euro area empirical version of the model described in Christiano, Motto and Rostagno (CMR, 2014), a NKM-type DSGE model of the monetary business cycle with a financial sector, to back out the sources of random shocks.

Why relying on the DSGE approach and using this model in particular, given the several shortcomings of a NK-type DSGE approach to the modelling and monitoring of the macro-economy that we have described in Chapter 2? There are two reasons that lead us to conclude that this approach is useful for identifying the shocks that have hit the economy. First, the shortcomings of the NK-type DSGE approach we have described pertain to global, not local analysis. When perturbations to the economy are reasonably small and fiscal policy can be abstracted from in the study of determinants of aggregate demand—in other words, when the economy can plausibly be assumed to be circling within a narrow neighbourhood around the 'virtuous steady state'—a DSGE model of the type we use here can provide useful insights into the underlying forces driving the economy. Second, alternative approaches to inference, such as the narrative approach and pure time series models (with some form of identifying restrictions), have their own drawbacks. The narrative approach is somewhat arbitrary and quite opaque in the way events are selected and assessed. Pure time-series models have troubles in providing those restrictions that are needed to identify the wider set of forces that arguably drive the economy at business cycle frequencies, beyond a handful of generic identified shocks such as monetary policy innovations and shifts in technology that vector autoregression models can support. DSGE models have at least the advantage of being fully transparent about the agents' preferences, technological possibilities, aggregate constraints, and market interactions in which the sources of macroeconomic motion are anchored. In any case, we cross-check our main findings with results derived in the literature on the basis of alternative approaches.

Within the DSGE approach, we choose to work with the CMR model. The model is well suited to capture the role of shocks originating within the financial side of the economy in the run-up to the global financial crisis and in its subsequent ramifications. The drawback is that the CMR is a closed-economy model. However, it should be able to capture to some extent the main global forces operating via trade and

---

[3] As we write above, such a level is approximately that of the longer-term inflation expectation measures shown by Otmar Issing at the press briefing of 8 May 2003.

financial markets during our review period. As regards trade, this is done by assuming in the CMR that net exports follow an exogenous process that replicates actual developments in trade. As regards global financial linkages, this is captured by the fact that financial factors in the euro area and internationally happened to exhibit a high degree of comovement during the period. Therefore, we should be able to correctly capture the dynamics of financial shocks even if we may miss their country of origin. This interpretation is also supported by a comparison of the inference made on the basis of the CMR with the one based on an alternative macromodel of the euro area that features a detailed international block, such as the New Area Wide Model (NAWM) maintained by ECB staff.[4] The empirical method involves extracting a full set of underlying shocks from the estimate: there are 16 of these in the CMR-based estimates, including shocks to households' preferences for current versus future consumption, technology shocks, monetary shocks, government spending shocks, price mark-up shocks, shocks to money demand and banks' deposit supply, shocks that affect the demand and supply of capital, including, in particular, a risk shock—anticipated and unanticipated.[5] As the composition of fluctuations is as critical to the success of monetary policy as their frequency and amplitude, we are particularly interested in the sources of those random impulses that generate fluctuations: whether these impulses originated predominantly in demand or supply. We therefore place the estimated shocks in five categories: aggregate demand; financial factors; aggregate supply; monetary policy surprises; and the shocks to the central bank inflation 'target'. Figure 3.2 A-B shows the historical decomposition for GDP growth and GDP-defined inflation, respectively. In essence, this is in-sample structural innovation accounting that quantifies the contribution to cyclical fluctuations in output and inflation received from the five groups of random structural forces identified by the model. Each group corresponds to a bar of a particular colour, and the algebraic sum of the bars assigned to each point in time corresponds to the observation on the solid line, GDP growth or inflation, at the same point in time. 'Aggregate demand' (green bars) and 'Financial factors' (grey bars) include shocks that, overall, move output and inflation in the same direction: the source of all these random shocks is 'demand'. Specifically, the green bars comprise the contribution of changes in households' intertemporal preferences for consumption and shocks to the government's and the foreign sector's absorption, while the grey bars group contributions of shocks to the funding conditions faced by financial intermediaries and, in particular, a shock that captures changes in the appreciation of market risk. This latent process is identified primarily by stock market and credit market information, notably the credit risk premium and the growth rate of credit to the private sector,

---

[4] See the model comparison of the CMR and NAWM, and the inference derived from the two models, in Smets et al. (2010).

[5] A property of these shocks is that, when they are fed simultaneously to our estimated model, the simulated observable variable coincides with the actual data (up to a small measurement error in some variables). Given the linearity of our approximation of the model's solution, the shocks therefore provide us with an additive decomposition of the data. In Figure 3.2, we show the decomposition of *demeaned* growth and inflation, respectively.

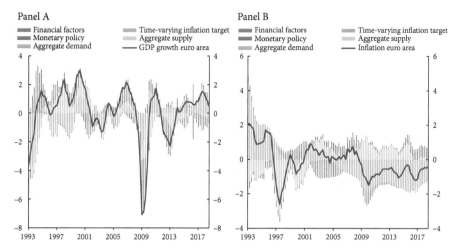

Figure 3.2 Shocks' contribution to (demeaned) euro area real GDP growth and inflation
Panel A: Real GDP growth (percentage points)
Panel B: Inflation (percentage points)
Source: CMR.
Notes: The solid line is the data. Data are in deviation from the mean.
Latest observation: 2018Q3.

and has two components: it is partly unanticipated and partly anticipated, in other words, reflecting news about its future evolution. Due to its powerful propagation properties, the evolution of the risk shock causes shifts in the uncertainty of the overall macroeconomic environment in the model, and it is interpretable as an underlying measure of systemic risk (for an analysis of the risk shock see Christiano et al., 2014). 'Supply' shocks move output and inflation in opposite directions. In the CMR model, a temporary total-factor-productivity (TFP) shock hitting intermediate-goods production, shocks to price mark-ups and changes in the price of oil all share this property. Their contributions to output and inflation are shown as yellow bars. Finally, innovations to monetary policy are in two different groups. The red bars stand for contributions coming from deviations of the policy interest rate from the typical Taylor-like reaction function that the model attributes to the central bank. The blue bars are shocks to the inflation 'target' that enters the reaction function. In other words, we allow for a time-varying process for the numerical objective.[6] We further elaborate on the reaction function and the latent process of the 'target' below.

The pictures support two observations. First, financial factors (the grey bars) lead or coincide with the peaks and troughs in GDP growth. They tend to dissipate quickly as a determinant of growth, while they introduce longer-lasting effects in inflation. Second, supply shocks (the yellow bars) are usually timely indicators and

---

[6] The target shock is treated as observed cum measurement error in the estimation of the CMR, where the observable variable is long-term inflation expectations from Consensus Economics. For the period prior to 1999, it is back-casted aggregating expectations in the largest euro area countries.

certainly extraordinarily persistent determinants of growth and inflation. They are unmistakably pro-cyclical, a feature that has been documented in previous research (Christiano et al. (2008) and Fahr et al. (2013)) and proved to be characteristic to the euro area structural environment. A close look at the boom-bust episode of the early years of monetary union, for instance, offers an instructive story. While financial markets were providing a robust spurt to growth during 1999 and much of 2000—after the short-lived Asian and Russian crisis-related deceleration of 1998—a pro-cyclical adjustment in productivity and mark-ups intervened to amplify the cycle. This appears to have damped the influences that the cyclical exuberance would otherwise have had on inflation (see Panel B). The bust phase that ensued and lasted until 2005 is the mirror image of the same pattern. Pro-cyclical adjustments in productivity aggravated the slump and kept inflation from falling. The finding of pro-cyclicality of supply forces in the euro area is not specific to the CMR, but robust across a wide range of models.[7]

In general, a structurally pro-cyclical supply side complicates the economic environment for monetary policy. There are two reasons for this. First, it de-synchronizes inflation and the economy. Provided inflation expectations are well anchored, pro-cyclical changes in inflation can work as automatic stabilizers and ease the task of monetary policy management. In booms, higher-than-normal inflation reinforces the signals that are released by the economy and thus encourages the tighter stance that can counter over-heating in the markets and in the broad economy. A counter-cyclical monetary policy restriction in those conditions is well understood and easy to communicate. In busts, a decline in actual inflation—relative to steady inflation expectations—can partly offset the cyclical fall in real incomes and thus sustain demand at a critical juncture. Our analysis indicates that neither of these equilibrating mechanisms seems to have been available in the euro area.

Second, supply-side pro-cyclicality makes the economic environment more difficult to interpret for the central bank itself. A typical demand shock poses little puzzle to a stability-oriented central bank: it puts it in front of a comfortable 'divine coincidence'. Because demand shocks induce a positive co-movement between inflation and output, a timely and determined response to restore price stability accomplishes output stabilization as a side effect. A supply shock, however, needs to be interpreted. It is not so much the supply shock per se that requires a monetary policy reaction, particularly if the shock is expected to be temporary and reverse itself before long. Rather, it is the implications that the shock is expected to have for

---

[7] The pro-cyclicality of supply forces in the euro area is a robust finding in the literature. It was detected in analyses based on DSGE models, such as Smets et al. (2010), who directly compare the CMR model with the New Area Wide Model developed by ECB staff in the context of the projection exercises, and Sahuc and Smets (2008), who compare the euro area with the United States. The latter paper finds that the pro-cyclicality of supply shocks is a euro area specific development, driven by technology and mark-up shocks, whereas in the United States supply shocks have behaved in counter-cyclical manner. The role of supply shocks in exerting upward pressure on inflation over that period is also found in Conti et al. (2017), who employ an identified Bayesian VAR. In addition, on the basis of industry-level data, Cette et al. (2016) document over that period the slowdown in total factor productivity in the euro area and the rise in the United States.

inflation expectations and for the self-sustaining momentum that expectations—once unsettled—can add to the inflation process going forward. Indeed, Begg et al. (2002) recognize this signal extraction problem as a major area of potential policy error: 'Can a central bank distinguish between permanent and temporary supply shocks? In practice this is difficult. Hence, inflation targeting may not prevent central banks from making policy errors. Moreover, the existence of temporary supply shocks (noise) reduces the quality of inflation as a signal of deflationary demand shocks.'

In summary, a cyclical environment such as appears to have prevailed since 1999—with supply factors 'oddly one-sided' and persistent—poses extra challenges for the monetary authority, even in regimes, like the ECB's, which give inflation an overriding status in the rank of the monetary policy priorities.[8]

We conclude this section by asking an obvious question: what would have happened if the ECB had used its policy instrument more aggressively to offset the inflationary shocks and produce an inflation rate that never exceeds 2%? To answer this, we use the same CMR model utilized to identify the structural disturbances, and construct a policy counterfactual. In other words, we change the history of the ECB's policy actions to the extent sufficient to keep inflation within the price stability zone throughout the decade. Figure 3.3 reports our findings for the counterfactual evolution of three key macroeconomic variables. GDP growth would have been 1.7 pp lower in 2001, 0.3 pp lower in 2002, 0.8 pp lower in 2006 and 1.4 pp lower in 2007. More importantly, starting in late 2005, inflation would have been put on a downward path that would have brought it to a level some 0.5 pp lower than it actually was on the eve of the Lehman crisis.

Whether such an inflation shortfall relative to the historical level of inflation just before the crisis would have been problematic is an issue we will return to in the concluding section of this chapter.

3.2 The Medium Term

The authors of the 2004 CEPR report felt the medium term concept often invoked in ECB communication to be particularly nebulous: 'What exactly is meant by the "medium term" at which the ECB wants to achieve its inflationary goal? [...] The

---

[8] This is because, as discussed in Chapter 1, it is never optimal to disregard secondary objectives, even if subordinated to the primary objective in a lexicographic fashion. We also acknowledge the arbitrariness of drawing a sharp line between 'demand' and 'supply' shocks on the basis of the sign of their respective impacts on prices and real income. As explained in Alesina et al. (2001) and Begg et al. (2002), the fact that a 'supply' shock might have a contractionary effect on spending does not rule out the possibility that it might be optimal for the central bank to completely offset the inflationary consequences of that shock, even at the cost of suppressing consumption and investment. If the 'supply' shock can be assumed to have negative implications for output potential, then such a monetary policy response would be welfare-improving as it would bring real output closer to a diminished level of the welfare-relevant full-capacity potential. The problem with this reasoning, however, is that the categorization of forces between those that do—and those that do not—have a bearing on the welfare-relevant potential is as arbitrary as the one based on our sign restriction.

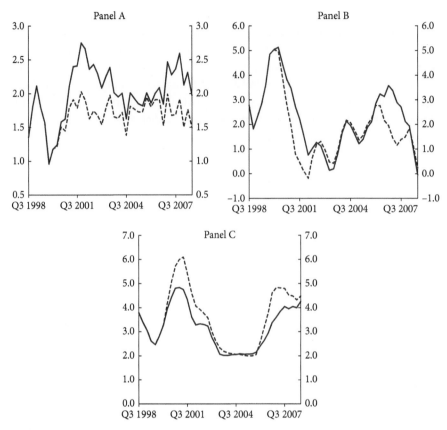

Figure 3.3 Counterfactual monetary policy in which the ECB does not let inflation rise above 2%

Panel A: GDP inflation (year-on-year % change)

Panel B: Real GDP growth (year-on-year % change)

Panel C: 3-month nominal interest rate (percentages per annum)

Source: CMR.

Notes: In each panel the solid line indicates historical data, while the dashed line indicates the counterfactual associated with the following experiment: the central bank uses its policy instrument more aggressively to produce an inflation rate that never exceeds 2%.

review of the monetary policy strategy could have clarified this important issue, but it did not' (Galí et al., 2004). In fact, the ECB had—and has since—been reasonably consistent in elucidating this notion. Duisenberg, as we saw above, was firm in the forward-looking interpretation of medium term and did not even shy away from mentioning a precise time interval which would bracket the medium term horizon: 'we are looking forward one-and-a-half to two years to vouch for the effects of monetary policy measures' (transcripts of his 28 May 2001 testimony to the ECON committee). Jean-Claude Trichet qualified Duisenberg's interval, but only at the margin to make it applicable to special circumstances, when a unidirectional sequence of shocks to the price of oil threatens to unsettle inflation expectations, and can thus transform into permanent *demand*-side pressure (positive or negative, depending on the sign of the primitive shock): '[T]he medium term should be taken to be at least as long as the average transmission lag for policy actions. While facing rises in commodity prices, the policy horizon could theoretically be more extended. But, […] the risk that a repeated sequence of supply-side shocks might turn into a demand disturbance with long-lasting implications for price stability has made our horizon shorter. It has made it closer to the average transmission lag' (Trichet, 2008a).

3.2.1 Why a Medium-Term Orientation

We try to summarize the thinking as follows. The medium-term horizon is the point in time, looking forward, by which the central bank has to be reasonably confident that it can deliver on its objective based on the current policy stance. The horizon should be short enough to be verifiable, but long enough to be consistent with inflation controllability. The standard transmission lag of monetary policy decisions, i.e. the length of time it ordinarily takes for a monetary policy impulse to exert its maximal impact on the economy and inflation, sets the minimum interval of time that quantifies the 'medium term'. Intuitively, a central bank can hardly control inflation at shorter horizons. In certain contingencies, however, the 'medium term' interval can stretch well beyond the standard transmission lag. These are times in which the economy is buffeted by supply-side shocks. As an example, think of cost-push shocks which make production costs sour, and thus promote a rise in prices—as firms seek to preserve their margins by passing the higher input costs onto the prices they charge—and a sag in activity—as firms curtail their demand for the more expensive inputs. Cost-push shocks are typically seen as less persistent than demand-side shocks, and this is the reason why they call for a longer visibility horizon—a medium-term end point that is farther away. Of course, the Trichet caveat is also relevant: if cost-push shocks become persistent, they may infiltrate inflation expectations and thus become permanent sources of higher-than-desired inflation, in other words they may affect the *underlying trend rate of inflation*. The policy horizon (medium term) then shrinks again towards the typical transmission lag that is most appropriate for demand shocks.

If the 'medium term' is flexible and shock-dependent, then a regime that instructs the central bank to stabilize inflation over that horizon can couple inflation discipline with shorter-term flexibility to counter economic weakness. This is because the central bank will modulate the vigour with which it will respond to inflationary or disinflationary shocks as appropriate to meet its objective by the end of a horizon whose end point may be more or less distant in the future, depending on the nature of those shocks. If cost-push shocks call for a longer horizon and indeed tend to be transient, then monetary policy can be more patient in reacting to their inflation implications—negative or positive. In fact, if well understood and accepted by the public, such a regime gives the central bank more rather than less latitude to minimize the amplitude of harmful cyclical fluctuations. If the public is confident that the central bank will always act as needed to nudge inflation towards its objective over time, then cost-push episodes will be fewer and less intense: at least bouts of demands for wage gains would be less in number and more moderate, if workers come to fear inflation less.

3.2.2 Medium-Term Orientation in Practice

So much for the theory. But where is the ECB's medium-term orientation most apparent? How should the medium-term orientation be measured anyway? What might have induced a medium-term oriented approach in real time? Has macroeconomic performance suffered or gained as a result of this approach—and the dampened reaction to the contemporaneous state of affairs that it might have induced—in comparison to a counterfactual 1999–2008 world in which the ECB had been more 'activist'? We turn to these empirical questions in the remainder of this section.

One place to start looking for evidence of the ECB's tendency to concentrate on a forward-looking medium term is a figure showing the time profile of its policy rate path compared with that of other central banks. Panel A of Figure 3.4 shows the path of the interest rate for the Eurosystem's main refinancing operations and the path of the federal funds rate over our sample period. Observationally, many economic commentators and market analysts had already remarked in the early days of the currency union, the ECB appears to have been relatively more circumspect in

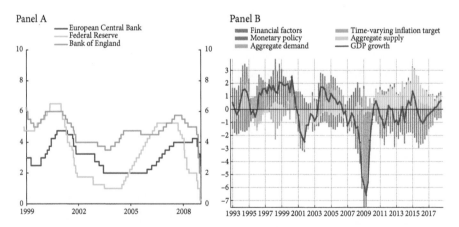

Figure 3.4 Policy rate adjustments and shocks' contribution to US GDP growth

Panel A: Policy rate paths (percentages per annum)
Sources: ECB, US Federal Reserve and Bank of England.
Latest observation: 31 December 2008.

Panel B: Shocks' contribution to US real GDP growth (percentage points)
Source: CMR.
Notes: Data are in deviation from the mean.
Latest observation: 2018Q3.

adjusting its policy instrument, at least between 1999 and 2007. It seems to have been considerably less 'activist' than the Fed or the Bank of England, despite facing an international landscape that was not markedly different (see Panel B of Figure 3.4 for a CMR-based decomposition of the US growth rate).

A variety of candidate explanations come to mind to explain this differential behaviour.[9] One could refer to underlying conditions that might be structurally more variable in the US economy than in the euro area. We take the variance of the CMR-generated structural (non-policy) shocks in the United States and euro area, respectively, as a summary statistic for the amplitude of the autonomous fluctuations that the two central banks had to control over this ten-year period. While we do find some differences across the two economic areas, they are not large. However, it is noteworthy that in the euro area the variance of the shocks generating a trade-off between output and inflation is found to be slightly larger than in the United States, while the opposite is true for shocks which do not give rise to a trade-off. We therefore conclude that a more benign cyclical environment, with disturbances that have less variance and persistence, cannot account for the ECB's dampened interest rate response.

A second explanation could invoke *policy inertia* narrowly defined. By this we mean the tendency of central banks—documented in a vast literature on empirical monetary policy reaction functions—to make their policy paths highly autoregressive processes and act in small steps in very persistent directions. Woodford (2003) finds that such a policy approach is optimal, as its persistence amplifies the impact of any policy action on those longer-term interest rates that are relevant for aggregate spending. Two of us have pursued this avenue in previous work (Christiano et al., 2008). So, here we looked in the same direction in order to understand the ECB's observationally sluggish policy path compared with that of the Fed. Table 3.1 below reports the estimated reaction coefficients of the two Taylor-like interest rate rules which (used to produce the shock decomposition of economic fluctuations in the euro area and United States in the CMR model) capture the empirical behaviours of

Table 3.1 Estimated policy rule parameters: ECB and Fed

	Autoregressive coefficient	Response to inflation	Response to GDP growth	Response to acceleration in inflation	Response to credit growth
Euro area	0.89	1.83	0.51	0.20	0.42
United States	0.92	1.85	0.61	0.25	/

[9] A further difference between the rate paths of the US Fed and the ECB is that changes in ECB interest rates generally occur about five months after changes in the fed funds rate. The main reason for this lies in the well-documented de-synchronization between the business cycles of the two large economies, with activity conditions in the United States found to lead those in the euro area by 4–12 quarters. See, Giannone et al. (2010) and Giannone and Reichlin (2004).

the ECB and the Fed, respectively.[10] The rules allow for a central bank response to inflation (in deviation from a numerical objective), to an acceleration in inflation and to GDP growth, and also incorporate a lagged interest rate term, which is a conventional measure of *policy inertia*. The ECB's policy rule also allows for reaction to credit growth, and we will expand on this extra reaction variable below. What is noticeable is that except for a reaction to credit that is positive and significant for the ECB, the estimated reaction parameters are otherwise very similar. In particular, there is no statistically meaningful difference in the inertia parameters. If anything, the Fed appears more persistent than the ECB.[11]

We therefore have to look elsewhere to help make sense of the dissimilar speed of policy reaction evident in Figure 3.4. We find two explanations attractive: one invoking uncertainty, and one invoking a differential way to manage expectations. We now turn to these two explanations sequentially.

Uncertainty about the underlying structure and state of the economy, compounded by the prevalence of supply-side shocks in the euro area, complicated the ECB's signal-extraction problem for much of its history. While the Fed and the Bank of England had a good understanding and proven record of controlling their economies, the ECB was *learning* about the euro area economy for a large portion of these years. If there is a large amount of uncertainty about the nature and sources of the macro-impulses and their propagation, Brainard's attenuation principle counsels caution. If there is also uncertainty about the stochastic properties of those impulses—their typical duration and volatility, for example—the option value of waiting increases. The relatively scant informative content of conventional measures of medium-term inflation expectations available to the ECB for much of this period lends this hypothesis some credence. In this respect, Figure 3.6 tells a tale of two sub-periods: 1999–2005 and 2005 until the end. In the first sub-period, there were no market-based measures of implied inflation expectations for the euro area as a whole, as the market for inflation protection was not sufficiently

---

[10] The Taylor rule in CMR calls for systematic adjustments in the instrument of policy relative to its expected longer-run neutral level in response to movements in GDP-deflator-defined inflation relative to a 'target' set at 1.83%. As for the assumptions made about the neutral value of the policy rate in the longer run, this is set at the steady state nominal short-term interest rate, which in the model is pinned down by the intertemporal discount factor, the permanent productivity growth factor and the inflation 'target'. However, since at least 2000 researchers and practitioners have markedly reduced their projections of the level of real short-term interest rates expected to prevail in the longer run. These revisions were made in response to accumulating evidence that lower real interest rates than those seen on average in the past would be needed permanently to keep the economy operating on an even keel. While such revisions should imply material shifts in the level of the Taylor rule's prescriptions, holding other factors constant, no such adjustments are made to the Taylor rule underlying the CMR model when the model is brought to the data. The model presumably seeks to compensate for this lack of down-step in the real natural rate of interest by generating a string of negative innovations to the latent process that governs the intertemporal discount factor, which is included in the 'consumption' category of our shock decomposition. This string of negative innovations turns out to have a differential impact on GDP and inflation. Whereas the near-term decline in GDP that the intertemporal-preference disturbance produces is soon reversed and GDP starts increasing, this is not the case for inflation. The propagation of a string of one-sided negative consumption shocks therefore appears to be mean-reverting on GDP but very persistent on inflation, as inspection of the two panels of Figure 3.2 suggests.

[11] This result is partly related to the estimation of the model over the full sample.

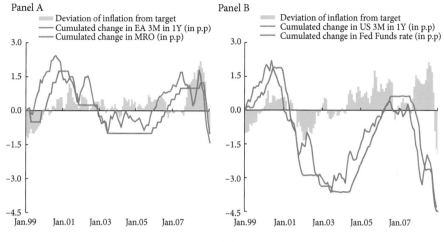

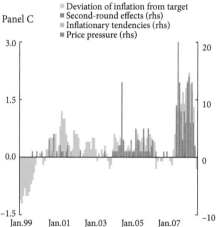

Figure 3.5 Rate action, rate expectations, inflation overshooting, and ECB communication over 1999–2008

Panel A: EA—Deviation of headline inflation from the central bank's inflation aim and (cumulated) change in near-term interest rates (percentage points)

Panel B: US—Deviation of headline inflation from the central bank's inflation aim and (cumulated) change in near-term interest rates (percentage points)

Panel C: EA—Deviation of headline inflation from the inflation aim and references to second round effects in ECB communication (percentage points (lhs axis) and number of occurrences (rhs axis))

Sources: ECB and US Federal Reserve.
Notes: The red, green and purple bars in Panel C report the number of occurrences of the phrases 'second round effects', 'inflationary tendencies', and 'price pressures' in the Introductory Statement to the Press Conference (with Q&A) over the period 1999–2008. For each occurrence, an additional filter is applied by checking neighbouring words to ensure that it refers to upside inflationary pressure. Latest observation: 31 December 2008.

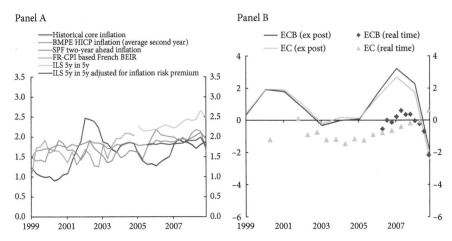

Figure 3.6 Measures of medium-term inflation expectations and of output gap
Panel A: Measures of medium-term inflation expectations (year-on-year % change)
Panel B: Real-time and ex-post measures of output gap (percentage)
Sources: Bloomberg, ECB projections, ECB Survey of Professional Forecasters, Eurostat and Refinitiv.
Notes: The model used for estimating the inflation risk premium is an affine term structure model,
see Camba-Mendez and Werner (2017). The FR-CPI based French BEIR depicts the difference between
a nominal and a (FR-CPI) inflation-linked French government bond both issued in 1998, both with an
original maturity of ten years.
Latest observation: December 2008.

developed. So, the question that springs to mind is: in the data-poor conditions of
the years prior to 2005, what was the measure of inflation of its 'own making' that
the ECB was able to consult looking into the 'medium term future'? There were
essentially four real-time indicators of trend inflation and Panel A of Figure 3.6
shows how they evolved in the observation period: the internal projections for
inflation two years out (red line), the SPF inflation two-years-ahead (green line),
the ten-year break-even inflation rate derived from contracts traded in French
OAT (and based on French realized inflation, light-blue line), and core inflation
(dark blue line). We also show the inflation-swap-derived longer-term inflation
expectations for the euro area as a whole, although these were not available in the
period prior to 2005 (yellow line).

As the picture suggests, between 1999 and 2005 three of the four readily accessible
indicators (SPF, French break-even, internal projections) displayed very modest
variability within a tight interval never exceeding 2%. Core inflation rose above the
2% threshold in mid-2001 and did not move back within the price stability zone
until early 2003. But the anticipatory properties of core inflation with regard to
medium-term inflation were dubious at the time, and in fact internal analysis had
pointed to a lagged—not leading—association between core and headline. These
empirical results suggested that core inflation was a problematic benchmark
for medium-term inflation, since it probably reflected *past* persistent shocks to

non-core prices rather than upward pressures that would result in permanent changes to underlying inflation.[12]

Real-time measures of economic slack could have served as a better guide to predicting where the rate of inflation was heading. Conventional Phillips curve specifications, in use at the ECB (as in virtually all policymaking institutions) at the time, provided a general framework for examining the link between underlying inflation and current resource utilization. However, as Panel B of Figure 3.6 shows, the European Commission measure of output gap available at any time before the second half of the decade did not indicate demand pressures which could have raised the odds of inflation settling at levels higher than desired. Quite the opposite is true: they were consistent with ongoing downside risks to inflation.

Around the end of 2004, high-frequency measures of euro area inflation expectations became readily usable for policy inference, and these measures revealed that inflation expectations had crept above 2%. Furthermore, internal inflation projections caught up with a history of almost systematic under-prediction of inflationary pressures.

3.2.3 Managing Expectations

The last competing explanatory hypothesis for the ECB's arguably high degree of policy inertia—and the one we find most appealing—stresses the different degree to which these two central banks whose policy path is described in Figure 3.4 might have resorted to, and been successful at managing the expectations of market participants, street experts and the wider public (as implied in Duisenberg's quote above). A stronger grip on expectations, this conjecture argues, could have determined shifts in the whole term structure of interest rates or in inflation expectations directly, well ahead of action, and these pre-emptive changes could have either complemented actual policy rate adjustments, or even made these adjustments superfluous ex post, at least to some degree. We defer to the next section a model-based analysis that can help to ascertain the merits of this hypothesis more robustly. Here we want to draw attention to Figure 3.5, which documents correlations that we find suggestive of the way rate action, rate expectations, central bank communication and inflation surprises co-moved in the pre-crisis era in the euro area and in the United States. Panels A and B in Figure 3.5 plot the cumulative changes in the policy rates and in the forward rates in the euro area and the United States, respectively, between 1999 and 2008 against the local overruns of headline

---

[12] Eurosystem-wide econometric analysis dated May 2001 came to the conclusion that core inflation measures were best used to help understand the inflation process but are not necessarily useful for forecasting inflation.

inflation with respect to 2%. The policy rate is the MRO rate for the euro area, and the fed funds rate for the US. In both panels, the forward rate is the three-month OIS forward rate in one year. Why do we choose this measure as representative of rate expectations? Because, as we shall argue in Section 5.4, that specific interest rate embodies rate expectations that stretch over horizons which, at each point in time, are particularly relevant for the pricing of credit to the economy. Comparing the two pictures, we offer a couple of observations that—we believe—are relevant to our expectations-management conjecture. To start, judging by the average level of the *forward* interest rate (the blue line), monetary policy in the euro area was more restrictive and more pre-emptive of positive inflation surprises, than one would conclude watching the evolution of the *actual* policy rate (the red line). By the forward rate metric, policy was distinctly tighter in the run-up to the burst of the dot.com bubble than measured by the MRO rate, and was hardly eased—compared to the stance prevailing in 1999—even over the following couple of years of economic slump. The US picture is manifestly different. Over the sub-periods in which the yellow bars point upward—headline inflation exceeded 2%—the spread between the forward rate and the actual policy rate was on net twice as large in the euro area as in the United States (30 basis points versus 15 basis points).

It is always misleading to measure the stance of monetary policy solely by the level and the actual path of the policy rate: the messaging and signalling released when communicating about policy or the state of the economy is as consequential—possibly, even more consequential—for shaping financing conditions than policy action itself. A comparison between Panel A and Panel C of Figure 3.5 supports the conclusion that this universal adage probably applies to the pre-crisis history of monetary policy in the euro area with greater force than anywhere else. Indeed, as shown in Panel C, the ECB official communication referring to inflation risks was quite dense during periods of inflation overshoots. The red, green and blue bars in the panel measure the frequency with which code phrases highlighting the presence and consequences of inflation pressures—'second round effects', 'inflationary tendencies', and 'price pressures'—were used in press conferences, either in the Introductory Statement read out by the President at the start, or during the questions-and-answers sessions that followed. Two facts seem to emerge: perhaps unsurprisingly, the ECB was expressing stronger alertness to inflation over periods of above-2% inflation readings, and the intensity of such expressions had a tendency to escalate, not only as a function of the severity of the observed overrun, but also through time, as the past record of relatively high inflation was gradually accruing. While correlation does not prove causation, the fact that the forward curve was steeper precisely during times of inflation overruns could partly owe to the pointed signals that the ECB was sending regarding the GC's growing concerns about inflation. As said, in Section 3.3 we offer a formal analysis that seeks to organize this evidence into a coherent interpretation.

3.2.4 A Medium-Term Compass

Jordi Galí and his co-authors correctly pointed out that on 8 May 2003 the role of money had been 'downgraded in importance'. Indeed, the time-perspective re-interpretation of the function of broad money could be seen as having de facto ejected money from the GC's day-to-day 'reaction equation'. The strategy review had redefined M3 as a sort of insurance mechanism, to which the central bank could resort for rescue in extreme events. But as with all insurance mechanisms, the relevance of money might actually never become visible in equilibrium, so the 'money monitoring' strategy might leave no evidence in time series data.[13] However, on 8 May 2003 the monetary analysis—as the former first pillar was renamed—was broadened in scope as much as it was re-ordered. As a matter of fact, emphasis on credit growth and its connection with the cycle and with asset price formation had also been increasing in internal discussions well in advance of the strategy review, in parallel and in proportion to the decaying quality of money growth as a conjunctural indicator. Public communication soon started to reflect the shift in focus and, as we shall see at the end of the chapter, the ability of credit growth to give advance notice about risks to financial stability became a regular feature of official descriptions of the role of monetary analysis in ECB policymaking.

Essentially, credit was studied for its good cyclical properties and its ability to provide some signals about the possible build-up of asset price misalignments that could pose threats to price stability down the road. For at least 15 years, bank loans in the countries that would join the euro had demonstrated regular early indicator properties relative to measures of economic slack (see Figure 3.8),[14] and credit flows were known to be in a tight coincidental connection with indicators of cyclical turning points such as capital formation (see Figure 3.9). These qualities of credit statistics—in addition, available at high frequencies and with very short lags—made them attractive sources for information in an environment in which severe data limitations meant the business cycle was difficult to decipher and internal forecasts potentially inaccurate.[15]

---

[13] Christiano and Rostagno (2001) draw a parallel between monetary analysis and a deposit insurance scheme: 'The government's commitment to supply liquidity in the event of a bank run eliminates the occurrence of bank runs in the first place. [Hence,] the government never actually has to act on its commitment. Similarly, [the central bank's] commitment to monitor the money growth rate and rein it in if necessary implies that money growth never gets out of line in the first place.'

[14] Credit leads unemployment by almost two quarters, GDP growth by slightly more, around three quarters. However, the correlation of credit vis-à-vis unemployment (0.8) is stronger than that for real GDP growth (0.58).

[15] In a series of contributions, Stock and Watson (1999, 2002) and Watson (2003) have confirmed the longstanding view of professional forecasters, that the use of large number of data series may significantly improve forecasts of key macroeconomic variables. Bernanke and Boivin (2003) find that the number and variety of series included in the forecasters' data set matters very much for forecasting performance.

Figure 3.7 Monetary and credit developments (year-on-year % change)
Source: ECB.
Latest observation: 2008Q4.

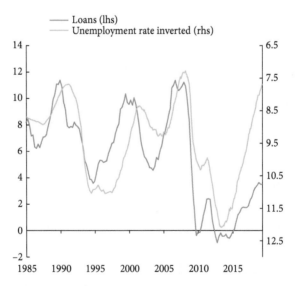

Figure 3.8 Credit developments and unemployment (year-on-year % change and percentage)
Sources: ECB, Eurostat and AWM database.
Latest observation: 2018Q4.

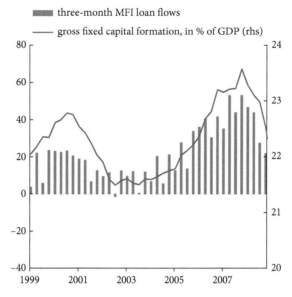

▬▬ three-month MFI loan flows

—— gross fixed capital formation, in % of GDP (rhs)

Figure 3.9 Credit flows and gross fixed capital formation in % of GDP (EUR billion and percentage)

Source: Eurostat, ECB, and ECB calculations.
Latest observation: 2008Q4.

Indeed, to appreciate the importance of monetary variables in the ECB's broad-based analytical framework one has to recall the exceptionally 'data poor' environment faced by the first generation of ECB policymakers: at the launch of EMU, area-wide time series were patchy, many statistical indicators were still under construction, and reliable measures of inflation expectations were lacking. More importantly, the creation of the euro area *itself* implied a major regime shift, meaning it could not be known with any degree of confidence whether the statistical regularities emerging from past data, once it was available, would be informative of the structure of the new monetary union, or whether past parameters and the model coefficients they yielded would in fact prove misleading.[16] Even some years after the establishment of EMU when the strategy review was being debated, extracting accurate signals from the economy remained more challenging for the ECB than for time-tested central banks. As Otmar Issing observed in 2002, 'we were studying the evolution of a moving object, which was changing for the very reason that it was being observed, as in the famous Heisenberg paradox' (Issing, 2002c). The situation facing policy-makers was, for large parts of the time, best described as one of Knightian

---

[16] Otmar Issing (1999) put it thus: 'nobody who is even superficially acquainted with the whole EMU process would deny but that the level of uncertainty which the ECB has to confront on account of the transition to Stage Three of EMU is substantially heightened relative to that which would face a central bank in normal times. The origins of uncertainty facing the ECB are many and varied. Some are broadly political while others remain in the arena of technical economic and data-related issues.'

uncertainty. In internal debates at the time staff therefore paid heightened attention to credit figures as a sort of real-time statistical instrument to capture the 'economic activity' latent factor of a large, but scarcely observable system.

Policymakers, for their part, included credit in their heuristic and judgmental analysis of the situation, as they considered information about output and prices too slow to appear and at risk of continuing revisions. The smooth, trend-like development of credit over this period is probably what lent it credibility in their eyes over other more volatile indicators, such as real-time activity gauges (e.g. PMI) and measured inflation itself. Credit dynamics also displayed the additional feature of providing some signals about the possible build-up of imbalances in financial and housing markets (see Figure 3.10).[17] This made credit a natural candidate for operationalizing the 'leaning against the wind' element of the money pillar.

As we have shown before, the CMR estimates assign credit a large explanatory value with respect to the interest rate decisions of the ECB over the entire period covered in this chapter (Table 3.1). An increase in credit growth of 1% above its trend, all other things being equal, was consistent with the ECB hiking its policy

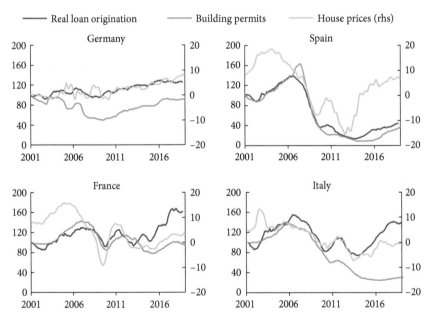

Figure 3.10 Loan origination, building permits, and house prices across countries (lhs: index, 2001=100; rhs: annual percentage changes)

Sources: ECB and ECB calculations.
Notes: Loan origination estimates deflated by house prices. Building permits and house prices based on monthly interpolated quarterly figures.
Latest observation: September 2018.

[17] For a more formal analysis, see for instance Detken and Smets (2004).

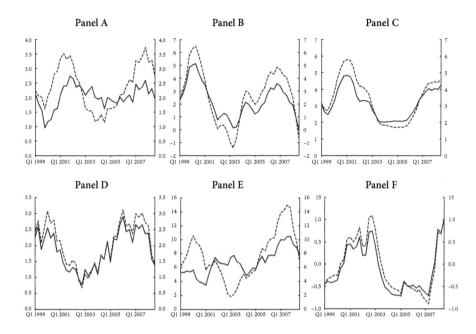

Figure 3.11 Counterfactual in which policy is assumed to disregard credit growth

Panel A: GDP inflation (year-on-year % change)

Panel B: Real GDP growth (year-on-year % change)

Panel C: 3-month nominal interest rate (percentages per annum)

Panel D: Nominal credit (q-o-q % change)

Panel E: Nominal M3 (year-on-year % change)

Panel F: Credit premium (percentages per annum)

Source: CMR.
Notes: In each panel the solid line indicates actual data, while the dashed line indicates the counterfactual associated to the experiment in which the economy is hit by the same historical sequence of non-policy shocks estimated in the baseline model, but the ECB disregards credit growth in its policy reaction function.

interest rate by about 40 bps on average. Motivated by the co-movements, we thus conduct a counterfactual historical exercise to test how history could have changed if the economy had been hit by the same historical sequence of non-policy shocks shown in Figure 3.2 A-B, but the ECB had not given large weight to credit growth in its reaction equation. The counterfactual history of some representative macroeconomic variables is shown as a dashed line in Figure 3.11 together with their actual history.

We find that fluctuations in euro area inflation and economic activity would have been much more ample both over upswings and in periods of downturn. While this model-based analysis cannot capture the richness of the ECB's monetary analysis, it is instructive that the superior stabilization properties of credit as a determinant of policy emerge particularly vividly if one studies selected episodes. We chose three of them. The first corresponds to the policy conduct over the first two and a half years of monetary union. Given the buoyancy of credit growth in the early phase of this period (see Figure 3.7), the CMR-estimated rule would have instructed the ECB to *tighten*—rather than ease—policy in April 1999. Unsurprisingly, the April easing shows up in large realized departures from the policy rule—and sustained policy support for both growth and inflation is associated with this surprise easing (policy shocks), as one can see in Figure 3.2 A-B. As it happened, the internal narrative at the time was that credit was distorted by one-off factors related to monetary unification, notably in Germany. These distortions were seen as reasons to downplay the observed dynamism in credit in the first half of 1999 and look elsewhere—including at the risks for the real economy still emanating from the global slowdown. As the year wore on, though, and—as we saw before—the clouds surrounding the global environment were rapidly dissipated, a credit growth picture stubbornly pointing to exuberance was one key factor that convinced the GC to reverse the April rate cut and tighten the stance in November. The tightening cycle lasted well into 2001. Had the ECB neglected credit growth, economic activity and inflation would have risen more strongly than previously, reinforcing the ongoing cyclical upswing.

The second episode refers to the easing cycle that followed. We find that the signal from weak credit growth that became apparent in 2001 is dispositive in explaining the policy easing of May and August 2001, in conditions in which actual inflation—measured both in terms of the GDP deflator inflation used in the CMR model and in terms of HICP headline inflation—was above the 2% price stability ceiling. Had the ECB ignored the decline in credit growth, the 2001–2002 economic slowdown would have been deeper and—unlike in actual history—the euro area would eventually not have dodged an outright recession (see Panel B of Figure 3.11).[18] The third episode covers the hiking cycle that started in December 2005. Circumstances at the time were almost opposite to those prevailing in mid-2001: credit growth had been accelerating since the beginning of the year and headline inflation was slightly above 2%, but core inflation was hovering around 1.5%. A lack of reaction to credit growth in those conditions would have added fuel to the cyclical upswing and financial market ebullience of 2006 and 2007.

The counterfactual documented in Figure 3.11 inspires the following conclusions. First, the ECB's reactions to the state of the economy cannot be accurately summarized by a simple forward-looking Taylor rule: over the phase of events covered in this chapter the ECB responded to variables other than real activity and actual or expected inflation. This was a wise practice as the inflation expectations available at the time were particularly uninformative about the state of the economy or the risks

---

[18] Interestingly, the more depressed macroeconomic conditions generated by the counterfactual would have called for a policy response via the systematic component of the policy rule, generating lower short-term interest rates in equilibrium. At the same time, we find that there were tightening 'policy shocks' over this episode in the euro area, suggesting that the ECB did not fully heed the prescriptions of the systematic component of its estimated rule and preferred to deviate in the more restrictive direction.

to price stability that lay ahead. Second, attention for extra variables such as credit with a proven steady correlation with the central tendency of a whole set of cyclical variables that are policy relevant but contemporaneously unobservable is likely to have been motivated by the need to avoid policy error. The GC feared costly errors could be incurred by over-reacting to a limited and noisy real-time information set, hence their search for additional cross-checks or medium-term compasses. We show here that credit performed acceptably if assessed in the light of these desiderata. The type of cross-check that monetary variables, and principally credit, were supposed to offer certainly had an unmistakably conjunctural perspective and motivation. And this contrasted somewhat with the cross-checking function assigned to money after the strategy review. In addition to serving as a cross-check between equilibria or time dimensions, monetary observables mainly became a way of validating the indications extracted from an incomplete information set.

3.3 Inattentive Policy and the Target

Here we address two important points raised by Galí et al. (2004), one positive and one normative. The positive judgement on how the ECB had handled policy-making in the five years prior to the report can be summarized by the following three sentences: 'The ECB may not have been overly concerned by inflation in the vicinity of, or just above, the 2% ceiling. Actual inflation appears to be adrift due to inattentive policy. This drift in inflation has undermined credibility, making it now increasingly difficult for the ECB to guide expectations in the future.' As we noted above, Geraats et al. (2008) largely confirmed this judgement looking back over the entire period that we cover in this chapter, so we take this description of the ECB's policy performance as representative of a consensus among expert ECB watchers. The normative advice was for the ECB to choose once and for all between two equally desirable options regarding its policy target: (1) either reconfirm the price stability range, but with 'an open recognition of failure based on the inability to meet its objectives, accompanied by a renewed determination to make the necessary changes to prevent a repetition of that failure in the future'; (2) or choose a higher target with a range around it, in order to adjust deeds and words 'to the realities of monetary policymaking in the euro area (and to actual ECB practice)'. Basically, the CEPR report portrays the selection of a 'target' as a neutral choice. A central bank should be largely indifferent between a higher or lower numerical value, insofar as either is communicated with clarity and trans-parency, and there is no residual ambiguity for the public concerning the genuine intentions guiding monetary policy.

In the remainder of this chapter, we seek to determine whether the data sup-port the positive assertion that the ECB was inattentive to inflation overshoots, and risks to price stability in general, over the ten years preceding the global financial crisis. This will also allow conclusions to be drawn on whether the genuine inflation 'aim' of the GC might have been outside, rather than inside, the price stability range, as implied by the CEPR report. From there, we will tackle the issue of the target choice.

To anticipate our results, and confirming the impression inspired by Figure 3.5, we don't find evidence of inattention to inflation. Quite to the contrary, we find that the ECB's policy focus was on hitting an inflation rate in the top quartile of the price stability range, although the econometrics that we employ cannot pinpoint the precise numerical value of that focal point. In fact, as shown in Box 3.1, the econometrics cannot quite discriminate between two observationally equivalent hypotheses: (1) the focal point was symmetric, particularly low and closer to 1.5% than to 2%, or (2) the point was indeed close to 2%, but the ECB was then penalizing inflation realizations above the 2% ceiling with a more aggressive reaction than it was applying to realizations below the ceiling. As for target selection, the results of our investigation suggest that the choice is very likely not a neutral one. In a world dominated by adverse supply shocks, trying to keep headline inflation from rising above the 2% line means pursuing a tighter policy on net than the central bank would follow if the ceiling had been set at a higher level or shocks had been of a different nature and sign. Systematically tighter policy due to a more ambitious policy 'target' is not neutral to the system. It can suppress underlying inflation, which in turn erodes space away from deflation and leaves the central bank in a less comfortable position in the face of a sharp downturn. We conclude that the ECB undoubtedly embraced the first of the two either/or alternatives put forward by Galí et al. (2004): to maintain the ambitious price stability range it had selected in 1998, and uphold its commitment to 'aim' for a medium-term inflation rate within the range.

3.3.1 A Story of Two Regimes

A medium-term perspective looking through supply-side disturbances may easily be mistaken for inflation forbearance and policy inattention. As a matter of fact, when the ECB lowered its main refinancing interest rate in the midst of a headline inflation surge in May 2001, the President in his introductory statement explained that:

> For some months to come, this medium-term trend [i.e. inflation of the ECB's own making] will be overshadowed by temporary developments in unprocessed food prices following the health concerns related to meat consumption and the consequences of the outbreak of foot-and-mouth disease. Moreover, the pass-through of the indirect effects of past rises in oil prices and the past depreciation of the euro is likely to continue for some months. The effects of these extraordinary factors should, however, gradually diminish over the course of this year, implying an improved outlook for inflation to fall below 2% in 2002.
>
> **(Duisenberg, 10 May 2001 press conference)**

These words raised almost no qualms at the time. But sure enough, as the ECB carried on loosening policy in the face of higher inflation and used similar words to explain this, some observers soon began to suspect that the ECB was neglecting inflation. But was it really a sign of forbearance? Was monetary policy pitched at a level that, if sustained, could have destabilized inflation expectations?

Our discussion around Figure 3.5 has argued in two directions: while observationally more inertial than the Federal Reserve, in fact the ECB might have made more extensive recourse to verbal guidance over periods of high inflation; and, by that channel, the ECB might have managed to influence rate expectations to an extent that, ex post, made the need for action less pressing. In the remainder of the section, we seek to test this argument by conducting an empirical exercise, in which we want to uncover and test the four-way interactions between monetary policy settings, realized headline and core inflation and inflation expectations in the euro area. The simple visual inspection of Figure 3.5 is one source of inspiration for the exercise below. The second source of inspiration is Figure 3.1, which documents the differential histories of inflation and the general price level in the euro area and in the United States, respectively, in the ten years prior to the crisis. Evidently, while the disturbances moving the non-core components of prices were to a great extent the same in the two economic areas, the dynamic association between the price of non-core components and HICP or CPI inflation was vastly different. Headline inflation and the price level moved broadly in lock-steps with price of energy and food in the United States.[19] But they were largely immunized from the swings in energy and food prices in the euro area. As we have already noted, other factors must have offset the inflationary pressure coming from the price of commodities this side of the Atlantic. Indeed, the model-based shock decomposition that we report in Figure 3.2 offers a perspective on which shocks pulled inflation down—including the central bank's deviations from its own standard monetary policy rule in the tightening direction—even as the supply side was mostly inflationary. But what about the role of the *systematic component* of monetary policy—the central bank's rule itself—and the degree to which the public's expectations internalized the rule? Did inflation expectations react in a compensating direction as well, so that the price level could keep sailing approximately along the (yellow) line traced by a trend consistent with average inflation of 1.9% per year until the crisis hit? The green and light-blue lines in Figure 3.6, which we discussed previously, seems to suggest that inflation expectations remained largely unperturbed by actual inflation overshoots, at least over the first six years of

---

[19] Unlike the ECB, through the years the Fed has emphasized its focus on core inflation, specifically the core personal consumption expenditure (PCE) deflator, which excludes food and energy prices. This approach has been motivated by the need to take into account not only the current inflation rate but also the prospects for inflation a few quarters ahead in the light of research using US data which has consistently shown that setting aside the most volatile prices leads to better predictions of headline future inflation. Therefore, during the crisis and before, the Fed communicated that neither the observed rise in oil prices nor increases in crop prices were likely to translate into persistently higher overall inflation, and thus did not call for a policy response.

monetary union. If the public experiences a spell of inflation higher than their long-run expectation, but their long-run expectation of inflation changes little as a result, then inflation expectations must be well anchored. And this is the legitimate guess that one makes when looking at that figure. One final observation which has persuaded us to conduct the exercise presented below is the behaviour of core inflation and the core level of prices over the history of monetary union. As a simple matter of accounting, Figure 3.1 illustrates that stabilization of euro area inflation in the face of upward pressures from its more volatile components can only mean one thing: that *core inflation* has to make space and adjust downward. This was a point made explicitly by ECB Executive Board member Lorenzo Bini Smaghi, who suggested that, in view of the persistent inflationary pressures triggered by the integration of emerging markets into the global economy, domestic inflation in the euro area might have to be *permanently* as low as 1% in order for headline inflation to remain consistent with the ECB's objective (Bini Smaghi, 2011a). The trade-off is quite evident in panel A and even more convincingly in panel C, where the light blue line corresponding to the core elements of the euro area price level departs from trend at an early stage and keeps diverging from it for the remainder of the sample period. Again, the difference compared with the United States is striking.

Figure 3.12 offers an alternative perspective over the same phenomenon. The figure shows rolling cross-correlations (calculated over moving windows of 50 months) between energy inflation—taken as representative of non-core imported inflation— at any time t and core inflation at time $t+k$. The time difference k can be positive (meaning that core inflation leads energy inflation) or negative (meaning that energy inflation leads core inflation). The prevalence of red and brown in the pre-crisis period indicates that the correlation was strongly negative over that phase. In other

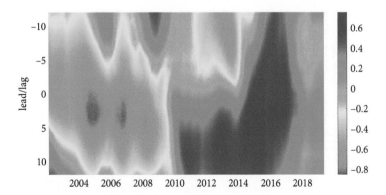

Figure 3.12 Euro area correlation between HICP energy and core

Sources: ECB and ECB calculations.
Notes: Centred rolling cross-correlation (moving window of 50 months) between Energy Inflation at time 't' and Core inflation at time 't+k'.
Latest observation: December 2018.

words, an episode of high energy inflation between 1999 and 2007 was followed by a period of rapidly softening core inflation.[20]

We suspect that the negative correlation apparent in the data between energy price shocks and core inflation might have had something to do with the way the ECB had expressed its price stability objective: as a range bounded upwards by a hard threshold, the 2% ceiling. Remember that in the ECB's framework 2% separates the price stability zone from inflation realizations that violate price stability. An inflation rate moving above the ceiling of the price stability range arguably holds far more meaning than a departure of inflation from a symmetric policy target in an inflation targeting regime: it basically signals that inflation has left the price stability comfort zone. As we saw, during the pre-crisis years the economy was hit by a long spell of cost-push shocks which more often than not drove inflation to test the upper boundary of the comfort zone. We conjecture that, in these conditions, agents might have internalized the sense of transgression that such overshoots could cause inside the ECB's Governing Council. Based on this, we conjecture that agents might have discounted the ECB's propensity to react vigorously to excess inflation, and accordingly might have revised their interest rate and inflation expectations in directions that eventually made the actual policy response necessary to bring inflation back into line less aggressive than it would otherwise have been in the absence of this self-correcting mechanism. Note that there are *two* thresholds intervening in such a mechanism: the 2% ceiling, acting as a 'reflecting barrier' for expectations in the way we have just described, and the effective lower bound (ELB) constraining the room for policy manoeuvre on the downside, in case inflation were ever to fall deep down within the price stability interval. This latter threshold was obviously not binding over the history of events prior to the crisis, but became a concrete possibility afterwards as the source and sign of shocks changed abruptly with the inception of the financial crisis.

With this in mind, to test our conjecture we are using an econometric approach that explicitly allows for changes in regime depending on which threshold is more likely to bind. We describe the regimes and the central prediction of our conjecture in the simple matrix below.

Regime	Thresholds		Expectations	
	2% ceiling	ELB	Policy action	Inflation
'high inflation & high interest rates'	Binding	Non-binding	Large	Small
'low inflation & low interest rates'	Non-binding	Binding	Small	Large

[20] As shown in Panel A of Figure 3.1, this negative correlation is a feature of all episodes of rise or decline of energy prices in the pre-crisis sample with the possible exception of the 1999 episode, in which core seems to have followed headline with a lag. Ultimately, the analysis of the transmission of shocks cannot rely on correlations, and for this reason we extend the analysis to identified shocks in a VAR setting in Figure 3.13.

In the (relatively) high inflation/high interest rate regime, the relevant threshold is the price stability ceiling, while ELB is not binding. This is the configuration prevalent for much of the period prior to the crisis, and in some respects even after the crisis, as cost-push forces continued to drive inflation above the ceiling until 2011. That was a world in which inflation was (at least potentially) high, and so too were interest rates. In this regime, policy is anticipated to respond with vigour to inflation overshoots, and as a result inflation expectations do not budge and remain well anchored. Conversely, in a low inflation/low interest rate regime, inflation is low and far from the ceiling, while policy interest rates are already testing ELB. In these conditions, agents expect a small monetary policy response because of the central bank's limited wiggle room. It is therefore inflation expectations that react to inflation realizations. We test the two predictions using both a single-equation-with-interaction method and a daily threshold BVAR. We start with a discussion of the single equation method. Equations (1) and (2) incorporate the two key predictions about interest rate and inflation expectations, respectively:

$$(1) \quad f_t = \alpha + \beta Core_t + \delta(1 - D_{ELB}) + \vartheta_m(1 - D_{Ceiling}) + \\ \varphi_m \left(Core_t \times (1 - D_{ELB}) \times (1 - D_{Ceiling}) \right) + \varepsilon_{m,t},$$

where

$$D_{Ceiling} = \begin{cases} 1 & \text{if Headline inflation} \leq 2\% \\ 0 & \text{if Headline inflation} > 2\% \end{cases} \quad \text{and} \quad D_{ELB} = \begin{cases} 1 & \text{if MRO} \leq 1 \\ 0 & \text{if MRO} > 1 \end{cases}$$

The prediction in equation (1) maintains that, when the price stability ceiling is binding (headline inflation is high) and ELB is not binding (interest rates are high), the policy response to core inflation is stronger. Therefore, we regress a measure of interest rate expectations—the three-month-in-one-year overnight index swap (OIS) forward rate at time t, which is the left-hand variable f_t, on contemporary core inflation ($Core_t$), a dummy variable that takes a value of 1 in a low interest rate environment and zero otherwise (D_{ELB}), another dummy variable that takes a value of 1 when headline inflation is below the 2% ceiling and zero when it is above ($D_{Ceiling}$), and a triple interaction term including the three variables. The key coefficient here is φ_m, a measure of the extra strength with which monetary policy is expected to respond to core inflation when headline inflation 'violates' price stability.

$$(2) \quad ILS_t = \alpha + \beta Core_t + \delta D_{ELB} + \vartheta_m D_{Ceiling} + \varphi_m (Core_t \times D_{ELB} \times D_{Ceiling}) + \varepsilon_{m,t},$$

where

$$D_{Ceiling} = \begin{cases} 1 & \text{if Headline inflation} \leq 2\% \\ 0 & \text{if Headline inflation} > 2\% \end{cases} \quad \text{and} \quad D_{ELB} = \begin{cases} 1 & \text{if MRO} \leq 1 \\ 0 & \text{if MRO} > 1 \end{cases}$$

The prediction in equation (2) maintains that, when the 2% ceiling is not binding (headline inflation is low) and ELB becomes binding (interest rates are low), the reaction of inflation expectations to core inflation is stronger. Accordingly, we regress a measure of inflation expectations—the ten-year inflation-linked swap rate ILS_t that appears on the left of the equal sign—on contemporary core inflation ($Core_t$), the D_{ELB} and $D_{Ceiling}$ dummy variables, and a triple interaction term including the three variables. Now φ_m is a measure of the extra sensitivity of inflation expectations to core inflation in the vicinity of ELB.

The left panel of Table 3.2 documents our results and indeed shows that the data are congruent with our first prediction. The high and statistically significant estimated value of φ_m corroborates the conjecture that in pre-Lehman times the ECB had a tendency to suppress core inflation whenever the upper pain threshold of the price stability range had been exceeded. Before turning to the discussion of the

Table 3.2 Regression estimates on the two-regime predictions
Regression results for prediction 1

	Coefficient	T-stat
α	−0.70	−1.66
δ	0.86	2.27
ϑ_m	−0.02	−0.06
β	1.29	2.78
φ_m	0.73	3.86

Notes: Prediction (1) maintains that, when the price stability ceiling is binding (headline inflation is high) and ELB is not binding (interest rates are high), the policy response to core inflation is stronger.

Regression results for prediction 2

	Coefficient	T-stat
α	1.31	12.30
δ	−0.18	−3.64
ϑ_m	−0.28	−6.28
β	0.63	8.91
φ_m	0.22	2.92

Notes: Prediction (2) maintains that, when the 2% ceiling is not binding (headline inflation is low) and ELB becomes binding (interest rates are low), the reaction of inflation expectations to core inflation is stronger.

results shown in the right panel, we carry out additional analysis based on a macromodel to firm up the inference we have drawn from the left panel. This type of analysis requires a model that allows for non-linearities while maintaining good empirical properties.[21]

To this end, we estimate a threshold BVAR (T-BVAR) model that includes energy inflation, core inflation, the three-month OIS forward in one year, the term spread (computed as the difference between the ten-year OIS spot and the three-month OIS forward in one year) and the inflation-linked swap rate:

$$Y_t \equiv [Energy_t, Core_t, Nominal\,rate\,forward_t, Term\,Spread_t, Inflation\,forward_t]$$

The threshold that separates the two regimes is governed by the value of headline inflation:

$$D_{Ceiling} = \begin{cases} 1 \; if \; Headline\,inflation \leq 2\% \\ 0 \; if \; Headline\,inflation > 2\%, \end{cases}$$

We report the impulse-response functions of the system in Figure 3.13. The results confirm our earlier findings. In the comparatively 'high inflation' regime that prevailed before the crisis, the policy rate was expected to rise whenever agents received a 'high-inflation' surprise (captured in the model by a shock to energy prices), but long-term inflation expectations were relatively insensitive to incoming data. Furthermore, core inflation had to adjust for the higher energy price inflation rate to be accommodated while keeping overall inflation within or not too far above the price stability ceiling.[22] We conclude this part of our analysis by arguing that the concerns expressed in the 2004 CEPR report—and in Geraats et al. (2008)—about the ECB's putative inattention to inflation were vastly exaggerated.

By contrast, the pre-crisis data confirm that the ECB's regime adhered to the principle that the stability of expectations rests on the central bank's strong long-term commitment to providing a nominal anchor. With such a commitment firmly established, and expectations well anchored, monetary policy does not need to respond as much to the temporary rise in headline inflation in order to stabilize inflation over the longer run. In turn, a more muted response to swings in inflation has first-order implications for the performance of the economy more generally.

---

[21] Our workhorse DSGE model is a linearized model which (by definition) does not allow analysing non-liner dynamics, and the model is too large to be solved in its fully non-linear form. Also, the model is quarterly, whereas the use of higher-frequency data becomes important here to study non-linear dynamics because the latter require ultimately to partition the data into separate regimes, whereby requiring a sufficient number of observations in each regime.

[22] The impulse response of HICP core inflation to HICP energy inflation depicted in Figure 3.13 stands on the low side of ECB internal model estimates.

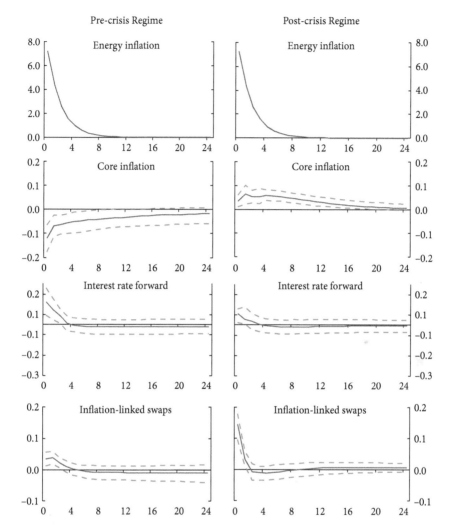

Figure 3.13 Impulse response functions to an energy price shock in the two regimes (year-on-year % change)

Source: ECB calculations.

Notes: The first column shows impulse response functions to an energy price shock in the pre-crisis regime, while the second column in the post-crisis regime. Results are computed using a threshold BVAR (T-BVAR) model that includes energy inflation, core inflation, the three-month OIS forward in one year, the term spread (computed as the difference between the ten-year OIS spot and the three-month OIS forward in one year) and the inflation-linked swap rate. The threshold that separates the two regimes is governed by the value of headline inflation, below or above 2%. The sample period spans from 2004 until 2018, at monthly frequency.

Looking at the specifics of the pre-crisis years, a lower sensitivity of long-run inflation to supply shocks implied that such shocks were much less likely to generate economic instability than they were only ten years earlier. And this dampened reaction of expectations and the underlying trend rate of inflation to the economic circumstances translated into a smoother path for the ECB's key interest rate (see Figure 3.4).

In short, in the pre-crisis era the ECB's price stability framework functioned in the way that theory predicts an ideal inflation targeting framework should behave when tested by unfavourable disturbances: automatic adjustments in underlying conditions, including expectations, should do a large part of the stabilization job. A credible monetary regime can improve the economy's ability to absorb shocks, meaning that monetary policy can afford more patience. If this is the case, better outcomes can be observed not only for inflation but for real activity as well, because a less activist central bank injects less volatility into the economy in such conditions.

Figure 3.14 does indeed support this last claim, by locating the euro area, along with other advanced economies, in a space defined by the realized variability of the level of activity and the realized variability of inflation over the ten-year period covered in this chapter. Variability is defined by the standard deviation of real per capita output and inflation in the left panel, and by level deviations from trend output and a 1.9% 'target', respectively, in the right panel. We discussed the simple idea behind this figure in Chapter 1: attempts to keep inflation from rising in the face of shocks to aggregate supply are likely to result in increased fluctuations in real GDP and employment—which are welfare-reducing.

Conversely, attempts to control business cycle fluctuations too closely in the face of these shocks are likely to lead to wider fluctuations in inflation, which are also very costly for society. Lower volatility of inflation improves market functioning,

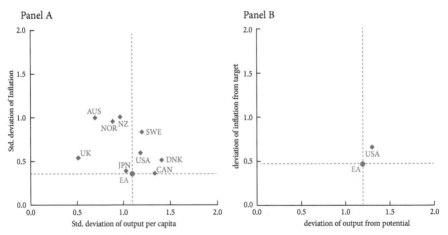

Figure 3.14 Macroeconomic volatility in the euro area and other advanced economies 1999–2007

Panel A: Variability of inflation and output (standard deviation)
Source: OECD.
Notes: The figure shows the standard deviation of annual CPI inflation and annual real GDP per capita growth at annual frequency from 1999 to 2007 for a panel of OECD countries.

Panel B: Deviations from inflation target and trend output (percentage points)
Sources: Eurostat and Haver.
Notes: The figure shows the deviation of CPI inflation from target (taken to be 1.9% for the euro area and 2% for the United States) from 1999 to 2007, and the deviation of real GDP growth from potential growth.

makes economic planning easier and reduces the resources devoted to hedging inflation risks. In addition, reduced volatility of output implies a reduction in the extent of economic uncertainty confronting households and firms. Supply-side shocks increase volatility on both dimensions: inflation and output. So, the periodic occurrence of shocks to aggregate supply (such as oil price shocks) confronts policy-makers with the choice between stabilizing output and stabilizing inflation: a clear trade-off. This trade-off can conveniently be depicted in what is known as the Taylor frontier (described in Taylor, 1994). In this trade-off space, economies located close to the origin of the graph perform better than those farther out, because they manage to squeeze volatility on both sides of the trade-off. By this metric, the euro area's record appears satisfactory. The euro area is positioned south-west of the other two or three major economies of comparable size, a sign that it managed to compress headline inflation variability without paying too high a price in terms of output stability. Low volatility did not suppress growth performance measured in levels. In fact, a comparison with the other two major economies based on per capita real income developments since the onset of monetary union (see Figure 3.15) shows that the euro area outperformed its peers.

3.3.2 The Regime Switch

Arguably, the 2% price stability ceiling played a decisive role in enabling the relatively good macroeconomic outcomes shown above. It did so by setting in motion the self-equilibrating mechanism that we tried to describe in the previous subsection. Seen as a pain threshold, it introduced the sort of non-linearity that contributed to

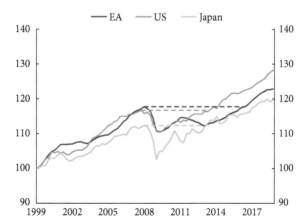

Figure 3.15 Real GDP per capita in the G3 economies (index, 1999Q1=100)

Sources: Bureau of Economic Analysis and Eurostat. *Notes*: Output per capita is real GDP divided by total population.
Latest observation: 2018Q4.

keeping inflation expectations—and inflation realizations—in check over those early years, despite repeated bouts of excess inflation. But clearly, as we remarked before, in a world hit by a long sequence of inflationary supply shocks, stabilization of head-line inflation comes at a cost: suppression of core inflation. Indeed, Figure 3.1 shows that core inflation has followed a downward path over the years leading up to the financial crisis, a path that seems to have been departing stepwise but sustainably over the years from the 2% line.

How might the mechanism linking sequential inflation surprises to expectations of an ECB's interest rate reaction to ultimately lower core inflation have worked in reality? A powerful link in this chain of reactions is typically the exchange rate. If the central bank is perceived to be permanently on alert because of upside inflation sur-prises and more likely to tighten in the near future than to ease monetary policy—like it appears to have been the case during the pre-crisis years (see Figure 3.5)—then the exchange rate tends to appreciate vis-à-vis foreign currencies. Indeed, over the pre-crisis period, and particularly starting in 2005, the euro was subject to marked and sustained appreciation pressures vis-à-vis the dollar (see Figure 3.16). The mechanic link is given by what is known as the 'covered interest rate parity' (CIP), an arbitrage condition that applies to international investors trying to exploit any

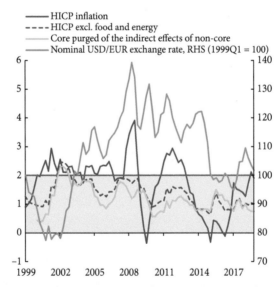

Figure 3.16 Inflation in the euro area, core inflation, core purged of the indirect effects of non-core, and exchange rate (annual % change and index)

Sources: ECB and Eurostat.
Notes: The horizontal line marks the ceiling of the ECB price stability range, while the shaded area marks the price stability range. Core purged of the indirect effects of non-core is computed by mapping at each point in time the historical realization of HICP energy into impact on core by employing elasticities commonly used in Eurosystem projection exercises, and then subtracting the resulting time series from actual core inflation.
Latest observation: 2018Q4.

difference in yields across currencies. On average, if cross-border capital mobility is unimpaired, there should be indifference between, on one hand, investing in dollar funds and earning the interest rate on the dollar and, on the other, converting those funds into EUR, investing in EUR funds and locking in an exchange rate at maturity by writing a forward exchange rate contract to return the funds into dollars at a pre-fixed conversion rate. This is what CIP is all about.[23]

Imagine that the ECB displays a strong conviction that policy should be firmed in the face of persistent upside inflation pressures. This pushes the interest rate on the EUR higher and, for a given value of the forward exchange rate between the EUR and the dollar, investors will find it convenient to move funds into EUR assets and earn the interest rate differential that has formed now between returns in EUR and returns in dollars. Accordingly, there will be an inflow of funds into EUR assets, which will put the euro on a sustained appreciation path. Is this an accurate description of the mechanism that appears to have been at work over those pre-crisis years? Figure 3.17 shows the spread between a representative interest rate payable on risk-free EUR assets and a representative interest rate with the same maturity payable on

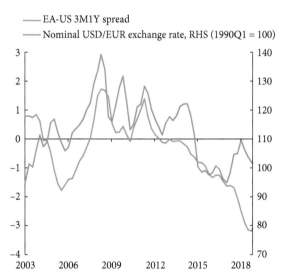

Figure 3.17 Exchange rate and euro area-US interest rate differential (index and percentages per annum)

Sources: ECB and US Federal Reserve.
Notes: The 3M1Y spread refers to OIS spread. The US 3M1Y series is calculated based on yield curve factors provided by the Fed.
Latest observation: 2018Q4.

---

[23] In formal terms, the Covered Interest Parity is defined in approximate terms as: $i_t^{\$} = i_t^{\epsilon} + \dfrac{(f_t^{h} - s_t)}{s_t}$, where $i_t^{\$}$ is the net interest rate on the risk-free dollar asset, i_t^{ϵ} is the net interest rate on the risk-free EUR asset, s_t is the spot exchange rate defined as the units of dollars per 1 EUR, f_t^{h} is the forward exchange rate defined as the units of dollars per 1 EUR.

risk-free dollar assets, where the interest rate is the three-month in one-year derived from OIS rates. As one can see, this spread moved in tight coherence with the spot exchange rate between the euro and the dollar.

A stronger euro, of course, has a direct dampening effect on headline inflation because of the imports component of the price index. In turn, the compression of import prices is expected to put downside pressure on domestic prices via the input-output structure of production and as result of domestic producers' attempt to maintain their market share in the domestic market. The situation was the opposite in the United States, with a depreciation of the dollar over the pre-crisis period creating strong inflationary pressure both on headline and core inflation (see Figure 3.18).

Probably, the decline in actual core inflation that we attribute to the observed combination between inflationary supply shocks and the ECB's anti-inflationary stance is an underestimation of the impact of that combination of factors on domestic inflation creation. The reason is that core inflation itself is affected by energy prices, albeit indirectly. To illustrate the quantitative importance of this effect we map at each point in time the historical realization of HICP energy into impact on core by using model-based elasticities, and then we subtract from actual core this estimated indirect effect from energy. The resulting time series is represented by the yellow line in Figure 3.16. It shows that over the period 2004–2008 the adjusted

Figure 3.18 Inflation in the US, core inflation, and exchange rate (annual % change and index)

Sources: Bureau of Labor Statistics and US Federal Reserve.
Notes: The horizontal line marks the value of inflation that the FOMC judges as most consistent over the longer run with the Federal Reserve's statutory mandate, as announced since January 2012. Latest observation: 2018Q4.

measure of core was on average 27 basis points lower than actual core inflation. This suggests that the weakness in the ability of the euro area economy to generate domestic inflation at the onset of the financial crisis was a more pervasive problem than suggested by actual core inflation.

Against this backdrop, the questions that we want to answer next are therefore the following. What happens in this world if shocks change signs and consumer price inflation starts to visit regions of the price stability range closer to zero? What lessons can we draw about the 'right' target in a two-regime world?

In searching for an answer to these questions, we return to the results of the regime-switching analysis expounded in the previous subsection. The key prediction we concentrate on here is the second one: when the ceiling ceases to bind, inflation falls and the policy rate reaches its ELB, inflation expectations start to react to observed inflation. Core inflation consequently follows actual inflation *downwards*, i.e. the key correlation between core inflation and innovations to headline inflation becomes *positive*. This last point is an important switch in this two-regime world. Remember that the *negative* correlation between core and observed inflation acted as a critical circuit breaker in the transmission of adverse inflation shocks for the best part of the ECB's first ten years. If the correlation becomes positive, however, then adjustments in inflation expectations and in core inflation become multipliers rather than dampeners of adverse disturbances.

This is indeed what the data tell us. First, look again at Figure 3.12 and notice the marked change in colour in the picture as the euro area economy enters the financial crisis. The prevalence of blue over the crisis and post-crisis years clearly indicates a change in regime compared with the pre-crisis period (when the dominant colours were red and brown), suggesting an entirely different dynamic connection between core and non-core inflation. Evidently, when the positive supply shocks of the previous ten years reversed signs and gave way to negative demand shocks in the immediate aftermath of the financial crash, the dynamic pattern of core inflation changed. And as Figure 3.1 indicates, the path of core inflation took another major leap down. Reflecting this evidence, the right panels of Table 3.2 and Figure 3.13 lend support to our second prediction. Figure 3.13 in particular shows the strong co-movement between core inflation and inflation expectations when the expected rate reaction by the central bank is nil—because of the lower bound.

We believe this evidence holds two important lessons. First, a clearly defined floor for the price stability range in the second, disinflationary regime would be as critical in breaking its perverse downward dynamics as the 2% upper threshold in the first regime is critical in preventing inflationary shocks from taking hold. A floor should be sharply defined and not too far below the ceiling, otherwise the ELB is reached before inflation hits the floor and the economy switches over to the second regime.

The second lesson is about the choice of a 'target'. We think that our analysis proves that a lower target is not equivalent to a higher target. A low target in inflationary conditions may unwittingly destabilize domestic inflation and cause its underlying rate to fall short of the objective in a lasting way. If this is the case, good macroeconomic performance in the first regime may be bought only at the price of particularly bad performance if the economy ever enters the second regime. There is a sort of intertemporal trade-off in the way the central bank delivers on its objectives. And assuming welfare can be measured in Taylor's inflation/output variability space, the result is a kind of intertemporal substitution in societal welfare. If price stability in the first regime causes a permanently weaker process for core inflation, then the first regime is essentially importing welfare—lower deviations of inflation from target—from the future.

We attempt to visualize this intertemporal trade-off by adding one dimension to the canonical Taylor frontier that we show above. In particular, we transform the right panel of Figure 3.14 into the tri-dimensional picture presented in Figure 3.19 by adding one more axis to that representation. Along the new axis, performance is measured by the average divergence of *core* inflation from the central bank's objective. Why do we add core inflation as an extra standard of measurement for welfare? It is because, over the time span relevant for this comparison, an economy whose macroeconomic outcomes appear superior if judged in the canonical headline inflation/output plane might have earned high marks at the expense of its future performance. Core inflation is an indicator of this intertemporal transfer. If we contrast the euro area with the United States only, we see from Figure 3.19 that the latter did indeed have a better record.

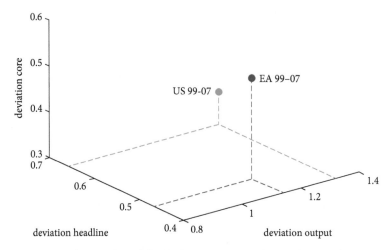

Figure 3.19 Macroeconomic stability in the euro area and United States (percentage points)

Sources: Eurostat and Haver.
Notes: The figure shows the deviation of headline inflation from target (taken to be 1.9% for the euro area and 2% for the United States) between 1999 and 2007, the deviation of real GDP growth from potential growth, and the deviation of core from target.

3.4 Competing Hypotheses

The above analysis tends to support the conclusion that the ECB considered that the costs of inflation escalate rapidly above 2%, while modest shortfalls below this rate were seen as less problematic. But, can real-time inflation expectations—stubbornly above the 2% line for much of the pre-crisis era—really support our conclusion? The yellow line in Panel A of Figure 3.6, which represents the evolution of the five-year in five-year inflation expectations implied by inflation-linked swaps between 2005 and the onset of the crisis, arguably tells a different story: investors in this market do not appear to have internalized a particularly aggressive anti-inflationary stance on the side of the GC over this period. In fact, on the face of it, the 2% line does not seem to bear any of the characteristics that one would associate with a 'reflecting barrier', at least in the way this expression has been used in the exchange rate target zones literature since the canonical model of Krugman (1991).[24] There is a second question: can data discriminate at all between the hypothesis that we favour and an alternative hypothesis contending that the ECB was indeed symmetric in its reactions to inflation departing from its 'aim', but the 'aim' itself was in fact not quite at the edge?

We first try to respond to the first objection: the observed state of inflation expectations as disproof of our 'reflecting barrier' conjecture. Indeed, a straight read of Panel A of Figure 3.6 might suggest that market participants expected inflation to significantly exceed 2%, even at long horizons. However, other factors in addition to genuine *expected inflation* likely affect the measure of inflation compensation that one can extract from inflation-linked swap contracts. An important component of that measure, beyond liquidity premia and a variety of transitory trading effects, is the *inflation risk premium*. Why do inflation-protected contracts incorporate such a premium over and above the return that is due to compensate for investors' pure inflation anticipations? Because assets like nominal bonds whose prices and returns suffer when inflation is *unexpectedly* high—even relative to what markets expect as the likeliest inflation realization at longer horizon—are viewed as risky by market participants, who then require an inflation risk premium, affecting long-term nominal yields. By arbitrage, this premium moves from the nominal fixed-income market to the market for inflation protection, of which inflation swaps are a branch. We note here that, in conditions of recurrent oil price shocks, this premium was positive and sizeable in magnitude over the period covered by Figure 3.6. Why was the

---

[24] In practice, there are important differences from a target zone regime and a price stability range framework. Notably, a credible target zone implies the presence of a hard ceiling that constrains the possible future paths of the exchange rate; a distinct manifestation of this mechanism is that the distribution of exchange-rate expectations tends to become negatively skewed as the exchange rate approaches the ceiling of the target zone. In the case of a price stability range, instead, the ceiling does not imply a similarly binding constraint, and so non-linearities in the distribution of inflation expectations might not at all emerge. In the price stability range regime, the mechanism at play may be more akin to one in which the central bank has an asymmetric loss function around its target, weighting overshootings more than undershootings.

inflation premium large over those years, and how large was it? On the underlying reason for observing a large inflation premium, one should simply resort to conventional asset pricing theory, which suggests that the sign of risk premia depends on the sign of the covariance of the returns of those assets with the typical investors' consumption or wealth. Inflationary supply-side shocks determine an environment in which inflation is high while output tends to be weak and consumption falls, so the correlation of long-run future inflation with long-run future consumption is perceived to be negative. This induces investors to demand extra compensation. Conversely, in an environment dominated by demand shocks, inflation tends to be procyclical and nominal bonds tend to embed a negative inflation premium.[25] We gauge the size of the premium by deploying the results of an affine term structure model estimated on the euro area inflation-linked swap curve, which allows separating the 'pure inflation expectations' component of the observed inflation compensation from the 'inflation risk premium'.[26] We show the evolution of the 'pure inflation expectations' component in Figure 3.6 (purple line). It is noteworthy that, as measured inflation surged past 4% in the summer of 2008, the observed ample overshoot above the 2% threshold spurred a widening in the inflation premium but no trespassing in point inflation expectations (see the expanding wedge between the yellow and the dark green lines in Figure 3.6). The latter came close to the barrier, but appears to have bounced back against it. The inflation outburst of 2011 gave rise to the same phenomenon (see Figure 4.8).[27]

To shed light on the second question (asymmetry versus distance from zero), we consider a more traditional approach to characterizing monetary policy conduct in the pre-crisis regime, namely through the lens of a Taylor-type feedback rule for the short-term interest rate. In its standard specification, the Taylor rule prescribes a response of the policy interest rate to deviations of inflation from target and output from potential. As investigated in Box 3.1, we consider an augmented Taylor rule specification to investigate possible asymmetric interest rate reaction to inflation realizations around the price stability ceiling. Overall, the analysis provides equal support for two distinct characterizations of the ECB's policy rule. The first entails an asymmetric reaction around a 2% point target, in the form of a more aggressive reaction to overshooting than undershooting. The second embodies a symmetric reaction around lower focal point(s) for inflation, i.e. levels of target inflation not

---

[25] See, e.g., Chen et al. (2016) and Campbell et al. (2009) on the economics of the sign of the inflation risk premium and for evidence that also in the United States the inflation risk premium has declined over recent years and has arguably turned negative.

[26] Specifically, the estimates are based on an update of the model expounded in Camba-Mendez and Werner (2017). The affine three-factor model is estimated on the ILS curve adapting the approach by Joslin, Singleton and Zhu (2011) to decompose the nominal yield curve. At each point in time, the model allows to produce a 'true' (i.e. under the so-called 'physical measure') expectation of average inflation, which is subtracted from the model-based expectation under the risk-neutral measure to obtain the inflation risk premium. Subtracting the estimated inflation risk premium from observed ILS rates delivers our measure of 'genuine' inflation expectation reported in the figure.

[27] On the presence and salience of inflation risk premia in measures of market-based inflation expectations, see Coeuré (2019c).

quite at the edge of the price stability comfort zone. In either characterization, and consistent with earlier findings, the Taylor rule analysis rejects the view that the ECB was inattentive to inflation. In fact, the characterization of the ECB's Taylor rule in the form of a stronger response to inflation overshooting the 2% ceiling is closely aligned with the earlier findings reported in Table 3.2 and Figure 3.13, and provides explicit support to our base-case hypothesis. Our results resonate with recent empirical work on estimated Taylor rules for the euro area. For instance, Hartmann and Smets (2018) find some empirical support for two alternative characterizations of the ECB's policy rule: one with an implicit symmetric reaction around an estimated 1.8% point target; and one implying an asymmetric reaction around the 1.8% point target, with the ECB tightening interest rates mainly in response to expected inflation above its inflation aim, and easing policy mainly in response to an expected slowdown in growth. Our results are close to those reported in Paloviita et al. (2019), from which we largely borrowed the empirical Taylor rule specifications described above and analysed in more detail in Box 3.1. The paper claims that its main result cast some doubt on the optimality of the ECB's price stability definition. Although our policy inference is similar to that of Paloviita et al. (2019), our conclusion is far less definitive. We limit ourselves to the following observation. The uncertainty involved in characterizing the precise features of the price stability definition is in itself problematic and, in particular, the difficulty of empirically pinpointing the floor of the interval targeting is worrisome. It might suggest that, faced with a seemingly minor outbreak of adaptive expectations, the economy may become vulnerable to self-sustained downward trajectories.

There are other competing hypotheses that could in principle help explain the conditions of persistent disinflation represented in Figure 3.13 and are not related to the formulation of the inflation objective. One alternative is a systematic misperception of the natural rate of interest (henceforth r^*).[28] Specifically, suppose r^* drifts down, in ways that are hard for the central bank to diagnose. Figure 3.20 shows that alternative econometric estimates of r^* for the euro area similarly feature a pronounced long-term downward trend, and a sharper fall during the financial crisis. The literature suggests that major driving forces behind the decline in r^* are secular in nature and include waning productivity growth, a climb down in population growth and demographic ageing, and a shift from physical to human capital-intensive industries. The sharp fall of r^* during the financial crisis is typically attributed to the surge in risk aversion and associated safe-haven flows around that period. While similarly pointing to a protracted fall in r^*, the estimates displayed in Figure 3.20 provide an indication of heightened uncertainty about the extent of the fall in r^*, and more prominently about its prevailing level. If the central bank misperceives the level of r^* and does not accommodate the protracted fall in r^*,

---

[28] Defined as the real rate prevailing when the economy is at its full employment equilibrium, with stable inflation close to the monetary authority's target, r^* should appear as the intercept in a traditional Taylor rule.

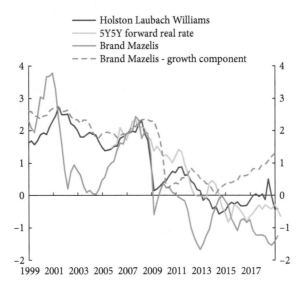

Figure 3.20 Estimates of the natural rate of interest for the euro area (percentages per annum)

Sources: Holston et al. (2017) and Brand and Mazelis (2019).
Notes: Estimate from Holston et al. (2017) is obtained from the homepage of the Federal Reserve Bank of San Francisco. Holston et al. (2017) based on filtered estimates and Brand and Mazelis (2019) based on smoothed estimates of states.
Latest observation: 2018Q4.

monetary policy would end up being tighter than intended.[29] In the pre-crisis period, this situation would have resulted in a compression of core inflation and some downward pressure on headline due to a stronger exchange rate, a constellation that might remain compatible with the observed negative correlation between headline and core over that period.[30] During the crisis, the misperception about r^* would have resulted in a less accommodative policy response to disinflationary global and domestic demand shocks than actually intended. This would have compressed core and helped put downward pressure on headline via the exchange rate. While it does in principle capture the correlation patterns between headline and core we observe in the data, this hypothesis remains vulnerable to the following criticism: if the central bank is committed to a symmetric reaction to overshoots and undershoots compared with its goal (say 1.9%), then observing that inflation remains persistently below the goal should lead over time to the signal extraction problem about the correct level of r^* being resolved, with the central banks taking

[29] Misperception about r^* would possibly translate into misperception about potential output, in a manner that in a Taylor-rule framework the two would partially offset each other. However, there are many forces that can affect r^* without affecting potential output, see for instance Laubach and Williams (2003).

[30] Headline would go up following the inflationary shocks hitting the euro area at the time, but by less than would otherwise have been the case, due to some downward pressure from a stronger exchange rate coming from a tighter policy than intended. So this constellation may still be capable of generating the negative correlation between headline and core inflation that we have documented over the pre-crisis period.

the necessary forceful policy actions. It is true that the process may take a very long time to converge if r^* keeps drifting down, but this should apply to all central banks in advanced economies, as they faced a similar challenge. From this perspective, it is then difficult to rationalize the distinct pattern of core and headline inflation in the euro area relative to the United States of the type documented above.

Another hypothesis may rest on the (perceived) lack of policy instruments when policy rates are approaching the lower bound. Assume a central bank is fully committed to a symmetric inflation goal (say 1.9%) and r^* is correctly measured. A situation is conceivable in which the global supply shocks in the pre-crisis period pushed up headline inflation and monetary policy reacted to them, thereby compressing core inflation. This would be consistent with the pre-crisis negative correlation we documented. With the outbreak of the crisis, the prevalence of disinflationary global and domestic demand shocks would have led to a decline in headline and core inflation, and the central bank was (or was perceived to be) constrained by the lower bound and the scarcity of other powerful policy instruments. This (perceived) lack of policy instruments would reinforce the adverse impact of the original demand shocks and make the disinflationary process more persistent. However, this does not seem able to account for the fact that the ECB has reacted forcefully to the crisis and adopted many new and powerful policy tools for the exact purpose of addressing the diminishing room for manoeuvre of the standard policy rate, as discussed in the next chapter.

Each of these alternative hypotheses may in reality have been conflated. And each may have interacted with some form of adaptive expectation formation for inflation, thereby increasing the likelihood of an enduring self-sustained downward trajectory in inflation following an initial decline in inflation caused by the large and persistent demand shocks that have characterized the crisis period.

Armed with the results of our empirical analysis expounded above, a bit of retrospection is in order regarding the outcome of the May 2003 strategy review. As we discussed at length in Chapter 2, the May 2003 announcement retained the price stability range but identified a focal point for policy within it, stating that policy would aim for a level of inflation somewhere in the upper quartile of the range ('below but close to 2%'). If the policy aim is the diamond in Figure 3.21 the innovation in the strategy announcement amounted to increasing the distance between the 'policy aim' diamond and the deflation zone.

However, nudging the policy aim towards the edge of the price stability range created the risk that—purely mechanically—inflation realizations might ultimately cluster almost half of the time outside what qualified as the price stability space, the 0% to 2% range. If an observer in May 2003 had imagined inflation realizations to be distributed according to a normal, bell-shaped distribution of the type we show in the figure, then assuming the central bank was completely indifferent to the sign of observed departures from the policy aim, the observer could have predicted very frequent inflation overshoots in the future. Indeed, a large portion of an unconditional distribution for inflation centred around the diamond lies above 2%. But did

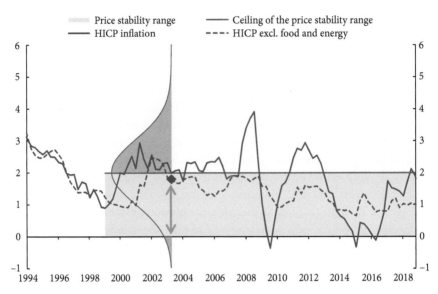

Figure 3.21 Hypothetical distribution of inflation outcomes centered around alternative inflation focal points (year-on-year % change)
Source: Eurostat.

the framework really encourage indifference about the *sign* of the inflation deviations from the aim on the side of the central bank? We doubt it. The combination of a timeless price stability range and a focal point close to the upper bound of the range is a framework that has an inherent tendency to focus policymakers' attention chiefly on inflation *overshoots* rather than *undershoots*. Consider the relative sizes of the two portions of the inflation density lying above or below the two boundaries. In other words, within this framework observed deviations of inflation on the upside might not be viewed as being equally costly as moderate deviations of inflation on the downside.

So, the 2003 decision might have brought with itself a trade-off between *safety* and *symmetry*. In the next chapter we contend that history resolved the trade-off against safety. In the early years of the crisis the costs of inflation were judged to escalate rapidly above 2%, while modest projected shortfalls below this rate were seen as less problematic.

3.5 The Conundrum

The euro area approached the onset of the global financial crisis (GFC) with a weakened objective and with less effective instruments. Although not yet apparent in the data of the time to the same extent as it is in retrospect today, the capacity of the euro area economy to generate domestic inflation consistent with the 'close to 2%'

Box 3.1 The ECB's interest rate policy and the definition of price stability through the lens of a Taylor rule framework

In this box we employ a Taylor rule framework to test whether the ECB policy reaction to inflation can be characterized as symmetric or asymmetric, and whether the inflation target can best be described as a point target or an interval. To increase robustness, we adopt a thick modelling approach that spans a wide range of different proxy variables for expected inflation and economic activity. Empirically, we find equal support for two distinct characterizations of the ECB's policy rule. The first entails an asymmetric reaction around a 2% point target, in the form of a stronger response to overshooting than to undershooting. The second embodies a symmetric reaction around an interval targeting between 1.6% and 1.9%, although the floor of this interval is difficult to pin down empirically. The uncertainty in characterizing the precise features of the inflation target that we uncover is worrisome, because it suggests that faced with a seemingly minor outbreak of adaptive expectations, the economy may become vulnerable to self-sustained downward trajectories.

Since Taylor's seminal 1993 paper, his eponymous interest rate rule has been widely used to describe monetary policy decisions, reflecting its good performance in explaining movements in the policy interest rate as well as its desirable properties when embedded into the New Keynesian framework described in Section 1.2. In its original specification, the Taylor rule prescribes a response of the short-term interest rate to deviations of inflation from target and output from potential. To characterize the ECB's policy rate conduct, we consider a variant of this rule modified along several dimensions intended to capture potential features of ECB policy:

$$R_t = \rho^* i_{t-1} + (1-\rho)^* \left(c + \phi_\pi^* (\pi_t^h - \pi^*) + \phi_y^* (y_t^h - \overline{y}) + \phi_m^* (m_t - \overline{m}) + \phi_{CL}^* CL_t \right) \qquad \text{(B.3.1.1)}$$

with CL_t defined as:

$$CL_t = \left(\frac{1}{q}\sum_{i=1}^{q} \pi_{t-i} - \pi^* \right) * \left| \frac{1}{q}\sum_{i=1}^{q} \pi_{t-i} - \pi^* \right|$$

where R_t is the policy-relevant interest rate, π_t^h is headline inflation, π^* is the inflation target, y_t^h is an indicator of economic activity, $\overline{y}$ is potential growth, m_t is a monetary indicator, $\overline{m}$ is the long-run value of the monetary indicator, and CL_t represents a 'credibility loss' term defined as signed squared deviations of inflation from target. The superscript h in the term for inflation and economic activity stands for the lead/lag horizon over which we measure those variables. In terms of policy interest rates,

(Continued)

Box 3.1 Continued

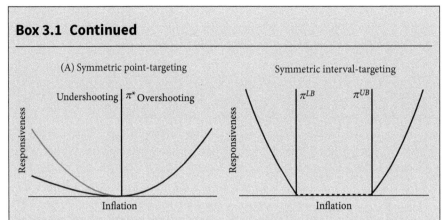

Figure B.3.1.1 (A) symmetric credibility loss terms in Taylor rule specifications
Notes: π^{UB} indicates the upper bound and π^{LB} the lower bound of the inflation targeting interval.

we consider two alternatives: the three-month EONIA as well as the three-month in one-year OIS forward rate. The specification of the credibility loss follows Neuenkirch and Tillmann (2014) and Paloviita et al. (2019). The non-standard terms of our Taylor rule specification are the monetary indicator, meant to capture the relevance of the monetary pillar in the ECB monetary policy strategy, and the credibility loss, meant to capture the ECB's concerns about missing its inflation objective. We further extend the baseline specification in two dimensions. First, we allow for an asymmetric response to persistent undershooting and overshooting of inflation (see Figure B.3.1.1, left panel) by partitioning the credibility loss term as follows:

$$\phi_{CL} * CL_t \equiv \phi_{CL}^P * d_t^P * CL_t + \phi_{CL}^N * d_t^N * CL_t$$

where $d_t^P \left(d_t^N \right)$ is a dummy variable taking the value of 1 (0) for inflation overshooting and 0 (1) for inflation undershooting. Second, we consider a specification of the inflation target, π^*, in terms of a point target and an alternative specification in which the target is formulated in terms of an interval as depicted in the right panel of Figure B.3.1.1. The different specifications are intended to allow us to test whether the ECB policy can be best described as symmetric or asymmetric around a point target or around an interval.

However, this approach entails a circularity challenge, whereby the response to undershooting and overshooting depends on the inference about π^*, and the inference about π^* depends in turn on the (a)symmetric reaction to the undershooting and overshooting. To address this problem, we estimate the regression parameters conditioning on alternative values for π^*. The regression sample spans the first decade of the euro, from 1999Q1 until 2008Q3; the estimation is carried out using the generalized method of moments (GMM) to address endogeneity of the regressors;

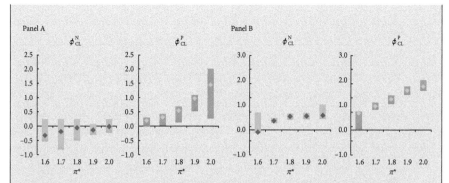

Figure B.3.1.2 Coefficient estimates under asymmetric point targeting under alternative proxies for policy rate (expectations): the three-month EONIA and the three-month in one-year OIS forward rate.

Panel A. Taylor rule specifications with three-month EONIA

Panel B. Taylor rule specifications with three-month in one-year OIS forward rate

Notes: The figure displays the coefficient estimates for ϕ_{CL}^{N} and ϕ_{CL}^{P} vis-à-vis alternative values of π^{*} under asymmetric point targeting (the coefficient estimates are scaled by the term $(1-\rho)$). The boxplots refers to the range of point estimates across Taylor-rule specifications. These specifications are identified following a thick-modelling approach combining a variety of economic indicators and are selected on the basis of their statistical fit. The economic indicators pertain to three blocks: inflation, real activity, and monetary developments. The number of Taylor-rule specifications identified in the case of the three-month EONIA (Panel A) is larger than in the case of the three-month in one-year OIS forward rate (Panel B), as reflected in the width of the respective boxplots. The estimation sample runs from 1999Q1 to 2008Q3.

this is particularly compelling in the case in which the policy rate is proxied by the OIS forward rate.

Figure B.3.1.2 depicts the parameter estimates associated to policy-rule specifications that allow for asymmetric point targeting, and defined respectively over the three-month EONIA (Panel A), and the three-month in one-year OIS forward rate (Panel B).

In both panels, the coefficient estimates attached to inflation overshooting (ϕ_{CL}^{P}) tend to be statistically higher than those attached to inflation undershooting ϕ_{CL}^{N} for values of π^{*} around 2%. The difference between the two sets of coefficients tends to recede for values of π^{*} around 1.6%.

Overall, our empirical results show that there is equal support for two distinct characterizations of the ECB's policy rule. The first entails an *asymmetric* reaction around a *2% point target*, in the form of a stronger response to overshooting than to undershooting. The second embodies a *symmetric* reaction around an *interval targeting between 1.6% and 1.9%*, although the floor of this interval is difficult to pin down empirically and visual evidence such as that shown in Figure 3.5 could tilt the balance of arguments in favour of the *asymmetry* interpretation.

(Continued)

Box 3.1 Continued

Our results resonate with recent empirical work on estimated Taylor rules for the euro area. For instance, Hartmann and Smets (2018) provide an assessment of the ECB's policy rate conduct within a Taylor rule framework, using an Orphanides rule specification (first-difference rule) linking the change in the main policy rate of the ECB to deviations of the one-year-ahead inflation forecast from the ECB's inflation aim and deviations of the one-year-ahead real GDP growth forecast from potential output growth. Their estimates provide some empirical support for two types of characterizations of the ECB's policy rule. The first implies a symmetric reaction around an estimated 1.8% point target. The second suggests that the ECB has tightened interest rates mainly in response to expected inflation above its inflation aim, where the latter is again estimated to be around 1.8%, and eased interest rates mainly in response to expected growth slowdowns. Our results on the (a)symmetry of ECB's policy rate conduct are also close to those reported in Paloviita et al. (2019), from which we largely borrowed the empirical specification.[31] They believe their results cast some doubt on the optimality of the price stability definition. Our interpretation is less definitive, although the ensuing policy conclusions are similar. In our view, the most important message coming both from our results and more generally from this strand of empirical literature is that the data do not seem to allow us to pin down a clear inflation attractor across various specifications, something that we believe is problematic per se. Assuming that economic agents are confronted with the task of learning the features of the central bank's inflation target (point vs. interval, level, symmetric vs. asymmetric), they may face an identification challenge similar to the one our results have uncovered. The upshot is that a seemingly minor outbreak of adaptive expectations may render the economy vulnerable to self-sustained downward trajectories.

topology was probably reduced. As for the instruments, between 2005 and 2007 the ECB had its fair share of a novel problem that complicated the conduct of monetary policy in a number of advanced economies during those years. The phenomenon was referred to by Alan Greenspan, then Chairman of the US Federal Reserve, as a *conundrum* in a famous testimony before the US Congress in February 2005. After a year of pause, with the federal funds rate held constant at the then exceptionally low level of 1%, in June 2004 the Fed had eventually started to raise its policy rate target, and since its first move in June had continued to firm its policy at each one of the following FOMC meetings. Yet in contrast to the established regularities governing

[31] Specifically, Paloviita et al. (2019) estimate a large number of competing specifications for the ECB's reaction function, using extensively the real-time projections from the Eurosystem/ECB staff macroeconomic projection exercises conducted in 1999Q4–2016Q4.

the relationship between short-term and long-term interest rates, long-term interest rates had responded to the policy tightening by trending lower. Greenspan concluded that: 'For the moment, the broadly unanticipated behaviour of world bond markets remains a conundrum.'

The *conundrum* was an unexpected complication for monetary policymakers, because a monetary policy tightening cycle is less effective in restraining spending if it is offset by an autonomous decline in long-term interest rates or in corporate credit spreads. The latter provides the financial stimulus that the former is meant to withdraw. Figure 3.22 shows that the euro area saw a bit of both reactions in the years preceding the financial crisis. Figures 3.23 and 3.24 document that this phenomenon was not confined to financial markets but also affected bank credit conditions. While monetary policy was being restricted after 2005 to respond to a resurgence in inflation (see Figure 3.25), the same financial factors that were moving inflation and real activity were causing countervailing adjustments in asset prices.

These uncontrolled adjustments worked against the inclinations of the GC. Panel A of Figure 3.22 shows the response of the spread between the long-term risk-free rate and the short-term rate. While a decline in the spread is typical in tightening phases—as the short end of the term structure rises relative to the long-end, which remains well-anchored by the price stability objective of policy—the pace of the decline was atypical. Long-term rates were easing the terms of long-term borrowing at a time in which the price of short-term borrowing was being raised. Developments

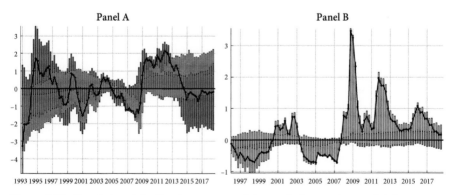

Figure 3.22 Shocks' contribution to euro area risk premia (percentage points)

Panel A: 10-year term spread

Panel B: credit spread

Source: CMR.

Notes: The solid line is the data. The red bars indicate the contribution from monetary policy; the blue bars the time-varying inflation target; the green bars aggregate demand; the yellow bars aggregate supply; the grey bars financial factors; the brown bars the term premium. The ten-year term spread is the difference between the ten-year yield and the three-month interest rate; the credit spread is the difference between a composite rate faced by the non-financial sector to borrow funds and the swap rate of corresponding maturity. The credit spread is displayed starting from the time in which euro area data are available. Data are in deviation from the mean.

Latest observation: 2018Q3.

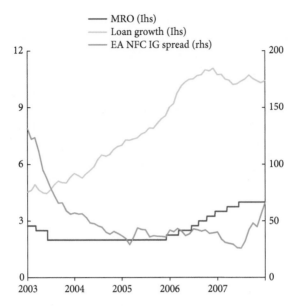

Figure 3.23 Policy rate, loan growth, and investment grade NFC corporate bond spread (percentages per annum and y-o-y % change, basis points)

Sources: ECB and Merrill Lynch.
Notes: The spread is computed as the average bond yield over the riskless rate. It only refers to investment grade bonds.
Latest observation: December 2007.

in private credit markets were adding further stimulus. Panel B shows that the credit spread which corporate borrowers were required to pay over and above risk-free rates also fell steeply. Market rates were falling rather than increasing in response to the monetary policy tightening. According to the evidence displayed in the figure, the grey bars caused the fall. Looking inside this group of shocks, one sees that the main explanatory force was a sharp revision in the appreciation of market and macroeconomic risk.

3.6 Leaning Against the Wind

In an article published in its Monthly Bulletin of April 2005, the ECB noted that: 'the volume of aggregate credit demonstrates a fairly systematic leading relationship with episodes of asset price turbulence. [...] Indeed, certain historical episodes suggest that major asset price escalations can be encouraged by lax monetary conditions which are not immediately reflected in an increase in consumer price inflation.' Based on that evidence, the article highlighted a relatively novel channel through which variables monitored in the monetary analysis, first and foremost credit, could regain the day-to-day conjunctural indicator function that M3 had lost: 'Monetary

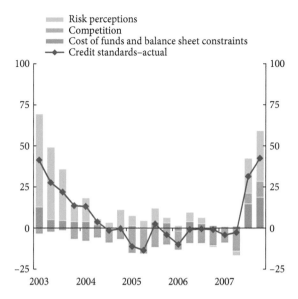

Figure 3.24 Changes in credit standards applied to the approval of loans or credit lines to enterprises, and contributing factors (net percentages of banks reporting tightening credit standards and contributing factors)

Source: ECB Bank Lending Survey.
Notes: Net percentages are defined as the difference between the sum of the percentages of banks responding 'tightened considerably' and 'tightened somewhat' and the sum of the percentages of banks responding 'eased somewhat' and 'eased considerably'. 'Cost of funds and balance sheet constraints' is the unweighted average of 'costs related to capital position', 'access to market financing' and 'liquidity position'; 'risk perceptions' is the unweighted average of 'general economic situation and outlook', 'industry or firm-specific situation and outlook/borrower's creditworthiness' and 'risk related to the collateral demanded'; 'competition' is the unweighted average of 'competition from other banks', 'competition from non-banks' and 'competition from market financing'.
Latest observation: January 2008 BLS.

analysis can contribute to assessing the extent to which generously valued assets can be traced to—and at the same time become a source of—excess creation of liquidity and over-extension of credit. Detecting and understanding this link helps the ECB form an opinion on whether an observed movement in asset prices might already reflect the inflating of an unsustainable bubble. [...] Early indications that a process of surging equity or house prices in the euro area might be interacting with conditions of abundant liquidity would lead to heightened vigilance.'

In fact, several lines of theoretical research had combined in the years prior to the *conundrum* to boost the case for incorporating asset prices more systematically into the policymaking process (Cecchetti et al., 2000). These proposals generally rested on the notion that asset prices contained information about the current and prospective state of the economy which was valuable, i.e. incremental relative to that conveyed by central bank macroeconomic forecasts. In the specific circumstances generated by the *conundrum*, having asset prices as an explicit right-hand term in

Panel A

Panel B

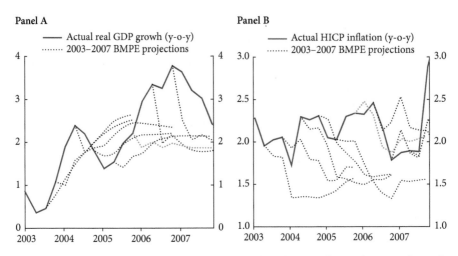

Figure 3.25 Actual and projected real GDP growth and HICP inflation (y-o-y % change)

Panel A: GDP growth
Sources: Eurostat and ECB projections.
Notes: Green dotted line indicates the December 2005 BMPE, which corresponds to the start of the 2005–2008 tightening cycle.
Latest observation: 2007Q4 for realized GDP growth.

Panel B: HICP inflation
Sources: Eurostat and ECB projections.
Notes: Green dotted line indicates the December 2005 BMPE, which corresponds to the start of the 2005–2008 tightening cycle.
Latest observation: 2007Q4 for realized HICP inflation.

the central bank reaction rule would offer the extra advantage of making the adjustments in the policy interest rate conditional on the extent to which it influenced key asset prices or longer-term interest rates.[32]

But this approach, known as the leaning against the wind strategy, posed some non-trivial questions (see Visco, 2014 for a review). How high a hurdle would a central bank facing a possible asset bubble have to surmount before it would be justified in tightening policy beyond what the outlook for inflation and output would require, after taking past and projected asset price developments into account? For adherents of conventional IT strategies, this hurdle is pretty high. A central bank should typically not attempt to use monetary policy to influence the speculative component of asset prices, based on the assumption that it has little ability to do so and that any attempt will only result in sub-optimal economic performance in the medium term. Advocates of a leaning against the wind strategy hold the opposite view. A central bank, upon perceiving the development of an asset bubble, should take extra action by tightening policy beyond what the conventional strategy would suggest, with the hope of limiting the size of the bubble and thus the fallout from its deflation.

---

[32] There was a large literature at the time debating the role of asset prices in the monetary policy conduct, see for instance: Bernanke and Gertler (2000) and Borio and Lowe (2004) for different views.

As shown above, the data support the inference that the ECB has reacted to developments in credit throughout its history. To the extent that credit growth helps identify ongoing perverse interactions between price formation in financial markets and investor leverage, credit can indeed signal and *stand in* for the most speculative component of asset prices and for pending risks to financial stability. Part of the reason we see credit as a significant right-hand variable in the ECB's 'reaction function' can therefore be attributed to an underlying leaning against the wind approach by the GC. But as we sought to argue before, credit also has good cyclical properties and might have given the ECB early information on the current level of resource utilization in the data-poor environment in which the central bank was operating during its early days. We ask whether a somewhat tighter monetary policy in the couple of years prior to the crisis, motivated by the ongoing credit boom, would have helped check at least some of the speculative activity in the markets and as a result produce an improved economic performance. In trying to answer the question, we eschew a number of real-time and analytical complications. First, we ignore the difficulty for monetary policymakers of identifying a bubble with sufficient confidence as it occurs. Second, although the housing market was obviously the trigger for the crisis and a key factor in its propagation to the real economy worldwide, the CMR model we use does not embody a mortgage market. We therefore concentrate on a key side aspect of the broader credit boom, namely the unusually low compensation for risk-taking which, at the time, became apparent in a sustained decline in underwriting standards and greatly compressed credit spreads. Specifically, we imagine an alternative world in which the ECB would have pursued a tighter monetary policy than it actually did in order to halt the sustained decline in credit spreads between 2004 and 2007, as shown in Figure 3.26, and keep them from falling below their historical average. In substance, the model suggests that, in the pursuit of this intermediate objective, the ECB would have had to raise its key interest rates two full years earlier than in December 2005 and should have implemented a steeper path than it followed over the next couple of years. Figure 3.26 documents the results of our counterfactual experiment. Credit spreads could indeed have been stabilized effectively at higher values than those prevailing during those years. However, the magnitude of the tightening necessary to achieve that outcome would have measurably restrained the economy, and notably would have caused large shortfalls in inflation relative to the below, but close to the 2% aim. We find that GDP growth would have been a full percentage point lower in each of the years 2005 to 2007 and the level of inflation more than half a percentage point lower when entering the 2008 financial crisis.[33] These sustained inflation undershoots would probably have weakened the underlying inflation process to a greater extent than we document in the next chapter. We also find that the less severe mispricing of financial risk during the pre-crisis years would not have

---

[33] Dokko et al. (2009) and Bean et al. (2010) derive similar conclusions for the United States and the United Kingdom regarding the strong decline in real economic activity and inflation had the central bank tried to stabilize credit growth and the housing market in the years preceding the global financial crisis.

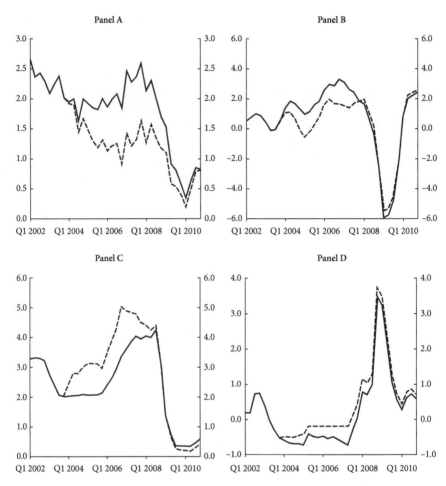

Figure 3.26 What would have happened to the economy and inflation had the ECB prevented credit spreads from declining in the run up to the financial crisis?
Panel A: GDP inflation (year-on-year % change)
Panel B: Real GDP growth (year-on-year % change)
Panel C: 3-month nominal interest rate (percentages per annum)
Panel D: Credit premium (percentage points)
Source: CMR.
Notes: In each panel the solid line indicates actual data, while the dashed line indicates the counterfactual in which it is assumed that the ECB would have stabilized credit spreads at historical mean from 2004 onward.

made the depth of the contraction less severe during the crisis years, as average GDP growth would have been only 0.3 percentage points higher in the years 2008 to 2010 than actually recorded.[34]

---

[34] As a caveat, while the model features a fully endogenous amplification mechanism via the financial side of the economy, the exercise is based on the linearized version of the model and the size of the original financial shock is treated as invariant to monetary policy.

4
The Crisis

The global financial crisis was born in the United States but came of age in Europe. A vast literature has investigated the long and circular causality chain that turned a high-risk segment of the US housing market into the epicentre of a financial panic, eventually pushing the major advanced economies into the deepest synchronized contraction seen since the 1930s. Box 4.1 recounts the antecedents of the crisis and provides a basic timeline.

Economists were also starting to debate whether the long stretch of stability in the world's mature economies and the rapid and seemingly painless integration of many emerging nations constituted a new normal, a quasi-permanent era of macro-economic resilience to shocks. There was a growing confidence that the quantum of risk produced by the world's leading economies had structurally diminished, and the financial innovations designed to hedge and distribute that residual risk had made its materialization less likely and less impactful anyway. In summary: risk was camouflaged and the dominant narrative was that, wherever it was hiding, it was borne by institutions and investors with large shoulders. But, in fact, the leveraged funds that ended up holding that risk had much-reduced capacity to absorb it. The reality was that the fundamental lack of visibility about the system-wide risk map was feeding inadequate risk diversification. As a consequence, few financial players were building adequate buffers against adversity.

Whether the economy had switched over to that second inflation regime—one where the policy rate is stuck close to its lower bound and inflation expectations become sensitive to deflationary shocks—did not immediately become apparent. In fact, inflation stayed at relatively elevated levels for more than four years past the date of Lehman Brother's demise. Should the European Central Bank (ECB) have reacted to deflation risks pre-emptively despite persistent upside inflation pressures, invoking evidence that inflation was being distorted by *transient* cost-push shocks? We try to answer this question by running stochastic simulations and measuring the probability of inflation falling below the upper half of the ECB's price stability comfort zone within a medium-term horizon, even abstracting from the supply-side shocks that, according to the model, were actively shaping the economic state during the early stages of the financial crisis.

In conditions of persistent monetary policy dilemma, the ECB concentrated on repairing the transmission process which had become highly dysfunctional. First, keeping the banking sector stable and intermediating required some marginal

Monetary Policy in Times of Crisis: A Tale of Two Decades of the European Central Bank. Massimo Rostagno, Carlo Altavilla, Giacomo Carboni, Wolfgang Lemke, Roberto Motto, Arthur Saint Guilhem, and Jonathan Yiangou, Oxford University Press (2021).
© Massimo Rostagno, Carlo Altavilla, Giacomo Carboni, Wolfgang Lemke, Roberto Motto, Arthur Saint Guilhem, and Jonathan Yiangou.
DOI: 10.1093/oso/9780192895912.003.0005

Box 4.1 Antecedents of the global financial crisis

After briefly recounting the antecedents of the global financial crisis, primarily in the United States, this box provides the basic timeline of the crisis with a particular focus on Europe.

Over the first half of the 2000s, declining discipline in mortgage lending in the United States, particularly in the subprime area, had made the US housing finance industry vulnerable and unstable under pressure. In those years, growing international demand for safe financial assets denominated in dollars and other prime currencies had given the financial sector the incentive to fragment the process by which a mortgage loan was extended and funded. Unlike in the past, lenders could sell their mortgages to third parties, which then packaged them together and sold newly created securitized bonds with various degrees of exposure to the underlying pool of loans to investors with different portfolio preferences. This new originate-and-distribute model of loan creation—as it came to be known—could indeed effectively increase diversification, and better tailor portfolios to the risk/return preferences of investors.

But there were two built-in defects hiding in the complex construction of the new model of loan origination that proved disastrous for the stability of the world financial system.

First, the surging demand for highly-rated mortgage-backed assets from residents and non-residents had offered US mortgage lenders access to an enormous global reservoir of savings. The surge in demand for safe assets denominated in dollars could be explained, in part, by the emergence of what Ben Bernanke had dubbed 'a global saving glut', namely by the transformation of many emerging-market economies—notably, rapidly growing East Asian economies and oil-producing countries—from net borrowers to large net lenders on international capital markets. These elastic funding conditions, in turn, had encouraged lenders to expand loan supply on progressively easing terms and conditions. The intrinsic quality of the underlying assets was deteriorating. At the same time, poor lending practices, such as defective underwriting standards (no verification of borrower income, for example), low down-payments, increased reliance on adjustable-rate mortgages (ARMs) with minuscule initial rates, and 'interest-only' mortgages—where borrowers did not have to pay down their loan principal –stoked the demand for mortgages. Expanding demand for housing finance pushed house prices higher. Subprime ARM lending was particularly dynamic and risky. Its fortunes were built on the flawed premise that house prices would continue to rise rapidly. Indeed, when house prices were increasing at double-digit rates, subprime ARM borrowers were able to build equity in their homes during the period in which they paid a low introductory (or 'teaser') rate on their mortgages. Once sufficient equity had been accumulated, borrowers were often able to refinance, avoiding the increased payments associated with the reset in the rate on the original mortgages. However, the mechanism had an in-built speed limit. As home prices were rising, declining affordability was bound to suppress demand for homes at some point, and falling demand would eventually halt and reverse the upward trend in home prices. The risk was that borrowers could no longer rely on home price appreciation to build equity and would therefore be unable to refinance.

The second defect that undermined the stability of the global financial architecture was widespread lack of visibility over concentrations of risk. The layered, tranched structure of the new securitized bonds made them into particularly complex and non-transparent assets. Besides asset-backed securities, a new class of asset in the shape of collateralized debt obligations (CDOs) was created, which facilitated a further layer of restructuring and redistribution of the risks embodied in an asset-backed security. These investment products, sometimes packaged with various credit and liquidity guarantees obtained from banks or through derivative contracts, were divided into portions, or tranches, of varying seniority and credit quality. The senior tranches were typically garnering high ratings from credit agencies, which made them a good match for the investors' search for safety. This was a new world, in which risk—notably related to the US subprime market—was 'sliced and diced', its fragments parcelled up and buried in complicated structures, and the instruments embodying these synthetic structures dispersed widely across markets and geographies. Hence, it was hard for investors and even for rating agencies to spot the ultimate location and concentration of risk. And it was difficult for the financial institutions involved in the supply chain of securitization to track their firm-wide exposures, including off-balance-sheet contingent commitments. Losses, rather than being dispersed broadly, proved in some cases to be heavily concentrated among relatively few, highly leveraged companies. Ultimately, these securities were purchased by investors ranging from US pension funds to German banks and Asian sovereign funds, few with a genuine understanding of the underlying risks they were acquiring.

As it happened, the cooldown in the United States housing market came in early 2006. On the way up, expansive subprime lending had increased the effective demand for housing, pushing up prices and stimulating construction activity. On the way down, starting in 2006, the withdrawal of this source of demand for housing exacerbated the downturn, adding to the sharp decline in new home-building and putting downward pressure on house prices. As was to be expected, past the peak in house prices, many of the subprime ARM borrowers found it difficult to make payments at even the very low introductory rate, much less at the higher post-adjustment rate. The result was an increase in delinquencies and foreclosures.

In late 2006 a new synthetic index became available for the first time which could be used to price subprime related tranches of credit derivatives. This new market price probably aggregated information about the quality of the underlying contracts,

(Continued)

Box 4.1 Continued

information that had previously been too dispersed or inaccessible. This may have brought awareness of the precarious bases of the financial structures being traded. A wide pool of borrowers and lenders were viewed as exposed to significant losses. By early 2007, declining house prices and rising rates of foreclosure were prompting increasing scrutiny and watchfulness among market participants. But by the summer the situation had visibly deteriorated further. As Tim Geithner put it: 'The subprime market was imploding. Borrowers with "no-doc-loans" (without proof of income) and " liar loans" (with inflated claims about income) and "NINJA loans" (No Income, No Job, No Assets) were defaulting in droves.' Standard & Poor's warned that many of those bonds could be downgraded. Some observers and policymakers welcomed the credit spread decompression as 'a generally healthy development',[1] but the burning question was: where were those losses—actual and potential—located?

As subprime mortgage losses rose to levels that threatened even the highly rated tranches, investors lost faith in the credit ratings and became increasingly unwilling to hold these products. Similar concerns arose in the market for asset-backed commercial paper (ABCP). In this market, various institutions established special-purpose vehicles to issue commercial paper to help fund a variety of assets, including some mortgage-backed securities and other long-maturity assets. Investors had typically viewed the commercial paper backed by these assets as quite safe and

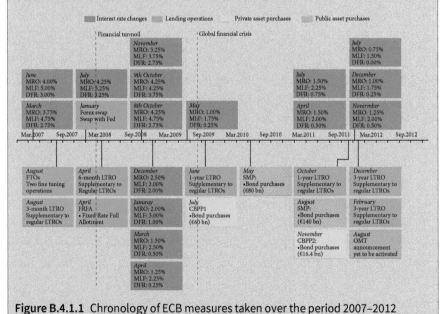

Figure B.4.1.1 Chronology of ECB measures taken over the period 2007–2012

---

[1] Geithner (2015), page 117.

liquid. But the concerns about mortgage-backed securities, and structured credit products more generally (even those unrelated to mortgages), led to great reluctance on the part of investors to roll over ABCP, particularly at maturities of more than a few days, leaving the sponsors of the various investment vehicles scrambling for liquidity. Those who could not find new funding were forced to sell assets into a highly illiquid and unreceptive market.

adjustments to the ECB's operating framework.[2] In this chapter we will quantify the effect of the ECB's decision to guarantee an elastic supply of liquidity through a fixed rate full allotment (FRFA) procedure in regular and extraordinary longer-term lending operations. Second, the asset and loan markets in vast regions of the euro area had lost their chief pricing kernel, because the sovereign debt crisis had undermined the benchmarking role of the sovereign yield curve. The ECB intervened in the most dysfunctional segments of the euro area sovereign debt market by activating two instruments: the Securities Market Programme (SMP) and the Outright Monetary Transactions (OMT) programme. In this chapter we will quantify the effects of the SMP and the OMT announcement.

As supply-side shocks gradually dissipated over the four years following the Lehman Brothers' default and through the ensuing sovereign debt crisis, negative demand shocks became the dominant source of macroeconomic fluctuations in the euro area. Inflation gradually drifted down towards the floor of the ECB's price stability definition, namely the border separating inflation from deflation. As we posited in the previous chapter, the result was a fundamental change in the dynamic properties of the inflation process which ultimately drove the ECB to the very aggressive response strategy unveiled in June 2014 and discussed in the next chapter.

---

[2] Adjustments were marginal compared to those made in other currency areas. The liquidity measures adopted from late 2008 until 2012 succeeded in lowering the cost of financing in specific financial market segments. For example, the full allotment policy, especially after the lengthening to one year of the maturity of longer-term refinancing operations, led to a persistent fall in the overnight interbank interest rate (as measured by the euro overnight index average, EONIA) below the levels of the ECB's main refinancing operation (MRO) rate. Allowing for a persistent spread to open between the overnight interest rate and the MRO rate—something unprecedented in the ECB's history—was the approach followed by the ECB to deal with the segmentation which had in the meantime materialized in the banking sector. Only some of the banks with liquidity needs could borrow funds from their counterparties at the EONIA; other banks were considered too risky and were therefore forced to obtain refinancing directly from the ECB at the higher MRO rate. The spread between the EONIA and the MRO rate had two effects. On the one hand, the lower refinancing rate (the EONIA) faced available to banks with access to the overnight market could be expected to influence other money market segments and ultimately the rates on loans to the non-financial sector. On the other hand, the MRO refinancing available for banks with larger perceived exposures to illiquid assets—together with the extension of the list of assets accepted as collateral—could be interpreted as a standard application of the Bagehot principle according to which, at times of crisis, the central bank should provide unlimited liquidity at a penalty rate. The unlimited provision of liquidity allowed solvent banks to overcome their liquidity problems, while the penalty at which they obtained central bank funds remained an incentive for them to restructure their balance sheets.

4.1 Spillovers to Europe

The pre-crisis situation in Europe was not quite the same as in the United States. Over the years prior to the crisis, credit extension in the United States had progressively migrated outside traditional banking to so-called shadow banking entities (or simply non-banks), bank-like entities with high leverage and short-term funding, and without a government safety net of the type that since the 1930s had made the banking industry a safe haven for depositors.[3] By contrast, in the euro area, financial intermediation had remained largely within the confines of traditional banking.

But three developments had made banks and the countries in which they were domiciled less impervious to a generalized loss of investor confidence than they had been for decades. First and foremost, since the birth of the euro, the banking system in the European Continent had been the hub of an intricate network of cross-border capital flows, whose direction was primarily from core economies (Germany, France, and the Netherlands in particular) to the periphery (specifically, Ireland, Portugal, Spain, and Greece). Citing from Baldwin and Giavazzi (2015), who identify in this bank-intermediated cross-national flow of funds the true Achilles' heel of Monetary Union,

> a major slice of these [funds] were invested in non-traded sectors—housing and government services/consumption...When the euro zone crisis began—triggered ultimately by the Global Crisis—cross-border capital inflows stopped. This 'sudden stop' in investment financing raised concerns about the viability of banks and, in the case of Greece, even governments themselves. The close links between euro zone banks and national governments provided the multiplier that made the crisis systemic.

Lane (2012, 2013, 2015a, 2015b) provide evidence that, for Ireland and Spain, debt inflows helped to fuel large-scale domestic property booms (with extrapolative behaviours of the real-estate investors amplifying the imbalance), while in Greece and Portugal they provided a cheap source of government funding. Overall, the interpretation of the European phase of the financial crisis as, ultimately, a current account crisis—made more severe by the zero currency risk that creditors were perceiving while building up their exposures—seems to be widely accepted among scholars, and has received further support in Lane and Milesi-Ferretti (2012, 2015).

In the lead-up to the crisis, the funding structure of many major banking institutions had undergone a remarkable evolution. Banks—even commercial banks that had traditionally relied on less flighty, insured deposits to finance credit—had been increasingly supplementing their funding sources with un-insured, mainly

---

[3] The so-called shadow banks are a diverse set of institutions and markets that, collectively, carry out traditional banking functions, but do so outside the traditional system of regulated depository institutions. Examples include money market funds, asset-backed commercial paper and securitization vehicles, repo markets, investment banks, and non-bank mortgage companies.

short-term borrowing in the interbank market. The advent of securitization had favoured and accelerated this trend. Banks had become accustomed to raising funds in the money market not only on unsecured terms—as had been typical in the early years of monetary union—but also by selling short-term asset-backed securities. By the summer of 2007, interbank lending in the form of repurchase agreements had doubled in Europe relative to its 2002 level, to reach €6.4 trillion (or around 71% of euro area GDP). Accordingly, banks' funding costs, and hence retail interest rates, had become more sensitive to developments in the market for structured finance products, for covered bonds and for sovereign bonds—assets that could be used in collateralized borrowing.[4] Excessive or abrupt changes in the value or availability of these securities could easily imply a sharp deterioration in banks' funding conditions, with adverse effects on both the supply of bank loans to the real economy and on their prices.

A second development that had undermined the long-term stability of the euro area banking sector was that large banks in Europe had created many of the structured credit products that were in high demand in the market. They had done so partly with a view to retaining selected tranches of those securities as valued collateral for their own funding. This had driven banks towards new lines of business in support of the whole securitization chain, including serving as advisers and providing standby liquidity facilities and various credit enhancements to the investment vehicles they were sponsoring. As the problems with these facilities mounted, banks came under increasing pressure to rescue the investment vehicles—either by providing liquidity or other support or, as had increasingly become the norm, by taking the assets of the off-balance-sheet vehicles onto their own balance sheets.[5]

A few observers and analysts had long warned about threats of an impending crisis. But few had imagined how all those scattered risks that could be detected in various pockets of the financial system would coalesce and interact to produce one of the most ruinous macroeconomic debacles on record. Jean-Claude Trichet, President of the ECB, had for some time been pointing with some force to the opacity of the credit derivatives market, and especially of structured synthetic instruments built on underlying pools of housing loans. More often than not, however, the knee-jerk reaction to such warnings from within the financial industry had

---

[4] Covered bonds are debt securities issued by a bank or mortgage institution and collateralized against a pool of assets that, in the event of the failure of the issuer, can cover claims at any point in time. Unlike with securitized products, the investor in a covered bond has 'double recourse' against the issuer and the collateral. Covered bonds had not only grown in importance as a source of direct funding for many financial institutions in Europe but had also come to be used increasingly as collateral in money market transactions. In a similar vein, with the rapid increase in secured interbank lending, the impact on money markets of developments in government bond markets had grown substantially. While government bonds had traditionally been an important element in the transmission process because they serve as a benchmark, or floor, for the pricing of other financial contracts and fixed income securities, they had also emerged as a prime source of collateral in interbank lending.

[5] More often than not, there was no legal obligation on the bank's part to bail out the off-balance sheet vehicles, as they were separately incorporated entities. But many parent banking institutions were concerned about maintaining good relationships with the lenders to the funds. So they were inclined to prop up the funds.

been denial. Financial innovation and even financial engineering were seen as the precondition for improving risk management at the level of the individual intermediaries, and for enhancing the resilience of the financial system in the aggregate. The exchange between Jean-Claude Trichet and participants at the annual meeting of the International Swaps and Derivatives Association in April 2007 is symptomatic. Speakers responded to Mr Trichet's remarks that 'opacity' had made it difficult to assess risks to the financial system by pointing to a reassuring antecedent: the large-scale collapse of large companies such as Enron, WorldCom, and Parmalat in the first half of the 2000s had had no adverse implications for banks. This was, in the prevalent opinion, proof that markets were functioning correctly.

4.2 The Summer 2007 Turmoil

In late July 2007, Rhineland Funding, an off-balance-sheet vehicle created years before by a small German bank, IKB Deutsche Industriebank, suddenly found itself unable to secure refunding for its asset-backed commercial paper (ABCP). There had been persistent rumours that Rhineland's paper was heavily collateralized by the riskier end of the US residential mortgage-backed securities, the mezzanine tranches of subprime mortgages.[6] Rhineland called on a line of credit promised by IKB and a handful of other banks. With the intervention of the German Federal Financial Supervisory Authority (Bundesanstalt für Finanzdienstleistungsaufsicht, BaFin) the Rhineland call prompted a bail-out, in which the state-owned Kreditanstalt für Wiederaufbau (KfW), the major shareholder of IKB, provided €8 billion of liquidity and covered €1 billion of the €3.5 billion of estimated paper losses on the IKB group's portfolio. The rapid, seemingly happy end of the Rhineland/IKB case calmed the markets. But the travails of IKB heightened lenders' concerns about the viability of other conduits funded by ABCP. Banks too became subject to valuation uncertainty, as could be seen in their share prices and other market indicators such as quotes on credit default swaps (CDS, see Figure 4.1).

4.2.1 9 August

On 9 August 2007, the temperature in the financial markets climbed higher. France's largest bank, BNP Paribas, froze redemptions by investors from three of its

---

[6] Since 2002, through Rhineland Funding, IKB had built up an off-shore and off-balance-sheet worth portfolio of asset-backed investments worth €12.7 billion. These were packaged into collateralized debt obligations (CDOs), a type of structured asset-backed security promising to pay investors in a prescribed sequence, based on the cash flow the CDO collects from the pool of bonds or other assets it owns. Superficially the portfolio appeared a safe investment, as 70% of its assets were rated double-A or above and only 10% of them were below investment grade. However, market insiders soon came to suspect that, owing to the particularly risky make-up of the portfolio, even the highest-rated triple-A tranches could be affected by losses in the less creditworthy parts.

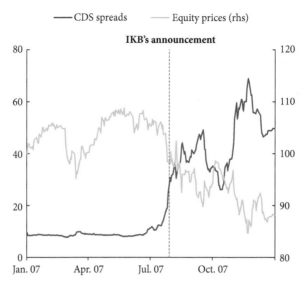

Figure 4.1 Bank CDS spreads and equity prices around the summer 2007 turmoil (basis points, index)

Sources: IBES and Refinitiv.
Latest observation: December 2007.

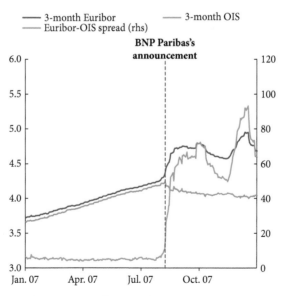

Figure 4.2 Stress in the money market term lending (percentage per annum, basis points)

Sources: IBES and Refinitiv.
Latest observation: December 2007.

investment funds that held securities backed by US subprime mortgages. BNP justified its decision with the fact that it could not determine the fair value of its funds because of 'complete evaporation of liquidity' in the markets for those securities.

Instinctively, banks with liquidity surpluses withdrew en masse from the money market for fear that their interbank loans might default. They became very protective of their liquidity and balance sheet capacity, and started to build liquidity buffers in their current accounts and deposit facility with the ECB. At the same time, banks with liquidity needs could no longer raise funds in the interbank market and thus found themselves on the brink of default. Turnover declined substantially as a result, and spreads between interest rates on secured and unsecured lending, particularly at longer tenors, rose to unprecedented levels.

One way to measure the stress in the money market term lending is to take the spread between the Euro Interbank Offered Rate (EURIBOR)—the average of the interest rates at which euro area banks offer to lend unsecured funds to other banks in the euro wholesale money market for a certain maturity—and the rate on euro overnight index swap (OIS) with a corresponding maturity. The swap rate is the fixed rate which banks engaging in swap contracts agree to pay in exchange for receiving the average overnight interest rate for the duration of the swap. Unlike an unsecured interbank loan, in which the lender is exposed to the full credit risk of the borrower, a swap contract is settled in notional amounts, namely without involving a physical exchange of principals, and thus it is considered near-risk-free. This explains why the spread between the two rates is seen as a measure of mutual trust in the market in which banks transact cash with each other. The EURIBOR-OIS spread had typically hovered around 5 bps. But on 9 August 2007, the spread surged to more than 60 bps, and fluctuated wildly, as Figure 4.2 shows.

The ECB had traditionally conducted monetary policy through collateralized refinancing operations—reverse transactions—executed primarily in weekly competitive tenders, referred to as the main refinancing operations (MROs). They were conducted each Tuesday and settled on the following Wednesday. As the euro area banking system as a whole was in structural liquidity deficit, and thus routinely needed central bank funds to fulfil its reserve requirements and accommodate other liquidity-absorbing factors, it had to borrow regularly from the Eurosystem. So, by adjusting the cost at which banks could borrow under the MRO—and under the ancillary three-month LTROs—the ECB could steer banks' marginal cost of refinancing and thereby influence the whole spectrum of market rates.

At each monetary policy meeting, the Governing Council (GC) of the ECB would set the MRO rate at the level that was judged to be most appropriate to enforce the intended stance of monetary policy. Based on that level, the amount of funds that had to be allotted in the weekly operations would then be determined so as to satisfy banks' aggregate demand for liquidity and keep the overnight interbank interest rate index representative of the prevailing money market conditions—the euro overnight index average (EONIA)—sufficiently close to the MRO rate for the period up to the settlement of the next weekly operation. While only a sub-group of the eligible banks

Box 4.2 The Eurosystem's operational framework

The sources of liquidity demand and liquidity supply in the euro area can be illustrated by the simplified balance sheet of the Eurosystem in Figure B.4.2.1. The coloured areas on the liability side of the Eurosystem's balance sheet (the negative portion of the figure) represent the two key sources of demand for central bank money from the euro area credit institutions: 'minimum reserve requirements' and 'autonomous factors'. Both items are non-discretionary because they originate from legal obligations to which banks are subject either vis-à-vis their NCBs or vis-à-vis their customers. This is why these two balance sheet items have traditionally been referred to as 'liquidity needs'. Both are liquidity-absorbing factors for the banking system as a whole, that is, they subtract cash that would otherwise be available for banks to transact freely in the daily interbank credit circuit.

The 'minimum reserve requirements' are related to banks' obligation to re-deposit a fraction of their own deposit base with their respective NCBs. They are calculated as the reserve ratio (originally set to 2% but reduced to 1% in early 2012) times the reserve base, which is comprised of a variety of short-term liabilities in the credit institutions' balance sheets. In the aggregate, the reserve base by and large coincides with the broad money measure of M3. An averaging mechanism allows credit

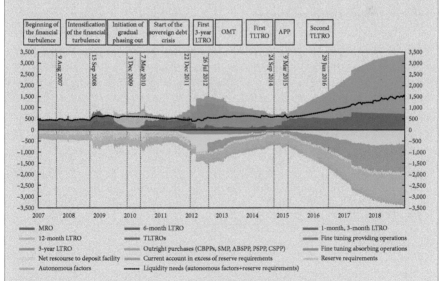

Figure B.4.2.1   Evolution of the Eurosystem balance sheet (EUR billion)
Source: ECB.
Notes: Autonomous factors are in net terms, and include the ANFA portfolio (i.e. holdings of financial assets which are related to national tasks of the NCBs but not related to monetary policy). Latest observation: 31 December 2018.

(Continued)

Box 4.2 Continued

institutions to fulfil these requirements on average over the one-month maintenance period, not necessarily on a daily basis. This gives banks a high degree of flexibility in managing liquidity and provides the system with an effective mechanism for keeping overnight conditions steady. Banks hold the funds related to their reserve requirements in 'current accounts', where they can also deposit any excess amount of liquidity which, by the end of the trading day, they have not lent out to other banks (see below).

The items collectively referred to as 'autonomous factors' represent the miscellaneous channels by which liquidity is drained from the system for reasons beyond the control of banks.[7] Government accounts and currency in circulation are examples of these liquidity-absorbing factors. For example, when the governments collect taxes, they generally deposit the tax revenue into special accounts they hold with their respective NCBs. The inflow of cash into those accounts corresponds to an outflow of cash from banks' accounts with the NCB, since banks act as paying agents for the taxpayers. Likewise, an increase in the demand for currency by the public determines a decline in the amount of cash which banks hold in their accounts with their NCB, as banks have to draw down their central bank reserves when paying out banknotes to their depositors. Besides through such non-discretionary channels, or 'liquidity needs', money can occasionally leak out of the system of interbank transactions because banks may be unable or unwilling to lend it out to other banks that need it—for example, to fulfil their own reserve requirements. In Figure B.4.3.1, such 'excess reserves' which sit 'idle' on some banks' books rather than flow through the interbank credit system to meet other banks' 'liquidity needs' appear as the part of banks' 'current accounts' that is not related to the fulfilment of their minimum reserve requirements, and those amounts of money that banks re-deposit with the Eurosystem in the deposit facility.[8]

Whether on account of genuine 'liquidity needs' or due to banks' decisions to hold cash in excess, until relatively late in the crisis, there was a structural 'liquidity deficit' in the system (the coloured areas pointing downwards in Figure B.4.3.1) which the Eurosystem had to make up for by conducting liquidity-providing monetary policy operations (all the coloured areas pointing upwards on the figure). These

---

[7] Autonomous factors are defined as the sum of banknotes in circulation plus government deposits minus net foreign assets plus other factors. Net foreign assets are liquidity-providing autonomous factors, i.e. they reflect Eurosystem assets that have been acquired by issuing money which is in the system. On balance, however, the liquidity-absorbing autonomous factors outweigh the liquidity-providing factors, so the net amount is a liability for the Eurosystem.

[8] Typically, excess reserves held in the current accounts are owned by credit institutions that have already fulfilled their reserve requirements or are not subject to such requirements because they are too small. Unlike the required reserves, excess reserves are not remunerated. However, since the deposit facility rate was cut to -0.10% in June 2014, excess reserves have been subject to negative remunerations to ensure the effectiveness of the negative DFR.

operations consisted exclusively of collateralized temporary refinancing operations with relatively short maturities.

At the time of turmoil—and for the previous eight years of history of monetary union—the MROs were the main sources of central bank money supply. These are reverse operations executed once a week with a maturity of two weeks. Over the first eight years of monetary union, the bulk of credit institutions' liquidity needs, on average a bit less than three-quarters—was met through this channel. The LTROs are conducted once a month and have a maturity of three months, with the intended size fixed in advance by the GC. Liquidity-providing fine-tuning operations (FTOs), which can be conducted daily on a discretionary basis, had traditionally paid a minor role in the management of aggregate liquidity, except on the eve of extraordinary events, such as the millennium changeover and the terrorist attacks in the United States on 11 September 2001. Individual banks can also draw central bank credit with an overnight maturity outside the Eurosystem's regular or discretionary operations on their own initiative by accessing the marginal lending facility (MLF).

The GC has traditionally signalled the desired stance of monetary policy by announcing three key interest rates: the interest rate to be used in the MROs, the interest rate on the deposit facility (deposit facility rate, DFR), which is lower than the MRO rate, and the interest rate on MLF, which is higher. In the summer of 2007, and for much of the past life of the monetary union, the MRO rate acted as the minimum bid rate for the weekly tenders. Before the introduction of the variable rate tender in June 2000, the signalling role was performed by the rate applied to the fixed rate tenders. In the weekly tenders, eligible counterparties would submit bids for up to ten different interest rate levels. In each bid they had to report the amount they were willing to borrow and the respective interest rate at which they were bidding. Bids at a rate below the minimum bid rate, namely the MRO rate, were discarded. In apportioning the pre-set allotment amount, the Eurosystem would list bids from the highest to the lowest offered rate and accept the bids until the total liquidity to be allotted was exhausted.

The interest rates on the standing facilities, instead, define the boundaries of the interest rate corridor, the range within which the daily fluctuations in the overnight money market rate are constrained and a fundamental instrument of monetary policy control in the ECB's operational framework. Banks transacting liquidity with an overnight tenor in the interbank money market are typically unwilling to borrow from other banks if the overnight rate charged in the bilateral trade is above the rate on the marginal lending facility (MLF), as in this case they would rather borrow from the ECB under the MLF. Conversely, banks would refuse to lend at overnight interest rates below the DFR because the alternative of depositing liquidity with the ECB under the deposit facility and receiving the DFR would be more attractive.

The ECB normally keeps a strict dividing line between the monetary policy decisions and the implementation of that policy through monetary policy operations.

(Continued)

Box 4.2 Continued

This 'separation principle' prevents the specification and conduct of refinancing operations from being interpreted as signals of future changes in the monetary policy stance. This procedure has proved to be a reliable way of ensuring that the GC's monetary policy stance is reflected appropriately in market interest rates and that credit markets function smoothly. The stable and predictable relationship between money market rates and the ECB's main refinancing rate that prevailed until the middle of 2007 underlines the effectiveness of the Eurosystem's operational framework in implementing the monetary policy stance as determined by the GC. A key role in monetary policy implementation has been played by the Eurosystem collateral framework, whereby all credit operations are carried against adequate collateral, as provided for by the Statute of the ESCB.[9] This concept of adequate collateral is aimed first at protecting the Eurosystem from incurring losses in its credit operations. It is also intended to ensure sufficient collateral availability to a broad set of counterparties, so that they can obtain the necessary amount of liquidity. Compared with other major central banks, the Eurosystem has, since its inception, been accepting a broad range of assets as collateral in all its credit operations, for reasons also rooted in the historical, structural and institutional set-ups of member countries. The breadth and flexibility of the collateral framework have proved to be important aspects in responding to disruptions in the interbank market. During the financial and sovereign debt crisis in particular, the Eurosystem promptly expanded the range of eligible collateral that could be pledged against central bank money.

would bid for liquidity at the weekly operations, the ECB relied on the daily interbank trades in the money market for cash to flow from banks with a cash surplus to those banks with a cash shortfall. This market mechanism ensured that all the banks—those borrowing and those not borrowing from the ECB—could seamlessly fulfil their reserve requirements and meet their other payments obligations. Ensuring that, on a net basis, the market interest rate in those interbank cash transactions would shadow the official MRO rate was instrumental in securing the ECB's control over the very first stage of monetary policy transmission. Indeed, since monetary union, banks with a surplus of liquidity at the end of a trading day had been happy to lend money to other financial institutions in need of funds on terms that closely reflected the intentions of the ECB. Accordingly, the marginal lending rate in the weekly tenders had kept close to the minimum bid rate (the MRO rate), and the EONIA index had remained firmly anchored around the MRO rate.

[9] See Article 18.1 of the Statute of the ESCB. For an extensive review of the role of collateral in monetary policy implementation and the design and evolution of the Eurosystem collateral framework, see Bindseil et al. (2017).

But in the early hours of 9 August 2007, the demand from banks for current account holdings with the Eurosystem surged and credit flows in the interbank money market seized up. The collapse of the money market had the potential to lead to a gridlock in the payments system.[10]

4.2.2 The ECB's Reaction

Falling on a Thursday, the 9 August breakdown in the money market could not be addressed via an ordinary weekly refinancing operation. The last such operation had been allotted two days before, on Tuesday 7 August, with settlement on the day before, Wednesday 8 August, in conditions that did not portend impending disruptions. So, in order to ensure that all banks had adequate access to short-term funds, on 9 August the ECB announced a discretionary fine-tuning operation (FTO) with same-day settlement and overnight maturity. Setting aside the consolidated practice of auctioning liquidity in variable-rate competitive tenders (see Box 4.2 for detail), the operation was conducted as a fixed rate tender at a 4.00% interest rate, which was equal to the prevailing MRO rate level. Most importantly—and, as we will see, this played a significant role in shaping developments at later stages of the crisis—the ECB pre-announced 'full allotment', namely the intention to meet all the bids in the FTO at a fixed rate. This new approach, which came to be known as 'fixed rate full allotment' or FRFA, offered a key advantage over alternatives as a crisis-fighting tool in a liquidity crunch situation. It did not necessitate complicated calculations to quantify the amount of liquidity that counterparties would demand in those highly perturbed conditions. It would simply establish a perfectly elastic supply of cash at auction and leave it to the banks' aggregate demand schedule to move along the horizontal supply and settle on an equilibrium quantity.

The injection of liquidity turned out to be massive. The 49 banks that participated in the FTO drew €94.8 billion in fresh liquidity, an unprecedented amount for a one-day refinancing operation. The extraordinary measure did not restore the market turnover to normality. However, after spiking in the early hours, the overnight rate rapidly moved back to levels not too far above the MRO rate, and stayed there for the remainder of the trading day. In the meantime, the liquidity stress had crossed the Atlantic and, when markets opened in New York, the Federal Reserve also engaged in overnight repurchase agreements worth US$24 billion.

On the following morning, 10 August, when the ECB's overnight repurchase agreements of the previous day rolled off, the operation was renewed at about two-thirds of its original size. In contrast to the FRFA modality of the previous day, the new operation was conducted by variable-rate tender procedure with a minimum bid rate and without a pre-announced allotment amount. The reason for the switch from elastic allotment was twofold. First, tensions had arguably abated and, second,

[10] For a far more exhaustive account of the liquidity crisis, see Papadia and Välimäki (2018).

the variable rate tender would bring to light valuable information regarding banks' underlying liquidity positions. Counterparties taking part in the FTO would have to post bids for volumes at corresponding rates, thus revealing the shape of their liquidity demand schedule.[11]

In the following weeks, the ECB stayed the course and used the MRO to inject more liquidity than was strictly necessary for banks to meet their reserve requirements and their other 'liquidity needs'. The tactic was to accommodate banks' desire to satisfy ('front load') their minimum reserve requirements as early as possible in the maintenance period. Doing otherwise might have exposed them to the risk of failing to meet that obligation in the event that renewed tensions in the market shut them out of private funding. So the surplus volumes of liquidity allotted in the weekly operations over and above the narrowly defined 'liquidity needs' were sizeable in the first week of turmoil but abated over the remainder of the month (see Figure 4.3).

The EONIA responded as expected and gradually converged back to the prevailing MRO rate. This was interpreted as a comforting signal that the funding stress

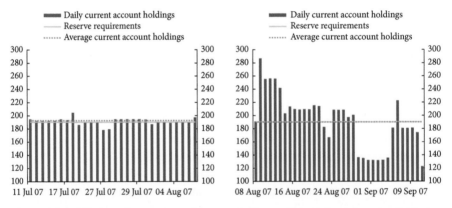

Figure 4.3 Fulfilment of reserve requirements in 'normal' times (maintenance period before 9 August 2007) and during the financial turmoil (maintenance period after 9 August 2007) (EUR billion)

Source: ECB.
Notes: The figure depicts the daily current account holdings and reserve requirements over the maintenance period. 'Average current account holdings' means the average of the daily current account holdings over the specified maintenance period.

---

[11] Somewhat disappointingly, the number of bidders increased to 62, with bids totalling €110 billion. But the range of interest rates that banks were ready to pay was relatively contained, varying from 4.00% (the minimum bid rate) to 4.15%. Consistent with Walter Bagehot's prescription that in a generalized scramble for liquidity a central bank should lend freely at a penalty, the ECB decided to allot liquidity to all bidders at or above 4.05%, i.e. one basis point lower than the marginal MRO rate in the regular weekly tender conducted three days earlier. Admittedly, the penalty was small, as the primary intention was to put into practice another piece of advice from Bagehot: 'Lend freely, boldly, and so that the public may feel you mean to go on lending.' The EONIA settled at 4.14% on that day, 0.14% above the prevailing MRO rate.

was easing in the shortest-maturity end of the money market. But tensions continued to be observed in the market where banks were transacting liquidity at longer maturities. Turnover was particularly compressed in that segment, and the spreads between banks' interbank bid rates and the swap rates remained stubbornly high. Therefore, on 22 August, a supplementary LTRO was announced, with a view to encouraging credit to flow at terms longer than overnight. In all, 146 counterparties bid for a total amount of €126 billion, with bids ranging from 3.8% to 5.0%. The abnormally large size of the bids and the dispersion of the interest rates that banks were willing to pay to secure term funding gave a sense of how deeply the 9 August tumult had shaken confidence in the markets. Investors remained reluctant to provide credit beyond the shortest of tenors and were shifting money into the safer and most liquid assets. The slump in confidence was evident across financial markets. In the week following 8 August, equities lost around 5% on both sides of the Atlantic, while an investor rush to safe haven investments caused a significant drop in short-term sovereign bond yields, with the two-year yields falling by 30–50 bps across issuer ratings.

4.2.3 The Efficiency of the Operational System

The central bank must keep financial markets functioning. Financial stability—liquid money markets with low price volatility and orderly payments—is a key short-term objective of most central banks. In fact, one of the most prominent central banks of the present day, the Federal Reserve System, for example, was originally designed to provide an effective backstop against the recurring episodes of financial panic that were relatively frequent in earlier days.[12] Even so, the interest of societies in having a central bank in place as a bulwark against financial panics was not financial stability per se. Rather, in establishing central banks, societies recognized that a stabilization of the financial system would lead to a stabilization of the whole economy—a goal which, since at least the end of the Second World War, has become part of the medium-term statutory objectives of most central banks. According to these medium-term objectives, the focus of central banks is on analysing whether current conditions are appropriate to attain their medium-term macroeconomic stabilization objectives. If so, the conclusion is that short-term interest rates are pitched at the appropriate level. Otherwise, a change to the central banks' key interest rates—which steer the market short-term interest rates—is necessary.

---

[12] The Federal Reserve System was created in 1913 'to furnish an elastic currency, to afford means of rediscounting commercial paper, to establish a more effective supervision of banking in the United States, and for other purposes'. As for the ECB, Article 127(2) of the TFEU states that one of the basic tasks to be carried out through the European System of Central Banks shall be 'to promote the smooth operations of payment systems', while Article 127(5) states that 'the ESCB shall contribute to the smooth conduct of policies pursued by the competent authorities relating to the prudential supervision of credit institutions and the stability of the financial system'.

The efficiency of an operational framework can be measured by two parameters: first, the degree to which the central bank can deal with emergency situations in the financial market—a prime concern under its first, short-term objective—in a timely manner and with minimal last-minute tweaks to the rules of the game; and, second, the extent to which decisions that are made to keep financial markets functioning serve the purpose of, or may interfere with, actions that are necessary for the central bank to meet its medium-term macroeconomic objectives. In this subsection we deal with the first issue: how many last-minute innovations are necessary for the system to respond quickly to a systemic liquidity shock in a stabilizing fashion? In the following subsection we move to the second question: how much separation between liquidity provision and adjustments to the stance of monetary policy does the system afford? How much separation is appropriate anyway?

The fewer the innovations to the operational rulebook, the more flexible, efficient and complete is the operational system in place. By this metric, when put to the first test of the crisis, the Eurosystem's operational framework proved more efficient and resilient than its equivalents elsewhere. For one thing, it was possible to make sufficient liquidity available to the system, and even to channel it to the corners of the system where cash shortages were most acute, relying entirely on existing facilities.[13] The jumbo FTOs of the first panicky trading days reversed the immediate consequences of the initial confidence shock. The attractive terms on which the operations were offered helped defuse the stigma that banks otherwise would have felt in accessing an emergency line of credit—for example a loan under the marginal lending facility (MLF). Then, as the panic psychology subsided, the MRO took over as the main instrument to normalize the overnight market. The breadth and flexibility of the collateral framework were instrumental in the reabsorption of liquidity-driven tensions in the interbank market (see Box 4.2). The averaging system applying to the minimum reserve requirements assisted in this healing process: banks could temporarily unfreeze part of the cash parked in their reserve accounts and use it for current payments, which helped alleviate the demand pressure that was unsettling the interbank market. Finally, as the functioning of the shortest-maturity end of the money market gradually resumed, the LTRO replaced the MRO as the system's main portal to central bank liquidity. There was a sense that term spreads still failed to reflect accurately the current uncertainties in economic fundamentals, and this called for the Eurosystem to lengthen the average duration of its credit to the banks (see Figure 4.4).

A noteworthy fact is that this shift in the maturity composition of the Eurosystem credit was achieved at a virtually constant size for the Eurosystem balance sheet

---

[13] This contrasts with the situation faced by other major central banks at the beginning of the crisis. For example, the Federal Reserve System had to create a number of new temporary liquidity programmes in 2007 and 2008 to provide financial institutions with necessary access to credit (e.g. the Term Auction Facility in December 2007), while its traditional facilities—in particular the discount window—were thwarted by concerns on the part of banks that borrowing might be perceived as a sign of financial weakness.

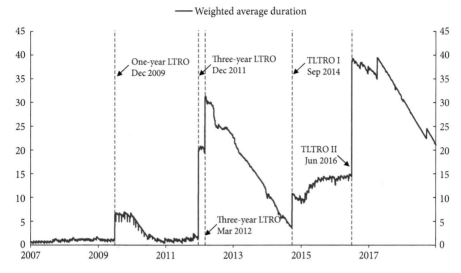

Figure 4.4 Average maturity of ECB liquidity provision (months)

Source: ECB.

Notes: The weighted average duration is calculated as the product of the outstanding credit operation times their residual duration, divided by the total outstanding credit operations at each period. The weighted average duration depicted is in months.

Latest observation: 31 December 2018.

(see Figure B.4.3.1). Throughout, the Eurosystem maintained reasonable control over the overnight interest rate. To be sure, the EONIA remained volatile until the end of the year. But, as evident in Figure 4.5, its oscillations around the prevailing MRO rate were contained. In sum: the liquidity crunch could be handled and partly reversed with minimal interference with established practices and with the stance.

4.2.4 The Separation Principle

The rate corridor, the reserve-averaging system and the possibility of conducting high-frequency (liquidity-absorbing and liquidity-providing) FTOs proved that the operating framework was particularly flexible to adapt in emergencies, without tweaks or last-minute additions. It also afforded a lot of space for the GC to keep distinct its two objectives—short-term and longer-term—and to target them separately. The separation principle—as it came to be known—referred to the intention and ability to keep liquidity management and stance considerations as two different things. The principle prescribed that the setting of the level of the policy rate should be done with an exclusive view to ensuring price stability in the medium term, while liquidity management had the ancillary function of guaranteeing that overnight market rates stayed sufficiently close to that policy rate for the monetary policy stance of the GC to be adequately reflected in short-term money market

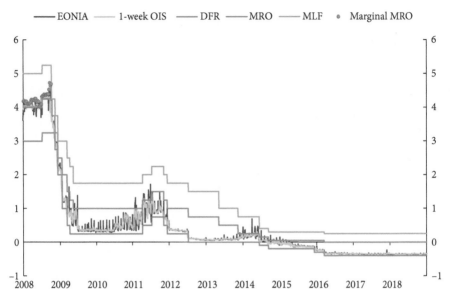

Figure 4.5 EONIA, 1-week OIS, and key ECB interest rates (percentages per annum)

Sources: Bloomberg and Refinitiv.

Latest observation: 31 December 2018.

conditions.[14] In essence, the principle encapsulates the raison d'être of modern central banks. Central banks can be assigned to macroeconomic objectives because they have the monopoly power over cash production, and so they possess the (liquidity) means to support the (rate) actions that are necessary to achieve those objectives. In crisis conditions, the significance of this principle is magnified: the central bank's power to create cash is the pre-condition to forestalling the implosion of the financial system, which in turn is an absolute pre-condition to support the stability of the macro-economy.

Communication about this principle could have highlighted this simple idea. But in fact, soon enough, the separation principle developed into one of the most cherished cornerstones of the way the ECB portrayed—in internal and external communication—its own modus operandi, its own approach to the handling of the financial crisis. Why? The reason might have been that, when communication started to

---

[14] The separation principle was first mentioned implicitly by President Trichet at the press conference following the GC meeting of 6 September 2007. He said: 'Again, let us not confuse the appropriate functioning of the money market and the monetary policy stance. I would say that, at whatever price, at whatever level of interest rates, the market has to function. And it is very important to make a clear separation between those two factors.' In a speech delivered in December 2007, José-Manuel González-Páramo, member of the Executive Board of the ECB, clarified: 'The need to understand the difference between technical liquidity provision measures and changes to the monetary policy stance is particularly important in the current environment, since the turmoil in money markets has occurred at a time of increasing concerns about rising inflationary pressures and deteriorating outlook for inflation. In this context, misunderstandings about the purpose of our liquidity interventions might adversely affect inflationary expectations' (González-Páramo, 2007).

develop in this direction in the second half of 2007, the two objectives mentioned above—short-term and medium-term—seemed to be pulling in starkly opposite directions. While few could have contested the merit of the ECB's decision to act on the basis of short-term financial stability considerations and offer itself as a safe port in the money market storm that was unfolding, it was highly debatable in the late summer and autumn of 2007 whether there was a need for the ECB to act on its medium-term price stability objective with a rate cut. In fact, as we document below, the base-case assumption was that policy needed *tightening*, not easing.

So the ECB faced a dilemma. And there was a sense that the separation principle could help to resolve it. The ECB could supply liquidity in elastic amounts as necessary to relieve the pressures in the market for interbank lending, and still restrict the stance—or at least take more time to assess the outlook—as required by its price stability objective. This notion that the separation principle had problem-solving qualities endured through the crisis.

4.2.5 Risk Management

At its teleconference meeting of 2 August, a few days before the market tumult began, the GC had decided to hint at the possibility of raising the ECB's key interest rates at its next meeting of 6 September. In its characteristic 'traffic-light' language that had become the conventional means of signalling imminent rate decisions, the GC had stated that 'strong vigilance is of the essence to ensure that risks to price stability over the medium term do not materialize'. Strong vigilance was code for signposting a likely policy shift at the next meeting. As a result of these signals, and despite the market gyrations, by the end of August the probability that investors were attaching to a 25 basis point interest rate hike on 6 September was still as high as 50%. In other words, throughout August, the stance traffic light was flashing yellow. The question was: should the ECB deliver a 'green' on 6 September?

The euro area economy had entered the new phase of financial instability in good health, with signs of hyperactivity. Growth in the first quarter of 2007, at 0.7% quarter on quarter, had been unexpectedly robust, the last in a succession of upside surprises and revisions to real GDP data. Even real-time confidence indicators compiled in August after the financial shock, the closely-watched PMI composite output index, came in only slightly below expectations, in a sign that activity might be weathering the financial storm relatively well. In fact, the component of the August PMI index that registers the rhythm of activity in the services sector was particularly robust, although optimism among survey respondents about the prospects of their companies looking forward was dwindling. Accordingly, the ECB staff's projections, which became available in the second half of August and were published in early September, continued to indicate growth rates hovering around potential until the end of the two-year horizon covered in the exercise (see Figure 4.6). A particularly comforting aspect of the new staff projections was that

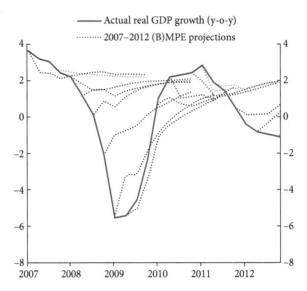

Figure 4.6 Actual and projected real GDP growth (y-o-y % change)
Sources: Eurostat and ECB projections.

the outlook seemed relatively immune to the recent market volatility.[15] Would financial intermediaries tighten terms and conditions on their own credit to the economy
to the point where consumption and investment would be hit?

The answer by the ECB forecasters was moderately negative, for essentially two
reasons. First, interest rates had certainly surged over the very short end of the
maturity spectrum in the money market, but the tightening in conditions was more
modest along longer-maturity segments, particularly those that served as a reference
for banks' adjustable-rate loans to the real economy. Long-term sovereign bond
yields, key benchmarks for pricing mortgages in Germany and France, had even
declined. Second, in the largest euro area economies at least, the recent corporate
investment boom was seen as being financed by firms' retained earnings. So, the
thinking was, capital formation was largely de-linked from developments in
the credit market.

While the growth outlook was relatively benign, inflation was seen as a persistent
source of worries. The rise in oil prices to a record US$78 per barrel at the end of July
had determined material upward revisions to the oil price assumptions embedded in
the August staff projections, not only for the current year, but for 2008 and 2009 as
well. These updates had worsened the prospects for headline inflation looking into
the medium term (see Figure 4.7). A matter of greater concern was that the ECB's

---

[15] The new forecasts were built on financial assumptions already reflecting the higher short-term interest rates which the early-August events had left as a legacy: three-month EURIBOR rates were now
expected to peak at 4.8% by the end of the last quarter of the year, as opposed to the level of 3.9% assumed
in the previous round of staff projections published in June. This was a material change in financial
assumptions that had rarely been larger from one projection round to the next.

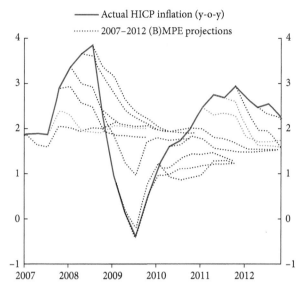

Figure 4.7 Actual and projected HICP inflation (y-o-y % change)

Sources: Eurostat and ECB projections.

Notes: The red dotted line indicates the September 2007 MPE. The green dotted lines indicate the March 2011 MPE and June 2011 BMPE.

Latest observation: 2012Q4 for realized GDP growth and HICP inflation.

preferred measure of core inflation—HICP inflation excluding the more volatile food and energy components—had remained at 1.9% since the beginning of the year, only a tenth of a per cent away from the 2% price stability ceiling. Market-based measure of inflation expectations, even when purged of the positive inflation risk premium, were bordering on 2% as well (see Figure 4.8 and our discussion about the inflation risk premium in Section 3.3). In an environment of rising energy costs, the risk was that overall inflation could at any time be pushed outside the GC's comfort area.

Indeed, echoing the logic that we sought to formalize with our regime-switching analysis in Chapter 3, all the conditions appeared to be in place for domestic price pressures to remain above levels of complacency.[16] If the financial tailwinds were to

[16] The sharp rise in oil prices over the year had boosted firms' costs and was seen as a major upside risk to the outlook for prices. Indeed, after a 1.6% inflation outturn in 2006, headline inflation was expected to average at 2.0% in 2007, 2008 and 2009. The last figure available at end-August was 1.8% for July, but the steep decline in unemployment to the historically low of 6.9% in June could be a harbinger of further pay rises. As for monetary variables, M3 had risen up sharply in July to reach 11.7%, a level unseen in the whole history of monetary union, on the back of double-digit annual rates of expansion for bank credit. M1, which includes bank sight deposits and currency and is the most liquid component of M3 had reversed its previous downward trend, as the financial market uncertainty had encouraged a flight to the safety offered by overnight deposits. Credit growth was buoyed by a further strengthening of lending to non-financial corporations, offset only in part by a continuation in the downward trend observed for the annual growth of loans to households. Looking ahead, the response of both money and credit to the turmoil was ambiguous. Money could keep accelerating as the inflow into the safest and most liquid

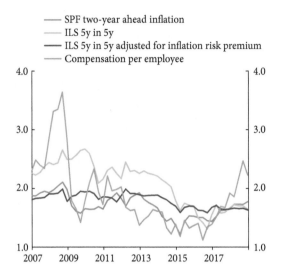

Figure 4.8 Medium-term inflation measures and wages per head (y-o-y % change)

Sources: ECB projections, ECB Survey of Professional Forecasters, Eurostat and Refinitiv.

Notes: The estimate of the inflation risk premium is based on an affine term structure model (Camba-Mendez and Werner, 2017).

Latest observation: December 2018.

prove ephemeral, inflation could well perk up, and the ECB would be in danger, some staff members feared, of having households and companies conclude that the central bank was not too serious about hitting its inflation objective.

Another central concern was about moral hazard. A price stability-oriented central bank does not target or try to steer asset prices. Attempts to do so are a recipe for promoting the kind of moral hazard that encourages excessive risk-taking among investors and thus increases the risk and intensity of future crises. In late August 2007 this argument had even greater force than at any other time: it was clear that the ongoing turmoil was the result of a long spell of 'financial exuberance' rather than adverse exogenous shocks—such as the sudden Russian default in 1998 or the terrorist attacks in the United States on 11 September 2001. During recent years, it had been the deliberate overexposure of much of the financial system to opaque and risky structured credit products that had created the conditions for the eventual mass withdrawal of investors as the extent to which they had misjudged the risk they were taking became more evident. This final moment of truth was to be expected, but it was not the task of the central bank to protect lenders and investors from the

instruments included in M3 was expected to continue. Credit was not easy to anticipate either. It could slow, as banks could become more conservative and tighten credit standards, amid growing uncertainties about the strength of their balance sheets. Furthermore, the growth rate of household borrowing could moderate as house price dynamics and real estate activity was slowing. But there was a chance that bank credit could even resume its vigorous expansion, as the flattening of the yield curve increased the attractiveness of monetary assets relative to less liquid longer-maturity instruments, and the contingent credit lines that banks had extended to separately incorporated off-balance-sheet entities were activated.

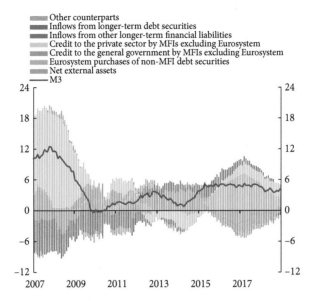

Figure 4.9 M3 growth and counterparts (y-o-y % change, contributions in pp)

Source: ECB BSI.

Latest observation: December 2018.

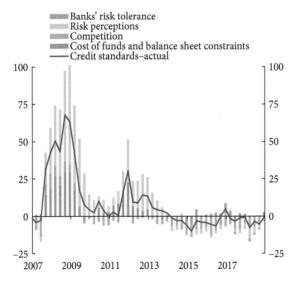

Figure 4.10 Changes in NFC credit standards, and contributing factors (net percentages of banks reporting tightening credit standards and contributing factors)

Source: ECB Bank Lending Survey.

Notes: See Notes to Figure 3.24.

Latest observation: 2018Q4 (January 2019 BLS).

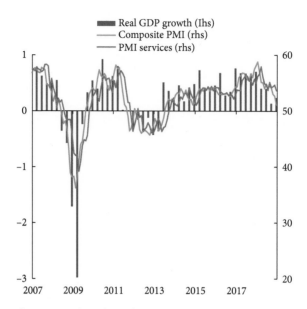

Figure 4.11 Real GDP growth and PMI (q-o-q % change, index)
Sources: Eurostat and IHS Markit.
Latest observation: December 2018.

consequences of their financial decisions.[17] These considerations supported the argument for following through on the early August signal. In the event, at its meeting of 6 September the GC confirmed that the 'outlook for price stability [remained] subject to upside risks' but noted that 'financial market volatility and reappraisal of risk' had injected enough uncertainty into the outlook to place a high option value on gathering additional information before acting on the August tightening bias. The financial uncertainty 'knock-out' used in the official statement as justification for suspending the rate hike that had been signalled before was rather unusual for the ECB. Ex post, it was a sensible course of action.

The fact was that quantitative risk analysis had been gaining prominence in the ECB's internal thinking. Risk analysis measures in statistical terms the possibility that the economy might derail from the path that is considered most likely over the foreseeable future. When central banks build forecasts about the future evolution of their economies, they usually seek to figure out the path the economy will most likely follow given the way shocks that have already materialized at the time of forecasting tend to play out and propagate through the economy. But the economy receives new shocks continuously. So it is always a good idea for policymakers to form an opinion on the degree to which what is considered the most likely, 'baseline' prediction might be robust to shocks that are not yet in sight at the time of the

---

[17] In internal debates in mid-2008, some staff members emphasized the principle that monetary policy was not the appropriate tool to address problems in the banking and financial sectors, and that banks themselves, supported by the relevant supervisory and regulatory authorities, were better equipped to find the necessary solutions.

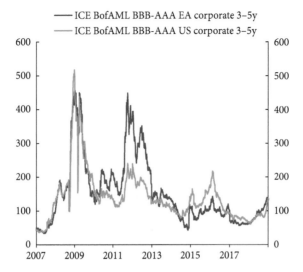

Figure 4.12 Non-financial corporate bond spreads in the euro area and the US three- to five-year maturity (basis points)
Source: Refinitiv.
Latest observation: December 2018.

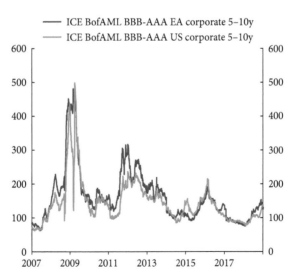

Figure 4.13 Non-financial corporate bond spreads in the euro area and the US five- to ten-year maturity (basis points)
Source: Refinitiv.
Latest observation: December 2018.

projections. A policy course that may be appropriate if the economy follows the baseline path may in fact turn out to be severely inadequate if the economy instead deviates in an unforeseen direction. Staff can assist in that search for robustness by feeding the policy process with the results of risk analysis. The protocol usually followed in the exercise is a multiple-stage procedure. First, a statistical model of the economy with good empirical properties is forced to match the baseline forecasts. Then, starting from that baseline scenario, the model is hit by shocks—to be realized at some future date—along dimensions that, looking into the proximate future, are considered relevant sources of uncertainty. The intensity and persistence of the hypothetical shocks assumed in the exercise reflect how frequently and strongly those shocks are estimated to have hit the economy in the past. Finally, the model is left free to adjust to those shocks, and the upside or downside deviations that the model generates away from the baseline path in responding to those impulses are a measure of risk.

In this endeavour, ECB staff had specialized in a particular corner of simulation methods that was not much practiced or researched during Great Moderation times among academics or policymaking institutions: the study of shocks originating in the financial system. The Great Moderation had inspired the view among many academic economists that the financial system was a 'veil'. NKM, in its canonical specification, abstracts from financial intermediaries and relies on the existence of a complete network of deep markets, in which consumers and investors are able to insure against any conceivable risk and take positions on any possible contingency. The financial industry is seen as a pass-through. It can hardly become an independent influence on the economy. The ECB had institutionally taken a very different perspective, though. As we saw in Chapters 2 and 3, the ECB had committed to keeping a window constantly open and focused in its internal analysis on phenomena, such as money and credit creation, which it considered informative of underlying trends in the economy. Thanks to the emphasis assigned to money and credit under the 'second pillar' of its strategy, the ECB had invested financial resources and human capital in building models fully in the NKM tradition, but with a non-neutral financial sector. That analysis was mobilized during the financial turmoil and the ensuing crisis to quantify the probability that a financial disruption would cause significant deterioration in the real economy. Box 4.3 shows a sample of such model-based exercises that were brought to the attention of the Executive Board of the ECB at the beginning of September 2007. This type of analysis available to ECB policymakers in real time disproves the claim that 'policymakers grappling with the crisis [...] found little to help them in the DSGE analysis' (Bean, 2010).[18]

---

[18] The view that central banks got little support from theory or econometrics during the crisis found some echoes among central bankers in the aftermath of the crisis. For example Mervyn King wrote in his 2016 book on the crisis (King, 2016): 'An abstract and increasingly mathematical discipline, economics is seen as having failed to predict the crisis. This is rather like blaming science for the occasional occurrence of a natural disaster. Yet we would blame scientists if incorrect theories made disasters more likely or created a perception that they could never occur, and one of the arguments of this book is that economics has encouraged ways of thinking that made crises more probable.'

Box 4.3   Risk analysis at the ECB

Baseline projections produced at policy institutions are usually based on a combination of models and judgement and are intended to describe the most likely path going forward. The Eurosystem/ECB (Broad) Macroeconomic Projection Exercise ((B)MPE) projections share these features. ECB staff have regularly complemented the base case with risk analysis.

Among the different types of risk analysis that have been prepared by ECB staff ahead of monetary policy meetings are model-based scenarios, which have been used to gauge the impact and transmission of events that could significantly alter the central view underlying the (B)MPE baseline.[19] This tool has made it possible to better understand risks of highly disruptive low-probability events and to plan possible policy responses in the face of different contingencies. While scenario analysis is a widespread practice in macroeconomic forecasting and strategic policy design, the focus in the profession has typically been on quantifying the sensitivity of baseline projections to alternative paths regarding real and exogenous variables (e.g. world demand, oil prices) with little attention to monetary and balance sheet variables. This has probably been due to the lack of models with good empirical properties able to combine real sector and monetary/balance sheet variables in a consistent setting. To fill this gap, ECB staff developed a relatively large DSGE model (the CMR model developed by Christiano, Motto, and Rostagno) combining these elements and displaying good forecasting performance, to be regularly used for constructing monetary/balance-sheet scenarios. In this box we review some real-time applications of model-based risk analysis focusing first on financial and monetary scenarios, and then on real-side scenarios and inflation risk assessment.

Monetary and Financial Scenarios

The methodology that was used in real time to construct financial and monetary scenarios is based on a two-stage approach. In the first stage, the data sample is extended forward with 'baseline projections', which, for the purpose of the scenarios, are treated as actual data. In other words, the model is forced to replicate the extended time series, including projections, thus treating the non-historical portion of the augmented sample as if it were 'in sample.' In building the scenarios, the projections for the variables that are fed into the CMR model were taken, as much as possible, from the ECB/Eurosystem's macroeconomic projections. Variables not included in the projections were forecast on the basis of several models, conditional

(Continued)

---

[19] Other forms of risk assessment regularly prepared by staff are: the quantitative risk analysis; average distribution constructed from survey responses (e.g. the ECB Survey of Professional Forecasters); option-implied distribution for inflation; risk distribution based on a BVAR with the first moments tilted to match the (B)MPE baseline; risk assessment based on quantile regressions.

Box 4.3 Continued

on the path followed by the variables included in the (B)MPE projections. In a second stage, once the augmented data sample has been replicated, monetary scenarios can be constructed in two distinct and yet complementary ways. The first is based on directly manipulating the string of innovations of monetary and financial shocks, for instance by assuming that the economy will be hit by a string of shocks which are broadly similar in magnitude and timing to those estimated to have occurred in a specific historical episode, so that staff may consider that it could repeat itself. The second type of scenario is based on assuming that some variables, for instance money and credit growth, could follow a certain path different from that in the baseline, where the alternative path is derived from, say, a past episode.

The scenarios discussed here are real-time applications prepared by ECB staff in 2007. At the time, the financial turmoil had just erupted, manifesting itself in August 2007 through distress in money markets. Initially, there was minimal spillover to other segments. However, it was not clear whether such distress would be reab- sorbed quickly or would initiate a cascade effect. There was also the question of whether it would affect only the financial markets, whether it would compromise the soundness of the banking system. It was still too early to see the macroeconomic impact of the financial turbulence in hard data or even in surveys. This had two implications. First, the (B)MPE baseline projections, based on the most likely out- come and rooted in models with no role for funding or lending channels, encoun- tered problems in taking on board the potential effects of the turmoil. Second, the assessment of the potential macroeconomic implications of the turbulence had to be addressed via scenarios, namely 'risks' around the baseline projections, and based on macro models with funding and lending channels.

The scenarios produced by ECB staff at the time (the perspective is that of the third quarter of 2007) explored the possible risks to the baseline were the turmoil to evolve in a manner similar to two historical episodes of financial distress. The first episode is the stock market correction between the second quarter of 2000 and the second quarter of 2001, which excludes the further collapse triggered by the terror- ist attack in the United States on 11 September 2001 and the subsequent prolonged phase of severe stock market declines in 2002. The second episode is the severe but temporary re-appreciation of the financial risk that occurred in August and September 1998, when the Russian default and devaluation exacerbated the ongoing Asian financial crisis and led in a matter of weeks to the collapse of the hedge fund Long-Term Capital Management. In both scenarios it was assumed that the estimated monetary policy reaction function would play out endogenously in reaction to the alternative state of the economy.

The results are reported in Figure B.4.3.1. The red dashed line with circles depicts the outcome of the first exercise. Here, the more protracted and severe destruction of stock market value, in conjunction with expectations of further stock market losses looking forward and the sharp re-appreciation of the investment risk that the model estimates to have occurred after the second quarter of 2000, determines an appreciable and steady decline in inflation. Credit growth also moderates as the anticipation of further losses on equity value and the concomitant widening of the credit risk premium—which tightens up the real credit conditions applying to corporate borrowing despite the endogenous easing of policy—discourages the assumption of loans. Annual real GDP growth declines by around 0.4/0.6 percentage points relative to the baseline in 2008 and 2009.

The 1998–1999 scenario is described in the figure with the dashed blue line. Here, after dropping initially beyond the negative levels incorporated in the baseline projections, the stock market stages a strong rebound boosted by the sharp turnaround in confidence that the model estimates to have occurred—after the initial two quarters of the 1998 episode—in the first quarter of 1999. As a consequence, after an early softening of real GDP growth in the third and fourth quarters of 2007, growth resumes and stays close to its baseline levels over the latter part of the projections horizon. Meanwhile inflation also recovers and eventually overshoots its baseline levels, propelled by the strong rebound in the stock markets, which—by the end of the projections—completely offsets the 2007 losses, and by a gradual decline in the credit risk premium. Tighter credit conditions persist for two quarters until the financial market uncertainty is resolved in the course of the third quarter. At that point, risk spreads and market volatility promptly retreat from crisis levels with moderate impacts on consumption and investment and therefore economic growth. The latter drop in spreads more than offsets the impact on credit tightness exercised by the endogenous firming of policy. Credit growth also recovers quickly and stabilizes at levels above baseline.

Several other scenarios of this type were carried out in real time in the attempt to assess the economic fallout and the implications for the risks to price stability that could materialize were the financial turmoil to end up in a full-blown banking crisis, such as those that unfolded in the worst banking crises of the last century. These scenarios became especially relevant after March 2008 and even more so after September 2008. They made it easier to cross-check the baseline projections with information obtained from monetary analysis, which in turn helped with the formulation of contingency plans.

Real-Side and Nominal-Side Scenarios and Risk Assessment

Staff assessment of the risks emanating from the real side and the external environment and their likely implications for the baseline projections has been a mainstay of all projection rounds. The model-based analysis has mainly been founded on the New Area-Wide Model (NAWM)[20] for the euro area and has taken the form of scenarios in which staff have investigated the impact of changes in the technical assumptions and unobservable variables such as the output gap. Examples of the

(Continued)

---

[20] See Christoffel et al. (2008) for a detailed description of the model and its use for forecasting and policy analysis.

Box 4.3 Continued

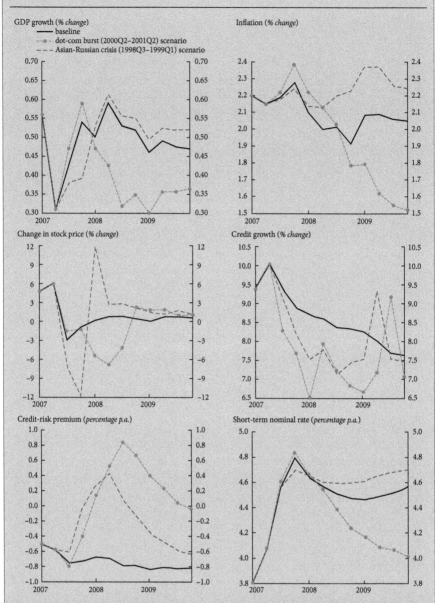

Figure B.4.3.1 Replicating the financial shocks that took place between the second quarter of 2000 and the second quarter of 2001

Source: CMR.

Notes: The solid line shows the CMR baseline macroeconomic scenario (MPE projections for inflation, GDP growth, the stock market and the short-term interest rate, and BVAR implied projections for credit growth and the credit risk premium) over the period 2007Q1-2009Q4. The red dashed line with circles is the alternative scenario constructed on the assumption that the innovations to the financial shock and the riskiness shock between 2007Q3 and 2008Q3 are the same as estimated for 2000Q2–2001Q2. The blue dashed line is the alternative scenario constructed on the assumption that the innovations to the financial shock and the riskiness shock between 2007Q3 and 2008Q1 are the same as estimated for 1998Q3–1999Q1.

former are scenarios regarding alternative paths of the exchange rate, sovereign yields, and the fiscal stance. For instance, in 2011 staff discussed the impact of an intensification of sovereign stress by quantifying the effects of alternative paths for the technical assumptions on the baseline projections for the real economy and inflation. Related to that, a recurrent discussion in 2010 and 2011 was the macro-economic impact of fiscal consolidation policies, disentangling short-term and long-run effects, including in relation to alternative configurations of the size and composition of fiscal adjustment plans.

As an example of the implications of the uncertainty surrounding output gap esti-mates in the light of the impact that the crisis may have exerted on the underlying forces determining the potential output, in mid-2010 the staff explored the sensitivity of the Eurosystem macroeconomic projections to alternative estimates of potential output. These estimates for potential output growth were based on the

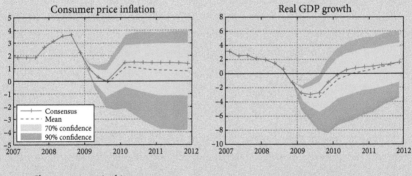

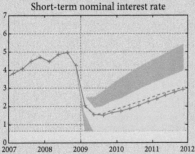

Figure B.4.3.2 Predictive distributions for consumer price inflation, real GDP growth, and the short-term nominal interest rate, March 2009 (percentage change and percentage per annum)

Source: Coenen and Warne (2014).

Notes: The predictive distributions are derived from stochastic simulations of the NAWM and are centred on the structural shocks that the model has identified for the March 2009 consensus forecast vintage. The lower bound is imposed at an interest rate level of 65 bps, reflecting the average spread between the EURIBOR and the EONIA over the horizon of the forecast vintage.

(Continued)

> **Box 4.3 Continued**
>
> NAWM and cross-check with partial-equilibrium approaches that incorporated expert judgement. Lower potential output growth was estimated to lead to a marked decline in expected real GDP growth, with a rather subdued closing of the output gap and limited impact on inflation.
>
> Model-based analysis also contributed to the summarizing of the risks to inflation via stochastic simulations.[21] This became particularly relevant when policy rates reached low levels as the presence of the lower bound on nominal interest rates generates non-linearities—even in a model that is otherwise linear, such as the NAWM. Stochastic simulations were carried out by drawing from the estimated distribution of shocks either prevailing over a long sample period or observed at the outbreak of the Great Financial Crisis. These model-based simulations made it possible to construct a measure of excess inflation risks (defined as the probability of observing at least four consecutive quarters of annual inflation above 2%) and deflation risks (defined as the probability of observing at least four consecutive quarters of negative annual inflation rates over the respective forecast horizon). By combining the two, it was possible to derive a model-based balance of risks, which represents a summary of the statistics that staff had been monitoring over time. Staff assessments and results were along the lines documented in Coenen and Warne (2014). They showed for instance that downside risks to price stability were considerably greater than upside risks during the first half of 2009, followed by a gradual rebalancing of these risks until mid-2011, and a renewed deterioration thereafter (see Figure B.4.3.2). Moreover, the perceived lower bound induces a noticeable downward bias in the risk balance because of the implied amplification of deflation risks.

More importantly, the GC's decision to hold off on the rate hike for the rest of 2007—despite prior signals—also helps to qualify the contention that the ECB was intellectually averse to a risk-management approach to monetary policy and only concentrated on the central tendency of likely future outcomes to assess whether the stance of monetary policy was properly calibrated.

4.3 The July 2008 Rate Hike

By the winter of 2007, the euro area economy had entered a state of 'meta-stability'—a term in fact coined later on by Jean-Claude Trichet to describe a state of affairs in which the economy was exceptionally vulnerable to shocks. In those conditions, perturbations that the overall economy would take in its stride in different

---

[21] For a description of the model simulation and the types of results see Coenen and Warne (2014).

circumstances have the potential for driving it to the brink of systemic failure.[22] In the end, a latent 'meta-stability' feeling within the GC tipped the balance of considerations in favour of a prolonged wait-and-see tactic. As a consequence, financial markets gradually ratcheted down expectations of rate rises through the end of the year and, by the May 2008 GC meeting, were already assigning a 40% probability to a rate cut by the end of 2008.

But the transition between the May and the July 2008 GC meetings was eventful. Brent crude prices, on a relentless rise since the summer of the previous year, were in a range of US$126–130 per barrel at the end of May. While the abrupt upward pressure on the spot price of oil throughout the spring had caused an inversion of the oil price futures curve, around the June GC meeting the curve was once more positively sloped, indicating that markets considered it increasingly likely that the price of energy would continue to rise in the foreseeable future. Internal analysis could explain only part of the increase by supply factors, including restraints in producer countries. So, the risk was that oil prices were merely a symptom of an overheating global economy and of underlying nominal trends that pointed to a more generalized inflationary trend at the global level. The high resilience of growth in emerging economies to the financial strains that had hit the advanced world was lending credence to the demand-side reading of the rapid increases in the prices of energy and other commodities. The aggressive easing by the US Federal Reserve System over the past nine months had determined a measurable widening in the cross-Atlantic rate differential. The euro was on a path of sustained appreciation. This notwithstanding, however, measured inflation in the euro area had been climbing since the turmoil of the past summer and had reached an all-time high of 3.6% (see Figure 4.7). Staff forecasts saw inflation declining below 3% only in 2009 and below 2% only by the end of 2010. The response of unit labour costs to high inflation was projected to be somewhat more muted than implied by historical patterns, as captured by the model equations used in the projections. But the projected path for productivity growth was viewed as subject to downside risks, owing to the well-known pro-cyclical behaviour of productivity in the euro area (see our discussion in Chapter 3). In this light, second-round effects could not be ruled out, particularly against the backdrop of underlying business conditions that looked robust. Indeed, in stark contrast to the slowing US economy—which was weighed down by a sharp housing contraction, and more stringent borrowing conditions—the euro area real economy had surprised on the upside in the first quarter and was seen as likely to land softly on its potential, from slightly below, looking into the future. Credit and broad money had been accelerating, although both were probably distorted by re-intermediation of finance that banks had spun off to ad hoc vehicles issuing structured products in the

[22] In the words of President Trichet, speaking in London in December 2009: 'The meta-stability of a system is a complex concept, which calls for analysis of the interplay between diverse phenomena. In financial systems, these phenomena include herd behaviour, complex networks of relationships between counterparties, and contagion from common or correlated exposures to particular asset classes. They also include the undesirable pro-cyclical effects of prudential rules, of accounting rules, of credit rating agencies, and of compensation systems that put undue emphasis on short-term earnings' (Trichet, 2009c).

years prior to the turmoil and were taking back on-balance-sheet as the demand for those products had dried up.

The wait-and-see tactic was still an option for the GC, primarily on account of the persistent strains in the money market. But credit was flowing to the real economy seemingly unimpaired, spreads were narrowing, and the liquidity pressures in the money market had ebbed to some extent. Against this evidence, risk considerations grounded exclusively on the lingering perception that the system was in a state of 'meta-stability' were being increasingly overshadowed by tangible signs that price stability might be endangered. In fact, looking backward, some in the staff were sounding a credibility alarm, emphasizing that inflation had exceeded the price stability ceiling on a year-on-year basis in each year since 2000, and was projected to do so again in both 2008 and 2009. While it was acknowledged that the accomplishment of the ECB's mandate could only be meaningfully assessed over the medium term and specific explanations could be offered for past performance, according to this view the credibility of the ECB's commitment to the definition of price stability was at stake.

At its 5 June meeting—falling in the week of celebrations of the tenth anniversary of the ECB—the GC left its key interest rates unchanged. At the same time, in his introductory statement at the press conference following the meeting, the President noted that risks to price stability over the medium term had 'increased further' and that the GC was 'in a state of heightened alertness' and ready to act in 'a firm and timely manner'. After almost a year, the traffic light had turned yellow again.[23] One month later, on 3 July 2008, the ECB finally increased its policy interest rates by 25 bps, bringing its main refinancing rate to 4.25% 'to prevent broadly based second-round effects and to counteract the increasing upside risks to price stability over the medium term'. Financial conditions had worsened in the course of June, and corporate bank borrowing was showing signs of retrenchment, although the net flow of loans to companies remained sustained (see Figure 4.9). Business confidence and consumer confidence were deteriorating moderately. However, some staff analysis had emphasized that price declines in the stock market, slowing business activity and subdued consumption were all to be associated with a clear common factor seeping through the broader economy: rapid increases in the prices of energy and other commodities, which sapped household purchasing power and undermined companies' earnings prospects. These experts were convinced that the biggest downside risk to growth was the erosion of purchasing power and consumer confidence that would follow from a failure to maintain price stability, and that by delivering price stability and solidly anchoring inflation expectations, the ECB could support consumer confidence, foster domestic consumption and thereby contain the downside risks to growth. In this environment, the so-called dilemma between anchoring inflation and supporting growth would disappear. Echoing the same conviction, in its official communication on 3 July the GC acknowledged that the rate hike would

---

[23] During the press conference on 5 June President Trichet was more explicit, remarking that the possibility of the GC deciding to move the policy rates at its next meeting had not been excluded. As a consequence, the probability of a 25 basis point rate hike by July—as embedded in EONIA swap rates—rose to around 85%. By the July meeting, markets were pricing in another rate hike before year-end.

'preserve purchasing power in the medium term and continue to support sustainable growth and employment in the euro area.'[24]

Although much hailed at the time by expert observers, this decision was denounced later as a hasty overreaction to oil price shocks that, in retrospect, proved short-lived. Above, we have tried to reproduce the thought process that at the time assessed the available information within the ECB and finally motivated the decision. All in all, one should not underrate the sense—ingrained in the GC in the first half of 2008—that the ECB had systematically miscalculated the likelihood of inflation staying durably above 2% and had underperformed on its mandate as a consequence.

Longer-term inflation expectations—with the preferred raw measure extracted from the five-year in five-year inflation-linked swaps approaching 2.5%—were seen as a vote of no confidence in the ECB's ability to steer inflation trends. A similarly worrying message was emerging from survey-based information available to monetary policymakers at the time, as the share of SPF respondents expecting inflation above 2.0% in the long-term was reaching its highest reading in the (short) history of the SPF precisely in the third quarter of 2008 (see Figure 4.14).

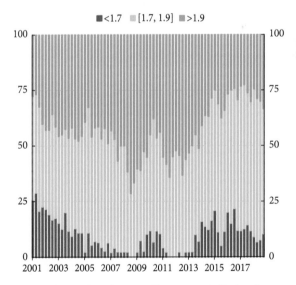

Figure 4.14 SPF respondents' distribution of long-term inflation forecast over selected bins (% of respondents)
Source: ECB Survey of Professional Forecasters (SPF).
Latest observation: 2018Q4.

---

[24] In the context of the monetary dialogue of September 2008, for which the European Parliament asked experts to examine whether 'the upward shift in inflation' was going to last, the then Chairman of the CEPR, Guillermo de la Dehesa neatly summed up the consensus that emerged from these various contributions (De la Dehesa, 2008): 'There are other less ambitious ways for the ECB to deal with this difficult dilemma. One is to continue to miss its low inflation target for several more years, which can also damage its reputation, but it may be understandable, given that it has consistently missed it before for years and given that most analysts believe is too ambitious.'

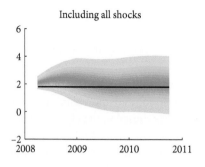
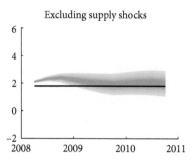

Figure 4.15 Stochastic simulations in 2008Q1: inflation looking forward (y-o-y % change)
Source: CMR.

In the light of this perceived credibility deficit, we ask a different question here, namely: what would stochastic simulations have advised, if the GC could have taken advantage of this analytical tool in the first half of 2008 to chart out the predictive distribution of inflation over the projection horizon? In stochastic simulations, analysts draw randomly from the estimated process that generates shocks according to a model and then apply these drawings back to the model to obtain simulated trajectories of key observable variables into the future. Were the oil price and other supply-side forces really the main source of upside risk for future inflation in 2008? We utilize the CMR model to shed light on this issue, and Figure 4.15 shows the result of CMR-based stochastic simulations.

The left-hand graphic depicts the predictive distribution for inflation, taking into account the entire spectrum of the shocks that the CMR estimates in sample and their stochastic properties. The right-hand graphic does the same but abstracts from supply-side shocks, those shocks that create opposing effects on inflation and real growth. The point of departure for both simulations is the first quarter of 2008, namely the model is asked to produce predictions as it had no knowledge of the following history. We note two features. First, risks to price stability were indeed skewed to the upside, with the likelihood of higher-than-ceiling realizations larger than that assigned to inflation undershoots. Second, the skewness of risks does not disappear—in fact, it is slightly accentuated—if one ignores the supply side. Even in the extreme case of a central bank attaching zero weight to risks coming from the supply side and simply looking through this type of shocks, one would have concluded at the time that the urge to act was very strong.

4.4 The Great Crash

During the summer of 2008, a slew of disappointing euro area macroeconomic data releases together with a material drop in oil prices and renewed concerns about the resilience of the US financial sector led investors to price out any ECB rate increase until well into 2009. Spreads between the interest rates paid on uncollateralized and collateralized transactions in the euro money market were widening again for maturities longer than three months. European banks had neither announced write-downs nor raised new capital to nearly the same extent as their US counterparts. This behaviour, traditionally interpreted in Europe as a sign of better health, looked increasingly like a strategy of procrastination. The rising spreads that banks were paying for borrowing funds in the money market, the creep-up in measures of bank default risk and a solidifying pattern of tightening conditions for bank loans (see Figure 4.10) were all indicators sending messages that banks' health was quickly deteriorating and that procrastination was a risky approach. All told, the conviction that the euro area had weathered the 2007 liquidity shock with composure was losing strength. Ahead of the GC's September meeting, ECB staff were advocating that monetary policy should be directed in a steady-handed manner—which meant staying the course chosen in July and reassuring the markets amid heightened volatility—but at the same time warning that any substantial financial risk, such as the failure of a systematically important US financial institution, would have profound implications for the euro area economy, even if its immediate cause were geographically remote.

The systemically important US financial institution, Lehman Brothers Holdings Inc, defaulted less than three weeks later and brought worldwide credit markets to a halt within hours. Tightening credit and falling asset values in a vast swathe of financial markets took a heavy toll on business confidence and consumer confidence and precipitated a sharp slowing in global economic activity. Over the following year, the damage, in terms of lost output, lost jobs, and lost wealth, turned out to be dramatic, making this the most severe macroeconomic debacle on record since the Great Depression of the 1930s.

The combination of widespread dependence on wholesale, short-term financing in the funding markets, excessive leverage among intermediaries, generally poor risk management, and the gaps and weaknesses in regulatory oversight created an environment in which a powerful, self-reinforcing panic could begin. Adverse selection, namely lenders' fear of engaging in transactions with borrowers who might be unable to reimburse them, fuelled 'counterparty risk', which in turn deterred banks from lending funds even at the shortest tenors. Repo transactions, which had become a major source of short-term credit for many financial institutions, were secured by collateral, and thus in principle protected from counterparty risk. But, once the crisis began, repo lenders became increasingly concerned about the possibility that they would be forced to receive collateral instead of cash, and that the securities to be received in payment would have to be sold in dysfunctional and illiquid markets. Lenders' response to such fears was an immediate increase in haircuts, a cut to the effective amount of funding available to borrowers, or an outright withdrawal from the market. Some borrowers lost access to repo financing entirely as a result, and some securities became simply unfundable in the repo market. As these borrowers were left with no option but to sell assets into illiquid markets, asset prices collapsed, volatility increased, and the financial positions of all participants weakened dramatically. Overall, the contemporaneous emergence of sudden stops across a variety of funding channels on which the financial system had become particularly reliant helps explain the remarkably sharp intensification of the financial crisis and its rapid global spread.

This situation also had great potential for destabilizing the overnight money market, the very first link in the monetary transmission chain. In the event, very short-term interest rates kept reasonably close to the MRO rate (see Figure 4.18) thanks to a series of ECB liquidity-providing FTOs. An increase in US dollar liquidity provided to euro area banks through the Term Auction Facility (TAF) helped soothe fears that European banks might become unable to refund their dollar-denominated exposures. Nevertheless, counterparty risk was showing up in the unprecedented level of tender rates at the weekly MROs (see the orange line in Figure 4.5) and in the widening spreads between the cost of obtaining funds in the unsecured versus the secured interbank market. The spread between the three-month EURIBOR and the OIS rate with the same maturity rose above 200 bps, a level unseen in the ten-year history of the euro money market (see Figures 4.16 and 4.17). Credit spreads paid by non-financial corporations moved in sympathy and reached levels in the history of monetary union (see Figures 4.12 and 4.13).

Against this backdrop, ECB staff prepared for the 2 October GC meeting with three broad scenarios in mind. The first scenario, reflecting the September baseline projections, was considered to be somewhat optimistic, so staff concentrated instead on the second and third possibilities: a prolonged period of sluggish growth, with activity doing little to weaken labour costs and bring down inflation, given the multitude of inflexibilities gripping the euro area factor and product markets; and a

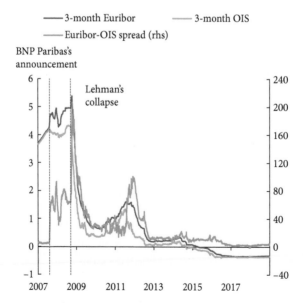

Figure 4.16 Stress in interbank market (percentages per annum, basis points)

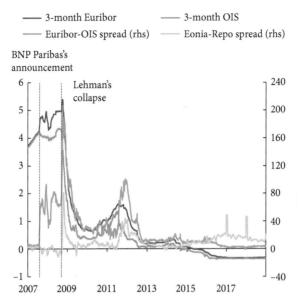

Figure 4.17 Stress in interbank market and EONIA-repo spread (percentages per annum, basis points)

Source: Bloomberg.

Latest observation: December 2018.

financial meltdown leading to a bank loan crunch, causing serial corporate bankruptcies and severe risks of self-sustaining deflationary pressures. While the second scenario was still considered the modal outlook, the probability of the third scenario was not negligible—and it was increasing. With this in mind, it was important to uphold two approaches that, in the view of staff, had served the ECB well in the recent past. One was the celebrated separation principle, whereby interest rate decisions should not be deflected from the pursuit of price stability by short-term considerations about market functioning for which other instruments were better suited. The second was the GC's principle of not pre-committing to any specific course for monetary policy with a view to not fine-tuning market expectations, which were ultimately the responsibility of market participants themselves.

In the end, the second scenario prevailed, and the GC held steady on 2 October, while it sought to gain greater insight into how the economy was performing. The market reaction to the decision was not positive, though. Tensions in the money markets escalated, and the EONIA reached levels of around 4.5%, a full quarter of a percent higher than the level of the MRO rate (see Figure 4.18).[25]

---

[25] As a matter of fact, markets had been in a state of panic since the US Congress had rejected the first bad asset purchase programme proposed by the Treasury Department on 29 September 2008. The following day Bloomberg reported: 'Wall Street was pinning its hopes on the government's $700 billion financial system rescue plan. But the fervently wished-for bailout was rejected Monday by the House of Representatives in a stunning turn of events, and investors reacted with a vengeance. Major US stock

4.5 The ECB Steps into the Breach

A few days later, by teleconference, the GC decided to join the Bank of Canada, the Bank of England, the Federal Reserve, Sveriges Riksbank and the Swiss National Bank in a coordinated bold interest rate reduction. The level of the interest rate corridor was cut by 50 bps, with the minimum bid rate on the MRO lowered to 3.75%. In order to remove the dispersion of tender rates at auction, the GC announced that the subsequent MROs would be carried out through fixed rate tender procedures with full allotment at the interest rate on the main refinancing operation. This move marked a return to the liquidity allotment modality tested with success on 9 August 2007, a practice that has been encoded in the Eurosystem operational framework since then and is still in place at the date of writing. The GC also reduced the width of the interest rate corridor from 200 bps to 100 bps around the MRO rate, with the intent to gain a better grasp over the EONIA and dampen its wide swings.

The markets remained unimpressed. The differential between the EURIBOR deposit rate and the OIS rate continued to climb and reached another all-time high on 10 October. It started to ratchet down only in the course of the following week, as two new developments occurred. First, a number of euro area governments announced comprehensive rescue packages meant to provide government guarantees and capital support to the ailing national banks.[26] Second, on 15 October the ECB decided on measures to expand the collateral framework and enhance the provision of liquidity. A number of new asset typologies were declared eligible in Eurosystem operations and, most importantly, the credit threshold for the marketable and non-marketable securities that could be pledged was lowered from A- to BBB-, with the exception of asset-backed securities (ABSs). While this measure was meant to expand the pool of assets that could be liquefied through collateralized borrowing from the Eurosystem, the ECB also extended the frequency and tenors of such liquidity operations. It decided that two three-month LTROs, one

---

indexes plummeted Monday in one of their worst sessions ever. The ugliness was widespread, with major indexes posting their worst percentage declines since the 1987 stock market crash. The Dow Jones Industrial average tumbled almost 7%, the S&P 500 sank 8.8%, and the Nasdaq plunged a jaw-dropping 9.1%. The Dow suffered its largest point drop in history.'

[26] European G8 members at their summit in Paris on 4 October 2008 jointly committed to ensure the soundness and stability of their banking and financial systems and to take all the necessary measures to achieve this objective. The leaders of all 27 EU countries agreed on a similar statement on 6 October 2008, also stressing that each of them would take the necessary steps to reinforce bank deposit protection schemes. At the ECOFIN Council meeting of 7 October 2008, the ministers of finance of the Member States agreed on EU common guiding principles to restore both confidence in and the proper functioning of the financial sector. National measures in support of systemic financial institutions would be adopted in principle for a limited time period and within a coordinated framework, while taking due regard of the interests of taxpayers. At the same time, the ECOFIN Council agreed to lift the coverage of national deposit guarantee schemes to a level of at least €50,000, acknowledging that some Member States were to raise their minimum to €100,000. Following the adoption of their concerted European Action Plan on 12 October 2008, the principles of which were endorsed by the European Council a few days later, euro area countries announced (additional) national measures to support their financial systems and ensure appropriate financing conditions for the economy as a prerequisite for growth and employment.

six-month LTRO, and one operation with a maturity corresponding to the length of the relevant maintenance period (approximately one month) would be carried out each month until and including March 2009 under FRFA.[27] The ECB's swap line with the Federal Reserve was enlarged, with provision of dollar liquidity with full allotment and at various maturities.

The ECB cut its key interest rates by 50 bps on 6 November and by another 75 bps—a rate adjustment of an unprecedented size for the ECB—on 4 December, thus bringing the MRO rate to 2.5% by year-end. Acting in this way, in the last two months of 2008 the GC demonstrated the collective strength of character necessary at the time to suspend to some extent its 'steady handedness' in the setting of interest rates and the medium-term assessment, and to practice risk management instead.[28] It was indeed an exercise in risk management, given the relatively light recession foreseen in the central scenario of the staff macroeconomic projections available for the December meeting (see Figure 4.6), and crude longer-term inflation expectations obstinately above 2% throughout this period. The rapid deceleration of money and credit was interpreted as an omen of dark clouds gathering on the horizon. And this led the GC to take out some insurance.

In the new year, as the perception that the economy was in free fall solidified, the GC continued to ease policy aggressively. After a series of three further rate reductions, on 7 May 2009 the MRO rate was finally lowered to 1%, at the time the lowest level for the monetary policy key interest rate observed in any single member of the monetary union in post-war times. Since the width of the rate corridor was narrowed to ±75 bps around the MRO rate, the floor of the corridor was decreased to 25 bps.

Besides its rate decision, on 7 May the GC made two other important announcements. First, it said it was launching a series of three one-year refinancing operations under FRFA procedures, indicating that the second and the third operation might be priced at the MRO rate plus a premium. Second, it announced its intention to purchase euro-denominated covered bonds issued in the euro area. In the event, the Eurosystem conducted the three LTROs at the prevailing MRO rate of 1%, without a premium. The injection of liquidity in the first operation allotted in June was deemed colossal at the time: €442 billion, at the top of the range that staff had expected. Together with the covered bond purchase programme, the measure spelled an unprecedented expansion in the size of both the asset and liability sides of the Eurosystem's balance sheet (see Figure B.4.3.1). The size of the balance sheet reached a local peak of €900 billion in June, as the first 12-month operation was settled.

---

[27] The extent to which the system was hunting for liquidity could be seen by comparing two successive Supplementary LTROs, one conducted at fixed allotment (of €50 billion) and at variable rate on 8 October with a maturity of six months, and the other conducted on 29 October at FRFA (with a fixed rate of 3.75%) and a maturity of three months. In the former operation, the marginal rate was as high as 5.36%. In the latter operation, the allotted amount was €103 billion.

[28] For most of this period, however, staff highlighted the risks that a frontloaded monetary policy response might restrict the space for future monetary policy action.

A few questions come to mind at this point. First, was the ECB's easing trajectory effective in easing the stance and providing adequate accommodation? Second, could the stimulus have been more effective?

4.5.1 What Determines the Stance?

Answering the first question requires giving some thoughts first of all to the precise definition of the monetary policy stance itself. As we saw before, the GC was wedded to the principle that the ECB should draw a sharp line between the setting of its interest rate and the provision of liquidity: in other words, the separation principle. In a corridor system with a deposit facility providing a hard floor to the level of the overnight interbank interest rate, such separation is always feasible. The issue is: at what level of interest rates within the corridor can this separation between liquidity volumes and the overnight interest rate be effected? In pre-crisis times, the Eurosystem supplied liquidity principally in weekly lending operations and, in those operations, actively adjusted the volume offered in order to keep the overnight money market interest rate, the EONIA, close to its pivot lending rate, the minimum bid rate in the MRO. This technique, as we saw, worked well before the financial crisis, when reserve demand was fairly stable in the aggregate and largely influenced by payment needs and reserve requirements. That was also a period in which the liquidity balances available to the system were just sufficient to meet banks' obligations in the aggregate, namely their 'liquidity needs', and any amount of reserves in excess of such 'needs' at individual banks was traded away in a fluid interbank money market. In those conditions, the rate within the corridor around which the overnight rate was oscillating was the MRO rate. However, with the increased use of reserves for precautionary liquidity purposes following the financial panic of September–October 2008, banks' demand for reserves in the weekly and longer-term operations had greatly increased in size (see Figure B.4.3.1) and had become nearly impossible to predict. So the Eurosystem found itself unable to precisely target an interest rate the old way, namely through the active management of liquidity at the auctions. The shift to an FRFA modality in all of its operations helped to ensure that, at auction at least, all participating banks would receive the liquidity needed at an interest rate not far away from—and, in the event, equal to—the targeted MRO level.

But the combination of this new approach with the longer maturities at which liquidity was being offered after the 15 October 2008 decisions led to structurally higher reserve holdings in the system. The end of the reserve scarcity regime, combined with the wide corridor, in turn, determined a situation in which the overnight interest rate, the EONIA, and the MRO rate departed from one another, with the former displaying a tendency to gravitate towards the floor of the corridor, the rate on the deposit facility (DFR). Stabilization of the EONIA around the MRO rate was still possible, had the GC decided to conduct frequent liquidity-absorbing FTOs at that rate. However, the GC wisely chose not to do so, and instead let the EONIA de-link and drift down within the corridor.

Accordingly, the separation principle had to be reinterpreted. It was duly redefined as implying that the MRO rate was the pivot of the monetary policy stance in the euro area, while the EONIA was merely a market reflection of the abundant excess amount of liquidity that was now floating around the system.

However, this reinterpretation was only partly warranted. It also encouraged some degree of neglect for the behaviour of the EONIA which, with the passage of time, proved to be harmful to the control of the monetary policy conditions in the euro area. To be sure, the idea that the MRO rate was the pivot of the stance was not a complete misconception. Indeed, the Lehman crisis had left behind a legacy of a banking system split into two sub-groups: 'ostracized' and 'non-ostracized' banks. The former group comprised credit institutions that either faced systematic credit rationing in the interbank market or were lacking sufficiently liquid collateral to engage in market trading. These 'ostracized' banks had become persistent bidders in the Eurosystem's lending operations because they had little or no access to alternative sources of funding. In fact, for them the MRO rate *was* the marginal cost of funding and thus a good proxy for the prevailing stance of monetary policy. But, for the 'non-ostracized' banks, which with the slow normalization of money market conditions had regained access to an interbank source of liquidity and in fact had accumulated comfortably large amounts of reserves, the relevant metric for the prevailing stance was closer to the EONIA—at which they could lend or borrow in the interbank exchange—than to the MRO rate. These banks had remained active participants in the money market. Through their lending and borrowing at a variety of maturities, this group of banks, together with other investors, was engaging in those key inter-temporal arbitrage activities that ordinarily help to bridge long-term yields and the very short-term interest rates in fixed income markets. A key market in which this intertemporal arbitrage takes place is a particular segment of the interest rate swap market, the so-called overnight index swap (OIS) market, where the periodic floating payment in the swap contracts is indexed to the EONIA.[29] Figure 4.18 shows the tight connection that existed at the end of 2008—as at most other times—between the overnight interest rate and the whole terms structure of swap interest rates. The level of the realized EONIA at the end of 2008 is the last blue point on the left-hand side of the graphic, the EONIA forward curve implied by the swap contracts in existence at the end of 2008 in this market is the blue line, and the contemporaneous term structure of the interest rates paid by the German Treasury—also tied to the

[29] The OIS contract is an interest-swap contract where two parties agree to exchange two cash flows: one party pays a fixed rate applied to some notional principal amount for the duration of the contract (this is the fixed rate leg of the contract) and the other party provides a floating rate payment applied to the same principal contract (the flexible rate leg). The periodic floating rate is indexed to the EONIA, so the fixed rate that is swapped has to be a good approximation of the parties' expectations about the evolution of the EONIA in the future. Technically, in an interest rate swap contract, at maturity the 'receiver' party of the swap contract will receive the initially agreed fixed rate of the swap contract and pays a geometric average of EONIA as realized over the lifetime of the swap; the reverse applies to the 'payer' of the swap contract. However, only the net cash flows are actually exchanged, i.e. if EONIA by chance turns out to be on average equal to the fixed rate, no payments change hands. The market-quoted (spot) OIS rate is the fixed rate of the contract. See ECB (2014) for more details on the OIS market and the role of the term structure of OIS rates as proxy for the euro area risk-free curve.

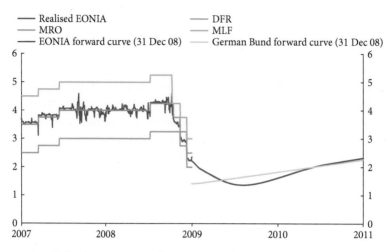

—— Realised EONIA	—— DFR
—— MRO	—— MLF
—— EONIA forward curve (31 Dec 08)	—— German Bund forward curve (31 Dec 08)

Figure 4.18 ECB key interest rates, short-term market rate and forward curves (percentages per annum)

Sources: ECB, EuroMTS and Refinitiv.

Latest observation: 31 December 2008 for realized EONIA and ECB key interest rates.

swap curve through financial arbitrage—is the yellow line. Owing to this close cross-asset association, by controlling the EONIA and influencing markets' expectations about its future evolution—expectations that are embedded in the OIS term structure—the ECB can typically determine to some extent the term structure of risk-free interest rates in the euro area. This risk-free curve, in turn, enters as the pricing kernel in all euro-denominated financial prices, and offers the benchmark that banks typically use to reset floating rate loans and price new loans. In other words, good control over the EONIA affords good control of the stance.

The fracture between the MRO rate and the EONIA, and the reinterpretation of the 'separation principle' that this phenomenon necessitated, were consequential. On the one hand, the effective stimulus injected between October 2008 and May 2009 was larger than registered by the series of discretionary reductions in the MRO rate over the same period. On the other hand, the ample swings to which the daily behaviour of the EONIA became subject to some extent diminished the power of propagation of the monetary policy loosening that was being applied. Below, we seek to quantify the extent to which these conflicting tendencies amplified and attenuated stimulus, respectively.

4.5.2 Stimulus Amplifiers

Between October 2008 and May 2009, the ECB cut its main refinancing rate by 325 bps. But, if measured by the concomitant drop of the EONIA, the easing of the stance was in fact more proactive, and closer to 400 bps. No doubt, the stimulus was massive and highly concentrated in time. Its propagation to the real economy faced two cross-currents, one amplifying the impact of the extraordinary monetary treatment that was being applied, and one restraining it.

The amplifier of transmission was certainly associated with the ECB's bold pledge that it would exercise the central bank's traditional role of last-resort provider of liquidity to sound financial institutions without restrictions. There were no restrictions on the amount of central bank credit that a solvent credit institution could secure in weekly operations against eligible collateral. And the ECB progressively extended the maturity at which such unlimited liquidity was made available to the counterparties. In doing so, the ECB enhanced the stability of the euro area financial system, defused the threat that financial institutions might respond to the funding crunch and lack of visibility about their ability in the future to borrow funds when necessary by curtailing credit to the broader economy and, indirectly, reduced the overall cost of capital to banks.

What would have happened if the demand for liquidity had not been satisfied unboundedly in the Eurosystem liquidity-providing operations? We simulate the extreme case, in which the Eurosystem—in keeping with the pre-crisis practice of variable rate tender procedures—would have allowed the preset allotments at its liquidity-providing operations to increase at the same pace as the estimated 'liquidity needs' narrowly defined. The latter aggregate quantifies the minimum volumes of liquidity borrowing that would have just enabled banks to fulfil their minimum reserve requirements and cover for changes in the public's demand for banknotes and for autonomous variations in the accounts held by some governments at their national central banks. As explained more extensively in Box 4.2, in pre-crisis times, such estimated 'liquidity needs' were the main reference statistic used to calibrate the preset volume of liquidity supply in the weekly refinancing operations.

Specifically, we run counterfactuals with the CMR model to assess the impact of the liquidity measures. To separate out the specific impact of FRFA from the concomitant expansion of the spectrum of maturities at which liquidity was provided in unlimited volumes we proceed in incremental steps: the first counterfactual singles out the impact of the maturity extension, and the second turns to quantify the impact of FRFA per se.

To assess the role played by the maturity extension we note that the announcement of the maturity extension has left an imprint in the model estimates in the form of an accommodative expected (signal) component of the monetary policy shock process, which also helps explain the smaller-than-usual increase in the spread between the ten-year long-term rate and the short-term rate. Typically, an expected policy shock has very little impact on the long-term interest rate in the euro area. We compute the impact of maturity extension by counterfactually assuming that the expected component of policy and the spread would have behaved as typically found in response to a decline in the short-term rate.

To assess the impact of the FRFA we assume that the Eurosystem would have allowed the preset allotments at its liquidity-providing operations to increase at the same pace as the estimated 'liquidity needs'. The latter aggregate quantifies the minimum volumes of liquidity borrowing that would just enable banks to fulfil their minimum reserve requirements and to cover for changes in the public's demand for banknotes and for autonomous variations in the account held by some governments at their national central banks. Before the introduction of FRFA, such estimated liquidity needs were the main reference statistic used to calibrate the preset volume of liquidity supply in the weekly refinancing operations. Specifically, the counterfactual is implemented as follows: (i) we consider the estimated structural non-policy shocks after the third quarter of 2008 as a description of the environment faced by the euro area in presence of FRFA, the main feature of which is that the ECB accommodates any liquidity shock and therefore the money market interest rate remains insulated from such liquidity shocks; (ii) the model is re-estimated up to the third quarter of 2008 under the assumption of variable rate tender procedures;[30] (iii) the structural shocks recovered in (i) are fed into the baseline model under the counterfactual assumption that FRFA is not introduced in the fourth quarter of 2008;[31] (iv) we manipulate the unexpected component of the policy shock process to generate an alternative for the outstanding volumes of Eurosystem refinancing operations, which are counterfactually forced to grow at a constant rate reflecting the average growth rate of the liquidity needs over the pre-crisis period.[32]

The results of the two scenarios are portrayed in Figure 4.19 and correspond to the dotted line (no-long-term-operation counterfactual) and the dashed-dotted line (no-FRFA counterfactual) in the panels. In particular, the difference between the solid line and the dashed-dotted line is our measure of the impact of the shift to an FRFA procedure for auctioning liquidity. The difference between the solid line and the dotted line measures instead the pure impact of the lengthening of the maturities of monetary policy operations, under the assumption that, had the maturity spectrum not been expanded, the ECB would have provided liquidity in unlimited amounts in its weekly operations nonetheless. According to the counterfactual exercises, the maximal impact of the non-standard policy interventions was associated with the switch to the FRFA tender procedure (the dashed-dotted line). Given the

[30] This is accomplished by modifying the policy rule in CMR in order to add a latent shock, which in the model captures banks' demand for central bank liquidity. In the estimation, this shock is identified with the total outstanding stock of Eurosystem refinancing operations, which is included in the set of observables. The coefficient attached to this shock in the policy rule thus measures the sensitivity of the money market rate to money market liquidity conditions. We find that this estimated elasticity is positive and significant in the pre-crisis period. However, in that sample we also find that the demand-liquidity shock (which by assumption would have no impact on the money market rate under the FRFA regime adopted in the fourth quarter of 2008) contributes very little to explaining the variance of the money market interest rate also in the pre-Q4 2008 sample, in the order of less than 0.5%. The reason is that shocks to liquidity were typically small in the pre-Q4 2008 sample at the quarterly frequency we use in the CMR. The implication is that the simplifying assumption we have made in our baseline specification of setting to zero the reaction of the money market rate to the demand-liquidity shock also in the pre-Q4 2008 sample does not affect the inference we have presented in this book. However, had the Eurosystem not adopted FRFA as of the fourth quarter of 2008, the impact would have been very adverse (as shown in the counterfactual) because the liquidity-demand shock during that period became very large.
[31] This is implemented by assuming that the elasticity of the money market rate to the liquidity-demand shock corresponds to the one estimated for the pre-Q4 2008 sample.
[32] We abstract from the possible role of the marginal lending facility rate in capping the EONIA, implicitly assuming that the path followed by the MRO would have been different.

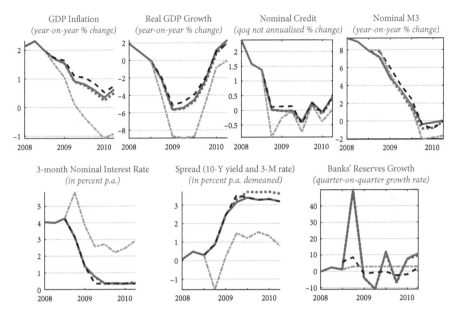

Figure 4.19 Impact of Eurosystem long-term and fixed rate full allotment (FRFA) operations: a model-based counterfactual analysis

Source: CMR.

Notes: The model simulations are carried out using the CMR. The blue line denotes the realized historical path; the red dashed-dotted line denotes the counterfactual path in absence of fixed rate full allotment (FRFA) operations; the blue dotted line denotes the counterfactual path in the absence of longer-term refinancing operations; the black dashed line denotes the counterfactual in which it is assumed that the ECB provides forward guidance.

Latest observation: 2010Q2.

positive elasticity of the overnight interest rate in the counterfactual feedback relationship underlying the dashed-dotted line, and the constraint forced on the model that, under variable rate tenders, liquidity supply should satisfy no more than the banks' 'liquidity needs', this result is perhaps unsurprising. Note that these two features of our simulations mean that the unprecedented increase in the demand for liquidity observed in the quarters following the financial collapse would have exercised strong upward pressure on the overnight interest rate. That upward pressure on the cost of borrowing and the lack of liquidity would have unleashed a severe deleveraging process (see the credit panel) through which banks would have sought to align their liquidity needs to the size of their balance sheets by shrinking the latter. This process would have resulted in severe downside risks to price stability and in a deeper contraction than was actually observed.

4.5.3 Stimulus Dampeners

The unpredictability of the EONIA was a factor that probably worked in the opposite direction, dampening transmission. As we saw before, the decline in the level of the

EONIA at times exceeded the decline in the MRO rate. But, due to the width of the corridor, the daily volatility of the EONIA increased measurably in the highly perturbed conditions of the months following the autumn of 2008. The effective federal funds rate—the EONIA's equivalent in the US money market—was very volatile at the start of the financial crisis too, but its volatility subsided before long, as massive injections of liquidity through the Federal Reserve's large-scale asset purchases soon saturated banks' reserve demand (see Figure 4.20 Panel A and B). In the euro area, by contrast, the excess reserves created in the Eurosystem longer-term operations were not sufficient to stabilize overnight conditions, and the erratic behaviour of the overnight index persisted.[33]

EONIA was erratic because the amount of excess liquidity available to the system as a whole was particularly variable—always conditional on banks' noisy bidding behaviours in the weekly and longer-term operations—and banks' willingness to transact that amount of excess liquidity in the interbank market was also subject to sudden turns in sentiment. Figure 4.20 shows that this enduring volatility of the EONIA was probably costly in terms of foregone accommodation. What does excess volatility in the overnight market have to do with accommodation? When marketeers are more exposed to unpredictable changes in returns, they require higher premia to bear this extra risk. *Ceteris paribus*, this pushes up the long-term interest rate, even if expectations of future short rates are unchanged. In other words, the so-called term premium on long-term bonds—the difference in expected returns between a buy-and-hold strategy for the longer-dated bond and an instantaneous roll-over strategy at the risk-free rate—increases.

In the specific case at hand, those OIS market participants paying the fixed interest rate leg and receiving a particularly unpredictable EONIA in exchange in swap contracts were carrying more risk than they would have been exposed to if the EONIA had been anchored more effectively at the floor of the rate corridor—or at any other level, for that matter. That extra risk was remunerated by a bigger term premium. As a result, the OIS curve—made of the fixed interest rate legs of those swap contracts indexed to the EONIA with various maturities—was probably steeper and noisier than would otherwise have been the case. Panel B shows how an erratic EONIA translates into more variable term interest rates, and Panel D shows the high correlation between the term premium embodied in long-term OIS rates and the volatility of money market rates.[34] Steeper and more volatile yield curves are undesirable when price stability is at risk, the economy is struggling, and the central bank thus wants to drive long-term interest rates lower.

---

[33] Developments following the 7 May announcement are revealing. In spite of a reduction in the MRO rate to 1% and the DFR being kept constant at 0.25%, EONIA jumped to a level of around 0.75% and continued to increase to reach 1.15% (above the MRO rate) at the end of May, a level that was 50 bps higher than two months earlier, when the MRO rate was still 1.5%. Note that the MRO rate was not providing an effective ceiling to the overnight market rate because the main refinancing operations were not a standing facility, i.e. they were not daily, but weekly backstops.

[34] For a given path of expected short-term interest rates, the term premium is a measure of the steepness of the term structure of interest rates.

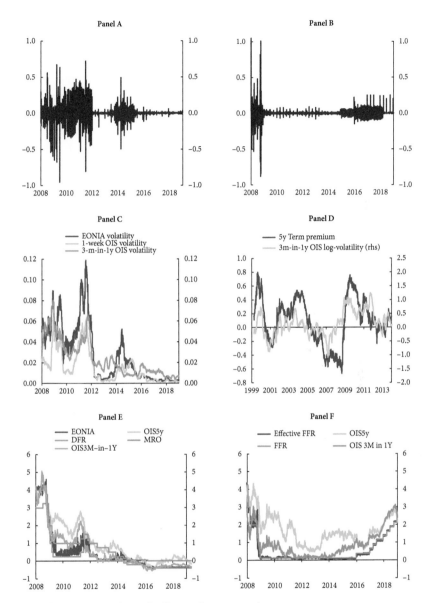

Figure 4.20 Money market volatility and term premium

Panel A: EONIA daily changes (percentage points)

Panel B: Effective FFR, daily changes (percentage points)

Panel C: Money market volatility in the EA (percentage points)

Panel D: Term premium vs money market volatility, conditional on general level or interest rate (percentage points)

Panel E: EA Short and longer-term money market rates (percentages per annum)

Panel F: US Short and longer-term money market rates (percentages per annum)

Sources: Bloomberg, ECB, and Refinitiv.

Latest observation: 31 December 2018 for Panels A–C, E and F; December 2013 for Panel D.

The sluggishness and mean-reversion of market participants' expectations of the future path of the ECB's policy rates also had the effect of diluting the stimulus that was being injected. The GC's commitment to 'never pre-commit' might have played a part in fostering expectations that the ECB would act to temper accommodation as soon as it saw nascent signs of an economic recovery. This effect might have worked through the expectations hypothesis component of long-term yields, namely the fraction of a term interest rate with a given maturity that reflects the average return that investors expect to earn by rolling over a series of, say, one-week bills for the same term to maturity.

In fact, after some initial downward reaction to the 7 May announcement, this measure of short rate expectations started to ratchet higher. The level of the three-month OIS rate one year forward—as we saw before, a good gauge of the level at which market participants expected to see the very short end of the OIS curve one year hence—reached 1.5% soon after, implying that the ECB was seen as likely to hike rates at least twice in the next 12 months. As long-term interest rates are made of the expectations hypothesis component plus the term premium, the restrictive potential of this knee-jerk response in rate expectations was compounded by the concomitant sharp increase in the term premium and pushed up the level of long-term interest rates, as shown in Figure 4.20 Panel D. This being said, one has to recognize two facts. First, on announcing what turned out to be the last of a series of emergency rate reductions in May 2009, President Trichet insisted that the GC decision did not imply that the ECB key interest rates had reached the 'lowest level that can never be crossed'. In other words, markets should not necessarily have inferred from the 7 May announcement that rates had reached their lower bound and could only be expected to rise from their current levels. As we shall see in the next chapter, this assumption of a non-negativity restriction constraining the rate path on the downside is typically a major factor that explains why the money market curve tends to steepen when central banks cut rates to levels close to zero. Indeed, market commentary at the time interpreted the introduction of non-standard measures such as the very long-term lending operation and outright purchases of securities as signalling that the rate corridor had reached its effective lower bound and that, moving forward from that point, any further easing would have to come solely through liquidity measures.[35] Second, the steepening of the expected path of interest rates was not a phenomenon exclusive to the euro area. It happened in the United States

---

[35] The low level of the EONIA aroused mixed feelings within the ECB. Some feared that very low interest rates would cause disruptions for money market funds and for money market activity in general, and that they would stoke financial stability risks, diminish the incentives for balance sheet repair and delay the necessary deleveraging by both the financial and non-financial sectors. They also foresaw negative implications for bank profitability and for the incentive of fiscal authorities to consolidate. Others saw the fall in the EONIA as adding accommodation almost by stealth, thus relieving pressure to reduce the pivot interest rate, the MRO rate, much further. All told, the balance of opinion was in favour of setting a floor for the MRO rate at 1%, the level that it actually reached on 7 May. Such a configuration offered a balance between, on the one hand, the need to provide stimulus to the economy via the interest rate channel (in order to improve the outlook for price stability) and, on the other, the need to limit the costs related to very low levels of interest rates.

as well, despite the Federal Reserve's generous use of rate forward guidance, if only qualitative in its formulation. Figure 4.20 Panel F shows that a similar bump formed in the time profile of forward interest rates nine months ahead in the US money market. The ongoing sharp appreciation of the euro was, however, a sign that, despite sticky anticipation of an imminent rate hike in the United States, the rate constellation was seen as favouring euro-denominated investments. An interesting question—in the light of the ensuing history of the ECB's policies—is the following: how could the economy have changed course if the ECB had utilized the novel 12-month operations as a 'signalling tool' to message an intention to maintain the policy rates at low levels for the entire life of the facilities? Figure 4.19 documents the result of a counterfactual in which it is assumed that the EONIA is stabilized at 0.35% and that the ECB signals that it will remain at that level over the following quarters. We find that this could have provided support to economic activity and inflation in the order of 0.5 and 0.2 percentage points, respectively.

In conclusion, the emergence of a positive—though by no means steady—spread between the MRO rate and the EONIA provided some middle ground on which two conflicting positions within the ECB could meet and reconcile: the position of those who thought that liquidity conditions might, in a scenario of rapidly rising inflation, have become too ample, sticky, and difficult to reign in; and those who looked favourably at the same situation, as it gave a freer hand to buy more time for the system to work off the destructive effects of financial instability.[36] Overall, the 'separation principle' contributed to—and was a reflection of—the conviction that liquidity measures could to some extent at least substitute for interest rate action, and that the demand for liquidity in the money market was a good gauge for evaluating whether the stance of monetary policy was adequate or otherwise.

4.6 Uneven Recovery

During the summer of 2009, many of the forces that had acted as severe headwinds for the euro area economy over the most acute phase of the financial crisis started to generate tailwinds. In the United States, consumption rebounded and the housing market stabilized, thus removing a factor that had acted as a major source of distress for the United States and the global economy over the previous two and a half years. In the meantime, reinvigorated global demand—boosted by expansionary monetary

---

[36] These two positions can be illustrated by two quotations. Speaking in Frankfurt in November 2010, Jürgen Stark said: 'Through the adoption of fixed-rate full allotment in the longer-term refinancing operations the EONIA has been deviating from the main refinancing rate and has been closer to the deposit rate. With a normalization in financial markets the demand for excess liquidity is dropping, so that the withdrawal of non-standard measures can proceed. As a result the EONIA will ultimately return to levels around the main refinancing rate. Hence, the separation principle will be fully re-established.' In reply to a question on 14 January 2010, President Trichet said, with reference to the drop in the value of the EONIA towards the DFR: 'As I have already said, it is obvious that this would be the case. We accept it fully. It is part of market functioning and we consider it to be fully in line with our monetary policy.'

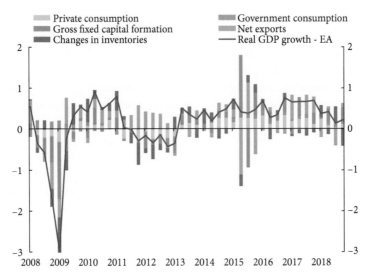

Figure 4.21 Contribution to euro area quarter-on-quarter real GDP growth (percentage points)

Source: Eurostat.

Latest observation: 2018Q4.

and fiscal measures in the United States and fiscal expansion in China—was providing strong support to the export-oriented euro area companies.

The upward revisions to the foreign economic outlook were also pulling forward expectations that the ECB would be quick withdrawing stimulus in reaction to positive macroeconomic spillovers from overseas, and this helps explain the relentless appreciation of the euro in the course of 2009 and 2010. But, the increasing international value of the single currency did not prevent net exports from becoming—together with a favourable turn in the inventory cycle—a key supporting engine of euro area growth throughout the recovery (see Figures 4.21 and 4.22). Despite some choppiness in financial markets, borrowing conditions in the capital market eased (see Figures 4.23 and 4.24), and the degree to which banks were tightening their credit terms fell steeply in the second half of 2009. The pass-through of the 12-month fixed rate operations of June and September became visible by year-end—including in a less noisy and lower average level of the EONIA, and a flatter term structure of money market rates. That evidence consolidated in the course of the following year.[37]

---

[37] The situation in financial markets and in the money market specifically looked sufficiently comfortable (albeit uncomfortably loose for some) to lead some of the staff to suggest in December 2009 that excess liquidity should be gradually phased out in line with the monetary policy strategy. According to this view, the provision of substantive longer-term refinancing operations would need to be scaled back gradually if the underlying reasons motivating them faded away, and the continuation of non-standard measures which were no longer needed might even be counterproductive, as they could hamper the functioning and delay the full recovery of the money market. It was thus important to return eventually to steering overnight interest rates with the MRO rate. In this regard, re-establishing over time a shorter

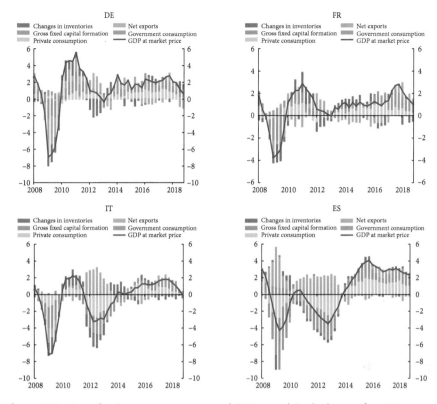

Figure 4.22 Contribution to year-on-year real GDP growth in the largest four EA economies (percentage points)

Source: Eurostat.

Latest observation: 2018Q4.

On the back of this heartening but still tentative evidence, the GC reassured the public on 3 December 2009 that the Eurosystem would continue to conduct its MROs as fixed rate tender procedures with full allotment for as long as needed, and at least until April 2010, a date that the GC extended to October 2010 at its meeting on 4 March 2010. At the same time, between December 2009 and March 2010, the number of three-month operations was reduced, the six-month operation was discontinued, and the interest rate to be applied in the last 12-month LTRO to be settled in December was fixed at the average minimum bid rate over the life of the operation. In other words, the signalling content of the previous two one-year fixed-rate operations was removed. Furthermore, on 4 March 2010, the GC announced

average maturity of the ECB's refinancing operations would help to regain flexibility, particularly with respect to the control of liquidity and the steering of short-term interest rates, and would ensure the efficient implementation of monetary policy. As for the pricing of the December 12-month LTRO, the case was made to index the cost of borrowing to the MRO rate prevailing during the life of the operation in order to avoid a situation where the use of the current MRO rate amounted to a downward movement in the money market yield curve and a loosening of the monetary policy stance, which was seen as unwarranted. A fixed rate LTRO, these experts argued, would send an undesired policy signal suggesting the policy rate would remain unchanged until the end of 2010.

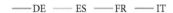

Figure 4.23 Equity prices in the largest four euro area economies (index)
Source: Refinitiv.

Latest observation: December 2018.

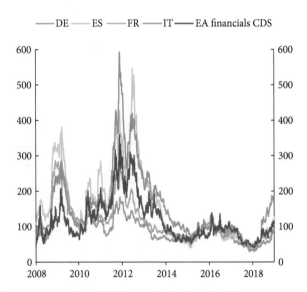

Figure 4.24 Corporate bond and CDS spreads (basis points)
Sources: IHS Markit iBoxx and iTraxx.

Notes: Country indices depict investment grade corporate bond spread indices from iBoxx, the EA financials CDS depicts the Europe Senior Financials CDS index from iTraxx.

Latest observation: 31 December 2018.

the return to variable rate tender procedures in the regular three-month LTROs, although with the pledge that 'allotment amounts in these operations [would] be set with the aim of ensuring smooth conditions in money markets and avoiding any significant spreads between bid rates and the prevailing MRO rate'. [38]

The brightening of the landscape was evident. At the same time, improvements in the euro area were uneven across market segments and member countries. We mentioned previously the split between those banks that had regained market access and those becoming chronically reliant on Eurosystem liquidity assistance, the 'persistent bidders'. Monetary developments also offered a contradictory picture, with loans to households expanding at a fair pace and loans to non-financial enterprises still contracting. But, at the turn of 2009 and 2010, fault lines started to form along country borders. Cross-country asymmetries, a phenomenon that had been contained for the first ten years of monetary union, were coming to analysts' attention and tempering optimism about the prospects of the euro area economy. The external impulse was asymmetric in the way it was reaching and stimulating different member countries, being very robust for Germany and muted for Spain (compare the contribution from net export across countries as shown in Figure 4.22). Credit easing by banks—both actual and expected—was very apparent in France, while Spanish banks continued to tighten conditions well into 2010 (see Figure 4.25).

The costs of borrowing in the bond market for fiscal authorities, once uniform across member countries regardless of the issuer's credit standing, started to diverge dramatically. The premium paid by Ireland—whose contingent liabilities vis-à-vis the teetering national banking system were seen as very sizeable relative to GDP—had widened since the Lehman crisis. But revelations from Athens in the course of October 2009 that Greece had grossly understated its debt and deficit figures for years—and, at 12.5%, the deficit was in fact almost twice as large as previously recorded—sent the euro area sovereign bond market into another acute phase of risk repricing. The news acted as a powerful crisis detonator: it alerted investors to the possibility that the EU cross-country peer surveillance architecture was a porous and fragile construction, and fiscal rules could be violated for long periods of time without setting off system-wide alarms. As a consequence of these revelations, the spread between the Greek and German bond yields surged to 275 bps by the middle of December, pulling the Portuguese bond yield differentials in the same direction.

On 3 March the Greek government unveiled a package of radical fiscal consolidation measures to reassure the markets, receiving official support on 25 March from the *college* of the Heads of States and Government of the Euro Area. The 25 March declaration stated that:

Euro area member states reaffirm their willingness to take determined and coordinated action, if needed, to safeguard financial stability in the euro area as a

---

[38] The ECB was not alone in feeling the urge to scale down its extraordinary liquidity measures in an attempt 'to avoid distortions associated with maintaining non-standard measures for longer than needed' (ECB, 2010). In parallel, the Federal Reserve System unexpectedly discontinued its own asset purchase programme, triggering a sharp strengthening of the dollar.

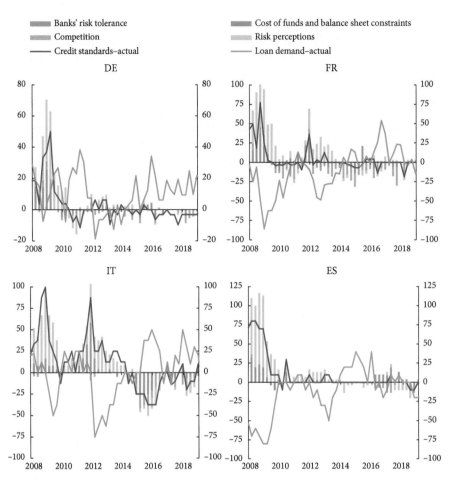

Figure 4.25 Changes in credit standards applied to the approval of loans or credit lines to enterprises, and contributing factors (net percentages of banks reporting tightening credit standards and contributing factors, and net percentages of banks reporting an increase in demand)

Source: ECB Bank Lending Survey.

Notes: Net percentages are defined as the difference between the sum of the percentages of banks responding 'tightened considerably' and 'tightened somewhat' and the sum of the percentages of banks responding 'eased somewhat' and 'eased considerably'. The net percentages for responses to questions related to contributing factors are defined as the difference between the percentage of banks reporting that the given factor contributed to a tightening and the percentage reporting that it contributed to an easing. 'Cost of funds and balance sheet constraints' is the unweighted average of 'costs related to capital position', 'access to market financing' and 'liquidity position'; 'risk perceptions' is the unweighted average of 'general economic situation and outlook', 'industry or firm-specific situation and outlook/borrower's creditworthiness' and 'risk related to the collateral demanded'; 'competition' is the unweighted average of 'competition from other banks', 'competition from non-banks' and 'competition from market financing'. Net percentages for the questions on demand for loans are defined as the difference between the sum of the percentages of banks responding 'increased considerably' and 'increased somewhat' and the sum of the percentages of banks responding 'decreased somewhat' and 'decreased considerably'. 'Risk tolerance' introduced in 2015Q1.

Latest observation: 2018Q4 (January 2019 BLS).

whole [...]. As part of a package involving substantial International Monetary Fund financing and a majority of European financing, Euro area member states are ready to contribute to coordinated bilateral loans. This mechanism, complementing International Monetary Fund financing, has to be considered ultima ratio, meaning in particular that market financing is insufficient. Any disbursement on the bilateral loans would be decided by the euro area member states by unanimity subject to strong conditionality and based on an assessment by the European Commission and the European Central Bank. We expect Euro-Member states to participate on the basis of their respective ECB capital key. The objective of this mechanism will not be to provide financing at average euro area interest rates, but to set incentives to return to market financing as soon as possible by risk adequate pricing. Interest rates will be non-concessional, namely not contain any subsidy element. Decisions under this mechanism will be taken in full consistency with the Treaty framework and national laws.

The declaration was important in that it established the principle of solidarity among members of the euro area. This was a principle that the ECB, as an active party to the negotiations, had been adamant in getting officially endorsed. In President Trichet's words: 'We all share a common destiny.'[39] And the statement was also significant because it carved out a unique role for the ECB within the European architecture, namely the role of principal technical adviser to the EU authorities in crisis management. It was a role that the institution maintained and strengthened throughout the sovereign debt crisis.

However, markets did not draw much comfort from the statement, and by mid-April, after the European authorities had agreed an assistance package, the spread of Greek yields over German yields reached 900 bps. The strains in the Greek bond market spread rapidly to the market for Portuguese bonds and generated some tremors in the Italian and Spanish sovereign debt markets as well (see Figure 4.26). The downgrade of Greece's credit rating by Standard & Poor's to below-investment grade at the end of April finally sent shockwaves across global asset markets. The financial turbulence that developed did not subside even as the parties, including the IMF, reached an agreement on a three-year financial assistance package for Greece worth €110 billion in an emergency Brussels summit on 2 May.[40] In fact, on Thursday 6 and Friday 7 May, the international financial markets went into a

---

[39] At the press conference following the GC meeting of 8 April 2010, President Trichet replied to a question in the following passionate way: 'We cannot run the euro area if there is no longer a responsibility on the part of the governments of the euro area countries, a responsibility, which is commanded by the Stability and Growth Pact. [...] It is essential that the governments fulfil their responsibilities. We are all interdependent. When there are important issues here or there, the euro itself moves. We all share a common destiny; wir teilen ein gemeinsames Schicksal.'

[40] Within the package, EU loans amounted to €80 billion, the rest being IMF credit. The loans were to be paid out in tranches until 2012, conditional on the implementation of a fiscal adjustment package of 11 percentage points of GDP over three years and structural reforms intended to restore competitiveness and growth.

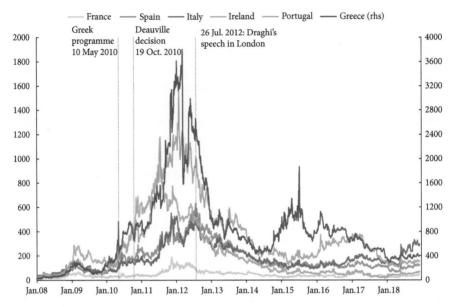

Figure 4.26 Ten-year sovereign spreads of selected euro area countries vis-à-vis the ten-year Bund yield (basis points)

Source: Bloomberg.

Latest observation: 31 December 2018.

tailspin, forcing a renewed round of declarations of intent and concrete policy initiatives worldwide.

4.7 The Spark Igniting the Debt Crisis

The ECB engaged in the last, tumultuous phase of initiatives at the European level with a threefold paradigm in mind (see González-Páramo, 2011a for a comprehensive description of the paradigm). First, the fiscal roots of financial distress were clear, and so was the ultimate remedy: fiscal consolidation. Second, if the debt crisis threatened the capacity of any Member State to remain up to date with its payment obligations in the near term, the community of peer Member States had to exercise euro-area solidarity and—under appropriate conditions—tide the country over until such time that fiscal stabilization was coming closer to fruition. Indeed, in the ECB's view, governments' creditworthiness was fundamental: it provided an unshakeable basis for the pyramid of credit in the nations and in the whole of the euro area. Third, if the new conditions should have any implications for the conduct of the ECB's monetary policy, that had to be judged on the basis of signs of financial contagion and on the potential for financial contagion to undermine the capacity of the ECB to transmit the monetary policy impulse adequately to the wider economy. Reflecting this principled orientation, the ECB took action in two directions. First, it joined the EU finance ministers who met in Brussels on 9/10 May in yet another emergency Economic and Financial Affairs (ECOFIN) Council summit with an elaborate proposal for a new institution, referred to by staff as the European Stability Mechanism (ESM). In the ECB's blueprint, the Member States would contribute capital to the new institution which, in turn, would issue bonds and extend credit to governments—in the form of bilateral loans or purchases of securities—under conditionality and seeking the co-participation by the IMF. The ECB would act as a facilitator for the activation of the ESM and could systematically participate in the monitoring of country compliance. The new institution would be designed in such a way as to forestall the risk of contagion, while fostering fiscal adjustment and preserving the integrity of monetary policy.[41] The intention guiding the ECB's proposal was to facilitate completion of the European construction, to render constructive actions by other policymakers in the fiscal and financial arenas outside the ECB's narrow remit more likely, and to make those actions more likely to succeed when undertaken. The scheme was debated at the summit, but legal impediments prevented the setting-up of a self-standing institution. Therefore, following frantic negotiations, in the early hours of 10 May the ECOFIN Council announced the creation of a pass-through mechanism called the European Financial Stability Facility (EFSF), based on Article 122.2 of the Treaty and on an intergovernmental agreement of euro area Member States.[42] The new facility had a lending capacity of €440 billion.

The other action by which the ECB sought to contribute to a constructive multilateral solution, and in parallel with the ECOFIN Council's declaration, was by issuing a press release on 10 May 2010 announcing 'several measures to address the severe tensions in certain market segments which are hampering the monetary policy transmission mechanism and thereby the effective conduct of monetary policy oriented towards price stability in the medium term' (ECB, 2010). The

---

[41] The proposal envisaged two alternative institutional structures. The first option was to establish the ESM—at least temporarily—under the aegis of the European Investment Bank (EIB). In this latter respect, note that Article 352 TFEU establishes a specific simplified amendment procedure for the EIB Statute, which could have provided the legal basis for enabling this new mechanism. A (preferred) alternative, however, was to establish the ESM as a new entity under the aegis of the Commission, on the basis of 'unused' funds (approximately, €60 billion). In order to lever up this limited amount of available resources to a scale that could help face the new wave of financial contagion effectively, these funds would be conferred to the ESM as own capital, thus allowing the new institution to build up a larger pool of resources to be mobilized in case of need. Staff argued that the new scheme offered the following advantages: (1) it would tackle the crisis at root, namely as a run on national debts originating in a loss of confidence in national fiscal sustainability rather than a negative demand shock giving rise to deflationary pressures, which would justify monetary easing; (2) it would establish a mechanism for the resolution of sovereign crises which could be activated at short notice in the immediate future but would be a lasting institution for the European Union in the future; (3) it would ensure that short-term intervention would not come at the price of generating moral hazard, if it were clear that the early release of funds would not lessen the willingness of national authorities to agree to and apply strong conditionality; (4) it could be achieved without a change to the Treaty.

[42] Article 122.2 TFEU states: 'Where a Member State is in difficulties or is seriously threatened with severe difficulties caused by natural disasters or exceptional occurrences beyond its control, the Council, on a proposal from the Commission, may grant, under certain conditions, Union financial assistance to the Member State concerned. The President of the Council shall inform the European Parliament of the decision taken.'

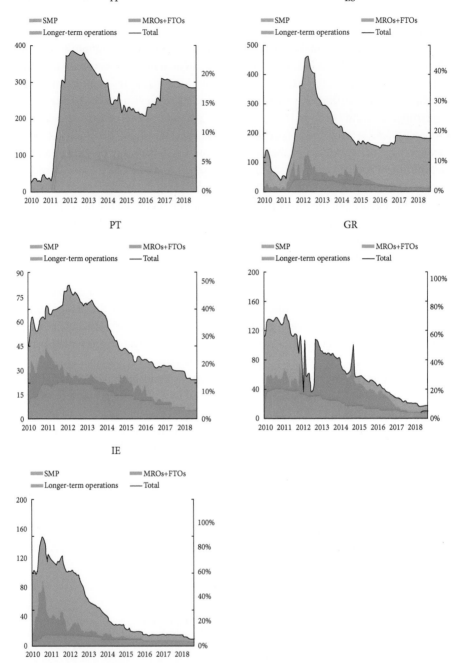

Figure 4.27 Eurosystem exposure to countries under the SMP (lhs in EUR billion; rhs in percentage of GDP of respective countries)

Source: ECB.

Notes: The item 'longer-term operations' includes all longer-term refinancing operations of maturity between one month and three years, together with TLTROs. The item 'MROs + FTOs' includes all Main Refinancing Operations with one-week maturity (MROs) and all Fine Tuning Operations (FTOs), but excludes Emergency Liquidity Assistance (ELA).

Latest observation: December 2018.

measures included going back to FRFA in the three-month operations, the conduct of a new six-month operation, reactivation of the temporary liquidity swap lines with the Federal Reserve and, most notably, interventions in the euro area public and private debt securities markets under (the new SMP) 'to ensure depth and liquidity in those market segments which are dysfunctional'. The press release adds:

Box 4.4 Impact of the Securities Market Programme—a literature review

Relatively few econometric studies focus exclusively on the impact of the ECB's Securities Market Programme (SMP), and only two of them work explicitly with Eurosystem-confidential data on country-specific purchase volumes. Eser and Schwaab (2016) deploy a dynamic factor model to capture ECB purchases of individual countries' bonds. The cross-section information and the factor structure help separate the impact of common trends from the impact of the SMP. Ghysels et al. (2016) tackle the econometric challenges of simultaneity (bond yields rising while SMP purchases are ongoing) and endogeneity (individual ECB bond purchases may have in principle reacted to specific yield constellations) by incorporating individual country SMP purchases in a high-frequency (intraday) VAR.

While those two studies (involving Eurosystem staff) were able to deploy granular data of Eurosystem holdings of government bonds purchased under the SMP, Eurosystem-external scholars had only the aggregate weekly holdings of the SMP at their disposal. As a proxy, De Pooter, Martin, and Pruitt (2018) and Jäger and Grigoriadis (2017) relied on country share estimates provided by commercial banks, while Trebesch and Zettelmeyer (2018) used Greek newspaper reports on the ECB's holdings of individual Greek bonds. Other studies used event study approaches, avoiding reliance on country-specific purchase volumes, and conducted a joint assessment of the SMP and other ECB non-standard measures. For instance, Krishnamurthy, Nagel, and Vissing-Jorgensen (2017) analyse the SMP, OMT, and LTROs, Szczerbowicz (2015) includes in addition the first and second covered bond purchase programmes, while Falagiarda and Reitz (2015) also consider announcements on fixed rate full allotment and the extended collateral framework as events. All empirical studies agree that the SMP had a significant announcement effect. They indicate that this effect was largest for bond yields and spreads of those jurisdictions for which purchases were expected to take place. Accordingly, a strong impact is found for Greece, Ireland and Portugal—and to a lesser extent for Italy and Spain—following the 10 May 2010 announcement, and for Italy and Spain following the 8 August 2011 announcement.[43] Purchase flows as such were found to matter as

(Continued)

---

[43] Eser and Schwaab (2016) document a five-year yield decrease of 773 (Greece), 139 (Ireland) and 226 (Portugal) bps upon the first SMP announcement and of 97 (Spain) and 93 (Italy) bps on the second announcement, whereas German Bund yields remained broadly unchanged.

Box 4.4 Continued

well, and the smaller the outstanding volume of bonds, the larger the yield impact per nominal purchase volume turned out to be.[44] Scaling SMP purchases accordingly, Eser and Schwaab (2016) find an approximately 3-basis-point yield reduction for five-year maturity bonds per 0.1 percentage point purchase of outstanding debt. A similar result is obtained by DePooter et al. (2018), while Trebesch and Zettelmeyer (2018) find somewhat weaker results in their analysis focusing on Greece. Those studies using dynamic time series models also allow for an assessment of cumulated yield reductions. For the overall duration of the SMP, Ghysels et al. (2016) estimate the yield impact on two-year Italian and Spanish debt to be about 3.2 and 1.8 percentage points respectively, and to be around 2.3 percentage points for the ten-year maturity. Eser and Schwaab (2016) report cumulative effects for the five-year maturity of 1.9 (Spain), 3.3 (Greece), 0.1 (Ireland), 2.1 (Italy) and 1.7 (Portugal) percentage points respectively. Taking a more detailed assessment beyond measuring the yield or spread effect, De Pooter et al. (2018) and Eser and Schwaab (2016) confirm that the SMP helped improve bond market liquidity conditions for the jurisdictions included in the SMP.[45] As regards a potential policy rate signalling channel, Eser and Schwaab (2016) do not find evidence of the SMP affecting short-term interest rate expectations. The same authors also evidence that volatility and priced tail risk have decreased on SMP intervention days.

Finally, those papers conducting a joint assessment on the SMP and other ECB non-standard measures confirm the yield compression effect for the selected countries. In addition, Krishnamurthy et al. (2017) note stock price increases concomitant with SMP, OMT and LTRO events. The authors take these increases to be as a token of 'beneficial macro-spillovers' of those non-standard measures. Szczerbowicz (2015) notes a spillover of SMP bond purchases (and OMTs) to covered bond spreads and concludes that the purchase programmes were effective in lowering banks' longer-term financing costs.

'The objective of this programme is to address the malfunctioning of securities markets and restore an appropriate monetary policy transmission mechanism.' Concerning the perimeter of the SMP interventions, in preparatory work staff had contemplated two options: outright purchases in the bond markets of *all* countries in proportion to the shares of the ECB capital held by the respective central banks; or purchases targeted at those debt markets that were seen as most affected by financial contagion. The former solution was preferred, although its 'monetary easing' side effects were to be avoided and the potentially large amounts of liquidity created in the process were to be sterilized. As it happened, the 10 May press release

---

[44] For instance, Eser and Schwaab (2016) find that for €1billion of SMP purchases, five-year yields decreased by 1 to 2 bps (Italy) and 16 to 21 bps (Greece).

[45] By contrast, Trebesch and Zettelmeyer (2018) do not find any impact on liquidity for Greek debt.

maintained some ambiguity regarding the perimeter of the programme, stating that 'the scope of the interventions will be determined by the Governing Council', although it added that the GC had 'taken note of the statement of the euro area governments that they "will take all measures needed to meet [their] fiscal targets this year and the years ahead in line with excessive deficit procedures" and of the precise additional commitments taken by some euro area governments to accelerate fiscal consolidation and ensure the sustainability of their public finances', thus hinting at the possibility that the programme was targeted at jurisdictions whose governments had committed to concrete macroeconomic adjustment measures.

The sterilization component of the staff proposal was retained, and the announcement made clear that 'specific operations will be conducted to re-absorb the liquidity injected through the Securities Markets Programme'. In line with the separation principle, the announcement went on to say: 'This will ensure that the monetary policy stance will not be affected.'

Markets greeted the new measures euphorically, and bond spreads for countries most affected by the debt runs plunged on Monday 10 May. But the respite was short-lived. Sovereign spreads for Greece, Portugal, and Spain resumed their widening trend throughout the month, and tensions moved, for the first time in a year, to the corporate bond segment and the money market, where the differential between the unsecured term EURIBOR and the OIS rate of matching maturities increased (see Figure 4.16). Fundamentally, analysts were having doubts that, despite the large assistance programme, Greece was on a clear path to debt sustainability, given that credit restrictions in the country and the sharp fiscal tightening had contributed to a recession in the Greek economy, with nominal GDP anticipated to fall steeply. Reflecting this scepticism, in June Moody's downgraded Greece citing substantial macroeconomic and implementation risks associated with the euro area/IMF support package. In parallel, bond traders began to learn about the ECB's actual presence in the market under SMP. As evidence accumulated about the likely size and time profile of the official interventions in the distressed jurisdictions, investors grew concerned that the programme might fall short of the minimal scale that, in their assessment, would be necessary to decisively eradicate the fear that was gripping the sovereign bond market (for a detailed literature review of the impact of SMP on financial markets, see Box 4.4).[46]

Most importantly, a vicious circle—once only apparent in Ireland—started to become visible in all the countries where the run on the local sovereign debt had caused losses in banks' bond portfolios. There were multiple feedback channels in the vicious circle. Balance sheet losses meant that credit institutions needed to draw

---

[46] At the press conference following the GC meeting of 10 June 2010, in response to a question about the size and jurisdictions of purchases, President Trichet replied: 'You could see that the first week we withdrew approximately €16.5 billion, the second week €10 billion more, the third week an additional €8.5 billion, in the fourth week €5.5 billion. So you have this information. We withdraw exactly the level of liquidity that we inject. No other indication.' Inside the ECB, views differed concerning the size and duration of SMP. While some were of the opinion that large demonstrative interventions were essential at an early stage to stem the crisis, others were convinced that the programme was to be seen as a temporary, auxiliary 'market making' device until a more fundamental solution could be found. According to this view, it would be preferable to reconsider continuing the programme once the EFSF was in place.

to a greater extent on existing government guarantees or were asking for new rounds of guarantees and capital injections. They were curtailing their exposures to the government to protect their credit standing. But the governments had seen their fiscal capacity shrink dramatically because of the debt runs, which had limited their ability to borrow. So, they had little budgetary space to deploy for the purpose of rescuing the banks. The fact that banks were disengaging—or planning to do so—from the national debt market was only aggravating their own funding crunch. Banks and sovereigns were locked in a deadly embrace, and the CDSs of banking institutions started to co-move one-for-one with the CDSs of their governments (see Figure 4.28). This was not the case in the US (see Figure 4.29). In the summer, this vicious circle began to affect the money market. The demand for liquidity in the Eurosystem refinancing operations from banks domiciled in Spain, Portugal, and Ireland increased materially (Figure 4.27), and their scramble for liquidity caused a renewed surge both in EONIA volatility and in the level and volatility of longer-term money market interest rates (see the bump in the one-week OIS rate in Figure 4.5 and the jump in the volatility of EONIA and term interest rates in Figure 4.20). Banks started to underbid in the weekly reserve-absorbing operations which had been set up to sterilize the SMP-generated liquidity.

At the German-French summit of 19 October 2010 in Deauville, Chancellor Merkel and President Sarkozy called for a permanent crisis resolution mechanism in Europe 'comprising the necessary arrangements for an adequate participation of the private sector'. In substance, they agreed that, after 2013, financial assistance to sovereigns would require that losses be imposed on their private creditors. The Deauville moment is clearly recognizable in Figure 4.26. Private investors, already

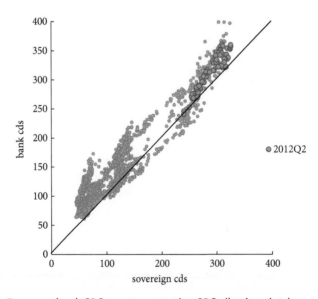

Figure 4.28 Euro area bank CDSs versus sovereign CDSs (basis points)
Source: Refinitiv.

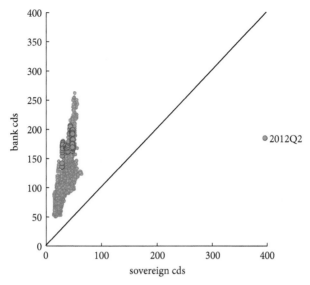

Figure 4.29 US bank CDSs versus sovereign CDSs (basis points)
Source: Refinitiv.

unnerved by the prospect of becoming increasingly junior to official creditors, inter-preted the announcement as an official signal that sovereign debt restructuring would henceforth be considered acceptable in EU countries. Bond yields of vulner-able sovereign issuers—now including also Spain and Italy—increased steeply on the news. The Irish sovereign bond yields rose above 7% over the following few days, making the further market borrowing necessitated by Ireland's bank bailout pro-gramme unrealistic at a time when the government deficit was already running at very high levels. Therefore, in November 2010 the Republic of Ireland became the second EU country to seek financial assistance from the EU, the EFSF, and the IMF. Portugal was to follow in April 2011.

4.7.1 The ESM Is Born

The ECB strongly disapproved of the Deauville approach to a crisis resolution mech-anism. As various ECB Executive Board members observed, it made no sense for the euro area to invent a doctrine for itself of automatic sovereign default that was not applied elsewhere in the world and would only be seen by investors as a self-imposed handicap (Trichet (2011a) and Bini Smaghi (2011b)).[47] Its vision for an institution

---

[47] At the 3 March Press Conference, President Trichet expressed frustration at the Deauville doctrine: 'Automaticity as regards private sector involvement is absolutely counterproductive. We have a global doctrine in this regard. If the Europeans were inventing a doctrine for Europe which put Europe in a

that could intermediate credit to distressed members with limited access to private refinancing had been articulated by staff ahead of the 9/10 May 2010 ECOFIN Council meeting. It did not contemplate a debt restructuring as a precondition for official lending. The May 2010 blueprint was further developed and refined in the context of the ECB's participation in the high-level Task Force on Economic Governance chaired by the then President of the European Council, Herman van Rompuy, and in the sherpa technical work that supported the Task Force during its lifetime between May and October 2010. So, when at the end of October 2010 President van Rompuy received a formal mandate from the Heads of State or Government of the EU Member States to undertake consultations on a limited Treaty change to establish a permanent crisis management framework to replace the EFSF, the ECB engaged in active promotion of its vision.[48] The new mechanism, according to the ECB, would be endowed with paid-in capital which it would lever up to provide financial assistance, in turn acting as a catalyst to restore vulnerable Member States' access to market financing and providing effective protection against market disruptions that were disconnected from underlying fundamentals. In the pursuit of this mission, the European Stability Mechanism (ESM)—as the new institution was to be named—would extend loans, including under precautionary arrangements, and make purchases of medium- to long-maturity bonds issued by the requesting Member State on the secondary market. The Eurogroup discussed the proposal throughout the first half of 2011, with broad endorsement but also with strong opposition expressed by a group of countries to precautionary lines and securities purchases. The opposition only relented as the debt crisis took a renewed turn for the worse in the summer of 2011.

4.8 2011

The year 2011 deserves a special mention in our (incomplete and partial) chronicle of the European debt crisis. As we saw, the year started under the worst auspices, with two more members under financial aid and surveillance. Although serious action was being taken to strengthen European economic governance, bond markets had become fundamentally disillusioned about the capacity of Europe to stabilize itself.

Faced with an outlook fraught with financial risks, over the last months of 2010 the ECB staff started to entertain the possibility of a double-dip recession. Past

vulnerable position by comparison with the rest of the world, this would be a very bad move. By the way, this has been avoided, because the doctrine adopted by European governments – which has been made public – sticks to the global doctrine, the IMF doctrine.'

[48] The view of staff, which shaped the position of the ECB on the crisis resolution framework, was that forcing a country into open default as a precondition for any type of assistance should not be part of any compromise scheme, as any such provision would fatally interfere with supervisory and Eurosystem collateral policies and would precipitate a financial crisis within monetary union, with uncontrollable ramifications.

experience suggested that in the aftermath of banking crises, wage pressures would be limited, low credit availability and high risk aversion would suppress investment, and consumption growth would be well below trend. Indeed, while euro area bank loans to non-financial enterprises were still running at negative annual growth rates, the strains in the money market and the effective closing-up of the traditional lender-of-last-resort channel of assistance from governments to banks in a group of countries were increasing the probability of an impending credit crunch in those economies.

However, the internal projections did not quite support either a negative base case or a bi-modal scenario. The economy was still judged a little less likely to grow faster than expected, than it was to face a new downturn. But the chances of a favourable outcome for growth had been consistently moving in the favourable direction. Although financial markets did not share this view, by the turn of the year, economic fundamentals appeared to be steadying in the euro area. Consumer confidence had recovered over recent months, and employment expectations were picking up (see Figures 4.31 and 4.32). In the first half of 2010, growth had vastly surprised on the upside, and the real-time composite PMI indicator in the second half of 2010 constantly ran ahead of expectations (see Figures 4.11 and 4.30). The euro area economy was seemingly disconnecting from the US economy—which was slowing as the fiscal stimulus faded—and was probably riding on the back of the strong revival of growth in China. Unsurprisingly, economic dynamism was concentrated in Germany, whose export penetration in the Chinese internal market had given the largest economy in the euro area a life jacket to keep it afloat in the turbulent waters of the unfolding European crisis. Overall, the gradual reintegration of unused resources into the production process in Germany and worldwide was starting to put pressure on the prices for raw material and energy. Headline HICP inflation was translating those pressures into an upward crawl so that, by the start of 2011, it had breached the 2% ceiling.

The fact that the landscape was fracturing across multiple dimensions—with even real-time conjunctural indicators exposing a deepening division between a 'core' and a 'periphery' within the euro area—was seen as a complication, not a reason to deflect from a euro area perspective. First, unlike in the midst of the worldwide synchronized macroeconomic collapse two years before, the euro area crisis in early 2011 was judged to be local and thus unlikely to spread or deepen. Second, to the extent that the macroeconomic malaise in the periphery was due to fiscal restriction, the slump in the peripheral economies was deemed to be transient and likely to be reversed as soon as the confidence effects associated with restored debt sustainability took hold among consumers, investors and market participants. Third, country heterogeneity encouraged analysts inside and outside the ECB to 'look to Germany as the reference or benchmark economy and to attribute underperformance in other euro area countries to self-imposed national policy errors', as Patrick Honohan—at the time a member of the GC—wrote recently (Honohan, 2018). National policy errors did not call for a monetary policy response. Finally, as is typical in post-crisis times, measurement of underlying activity was complicated by an exceptionally noisy inventory cycle (see Figures 4.21 and 4.22). Together with the long lags with which key real-economy information was available to the ECB decision-makers for their monetary policy deliberations, this led at times to inaccurate judgement about the genuine state of the economy. It unwittingly made the course of policy backward-looking rather than focused on the present- or forward-looking.

In those conditions, the potential asymmetry in the assessment of the relative costs of an observed inflation rate rising above 2% versus an inflation rate seen declining within the price stability range, which we discuss in Chapter 3, took hold and shaped policy to an extent that remains unparalleled to this date. The month-after-month climb in headline inflation attracted an outsized share of attention. Core inflation, steady at around 1%, and other measures of underlying inflation were still quiescent, with pay growth hovering around 2% (see Figure 4.33). Staff projected headline inflation to peak at 2.6% over the near term, but dip below the 2% line by the turn of the year and to stay within the price stability zone for the rest of the projection horizon (see the two green dotted lines in Figure 4.7).

Our ex post stochastic simulations confirm the staff assessment of the time. Figure 4.34 below shows the predictive distribution for inflation, taking into account the information available in the first quarter of 2011. As we did previously with respect to the quantification of risks to price stability at the start of 2008, we provide both the entire predictive distribution and one derived by removing the supply-side

Figure 4.30 PMI composite (index)
Source: IHS Markit.
Latest observation: December 2018.

Figure 4.31 EC Consumer confidence (index)

Source: European Commission.

Latest observation: December 2018.

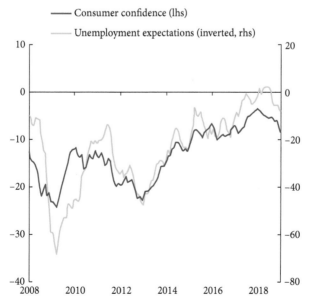

Figure 4.32 European Commission Consumer Survey (index)

Source: European Commission.

Latest observation: December 2018.

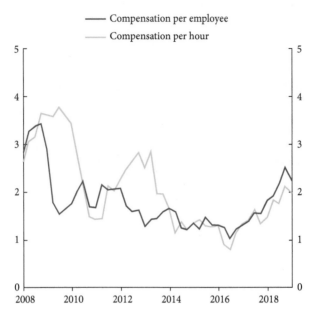

Figure 4.33 Measures of wage pressures (year-on-year % change)
Source: Eurostat.
Latest observation: 2018Q4.

forces that, according to the CMR model, were at work at the time. Unlike in the assessment for 2008, we fail to detect a positive tilt to either distribution. And we can confirm the view that the central tendency was indeed for the inflation path to turn downward and gently converge towards levels eventually below 2%, although over a more extended horizon—three years—than was relevant for the staff projections of the spring of 2011.

But staff had been under-predicting inflation in their forecasts, citing low domestic price pressures, ever since the summer of 2009 (see, again, Figure 4.7). Upstream inflation pressures were material—with producer prices increasing at an annual rate close to 6%—and were threatening to roll down and reach consumer prices sooner than probably was forecastable by the internal mechanical pass-through models. Furthermore, when run through the structural models used in internal risk analysis in real time, the inflationary environment of the early months of 2011, combined with a firming-up in domestic and foreign demand, was interpreted as entailing a distinct 'excess inflation risk' (see Box 4.3).

Therefore, in the run-up to the March GC monetary policy meeting, the upward path of inflation in the recent months and the prospects of further acceleration due to the upsurge in the price of oil swayed the balance of arguments in favour of bringing forward the start of policy normalization. To prepare the markets for the imminent move, in March the GC removed the downside skew to its assessment of the distribution of risks to future growth, something that had been a mainstay of the ECB's post-meeting communication ever since the Lehman crisis. The GC, however,

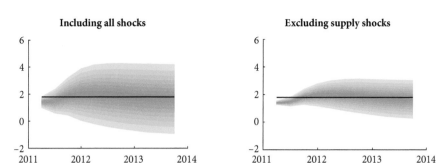

Figure 4.34   Stochastic simulations in 2011Q1: inflation looking forward (y-o-y %
change)
Source: CMR.

still recognized that the absolute dispersion of risks remained elevated. Most significantly, the GC tilted the balance of risks to prices to the upside. It was 'paramount
that the rise in HICP inflation [did] not lead to second-round effects and thereby
give rise to broad-based inflationary pressures over the medium term' in conditions
in which the large amounts of monetary liquidity accumulated in the economy prior
to the period of financial tensions might 'facilitate the accommodation of price pressures currently emerging in commodity markets as a result of strong economic
growth and ample liquidity at the global level'. Therefore, 'strong vigilance [was]
warranted with a view to containing upside risks to price stability'. Then, following
through on the March 'strong vigilance' pronouncement, on 7 April 2011 the GC
eventually increased the key ECB interest rates by 25 bps, 'after maintaining them
unchanged for almost two years at historically low levels', as it was acknowledged in
the President's introductory statement. Expectations had already converged on a 25
basis point rate hike in the month before the meeting and the reaction to this latest
decision was a further clustering around another hike by July.

Why did the ECB hike rates in the spring of 2011? The concern expressed by
many in internal debates was that yet another inflation overshoot would have
widened further the 'credibility deficit' that the ECB had been accumulating since its
inception. In July 2011, and despite the deep plunge in headline inflation in 2009,
average inflation since 1999 was hovering above 2%. The risk-neutral probability
density function—which staff were extracting from the prices of zero coupon inflation floors—indicated in July that the probability of observing inflation above 2%
over the next five years was nearly 50% (see Figure 5.2 in the next chapter). It was
not hard to claim at this point that the ECB's record of inflation misses went back far
enough to disqualify it as a central bank seriously striving to deliver inflation outcomes in line with the price stability definition.

Does this episode hold any lessons concerning the workings of a monetary policy
strategy founded on a price stability definition? We note a parallel between the price
stability definition strategy and a price level targeting framework. Contrary to an
inflation targeting regime, which would have required the ECB to simply guide

inflation back to target over time when faced by a string of one-sided supply shocks that temporarily drove up inflation, a regime based on a 'below 2%' price stability definition, when put under such stress for a sufficiently long period of time, de facto required the ECB eventually to seek policy settings that would reverse and neutralize such shocks in an attempt to demonstrate its commitment to the strategy. This approach made the ECB more akin to a price level targeting central bank than to one targeting forecast inflation. To be sure, to claim that the approach taken by the ECB in the spring of 2011 worked in the same way as it would have if the institution's strategy had *explicitly* required it to make up for past inflation misses would be to overstate the case. A price level targeting regime would have functioned differently at least in one regard: its ability to steer expectations. A full-blown, well-internalized version of price level targeting would probably have created the expectation among market participants and the public at large that episodes of inflation misses—both overshoots and undershoots—would lead in the future to 'make-up' monetary policy actions that could generate deviations in the other direction. This would have introduced a kind of 'history dependence' into policymaking which, as Woodford (2003) and many others have demonstrated, could have induced re-equilibrating adjustments in expectations. On the question of how a make-up strategy might work in practice, see Svensson (2019). Undeniably, the price stability definition frame-work lacked such types of self-correcting mechanisms. This being said, we believe that the price stability range regime might have yielded a history of inflation and macroeconomic outcomes on which analysts will be able to look back to form predictions as to how a price level targeting regime could work in practice when put under strain by sustained adverse shocks to supply.

4.8.1   Financial Instability

Historically, recessions tend to sow the seeds of their own recoveries, as reduced spending on investment and consumer durables generates pent-up demand. When the business cycle bottoms out and confidence returns, this pent-up demand is met through increased production and hiring. Increased production in turn boosts business revenues and increased hiring raises household incomes, providing further impetus to business and household spending. Improving income prospects and balance sheets also make households and businesses more creditworthy, while financial institutions become more willing to lend. In the spring of 2011, the business cycle had seemingly bottomed out and turned, but two critical elements in the typical progression from a recession to a self-sustained recovery were missing or fading in large regions of the euro area: balance sheet repair and confidence. The balance sheets of households and firms (notably in the construction sector) and credit institutions had worsened—not improved—in Spain. This was essentially due to the depressed conditions of the local housing market.

At the same time, the deep economic contraction had decimated Italy's fabled legions of small and micro-enterprises, many of which had been operating too close to break-even even in the tranquil years prior to the crisis, and thus were all too vulnerable to the subsequent major collapse in demand that came after. Consequently, Italian banks were accumulating bad loans at a rate unseen since the recession in the early 1990s.[49] Overall, balance sheet repair was going into reverse in those two countries, and the banks—the linchpins of financial intermediation—were reflecting the general deterioration in many agents' repayment capacity. Indeed, evidence provided in Albertazzi et al. (2016) and Angelini et al. (2017) using Italian data indicates that the steep deterioration in the balance sheet conditions of the banks was for the most part attributable to the recession. Accordingly, banks both in Italy and Spain started to report major obstacles to their access to funding, so that their borrowing in the Eurosystem operations increased steeply and reached unprecedented peaks, both in euro terms and as a percent of GDP (see Figure 4.27). Meanwhile, confidence was undermined by the persistent talk of an impending debt restructuring in Greece. Consultations to explore a 'reprofiling'—as the restructuring was referred to—of the Greek debt still in private hands had started in earnest at the European level, and the IMF had embarked on a softer initiative, called 'Vienna-II', to promote a voluntary roll-over of maturing Greek government securities by private sector holders. Despite official reassurances, the signal was unmistakable: the fear of 'private sector involvement'—code for haircuts on the nominal value of sovereign bonds outstanding—led bondholders to disinvest and market yields on Greek, Portuguese and Irish securities to soar. Indeed, Fitch and Moody's cited the increasing possibility of private sector involvement as a reason for the downgrades of the sovereign ratings of Portugal, Ireland and Greece on 5, 12 and 13 July respectively. Spain was affected too, and Italy, which had largely defied the contagion throughout most of 2010, finally recoupled to the trend in June 2011. The issuer of one of the largest and most liquid debts in the world, Italy faced a variety of domestic frailties, including a decade-long record of slow growth and entrenched political instability. In June, the daily infighting within the government of the time around the size and composition of a fiscal package big enough to reassure creditors heated up, and investors took note. On Thursday 7 July the ECB announced the second rate increase of the year, arguing that it remained 'of paramount importance that the rise in HICP inflation does not translate into second-round effects in price and wage-setting behaviour and lead to broad-based inflationary pressures'. With regard to the Greek debt restructuring, President Trichet, at his press conference, gave the follow-ing clarification: 'We are giving our own advice to governments as clearly as possible on the subject of private sector involvement, namely: "Don't depart from the global doctrine. If you depart from the global doctrine, you are weakening what you are

---

[49] The stock of non-performing loans rose precipitously between 2011 and 2015, reaching a peak in the latter year at €360 billion in gross terms (see Figure 4.35) and €200 billion in net terms.

aiming for—namely maintaining financial stability in Europe as a whole and in the euro area as a whole."[50]

The run on the Italian debt started in earnest on Friday 8 July and, on that day, the European crisis took on a systemic dimension. Contagion to Italy was a matter of grave concern to investors all over the world because of the sizeable international exposures to the country, and the multiple channels through which an Italian sovereign default could penetrate and destabilize the global financial system. Italian banks, despite their relatively good performance in the EBA stress test published on 15 July, came under intense selling pressure as market participants evaluated their exposures and vulnerabilities to a potential local default event. The decline in their shares led to a more general fall in European equities while the European iTraxx CDS Senior Financial Index—a broad index of financial credit default swaps—rose above the levels seen after the bankruptcy of Lehman Brothers and not far from the all-time high of 210 bps reached in March 2009, indicating that the cost of insuring bank debt had increased substantially (see Figure 4.24). The funding conditions of euro area banks, both in euro and dollars, in bond markets as well as in the money market, deteriorated materially as a result. But the contagion did not remain confined to the private credit markets. Soon, the CDS spreads of France, the Netherlands, Belgium, Austria, and Finland started edging up—a sign that the dissolution of the euro area was considered a likely contingency. Longer-term, so-called real-money investors such as pension funds and insurers were actively disinvesting from euro area sovereigns, including from France and Belgium.

Under pressure from the escalating tensions in the financial markets, the Heads of State or Government bowed to the inevitable and, at their summit of 21 July, approved the ECB's long-standing proposal to broaden the set of instruments available to the ESM to halt contagion. They allowed the ESM to grant a precautionary programme, to intervene in the secondary markets on the basis of an ECB analysis recognizing the existence of exceptional financial market circumstances and risks to financial stability, and to extend loans to governments earmarked for recapitalization of financial institutions. While the first two instruments were never activated, the last one was utilized—very successfully—in July 2012 to support Spain in its attempt to shore up the Spanish banking system. Upon President Trichet's insistence, the EU Council accepted de facto to shelve the Deauville agreement. The Private Sector Involvement (PSI) paragraph stated explicitly that

> we would like to make it clear that Greece requires an exceptional and unique solution. All other euro countries solemnly reaffirm their inflexible determination to honour fully their own individual sovereign signature and all their commitments to sustainable fiscal conditions and structural reforms. The euro area Heads of State or Government fully support this determination as the credibility of all their

---

[50] On the dynamics of contagion, by which an idiosyncratic fiscal crisis was mutating into a systemic threat, see Constâncio (2011), González-Páramo (2011b), and Bini-Smaghi (2011c).

sovereign signatures is a decisive element for ensuring financial stability in the euro area as a whole.[51]

Financial prices rebounded in response to the European Council announcement, but soon the sell-off resumed.[52] The ECB responded by conducting a supplementary six-month LTRO and extending assurances that FRFA would be applied in MROs and in the special-term refinancing operations with a maturity of one maintenance period until at least the end of the year. But the broadening of financial contagion and its increase in intensity raised the question of whether the SMP should be extended in scope.[53] So, after Spain and Italy announced fiscal measures and

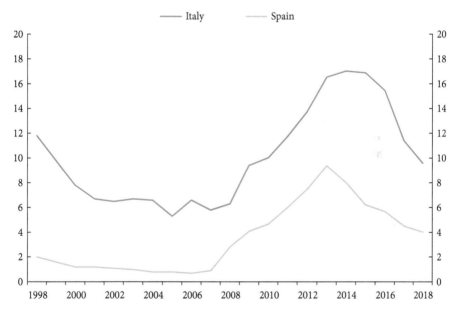

Figure 4.35 Bank non-performing loans to gross loans (percentage)
Sources: ECB Consolidated Banking Data and World Bank retrieved from FRED, Federal Reserve of Saint Louis.
Latest observation: 2018.

[51] They also supported a new programme for Greece which, together with the IMF and the voluntary contribution of the private sector, would fully cover the financing gap that had arisen in implementing the existing programme. Finally, they decided to lengthen the maturity of future EFSF loans to Greece from 7.5 years to a minimum of 15 years and up to 30 years with a grace period of 10 years.
[52] Market participants welcomed the significant broadening of the mandates of the EFSF and ESM, which would allow them to intervene in the secondary markets and act on the basis of a precautionary programme. This was seen as an important tool in stemming contagion. However, it was also noted that the size of the EFSF had not been increased and some cautious statements made by the German Finance Minister Wolfgang Schäuble were interpreted as implying that Germany was opposed to secondary market purchases. More broadly, the lingering concern was about the very high implementation risk and the uncertainties related to the parliamentary approval of and potential legal challenges to the decisions.
[53] In fact, in line with the general design of the programme, interventions under the SMP had been put on hold—except in the case of Portugal—since the beginning of the year (see Figure 4.27).

structural reforms in a variety of domains, after a joint Franco-German communiqué in which President Sarkozy and Chancellor Merkel reiterated their commitment to fully implement the decisions taken by the Heads of State and Government, and after hectic consultations between the ECB and a number of euro area Heads of State and Government, on Sunday 7 August—following a tense GC meeting by teleconference—President Trichet published a statement in which he for his part welcomed the measures.[54] In the same statement he called on the governments to implement in full the plans announced at the 21 July summit and to stand ready to activate secondary market purchases through the EFSF. Finally, he wrote that the ECB would 'actively implement its Securities Markets Programme. This programme has been designed to help restoring a better transmission of our monetary policy decisions—taking account of dysfunctional market segments—and therefore to ensure price stability in the euro area.' The second sentence marked a subtle departure from the strict doctrine of the 'separation principle' as it had been applied to SMP—and to longer-term refinancing operations—since the launch of the new programme in May 2010. It recognized that the achievement of price stability might at times necessitate activation of more than one instrument. In those circumstances, it was hard or impossible to segregate the unconventional tools from the ancillary function of ensuring an orderly transmission of the impulse provided by the conventional tool. Bond purchases could be part of the more holistic toolkit deployed to achieve the ultimate objective of price stability.

In any event, the announcement of a more active deployment of the SMP signalled two decisions, both strongly advocated by President Trichet. First, the SMP would be revitalized after five months of inaction. Second, the perimeter of the SMP would be enlarged to include interventions in the Italian and Spanish sovereign bond markets (see Figure 4.27). SMP transactions would contribute to re-establishing a two-way risk in the market and would be a bridging measure to remain in place until such time as the EFSF's newly legislated ability to intervene in the secondary market for euro area sovereign securities was made fully operative and actionable. Despite the criticism to which the Eurosystem would be exposed on account of its resumption and extension of SMP, this decision was an act of

---

[54] On Friday, 5 August, Italy's Prime Minister and Finance Minister had announced, in a press conference, measures to address concerns on the financial markets about the outlook for growth and public finances in the country. Four elements had been presented. First, the Italian government would bring forward to 2013 the balanced budget target initially intended to be reached only in 2014. Second, a balanced budget rule would be introduced into the constitution. Third, the liberalization of all economic activities would be introduced in the constitution. Finally, a reform of the labour market, agreed with the social partners, would be presented for parliamentary approval during the following week. In the case of Spain, the country's Finance Minister had given a press conference earlier in the day of the teleconference (7 August), spelling out some of the measures envisaged, or already implemented, by the Spanish government. These entailed reassurances that, for 2011, about 0.5% of GDP consolidation measures would be approved in order to reach a deficit target of 6% in 2011. Progress on labour market reform was also envisaged. The aim was to approve all the measures in the extraordinary Council of Ministers meeting on 19 August 2011.

responsibility on the part of the GC to mitigate the destructive fallout of a speculative attack that was directed at the system, and not at any single country.[55]

4.8.2 A New Phase

In the autumn, with the financial crisis in full swing, the general landscape darkened. In September and October, markets grew exceptionally disillusioned with the EU Council's pledge that the Greek default would be no precedent for the handling of other distressed situations, and the ECB—with its revamped SMP and longer-term refinancing operations—remained the only bulwark against a complete breakdown of the financial system. At the Euro Summit on 26 October, the Heads of State or Government agreed on yet another 'comprehensive set of additional measures'. As part of this package, the EU leaders invited Greece and its private creditors to develop a voluntary bond exchange with a nominal discount of 50% on the notional value of Greek securities held by private investors. After initial relief in the bond market, sovereign spreads widened to new highs, this time with a sizeable reaction in the Belgian and French debt markets as well.[56] In early November, as a paralysed government in Rome was approaching resignation, the Italian long-term yields reached a threshold that had previously heralded an imminent start of negotiations for an international rescue programme. Bank credit conditions in the country were tightening dramatically (see Figures 4.25 and 4.36).

In the meantime, the euro area economic recovery, the pace of which had visibly softened in the summer, ground to a halt, and analysts within and outside the ECB started to talk about outright recessionary risks.

At the end of October, the worst possible time, Jean-Claude Trichet handed over the ECB presidency to Mario Draghi. Two months later, following Jürgen Stark's

---

[55] The impact of the announcement was material. On Monday 8 July, yields on ten-year bonds decreased by 79 bps to 5.29% for Italy, and by 88 bps to 5.15% for Spain. Portuguese yields also declined by 35 bps, while Irish yields declined by 7 bps. The total amount of the Eurosystem purchases for the day was €16 billion. The results were somewhat better, if one adjusts for the fact that S&P downgraded the United States on the same day and if one takes into account the very high inverted correlation between the stock markets—which plunged in reaction to the S&P decision—and the spreads of peripheral countries.

[56] After a brief relief in August, and in spite of the Eurosystem's continued SMP purchases, Italian ten-year yields had increased back to a level of 6% and, at the 28 October auction, reached 6.06%, the highest level for Italy since the advent of the euro. Many of the conservative 'real money' investors regarded the 6% level as a point of no return beyond which a snowball effect would set in and precipitate an unsustainable fiscal situation. The rise in Italian government yields was having an adverse impact on the funding conditions of Italian banks and corporates, which related not only to higher funding costs but also to a decline in the outstanding amounts of short-term paper. The bankruptcy of a US broker, MF Global, had also triggered concerns that its large long positions in short-term euro area government bonds, including peripheral bonds, might need to be liquidated. In the meantime, the ten-year spreads between French and German government bond yields rose to fresh euro era highs of around 120 bps. Some of the main drivers behind these developments had been the actions/statements of the rating agencies, with Italy downgraded by Moody's and Fitch at the start of October, Spain downgraded by Fitch and S&P in the first half of October, Belgium placed on negative credit watch by Moody's and France warned by Moody's (on 18 October) that the outlook for its Aaa rating might be changed to negative in the next three months.

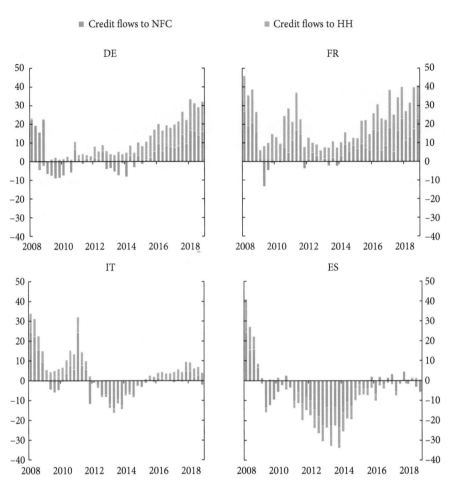

Figure 4.36 MFIs credit flows to NFCs and households (EUR billion)

Source: BSI.

Notes: MFIs excluding Eurosystem. Adjusted loans to NFCs and HH (i.e. adjusted for loan sales, securitization and notional cash pooling) and seasonally adjusted.

Latest observation: 2018Q4.

resignation, Peter Praet took over the key role of Chief Economist. As of 1 March 2012, Benoit Coeuré became the Executive Board Member in charge of the Market Operations department. Together with the sitting Vice-President, Vítor Constâncio, the new leaders were to develop a new strategy. This strategy was, first, to quell the spread of uncertainty and panic and, later, to enact decisive policies to halt disinflation and reignite growth in the euro area. In relation to the traditional triad of ECB crisis resolution principles—a fiscal crisis needs primarily fiscal solutions, there is a deficit of cross-country solidarity in euro area governance, and the role of monetary policy in a period of financial panic is confined to preserving the integrity of the transmission mechanism—the new leadership showed continuity and brought innovation at the same time. What changed most was the conception of the central bank's role in a financial, macroeconomic and institutional meltdown. The new leadership embodied the growing conviction within the GC that the ECB bore full responsibility for inflation determination in the euro area, and that inflation would be indeterminate, or irrevocably destabilized, in a macroeconomic system under constant threat of dissolution.

At Mario Draghi's first monetary policy meeting as President on 3 November 2011, the GC decided to reduce the ECB's rate corridor by 25 bps. On 8 December, it decided on a second rate reduction of the same size, bringing the ECB's key interest rates back to the level at which they were a year earlier. Concurrently, in December the GC launched two very long-term refinancing operations with a maturity of three years, and with the option of early repayment after one year. The operations were to be conducted in FRFA modality, with the rate fixed at the average MRO rate over the life of the operation. The first operation was allotted on 21 December 2011 and the second operation on 29 February 2012.[57] The amount of liquidity provided to euro area banks in the two operations was enormous: €489 billion and €529 billion, respectively. While roughly half of the allotted amount was used by banks to repay outstanding shorter-term borrowings, the total size of the Eurosystem's balance sheet increased by some 12% net. Participation was ample, with the number of bidders equal to 523 and 800 for the first and second operation, respectively.

The immediate impact of the announcement on financial markets can be appreciated by looking at two different indicators of stress (see Figure 4.37): the

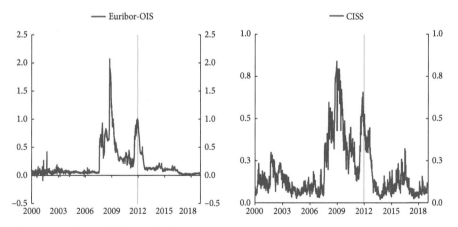

Figure 4.37 Stress indicators in the euro area
Sources: Refinitiv, Bloomberg, and ECB calculations.
Notes: The vertical line indicates the date of the first three-year LTROs.
Latest observation: 28 December 2018.

---

[57] In addition, the GC increased collateral availability by reducing the rating threshold for certain ABSs and authorized the NCBs to accept as collateral additional performing credit claims (namely bank loans) that satisfied specific eligibility criteria. They also freed up collateral and supported money market activity by reducing the reserve ratio from 2% to 1%.

EURIBOR-OIS spread, which we commented on previously, and a composite indicator of systemic stress (CISS) elaborated by ECB staff. Both indices reached a local peak immediately prior to the announcement and dropped to local minima following the announcement.

4.9 'Whatever It Takes'

The very long-term operations, combined with energetic corrective action taken in Rome by the new government and new elections in Spain giving a large majority to the opposition, restored some order in financial markets. The risk premium paid on the Italian and Spanish bonds deflated somewhat. The downtrend in bond spreads (see Figure 4.26) continued into the new year, as the Italian and Spanish banks participating in the three-year LTROs diverted the borrowed funds into generous purchases of securities issued by their respective sovereigns. The economics of such a diversion of central bank borrowings into bond holdings were twofold. First, the risk-adjusted return on domestic loans for banks operating in Italy and Spain had worsened dramatically. The fear factor had left the financial sphere and was feeding on itself in the wider economy. If frightened households and companies spend less, the resulting loss in growth nourishes the fear of a deeper downturn, which in turn depresses spending even further. Lending into an economy gripped by such a perverse cycle was utterly unprofitable for banks. Indeed, the differential that could be earned from lending to firms and households as opposed to receiving coupons on bonds had been negative—if risk-weighted—since the financial crisis, and had been falling to ever more negative values throughout 2011 (see Figure 4.38). Second, as regards the expected return on public bonds, the literature has drawn attention to a 'gamble for resurrection' psychology setting in among lenders. In conditions in which the sovereigns faced a growing probability of defaulting on their obligations, bond yields were offering rich returns in a scenario—still considered the baseline—of no default. But the tail event of a default carried less relevance in the banks' cross-asset evaluation, as a 'public default' state of the world would spell bankruptcy for the national banking system anyway.

In any event, banks' hefty bond purchases supported private demand in the primary market for peripheral debt through the first quarter of 2012, and the lower bid rates at auction were reflected in lower yields in the secondary market. In retrospect, the impact of the three-year LTROs on bank lending to firms was not negligible either. Garcia-Posada and Marchetti (2016) for Spain, Andrade et al. (2018) and Mésonnier et al. (2017) for France, Carpinelli and Crosignani (2018) for Italy, and Crosignani et al. (2019) for Portugal study the transmission and find positive effects, namely that: i) the three-year LTROs enhanced loan supply; ii) the first operation, allotted in December 2011, was the one with the largest positive impact on transmission to the real economy; iii) the opportunity offered to banks to engage in funding substitution (see Figure 4.39) and replace long-term for short-term central bank

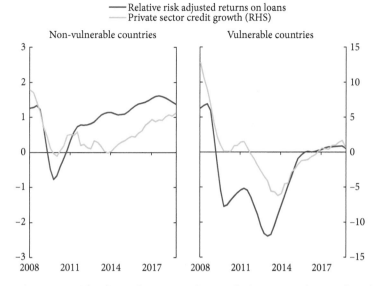

Figure 4.38 Ex-post risk-adjusted returns on loans relative to securities and credit growth in selected euro area countries (percentage points and y-o-y % change)

Sources: Moody's, ECB, and ECB calculations.

Notes: Risk-adjusted return on loans (lending rate net of expected losses and capital requirements) relative to the yield on 5-year government bonds. Yearly credit growth, private sector excludes loans granted to MFIs. 'Non-vulnerable countries' are Germany and France. 'Vulnerable countries' are Italy and Spain. Quarterly data.

Latest observation: December 2018.

credit was an amplifying factor which discouraged banks' disengagement from loan origination; iv) the operations benefited larger borrowers more and did not lead banks to increase their lending to riskier firms; v) the operation gave public banks in stressed countries the incentive to divert the borrowed funds to domestic sovereign debt purchases (see Figure 4.40, and Altavilla, Pagano, and Simonelli 2017 for an in-depth analysis), a fact to which we will return in the next chapter.

The powerful injection of liquidity—a side effect of the two three-year operations—also suppressed the chronic volatility in the EONIA, and the steadier conditions in the overnight money market helped to stabilize short-term rate expectations and to steer them towards more accommodative expected paths. The three-month OIS rate expected to prevail in one year had been falling since the summer in tandem with the worsening outlook for the economy (see Figure 4.20, Panel E). In late 2011, that indicator of near-term rate expectations converged to the current prevailing level of the EONIA and, from that point in time, it started to shadow the EONIA and the DFR, indicating that the ECB had regained the capacity to be in control of monetary conditions.

The very long-term liquidity measures ushered in an interlude of financial stability that lasted for approximately one quarter. The provision of long-term central

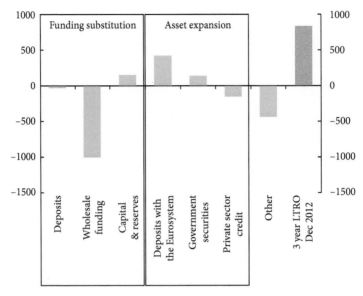

Figure 4.39 Developments in assets and liabilities of three-year LTRO bidders (from December 2011 to December 2012, EUR billion)

Sources: ECB IBSI and ECB MOPDB.

Notes: The figure shows the cumulative flows in the main assets and liabilities from December 2011 until December 2012 for three-year LTRO bidders. The three-year LTRO is the gross take-up in this operation for the IBSI sample of banks. Deposits are vis-à-vis non-MFIs; wholesale funding includes debt securities issued and loans from other MFIs excluding the Eurosystem; capital and reserves is at book values. The category 'Other' includes developments in all other asset and liabilities that are not shown.

bank credit reduced liquidity premia and thus helped discourage panic-driven fire sales of assets. But financial strains returned with a vengeance in April 2012 and became more acute moving into the summer. There were two proximate causes for the renewed surge in financial instability. As the opportunity to borrow money with a three-year maturity ended in February, fresh long-term funding was unavailable for banks to help fill the void left by private—particularly foreign—investors at auction. In addition, fundamentals were manifestly deteriorating in Spain. The country was the only one among the big four members of the euro area clearly in contraction and with an unemployment rate close to 25%. According to estimates by market commentators and specialist analysts, Spanish banks' capital shortfalls were at exorbitant levels, well in excess of the assumed capacity of the Spanish Treasury to raise extra funds in the market—namely beyond what was already required to roll over maturing debt and finance the new deficit figure, which had been revised to a shade below 9% of GDP. On 26 May, BFA-Bankia, a large and fragile Spanish bank created in 2010 by consolidating the operations of seven regional savings banks, presented a financing, restructuring, and recapitalization plan requesting an injection of an additional €19 billion for extra provisioning of real estate exposures and to recognize the lower values of foreclosed real estate assets. The operation sparked a new bout of

Figure 4.40 Holdings of domestic government bonds by euro area MFIs (percentage of main assets)

Source: ECB BSI.

Notes: The vertical gridline indicates the date of the settlement of the first operation of the three-year LTRO.

Latest observation: December 2018.

sharp volatility and risk aversion in the markets, and bond spreads for so-called vulnerable countries surged to new highs. In June the Spanish government requested the assistance of the EFSF/ESM for bank recapitalization purposes amid incipient signs of a deposit run targeting Bankia and other vulnerable credit institutions in the country.

Frighteningly, the severity and persistence of the debt crisis was stirring up fears that the governments targeted by the ongoing debt runs might be brought to the brink of default and, in those circumstances, might choose to leave the euro area and redenominate their liabilities into a successor currency. A large 'redenomination risk' started to emerge and absorbed a fraction of what was previously seen as a pure 'credit risk', namely the risk that bonds issued by the government might still be paid in euro, though not in full. Figure 4.41 documents how a measure of the redenomination risk for Spain, Italy and even France had a tendency to increase in late 2011 and surged in the first half of 2012.

On Sunday 17 June, at an emergency meeting, ECB policymakers met with staff to discuss all necessary and appropriate steps to address the situation effectively and comprehensively. The brainstorming session was an opportunity to explore schemes for the ECB and the newly created ESM to form a partnership and thus jointly try to

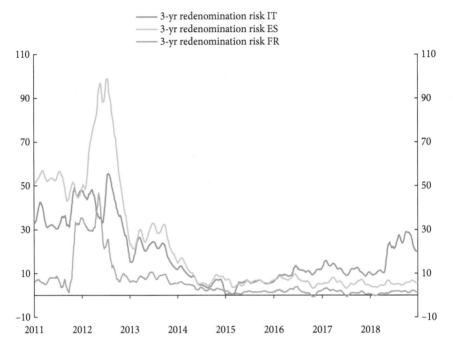

—— 3-yr redenomination risk IT
—— 3-yr redenomination risk ES
—— 3-yr redenomination risk FR

Figure 4.41 Redenomination risk in selected euro area countries at three-year maturity (basis points, 20-day forward moving average)

Source: Refinitiv and De Santis (2018).

Notes: Redenomination risk is measured as a difference between Quanto CDSs for Italy/Spain/France and for Germany. The Quanto CDS is computed as difference between the sovereign CDS quotes in dollars and euro.

Latest observation: 31 December 2018.

stem the contagion and restore confidence on a lasting basis. The meeting could bring to fruition the previous action taken by the ECB to promote the creation of new EU institutions—the ESM specifically—which could provide the enabling conditions for the ECB to engage in that sort of monetary policy initiatives that had proven decisive elsewhere. Soon, the attention of the group was focused on one such scheme which envisioned the following sequence of actions taken by different decision-makers: (1) to begin with, a vulnerable country—close to losing market access—would apply for EFSF/ESM financial assistance; (2) in response to the request, the EFSF/ESM would grant assistance either in the form of a standard macroeconomic adjustment programme, or as a self-standing secondary market purchase programme, a line of official assistance that—as we mention above—was ready for use, although untested thus far; (3) conditional on approval of and compliance with the programme, the ECB's Governing Council would assess the financial conditions and evaluate whether a monetary policy intervention was justified. If the GC gave a positive assessment, the ECB would engage in purchases of bonds issued by the distressed government in the secondary market; (4) and, finally, the ECB would swap a predefined share of a portfolio of securities acquired under the programme with the EFSF/ESM in exchange for EFSF/ESM notes. In the following days and weeks, all the legal aspects and likely implications of the scheme were studied further. In successive refinements, step (4), viewed as a potential handicap to the efficacy and efficiency of the scheme, was removed, and the issue of credit subordination was addressed. The bonds acquired by the ECB under the scheme would be held to maturity, and the ECB would not be senior to other creditors. The scheme would still be triggered upon a country's initiative to request a programme, and would be conditional on the country's continuing compliance with the conditions agreed under the programme. But its firepower would not be constrained by the maximum lending potential of the EFSF/ESM, as would have been the case if step (4) had been retained.

Armed with this general blueprint, which was slowly maturing into a fully specified programme, at the Global Investment Conference in London on 26 July, President Draghi gave an account of the euro area economy (Draghi, 2012a). Bond yields of vulnerable euro area member governments were soaring in the market, and the perception in the audience—mostly made up of financiers and traders—was that time was running out for the euro area authorities to avert a break-up. President Draghi's off-the-cuff remarks started with an analogy which sounded like a cryptic utterance when it was pronounced: 'The euro is like a bumblebee. This is a mystery of nature because it shouldn't fly but instead it does.' From that analogy, he moved to another seemingly cryptic observation: 'The bumblebee would have to graduate to a real bee. And that's what it's doing.' He then praised the progress made recently by the distressed countries to return their economies to solvency and lasting growth, and the progress made at the last summit of the Heads of State or Government a month before, on 29 June, where all leaders had agreed that 'the only way out of this present crisis is to have more Europe, not less Europe', where they had pledged to break the vicious circle between banks and sovereigns by establishing a single supervisory mechanism, and where they had pledged to use the existing EFSF/ESM instruments in a flexible and efficient manner in order to stabilize markets. At the end, he added: 'But there is another message I want to tell you. Within our mandate, the ECB is ready to do whatever it takes to preserve the euro. And believe me, it will be enough.' The remark was indeed enough to jolt the equilibrium in the market from one in which the conformist view expressed in the median trade was to be short the euro area regardless, to one in which investors returned to euro area exposures in flocks. As they looked at their smart phones for the instant reaction of the market to the speech, the bumblebee analogy became suddenly clear to the audience. Figure 4.42 shows the immediate reaction of the two-year and ten-year sovereign yields of Italy and Spain to the 'whatever it takes' sentence.

Estimates of redenomination risk for Italy and Spain started their steep decline too. Unlike in previous episodes, the correction was not ephemeral. By the end of

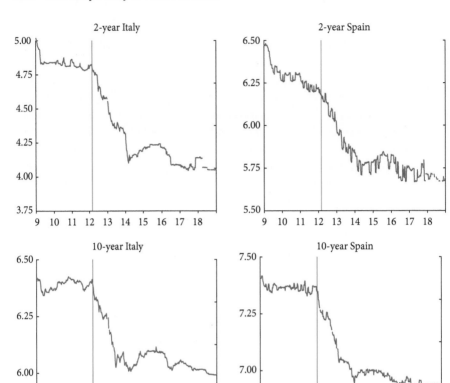

Figure 4.42 Reaction of the two-year and ten-year sovereign yields to the 'whatever it takes' speech (percentages per annum)

Source: Bloomberg.

Notes: Horizontal axis refers to trading hours. The vertical lines indicate the time in London when the ECB's President, Mario Draghi, said that the ECB would do 'whatever it takes' to preserve the euro (12:09 p.m.).

the year the two countries' sovereign yield spreads versus Germany had declined by 200 bps, and the estimated compensation for the risk of a break-up went back to levels not seen in many years (see Figure 4.42).

The introductory statement to the press conference following the 2 August monetary policy meeting included the following announcement: 'The Governing Council, within its mandate to maintain price stability over the medium term and in observance of its independence in determining monetary policy, may undertake outright open market operations of a size adequate to reach its objective. In this context, the concerns of private investors about seniority will be addressed.' Finally, on 6 September, the GC disclosed the design of the new Outright Monetary Transactions (OMT) programme, an instrument 'to address severe distortions in government bond markets which originate from, in particular, unfounded fears on the part of

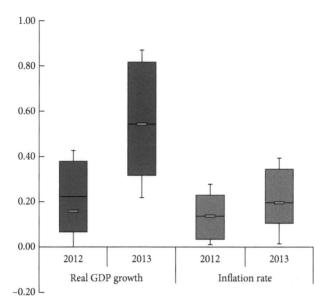

Figure 4.43 Impact of OMT announcements on real GDP growth and inflation (percentage points)

Source: ECB calculations.

Notes: The figure shows the effects for real GDP growth (blue) and inflation (red) associated with the OMT announcements in terms of percentage deviations in the OMT scenario relative to the no-OMT scenario for the two-year projection horizon.

investors of the reversibility of the euro'. The GC added: 'Hence, under appropriate conditions, we will have a fully effective backstop to avoid destructive scenarios with potentially severe challenges for price stability in the euro area.' Strict and effective conditionality attached to a full macroeconomic adjustment programme or an Enhanced Conditions Credit Line of the EFSF/ESM—provided that they included the possibility of EFSF/ESM primary market purchases—would be the precondition for activation. The ECB purchases would be focused on the shorter part of the yield curve, and in particular on sovereign bonds with a residual maturity of between one and three years, the segment of the yield curve most affected by market expectations of an upcoming default of the issuer.[58] There would be no ex ante limits to the purchases. The ECB's holdings of securities acquired under OMT would be treated *pari passu* with the bonds held by other investors.[59]

---

[58] In fact, when investors' risk perceptions are at extreme levels, the term structure of sovereign bond spreads typically flattens and may become inverted, with high spread levels at the short end of the curve. For example, for Spain, the term structure of sovereign bond spreads (over Germany) saw a distinct inversion at the end of July 2012, with two-year spreads standing at around 710 bps while ten-year spreads were at 640 bps. This inverted spread curve can be interpreted as investors pricing in a high probability of an extreme event taking place in the short term, while assuming that the situation would be more benign once the 'critical' years had been survived.

[59] The technical features of Outright Monetary Transactions are outlined in a press release of 6 September 2012; see https://www.ecb.europa.eu/press/pr/date/2012/html/pr120906_1.en.html

Several studies (Altavilla, Giannone, and Lenza (2016) and Szczerbowicz (2015)) found evidence that the OMT announcement significantly lowered spreads of sovereign bonds issued, especially for stressed euro area countries, thereby increasing these bonds' prices. But the transmission of the announcement went beyond the bond market. Banks with significant holdings of sovereign and privately issued bonds experienced substantial valuation gains. Accordingly, Acharya et al. (2018), and Krishnamurthy et al. (2017) document significantly positive effects on banks' equity prices after the OMT announcement. The effectiveness of the announcement of OMTs in influencing financial market conditions (especially if compared with the SMP) is probably related to the fact that purchases are in principle unlimited, subject to conditionality on compliance with a macroeconomic adjustment programme, and have greater transparency.

Moving to the real economy, Altavilla et al. (2016), show that OMT had statistically significant and economically relevant effects on credit, as well as on economic growth, especially in Italy and Spain, with more limited spillovers in France and Germany. More precisely, translating the financial market effects into real economic activity through the lens of the BVAR model used in Chapter 5 gives the impact depicted in the Figure 4.43. In the absence of the OMT announcement, real GDP growth and inflation in the euro area would have been about 1 and 0.3 percentage points lower respectively (median effect (cumulative) over two years).[60]

---

[60] The overall effects are very similar to that obtained by aggregating the euro area countries included in the analysis by Altavilla et al. (2016) and rescaling the impact for the whole euro area.

5
The Second Regime

Deflation Risks

The ECB entered the last phase of the crisis—the subject of this chapter—facing a
weakened inflation process and with less effective policy instruments to shore it up.
Although not yet apparent in the data at the time to nearly the same extent as it is
today in retrospect, the capacity of the euro area economy to generate domestic
inflation consistent with the 'close to 2%' pledge was probably already much
diminished by 2012. At the same time, after the July 2012 rate cut, the deposit facility
rate (DFR) had reached zero, a level universally regarded at the time as the lower
bound for the policy interest rate. The DFR sets the floor of the Eurosystem rate
corridor and, if there are ample excess reserves (such as those prevailing in 2012 and
part of 2013), it exerts a sort of gravitational pull on the overnight interest rate, the
EONIA. At the start of 2013, the EONIA was therefore attracted to the floor of the
corridor while also being stuck at or near the zero lower bound (ZLB) (see Figure 4.5).
The overnight rate also pins down the whole term structure of risk-free interest
rates, as it anchors the near-maturity segment. Barring ways for the central bank to
influence the slope of the curve, namely the spread (or distance) between longer-
term interest rates—those that matter most for pricing credit to the wider economy—
and the overnight rate, reaching the lower bound on very short-term interest rates
meant, at the time, reaching the limit of monetary policy easing. If, in addition, the
financial intermediation channel happens to be clogged, as was the case in 2013, the
insufficient stimulus that originates in the early stages of transmission is further
dampened as it filters through unresponsive financial intermediaries.

This is a summary description of the landscape that faced the ECB over the two
years, 2013 and 2014, covered in this chapter. By the end of 2014, it was clear that the
euro area had switched over to the second regime described in Chapter 3: downside
risks to inflation and the economy had replaced cost-push factors as the dominant
drivers of the macro-economy. With conventional policy unavailable, the ECB
launched a sequence of unconventional policy interventions to avert a multi-year
depression and the deflation scenario that would have accompanied it. The measures
were further elaborated, coordinated, and unified into a 'combined arms strategy'
through the learning process that we describe in this chapter and with the results
that we document in Chapter 6.

Monetary Policy in Times of Crisis: A Tale of Two Decades of the European Central Bank. Massimo Rostagno, Carlo Altavilla,
Giacomo Carboni, Wolfgang Lemke, Roberto Motto, Arthur Saint Guilhem, and Jonathan Yiangou, Oxford University Press (2021).
© Massimo Rostagno, Carlo Altavilla, Giacomo Carboni, Wolfgang Lemke, Roberto Motto, Arthur Saint Guilhem, and Jonathan Yiangou.
DOI: 10.1093/oso/9780192895912.003.0006

5.1 The Long Slide in Inflation

After peaking in mid-2011, headline inflation had gradually begun to fall. Initially, disinflation did not worry experts either within or outside the ECB, for a number of reasons. First, the slide in headline inflation (the dark blue line in Figure 5.1) was ascribed to the fading effects of earlier increases in energy prices and the prices of non-energy imports. These so-called base effects—strong increases in monthly price inflation washing out the annual statistics after 12 months—could pretty much explain the bump in annual inflation figures between 2011 and 2012. Second, over the course of 2012, measures of underlying inflation remained centred on levels below but not too far from 2%, even as headline inflation had begun its sustained descent. The green range in Figure 5.1 encompasses a set of underlying inflation measures in use at the ECB that identify an 'inflation trend' by extracting a low-frequency momentum from within measured inflation.[1] If, at any point in time, contemporary measures of underlying inflation pressures can be interpreted as an early guess about the level around which inflation will settle in the medium term—when short-term shocks that may influence headline inflation have faded away—the central tendency of that range may help judge whether the inflation objective is likely to be met on a sustainable basis. Indeed, underlying measures are a useful cross-check to the projections precisely because they give an idea of sustainability. Third, longer-term inflation expectations, both derived from inflation protection contracts and from surveys, were holding steady with the former in particular showing no signs of softening from the levels well above the 2% price stability ceiling around which they had been hovering since 2011. Purged of the inflation risk premium (see Section 3.2), inflation-linked swaps implied long-term levels of inflation expectations that were well in line with the ECB medium-term aim (see Figure 5.1). As became evident only later, resilience in financial market measures of inflation compensation in 2012 and early 2013 was probably driven by an adaptive approach to pricing longer-term inflation risk in inflation protection markets. By this we mean a tendency among participants in these markets to project forward the level of underlying inflation that happens to be registered in the current period, while also taking into account recent surprises to headline inflation and, notably, the

---

[1] The green range includes four statistical metrics of underlying inflation that are regularly maintained by ECB staff. These comprise the two exclusion indicators, of HICP inflation excluding food and energy (HICPX commonly referred to as 'core inflation') and HICP inflation excluding food, energy, travel-related items, and clothing, as well as two more elaborate statistical indicators, U2 Core and Supercore. U2 Core is based on a dynamic factor model using all (93) HICP items from 12 euro area countries. It combines cross-sectional with frequency domain smoothing techniques (see Cristadoro et al., 2005), and has the characteristics of both a core (as it applies cross-sectional smoothing) and a trend measure aiming at a medium- to long-term horizon (by eliminating cycles with a period of less than three years). It demonstrates leading properties for HICPX. Supercore is based on those items covering the euro area HICPX that are sensitive to slack as measured by the output gap. The items are selected based on a forecast performance test, using a type of Phillips curve equation for each of the (72) HICPX items and choosing only those items for which the Phillips curve provides a forecast superior to one based on a simple autoregressive model (with 49 items).

futures-implied price of oil in the more distant future. The dotted lines in Figure 5.1 correspond to the inflation forward curves recorded at selected dates.[2] As shown, underlying inflation—proxied by the position of the green range at any point in time—acts as a local attractor for inflation expectations, despite its anchoring role decreasing along the horizon.[3]

Finally, deflation risks seemed particularly remote. Figure 5.2 documents the implied risk-neutral probability density functions computed from five-year maturity zero-coupon inflation option floors at the end of 2012 and 2013. These bell-shaped distributions are helpful in gauging both the central tendencies in the inflation process, as assessed by investors, and the tail risks that investors are ready to entertain when engaging in these contracts. The price stability range provided analysts with a particular lens through which they could look at the distributions. And the lens was a magnifier of those portions of the distribution falling outside the price stability zone. As shown, provided the distribution is reasonably symmetric and centred around a level not too far from the 2% ceiling, the measure of upper tail risk is always bound to dominate the measure of lower tail risk. This was particularly the case throughout 2012 and for a good portion of 2013.

The inflation landscape changed dramatically in the second half of 2013. The euro area had remained entrenched in contraction territory for the whole of 2012, though with cross-country disparities larger than ever. While Italy had been mired in a deep slump since mid-2011 and Spain had never quite returned to positive growth since the global financial crisis, Germany only tiptoed into mild negative growth in late 2012 and France, after emerging from the post-Lehman economic collapse, never really experienced a technical recession. When the euro area finally bounced back to positive growth in the second quarter of 2013, the impetus that aggregate demand could have received from the typical drivers of economic expansion that materialize after protracted periods of economic duress was curbed by enduring malaise in some peripheral countries. There, economic slack kept rising, even as the economy stabilized, owing to subpar growth.[4] The accumulating slack, combined with the ripple effects that weak energy prices were having further down the supply chain, started to exert a constant downward pull on underlying inflation, which became

---

[2] The inflation forward curves are derived from inflation-linked swap (ILS) rates. An ILS is a derivative contract that involves an exchange of a payment defined in terms of a fixed rate on a notional amount (the 'fixed leg' of the swap) for a payment defined in terms of the realised inflation rate over a predetermined horizon on that same notional amount. Thus, the ILS rate on the contract is indicative of the market's expected inflation rate over the relevant horizon. The swap contract is usually linked to a non-seasonally adjusted consumer price index (CPI). In the euro area, the relevant index is the HICP excluding tobacco (HICPxT), while in the United States it is the Consumer Price Index for All Urban Consumers (CPI-U) and in the United Kingdom it is the Retail Price Index (RPI).

[3] The econometrics supporting this statement is available upon request.

[4] The OMT announcement in September 2012 had revived international investors' appetite for euro area risk, and the robust financial inflows into euro area assets had pushed up the external value of the euro at the turn of the year as a result. This did not sap demand for German exports, as the country's competitive edge in the dynamic emerging market world was consolidating, while it held back recovery in the periphery, where firms had lost competitiveness through low productivity and sustained nominal wage gains throughout the crisis.

more and more apparent as 2013 wore on. In October, headline year-on-year inflation recorded an unusually large fall that brought it below 1%, marking the lower boundary of the green range of underlying price pressures shown in Figure 5.1. Even before October, the genuine inflation expectations component implicit in inflation-linked swap measures of inflation compensation had started to edge down (see Figure 5.1).

Measured and trend inflation seemed to have joined the same path, and were heading with unanticipated speed towards levels that would test the significance of the 'close to 2%' focal point within the ECB's price stability definition. As we sought to clarify in Chapter 2, the 'close to 2%' clarification of May 2003 had two rationales: to provide a cushion against euro area-wide deflation risks, and to set a sufficiently high bar around which the rebalancing of cross-country relative prices—an ongoing process in a currency union as heterogeneous as the euro area—could take place without forcing national inflation rates to excessively low or even negative values. Both rationales were being challenged at the end of 2013. Anaemic growth was raising concerns about the direction of travel underlying domestic euro area inflation formation (see Figures 5.3 and 5.4), while rising economic slack (see Figures 5.5, 5.6, and 5.7), together with deliberate national strategies to regain competitiveness after years of excess nominal wage gains were suppressing inflation in the countries hit hardest by the sovereign crisis. By the end of 2013 and during 2014 a few of them were in outright deflation.

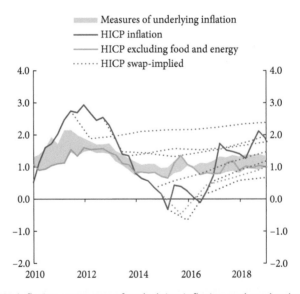

Figure 5.1 HICP inflation, measures of underlying inflation and market-based inflation expectations (year-on-year % change)

Source: ECB.

Notes: The red dotted line indicates the HICP swap-implied curve as of the end of December 2014. Measures of underlying inflation include HICP inflation excluding food and energy, HICP inflation excluding food, energy, travel-related items and clothing, U2 core and super-core.

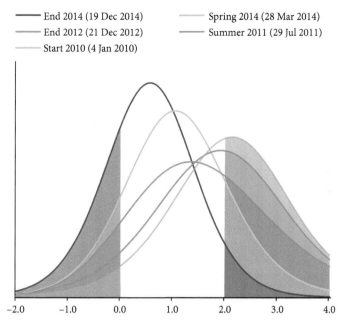

Figure 5.2 Option-implied risk-neutral distribution of average inflation over the next five years (density)

Sources: Bloomberg and Refinitiv.

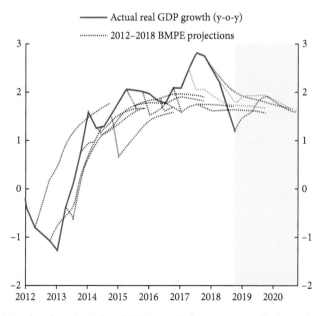

Figure 5.3 Actual and projected real GDP growth (year-on-year % change)

Sources: Eurostat and ECB projections.

Notes: The red dotted lines indicate the June 2017 and June 2018 BMPEs.

Latest observations: December 2018 for historical data and December 2020 for ECB projections.

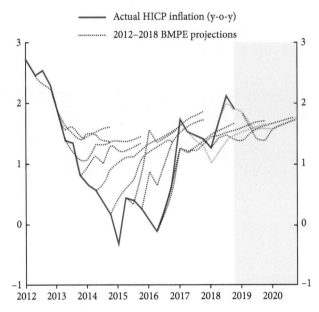

Figure 5.4 Actual and projected HICP inflation (year-on-year % change)

Sources: Eurostat and ECB projections.
Notes: The red dotted lines indicate the June 2017 and June 2018 BMPEs.
Latest observations: December 2018 for historical data and December 2020 for ECB projections.

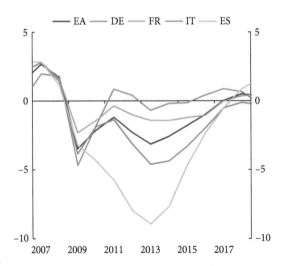

Figure 5.5 Output gap in the euro area and four largest euro area countries (percentage)

Source: Ameco.
Latest observation: 2018.

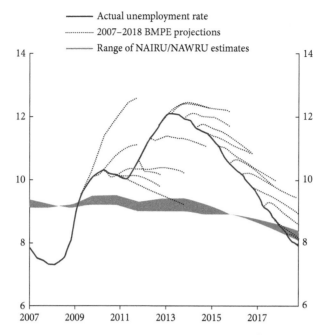

Figure 5.6 Actual and projected unemployment in the euro area and estimates of NAIRU/NAWRU (percentage)

Sources: Eurostat, ECB projections, European Commission, and OECD.
Latest observation: 2018Q4 for realized unemployment rate.

5.2 The Instruments of Monetary Policy

On 2 May 2013 the Governing Council (GC) lowered the interest rate on the MRO by 25 bps to 0.50% and the rate on the marginal lending facility (MLF) by 50 bps to 1.00%, while leaving the DFR unchanged at 0.00%. The move was supposed to bring relief to the banks that had borrowed heavily under the two three-year LTROs, as the interest rate applied in those operations was indexed to the pro tempore MRO rate. The deep cut in the rate on the MLF was also meant to alleviate the borrowing costs applied to those banks—mainly in programme countries—that were receiving emergency liquidity assistance (ELA), as the rate applied by the NCBs on those emergency operations was indexed to the MLF rate.

For all practical purposes, however, monetary policy at the beginning of 2013 was operating through a de facto floor system, where the MRO rate acted more as a weekly backstop than as a steering rate and the DFR was the instrument with the tightest grip on the stance. Having de-emphasized the 'separation principle', the new ECB leaders and their staff were concentrating on the overnight interest rate and its forward curve as the most relevant and informative indicators of the monetary

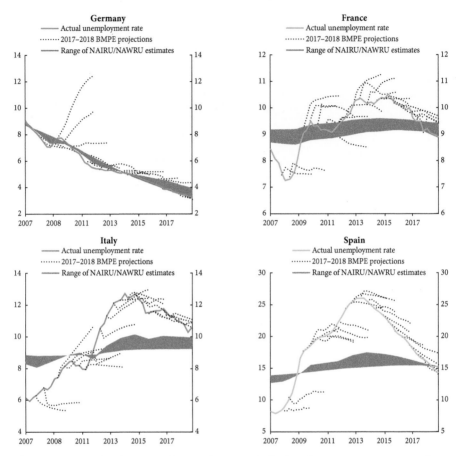

Figure 5.7 Actual and projected unemployment in the four largest euro area countries and estimates of NAIRU/NAWRU (percentage)

Sources: Eurostat, ECB projections, European Commission, and OECD.
Latest observation: 2018Q4 for realized unemployment rate.

policy stance.[5] From that point of view, securing a fair degree of control over the stance was premised on two conditions: first, stability in the overnight interest rate and, second, steady expectations among market participants of the future path of the monetary policy instruments. The former condition was key to anchoring the level

---

[5] We refer to our description of the OIS spot market in Chapter 4. We add that the OIS market is very liquid, as a very large number of players can participate in it over the counter at low cost, even though the underlying market—the EONIA—is very thin. Therefore, the forward rates that are derived from the spot OIS curve have easily established themselves as benchmarks for the pricing of a whole menu of financial contracts that investors enter into for a number of reasons, hedging or position-taking being the most important. Through arbitrage activity, these indicators have thus become benchmarks for pricing in the bond market and for the EURIBOR, namely for unsecured term deposits among banks. The EURIBOR, in particular, is a critical link in the chain of transmission between the forward curve and the economy, as it acts as a benchmark in its own right. Bank lending contracts, for example, are very often priced on the basis of the 3-month or 12-month EURIBOR. This applies primarily to adjustable rate loans. But also banks that offer fixed rate loans use the EURIBOR when they set the loan terms at the start of the contract.

of the curve and containing the size of term premia across all maturities. As we showed in Chapter 3, compensation for risk is a multiple of the variance of the interest rate risk, and thus a volatile EONIA invites higher premia to compensate money market participants for the heightened uncertainty that it generates. The GC's decision in May 2013 to narrow the corridor, and particularly the distance between the MRO rate and the DFR, was taken also with a view to containing the amplitude of the weekly fluctuations in the EONIA.

Fostering the latter condition (steady rate expectations), in turn, was necessary to ensure that the shape of the curve consistently reflected the GC's resolve to lock in enough accommodation in conditions of rapid disinflation and subpar growth. Indeed, abstracting from term premia, the steepness of the curve and, hence, the level of longer-term interest rates, are the reflection of agents' expectations of the central bank's future moves. The EONIA forward curve crystallizes the expectations of the overnight rate in the market and, in a floor system where the overnight rate shadows the DFR, the EONIA forward curve registers the market participant's best guess about the level of the DFR at future dates.

Over the course of 2013, both key conditions for efficient monetary control were increasingly challenged. Below, we review the three factors that during 2013 combined to make the monetary policy stance, as measured by the EONIA forward curve, less supportive and predictable than it otherwise could have been.

5.2.1 The ZLB Steepens the Curve

Ceteris paribus, as central banks drive the very short-term money market interest rates towards zero, the forward curve tends to steepen. Why? Imagine a world in which investors expect monetary policy to be constrained at present and at all future dates by the ZLB. As the central bank brings the short-term interest rates closer and closer to the ZLB, investors and lenders of all types reasonably start to fear a reversal of the easing process. Those assigning a high probability to seeing further rate cuts in the future become fewer, and those expecting the central bank to hike rates grow in number. When the overnight interest rate finally reaches the ZLB, nobody in the marketplace is left assigning any probability to a future cut: all investors expect either a flat or rising path for the overnight rate looking forward. In other words, in ZLB conditions, the non-negativity restriction on future expected short rates imparts an upward skew on the bundle of rate paths that investors bet on when they engage in forward contracts. As the forward EONIA curve computed at each point in time is the probability-weighted average of all the hypothetical paths priced in the market, the upward asymmetry in the distribution of these paths translates into a steeper forward curve. The economics of term lending is also affected: as short- and long-term yields decline, the return on term lending in all markets is seen as too low to compensate for the potential future volatility (or backup) in yields, so investors and lenders will prefer to invest and lend only at the shortest of maturities. Importantly, most financial intermediaries are volatility constrained: they cannot allow the price movements in their assets and liabilities to be too far out of alignment over relatively short periods of time. As the nominal coupon on long-dated bonds is driven down, it no longer compensates the intermediary for the potential future volatility.

Indeed, after the last reduction of the DFR to zero in July 2012, the forward curve displayed a distinct tendency to steepen. Figure 5.8 shows the forward EONIA curve at the beginning of 2013 together with the 15th–85th percentiles of the predictive density of future interest rate paths, generated using linear interpolation though risk-neutral option-implied distributions around the three-month EURIBOR at a 6, 9, 12, and 18-month horizon.[6] Essentially, the ZLB restriction likely prevented the long end of the curve from coming down at the same rate at which it would have declined otherwise.

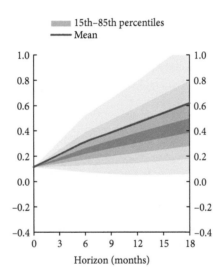

Figure 5.8 EONIA forward curve and its risk-neutral density in January 2013 (percentages per annum)

Sources: Bloomberg and ECB.
Notes: Risk-neutral densities as of 29 January 2013 derived from options on EURIBOR futures. The mean and the percentiles are shifted to the EONIA space by subtracting the EURIBOR3M-OIS3M spot spread. Latest observation: January 2013.

---

[6] More specifically, risk-neutral densities are derived by the ECB using options on EURIBOR futures for fixed expiration dates and then interpolated for fixed horizons, between which Figure 5.8 in turn interpolates. As usual, risk-neutral probabilities typically differ from actual or physical probabilities. For further information, see the notes beneath Figure 5.8. See Chapter 6 for an explanation of how densities such as the one displayed in Figure 5.8 are constructed and can be interpreted.

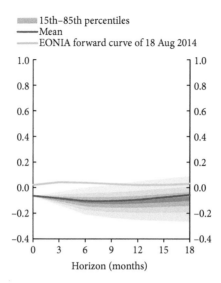

Figure 5.9 EONIA forward curve and its risk-neutral density in September 2014 (percentages per annum)

Sources: Bloomberg and ECB.
Notes: Risk-neutral densities as of 5 September 2014 derived from options on EURIBOR futures. The mean and the percentiles are shifted to the EONIA space by subtracting the EURIBOR3M-OIS3M spot spread.
Latest observation: September 2014.

5.2.2 LTRO Reimbursements

At the end of January 2013, banks that had borrowed funds under the first three-year LTRO allotted in December 2011 could start availing themselves of the early repayment option. On that occasion, as banks chose to reimburse as much as €137 billion—an unexpectedly large volume—an equal amount of excess liquidity was withdrawn from the system. Over the following weeks, and for the remainder of the year and the following one, liquidity kept trickling out of the system as banks continued to shed central bank credit at the weekly frequency foreseen for voluntary repayments under the two three-year operations.

Commentators within and outside the ECB were divided in their interpretation of the sustained early repayment phenomenon. Some thought the robust early reimbursements were a sign that the banking sector was healing and that the stance was more permissive than the system needed. Others viewed the process with growing anxiety. First, from a micro-economic perspective, in their opinion banks might have chosen an accelerated schedule of repayment for reasons unrelated to their economic health: they might have started to clean up their balance sheets in anticipation of the comprehensive assessment exercise that the ECB would have to conduct in 2014 before taking up its novel supervisory responsibilities;[7] in programme countries, they might have been following through on the deleveraging obligations imposed on them by their restructuring plans; or, they might simply have been using accelerated repayments as a signalling device to reassure investors about their restored viability, whether real or pretended. Second, from a macro-economic view-point, individual decisions to reimburse were having sizeable externalities. When aggregated system-wide, reimbursements were destroying excess liquidity, and the increasing scarcity of liquidity in the circuit of interbank credit had the potential to destabilize the daily fixing of the EONIA and keep money market interest rates higher than the subdued state of the economy was demanding. In any event, beyond the implications for the EONIA—which materialized to a measurable degree only in late 2013 and early 2014—the fact that banks were shedding liquidity was an omin-ous sign. It was a reflection of a deliberate strategy by banks to deleverage and, par-ticularly, shrink their exposures to the real economy. Leaner balance sheets for banks meant lower volumes of assets to refinance and thus necessitated a lower buffer of reserves to cover their day-to-day operations. Indeed, after a short-lived recovery in late 2012, credit flows had turned negative (see Figure 5.13). Fundamentally, this group of observers took aim at the conclusion implied by the opposing view that a system regurgitating liquidity was necessarily a system that *did not need* liquidity. In their opinion, this was unwarranted and reminiscent of the misguided implications drawn by members of the Board of the Federal Reserve System in the midst of the Great Depression when confronted with similar conditions of abundant liquidity com-bined with a depressed economy.[8] They saw LTRO pre-payments as a symptom of bank deleveraging, and bank deleveraging as a harbinger of a credit crunch.

---

[7] The ECB together with national supervisors carries out regular financial health checks of the banks it supervises directly. These comprehensive assessments help to ensure that the banks are adequately capitalised and can withstand possible financial shocks. The first such exercise was conducted between November 2013 and October 2014 on 130 banks in the euro area (including Lithuania, then not yet a member) with total assets of some €22.0 trillion, and was an important step in preparing for the Single Supervisory Mechanism (SSM) to become fully operational (the SSM took up its day-to-day supervis-ory activities on 4 November 2014). The exercise consisted of two components. The first component was an asset quality review (AQR), a point-in-time assessment of the accuracy of the carrying value of banks' assets as of 31 December 2013. The AQR was undertaken by the ECB and national competent authorities, and was based on a uniform methodology and harmonised definitions. It provided a thor-ough health check of the banks that would be subject to direct supervision by the ECB. Under the AQR, banks were required to have a minimum Common Equity Tier 1 (CET1) ratio of 8%. The second component, taking the AQR as a starting point, was a stress test, a forward-looking examination of the resilience of banks' solvency to two hypothetical scenarios. The stress test was undertaken also in cooperation with the European Banking Authority (EBA), which designed the methodology along with the ECB and the European Systemic Risk Board (ESRB). Under the baseline scenario, banks were required to maintain a minimum CET1 ratio of 8%; under the adverse scenario, they were required to maintain a minimum CET1 ratio of 5.5%. The results of the comprehensive assessment, with an aggre-gate disclosure of the overall outcomes as well as bank-level data, together with recommendations for supervisory measures, were published on 26 October 2014.

[8] This view which was predominant among Federal Reserve System officials in the 1930s was famously captured in the testimony of Marriner Eccles—then Governor of the Federal Reserve Board—on the Banking Act of 1935, in which he compared monetary policy in a depression to 'pushing on a string': 'Under present circumstance there is very little, if anything, that can be done [...] one cannot push on a string. We are in the depths of a depression and...beyond creating an easy money situation through

5.2.3 Transatlantic Spillovers

When Ben Bernanke, then Chairman of the US Federal Reserve, indicated in testimony in late May 2013 that the Federal Open Market Committee (FOMC) was considering slowing asset purchases if economic conditions improved sufficiently, the markets responded with a 'taper tantrum' that included sharp increases in volatility and a rise in longer-term rates. The Treasury bond sell-off was particularly acute, but the selling wave spread to markets worldwide and reached the euro area fixed income market as well. The EONIA forward curve, which had moved down and flattened distinctly after the GC's meeting in May, backed up sharply and steepened in sympathy with similar adjustments in the US yield curve (see Figure 5.10). A widely discussed amplification mechanism during the 2013 taper tantrum was the activity of risk-parity funds, which had held leveraged positions in US Treasuries. They had probably been encouraged to build such long positions by expectations that the open-ended programme of bond purchases announced in September and December 2012 by the Fed would extend indefinitely into the future. But, when those expectations were truncated by the Fed's pre-warning of a taper and volatility picked up, the risk-parity funds became forced sellers on a large scale. As can be expected in a highly integrated global financial system, forced selling extended to

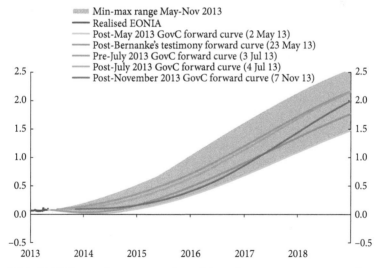

Figure 5.10 EONIA forward curves on selected dates (percentages per annum)
Sources: Bloomberg and Refinitiv.
Notes: The grey range spans the forward curves observed between May and November 2013, with the upper bound in the range marking the forward curve of 21 June 2013 for short maturities (up to two years) and the curve of 5 September 2013 for longer maturities (from three to ten years).
Latest observation: November 2013.

reduction of discount rates, and through creation of excess reserves, there is very little, if anything, that the reserve organization can do toward bringing about recovery.'

euro-denominated bonds, and the repricing spread to all segments of euro area rate and credit products, including the OIS market.

While the international propagation of the US disturbance was broad and powerful, the generally loose control over money market conditions in the euro area made them particularly vulnerable to extraneous shocks. The backup in the EONIA forward curve blurred the monetary policy signal that the GC considered appropriate and commensurate with the euro area domestic conditions.

5.3 Forward Guidance

The confluence of the three factors mentioned above, and particularly contagion from the US tapering indications, had the potential to perturb the first stage of transmission, the near-term portion of the term structure of risk-free interest rates. The risk of 'instrument instability' raised the need for communication and explanation by the ECB Governing Council to a new level. One option was to put more emphasis in official communication on the connection between the long-run objectives of monetary policy and the path of interest rates most consistent with achieving those objectives. While at risk of being seen as a departure from its traditional insistence that 'we never pre-commit', forward guidance was an approach that the GC could utilize to provide that link. Forward guidance could increase the transparency of monetary policy deliberations and plans at a time of heightened uncertainty. It could solidify—in the public's perception—the ECB's commitment not to a particular path for its rate instruments but to a policy approach that considered the stability of, and control over, the short segment of the yield curve as an indispensable precondition for steering the stance of monetary policy.

But design issues were not trivial. Foremost among them was enforcement. In a rate corridor system, there was no such thing as a single very short-term interest rate on which the central bank could unambiguously give guidance. The ECB could choose from a variety of money market rates or, alternatively, the three key policy interest rates defining the corridor. Among market rate solutions, issuing guidance with reference to the EONIA was the most obvious, not least because the forward curve—the object that forward guidance would be trying to influence—reflects the expected evolution of the EONIA. However, the way in which the ECB could enforce such a solution was not obvious. With liquidity supply endogenous in the euro area, namely provided on banks' demand, and a still relatively wide corridor, there was no guarantee that the EONIA would follow the intended path within the corridor, unless there was an implicit commitment by the ECB to keep excess liquidity at a level sufficient to push the EONIA down against the DFR for any foreseeable horizon, or unless there was a decision to narrow the corridor much further. Reference to the ECB's key policy interest rates was a safer way to go, because steering expectations of the policy instruments would not encounter implementation or control issues. But the policy rate avenue raised an additional question: whether the ECB should first reach the effective lower bond (ELB) on all of its policy rates, including the MRO rate, before starting to guide rate expectations, or whether forward indications over their likely future rate path could start with any of the three key interest rates still some distance above their respective ELB.

Finally, the GC had to deliberate over the appropriate conditionality of the statement on future rates and decide whether conditionality was to be made explicit, possibly expressing a link between future rate decisions and a numerical value for medium-term inflation, or more qualitative in nature.

After careful debate, the GC issued the following statement on 4 July 2013: 'The Governing Council expects the key ECB interest rates to remain at present or lower levels for an extended period of time. This expectation is based on the overall subdued outlook for inflation extending into the medium term, given the broad-based weakness in the real economy and subdued monetary dynamics.' The selected formulation offered several advantages. First, it made reference to policy rates only, thus making the GC's expectations of future interest rates credible. At the same time, the lower bound and sequencing problem was solved by introducing an easing bias: rates were expected to either remain constant or decrease, thus retaining the option of future actions to test the specific ELB applicable to each of the three key interest rates delimiting the corridor. Furthermore, the conditions on which the policy direction was predicated were made explicit by the second sentence describing the macroeconomic circumstances that warranted an easing of the interest rate outlook. By contrast, establishing a more direct link between the rate path and a numerical value for inflation would have been unduly deterministic and risky. If recent experience was any guide for the future, in a world often buffeted by inflationary—and recessionary—cost-push shocks, as the euro area had been over the previous 15 years, inflation could spike abruptly to high levels. Making the direction of monetary policy conditional on any specific value for inflation would, in those conditions, lead market participants to expect an imminent rate hike, and this anticipation would likely reintroduce the volatility in longer-term interest rates that forward guidance was supposed to limit.

5.3.1 Impact

The effect of the new communication on market interest rates was substantial on the front end of the curve and much less visible over longer maturities (see Figure 5.10). In line with the GC's aspirations, it also inoculated forward rates against adverse contagion from overseas and against excess sensitivity to domestic macroeconomic news. The latter outcome was particularly welcome in a phase in which data releases were more likely than not to point to a cyclical improvement, if only gradual.[9]

---

[9] During the summer of 2013 incoming data proved to be positive. While the GDP figure of the second quarter—marking the end of the second recession in five years—was somewhat stronger than expected, HICP inflation seemed to have stabilised around 1.5% and financial market sentiment had continued to improve on the back of the OMT announcement and the recovery.

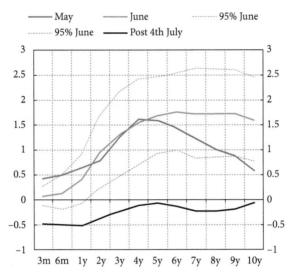

Figure 5.11 Term structure of sensitivity of forward rates to macro news

Source: ECB.

Notes: Estimated above-average sensitivity (when line is positive) and below-average sensitivity (line is negative) of forward rates to surprises in May (solid blue line), June (solid red line) and in the period after the 4 July (solid black line). The dashed red lines are 95% confidence bands for June. Latest observation: 28 August 2013.

During that phase, it was critical to ensure that market prices would not run ahead of the economy and, by doing so, unsettle an orderly pace of macroeconomic convalescence. The incipient return to growth had to be given time to consolidate and extend. Figure 5.11 documents the term structure of measures of sensitivity of forward rates—relative to historic regularities—to a composite indicator of surprises. A line in the figure corresponds to a particular date: when the line is above zero, it means that the sensitivity of forward rates on that date is abnormally large; when it is below zero, it means the opposite. We discriminate in the figure between sensitivities before the 4 July announcement of forward guidance (the red and blue lines refer to June and May 2013, respectively) and after the announcement (the black line). The three measures of sensitivity are given in deviation from normal historical sensitivities. Indeed, while markets happened to receive a series of (moderately positive) surprises during the summer, forward guidance greatly moderated the responsiveness of forward rates throughout the maturity spectrum to the flow of news. Arguably, the novel communication was successful in drawing more market attention onto the overall outlook for price stability than to any incremental piece of information that might become available from time to time.

5.3.2 Activating the Easing Bias

The muted responsiveness of market rates to surprises notwithstanding, as shown in Figure 5.10, market rates kept trending upward over the summer and early autumn,

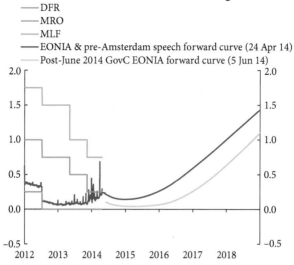

Figure 5.12 Key ECB interest rates, EONIA, and EONIA forward curves on selected dates (percentages per annum)
Sources: Bloomberg and Refinitiv.

in synch with longer-term yields in the United States. After the tantrum episode, long-term interest rates in the United States stabilized at higher levels and provided a gravitational pull for longer-term yields in the euro area as a result (compare the yellow lines in Panels E and F of Figure 4.20). By the autumn, these movements had tightened financial conditions to a measurable extent, and the tightening had occurred in conditions in which inflation was dropping more than anticipated, and real sector indicators were pointing to a slackening pace of economic recovery.

Amid signs that excess liquidity was evaporating at an accelerated clip and reserve scarcity was once more putting upward pressure on the EONIA, in November 2013 the GC decided to compress the rate corridor further and extend by 1.5 years the horizon of the FRFA mode in the Eurosystem credit operations. The MRO rate was reduced to 0.25% which, with an unchanged DFR of 0%, was expected to put a lid on the fluctuations in the overnight rate and, as a consequence, in combination with forward guidance, on term money market rates as well. The extension of the FRFA horizon was meant to reassure banks that access to liquidity would not be impaired at least until maturity of the outstanding three-year LTROs, and as they were entering the delicate phase marked by the first asset quality review and stress-testing exercise conducted by the ECB.

5.4 Credit Crunch

A disquieting feature of late 2013 and early 2014 was the pace at which banks were running down the scale of their balance sheets and the nature of the operations that they were curtailing in the process. Of course, there had been one notable precedent

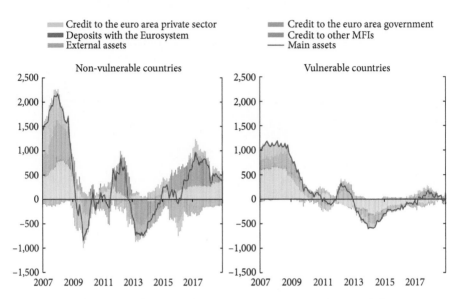

Figure 5.13 Main assets of MFIs resident in euro area countries (12-month flows in EUR billion)

Source: ECB BSI.

Notes: 'Vulnerable countries' comprise Cyprus, Greece, Ireland, Italy, Portugal, Slovenia, and Spain, while 'Non-vulnerable countries' refer to remaining euro area countries. Data are not seasonally adjusted. Latest observation: December 2018.

to the current phase of bank deleveraging: the rapid balance sheet contraction immediately following the Lehman crisis. Figures 5.13 and 5.14 show the expansions and reductions of banks' balance sheets, measured as 12-month euro flows, for core and vulnerable countries, respectively. Looking at the left-hand panel of Figure 5.13, it is easy to discern, in both episodes, the same behavioural pattern for banks domiciled in non-vulnerable countries. When put under pressure to retrench, banks there followed a clear pecking order in adjusting their business operations: they wound down non-core operations—exposures to the rest of the world ('external assets') and to the rest of the euro area banking system ('credit to other MFIs')—and chose to protect core assets, such as loans to the economy and securities holdings. Indeed, the yellow bars, corresponding to flows of credit to the private sector, never turned negative in either episode. By contrast, the strategy followed by banks in the periphery was quite different, with the balance sheet adjustment pursued between 2011 and 2013 playing out in two phases. First, note how banks' liabilities developed in the early, most acute phase of the sovereign debt crisis, between mid-2011 and 2012 (right-hand panel of Figure 5.14). In this time window, banks in vulnerable countries borrowed heavily from the Eurosystem principally under the two three-year LTROs (see the spike in the purple bars) and used the massive borrowed amounts for emergency liability substitution. Consistent with this strategy, the figure shows that the positive spike in central banks' credit to this group of banks is the

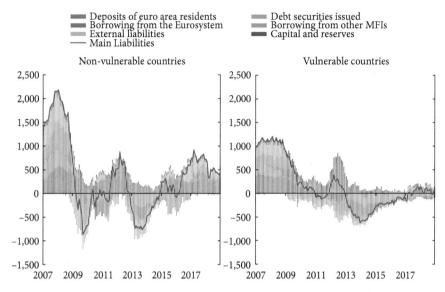

- Deposits of euro area residents
- Borrowing from the Eurosystem
- External liabilities
- Main Liabilities

- Debt securities issued
- Borrowing from other MFIs
- Capital and reserves

Non-vulnerable countries

Vulnerable countries

Figure 5.14 Main liabilities of MFIs resident in euro area countries (12-month flows in EUR billion)

Source: ECB BSI.
Notes: 'Vulnerable countries' comprise Cyprus, Greece, Ireland, Italy, Portugal, Slovenia and Spain, while 'Non-vulnerable countries' refer to remaining euro area countries. Data are not seasonally adjusted. Latest observation: December 2018.

mirror image of a concomitant, equally sized plunge in private sector credit to the same group of banks. By and large, this means that over this first phase of the sovereign crisis, Eurosystem credit to banks in vulnerable countries was used to plug a loss of deposits (the dark green bars) and a withdrawal of credit from other banks domiciled either in core countries (the light green bars) or in countries outside the euro area (the light blue bars). One can even trace this stream of liquidity flowing from the Eurosystem to the periphery (see the purple bars in the right-hand panel of Figure 5.13), and from there finally to the core (see the purple bars in the left-hand panel of Figure 5.13), as peripheral banks were paying down their debt obligations vis-à-vis banks in that area or were funding deposit flights to the core, and their non-retail depositors in the periphery were seeking a safer place to park their cash. The drain of cash from periphery to core had two implications: it changed the liability mix of banks in the periphery—from private to official funding—and the asset mix of banks in the core—from cross-country interbank credit to liquid claims vis-à-vis the Eurosystem. The glut of excess reserves that formed in the books of core country banks made them scramble to reduce it through advance payments of three-year LTRO money.

But the 2011–2012 liability substitution phase in the periphery did not last for long. Soon, distressed banks in vulnerable countries turned to their assets for a further and more decisive margin of adjustment. The damage wrought—primarily in Spain and Ireland—by the burst of the local housing bubble, together with the long-standing need for all these overleveraged economies to scale down debt, inter-acted with the massive blow delivered by the sovereign crisis to the balance sheet position of the banking system in ways that forced these banks to reduce the riskier portion of their assets (see yellow bars in the right-hand panel of Figure 5.13). Saddled with loans going bad at record rates (Figure 4.35), the higher gains in terms of balance sheet repair were to be had from drastic reductions in this particularly risky category of exposures.[10] The vicious deleveraging process taking hold in many banking sectors between 2012 and 2014 is evident in Figures 5.13 and 5.14.

The dual reflection of the same deleveraging phenomenon was the extraordinary sluggishness with which the lending rates applied by banks on loans to their commercial clients declined—if at all—in response to the repeated monetary policy easing adjust-ments made by the ECB between late 2011 and 2014. To document this sluggishness—a sign of profoundly dysfunctional transmission in a bank-based financial system such as Europe's—we use Figure 5.15, which codifies the state of monetary policy transmission at any point in time between 2007 and 2018. The figure is a stylized—but realistic—representation of the loan pricing formula used by the banks in the euro area. The lower boundary of the multi-coloured area is marked by the time series of the specific interest rate along the OIS spot curve that the banks in the euro area select as the benchmark (or base) for fixing the interest rate on a typical commercial loan. It turns out that banks in both core and peripheral economies refer to a spot OIS rate with a maturity of approximately (1 to) 2 years as the base rate. So the floor of the multi-coloured area is the time series of the 2-year OIS spot rate. The rate applied on that typical loan to enterprise—or, more precisely, to a non-financial corporation (NFC)—is the thick black line that marks the upper boundary of the multi-coloured area. The multi-coloured area itself is therefore a straightforward measure of the time-varying 'intermediation wedge': the spread that banks charge over and above the inter-est rate on a risk-free contract to extend a risky loan to their commercial customers.[11]

The loan pricing formula that we assume in constructing the figure is simple. We imagine that the intermediation wedge, namely the difference between the lending rate (i^L) and the 2-year OIS base rate (i^{OIS}), can be decomposed as follows: $i^L - i^{OIS} = spr^{EUR} + spr^D + spr^B + CK + margin$. In other words, the wedge in Figure 5.15 is the sum of spreads that banks charge their clients to remunerate a

---

[10] We calculate that the initial, liability substitution phase lasted roughly 12 months between July 2011 and June 2012. During this period, banks in Spain and Italy increased their Eurosystem borrowing by almost €600 billion. This amount was used in part (€120 billion) to cover a loss in retail deposits—par-ticularly from Spanish banks—but mainly to replace wholesale funding (€350 billion) that was not being rolled over. Loans were also reduced, but the reduction over these first 12 months was only by €20 billion. The anatomy of the balance sheet adjustment changed after July 2012. Between July 2012 and September 2013, banks in Spain and Italy reimbursed Eurosystem credit by almost €200 billion. And the main source of funds for repayments was now asset reduction, mainly loans to the economy. That source alone brought almost a €300 billion reduction in banks' total assets and in the size of their total balance sheet.

[11] What we call the intermediation wedge bears a close resemblance to—and in fact is a specific incar-nation of—what Chari et al. (2007) term the 'investment wedge', a spread that, inter alia, distorts the equilibrium decisions of agents operating in otherwise competitive markets. The intermediation wedge, like the more general investment wedge, is rooted in credit market frictions.

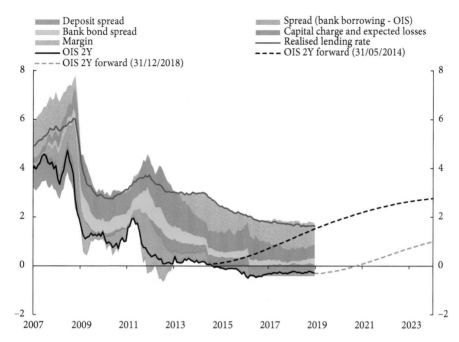

Figure 5.15 Euro area bank lending rates on loans to NFCs and intermediation wedge (percentages per annum)

Sources: ECB, Moody's, Merrill Lynch Global Index, and ECB calculations.

Notes: The intermediation wedge is the distance from the base rate (OIS 2Y, black solid line) to the realized lending rate, as measured by the observed lending rate on loans to NFCs. The light-blue area shows the spread between the rate faced by banks from borrowing from other banks and from the Eurosystem, and the swap rate. As a proxy for the most relevant borrowing rate, we consider the Euribor before June 2014, the MRO until March 2016, and subsequently the DFR. The red area and yellow areas comprise the bank deposit and bank bond spreads, respectively, both weighted by their share as funding sources in banks' balance sheets. The components of the green area are computed based on Basel II risk weights, with probability of default (PD) proxied by Moody's expected default frequencies (EDF). The margin is computed residually, as the difference between observed lending rates and all the other cost components. The OIS 2Y rate is approximately the swap rate that banks in the euro area take a base for NFC loan rate fixation.

Latest observation: December 2018.

variety of loan production factors. The spread between the EURIBOR of corresponding maturity and the OIS base rate (spr^{EUR}, the light blue area), the spread between the EURIBOR and the deposit rate (spr^{D} the red area), and the spread between the EURIBOR and the bond rate (spr^{B}, yellow area) all pay for funding sources. The green layer corresponds to the cost of capital and expected losses, as the bank has to set aside a certain amount of money to meet the regulatory capital charges on the new loan and to cover average loss due to defaults. Finally, the purple area is a residual margin which helps to pay for overhead costs and, as a true economic mark-up, remunerate the bank's equity.[12] We show the intermediation wedge

---

[12] For a description of the empirical counterparts of lending rate decomposition layers, see the notes beneath Figure 5.15.

together with the 2-year OIS forward curves prevailing at end-May 2014 (black dashed line) and at end-2018 (red dashed line), respectively, as proxies for the state of expectations about the future evolution of the banks' base rate entertained in the market at those two points in time. The picture gives an informative summary of the stance of monetary policy and the contemporary state of financial transmission over time. Indeed, if the base rate is high and expected to be high and higher in the future—as indicated by the forward curve corresponding to the 2-year OIS rate— then lending rates tend to be high. If the intermediation wedge is fat, inflated by high costs for banks to borrow and attract capital, then the tax that the banking system is imposing on the economy is large and, again, lending rates tend to be high.

Looking at the evolution of the wedge and its individual components over time, we note two things. First, as one might expect, the global financial crisis marks a major rupture in the intermediation mechanism in the euro area. All loan production cost factors and the wedge as a whole widen measurably from 2009 onwards. Most notably, deposit funding turns from a source of rent for banks engaging in loan creation—a funding component that detracts from the intermediation wedge—into a factor that increases the wedge and the cost of lending overall. This is because, in normal times, banks can ordinarily collect a yield premium—in fact, a generalized form of seigniorage—on their supply of deposits: as deposits confer a bundle of convenience services and monetary benefits to their holders, banks can pay for this source of funding at below-market interest rates.[13] Indeed, before the financial crisis, the red area was steadily below the OIS rate basis. In times of crisis, however, when a systemic banking crisis becomes a concrete possibility, deposit rates incorporate a premium to compensate depositors for the risk that their bank might default. Accordingly, the switch from normal to crisis times is marked by the red area in the figure moving above the OIS base rate (or, equivalently, the spread between deposit rates and the OIS becoming positive).

Second, margins eroded dramatically between 2011 and 2014, as all cost components rose more steeply and quickly than banks could adjust the rates on their clients' loans, given the rate fixation inertia implicit in loan pricing. As the favourable bond repricing spurred by the 'whatever it takes' approach started to compress funding costs, and as the comprehensive assessment contributed to a cheapening of capital, banks took the opportunity to reduce all of their loan cost components in order to expand margins (as shown by the widening of the purple area around 2013, a development due primarily to banks located in the periphery, see Figures 5.16 and 5.17). This meant that lending rates did not follow the steady loosening of the monetary policy stance, represented in the figure by a decline in the OIS rate basis. The pass-through efficiency of monetary policy degraded severely as a consequence.

---

[13] Among the benefits accruing to deposit holders are: the security of money balances convertible into cash on demand at any time to accommodate unpredictable needs, deposit insurance and a reduction in transaction costs.

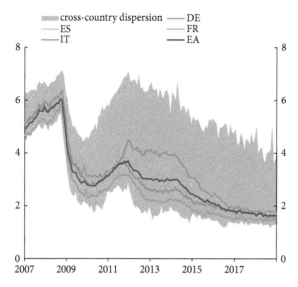

Figure 5.16 Composite indicator of the cost of bank borrowing for NFCs (percentages per annum)

Source: ECB MIR.
Notes: The indicator for the total cost of borrowing for NFCs' new loans is calculated by aggregating short- and long-term rates using a 24-month moving average of new business volumes. The cross-country dispersion displays the minimum and maximum range over a fixed sample of 12 euro area countries.
Latest observation: December 2018.

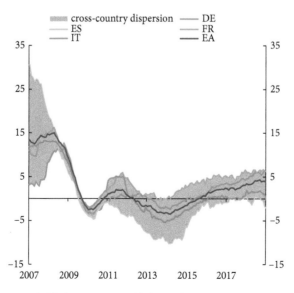

Figure 5.17 Loans to NFCs (year-on-year % change)
Source: ECB BSI.
Latest observation: December 2018.

Figures 5.18 and 5.19 offer a complementary perspective on the same phenomenon.[14] In the periphery, banks' losses on some of their most critical asset portfolios, loans, and government securities, could have been compensated for effectively if the banks in those countries had received immediate and robust injections of fresh capital, including from public sources—national or euro area-wide. But, before 2014, no euro area agency possessed the authority to spearhead and enforce the sort of stress tests and injections of funds that in the United States had proven decisive in reassuring current and prospective shareholders and restoring confidence in the banking system. The rapid launch of euro area-wide stress tests applying uniform standards as early as 2011 would probably have helped make it possible for banks—particularly those based in the periphery—to raise fresh equity from the market. This likely would have preserved the integrity of their operations, kept credit flowing to their

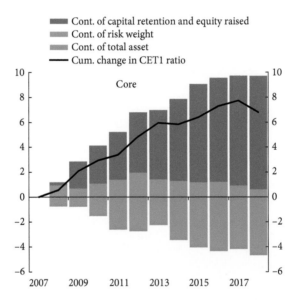

Figure 5.18 Cumulative change in banks' capital ratios in euro area non-vulnerable countries over 2007–2018 and contributing factors (percentage points)

Sources: S&P Market Intelligence (SNL Financial) and ECB.
Notes: December 2007 represents the starting point for cumulating capital changes and its components. Latest observation: December 2018.

---

[14] Note that while both the purple areas in Figures 5.15, 5.18, and 5.19 are related to bank profitability, they refer to distinct concepts. Figure 5.15 shows a margin which, conceptually, is a contribution to profits. However, there are important differences between this margin and actual accounting profits. First, this margin focuses only on lending activity, thereby abstracting from other sources of income—such as interest income on securities held and fee and commission income. Moreover, depending on the business model of the bank, this margin may be more or less representative of the bank's overall income. Finally, on the cost side, this decomposition only considers funding costs, thereby abstracting from operational costs. In Figures 5.18 and 5.19, the purple area shows the contribution to changes in the capital ratio of the amount of banks' equity. This can change either due to issuance of new equity or due to retained earnings. The latter corresponds to capital generated organically and therefore represents a share of total accounting profits.

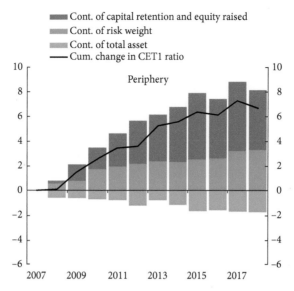

Figure 5.19 Cumulative change in banks' capital ratios in euro area vulnerable countries over 2007–2018 and contributing factors (percentage points)

Sources: S&P Market Intelligence (SNL Financial) and ECB.
Notes: December 2007 represents the starting point for cumulating capital changes and its components. Latest observation: December 2018.

customers and reduced interest rates. As for national sources of capital, as we outline above, the vicious loop largely prevented sovereigns in those countries from coming to the rescue of their national banking systems with the same vigour with which the governments of Germany and the Netherlands, for example, had intervened just a few years earlier.[15] In Spain, a thorough stress test and a systemic injection of public funds occurred only in the second half of 2012, in the context of the EFSF/ESM financial assistance programme designed to recapitalize the Spanish banks. In Italy, the same exercise never happened on a scale that could have cushioned loan origination (see Visco, 2018 for a thorough recounting of the banking crisis in Italy).[16]

In these conditions, as shown in Figure 5.19, few options were left available to banks in vulnerable countries to arrest the erosion of their capital base and build more capital. Specifically, these remaining options comprised deleveraging and/or de-risking, namely cutting down the scale of their overall operations, or the scale of their operations weighed by regulatory risk. Deleveraging on the loan book was an

---

[15] See Gropp, Hakenes, and Schnabel (2010) for an empirical analysis of the competitive effects of government bail-out policies.
[16] Visco (2018) argues that two factors prevented a large-scale public recapitalization of Italian banks: lack of fiscal capacity and the Italian government's funding problems before 2014, and the significant recasting of the European regulatory framework after 2013. As concerns the latter, he identifies a decisive turning point in EU regulation at the time when, in the summer of 2013, the EU Commission published a Communication on State aid for banks which conditioned the use of public funds on the preventive burden-sharing by the banks' shareholders and subordinated bondholders.

effective way for these banks to achieve both objectives. As evident in the figure, the contribution of balance sheet deleveraging (the red and green bars) to balance sheet repair (the rise in the black line) was much larger in the periphery than in the core (see Figure 5.18).

Financial rebalancing pursued in the periphery on the assets side—via deleveraging and the recuperation of margins—rather than the liabilities side—via capital raises—was equivalent to imposing a tax on those economies. As a result, the period of deficient demand was longer and more painful in that region than likely would have been the case had the adverse financial amplifier been arrested by an earlier infusion of capital into the banks.

5.5 Amsterdam

ECB staff and policymakers were looking at these developments with apprehension. The time was ripe for further action. Instability in the unsecured money market called for reconsidering the width and position of the rate corridor and for instruments to solve once and for all the recurrent problem of reserve shortage. Dysfunctional bank-based intermediation in large regions of the euro area demanded that the ECB searched for new ways to give banks incentives to re-engage in credit creation. While part of the contraction of loans in the periphery could no doubt be explained by a deficit in aggregate demand, the central bank could find new instruments to revive the supply of loans. These new instruments would push down the offered lending rate, thereby compressing the borrowers' hurdle rate below the expected rate of return on marginal investment projects in those economies. These relative adjustments would also stimulate loan demand and ultimately aggregate spending. In the meantime, the remorseless fall in inflation was hinting at a more general issue with the stance.

In April 2014, President Draghi took the opportunity of a speech in Amsterdam to set out contingencies and a detailed road map for action (Draghi, 2014a). While the speech was primarily about central bank communication and transparency in general, he turned it into an act of transparency and disclosure about the contingent plans themselves, unprecedented for an institution like the ECB that had traditionally spoken sparingly about scenarios in public and had been non-committal about its future steps. He identified three contingencies. First, domestic financial conditions—the broad spectrum of market interest rates, asset prices and the exchange rate—might continue to tighten, be it because of the receding excess liquidity, international factors pushing up bond yields or the persistent appreciation of the euro. Indeed, since the London speech in July 2012 had triggered a massive repatriation of capital into the euro area, the euro had appreciated by 12% in nominal effective terms, a cumulative exchange rate adjustment that was clearly restraining the economy. In Mr Draghi's words, this constellation of developments might call for protective measures to shield the money market from adverse influences: a further reduction in the width of the rate corridor with a possible cut of its floor, the DFR, to negative levels, and further liquidity injections to curb the variability of the overnight rate.

The second contingency was an exacerbation of impairments in the transmission of the stance through the banks. To be sure, the President mentioned that the reduction in bank funding costs over the last year and the ongoing clean-up of the banking sector through the ECB's comprehensive assessment exercise represented upside potential, which could revitalize bank credit even in the absence of monetary policy interventions. But, if the upside scenario did not materialize, the ECB would deploy 'a longer-term refinancing operation targeted towards encouraging bank lending or an ABS purchase programme, supported by the necessary regulatory changes aimed at revitalizing high quality securitization in Europe.'

Finally, a 'third contingency would be a worsening of the medium-term outlook for inflation. One cause for this could be by a broad-based weakening of aggregate demand that derails our baseline scenario of a moderate recovery. Another cause could be a substantial positive supply shock that, given the current low level of inflation, loosens the anchoring of medium-term inflation expectations. Unlike the other contingencies, the objective here would not be to defend the current stance, but rather to increase meaningfully the degree of monetary accommodation. Hence, the limited margin for manoeuvre that remains over short-term interest rates would not be sufficient. This would be the context for a more broad-based asset purchase programme.' Besides technical tweaks to secure better control over the front end of the curve and align investors' expectations embodied in those interest rates with the near-term orientations of the GC, the question was whether longer-term yields were not too far out of line with levels that would durably contribute to the attainment of the policy objective. A de-anchoring of the far end of the curve would only be amenable to central bank purchases of long-dated assets.

5.6 The Summer Package

The strategy laid out in Amsterdam was modular. It was not designed to be deployed in unison, but to be rolled out as new information was received and was judged to necessitate moving to the next stage of implementation. For all practical purposes, however, when the President spoke in Amsterdam, the ECB was convinced that the first contingency—a passive tightening of financial conditions—was already a fact. By early 2014, the constant drain of aggregate cash balances in the money market due to the early repayments of LTRO funds had reduced excess liquidity to a level of scarcity, at which an increasing number of banks each day were finding themselves short of reserves and had to borrow them from other

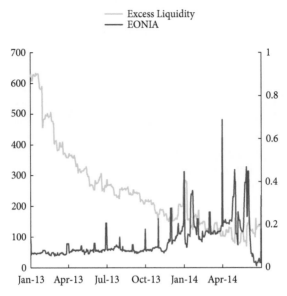

Figure 5.20 Excess liquidity and the EONIA (lhs in EUR billion, rhs in percentages per annum)

Source: ECB.

Latest observation: 30 June 2014.

banks. The upward swings in the level of the EONIA had thus become wider, more frequent and less predictable (see Figure 5.20).[17]

As for the second contingency—a clog in the downstream stages of transmission—the fear was that the damage wrought by banks' aggressive deleveraging in the periphery was already sizeable, was spreading to the core via the intimate intra-euro area trade and financial links, and still had some way to run. Quantitative internal analysis based on a multi-country BVAR showed that total lending to NFCs (the volume of loans plus NFC security issuances) was lower than one would have expected in similar cyclical and financial conditions. In other words, the 'credit gap' was negative. Furthermore, a counterfactual exercise with the same BVAR pointed to a negative contribution of the credit gap to the output gap, which was particularly large for Italy and Spain and already borderline statistically significant for Germany (see Figure 5.21). While the deleveraging process was currently helping to normalize the financial markets, as it was making banks less dependent on wholesale financing, funding pressures could return in the future, as banks were facing a sizeable hump in bond redemptions (see the red bars in the right-hand panel of Figure 5.14). This

[17] Frequent spikes of EONIA trading above the MRO rate had become persistent features amid low and volatile excess liquidity, possible regulatory stigma and coordination challenges. The banks were slow to converge to an established tactic to properly manage their liquidity needs in an environment of lower and more volatile excess liquidity and, on aggregate, were rather reluctant to take up sufficient liquidity in the weekly operations to hedge against liquidity accidents.

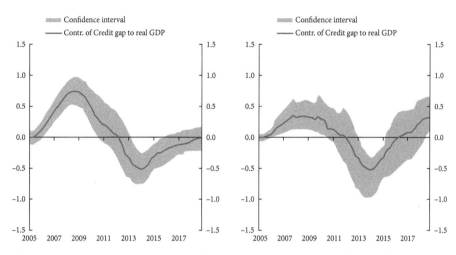

Figure 5.21 Contribution of total credit gap to output gap: Italy and Spain (lhs) and Germany (rhs) (percentage points)
Source: ECB calculations.
Latest observation: December 2018 for underlying data.

hump could determine supply congestion in the bank bond market. Depressed bond valuations would cause banks' borrowing costs to surge and thus force further deleveraging.

In May, after the monetary policy meeting held in Brussels, Mr Draghi signalled that the GC was 'unanimous in its commitment to using also unconventional instruments within its mandate in order to cope effectively with risks of a too prolonged period of low inflation. Further information and analysis concerning the outlook for inflation and the availability of bank loans to the private sector will be available in early June.' This language highlighted two novel elements of inflation monitoring that were absent from previous versions of verbal guidance: a notion of distance from 2% and a time dimension ('low for too long'). At the same time, by referring to the early June arrival of new information on the objective and state of transmission, the GC all but signalled a predisposition for imminent action.

Eventually, at its monetary policy meeting of 5 June 2014, the GC took the decision to act on the first two contingencies. The suite of policy actions that it disclosed was elaborate, innovative and, in no small part, courageous. It comprised a reduction of the DFR to a negative level, −0.10%, a step that no major central bank had ever taken in hundreds of years of central banking history.[18] The MRO rate was

---

[18] Experiences with negative interest rates prior to June 2014 include Switzerland in the 1970s, when a de facto negative interest rate regime was enforced from 1972 to 1978 to defend the Swiss franc against excessive appreciation due to capital inflows, especially from oil-exporting countries; and Denmark from July 2012 to April 2014, when Danmarks Nationalbank reduced the certificates of deposit rate to −20 bps as a way of discouraging capital flows from putting upward pressure on the krone. In Sweden, Sveriges Riksbank also introduced negative interest rates in 2009–10, cutting its repo rate to 0.25% in July 2009

also reduced by 10 bps to a record low of 0.15%. Furthermore, in an official recognition that the 'separation principle' had been more a distraction than a constructive element of the ECB's approach to policy management, the GC decided to suspend the weekly fine-tuning operation sterilizing the liquidity injected under the SMP. Sterilization had contributed to the drying up of free reserves in the overnight market circuit, allowing the new measure to unfreeze some €160 billion in cash and thus contribute to a better anchoring of the EONIA around the new rate floor.

With the second contingency in mind, the GC launched a new series of targeted long-term refinancing operations, TLTROs, embodying conditions to encourage banks to lend to the real economy. It also announced that, subject to further preparatory work, it was prepared to purchase simple and transparent asset-backed securities (ABSs) with underlying assets consisting of claims against the euro area non-financial private sector. The overarching consideration behind the combined TLTRO and ABS initiatives was to utilize banks as pass-through mechanisms of sorts, which—unlike in recent history—would elastically transmit as much stimulus to the real economy as the ECB was putting into the pipeline. The TLTROs were to operate on the banks' liabilities side, establishing tight incentives for banks to pass the funding relief they would receive through TLTROs along to borrowers in the form of lower lending rates. ABS purchases were to act on the assets side: the presence of a new, deep-pocketed buyer in the primary and secondary market of ABSs would encourage banks to originate more loans with a view to bundling and selling them on attractive terms into a revitalized market for securitizations.

5.6.1 TLTRO-I

What would become known as TLTRO-I, the first of three rounds of TLTRO recalibrations, went through a fair amount of cross-examination and debate at the technical level. Two parameters, among a multitude, were key to determining the accommodative potential of the operations: how to evaluate the lending performance of participating banks, and how to reward the good performers. On the metric for lending performance (the 'benchmark'), there were two options: either project forward the stock of eligible loans, as recorded at some reference date prior to the onset of the operations, and demand that banks at least maintain that stock until the end of a certain observation period during the life of the operations; or, make a distinction between those banks—primarily located in the core—that had been expanding their eligible loan book prior to the operation ('positive net lenders'), and those banks—mainly in the periphery—that had been contracting their loan book

and the overnight deposit rate to −0.25% in order to keep the interest rate corridor symmetrical. Nevertheless, the amount of funds on deposits overnight was at the time negligible, as the central bank typically used daily fine-tuning operations to drain most excess liquidity from the market. As a result, the regime was still that of positive interest rates, with the repo rate as the main policy rate steering money market conditions.

('negative net lenders'). In this second case, positive net lenders would be evaluated against a benchmark equal to the stock of loans recorded at the reference date, while negative net lenders would be allowed some further room for deleveraging, with the benchmark projecting the declining trend observed in history into the life of the operations.

Once the benchmark for lending performance was set, a system to reward those banks meeting or exceeding their benchmark had to be identified so as to provide a sufficient incentive for them to expand credit to the economy. The built-in incentive for banks to lend could be provided by varying prices or quantities. In the former price-based version, one could adopt a pricing schedule for the operation starting from an unconditional borrowing rate above the prevailing MRO rate—offered to all banks regardless of their final lending performance—and granting those banks outperforming their lending benchmark a discount relative to that entry rate. In the latter quantity-based version, banks would instead be granted an initial maximum borrowing allowance sufficiently low, and a borrowing rate fixed for all participants at a flat level sufficiently attractive, to generate TLTRO rationing and thus stimulate demand for extra borrowing. In this case, the targeting feature of TLTRO-I would be associated with the incentive for banks to earn additional borrowing allowances by expanding lending beyond their benchmark during the life of the operation.

Eventually, after considered analysis, the GC chose a combination of parameters that would contribute to levelling the playing field across banking systems to the maximum extent possible. The setting of the bank-specific benchmarks would allow for a distinction between positive and negative net lenders. The pricing would be uniform across banks, and incentives would work through tailoring borrowing allowances to the individual banks' ex post loan performance. Specifically, the ECB pledged to conduct a series of eight quarterly TLTROs, all maturing in September 2018, at a uniform borrowing rate fixed over the life of each operation and equal to the MRO rate prevailing at the time of take-up plus a flat fee of 10 bps.[19] The attractive borrowing rate—and more attractive the earlier the borrowing date—was meant to frontload take-up in 2014, when the reserve scarcity problem was particularly acute. Under the first two operations in September and December 2014, banks could draw-down only up to an initial entitlement equal to 7% of their eligible loan book—comprising loans to the private sector outstanding at the end of April 2014 (the reference date), but excluding loans to households for house purchase. However, participating banks would be granted additional draw-down entitlements in the form of extra borrowing allowances in the first two years of the programme on condition that, over that period, they expanded their eligible loans above their benchmarks. The benchmark would be flat at the pre-TLTRO stock of eligible loans for positive net lenders, and projected through a declining

[19] Starting from the third operation, the spread of 10 bps was abolished.

trend 'with a kink' for negative net lenders.[20] Figures 5.22 and 5.23 show how the benchmark was to be constructed for two hypothetical banks representative of positive and negative net lenders, respectively. The 'kinked trend' was conceived to account for the disadvantaged starting positions of negative net lenders, thus granting them more time to adjust their lending strategies with respect to their deleveraging past while at the same time strengthening their incentives to make an extra effort to expand loans further down the line. There would be an advance repayment option 24 months after take-up and a forced repayment obligation in September 2016 for those banks whose eligible net lending provided between April 2014 and the end of April 2016 was below the benchmark. Most importantly, those banks whose eligible loan volumes would outpace the benchmark during the observation period would be able to claim additional borrowing allowances equal to three times the distance between actual and benchmark loans.

Figure 5.23 shows the specific case of a negative net lender, which after the inception of the programme, managed to keep its lending to the private sector excluding mortgages above its benchmark. In March 2015, the bank exceeded its benchmark

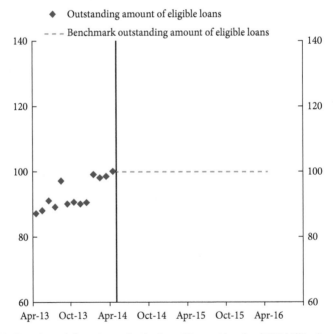

Figure 5.22 Benchmark for a hypothetical positive net lender (EUR billion)
Source: ECB.
Latest observation: April 2016.

---

[20] The initial stock of loans and banks' lending behaviour prior to the onset of the operations were to be converted into notional measures in order to remove the impact on observed stocks arising from loan sales and securitizations, revaluations, exchange rate variations and statistical reclassifications.

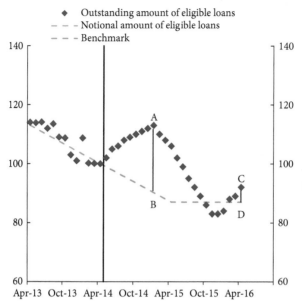

Figure 5.23 Benchmark for a hypothetical negative net lender (EUR billion)
Source: ECB.
Latest observation: April 2016.

by the segment AB, which entitled it at that point in time to borrow an extra amount equal to three times AB. By the end of the observation period (April 2016), however, the lending overshoot had shrunk to CD. As such, the bank had to reimburse a fraction of the additional allowance that it drew down in March 2015. That fraction is proportional to the difference between its net lending in September 2016 and its net lending in 2015—when the additional allowance was claimed.[21]

TLTRO-I was an innovative instrument: very dense in its parameters, challenging to communicate, bordering on the micromanagement of banks' business operations, but no doubt breaking new ground in terms of potential for conjuring up a variety of easing channels. Assuming a take-up of no less than €400 billion, staff estimated that the possibility for participating banks to substitute expensive private funding with TLTRO liquidity would foster a decline in lending rates by more than 10 bps—what they called a 'direct pass-through channel'. But the beneficial effects would extend far beyond the pool of participants. As the banks taking part in TLTRO-I would likely

---

[21] Additional operational features of TLTRO-I included the possibility for banks to form a 'TLTRO group' if they fulfilled specific conditions (for details, see the press release of 3 July 2014). They could then participate in a TLTRO through one member of the group, the 'lead institution'. In this case, the calculation of the TLTRO group's benchmark and borrowing allowances was based on aggregated loan data for the TLTRO group. Counterparties participating in TLTRO-I (individually or as the lead institution of a TLTRO group) were also subject to reporting obligations, having to submit reporting templates to their home NCB on a quarterly basis until the programme's end in September 2018, and being required to have an annual examination of data accuracy conducted by an audit firm (which could be carried out in the context of the regular annual audit exercise) or on the basis of an equivalent arrangement.

cancel or postpone plans to issue bonds on the market, bank bond scarcity would bring funding cost relief even to those banks that were to shun the operations—in other words, a 'portfolio rebalancing channel' would operate indirectly and across the board. An additional 'signalling channel' was also to be expected if a large injection of TLTRO liquidity determined a shift in investor expectations concerning the future policy path. The two latter effects combined would cut lending rates for banks' clients by another 10 bps.

The strength of all of these channels was conditional on a robust and early take-up, itself a function of banks' expectations concerning the likely evolution of the economy. The more optimistic the outlook, the more banks would be driven to the operation in anticipation of a pick-up in loan demand and a decline in risk. But, in the spring of 2014, sentiment was flimsy and—after the heavy sanctions imposed by the EU on the Russian Federation following its annexation of Crimea—expectations were being marked down as summer approached. There was probably room for disappointment in terms of both the TLTRO-I volumes and its effects.[22]

5.6.2 ABSPP, CBPP-3, and the Balance Sheet Target

This is why combining TLTRO-I with a programme of outright purchases of ABSs was an attractive strategy. It could strengthen in a meaningful way the direct pass-through channel arising from TLTRO-I. Financial normalization had never progressed in the secondary market for ABSs to nearly the same extent as it had done in the markets for other debt instruments competing with ABSs in terms of risk characteristics and investment base. Figures 5.24 and 5.25 contrast the broad index of spreads on high-rated senior tranches of various typologies of European ABSs with similar composite indices of spreads that issuers had to pay in the markets for covered bonds and non-financial corporate bonds, respectively. As shown in Figure 5.24, the slight compression in spreads that had occurred in the ABS space had gone hand in hand with—and probably was largely explained by—the collapse in ABS issuance. Note that the relevant measure of issuance in this figure is the red bar, which represents the fraction of new supply placed with final investors, as opposed to the yellow bar, which represents ABSs retained by originators for use as collateral in Eurosystem refinancing operations. Overall, all the conditions seemed to be in place in 2014 for a large and persistent bidder like a central bank intervening in this market to be able to turn around the market substantially, which was the essential precondition for setting in motion a powerful pass-through effect.[23]

---

[22] In terms of volumes, the size of the overall take-up was influenced by the envisaged price structure which was fixed at inception and initially set at MRO plus a spread amounting to 10bps. Starting from the third operation, the spread of 10 bps was abolished thereby making the operation more attractive.

[23] Besides remaining impaired overall, the ABS market in the euro area was segmented across geographies and typologies. Public issuance and secondary market trading of ABSs had failed to recover, except moderately in Germany, the Netherlands and France. Deals from stressed economies either involved short-maturity, high-yield assets (such as auto, credit card or leasing receivables) or SME

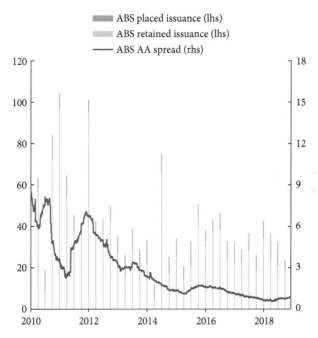

Figure 5.24 Quarterly gross issuance and spreads in the ABS market (EUR billion and percentages per annum)

Source: ECB.

Notes: The spread is the Barclays Euro Asset-Backed Security AA Index relative to the four-year OIS rate. Latest observation: December 2018.

The second reason to expect a powerful pass-through effect from an ABS initiative was that the link between a given change in the spread paid on a certain ABS tranche by the originator and the rate charged by the bank on the primary market for the credits that collateralized the ABSs was judged to be stronger. First of all, the internal

transactions with specific support from the EIB. Analysts described this market as bipolar: a 'rate product'—namely a good substitute for highly rated sovereign securities—in core jurisdictions and a 'credit product'—meaning something similar to speculative-grade securities—in peripheral countries. The amount of subordination (credit enhancement) that originators had to build into the structure in order to attract a prime rating for the most senior ABSs had evolved over time. Before the crisis, it was sufficient for Spanish banks to build a buffer of no more than 5 to 10% to manufacture a senior piece with an AAA rating. In 2014, the subordinated buffer ranged between 10 and 30% but, despite this enhancement, Spanish banks were not able to attract an AAA rating on the most senior tranche of their securitizations. As such, the cost tripled and the return for originators to place the highest-grade tranches declined. For this reason, ABS structures for which deal economics did not work in market terms were fully retained by the originators and only used as collateral for Eurosystem operations. By fully retaining, the originators did not need to pay yields on ABSs that would imply upfront losses. However, this situation was difficult to justify on the basis of actual performance. In fact, a number of securitization products had established a long track record of solid performance, including through the trough of the crisis. For example, data from Standard & Poor's indicate that by end-2011, only 0.07% of the balances underlying European residential mortgage-backed securities (RMBSs) had defaulted (AFME, 2012). Moreover, during the period of market turmoil in 2011, European RMBSs had a superior marked-to-market performance to most EU sovereign debt and senior bank debt, including a high number of covered bonds (with the exception of Pfandbriefe).

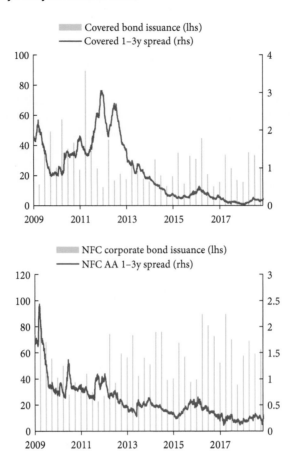

Figure 5.25 Quarterly gross issuance and spreads in the covered and NFC unsecured bond market (EUR billion and percentages per annum)

Sources: Dealogic and IHS Markit iBoxx.
Notes: The spreads are computed as the respective iBoxx bond index yields over the two-year OIS rate. Latest observation: December 2018.

view was that so-called patient investors, essentially insurance companies and pension funds, had a relatively inelastic demand for high-grade securitization tranches. These investors had a low demand for liquidity—because they mostly held bonds to maturity—but a high demand for safety. Seen from this angle, highly rated securitization tranches offered slightly more illiquidity—compared with competing investments—in exchange for greater safety: because the exposure to any default in the underlying pool of loans was minimized by diversification and subordination. Therefore, the reasoning was, if the central bank were able—through its purchases—to create relative scarcity in the ABS investment bucket, and there was a pool of investor capital dedicated to relatively high-quality debt instruments, originators would be incentivized to manufacture new ABSs, which in turn could expand loan supply and force down bank lending rates. Indeed, this was one of the prime channels through which the purchases of mortgage-backed securities (MBSs) by the Federal Reserve System under its large scale asset purchase programme was supposed to work: it created a scarcity of MBSs and induced banks to generate mortgages on the margin, which in turn established a tight connection between the evolution of the yield on the MBSs purchased by the Fed and the mortgage rate in the primary market for conformable mortgages.[24]

As a positive side effect, a revitalized ABS industry could promote a more balanced financial structure for the economy as a whole. In this respect, more than half of mortgages were securitized in the United States, either through government-sponsored enterprises (GSEs), or without GSE intermediation. In the euro area, the proportion was extremely limited even for mortgages and almost irrelevant for other loan categories. This structural difference could put European banks at a great disadvantage relative to US banks and other international competitors in terms of possibilities to deconsolidate loan portfolios, that is, to shed loans—once they had originated them—and to conserve on balance sheet capacity. If market conditions could be created for European banks to be able to securitize more actively, this would be beneficial both for those banks that had to deleverage aggressively—without hurting loans—and those that wanted to expand activities—because, via securitization, they could spare balance sheet capacity that they could then reuse for yet more credit intermediation.

However, for banks to be able to transfer risk and deconsolidate, the originators needed to be able to place at least the mezzanine or the full capital structure of the ABSs, respectively, in the market. Mezzanine and junior bonds were competing with asset classes such as senior unsecured bank bonds, corporate bonds, and high-yield bonds. Accordingly, 'fair' treatment of non-senior securitization bonds compared with these other asset classes was necessary to spur investor demand and, in turn, enable securitization to achieve the credit risk transfer from the originator to other

---

[24] See Hancock and Passmore (2011) and Krishnamurthy and Vissing-Jorgensen (2013). The latter paper writes: 'The MBS purchases lower MBS yields because of capital constraints in the MBS market and because the Fed's purchases are concentrated in the production coupon MBS where the Fed's purchases create a shortage of the cheapest-to-deliver MBS. ... the shortage of the current coupon MBS induces the private sector to create more of the scarce asset. That is, banks have an incentive to make new mortgage loans...' Other forms of super-safe investment than securitization, say prime corporate bonds, have adversely skewed risk. The probability of a prime corporate bond being paid off in full is high, but the value of its principal is roughly reduced by half in default. Securitization payoffs, meanwhile, are not so adversely skewed because investors' exposure to any one default is normally a small fraction of the total securitization principal. In perfect capital markets, the pricing of risk is identical across all assets. Issuing high-quality debt and retaining the residual has no benefit over the converse issuance strategy, along the lines described in Modigliani and Miller (1958). If, however, there is a pool of investor capital that is dedicated to relatively high-quality debt instruments, the supply of such instruments to the market can lag demand, and, in the meantime, an issuer of ABSs can earn attractive returns. Judging by what happened in the wake of the FOMC's policy announcements, this segmentation condition seems to be clearly satisfied. For example, following the 13 September 2012 announcement (that it would purchase $40 billion in MBSs per month in tandem with an ongoing maturity extension programme for US Treasuries), long-term Treasury yields were roughly unchanged but yields on MBSs fell dramatically. Moreover, the pass-through to primary mortgage rates was significant too. According to Freddie Mac's primary mortgage market survey, the rate on 30-year fixed-rate mortgages came down by more than 20 bps in just two months to reach historic lows.

banks or to other sectors, for example insurance companies. In the absence of banking and insurance regulatory frameworks actively promoting such a level playing field across investment typologies with similar risk characteristics, relying too much on an ABS purchase programme as a strategy for transforming banks into vehicles for credit creation and disposal was hazardous.

All in all, there was a choice to be made between being even more targeted than under the TLTROs and focusing on ABSs backed by very specific types of loans, such as commercial loans to NFCs and SMEs. Or, rather intervening in a much more inclusive pool of ABS typologies. Arguing for the former option was the consideration that the limited ABS supply and scarce liquidity observed in any particular niche of the ABS market did not necessarily mean that the supply of new ABSs might not respond to the ECB programme dynamically. After all, the market for MBSs—which had largely dried up with gross issuance collapsing—had reacted robustly to the Fed's November 2008 announcement that it would commence an MBS programme. Then again, this strategy of relying on a dynamic expansion of the market was extremely risky. To be sure, a very targeted ABS programme could maximize the stimulus per each euro spent. The risk, however, was that the overall amount of stimulus that could be introduced would probably be very weak, particularly at the outset, given the limited outstanding stocks.

Ultimately, the GC opted for broader coverage, not only including residential mortgage-backed securities (RMBSs) in a dedicated ABS purchase programme (the ABSPP), but pushing out the perimeter of the purchase programme targeting non-financial, privately issued securities to include covered bonds. This was viewed as a safer strategy. While the inclusion of RMBSs in the purchasable pool of ABSs could make the notional size of the programme as large as €250 billion, the realistic possibilities for the ECB to source those bonds in the market were difficult to estimate. The purchasable stocks of covered bonds were sufficiently vast (some €1.2 trillion) to provide the insurance that the GC was seeking. A new round of the covered bond purchase programme (CBPP-3) could easily bring the overall envelope to €500 billion.[25]

---

[25] Further technical details of the ABS purchase programme, as communicated in the press release of 2 October 2014, consisted of the following elements. First, it was decided to purchase senior and guaranteed mezzanine tranches of asset-backed securities in both primary and secondary markets. Second, in order to qualify for purchases under the programme, ABS senior tranches had to be eligible under the collateral framework for Eurosystem credit operations, be denominated in euro and have issuer residence within the euro area, be secured by claims against non-financial private sector entities resident in the euro area, and have a second-best credit assessment of at least CQS3. As regards mezzanine tranches, it was communicated at a later stage that the Eurosystem could purchase mezzanine tranches of ABSs provided that those mezzanine tranches would be subject to a guarantee complying with the criteria for guarantees in the Eurosystem collateral framework, meaning that the guarantee had to be unconditional and irrevocable, payable on first demand, and cover principal, interest and any amounts due under the ABSs. Third, the Eurosystem was to conduct appropriate credit risk and due diligence procedures on the purchasable universe on an ongoing basis. Fourth, it was decided to apply an issue share limit of 70% per ISIN. Last, it was decided that for fully retained securities, purchases by the Eurosystem would be possible subject to some participation by other market investors.

Overall, ex ante certainty about the size of the programme was increasingly seen as a prerequisite. To be sure, taking out insurance against TLTRO underperformance by adding an ABSPP and CBPP programme was primarily motivated by the desire to enhance the direct pass-through potential of the combined credit easing initiative. But the idea that, unlike under a temporary lending programme, outright purchases would afford the extra dividend of being in command of the overall size of the Eurosystem balance sheet was a consideration that had risen in prominence in the run-up to the decisions. In assessing the repayments-induced sustained contraction of the Eurosystem's balance sheet that is apparent in Figure B.4.2.1 of Chapter 4, the view was that the ECB could not afford to scale down its exposures to an ailing economy. That view had quietly displaced the contrarian view that the reduction in Eurosystem exposures was endogenous and warranted by the euro area's return to financial stability. In conditions in which the ECB had all but exhausted its capacity to seek a more accommodative policy through conventional instruments, a 'balance sheet policy' was the next line of attack. As economic recovery was lacklustre at best, losing momentum and facing the risk of relapsing into contraction, with an inflation rate heading towards outright deflation (see Section 5.8) and dismal money and credit creation, the ECB needed to find an 'optimal' commitment policy promising that the stimulus would be locked in for as long as necessary to accompany the economy to a safer place. A deliberate expansion of the balance sheet through the acquisition of long-dated assets that would take a long time to redeem was the closest to such a commitment strategy that the ECB at the time judged consistent with its framework.

So, while communicating the decisions that the ECB would 'purchase a broad portfolio of simple and transparent asset-backed securities (ABSs) with underlying assets consisting of claims against the euro area non-financial private sector under an ABS purchase programme (ABSPP)' together with 'a broad portfolio of euro-denominated covered bonds issued by MFIs domiciled in the euro area under a new covered bond purchase programme (CBPP3)', the GC on 4 September 2014 added an important and consequential line: 'The newly decided measures, together with the targeted longer-term refinancing operations which will be conducted in two weeks, will have a sizeable impact on our balance sheet.' A fortnight later, President Draghi used his quarterly testimony to the EU Parliament to expand on the balance sheet sentence in an unequivocal direction. He said:

> The Governing Council has emphasized that the combination of measures announced between June and September will have a sizeable impact on the ECB balance sheet, which is expected to move towards the dimensions it used to have at the beginning of 2012. With the purchase programmes, we are starting a transition from a monetary policy framework predominantly founded on passive provision of central bank credit to a more active and controlled management of our balance sheet. **(EU Parliament, 22 September 2014)**

He used similar words airing the notion of an informal 'balance sheet target' in replies to questions at the regular post-meeting press conference of 2 October 2014. Finally, the target was officially sanctioned by the GC and included in the introductory statement following the November monetary policy meeting.

5.7 The Effective Lower Bound

Throughout this chapter, we will refer to negative rates as 'NIRP', an acronym for 'negative interest rate policy'. But have negative rates been part of an intentional policy to ease credit conditions since the very beginning? No, negative rates were conceptualized into a deliberate credit easing policy, into a goal-bound 'NIRP', only as the ECB gained more experience of how the money market was adjusting to the negative rate environment, and more and more data were testifying to the potency of negative rates in shaping rate expectations and the yield curve more generally. For much of 2014—as the Amsterdam speech had made explicit—lowering the DFR into negative territory was largely viewed as a technical tweak opening the door to a reduction in the MRO rate further towards zero. Staff saw a distance between the DFR and the MRO rate of at least 25 bps as necessary to safeguard a minimal quantum of activity in the interbank overnight money market. The view was that banks' incentives to engage in liquidity trades with their peers would likely have been suppressed by the reduced trading spreads that too narrow a corridor would bring with it. In those conditions, the return that banks could earn from lending liquidity to other banks—and exposing themselves to some counterparty risk— would be too small compared with the return from holding liquidity idle in the deposit facility. Incidentally, a scenario in which banks would massively withdraw from trading liquidity in the market was made likelier by the scant signs of defragmentation in interbank transactions, with overnight activity still concentrated within banks of the same rating group and in the same jurisdiction. Reflecting these views, President Draghi at the press conference of June 2014, just few minutes after announcing a negative DFR, remarked that: 'I would say that for all the practical purposes, we have reached the lower bound. However, this doesn't exclude some little technical adjustments and which could lead to some lower interest rates in one or the other or both parts of the corridor' (Draghi 2014c). In the introductory statement to the July press conference, the same concept was codified in a formal amendment to the GC's forward guidance. The new formulation mentioned that 'the key ECB interest rates will remain at present levels for an extended period of time', thus eliminating the easing bias ('at present or lower levels') that had been used for the past year (Draghi 2014d). Despite the removal of the easing bias, the forward curve moved lower in reaction to the June decisions (see Figure 5.12).

Consequently, markets were surprised when the GC on 4 September took the decision to lower the MRO rate by another 10 bps to 0.05% and, most notably, the DFR to a more negative figure, –0.20%. The chief motivation for the decision was to make the upcoming first TLTRO more price-attractive through a lower benchmark rate (the TLTRO borrowing rate was the sum of the MRO rate and a 10-basis-point spread), with a view to enhancing the fire power of the new targeted loans to banks. Lowering the MRO rate, in turn, necessitated that the DFR be cut by an equal margin, if a meaningful width of the rate corridor was to be maintained. But, in the light of the June communication that had stressed that the lower bound was probably nearby, the further 'technical adjustment' to the floor of the corridor required a comment on the putative position of the effective lower bound. Internal analysis had tentatively placed the lower bound at around −0.25%. Those computations were based on an estimate of the cost of storage, transportation and security related to the hoarding of physical currency conducted by the two central banks that had introduced negative rates in the past, Danmarks Nationalbank and the Swiss National Bank. These studies suggested that storage and insurance costs for banknotes moderately exceeded 0.25%. Of course, whether those fixed costs were to prove sufficiently strong deterrents to discourage banks from converting electronic reserves into paper currency in material volumes could not be assessed in a timeless way. Banks would probably be reluctant to face the significant operational changes and bear the fixed costs of the massive conversion if the negative rate period was anticipated to be short, but would be much more willing to consider the conversion option otherwise. However, the experience gleaned in Denmark, where the seven-day DPR had been negative since July 2012—initially at a level of −0.20% and later increased to −0.10%—suggested that an effective lower bound of around −0.25% was a safe bet, even if one was ready to entertain the possibility that the DFR might have to be held at that level for a long time. In any event, the precise location of the lower bound for the DFR was not so relevant after all, given that there was no recognizable rationale—at the time—for moving the DFR independently of the MRO rate. And the MRO rate itself was thought to be downwardly constrained by a hard zero bound anyway, because it was hardly conceivable—at the time—that the ECB could ever apply a negative rate on a loan to a bank. All that mattered was to preserve some space for banks to keep transacting with each other. And that minimal space was going to be preserved even in the hypothetical case of an MRO rate at 0% and a DFR rate at −0.25%.

It was reflecting on these thought processes and background analyses that the President, when asked about the position of the lower bound at his post-meeting press conference on 4 September, answered: 'And now we are at the lower bound, where technical adjustments are not going to be possible any longer.' What changed over the following year or so that made the ECB reconsider the exact location of the effective lower bound and the desirability of lowering the DFR to even more negative levels? Two things changed: the assessment of the costs for banks to engage in wholesale tax avoidance strategies when confronted with a negative rate 'tax' on their free reserves; and the estimated amount of extra stimulus that further reductions in the DFR could deliver. Further analysis on the distribution of excess liquidity across counterparties demonstrated that liquidity holdings in excess of reserve requirements were quite concentrated among relatively few banks, with the vast majority of banks instead holding less than €1 billion. For banks in this latter group, the fixed costs of storage, security and transportation services associated with hoarding currency in their vault space were sufficiently large to make even a 0.5%–0.6% negative rate charge applied to their (limited) taxable pool of reserves look tolerable in comparison. These fresh calculations moved the estimated effective lower bound deeper into negative territory. But what convinced the ECB that it was in fact desirable to bring the DFR closer to that (more negative) threshold was the realization that the monetary policy benefits of a negative DFR were more material than previously imagined. The dispositive fact was the observed reaction of the yield curve—both the EONIA forward curve and the cash sovereign curve—to the unexpected rate cut of September 2014 and its further adjustments over the following months. First, it was remarkable that—notwithstanding the President's observation regarding the lower bound having been reached—the forward curve developed the mild inversion over short to medium-term maturities that is visible in Figure 5.9. Evidently, the very fact that the DFR had been reduced a second time to a more negative value was seen as an indication that it could be reduced yet again. The 'negative belly'—a low level of the forward EONIA over intermediate maturities relative to the actual EONIA—and the negative skew of the density around the most likely EONIA path embedded in the forward curve would become more pronounced in the course of 2015. But, in the autumn of 2014, such a configuration of forward rates already suggested that investors were placing considerable odds on scenarios that would necessitate a lower and flatter trajectory of the DFR than envisioned in market surveys at the time, which were more aligned with the ECB's official communication about the lower bound. Second, the term structure of impacts on the sovereign curves was peculiar. Whereas a rate cut in normal times typically had a distinctly larger downward effect on the front end than on the back end of the curve, with the impacts declining monotonically with maturities (sometimes referred to by market participants as a 'bull steepening' shift), a cut from a negative level to a more negative level had the puzzling bell-shaped profile of impacts that is illustrated and documented in Section 6.2. This was a symptom that negative rates influenced rate expectations to an extent undocumented by event studies conducted around conventional and unconventional policy announcements. We will return to the characteristic pattern of NIRP transmission through the expectations component of longer-term interest rates in the next chapter. Here, suffice it to say that the surprisingly pronounced responsiveness of the mid-segment of the yield curve to the September cut meant that swap rates with approximately one to two years to maturity—which, as we argue above, happen to be pivotal in the pricing of bank loans in the euro area—were pushed lower by a bigger margin than the adjustment in the DFR itself, both in core and peripheral countries. Accordingly, the time-varying swap rate relevant for loan rate fixation in the euro area dived below the zero line and pulled down the whole spectrum of rates and other factors that determine the cost of loans originated by banks. See how the lower boundary of the bank intermediation wedge shown in Figure 5.15—the time-varying benchmark rate for loans—turned negative and pulled the representative lending rate and all the coloured areas—the cost components of loan origination—down with it around September 2014.

5.8 The 'Third Contingency'

After four quarters of lacklustre expansion, euro area growth came to a halt in the second quarter of 2014. Throughout the summer and autumn, business and consumer sentiment continued to decline, weighed down by geopolitical tensions, in particular the Ukraine crisis. Uncertainty about the strength of recovery was dampening the propensity to invest. In fact, following four quarters of mild growth, total capital formation had fallen in the second quarter. Germany was running on one engine, services, as manufacturing was feeling the pain of the international sanctions against the Russian Federation. In the third quarter, German car production lost almost 7% on the back of faltering industrial and export orders. France and Italy—the latter hit particularly hard by the loss of exports to Russia—were clearly falling behind. The OECD forecasts for euro area growth, at 0.8% for 2014 and 1.1% for 2015, were even more pessimistic than those produced by the September ECB projections (0.9% and 1.6%, respectively).

The nagging concern at the ECB was the state and dynamics of longer-term inflation expectations. The five-year, five-year forward inflation rate had always featured prominently in the arsenal of metrics that the ECB had regularly consulted to test the solidity of longer-term expectations among investors seeking inflation protection. The measure was an attractive test for anchoring because it was an average—and thus little influenced by point expectations pertaining to any specific horizon—and was far removed from the present—making it less susceptible to shocks that might influence realized inflation on the date of measurement. Since the spring of 2014, the five-year forward inflation rate five-year ahead as well as a basket of market-based measures of forward inflation compensation one to five years ahead had been sliding down, had quietly decoupled from the observed developments in the price of oil, and had shown an increasing coherence with the negative trend in the macro-surprise index—a bellwether aggregate indicator of the flow of data releases for business activity, orders and consumer sentiment (see Figure 5.26). In August, the slide gathered pace and the forward inflation rate unexpectedly dropped below 2% for the first time since the height of the sovereign crisis. The credit easing measures announced in June, as critical as they were in repairing transmission and promoting a change in borrowing conditions, were slow to show through in the stream of data and change the general tone of macro-news.

President Draghi, in a speech delivered in Jackson Hole at the flagship annual conference of the US Federal Reserve on 22 August, drew attention to the phenomenon and the risk that, though partly due to temporary influences,

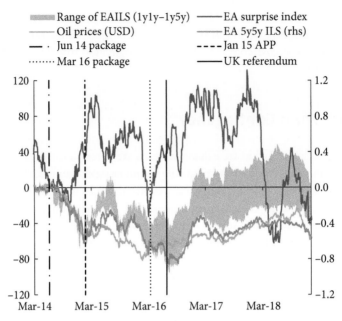

Figure 5.26 Flow of macro-news, market-based inflation expectations, and oil prices (normalized, 4 June 2014=0)

Sources: Bloomberg and Refinitiv.
Latest observation: 31 December 2018.

disinflation might become entrenched (Draghi 2014e). He commented that 'the Governing Council will acknowledge these developments and within its mandate will use all the available instruments needed to ensure price stability over the medium term'. Unlike in the rare prior episodes of below-2% readings, the drop in the five-year in five-year forward inflation rate did not prove temporary and in fact deepened a few days later, around the time the ECB unveiled the full scope of the summer package. The renewed decline following the 4 September announcement was particularly troubling. Markets had remained unimpressed by the size of the package, and the conviction was rising and spreading among traders and ECB observers that, overall, the package fell short of what was needed for the ECB to make good on the GC's pledge to bring the Eurosystem's balance sheet back to its 2012 levels, let alone address the worsening inflation outlook. Internal econometric analysis, exploring the connection between market-based measures of longer-term inflation expectations and the price of oil, rejected the thesis that the negative trend in the former was simply a reflection of the contemporaneous fall in the latter. Rather, it identified movements in macro-financial factors, such as weak credit dynamics, feeble economic conditions and fragile confidence, as the main factors driving down the five-year in five-year forward inflation-linked swap rate. As for the price of crude oil, its sharp decline in US dollars was seen as being due to a mix of supply and demand determinants. Supply was supported by a continued surge in US shale oil production and the recovery in the production capacities of Iraq and Libya. But global oil demand, notably from China and Europe, was faltering in synch. Ample near-term supply, in combination with weak demand, was causing oil inventories to rise, suggesting that even a brisk cyclical turnaround would not be enough to boost prices. Refining margins were being squeezed as well, as excess production and high storage rates rippled down the supply chain. The glut of oil production was translating into a glut of refined products and persistent downside pressures to consumer prices. In December, measured year-on-year inflation fell below 0% for the first time since 2009. These trends were infiltrating expectations. The Survey of Professional Forecasters (SPF), typically impervious to short-term negative inflation surprises, recorded a fall in medium-term inflation expectations to a historic low of 1.8%. Expectations for 2016 were revised down by nearly 20 bps to 1.35% compared with the previous round. By December, the entire inflation-linked swap curve had sunk in tandem with realized inflation and was predicting that inflation would not be in line with the ECB's 'close to 2%' aim before 2023. For the first time in the history of monetary union, the probability mass assigned by the risk-neutral density computed from five-year maturity zero-coupon inflation option floors to observing deflation over the next five years was larger than the probability of observing an inflation rate higher than 2% (see Figures 5.2 and 5.27).[26]

The downdrift in long-term inflation expectations was accompanied by an increasing degree of co-movement between long- and short-term inflation expectations, a phenomenon that was not observed before and was pointing to rising risk of de-anchoring of inflation expectations. Cecchetti et al. (2015) had been pointing to an emerging asymmetry in the impact of macroeconomic news on long-term inflation expectations and measures of uncertainty: negative tail events affecting short-term inflation expectations had acquired a tendency to affect long-term views negatively, whereas positive short-term tail events had no such impact. They concluded that 'this asymmetric behaviour may signal a disanchoring from below of long-term inflation expectations'. Natoli and Sigalotti (2018), in later research, also detect an increase in the risk of de-anchoring during the last quarter of 2014 for the euro area.[27]

There was a non-negligible probability that negative inflation could develop into a grinding process of self-perpetuating deflation. The GC was clearly confronted with the issue of whether the quantitative perimeter of the measures decided over the

---

[26] The bell-shaped probability density functions shown in Figure 5.2 and the time series of different probability buckets shown in Figure 5.27 are computed from the prices of zero-coupon inflation floors of five-year maturity. The various prices relate to strike prices for the floor, ranging from −1.0 to 2.5. The computation relies on the well-known finding from the finance literature that the second derivative of the price of an option with respect to the strike price is equal to the density function. The derivation method relies on fitting the volatility smile with a polynomial of order two and computing the implied volatilities from the standard Black-Scholes formula. From the fitted volatility smile, one can then compute a continuum of option prices from the Black-Scholes formula and, interestingly, analytical second derivatives which give the desired density.

[27] See ECB (2017), especially Section 3 and the references quoted there.

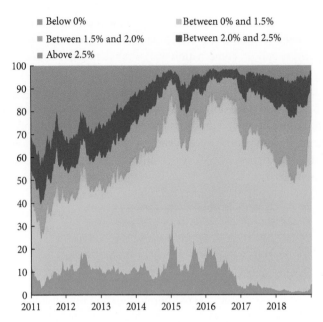

Figure 5.27 Option-implied distribution of average inflation over the next five years (%)

Sources: Bloomberg, Refinitiv and ECB calculations.
Notes: Probabilities implied by five-year zero-coupon inflation options. Risk-neutral probabilities may differ significantly from physical, or true, probabilities.
Latest observation: 31 December 2018.

summer—to normalize the money market and revitalize the credit channel—was adequate to fend off that risk: what in Amsterdam, a few months before, had been dubbed the 'third contingency'.

5.9 The Asset Purchase Programme

Starting in November, through a series of dedicated sessions, staff briefed the GC on their evolving diagnosis of the state of the macro-economy, risks to price stability and options to counter the threat of deflation. The dashboard reported in Figure 5.28 was particularly effective in filtering and summarizing a vast wealth of information relevant for quantifying the risk that the euro area might have already entered the 'third contingency'.

From left, the figure lined up a number of measures of price pressure: average realized inflation over the previous six months, both for headline and core HICP, GDP deflator-based inflation, market-based (forward) measures of inflation expectations, and so on. The red line connected the dots across the most recent updates of the individual indicators relative to the June 2014 observation (in yellow). The grey box plots indicated the 10th–90th percentiles of the historical distributions of each

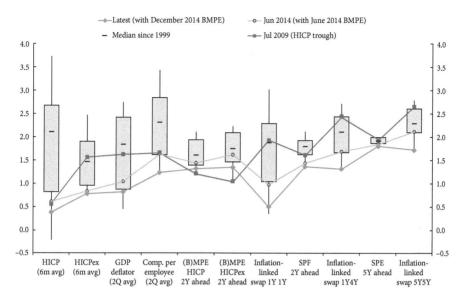

Figure 5.28 Euro area inflation dashboard as of end-2014 (year-on-year % change)
Sources: Eurostat, ECB, Refinitiv and ECB computations.
Notes: Box plots cover the 10th–90th percentiles of historical distributions since January 1999.
Inflation-linked swaps are monthly averages of daily observations up until 31 December 2014. HICPex
refers to HICP inflation excluding food and energy as a six-month average, and to HICP inflation
excluding energy for the (B)MPE values.
Latest observation: November 2014 for inflation rates; 2014Q3 for GDP deflator and compensation
per employee (the value is a two-quarter average of 2014Q2 and 2014Q3); the latest projections are
from December 2014 for BMPE and 2014Q4 for survey-based (SPF) inflation expectations.

indicator since January 1999. The figure carried two messages: the line connecting
the dots had been sinking relative to the bulk of the post-monetary union distribution of price pressures; and, while oil had a part to play in that downward shift, the
present episode was dramatically different from that following the Lehman crisis in
2009 (the green line). In the 2009 episode—probably because disinflation at the time
was so abrupt and self-correcting—none of the indicators measuring persistence
were atypically compressed compared with their history. Most importantly, core
inflation in 2009 was very sticky and lagging behind headline inflation, which at the
time provided a valuable buffer against second-round effects. That buffer was simply
unavailable at the end of 2014.

The Amsterdam road map had charted a course for policy options conditional on
the economy entering the 'third contingency': a broad-based asset purchase programme. But its size and composition remained undetermined. To help anchor the
decision process, staff reverse-engineered the textbook impact analysis used by generations of economists to trace the macroeconomic propagation of a monetary policy impulse. Whereas the canonical exercise ran from a standardized adjustment to
the instrument of monetary policy—say, a 25-basis-point cut to the policy rate—to
the response that that action would induce in real and nominal variables—say, an

increase in inflation by 20 bps relative to the baseline over a two-year horizon—the problem at hand implied running the exercise in reverse order: from a measure of macroeconomic underperformance, an 'inflation gap', back to the requisite instrument adjustment to offset it. The notion of an 'inflation gap' was new, of course, and partly alien to a framework that, as we saw before, comprised a sharp understanding of excess inflation (a rate bigger than 2%) but an ill-defined concept of inflation deficit. The very notion of a negative 'inflation gap' would have been unthinkable, even in 2014, had the GC not converged in the meantime to a new paradigm composed of two convictions. First, severe and persistent departures of inflation from the level defined by the GC as most desirable in the medium term were entirely a matter for monetary policy to address. The GC, in other words, had grown disinclined to shift the blame for inflation misalignments to outside forces (oil, structural factors) or other agents (fiscal, income policymakers) and had reasserted the belief that inflation was indeed 'always and everywhere a monetary phenomenon'.[28] Second, the policy aim was symmetrical, with large and persistent deviations of inflation on the downside as undesirable as large and persistent deviations on the upside. Backed by this new intellectual orientation, staff in December 2014 derived the 'inflation gap' as the difference between the inflation rate projected for the outer year (2016) by internal forecasts in a constant-policy scenario, and 1.9%, a number exemplifying staff's reading of the 2003 'close to 2%' medium-term policy aim. Further, based on elasticities of inflation to interest rate changes, and of interest rate changes to purchases of long-dated assets, they derived the 'missing stimulus' and the Eurosystem balance sheet expansion that was necessary to correct the inflation shortfall.

Figure 5.29 offers a visualization of the thought process that inspired the calibration. The horizontal dashed blue lines represent the inflation projections for 2015 and 2016 available at the time of the exercise, December 2014. The brown bars indicate the contribution to the projections that TLTROs were expected to deliver over the horizon. By the end of the year, that contribution had been materially dialled

---

[28] Mr Draghi expressed his unease with theories of inflation forbearance—justified on the grounds that 'structural' or 'political' factors, rather than monetary policy, move inflation—in a speech on the causes of low inflation delivered at a conference organised by the Deutsche Bundesbank on 4 February 2016. Quoting from the speech: 'If we do not "surrender" to low inflation – and we certainly do not – in the steady state it will return to levels consistent with our objective. If on the other hand we capitulate to "inexorable disinflationary forces", or invoke long periods of transition for inflation to come down, we will in fact only perpetuate disinflation. This is the clear lesson of monetary history, especially the experience of the 1970s. At that time, many policymakers argued that persistently high inflation was structural and central bankers could do little to reduce it. For example, in May 1971, when Arthur Burns was Chairman, the official staff presentation to the FOMC declared – like some of our critics today – that "the question is whether monetary policy could or should do anything to combat a persisting residual rate of inflation . . . the answer, I think, is negative . . . it seems to me that we should regard continuing cost increases as a structural problem not amenable to macroeconomic measures." Later in the speech: 'Similarly, Fed Chairman William Miller observed in his first FOMC meeting in March 1978 that "inflation is going to be left to the Federal Reserve and that's going to be bad news. An effective program to reduce the rate of inflation has to extend beyond monetary policy and needs to be complemented by programs designed to enhance competition and to correct structural problems." It was only when Paul Volcker arrived as Chairman in 1979 and shortened the policy horizon that the Fed took ownership for controlling inflation. Inflation, which peaked at around 15% in March 1980, fell below 3% by 1983.'

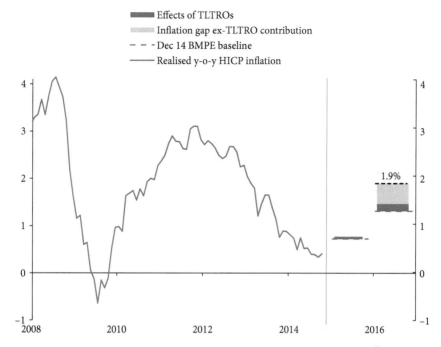

Figure 5.29 Inflation gap as of end-2014 (year-on-year % change)

Source: ECB computations.

Notes: The impact on inflation was reported for a TLTRO take-up of €436 billion, corresponding to the latest ECB-internal estimates. The size of the private sector asset purchase programmes (combining ABS and covered bond purchases) was normalized at €500 billion.

back relative to staff's prior expectations.[29] The 'inflation gap' was the difference between the current-policies projection for medium-term inflation and 1.9%.

5.9.1 Size and Composition

As to the Eurosystem balance sheet expansion that would deliver the missing stimulus, policymakers faced a three-dimensional grid of options, in which size interacted with composition and risk-taking, with potentially infinite permutations of the three parameters yielding the same impulse. On one side of the grid, purchases of a representative portfolio of sovereign securities of the highest credit rating would have minimized the Eurosystem's risk exposure, but would have necessitated a larger effort. In other words, a more restricted portfolio composition, with a lower risk

---

[29] The easing potential of TLTRO-I turned out to have been largely overstated. At the beginning of September 2014, the average take-up expectation among market analysts was around €650 billion, while ECB staff were expecting a figure closer to €600 billion, of which about half was to be allotted in the first two operations. In reality, the first two operations allotted €212.4 billion, while banks borrowed a total amount of €425 billion over the entire cycle of TLTRO-I.

content, would have called for a larger programme, because the efficacy of the policy intervention per each euro spent would have been diminished. The reason for this risk/size trade-off is that, with an asset purchase programme, a central bank extracts financial risk from the market. Consequently, the more diversified the typologies of risk that are absorbed and warehoused in a central bank portfolio, the more risk-bearing capacity is freed up in the market for investors to be able to engage in different risky activities, including the build-up of production capacity and job creation. By targeting AAA–AA securities only, the ECB would have extracted pure 'duration risk' and this would have activated the 'duration channel' of monetary policy. But other channels, which could have empowered the impact of the initiative through the extraction of other types of risk, would have lain dormant.

What is the 'duration channel'? The duration channel works through the market price of duration risk, which is the interest rate risk borne by an investor in long-term bonds: the longer the maturity of the bond, the larger the duration risk that the investor bears. By purchasing long-dated assets, a central bank reduces the amount of duration risk that is borne in aggregate, while simultaneously increasing the amount of short-term risk-free bank reserves in the system. In order for investors to be willing to make those portfolio adjustments, the expected return on the purchased securities has to fall relative to the expected return that investors can earn on an alternative rollover strategy at the risk-free rate for the same term to maturity. This excess return is called the 'term premium', and the duration channel operates through a compression of such a premium. The theory positing the existence of a duration channel for central bank asset purchases argues that, by extracting long-term bonds from private hands, a central bank not only impacts the price and yield of the asset class it targets, but also the price and return of a variety of other risky assets that embed duration risk. Because bonds are owned by the same risk-averse investors who also demand a large equity premium as compensation for holding risky stocks, the impact of bond purchases traverses markets and asset categories. So, a large-scale asset purchase program—even one targeted at high-quality bonds only—makes some of the risk tolerance that would otherwise be soaked up bearing undifferentiated duration risk free to bear other kinds of risk. More risk-taking is a precondition for igniting growth and job creation, and is thus an insurance against macroeconomic risk.

Against this conceptual background, an AAA–AA-only portfolio policy would have influenced macroeconomic risk only indirectly and rather tenuously. First, super-safe securities were already viewed—in the conditions of financial fragmentation prevailing in late 2014 dominated by the pervasive search for safety—as money-like, very close substitutes for cash. The Eurosystem would have been replacing quasi-cash securities for cash, and therefore the impact of the transaction on the yield of these securities would probably have been muted. Second, the macroeconomic risk was concentrated in parts of the euro area that would have been exempt from this type of intervention. Those geographies were also the ones where heightened risk aversion was impeding normalization most, and where risk absorption could have had the strongest traction. This perspective argued for broadening the portfolio to sovereign securities that retained an investment-grade rating but were considered as very imperfect substitutes for cash.

Having identified the universe of eligible assets, the next steps were to compute an elasticity converting a normalized quantum of purchases of those assets into a yield effect, and to quantify the response of inflation, over a horizon of two to three years, to a standardized adjustment in yields. Run in reversed order, from the 'inflation gap', this two-stage procedure would allow the size of the quantitative programme to be determined with some precision. For lack of first-hand experience with quantitative interventions, no event studies were available to pin down the effect of the announcement of a quantitative programme of a given size in terms of an interest rate equivalent. As a result, staff had to borrow from the recent Fed experience with its second round of quantitative easing. The long-term yield effect drawn from the US experience, appropriately rescaled to the size of the euro area debt market, was fed into a suite of macroeconometric models where a given long-term interest rate impulse could be interacted with macroeconomic variables, including inflation.[30] The exercise indicated that, assuming no further adverse shocks, a total envelope of €1.1 trillion, comprised of a balanced portfolio of euro area sovereign securities, would have been sufficient to bring inflation closer to 2% by the end of the projection horizon.

5.9.2 Sustained Adjustment

The GC announced the decision to 'launch an expanded asset purchase programme, encompassing the existing purchase programmes for asset-backed securities and covered bonds' on 22 January 2015. In practice, a new programme to purchase in the secondary market euro-denominated investment-grade securities issued by euro area governments and agencies and European institutions (the PSPP) was added to the existing ABSPP and CBPP to form a new encompassing purchase package that came to be referred to simply as the asset purchase programme (APP). The share of each jurisdiction in the portfolio would be based on the respective NCB's share in the ECB's capital key. The execution of the purchases would be mostly conducted by the NCBs in a decentralized manner, but the GC would retain control over all the design features of the programme and the ECB would coordinate the transactions.

---

[30] In practice, staff made a distinction between buckets of purchasable securities with a different credit standing. The yield elasticity borrowed from the US event studies was applied to the AAA–AA bucket only. For purchasable securities of lower rating, staff used the observed elasticity of the market yield on such securities to changes in the market yield of AAA securities. The overall impact on inflation was derived by first aggregating the yield results and then feeding this average yield impact into a suite of macroeconometric models. The suite of models encompassed two DSGEs—the CMR and Darracq-Pariès et al. (2011)—and a large-scale BVAR, documented in Altavilla et al. (2016). Results were averaged across models and cross-checked against the elasticity computed by averaging across the macroeconometric models used by the NCBs in the Eurosystem projection exercises.

With regard to risk management, full risk sharing would apply to the securities purchased directly by the ECB (8% of the total envelope) and to the securities issued by European institutions (12% of the envelope, purchased by NCBs). The rest of the NCBs' purchases would not be subject to loss sharing. The PSPP would be subject to an issue share limit and an aggregate holding limit designed to preserve market functioning and allow the formation of a market price for the purchased securities. In its decision published on 4 March, the GC provisionally set the issue share limit at 25%, subject to revision after the first six months of operations, and at 33% for the aggregate holdings of a single issuer's outstanding securities. The decision also clarified that the securities purchased under the PSPP would have a minimum remaining maturity of two years and a maximum remaining maturity of 30 years, and 'in principle, purchases of nominal marketable debt instruments at a negative yield to maturity (or yield to worst) above the deposit facility rate are permissible', thus excluding securities trading at a yield to maturity below the DFR.[31] In September 2015, following the announced review of the issue share limit under the PSPP, the GC decided to increase the issue share limit from 25% to 33%, 'subject to a case-by-case verification that this would not create a situation whereby the Eurosystem would have blocking minority power, in which case the issue share limit would remain at 25%'.

The novelty of the 22 January 2015 announcement was the three-way connection that it established between conditionality, horizon and the size of the interventions. In preparing for the announcement, the ECB had been weighing the advantages and drawbacks of disclosing an overall envelope upfront—shadowing the Fed's approach for the first and second rounds of its QE programme in 2009 and 2010, respectively[32]—or rather committing to a monthly flow of purchases that would continue unless certain conditions were realized to warrant their phasing out. While the former template would have helped investors appreciate the

---

[31] The 4 March decision also stipulated that 'to permit the formation of a market price for eligible securities, no purchases shall be permitted in a newly issued or tapped security and the marketable debt instruments with a remaining maturity that are close in time, before and after, to the maturity of the marketable debt instruments to be issued, over a period to be determined by the GC ("blackout period")'. Furthermore, starting on 2 April 2015, the Eurosystem has made the securities purchased under the APP (both under the private- and public-sector leg) available for securities lending. While creating scarcity in certain bond market segments is arguably a natural and intended part of the transmission of central bank bond purchases, at the same time the central bank may need to be cautious to avoid shortages of papers in certain market segments, which may hamper the price discovery mechanism and may curtail the availability of collateral or impair the functioning of repo markets: see Coeuré (2015) on the distinction between scarcity and shortage. The securities lending scheme is intended to avoid such frictions.

[32] QE1 was announced in November 2008, and was initially supposed to purchase $100 billion of debt issued by the government-sponsored enterprises Fannie Mae, Freddie Mac, and Ginnie Mae, plus $500 billion in agency-backed MBSs. Its stated purpose was to 'reduce the cost and increase the availability of credit for the purchase of houses'. In March 2009, the FOMC announced that it would expand its purchases of agency debt and MBS, and would also purchase $300 billion of longer-term US Treasury securities 'to help improve conditions in private credit markets'. QE-2 was announced in November 2010. The programme entailed the purchase of $600 billion in longer-term Treasuries. QE-3 started in September 2012 as an open-ended program with no ex ante limits. Initially, it was intended to purchase $40 billion per month of MBSs to 'support mortgage markets'. In December 2012, the programme was expanded to include $45 billion per month of US Treasury securities.

scale of the policy stimulus being injected, the latter would have manifestly tied the programme to the ultimate objective of the ECB and thereby hardened the perception that the GC was resolute in executing the programme until reflation was secured. The 22 January announcement combined features of both formats. It said that: 'the combined monthly purchases of public and private sector securities will amount to €60 billion. They are intended to be carried out until end-September 2016 and will in any case be conducted until we see a sustained adjustment in the path of inflation which is consistent with our aim of achieving inflation rates below, but close to, 2% over the medium term.'

In practice, forward guidance migrated from policy rates to the APP, and the APP was designated as the principal tool to set and telegraph the monetary policy stance. For the foreseeable future, any future policy step to guard against the asymmetric risks associated with the effective lower bound would have to be framed as a recalibration of the APP, in its size and duration. In this light, the APP forward guidance was given two legs: a calendar-based and a state-contingent leg. The date-based element (the monthly purchases were 'intended to be carried out until end-September 2016', a date that was subsequently postponed) was meant to indicate the minimum amount of stimulus that the programme could be expected to deliver. Placing a hard floor on the distribution of market opinions about the actual scale of the programme was felt to be a critical parameter to help coordinate expectations upon announce-ment and curb the potential hypersensitivity of bond yields and financial conditions to the flow of macroeconomic news over the ensuing months. The outcome-based element (monthly purchases 'will in any case be conducted until we see a sustained adjustment in the path of inflation which is consistent with our aim'), very funda-mentally, served the purpose of linking the programme to the ECB's inflation aim. The GC made the connection between the programme and the primary objective by using the characteristic formulation that became known as SAPI, an acronym for the phrase 'sustained adjustment in the path of inflation'.

The SAPI formulation was highly qualitative. Obviously, a sustained adjustment signified a process for headline inflation to converge towards the 'below but close to 2%' target that was not easily reversible. But, beyond the notion of durability, the residual room for ambiguity and misreading was probably large. Was it the path of realized inflation or projected inflation that had to converge in a sustained manner? And how long a period would inflation have to spend around levels close to 2% for the condition to be deemed satisfied? President Draghi seized the opportunity of his quarterly hearing before the ECON Committee of the EU Parliament on 23 March 2015 to cast some more light on the concept of inflation convergence (Draghi 2015c). He said that:

> The Governing Council will take a holistic perspective when assessing the path of inflation. It will evaluate the likelihood for inflation not only to converge to levels that are closer to 2%, but also to stabilize around those levels with sufficient con-fidence thereafter. When doing this assessment, the Governing Council will follow

its monetary policy strategy and concentrate on inflation trends, looking through any surprise in measured inflation (in either direction) if judged to be transient and with no implications for the medium-term outlook for price stability.

Essentially, he conveyed the notion that SAPI had to be assessed looking forward rather than backward, and that the GC would want to be reassured that the inflation condition was being met not solely as the result of a transitory shock or measurement error before discontinuing its monthly bond buys. Subsequently, staff articulated the 'holistic approach' in three precise criteria: (1) convergence: headline inflation should be on course and likely to reach levels below, but close to, 2% by the end of a meaningful medium-term horizon. The philosophy behind this criterion was that the full effects of monetary policy are felt only after long lags. Therefore, policymakers cannot wait until they have achieved their objectives to begin adjusting policy: they have to look into the future and make predictions; (2) confidence: relying on a single forecast for inflation would not be prudent. The GC would have to cross-check the inflation projections with multiple measures of inflation expectations and underlying price pressures, including those shown, respectively, as dotted lines and a green range in Figure 5.1; (3) resilience: the path should be maintained even after the end of the net asset purchases. In other words, the cyclical conditions calling for normalization should be reasonably mature for inflation convergence to be self-sustained.[33]

5.9.3 Immediate Impacts

The launch of the APP has had significant impact on financial markets, lowering yields and premia for a broad set of market segments, with effects that generally rise with maturity and riskiness of assets. Here, drawing on Altavilla et al. (2015), we document this finding using a traditional approach to assess the financial market impact of monetary policy decisions, namely an event study methodology.[34] In Chapter 6, we perform a structural analysis that keeps track of the evolving impact of the launch of the APP, and its subsequent recalibration, on the term structure. At the heart of the event study methodology is the market reaction following the announcement dates. Provided that policy announcements are unanticipated and the markets are liquid, the narrower the window around these announcements, the sharper their effects on asset prices tend to be, primarily because the arrival of con-

---

[33] For a complete exposition of the three SAPI criteria, see Praet (2018a) and Draghi (2018b). Note the difference between the SAPI-based conditionality for ending the APP and the formulation used by the FOMC in December 2012 to spell out the conditions that would lead to LSAP termination. The FOMC wrote: 'If the outlook for the labor market does not improve substantially, the Committee will continue its purchases of Treasury and agency mortgage-backed securities, and employ its other policy tools as appropriate, until such improvement is achieved in a context of price stability.'

[34] Andrade et al. (2016) also document how the January 2015 announcement of the APP has significantly and persistently reduced sovereign yields on long-term bonds and raised the share prices of banks holding more sovereign bonds in their portfolios.

comitant economic releases that may have independent effects on the constellation of market prices and yields is less likely. Figure 5.30 displays high-frequency intraday movements of sovereign yields for the largest euro area economies on the two GC event dates on which the launch and the timing of the asset purchases were announced (22 January and 5 March 2015).[35] Denoted by the vertical dashed lines, the two APP announcements mark a significant step decline in ten-year sovereign yields on both event dates and across euro area countries. This impact is more pronounced for lower-rated Italian and Spanish bonds, whose yields plummeted immediately after the policy announcements and continued to recede further in the course of the day.[36] Nonetheless, if an upcoming quantitative easing programme is inferred—or leaked—prior to its official announcement, the event study will underestimate the full effect of the programme. Indeed, since September 2014, an increasing number of articles published in international newspapers explicitly elaborate on a forthcoming QE-type programme to be launched by the ECB.[37]

Survey-based information consistently documents that market respondents were unanimously expecting the announcement of the APP ahead of the December 2014 GC meeting, with the median size of the programme mooted to be around €600 billion. Motivated by these considerations, our event-study impact assessment rests on a regression analysis that (i) considers a broad set of event dates, identified on the basis of interventions by the ECB officially hinting at a possible purchase programme[38]; and (ii) controls explicitly for concomitant macroeconomic releases. The empirical results indicate that the APP has significantly lowered yields for a broad set of market segments, with effects that generally rise with maturity and riskiness of assets. A sizeable impact is estimated, for instance, for long-term sovereign bonds, with ten-year euro area yields declining by 30–50 bps (depending on the approach), and by roughly twice as much for higher-yield member countries such as Italy and Spain. At 20-year maturity, the effects tend to be more persistent with the two-day window changes ranging from 30 bps in Germany to 80 bps in Spain. Moreover, the

[35] Because euro area sovereign bonds are relatively highly liquid, to isolate the effects we identify a narrow communication window of 60 minutes around (20 before and 40 after) the GC's press conference, where the latter is indicated in the figures by the vertical dashed lines.

[36] Interestingly, a specific feature of the ECB policy communication process that means the decisions on key policy rates are announced at 13:45, namely in advance of the press conference at 14:30, allows us to attribute these market reactions around the press conference to APP-related news, rather than to any interest rate decisions.

[37] Just to name few examples, on the 20 September 2014 the Financial Times published an article entitled 'Weak ECB loans take-up paves the way for QE', where 'weak loans take-up' refers to the lower than expected allotted volumes in the first TLTRO which, at €82.6 billion, had been roughly in line with ECB staff expectations, but had greatly underperformed market anticipations. On the 27 November 2014, again the Financial Times published an article entitled 'US data disappoint as possibility of European QE comes into focus', and a couple of days later it qualifies the message with the article 'Draghi needs support on QE in the Eurozone'. About one month later, on 3 January 2015, the Economist published an article on 'Euro-Zone Quantitative Easing. Coming Soon?'.

[38] As a robustness check, we compare this 'narrative approach' in dating events with a more agnostic approach based on an index of intensity of news coverage on possible purchase programmes in the euro area. This index of news coverage is derived by making use of an extensive range of different news sources from the Dow Jones' news database, Factiva. Overall, the news index supports our baseline 'narrative approach', spiking up around the identified event dates, and in particular around the six GC meetings.

launch of the APP had spillover effects to assets that were not initially targeted by the programme. For instance, we find that euro area corporate bond spreads have declined by about 20 bps for both financial and non-financial corporations, a sizeable spillover intensity when viewed through the lens of historical regularities.

What type of information did the January 2015 announcement convey? As emphasized by Campbell et al. (2012), there are both Delphic and Odyssean interpretations of the signal released by such announcements. If the Delphic interpretation prevails, asset purchases might be seen as revealing central bank proprietary information about the dire conditions of the economy. To the extent that this is the main signal, the announcement should compress yields and encourage a sell-off in the stock market as well as possibly a downgrade in market-based inflation expectations. The Odyssean interpretation would see the announcement as a pure statement of policy intentions regardless of the state of the economy: an almost unconditional pledge to maintain a highly expansionary policy for a longer period of time. In this case, yield compression should come together with a stock market boom and an upgrade in inflation expectations. Judging from the cross-asset-market reactions, was the January announcement predominantly Delphic or Odyssean? The reaction in the inflation protection-based measures of inflation expectations shown in Figures 5.26 and 5.27 and the stock market reaction visible in Figure 5.30 help answer the question. Inspection of the first figure demonstrates that the APP spurred a robust and sustained response in the euro area surprise index over several weeks and halted the fall in inflation expectations. More specifically, the event study evidence mentioned above suggests that the inflation spot curve shifted up by 35 bps at one-year maturity, by 26 bps at five-year maturity and by 5 bps at ten-year maturity. Figure 5.27 shows that the announcement instigated a shift of mass in the probability density of option-implied long-term inflation expectations away from deflation or very low inflation towards intervals more in line with the ECB's medium-term inflation aim.

Subject to the proviso that any inference drawn from an observation time around an event that is longer than the standard one- to two-day window typical of event studies may conflate different sources of news, we conclude that the Odyssean content of the 22 January communication likely prevailed over any other side message it may have carried.

5.9.4 APP and TARGET2

APP and the uneven pattern of liquidity creation to which it gave rise soon led to a sustained rise in TARGET2 balances. Why? TARGET2 is the set of financial market infrastructures through which the Eurosystem settles, in real time, euro-denominated payments in the form of central bank money (predominantly, bank reserves). TARGET2 is integral to the economic and monetary union as it ensures the full fungibility of reserves across borders and thereby supports well-functioning

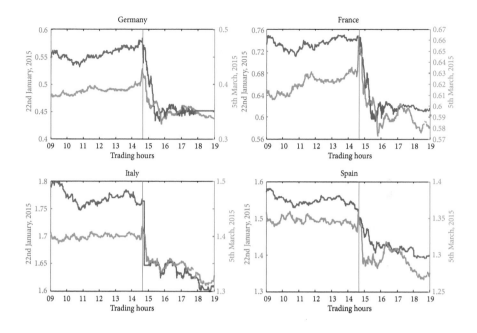

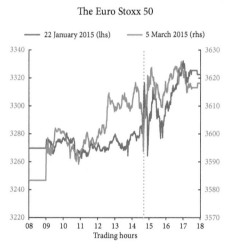

Figure 5.30 Intraday movements in asset prices on selected APP announcement dates

Notes: The dashed vertical line denotes the ECB press conference.

financial markets, economic activity, and financial stability. At the end of each TARGET2 business day, all bilateral transactions among NCBs are netted and give rise to aggregate TARGET2 claims and liabilities of each NCB against the ECB. TARGET2 balances are intra-Eurosystem claims and liabilities that arise from net cross-border payments in TARGET2. A high level of excess liquidity is a necessary—but not sufficient—condition for large, growing and persistent TARGET2 balances.

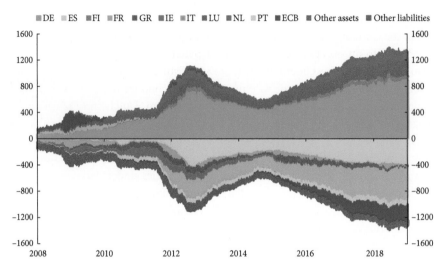

Figure 5.31 TARGET2 claims and liabilities (EUR billion)
Source: ECB.
Latest observation: 31 December 2018.

They may arise when the amount of central bank liquidity created by one NCB does not equate with the amount of central bank liquidity deposited by the banks at that particular NCB.

Two phenomena in the history of Monetary Union encouraged an expansion of TARGET2 balances (see Figure 5.31). The first episode is the capital flight from peripheral countries to the core economies that we commented on in Section 5.4. As the non-resident private sector withdrew credit from Italian and Spanish banks in 2011, banks in the two countries embarked on a massive liability substitution operation, using Eurosystem credit—extended by their respective NCBs, Bank of Italy and Bank of Spain—to reimburse liabilities (interbank credit, bank bonds, and deposits) which non-residents were demanding to be repaid. In that instance, the euro cash created under the weekly and longer-term lending operations by the Bank of Italy and Bank of Spain to fund the local banking system was leaving the two jurisdictions and flowing into core countries where the Italian and Spanish banks' creditors were located. This created a mismatch in the NCBs' balance sheet between their assets (credit to the banks) and their liabilities (banks' reserves deposited at the NCBs), with the increase in the latter falling short of the increase in the former. Symmetrically, Bundesbank was recording a similar mismatch, with its liabilities (in the form of banks' reserves) growing by more than its assets (credit to the local banks). In a currency union, in which money can flow freely across borders, whenever such mismatches arise in an NCB's balance sheet, an item needs to bring the books back to balance. This item is a TARGET2 balance. Over 2011, Bank of Italy and Bank of Spain were bleeding reserves toward Germany, and these capital outflows were recorded as an increase in their TARGET2 balances vis-à-vis the system. Both the expansion in the Italian and Spanish negative balances and concomitant expansion in the German positive balances over 2011 are evident in Figure 5.31.

APP led to an observationally equivalent pattern of divergence across country balances, although the underlying factors were distinctly different. The underlying factor was that a large share of APP purchases was conducted by NCBs with non-residents holding corresponding accounts with German, Dutch and French banks. Imagine the Bank of Spain buys a government bond from a London-based bank that accesses the TARGET2 payments system via Germany, the liquidity created by the Bank of Spain (to 'fund' the purchase) tends to flow to Germany, as Bank of Spain grows its balance sheet by purchasing Spanish securities under APP. Again, much like the 2011 episode, a difference in the location of liquidity creation and liquidity storage at settlement gives rise to changes in TARGET2 balances. But the underlying factor is not a capital flight, but a large incidence of euro area non-residents in the pool of bond sellers, and their preference for holding exposures to banks in core— rather than peripheral—economies. The expansion of the balances as from the date in which the purchases started, and their levelling off as net purchases were tapered in the course of 2018 (see Section 6.1) is very evident in Figure 5.31.[39]

5.10 The Law and Economics of Euro Area Sovereign Bond Purchases

The means and ends of central bank asset purchases have attracted ample attention, not only in the economics profession but also in the legal domain.[40] Most prominently, the APP—and, prior to it, the OMT—have been subject to constitutional complaints, centring on their compatibility with the monetary financing prohibition and the scope and limits of the ECB's monetary policy mandate, as laid down in the EU Treaties. Notwithstanding some differences in vocabulary and vantage points, the ensuing constitutional court cases offer an interesting perspective on central bank asset purchases in the euro area, which complements the above economic reasoning. The current section reviews these constitutional challenges, explains how the ECB's asset purchase programmes have accounted for the legal constraints within which the ECB operates, and highlights the key economic questions at the heart of the debate on the legality of ECB sovereign bond purchases.

5.10.1 Chronology and Issues at Stake

The legal challenges against the APP originated in a set of constitutional complaints brought before the German Federal Constitutional Court (GFCC), soon after the

---

[39] For an in-depth analysis of the link between APP and TARGET2 balances, see Eisenschmidt et al. (2017) and Hellwig and Schnabel (2019). For a discussion of TARGET2 balances in the context of the euro area sovereign debt crisis, see Bindseil and König (2012).

[40] This section was authored by Frédéric Holm-Hadulla.

inception of the programme in 2015. The complaints were directed against the German Federal Government, the German Parliament (Bundestag), and the German Bundesbank. On substance, they mainly pertained to the failure of these institutions to take appropriate action against the APP legal acts and, in the case of the Bundesbank, against its continued participation in the purchases under this programme on account of alleged violations of the complainants' rights under the German Basic Law.[41]

In terms of procedure, the case exhibits a somewhat peculiar constellation in that the constitutional complaints were directed against national bodies under the jurisdiction of the GFCC, whereas the measures being challenged had been adopted by an EU institution under the jurisdiction of the Court of Justice of the European Union (CJEU). But prior cases with similar features, including the constitutional complaint against the OMT, have provided a blueprint on how the GFCC may navigate this tension, specifically by: first addressing a request for a preliminary ruling to the CJEU in which it lays out the potential concerns that it sees emanating from the respective measure adopted by an EU institution; and, second, once the CJEU has issued its ruling, by determining whether the measure, also in light of the CJEU's jurisprudence, is consistent with German Basic Law.[42] In line with the first step in this sequence, the GFCC in July 2017 issued a request for a preliminary ruling to the CJEU, focusing on the PSPP as the APP constituent that foresees the purchase of public sector securities.[43]

On substance, the legal challenges to the PSPP have revolved around two core EU Treaty provisions—the monetary financing prohibition and the scope and limits of the ECB's monetary policy mandate. Both aspects had already featured prominently in the legal challenges against the OMT a few years earlier, as apparent from the request for a preliminary ruling in that case, the respective CJEU ruling, and the subsequent final ruling by the GFCC.[44] Accordingly, and notwithstanding some relevant differences in the design features of the two programmes,[45] the legal discourse on the PSPP has largely represented a continuation of the OMT case. The following considerations thus focus on the key arguments at the centre of the constitutional challenge against the PSPP, henceforth referred to as the *Weiss* case.

---

[41] See Bundesverfassungsgericht (BVerfG), Order of the Second Senate of 18 July 2017—2 BvR 859/15.
[42] See BVerfG, Judgment of the Second Senate of 21 June 2016—2 BvR 2728/13.
[43] See BVerfG, Order of the Second Senate of 18 July 2017—2 BvR 859/15.
[44] See BVerfG, Judgment of the Second Senate of 21 June 2016—2 BvR 2728/13.
[45] The OMT follows a distinctly different policy rationale, seeking to correct impairments in monetary policy transmission, as opposed to the APP's aim of injecting additional monetary policy accommodation. Reflecting these differences, the OMT for instance foresees selective interventions only in those parts of the euro area sovereign bond market that are subject to severe distortions, whereas the APP is expressly aimed at covering a broad universe of sovereign issuers (see Sections 4.9 and 5.9 for further detail). Vice versa, the OMT framework predicates any potential ECB intervention on a country being subject to strict and effective conditionality in the context of an appropriate ESM programme, whereas this eligibility criterion applies only in exceptional cases under the APP, namely if a country's credit ratings fail to meet a certain threshold (see Article 3 of Decision (EU) 2020/188).

5.10.2 Monetary Financing Prohibition

As to the PSPP's compatibility with the monetary financing prohibition in the Treaty on the Functioning of the European Union (TFEU), the CJEU judgment emphasizes a set of 'safeguards' hardwired into the design of the programme.[46] By its very nature, the PSPP is confined to the secondary market of sovereign debt securities. Its compatibility with the monetary financing prohibition is therefore evident in the narrow sense that the ECB shall not 'purchase directly' any debt instruments from public sector entities on the primary market (Article 123(1) TFEU). However, as detailed in Section 1.6, the monetary financing prohibition has a broader application. In particular, it also encompasses those types of secondary market purchases that lead to a circumvention of the objective of Article 123 TFEU by undermining the disciplining function of financial markets vis-à-vis public creditors.

To assess such circumvention, the CJEU relies on two criteria. The first is whether the effects of the PSPP are, de facto, equivalent to primary market purchases. Such equivalence may arise if private investors, when purchasing sovereign bonds in the primary markets, can count on the ECB's readiness to acquire these same bonds with certainty and in short order. In this case, private investors merely act as conduits between the sovereign issuer and the central bank, thus undermining their incentives to carefully assess the riskiness of the securities they transact in and to reflect this assessment into the returns they demand. The second criterion is whether the PSPP reduces the impetus for Member States to pursue sound budgetary policies. If sufficiently pronounced to raise fiscal sustainability concerns, such reduced impetus would put in doubt a core prerequisite for the central bank to be able to pursue an independent monetary policy geared towards price stability (see Box 1.2 for a review of the theoretical foundations of the nexus between central bank independence and fiscal solvency).

In its legal appraisal of the equivalence criterion, the CJEU ruling makes an important economic distinction between different types of certainty that market participants could, in principle, benefit from in the presence of a central bank asset purchase programme. The first type of certainty pertains to the overarching programme parameters—including, for instance, the overall purchase envelope that the central bank expects to accumulate in the course of the programme, the time period over which it expects the programme to run, and the set of securities and issuers that are eligible under the programme. The second type of certainty pertains to the specific circumstances that investors face when transacting in the market. Even with the overarching programme parameters known, the precise design and implementation of the purchase modalities may preserve uncertainty on whether and when the central bank would acquire a specific security. Such uncertainty, in turn, would avoid that investors might be consigned to the status of mere

---

[46] See Judgment of the Court of Justice of 11 December 2018, Weiss v ECB, C-493/17 (henceforth *Weiss* ruling).

pass-throughs between sovereign issuers and the central bank, in which case the prohibition of primary market purchases would be hollowed out.

In the CJEU's appraisal, the PSPP design and implementation eliminate any equivalence to primary market purchases. Via its forward guidance, published legal acts and other communication channels, the GC chose to disclose important information concerning the overarching programme parameters to the financial markets and the public at large. This choice was guided by academic literature, as well as the experiences of other central banks, pointing to the capacity of such communication to reinforce the key impact channels of asset purchases on financial market conditions, and consequently on the broader economy (see section 5.9). The resultant certainty, corresponding to the first type in the CJEU's taxonomy, has therefore reflected the intention 'to contribute to the effectiveness and proportionality of the programme, by limiting the volume of bonds that actually have to be purchased to achieve the objective sought' (*Weiss* ruling, para 111).

At the same time, the CJEU ruling emphasizes several programme features that avoid this 'macroeconomic certainty' from translating into equivalent certainty at the level of individual market participants transacting in specific securities.

First, the PSPP modalities comprise a 'blackout period' that specifies a certain time interval around the issuance or tapping of debt securities in the primary market within which the ECB refrains from purchasing securities with a similar remaining maturity in the secondary market. Thus, it establishes a temporal distance between these two types of markets and pre-empts strategies by which investors acquire securities in the primary market just to pass them on to the central bank a 'logical second' later.

Second, the PSPP purchase pace exhibits substantial variation over time—first because of fluctuations in the overall monthly APP envelope, and second because of fluctuations in the PSPP share in that envelope—and so does the monthly allocation of purchases across issuers. These different sources of variation in turn hamper attempts to predict the exact extent of central bank presence in specific market segments at a monthly frequency—let alone at higher frequencies, on which the PSPP communication has not provided any guidance.

Third, the universe of eligible securities covers a broad range of issuers, maturities, and jurisdictions, whereas the central bank exposure vis-à-vis specific issuers and securities is capped at certain upper limits. This combination thwarts potential efforts by market participants to identify individual securities in the eligible universe that predictably will end up on the central bank balance sheet. Instead, the programme features preserve ample uncertainty as to whether this will ever occur—and, if so, when—thus incentivizing market participants to apply diligence in managing their sovereign portfolios.

As a consequence of these features, the ruling concludes that ECB purchases 'of a significant volume of bonds issued by public authorities and bodies of the Member States does not afford a given private operator such certainty that he can act, de facto, as an intermediary of the ESCB for the direct purchase of bonds from a Member State' (*Weiss* ruling, para 128).

The concept of certainty also features prominently in the CJEU's assessment of the incentives for sound budgetary policies, the second criterion for ruling out a circumvention of the monetary financing prohibition. Here, the emphasis rests on the economic calculus of the public sector entities eligible under the programme and specifically whether the presence of the purchase programme induces them to disregard their solvency constraints in the expectation that the central bank would stand ready to act as the 'unconditional buyer of last resort' in case debt sustainability problems were to arise.

As the CJEU notes, the PSPP design also caters for this concern. Since its inception, the programme has embedded a 'sunset clause'. In particular, its link to a particular macroeconomic outcome, consisting in the 'sustained adjustment in the path of inflation', implies a phasing-out of net purchases once this outcome has materialized, followed by an eventual unwinding of the ECB's sovereign portfolio as provided for by the forward guidance on reinvestment (see section 6.1). Inter-temporal fiscal policy choices hence remain subject to the prospects of an eventual reversal of any favourable PSPP effects on debt servicing costs. While public authorities may partly discount that future scenario, the aforementioned exposure limits embedded in the PSPP also force them, at present, to submit to the disciplining role of financial markets, as 'in every case only a minority of the bonds issued by a Member State can be purchased by the ESCB under the PSPP, which means that that Member State has to rely chiefly on the markets to finance its budget deficit' (*Weiss* ruling, para 141).

A further alignment of fiscal incentives derives from the modalities for allocating purchases across jurisdictions and the consideration of creditworthiness among the eligibility criteria for the PSPP. As the allocation of the PSPP across countries is governed by their shares in the ECB's capital key, and the allocation across sovereign and supranational issuers is superimposed, the programme places that aspect of the purchase composition outside the influence of public authorities.[47] In addition, the PSPP is restricted to issuers demonstrating their creditworthiness, either by exceeding credit rating thresholds or, if they fail to meet these thresholds, by complying with a financial assistance programme that serves as an alternative route to anchor and enforce the commitment to fiscal sustainability. These restrictions in turn force fiscal authorities to preserve their solvency, lest they risk losing eligibility under the programme.

In summary, the CJEU hence concludes that, given the safeguards embedded in the programme design, the PSPP 'does not reduce the impetus of the Member States concerned to conduct a sound budgetary policy' (see *Weiss* ruling, para 144). Together with the clarification that '[t]he safeguards which the ESCB must provide

---

[47] In particular, it avoids any mechanical link between purchase allocations and indebtedness, as would be the case for instance if purchase allocations were calibrated on the relative stocks of outstanding debt per country. As a consequence, the PSPP does not accommodate any adverse yield impacts that may accompany an expansion in the respective supply of securities, nor from deteriorating investor risk perceptions that may result from it.

(...) will depend both on the particular feature of the programme under consideration and on the economic context in which the programme is adopted and implemented' (*Weiss* ruling, para 108), it thus reconfirms the key tenets of central banking on which the ECB has been founded (section 1.1): to enable the pursuit of price stability, central banks need to be equipped with a high degree of statutory instrument independence, allowing them to decide the appropriate settings of their policy measures so as to address the specific challenges at hand. But to safeguard instrument independence also in practice, central banks need to be shielded from potential sovereign solvency concerns that may arise from a lack of fiscal discipline.

5.10.3 Scope and Limits of the Mandate

The requirement for the ECB's monetary policy to operate within the scope and limits of its mandate reflects the assignment of competencies in the EU's institutional architecture, by which: (i) EU institutions should only act within the competencies explicitly assigned to them in primary EU legislation (as per the principle of conferral in Article 5(2) TEU); (ii) in the case of shared or overlapping competencies, they should act 'only if and in so far as the objectives of the proposed action cannot be sufficiently achieved by the Member States' (principle of subsidiarity; Article 5(3) TEU); and (iii) their actions 'shall not exceed what is necessary to achieve the objectives of the Treaties' (principle of proportionality; Article 5(4)). This assignment mechanism, in turn, provides the relevant context for interpreting the Treaty provisions governing the overarching economic and monetary policy framework in the EU—including for instance the principle of an open market economy with free competition (Article 119(1) TFEU) and the establishment of the euro as the single currency (Article 119(2) TFEU)—as well the specific objectives assigned to the ECB, among which price stability has primacy (Article 127(1) TFEU and Articles 17 to 24 of the Protocol on the ESCB and the ECB).

Among these assigment principles, proportionality has received particular attention in the debate on the PSPP's conformity with the ECB's mandate. In market economies like the euro area, the link between monetary policy decisions and the price stability objective is indirect and relies on the changes that monetary policy induces in the behaviour of a vast range of economic sectors. Reflecting this basic insight, the mere existence of monetary policy effects on variables other than those included in the ECB's objectives does not imply that it acts outside the competencies conferred upon it by the EU Treaties.[48] In fact, the reverse case would force central banks into inaction as any monetary policy measure, including standard policy rate changes, operates via indirect transmission channels. Instead, the CJEU clarifies that the ECB's measures comply with the principle of conferral as long as they pursue a

---

[48] See Judgment of the Court of Justice of 16 June 2015, Gauweiler v ECB, C-62/14 (henceforth *Gauweiler* ruling).

monetary policy objective and resort to instruments provided for in EU legislation, both of which is evident for the PSPP. At the same time, identifying the PSPP as a monetary policy measure is not a sufficient condition for its legality: to meet this standard, it also needs to qualify as a *proportionate* monetary policy measure.

The legal assessment of proportionality in turn is organized along three criteria. The first criterion, *suitability*, pertains to whether the measure is capable of supporting the pursuit of its objective. The second criterion, *necessity*, pertains to whether the objective of the measure could not be achieved by an alternative policy configuration that exerts less intrusive effects on aspects of economic life other than price stability. The third criterion pertains to whether the ECB 'weighed up the various interests involved so as effectively to prevent disadvantages which are manifestly disproportionate to the PSPP's objective from arising on implementation of the programme' (*Weiss* ruling, para 93).

These criteria allow for a direct translation of the proportionality principle into the language of economics. The natural economic analogue to the suitability criterion is the *effectiveness* of the measure, which may be assessed based on well-established quantitative models that facilitate the estimation of causal relationships between monetary policy measures and the variables they seek to influence. The analogue to the necessity criterion is the *efficiency* of the measure, the assessment of which may rely on these same models, but reversing the logic of the exercise. Rather than asking how a given monetary policy measure, such as the PSPP, is likely to affect key outcome variables, such as inflation, this alternative exercise would: first, back out the PSPP calibration required to achieve a given impact on inflation; second, estimate the (potentially detrimental) effects of that calibration on other relevant economic outcome variables; and third, repeat this exercise for alternative policy measures that the central bank could have resorted to, instead of asset purchases, to ease the stance. Efficiency would then argue for those policy measures among a set of conceivable alternatives that achieve the same inflation impact with weaker detrimental effects on other relevant variables.

While these first two criteria pertain to the benefits of a measure—in absolute terms in the case of effectiveness and in relative terms in the case of efficiency—the weighing-up criterion refers to the cost-side of the *cost-benefit* calculus embedded into the ECB's monetary policy deliberations. Although adjustments in the broader economic environment are a necessary condition for monetary policy transmission to operate, there is no guarantee for them to not also go along with the build-up of imbalances and vulnerabilities, for instance in the financial system. To identify such risks and to ascertain the orderly transmission of its measures, the ECB's economic and monetary analysis relies on an extensive and diverse set of indicators, models and judgements that are suited to detecting, at regular intervals, whether the adverse consequences of a given monetary policy configuration are disproportionate to its objectives (see Section 2). If a measure risks violating this condition, the ECB has two margins of adjustment to preserve proportionality. The first is to establish appropriate safeguards in the design of its monetary policy measures, thus making use of its well-established and far-reaching instrument independence (see Section 1.1). The second is to account for such risks in the calibration of the amount of monetary easing or tightening it injects at a given point in time, thus making use of the flexibility afforded by the medium-term orientation of its inflation aim. The latter, for instance, allows for a more delayed return of inflation to levels below, but close to, 2%, provided this does not compromise the anchoring of inflation expectations and thereby jeopardizes the pursuit of its primary objective.

Based on both, the design and the calibration of the PSPP, the CJEU ruling also confirms the PSPP as a suitable monetary policy measure that 'does not manifestly go beyond what is necessary to achieve [its] objective' (*Weiss* ruling, para 81). Its assessment of the PSPP's suitability rests on prior evidence regarding the effectiveness of central bank sovereign bond purchases, as well as the severe downside risks to the price stability objective that emanated from the very low realized and projected levels of inflation around the onset and later recalibrations of the programme. Its assessment of necessity, in turn, builds on the observation that policy-controlled short-term interest rates already stood 'at levels close to the bottom of their conceivable range' (*Weiss* ruling, para 80); and that previously adopted measures, including the then-existing private sector purchase programmes, did not supply sufficient accommodation to counter the prevailing downside risks to price stability. Further supporting the assessment of necessity, the ruling refers to many of the same safeguards as it does in relation to monetary financing. In this regard, it maintains that the stringent eligibility criteria, the explicitly limited nature of the PSPP on account of its link to a particular macroeconomic outcome and the self-imposed exposure limits, as well as the evident counter-cyclical link between the repeated and frequent programme recalibrations and the evolution of the inflation outlook, have all contributed to ensuring that the programme meets the necessity criterion.[49]

Finally, in the concluding step of its proportionality assessment, the CJEU subscribes to the view that the ECB 'weighed up the various interests involved so as effectively to prevent disadvantages which are manifestly disproportionate to the PSPP's objective from arising on implementation of the programme' (*Weiss* ruling, para 93). This assessment is based on both procedural and substantive considerations. Procedurally, EU institutions are required to demonstrate that the deliberations leading up to their policy measures include the act of 'weighing-up the various interests involved'. This requirement is grounded in the obligation for EU institutions to state the reasons on which their legal acts are based (Article 296 TFEU, second paragraph); and it assumes particular relevance in view of the necessarily complex

---

[49] Further to these safeguards, which the Court also refers to in relation to the monetary financing prohibition, the proportionality assessment accounts for further programme features, including the priority given to the private sector constituents of the APP in the monthly purchase volumes and the non-selective incidence of purchases across issuers. Selectivity is also one of the few aspects on which the rulings differ between the PSPP and OMT cases in relevant ways: since selectivity is one of the integral features of the OMT, it cannot act as a safeguard here; but the absence of this specific safeguard is compensated by other OMT features, including its reliance on strict and effective conditionality as an eligibility criterion (*Gauweiler* ruling, paras 60 and 120).

and technical nature of the design and calibration of non-standard monetary policy measures. In view of this complexity, the court holds that the ECB 'must be allowed a broad discretion' in preparing and implementing programmes such as the PSPP (*Weiss* ruling, para 24), combined with the requirement to 'show clearly and unequivocally the reasoning (…) of the measure in question' (*Weiss* ruling, para 31). As the ruling sees this requirement as met, its substantive assessment of the PSPP's side effects restricts itself to a particular focus, consisting of the financial risks that the ECB assumes via its securities portfolio under the programme. Besides the aforementioned safeguards, some of which limit the amount of securities on the central bank balance sheet while others, such as the eligibility criteria, limit the risk of a given portfolio, the ruling in this regard emphasizes the risk sharing modalities of the PSPP, which ensure that the bulk of the exposure to a given sovereign issuer is borne by the National Central Bank of the same jurisdiction.

Taken together, the ruling thus confirms the proportionality of ECB sovereign bond purchases, provided they satisfy the conditions laid out in the relevant CJEU case law. Given the prominent role assigned to the duty for the ECB to analyse and explain the features and implications of its measures, the following section presents a set of key analytical tools by which staff have assessed these aspects, zooming in on the effectiveness, efficiency and potential side effects that have accompanied the PSPP since its inception in Sections 6.3, 6.4, and 6.5, respectively.

Before going into the details of that analysis, a final conceptual remark is in order. The ECB's objective function entails a lexicographic ordering, in which price stability ranks first and other policy considerations are only to be pursued 'without prejudice to this objective' (Article 127(1) TFEU). At the same time, the condition to *weigh up the various interests involved* is highly abstract and may comprise an almost infinite number of criteria in the allocation, distribution and stabilization domains of macroeconomic policy. A natural question is whether this constellation, in practice, creates a tension by which the proportionality condition may force the central bank, at the margin, to compromise its price stability objective in favour of other considerations. The answer is no. In fact, the ECB's instrument independence and medium-term policy orientation resolve this tension. Under normal circumstances, it is indeed feasible for the ECB's measures to be designed and the medium-term horizon to be calibrated in a way that mitigates potential side effects. But this holds only up to the case in which further extensions of the policy horizon or the introduction of further safeguards into the design of its measures do not jeopardize the pursuit of price stability—for instance by dis-anchoring inflation expectations and fundamentally hampering policy effectiveness. In this case, the marginal benefit of price stability in the lexicographic objective function would go to infinity so that the disadvantages of policy measures helping to preserve price stability cannot be disproportionate to their objective.

6
A Combined Arms Strategy

In this chapter we review the evolution of the package of measures described in the previous chapter, as the euro area economy gradually moved away from the brink of deflation—with which it was flirting in 2014—toward the vigorous expansion of 2017 and the more balanced growth path of 2018, when our story ends. During the years covered by this chapter, the package matured into a unified policy strategy in which the targeting features of each instrument were perfected, integrated, and calibrated to achieve mutually complementary effects. After recounting the sequence of recalibrations that took place between December 2015 and June 2018, we end the chapter with an impact analysis where we seek to isolate and examine the contribution to financial conditions and macroeconomic outcomes. The novelty of our analysis lies both in our methodological approach and in its diagnostics.

Methodologically, we propose an identification scheme that assigns instruments to segments of the risk-free yield curve or credit spreads, and then constructs counterfactuals—worlds in which the ECB would not have activated all or any of the tools in the package—by simulating alternative configurations of the yield curve or the 'intermediation wedge'. We simulate counterfactual configurations of the yield curve by manipulating the predictive densities of the future rate path derived from rate options, from the vantage point of any date between 2014 and 2018. The manipulation is informed by the way in which the observed predictive densities tend to react to policy innovations. We find that at least a fifth of the overall impact of the policy package on the 2017 (i.e. peak-year) growth rate is attributable to the NIRP as a standalone instrument, a surprisingly elevated contribution given the contained size of the cumulated rate adjustments in negative territory (a spread of only 40 bps over the previous two years). Our estimates show that the APP explains the lion's share of the overall effect on output growth in 2017. Compared with available studies, our estimate of the impact of FG considered in isolation is relatively moderate. One could invoke two explanations for this finding. The methodology we use to disentangle rate adjustments that are due to the negative interest rate policy (NIRP) and rate adjustments that are due to FG might fail to isolate precisely the 'tax avoidance' effect coming from the NIRP—an enhanced incentive for banks to shed liquidity and seek longer-term or riskier investments in an attempt to avoid negative nominal returns—and the pure expectations-hypothesis effect coming from FG. A second reason has to do with the model that we utilize to convert shifts in the term structure

Monetary Policy in Times of Crisis: A Tale of Two Decades of the European Central Bank. Massimo Rostagno, Carlo Altavilla, Giacomo Carboni, Wolfgang Lemke, Roberto Motto, Arthur Saint Guilhem, and Jonathan Yiangou, Oxford University Press (2021).
DOI: 10.1093/oso/9780192895912.003.0007

of interest rates into macroeconomic impacts: a BVAR where announcement effects have notoriously more limited propagation.

We conclude the chapter with considerations on scenarios. The impact of the ECB's measures on the economic well-being of society in the euro area has been material. It is remarkable that these favourable effects were achieved in contexts in which the economy was facing persistent inertia in, or cross-currents from other policies. We document how fiscal policies, for example, turned sharply restrictive as early as 2010 and remained contractionary until 2014 when the fiscal stance became roughly neutral. This odd combination of an expansive monetary policy and a restrictive fiscal stance in years marked by economic contraction and looming deflation did not impede the robust expansion that started in late 2016 and reached a climax in 2017. We view this evidence as testimony to the potency of monetary policy instruments, when a central bank is determined to deploy them with the necessary vigour and conviction. However, building on the model analysis expounded in Chapter 1, one cannot rule out more extreme scenarios than those faced by the ECB in the years following the financial crisis, in which the economy sinks into an even deeper and more lasting contraction, and ingrained disinflation takes hold. In follow-up model-based analysis, we show that, should the economy ever find itself in such a predicament, a more policy-enabling environment—including a comprehensive set of non-monetary policies—would be necessary for monetary instruments to be able to exert the favourable knock-on effects that we document in this chapter.

6.1 Recalibrations

In the remainder of this chapter, we concentrate on the four elements of the policy strategy that was launched between June 2014 and January 2015—the NIRP, the APP and FG, complemented by TLTROs—and document their evolution and serial recalibrations until the end of 2018, when our story ends. The NIRP soon 'reached adulthood' as a self-standing, active tool to ease credit conditions in the course of 2015, as the ECB observed its powerful interactions with the APP. The size of the APP was repeatedly redefined, as the ECB saw a need, first, to upscale the stimulus, then to renormalize it, and finally to phase out the monthly pace of net purchases. Then, in March 2016, FG bifurcated, as the outlook for the policy rate had to be coordinated with the FG on the duration of the asset purchases in order to communicate an optimal sequencing for policy normalization. Finally, in June 2018 FG reverted from referring to the duration of the APP back to a statement of intent on the future path of the policy rates. The main difference with the pre-June 2018 formulation is that the policy rate path communicated as part of the post-June 2018 FG was made more explicit and was made the primary channel for conveying information about the likely evolution of the overall stance. Otherwise, the post-June 2018 FG maintained its characteristic two-leg conditionality: a calendar time to signal the nearest date for a lift-off, and a 'sustained adjustment' condition for the inflation outlook. TLTROs, on their part, were rejuvenated in March 2016 and turned into powerful amplifiers of the NIRP.

6.1.1 Deferred APP Expansion: December 2015

Following a turbulent summer in which a return of euro-area existential anxiety—related to the orientations of the Greek government at the time—combined with the bursting of a financial bubble in China and its local and global ramifications, the euro area economy lost steam.[1] In the autumn, fears of a hard landing in China in particular prompted scenario analyses at the ECB to estimate the potential fallout of the Chinese malaise for the euro area. Staff concluded that, should the slowdown spread from China to other emerging market economies (EMEs) and be accompanied by depreciation of the renminbi and other EME currencies, GDP growth in the euro area would decline by 0.5 pp in 2016 relative to the staff's base case. While this scenario was hypothetical, there were concrete signs that the global economy was slowing rapidly. The fall in oil and non-fuel commodity prices following the Chinese financial shock in August (see Figure 5.26) came in tandem with a decline in stock market indices (see Figure 4.23), hinting that global demand concerns might have become the dominant driver across markets. Model-based evidence in Haldane (2015), exploiting cross-asset correlations from a broad array of asset prices, had concluded that nearly three-quarters of the observed fall in oil prices since early May 2015 had been demand-induced. Reinforcing this inference, in the autumn inflation expectations eased back to their pre-APP trough (see Figure 5.26) and observed inflation, which had increased steeply in the first half of the year, fell towards zero.

From the point of view of the state of the domestic economy, the APP had clearly operated as a circuit breaker for the general macroeconomic tone, and the sense was that the economic situation was much better in the autumn than it had been for a long time, despite the global growth scare and the attendant stream of disappointing data releases. Financing conditions since the launch of the new easing strategy in June 2014 had loosened to a measurable degree. Bank lending rates for euro area

---

[1] On 5 July 2015, in a referendum to decide whether Greece should accept the terms for an extension of the country's financial assistance, the conditions were rejected by a majority of over 61% to 39%. Three days following the referendum, the Tsipras government 'formally asked for a three-year bailout from the eurozone's rescue fund and pledged to start implementing some economic-policy overhauls' which however fell short of the conditions proposed by the EU Commission. After frantic negotiations in which Greece reportedly went close to leaving the euro area, at a Summit on 12 and 13 July the Tsipras government finally reached an agreement with the European authorities for a three-year extension of the program. Almost coincidentally, the Chinese stock market suffered heavy losses which continued through the month of August, despite efforts by the government to contain the fall. On 11 August, two months after the start of turbulence, the People's Bank of China devalued the renminbi and three days later it devalued it again, sparking widespread concerns around the world about the health of the Chinese financial system. At the same time, the closely-watched Chinese PMI declined to 51.5, starting a slide that brought it to breaking through the 50 threshold marking a separation between expansion and contraction.

NFCs had fallen by approximately 80 bps—and by some 110–140 bps in Italy and Spain (see Figure 5.16). In normal times, such a sizeable reduction over a period of less than 18 months would have necessitated a hefty initial cut to the standard policy rates of around 100 bps. With bank lending rates lower, the volume of loans to NFCs had stopped dropping. In May 2014, before the announcement of the credit easing measures, loans to NFCs were contracting at an annual rate of 2.9% in the euro area as a whole. Since July 2015, loans had started to grow at a very modest but at least positive rate. Overall, internal analysis designed to assess the actual impact of the measures on inflation, given the way financing conditions had changed in reality, had led to the conclusion that, in the absence of the measures, inflation would have been −0.25% instead of the 0.1% rate that was projected as an average for 2015 as a whole, and 0.25% instead of the 1.0% rate projected in the December forecasts for 2016.

This being said, in view of the many positive forces—including low commodity prices and the monetary stimulus—that were lining up behind growth, one would have expected to see a much more convincing economic recovery. There was a lot of ground to be regained, as the euro area was the only major economy in the OECD group still short of pre-crisis real GDP levels. But the economic momentum was weaker than in all previous recoveries on record. While staff projections in December 2015 saw inflation averaging 1.6% in the terminal year (2017), taking into account the pronounced skew in the distribution of risks to the outlook, the 'inflation gap'—the difference between the policy aim of 1.9% and the inflation projection for 2017—could have been anywhere between a quarter and more than half of a percentage point.

President Draghi summarized the overall assessment in a speech in Frankfurt on 20 November 2015: 'The ECB's monetary policy measures have clearly worked, in fact they are probably the dominant force spurring the recovery. They have been instrumental in arresting and reversing the deflationary pressures that hit the euro a year ago. Yet growth momentum remains weak and inflation remains well below our objective of below but close to 2%.' He concluded:

At the December Governing Council meeting we will thoroughly assess the strength and persistence of the factors that are slowing the return of inflation towards 2%. If we conclude that the balance of risks to our medium-term price stability objective is skewed to the downside, we will act by using all the instruments available within our mandate. We consider the asset purchase programme to be a powerful and flexible instrument, as it can be adjusted in terms of size, composition or duration to achieve a more expansionary stance. The level of the deposit facility rate can also empower the transmission of APP, not least by increasing the velocity of circulation of bank reserves. If we decide that the current trajectory of our policy is not sufficient to achieve our objective, we will do what we must to raise inflation as quickly as possible.

(Draghi 2015e)

Why should a further reduction to the DFR have empowered the transmission of the APP? Because fresh evidence was supporting the view that negative rates in the money market indeed reinforced banks' and other investors' incentives to reallocate their cash holdings towards more productive uses. The ECB's bank lending survey (BLS), for example, had demonstrated that banks receiving comparatively larger net inflows of excess liquidity—because of the Eurosystem purchases—were also reporting greater reductions to margins on loans to enterprises (see Figure 6.1). As a result, there was room for exploiting complementarities between the NIRP and an APP extension.

On 2 December, the Governing Council (GC) 'conducted a thorough assessment of the strength and persistence of the factors that are currently slowing the return of inflation to levels below, but close to, 2% in the medium term' and, as a result, decided to lower the DFR by 10 bps to −0.3% and extend the time-based leg of forward guidance on the duration of the APP—the minimum expected horizon for the monthly purchases worth €60 billion—from September 2016, the date indicated in January, to March 2017. Importantly, the GC decided to reinvest the principal payments on the securities purchased under the APP coming to redemption 'for as long as necessary' adding that reinvestments 'will contribute both to favourable liquidity

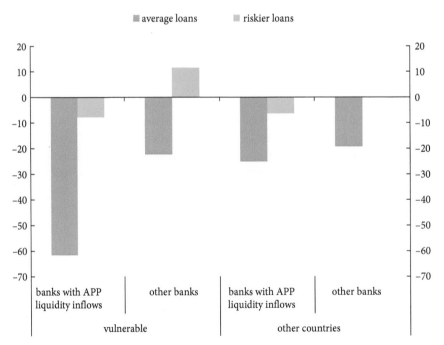

Figure 6.1 Changes in margins on average and riskier loans to NFCs across banks with different APP-related liquidity inflows (Net percentages of banks reporting a tightening of margins on riskier loans and average loans)

Source: ECB Bank Lending Survey.
Notes: Based on unweighted individual data. Net percentages for banks indicating APP-related liquidity inflows and other reporting banks. Margins on average and riskier loans are obtained from the sample of banks participating in the BLS. Data as of October 2015 BLS round.

conditions and to an appropriate monetary policy stance', and to include 'euro-denominated marketable debt instruments issued by regional and local governments located in the euro area in the list of assets that are eligible for regular purchases by the respective national central banks'.

6.1.2 TLTRO-II: March 2016

Markets were underwhelmend by the December 2015 decisions. Surveys and anecdotal evidence show that investors had expected a larger reduction of the DFR. In the event, they also heavily discounted the announcement of an expansion in the Eurosystem's bond portfolio relative to its current size because they had anticipated a near-term €15 billion increase in the *monthly pace* of net purchases, whereas the announced overall increase of the Eurosystem portfolio would start only at some distant point in the future and would take a long time—six to nine months—to execute. Disappointment over the size of the DFR cut, together with the pricing out of the prior anticipations of higher monthly buys, led to a sharp repricing in the EONIA forward market and a backup in longer-term yields across the curve.[2] The euro appreciated by nearly 3% against the US dollar to around $/€1.09, a level around which it oscillated for the rest of December.

Past the immediate market response, trading around the turn of the year became dominated by a general risk-off sentiment—mainly reflecting renewed sharp falls in international stock markets, in China in particular.[3] From 2 December to 11 February (the date of a local trough), the Dow Jones Euro Stoxx and Shanghai Composite indices fell by 21% and 22%, respectively. Market volatility, as measured for example by the VIX and the VSTOXX, also spiked, reaching the peak registered in August 2015. Two factors were seen as particularly disconcerting. One was the persistence of an atypically positive correlation between stock indices and the price of oil (compare Figures 4.23 and 5.26). In the rare past instances in which this association had endured for longer than a few months, the evidence had been a

---

[2] Two—observationally equivalent—hypotheses may explain the perverse reaction to the APP recalibration: (1) markets may strongly discount future purchases. The net present value of future purchases, such as those under the reinvestment policy, would hence be considerably lower than that of earlier purchases; (2) the fear that the decision would de facto lead to the ECB extracting less duration than expected by the market, as the sharp increase in market rates over the front-end of the term structure would alleviate the constraint on the eligibility of securities with a yield to maturity lower than the DFR—predominantly shorter-term securities—and, hence, imply that the Eurosystem would shift from targeting long maturities to targeting shorter maturities in its asset purchases.

[3] The sell-off in China was likely the result of two factors: (i) speculation that state-sponsored funds might rush to sell their equity holdings as soon as the ban on selling, which had been announced in July 2015, would expire; (ii) a negative feedback loop between the stock market and the currency, reminiscent of a similar association apparent in August 2015. In particular, the marked depreciation of the renminbi in mid-January 2016 raised speculations about either growing capital outflows, or a desire on the side of Chinese authorities to use a more aggressive foreign exchange policy as an additional means of policy easing. The Chinese authorities reacted to the market turmoil with administrative measures meant to stabilize the stock markets, including a suspension of a new circuit-breaking mechanism.

harbinger of an imminent significant international slowdown, if not a recession. The second feature of the market turbulence which aroused broad apprehension was that the stress was concentrating on banks, a phenomenon that many—projecting recent memories—associated with the risk of a systemic crisis. Part of the decline in bank stocks and in the price of junior bank bonds was ascribed to investors assigning a higher probability to bailing-in initiatives after the entry into force of the European Bank Resolution and Recovery Directive (BRRD) in January 2016. Another part of the decline, however, was related to the alleged adverse implications of a 'lower for longer' interest rate outlook for banks' bottom lines, with some observers pointing to the NIRP in particular as to a 'calamitous misadventure'.[4] Of course, the reality was that low rates suppressed banks' funding costs because banks were not only *receivers* of low interest but also *payers* of low interest, especially if they relied heavily on the wholesale market for funding. However, reports were pointing to 2017 as the year by which deposits should have repriced to near their lower bound—widely assumed to be a zero rate—meaning that banks would run out of space to offset rate pressure on the asset side with a further substantial cut in funding costs on the liability side. Banks with lower loan-to-deposit ratios—namely banks reliant on customer deposits to finance loans—and banks with a lower incidence of interest expense over total assets would be more adversely exposed to the NIRP. In summary, at the heart of the market concerns was an alarming conundrum: weakening economies badly needed lower rates, but hobbled banks were seen as unable to tolerate them. In late January, the Bank of Japan's surprise decision to cut its benchmark rate to −0.1% met with widespread scepticism. In reaction to this event, having observed how the Japanese measure had failed to impress investors, a rising tide of market reports began to express an exceptional degree of disbelief that the policy instruments being deployed by central banks could still be considered effective enough to assist in their efforts to revitalize their economies, arrest the process of disinflation and preserve a minimum degree of financial stability. The sense that the Bank of Japan and the ECB faced hard limits to further monetary policy easing led to a marked appreciation of both the yen and the euro: in the four days following the Bank of Japan's decision, the yen and the euro rose by nearly 5% and 2.5%, respectively, against the US dollar.

At the start of the year, inflation in the euro area was projected to remain close to 0% for the next six months, and the risks were mounting that very low anticipated inflation rates could increasingly be viewed as a substitute for ex-ante nominal salary concessions at the negotiating table between social partners. This practice had the potential to hold back price pressures via second-round effects and create an inertial process by which low inflation would perpetuate itself through backward-looking expectations. In this climate—and against the backdrop of a further surprise drop in annual headline inflation to −0.3% in February—the ECB started preparations for the 10 March meeting of the GC. The post-meeting introductory

---

[4] This was the headline of an article by Ambrose Evans-Pritchard in the British *Telegraph* from 17 February 2016.

statement in January, citing 'heightened uncertainty about emerging market economies' growth prospects, volatility in financial and commodity markets, and geopolitical risks', had disclosed plans to 'review and possibly reconsider' the monetary
policy stance at the next policy gathering in March. So, in the six weeks separating
the two consecutive meetings, staff set out to, first, review the experience garnered
on the efficacy and potential costs of the existing policies, notably the controversial
NIRP;[5] and, second, to consider a rescaling of the stimulus as adequate to address
the contingencies.

These considerations and studies led to an ambitious set of decisions, which
recalibrated the outstanding measures and provided safeguards against their potential costs. Among them, a new generation of TLTROs, TLTRO-II, was created and
launched to function in a dual capacity: as an amplifier of the stimulus *through*
banks, and as a safeguard against the side effects of the negative rate environment *for*
banks. On 10 March, the GC announced that there would be a new series of four
operations starting in June 2016, in which banks could borrow up to 30% of the
stock of eligible loans registered as at 31 January 2016. Each operation would have a
maturity of four years, and offer an 'entry' borrowing interest rate fixed at the MRO
rate prevailing at the time of take-up for the entire life of each operation. Importantly,
for banks whose net lending would exceed a benchmark the actual borrowing rate
would be lower than the entry rate and could be 'as low as the interest rate on the
deposit facility prevailing at the time of take-up'. The guiding idea behind TLTRO-II
was to create conditions in which banks could continue reducing their lending rates
without suffering too large and drastic a compression in their lending margins,
which—over the long haul—would have crippled their capacity to generate capital
organically. In the optical terms of Figure 5.15, the hope was to drive the benchmark
rate at which banks could fund themselves (the lower countour of the intermediation wedge in the figure) deeper into negative territory, so lending rates (the upper
contour) could continue along their sliding path without squeezing banks' margins
(the purple area) any further. Essentially, this required expanding the pool of banks
that could borrow term funds at a rate as negative as the DFR. In line with this overarching goal, it is easy to detect in the figure an inflection point roughly corresponding to the March 2016 decisions for both the benchmark rate and the lending rate.

Operationally, under TLTRO-II—not unlike under its predecessor—banks were
divided into two groups for the purposes of measuring their lending performance: a
group of 'positive net lenders'—those banks that over an observation period prior to
the start of the operations had increased their stock of eligible loans, and a group of
'negative net lenders'—banks that over the observation period had deleveraged. Two
hypothetical representative banks belonging to each of the two groups are shown in
the two panels of Figure 6.2. For positive net lenders, the benchmark for loan performance (the dashed horizontal lines in the panels) was simply a flat forward projection of the initial stock of eligible loans. For negative net lenders, this benchmark

---

[5] We report the thrust of the cost analysis on NIRP in Section 6.5.

was lower than the stock of eligible loans at the start of the operations, allowing for some further deleveraging. Banks in this group were assessed against a benchmark equal to the stock of loans at the end of the observation period minus the negative net lending recorded over the observation period. A further key parameter in TLTRO-II was the threshold for loan growth during the life of the operations (the dotted lines in the two panels), beyond which banks could claim full discount with respect to the MRO entry rate. Said differently, those banks which, by the end of a certain period during the life of the operations, exceeded the blue dotted line ('high performers') were able to borrow at the DFR, that is, were granted full discount with respect to the MRO entry rate. Conversely, those banks which fell below the benchmark ('low performers') had to borrow at the full entry rate. For 'intermediate performers', meanwhile, the borrowing rate was equal to the MRO rate minus a discount that varied as a linear function of the shortfall between the final stock of loans and the target (the dotted line).

The incentives provided by the pricing schedule described in Figure 6.2 have proven powerful. Nearly 80% of the borrowed amounts under TLTRO-II (around €740 billion) were charged (or rather remunerated) at the DFR (see Figure 6.3), as most participating banks were able to beat the performance threshold over the life of the operations.

Most importantly, the evidence shown in Figure 6.4 supports the conclusion—which is further corroborated by the formal econometric tests documented further

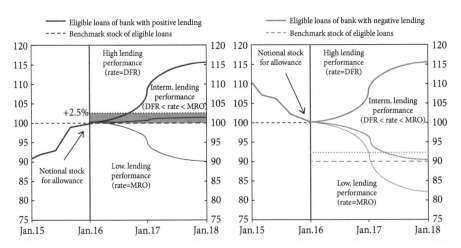

Figure 6.2 Benchmark and effective lending performance

A. Banks with positive net lending (notional stocks; 31 January 2016=100)
Source: ECB.
Notes: The reference period started in January 2016. The three curved lines are illustrative of possible scenarios of lending performance leading to different costs for borrowed funds.

B. Banks with negative net lending (notional stocks; 31 January 2016=100)
Source: ECB.
Notes: The reference period started in January 2016. The three curved lines are illustrative of possible scenarios of lending performance leading to different costs for borrowed funds.

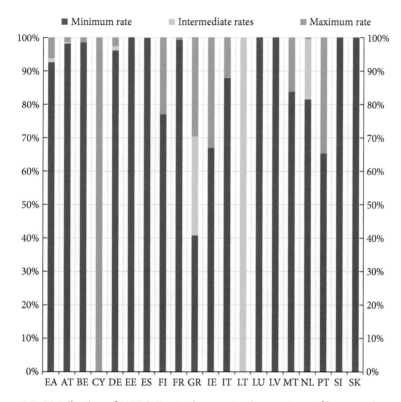

Figure 6.3 Distribution of TLTRO-II rates by country (percentage of borrowed amounts)

Sources: ECB and ECB calculations.
Notes: The figure displays the share of TLTRO-II uptake of banks whose eligible lending growth over the period 2019Q1-2021Q1 is projected to lead to each TLTRO rate. Bank-level projections are based on the latest round of the June 2019 BMPE and assume a constant growth difference, computed over 2018Q1-2019Q1, vis-à-vis country averages. Different lending targets apply depending on past positive or negative eligible lending growth.

below—that banks bidding in TLTRO-II have chosen to expand credit to the economy by more than banks which did not participate in the operations, and have reduced their sovereign debt holdings at a faster rate. It is also interesting to contrast the behaviour of bidders and non-bidders under TLTRO versus the untargeted 3-year LTROs of 2011–2012, with banks that borrowed in the latter operations expanding their holdings by significantly larger volumes than banks that did not borrow in the operations, and the opposite occurring in the TLTRO case (see Figure 6.5).

6.1.3   The APP and Rate Forward Guidance: March 2016

Besides TLTRO-II, the most salient elements of the March package to reinforce the easing impulse were three: a rate reduction, with the MRO rate cut to 0% and the

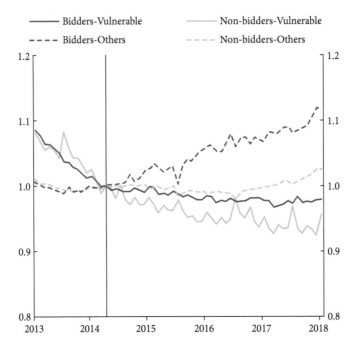

Figure 6.4 Lending volumes to NFCs of TLTRO bidders and non-bidders (notional stocks; Sept 2014=1)

Sources: ECB and ECB calculations.
Notes: The figure shows the notional stock of loans to NFCs across bidders and non-bidders relative to September 2014. Vulnerable countries are Ireland, Greece, Spain, Italy, Cyprus, Portugal and Slovenia. Other countries are all the remaining euro area countries. Data start in 2013Q2. Latest observation: June 2018.

DFR to −0.40%; an increase in the monthly pace of purchases from €60 billion to €80 billion; and a new 'chained' structure of forward guidance. In order to make the higher pace of asset absorption feasible, the GC lifted the issuer and issue share limits for the purchases of securities issued by eligible international organizations and multilateral development banks from 33% to 50%. With the same intent, and with a view to enhancing the pass-through of the APP to the wider economy, the new corporate sector purchase programme (CSPP) was designed to target investment-grade euro-denominated bonds issued by non-financial corporates.

FG on the policy rates had remained dormant for a long while, as the GC's indications on the likeliest outlook for APP size and duration had taken centre stage as the principal channel for telegraphing the stance. In the January policy statement, however, the conventional phrase that the key ECB interest rates were expected 'to remain at their present or lower levels for an extended period of time' had resurfaced as part of a broader signalling tactic to prime the markets for the March announcements. The reinstatement of an explicit form of rate guidance in the January communication, together with the GC's pledge to 'review and reconsider' the stance at

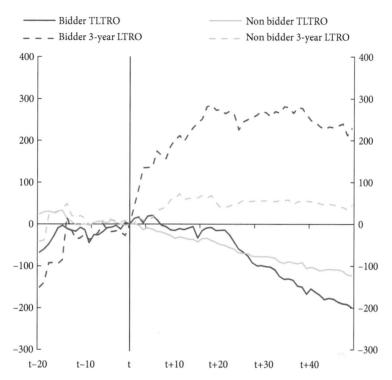

Figure 6.5 TLTROs vs 3-year LTROs: domestic sovereign bond exposures for bidders and non-bidders (EUR billion)

Sources: ECB and ECB calculations.
Notes: The figure shows the change in holdings of domestic sovereign bonds relative to the outstanding amounts at the beginning of each programme. For 3-year LTROs the month of the announcement 't' is equal to December 2011 and for TLTROs 't' is equal to September 2014. The time window considered goes from 20 months before (t-20) to 50 months after (t+50) the announcement of each programme.

the next meeting, had exerted a meaningful impact on market interest rates, so much so that, heading into the March meeting, the EONIA forward curve implied a 10 bps cut in the DFR for March and assigned some probability to further cuts in the near future. Those adjustments had corrected the sharp backup in the curve observed in the aftermath of the December 2015 press conference, and in particular its marked steepening over maturities corresponding to dates soon after the intentional end-point of the APP (March 2017). The January messages had successfully coaxed rate expectations toward a more plausible and desirable path, but there was no guarantee they would settle there durably, unless the new path was codified in official communication. More generally, the ECB did not want to find itself in a situation in which renewed uncertainty over the future path of the policy rate—a higher interest rate or duration risk—might augment the term premium at a time in which it was actively seeking to suppress the term premium by purchasing long-dated assets in the market. In fact, anticipations of a flat—or even downward-sloping—path for the policy interest rates over the life of the APP were a precondition for the APP to have an impact in the first place. For, while asset purchases put downward pressure on long-term rates by reducing term premia, thus stimulating the economy, investors' expectations that the central bank will respond to the better outlook with higher policy rates will push long-term interest rates back up, which will tend to offset the effects of the programme. There was a clear case for pledging to not raise the policy rates for an interval of time stretching beyond the terminal date of the net purchases.

Therefore, in the March post-meeting statement, FG became 'chained' (see Praet, 2017c). The rate guidance was made a derivative of and 'chained to' the principal formulation, still pertaining to the duration and size of the APP. The GC said that 'looking ahead, taking into account the current outlook for price stability', it expected the key ECB interest rates 'to remain at present or lower levels for an extended period of time, and well past the horizon of our net asset purchases'. How

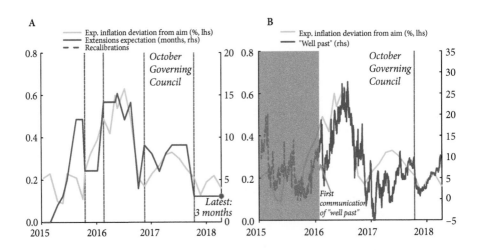

Figure 6.6 APP extensions, 'well past' horizon, and inflation undershoots

A. APP extension expectations and inflation undershoots (left axis: pp; right axis: months)

Sources: Bloomberg and ECB.

Notes: APP extension expectations are defined as the difference between the median expected APP end date according to Bloomberg surveys and the publicly announced intentional horizon at the time of the survey. Inflation expectation deviations from aim are derived as the difference between 1.9% and the 5year-5year inflation expectations implied by inflation-linked swap rates. Dashed vertical lines mark the first survey following each of the four APP recalibrations.
Latest observation: 8 June 2018 Governing Council.

B. 'Well past' horizon and inflation undershoots (left axis: pp; right axis: months)

Sources: Bloomberg and ECB.

Notes: The 'well past' horizon is derived as the difference between the date at which the forward curve prices in a full 10bp hike and the median expected APP end date based on successive Bloomberg surveys. The dark-grey area refers to the period prior to the announcement of the 'well past' formula on 10 March 2016. Inflation expectation deviations from aim are derived as the difference between 1.9% and the 5year-5year inflation expectations implied by inflation-linked swap rates.
Latest observation: 8 June 2018.

did FG imprint expectations about the future course of policy and by which channel? Figure 6.6 helps form an opinion about the efficacy of the chained structure of the APP and rate FG in steering the formation of market expectations, pending a more formal analysis, to which we will turn in the next subsections.

In Panel A, we plot two lines. The blue line measures the expected residual horizon for the APP over the period covered and, more specifically, is the difference between the median market expectation of the *effective* residual horizon and the *nearest date* indicated by the ECB FG (in the date-based part of the formulation) for the end of the monthly purchases, both measured in terms of additional months from present. The yellow line represents the difference between the five-year in five-year forward inflation rate implied by inflation swap contracts and the staff's working definition of the ECB's medium term policy aim of 1.9%. The tight correlation between the two lines is evident. Over periods such as the first half of 2016, in which the shortfall of inflation expectations relative to the policy aim was widening, so was the residual horizon of the monthly purchases that markets were factoring into their expectations. The reverse is also true: as inflation started to perk up toward the ECB's policy aim in the second half of 2016, which reduced the shortfall shown in the figure, expectations were building that the ECB might pare back its purchases and cut the duration of the programme. We interpret this association as a sign that the inflation contingency governing the APP, the 'sustained adjustment' condition, was well-internalized by market participants for the most part (see also Praet, 2018b).

As we show in Panel B of the same figure, one finds a similar process of co-movement between inflation expectations and markets' views concerning the length of the 'well past' interval, namely the time that would likely separate the date of APP termination and the first rate hike. As one can see, except for some limited episodes of disorientation, markets have tended to believe the sequenced guidance since March 2016. Barring those episodes, the horizon to a first rate hike has more often than not been longer than the time to the expected end of net purchases and the line has held above zero. What also emerges from the picture is that swings in market perceptions about the interval have correlated strongly with inflation undershoots relative to the 'aim'. Again, a significant share of the time variation in the markets' representation of the 'well past' phrase can be explained by changes in the inflation outlook.

6.1.4 The APP and the Scarcity Problem: December 2016

NFC and bank bond spreads declined substantially in reaction to the March decisions, and volatility fell in fixed income and equity markets, supporting a more benign market sentiment which consolidated as the euro area approached the Brexit referendum. In the event, while the UK electorate's vote to leave the EU initially triggered a bout of risk aversion across the globe, financial markets weathered the Brexit storm with unexpected resilience. The readiness of central banks worldwide to provide liquidity if needed, a more stringent regulatory framework, including a common euro area banking supervisor, as well as the two prior rounds of recalibrations of monetary policy all contributed to keeping market stress at bay. A temporary suspension of APP purchases in safe-haven jurisdictions served as an important backstop against potential liquidity shortages in the periphery, while alleviating bond demand pressure in the core.

Despite the limited damage it wrought to financial and macroeconomic stability, Brexit had an enduring after-effect on the term structure of interest rates in the euro area and worldwide. Both the EONIA forward curve and the yield curve of the Bund plunged to previously unseen levels in the few days following the leave verdict of the UK referendum on EU membership (see Figure 6.7). This was a reflection of anticipations that central banks would be forced to take further accommodative measures to contain the impact of Brexit on their economies, and the rush to safety that the news initially spurred. For the ECB, the fall in the short to intermediate maturities of the Bund curve was a headache. The legal framework governing the PSPP stipulated that no purchases would be made of securities with a yield to maturity below the DFR (−0.4%), so the post-Brexit yield curve adjustments made a large share of the otherwise purchasable German universe ineligible (Panel B of Figure 6.7 shows the distribution of the German securities bought under the PSPP by residual maturity bucket). Furthermore, the ineligibility of the shorter-dated securities was shifting the composition of the monthly purchases toward longer and longer maturities, thus

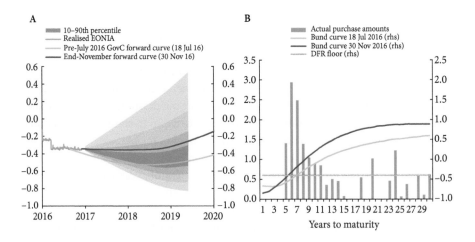

Figure 6.7 EONIA forward curve and Bund term structure in the aftermath of the Brexit referendum

A. EONIA forward curve after Brexit (percentages per annum)
Sources: Bloomberg and Refinitiv.

B. APP purchases and Bund term structure (EUR billion and percentages per annum)
Source: ECB.
Notes: Actual purchases are based on the monthly average between 12 September and 10 November 2016. Purchases of German agencies with residual maturities of up to four years are not included.

pushing more securities below the −0.4% threshold and contributing endogenously to the shrinkage of the purchasable pool of German public assets. The problem was aggravated by the significant presence of specialized clienteles with a rigid demand for long-term, near-zero-default-risk assets: any euro increase in the official demand for long-term Bund securities induced by the re-composition of the flow of purchases under the PSPP described above had the potential to trigger an outsized yield effect.

Staff studied options to alleviate the scarcity problem in the late summer and early autumn of 2016. A new format for the PSPP which attracted a fair amount of analysis was a form of flexible, yield-contingent approach to interventions, whereby the Eurosystem would suspend purchases in buckets of bonds whose yields had fallen below the DFR, but would not redirect those purchases to bonds (in the same jurisdiction) still paying more than the DFR. This new approach would have curtailed the volumes raised in jurisdictions where rate distortions were stronger, but the reduction in volumes would have remained contingent on market interest rates: purchases earmarked to be made in segments of the curve becoming ineligible because of a temporary decline in yields below the −0.4% threshold would have resumed subsequently and made up for the previous shortfall in volumes, should those yields ever have backed up above the DFR.

At its 8 December meeting, the GC decided to maintain an interventionist approach to monetary policy management and recalibrate the monetary policy impulse. Smoothing out the ups and downs of the news flow—which had been favourable over the past month or so—it appeared that the economy was growing at a fundamental pace such that, absent continuing assistance from policy, progress on reflation would have been exceedingly slow and vulnerable to setbacks. As for the operational modalities of the recalibration, two considerations held sway in the discussions: they had to be straightforward to communicate and they ought to be evolutionary, namely carrying the reassuring message that conditions—in the financial markets and the broader economy—were steadying. Both considerations argued for going down the path followed consistently in the past, that is, adhering to the well-tested strategy of APP recalibrations by extension. At the same time, the recalibration by extension should be unveiled jointly with the announcement of a reduced envelope for the monthly intake of bonds. There was general agreement that conditions indeed had evolved in a favourable direction since December 2015.

Whereas a year before markets were still focused on the ECB's bidding power at each given point in time, and thus (myopically) valued the size of the *flow* of monthly purchases in the near term much more than a promise by the Eurosystem that it would accumulate a larger portfolio of bonds over many more months, they currently appeared to be more appreciative of persistence—rather than intensity—in the Eurosystem presence in market trading. Indeed, staff had identified a sort of frontier which entailed different combinations of programme horizons and monthly purchase paces that delivered the same downward pull on interest rates. The frontier depicted in Figure 6.8 illustrates such a 'menu' of persistence versus intensity. The

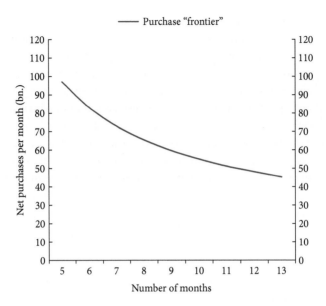

Figure 6.8   The constant-term-premium frontier: Illustration of combinations of APP monthly pace and number of months consistent with same ten-year term premium

Source: ECB calculations

Notes: The constant term premium frontier captures combinations of the APP net monthly purchase envelope and the number of months of the APP net purchases, leading to the same level of the 10-year yield (debt-weighted average of DE, IT, FR and ES sovereign). Results based on the Eser et al. (2019) model.

interesting fact was that the frontier had probably not remained steady but rather had been shifting over time depending on the prevailing market conditions.

In an early stage of the APP, the frontier was likely to be relatively high in the persistence/intensity space. In those early phases, in order to deliver a certain impact on the term premium and the yield, the Eurosystem had to increase the intensity of purchases per month for any programme horizon chosen. Or, equivalently, the Eurosystem had to announce a longer extension of the program for a given amount of monthly purchases chosen. Markets used to value relatively more a 'near term' rather than a 'sustained' presence of the Eurosystem for any given size of the programme announced, as the ECB had learned the hard way in December 2015. But, as conditions normalized, market participants de-risked, so their balance sheet capacity to hold duration was gradually augmented. They became better able and willing to deploy their balance sheet to arbitrage away misalignments in market prices and, commensurately, there was more scope for the Eurosystem to change the persistence/intensity combination in a more favourable direction.

In line with this analysis, the introductory statement announced that the Eurosystem would continue to make purchases at a monthly pace of €80 billion until the end of March 2017, as indicated before, but that the programme would keep running beyond that date and at least until December 2017, subject to the standard SAPI condition, at a reduced pace of €60 billion. To dispel perceptions that the ECB was in a hurry to dial back its programme regardless of progress towards a 'sustained adjustment' of the inflation path, the GC added a key sentence: 'If, in the meantime, the outlook becomes less favourable, or if financial conditions become inconsistent with further progress towards a sustained adjustment of the path of inflation, the GC intends to increase the programme in terms of size and/or duration.' It also opted to address the scarcity of safe-haven securities by lowering the minimum residual maturity for eligible securities from two years to one, and by allowing purchases of bonds yielding less than the DFR 'to the extent necessary'. The yield-contingent option was put aside as it was found to score particularly badly on the simplicity requirement. The intrinsic dynamic circularity of the scheme—volumes would be endogenous and contingent on yields, but yields would be contingent on perceived volumes—was judged to be a factor that could slow the convergence of market expectations toward reasonable predictions about the Eurosystem's demand for securities, thereby hampering price formation in the market.

In any event, an important helping hand for reconciling the multiple trade-offs facing the GC in the late autumn of 2016 came from investors themselves. The debate at the December meeting took place against the backdrop of rising market yields and investor expectations that, at least since the US presidential elections a few days before, had dialled back the probability of an imminent rate cut (see the EONIA forward curve and the Bund curve at the end of November 2016 in Figure 6.7).

6.1.5 Renormalization: June–December 2017

The presumption that markets were mature enough to favour longevity—over intensity—with respect to the outlook for the APP was substantiated by the positive reactions to the December 2016 decisions. The 8 December 2016 announcement led to a broad-based easing of euro area financial conditions: the sovereign term structure shifted lower, stock markets rallied and the euro depreciated measurably. The post-meeting message was that the Eurosystem would continue to suppress excess volatility even at a time in which the ongoing firming in consumer and corporate sentiment, as well as an economy that was expected to gradually gain speed, could otherwise have led to a fair amount of second-guessing in the market about the ECB's plans for an early exit from its accommodative stance, and could have destabilized the financial conditions as a result. The chained guidance—and the optimal sequencing for policy normalization that it entailed—gave reassurances that a supportive monetary policy would remain in place for as long as necessary to give the economy time to complete a safe transition to a higher growth path and for inflation to edge up towards levels more in tune with the GC's medium-term preferences.[6]

Indeed, by the end of May, the resynchronization of business cycles on a global scale—an event unseen since the ephemeral upswing in 2010—bolstered confidence that the economic recovery would continue to firm and spread across euro area countries and demand components. With the outcome of the French presidential elections removing a major source of political risk in the euro area, economic surprises had continued to be on the upside (see Figure 5.26). Real GDP had gained 0.6% quarter-on-quarter in the first three months of the year, after a 0.5% growth in the fourth quarter of 2016 (see Figure 4.21), and staff were projecting growth to continue above potential, at an annual pace of 1.9% for the current year, 1.8% in 2018 and 1.7% in 2019 (see Figure 5.3), as shown in the closing of the output gap in the euro area and the four largest euro area economies (see Figure 5.5). Domestic demand was consolidating its role as the mainstay of the economic expansion, but extra euro-area exports were adding to the upswing, as the global tailwinds were strengthening. By year-end, unemployment was expected to hit the upper range of the NAIRU measures maintained by a variety of international organizations (see Figures 5.6 and 5.7). In the meantime, coincidental gauges of firms' operating conditions, such as the composite output PMI, had risen from 55.6 in the first quarter of the year to 56.8 in April and May, indicating the strongest private sector activity since 2011.

This being said, inflation developments remained difficult to reconcile with the strengthening of economic activity. Underlying inflation remained subdued amid significant volatility in core inflation, while headline HICP inflation was heading down (see Figures 5.1 and 5.4). The upward trend in core inflation and wages foreseen in the June staff projection was still subject to antagonistic forces. On the positive side, pipeline pressures continued to rise at the early stages of the pricing chain and the expected rise in core inflation had become likelier in the light of the observed developments in slack. At the same time, growing evidence of backward-lookingness in wage and price setting remained a relevant drag.

For its June policy deliberations, the GC faced a harder set of questions: not about the value of the outstanding package of measures, which was uncontested, but about the most adequate constellation of instruments within the package, as the euro area was moving into a more ambivalent world than had been observed at any time since

---

[6] Occasionally, the message got lost in unorderly market noise. For example, in the aftermath of the March 2017 monetary policy meeting, news reports suggested that the Governing Council was considering the possibility to hike the DFR *before* ending the net asset purchase program. While President Draghi and chief economist Praet pushed back forcefully on those speculations on the occasion of their respective contributions to the *ECB and Its Watchers* XVIII Conference on 6 April 2017 (see Draghi (2017a) and Praet (2017a)), the episode offered something that came close to a true controlled experiment on what might be the consequences of an inverted sequencing of policy normalization. DFR expectations reacted violently to the news reports, and the whole yield curve backed up in sympathy through its very long maturity segments. Obviously, during the market correction, part of the impact of the on-going purchases was being undone.

the financial crisis, where economic dynamism combined with an absence of price pressures. The bundle of measures that had been deployed was highly multidimensional, with scope for infinite permutations of parameters. The sense was that not all parameters had the same status, however. For example, SAPI conditionality was among those parameters seen as lying at the heart of the package, as it established the foundational link between the stance and the objective of price stability. Sequencing was seen as a 'deep' parameter too. Deep parameters could obviously still be changed if conditions demanded a radical turn in policy, but the hurdles to tinkering with them were definitely higher. 'Soft' parameters were viewed as more data-dependent and evolutionary. The two easing biases were included in this latter category: one easing bias was attached to the expected future sign of rate changes (the GC's anticipation that the future policy rates would be at 'present or lower levels' for an extended period of time), and one to the size and duration of the APP (the sentence added in December 2016 to signal readiness to scale up the pace of monthly purchases if necessary). Therefore, at its June meeting, the GC parsed the available evidence relevant for deep and soft parameters in minute detail. The overarching precept was the one that had been applied successfully in December 2016: one should seek to combine persistence—inertia in the general posture of the monetary policy stance—with evolution—incremental adaptations to the shifting balance of risks—and calibrate the deep and soft parameters of the package accordingly.

The three SAPI criteria were diagnosed with great care. The staff analysis of *convergence* was moderately reassuring: despite a marked downward revision in the near term inflation path, and a rate of inflation still insufficiently close to 2% at the end of the horizon, comparing the June projections for inflation with those of the previous few rounds, evidence was building that the prospect of achieving a medium-term inflation rate more in line with the GC's aim at the end of the projection horizon was not receding further into the future (see Figure 5.4). Indicators of *confidence* that inflation convergence had strong legs gave less cause for optimism. There were scant signs of turn up in the inflation trends across contemporary measures of price pressures, and medium- to long-term expectations extracted from inflation protection contracts had softened again in the recent past and were flatlining around levels that seemed to just project the contemporaneous range of underlying inflation into the far future (compare the green range with the dotted lines in Figure 5.1). Finally, looking at the estimated contribution of monetary policy to the projected inflation path, the *resilience* criterion, the path was still judged to be conditional on a significant amount of policy stimulus being kept in place. Inflation would have been measurably lower without the amount of monetary policy support that staff attributed to the measures in place, notably the APP.

Overall, progress towards SAPI was judged to be insufficiently mature to substantiate a change in any of the deep parameters of the programme. But soft parameters, such as the two easing biases, appeared less attuned to how conditions had evolved since the time of their respective adoption. At the staff level, the debate around the opportunity to retain, alter or remove either or both of the biases revolved around two questions: whether the policy disposition that they signalled—to lower the DFR or ramp up the pace of net purchases—was likely to be acted upon in the new environment; and whether the tightening of financial conditions that the removal of any of these biases would most likely prompt was really affordable in the light of the SAPI outlook. One set of arguments stressed that, at 'turning points' in monetary policy cycles after a long period of extraordinary monetary accommodation, when confronted with central bank announcements concerning either the rate path or the size, pace or duration of quantitative interventions, markets had revealed a tendency to respond indiscriminately with a general sell-off, leading to a repricing of the entire yield curve. Given this amplifying tightening mechanism at 'turning points', it seemed sensible that the impulse itself should—all else being equal—be kept small. And this argued for removing only one bias at a time. Another set of arguments contended that removing the easing bias on the policy rates as a first step was preferable, for two reasons. First, the rate bias signalled the likely direction of response in the face of adverse tail events. But, insofar as the probability of very adverse events was judged to have diminished, there was a case for reassessing the likelihood that it might become necessary in the near future to reduce key interest rates further. Removing the 'lower' qualification could therefore more tightly align words with intentions. Second, leaving the door open to further DFR reductions had encouraged investors to assign some probability to an event of a DFR cut, and this near-term possibility had helped keep the forward curve flatter than it would have been if the probability distribution had shown more upward skew. Figure 6.9 shows the entire risk-neutral probability distributions corresponding to 18 April 2017 and 15 May 2017, respectively, derived from options contracts up to 18 months in the future together with the Bloomberg survey of market panellists about their expectations of the future level of the DFR. Even though the expectations of the mean and median panellists in the survey were for a flat level of the DFR well into 2018 according to both rounds of surveys, rate option contracts in April were still assigning some sizeable probability to EONIA rates below the current level of the DFR. However, already in mid-May, the mass of the predictive density around the rate path assigned to a rate cut had already pulled back quite substantially. The conclusion was that, should the easing bias to the rate path be removed in June, and should this lead to a complete disappearance of any residual probability assigned to a lower level of the DFR, the sensitivity of the forward curve to this shift in expectations would probably be rather small. See Section 6.3 for an explanation of how the densities displayed in Figure 6.9 are constructed and interpretable.

As for the bias concerning the size of the monthly purchases, staff noted that it was contingent on a set of potential facts and conditions that could not quite be characterized quite as 'tail events', as the language of the bias referred to the outlook becoming 'less favourable'—a relatively mild condition—or to financing conditions becoming 'inconsistent with further progress towards a sustained adjustment', which might be seen as replicating the SAPI conditionality. So, the case for removing that bias was much weaker.

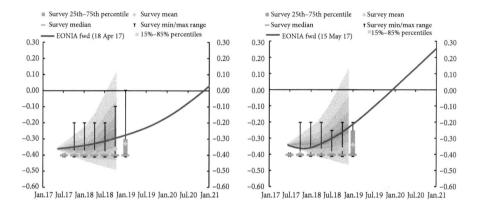

Figure 6.9 EONIA forward curve, option-implied densities and survey on DFR expectations

Evaluated on 18 April 2017 (percentages per annum)
Sources: Refinitiv, Bloomberg and ECB calculations.
Notes: The 15-85% percentiles refer to the option-implied distribution of the future 3m EURIBOR shifted to the EONIA space and the current difference between them. The survey refers to the Bloomberg survey published on 18 April on the expected level of the DFR.

Evaluated on 15 May 2017 (percentages per annum)
Sources: Refinitiv, Bloomberg and ECB calculations.
Notes: The 15-85% percentiles refer to the option-implied distribution of the future 3m EURIBOR shifted to the EONIA space and the current difference between them. The survey refers to the Bloomberg survey published on 15 May on the expected level of the DFR.

Eventually, at its 8 June meeting held in Tallinn, Estonia, the GC removed the negative skew from its own representation of the balance of risks around the growth outlook and, correspondingly, withdrew the easing tilt from its rate guidance. However, it retained the pledge that it would increase the pace of purchases if conditions warranted it. The APP easing bias was maintained even as the GC, at its 26 October meeting, decided to extend the minimum horizon for the purchases by nine months to September 2018, but at a pace reduced to €30 billion. A longer extension of the APP—even at a much-diminished monthly rhythm—carried a valuable signal about a 'lower for longer' rate setting. In the much-improved conditions prevailing in late 2017, that signal was seen as the dominant channel of the APP.

6.1.6 Rotation: June 2018

The easing impact of the October 2017 announcement was material: the 10-year OIS interest rate declined by 6 bps on impact. It came mostly from the informative content that the APP extension carried with respect to the future rate path, via the 'well past' sequencing pledge. While the minimum residual life of the APP was extended by nine months, lift-off expectations were pushed out to the second quarter of 2019. However, there was a non-trivial additional impact coming through a downward

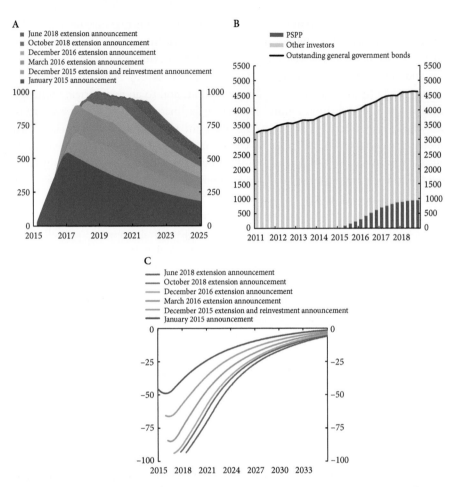

Figure 6.10 Eurosystem portfolios, stock of outstanding bonds, and estimated effects of the APP on euro area ten-year term premium

A. Projected evolution of the PSPP portfolio of the four largest euro area countries in maturity-adjusted terms (EUR billion 10-year equivalents)

Source: ECB.

Notes: For selected dates, corresponding to recalibrations of the APP, the figure shows the projected evolution of government bond holdings, based on an ISIN by ISIN simulation of APP purchases, for the four largest euro area countries in terms of nominal ten-year equivalents. The June 2019 Bloomberg survey calibration is based on a Bloomberg survey, published on 31 May 2019, indicating a median reinvestment horizon of four years.

Latest observation: December 2018 for realized data.

B. Outstanding quantity of duration in the four largest euro area countries: Eurosystem holdings under the PSPP and holdings by other investors (EUR billion 10-year equivalents) adjustment in the term premium, as the GC, in its post-meeting introductory state-ment, had clarified that 'the Eurosystem will reinvest the principal payments from maturing securities purchased under the APP for an extended period of time after the end of its net asset purchases, and in any case for as long as necessary. This will contribute both to favourable liquidity conditions and to an appropriate monetary policy stance.' Furthermore, adding a sentence destined to remain a constant part of the official statements in the following years, the GC emphasized that 'continued monetary support is provided by the additional net asset purchases, by the sizeable stock of acquired assets and the forthcoming reinvestments, and by our forward guidance on interest rates', a list reiterated and commented upon extensively by the President in his post-meeting Q&A session.

All told, the focus in public communication was gradually shifting from the APP to the policy rate path, and from net purchases to the sizeable stocks accumulated in the monetary policy portfolio and the reinvestment policy that would help maintain it over time. Panel A of Figure 6.10 visualizes the sequential recalibrations of the APP as coloured layers piling one on top of the other since the launch of the pro-gramme in January 2015. Panel B shows the aggregate portfolio of public bonds issued by the governments of the four largest euro area economies in relation to the outstanding universe of bonds by the same issuers, weighing bonds by their matur-ity, namely giving more weight to longer-dated than to shorter-maturity securities. By end-2017, the total outstanding debt issued by the four governments was around €6.4 trillion. As these bonds had an average weighted maturity of around seven years, the nominal amount in terms of ten-year equivalents was just under €4.5 tril-lion, as indicated by the black line in the figure. At the time, the Eurosystem PSPP portfolio for these four jurisdictions had reached a euro value of €1.1 trillion, with an average maturity of 7.7 years. Hence, in duration-adjusted terms, the Eurosystem PSPP portfolio was subtracting a bit less than 900 billion, or roughly 20% of the stock of duration otherwise available to private investors. Finally, Panel C reports the

Figure 6.10 (*Continued*)

Sources: Securities Holdings Statistics, GFS and ECB calculations.
Notes: The figures show the stock of debt securities issued by each general government of the four largest euro area jurisdictions, and the Public Sector Purchase Programme (PSPP) holdings for the same jurisdictions in terms of 10-year equivalents. 'Other investors' comprise all other financial and non-financial investors.
Latest observation: 2018Q4.

C. Estimated effect of APP recalibration vintages on euro area ten-year term premium (bps)
Sources: ECB, based on Eser et al. (2019).
Notes: For selected dates, corresponding to recalibrations of the APP, the figure shows the impact of the APP through the duration channel on the term premium component of the ten-year sovereign bond yield (averaged across the four largest euro area countries) over time. Estimates are based on a no-arbitrage term structure model incorporating the relative bond supply held by price-sensitive investors ('free-float').
Latest observation: December 2018.

term structure of the effects of the various vintages of APP recalibration on the term premium paid by euro area government bonds, as estimated by an arbitrage-free term structure model documented in Eser et al. (2019). For each recalibration, the picture shows the cumulative effect on the term premium, and its subsequent gradual reabsorption over time. Accordingly, the impact differentials across recalibration dates signify the incremental effect of the respective changes to APP parameters.[7] The three panels of Figure 6.10—much discussed and commented on internally— conveyed three important messages.

First, it was the size of the central bank portfolio weighted by its maturity relative to the total stock of maturity-weighted outstanding bonds, not the act of adding to the portfolio, that mattered for the term premium. This reflected the 'stock view' behind the duration channel, as embedded in the term structure model used internally.[8] Second, a pledge to maintain the APP portfolio constant at a certain euro billion amount by means of reinvestment of the principal payments received from the redeeming securities could not prevent an ongoing weakening of duration extraction and, correspondingly, a gradual lifting of the downward pressure on the term premium moving forward. The phenomenon, known as 'portfolio ageing', is due to the natural loss of residual maturity—and thus of overall duration—as the securities approach redemption month after month. Seen from the vantage point of end-2017 and the first half of 2018, the two messages were reassuring overall: the cumulative impact of the Eurosystem asset portfolio was very sizeable and expected to remain a major contributor to an easy stance for quite some time in the future. A decision to end the net purchases would set in motion a process of passive removal of accommodation, but that process would be slow-moving and proceed in tune with the consolidation of the recovery. Third, the incremental effect on long-term yields was diminishing. The asset price reaction to the October 2017 decisions had highlighted the importance of the rate expectations aspect of an APP extension, given the way the rate forward guidance was chained and sequenced to the end of the APP. The question was whether such evidence should counsel revisiting the hierarchy of instruments in the package.

When the GC met in Riga, Latvia, on 14 June 2018, these considerations occupied centre stage in the debate over whether the time was ripe to wind down net purchases. Euro area growth had moderated to a quarterly figure of 0.4% in the first quarter of 2018 after running at a rate of 0.7% in the previous three consecutive quarters, as net trade had been a drag. The pull-back from the exceptional growth rates registered in 2017 had come earlier than previously projected. The global

---

[7] An alternative and more indirect approach to tracing the impact of APP recalibrations on the stance is presented in Hartmann and Smets (2018). Based on the idea that a 'shadow rate' (hypothetical short-term rate in the absence of the lower bound) may summarize the stance of the economy, they bundle several such shadow rate estimates following Mouabbi and Sahuc (2019) and show that the resulting summary statistic captures the re-scaling of the ECB's non-standard measures fairly well.

[8] As regards possible flow effects of asset purchases, most studies find them to be small, yet sometimes statistically significant, see, e.g., the summary in Arrata and Nguyen (2017) and the references given therein, as well as De Santis and Holm-Hadulla (2020) and Schlepper, Ryordan, Hofer, and Schrimpf (2017).

factors at play, related to trade tensions, were already casting a shadow on business sentiment. However, a meaningful contribution to the observed moderation in the pace of the economic expansion had come from the confluence of temporary and/or supply-side factors. While the former were expected to wane quickly, the latter—related to increasing capacity limitations in some core economies—were likely to be resolved in the not-too-distant future by an expansion in the productive capacity of euro area firms, and through price adjustments. Both channels would be favourable for the outlook. On net, the medium-term prospects for growth remained solid, broad-based and arguably less vulnerable to setbacks than in the past, with the June BMPE marking down growth for 2018 but indicating a mild upgrade of the growth projections for 2019.

Most importantly, progress towards SAPI to date had been substantial. Headline inflation and core inflation were expected to reach 1.7% and 1.9%, respectively, by the fourth quarter of 2020, confirming a pattern of convergence to levels closer to 2% that had become more and more robust through a sequence of projection vintages. Confidence in the baseline path was bolstered by diminished uncertainty around the most likely inflation trajectory. The dispersion of possible outcomes had shrunk close to pre-crisis levels, and the negative tail of the forecast distributions had disappeared. Staff had sought to aggregate a voluminous amount of information from a variety of measures of price pressure, and had elaborated the summary confidence interval that is shown in Figure 6.11, Panel A.

The distributions shown in the picture—each one corresponding to a different date—combined the predictive density functions of two-year ahead HICP inflation drawn from the (B)MPEs, the SPF, the large BVAR that we use in the next section, and the inflation-linked swaps, averaging them across densities and weighing them by a coefficient reflecting their respective forecasting performance. The exercise was designed to inform the SAPI assessment by providing a measure of distance between the aggregate distribution of inflation outcomes two years ahead at different dates, and a distribution representative of more 'normal' conditions. Staff selected the distribution observed in 2006–2007 as the benchmark, as in those years the economy was growing at potential with inflation expected to be around the GC's aim. Clearly, the average distribution had migrated to the right since the start of the programme, and had moved closer to the benchmark density, both in term of central tendency and dispersion.

Resilience—the third criterion to assess progress towards SAPI—was measured by the extent to which the current inflation outlook was conditional on expectations of further APP extensions. The idea behind this test was simple. Disappointing expectations of a larger APP portfolio, which might have been factored in asset prices, thus contributing indirectly to the inflation path embedded in the staff projections, would determine a market correction and a tightening in financial conditions which, in turn, would have derailed inflation from its SAPI trajectory. In Panel B of Figure 6.11 we show the market expectations of further APP extensions as

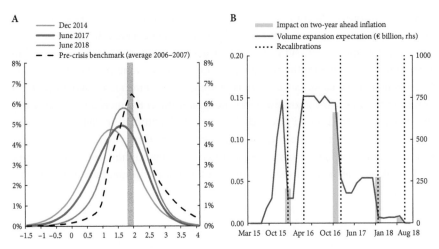

Figure 6.11 Sustained adjustment in the path of inflation (SAPI) criteria

A. SAPI confidence: aggregate probability distribution of two-year ahead HICP inflation expectations (density)

Source: ECB calculations.

Notes: The density combines a range of predictive density functions of two-year ahead HICP inflation based on: the (B)MPE, the SPF, a large macro-finance BVAR model which incorporates Nelson-Siegel term structure factors, and the inflation-linked swaps. The shaded area denotes the range of values for inflation from 1.8% to 2%.

B. SAPI resilience: APP expansion expectations and impact on two-year ahead inflation (left axis: pp; right axis: EUR billion)

Sources: Bloomberg and ECB.

Notes: APP expansion expectations are defined as the difference between the median expected APP volumes according to Bloomberg surveys and the publicly announced overall envelope at the time of the survey. Dashed vertical lines mark the first survey following each of the four APP recalibrations (survey dates: 14/12/2015; 18/04/2016; 16/01/2017; 11/12/2017). Impact estimates on inflation are based on a suite of simulation exercises comprising SAPI models, Expert Group elasticities, and BMEs.

Latest observation: 8 June 2018 for expansion expectations.

recorded by the latest Bloomberg survey available at the time of the Riga meeting. As evidenced by the steep decline in the blue line, the extra purchase volumes expected by the median panellist had fallen to €40 billion. Applying the elasticity that staff had consistently used to convert expected and realized volumes of the APP into impacts on inflation 2 years ahead (the yellow bars in the picture), one could infer that a €40 billion extension of the purchase programme gave an extremely small contribution to the inflation outlook. In other words, the inflation outlook that staff entertained in its forecasts in June 2018 did not appear to embody a meaningful contribution from further APP extension beyond September. Barring an outsized reaction in the market to a 'taper' announcement or the arrival of further disinflationary shocks down the line, the apparent robustness of the projections to a partial unwinding of the purchases eased worries that the inflation outlook might be thrown off course if net purchases were to stop.

Building on this evidence, a decision to phase out the net purchases emerged as the dominant strategy. Prudence spoke in favour of a technical extension of net asset purchases beyond September 2018 until year-end at a monthly pace of €15 billion. Furthermore, in line with the probabilistic, non-binary framework in which a SAPI assessment had been cast, the announcement had to be framed in terms of an *expected* course of action—subject to new data confirming the current outlook—rather than one that was irrevocably set. While the ECB could legitimately claim that the programme had achieved its purpose and that progress toward SAPI had been satisfactory to date, the language ought to be open and not sound irreversible, because progress itself might be reversible. Finally, the June meeting had to formalize the de facto role of forward guidance on the path for policy rates as the new active margin for steering and communicating about the monetary policy stance. Predicting what market participants might infer about future policy from the GC's announcement—the signalling effect—was particularly challenging. The 'taper tantrum' episode around Chairman Bernanke's testimony in 2013 disclosing plans to slow asset purchases in the near future if economic conditions improved sufficiently was a precedent warning about the risks and potential consequences of such incorrect inference. Re-anchoring the rate guidance immediately to the same SAPI conditionality that had governed the APP since 2015 would provide reassurances that the change in the hierarchy of instruments in the ECB's toolkit would not amount to a claw-back of stimulus, and would not frustrate progress toward inflation normalization.

The introductory statement which the President read out at the end of the Riga meeting was quite elaborate on the GC's deliberations and the outcome of the decisions. It first established a bridge between the announcement and past communication, acknowledging the central role of the SAPI assessment in steering the debate:

> Since the start of our asset purchase programme (APP) in January 2015, the Governing Council has made net asset purchases under the APP conditional on the extent of progress towards a sustained adjustment in the path of inflation to levels below, but close to, 2% in the medium term. Today, the Governing Council undertook a careful review of the progress made, also taking into account the latest Eurosystem staff macroeconomic projections, measures of price and wage pressures, and uncertainties surrounding the inflation outlook.

The text then proceeded to certifying that cumulative progress toward SAPI had been meaningful, also expressing confidence that progress was likely to advance further on the back of the 'underlying strength in the euro area economy' together with 'well-anchored longer-term inflation expectations'. Very importantly, it stated that progress would not be halted or reversed 'even after a gradual winding-down of our net asset purchases'. The conditional nature of the phasing out came next: 'we anticipate that, after September 2018, subject to incoming data confirming our medium-term inflation outlook, we will reduce the monthly pace of the net asset purchases to €15 billion until the end of December 2018 and then end net purchases'.

Finally, the dual-key FG was 'rotated' from the APP to the rate path: 'we expect [the key ECB interest rates] to remain at their present levels at least through the summer of 2019 and in any case for as long as necessary to ensure that the evolution of inflation remains aligned with our current expectations of a sustained adjustment path'.

The intended message sank in quite smoothly and market reactions were benign. Upon announcement, financial conditions eased mildly, as the enhanced formulation of rate guidance cushioned the potentially tightening connotation of the pre-announcement of an end for net purchases. Between the press release—published at 14:45 on 14 June—and the start of the press conference, the 10-year OIS rate fell by 4bp, the euro exchange rate depreciated by 1% against the US dollar and equity prices increased by about 0.8% (see Figure 6.12). During the press conference, the euro depreciated further (−0.4%) and equity prices continued to increase (+0.5%). Moreover, the forward curve flattened markedly as markets appeared to cut down the likelihood of steep rate hikes in the near future. Specifically, options on interest rate futures suggest that the probability of the short-term rate in one year's time exceeding current (June-2018) levels decreased by around 15 percentage points between 13 and 14 June.

While the upper percentiles of the risk-neutral predictive densities declined significantly, the lower end of the spectrum remained fairly stable, implying the observed flattening of the curve, see Figure 6.13. At the end of the trading day, the forward curve was pricing a first rate increase in October 2019, broadly cementing the 'through the summer of 2019' calendar-based indication used in the Introductory Statement (on the notion of rotation, see Praet, 2019).

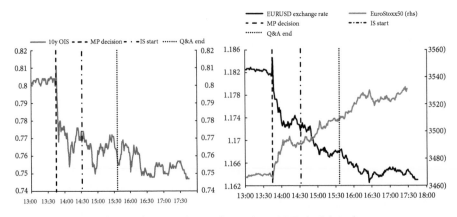

Figure 6.12 Intraday market reaction to the 14 June 2018 decisions (percentage per annum and index)

Source: Bloomberg.

Notes: 'MP decision' refers to the time of publication of the monetary policy decisions via the press release, 'IS start' denotes the start of the press conference with the Introductory Statement read out by the President, 'Q&A end' marks the end of the Q&A session and hence of the press conference.

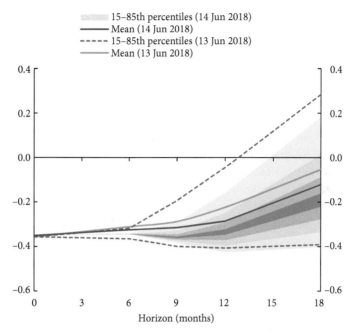

Figure 6.13 Change in risk-neutral density of future short-term rate between 13 and 14 June 2018 (percent per annum)
Sources: ECB and ECB calculations.

6.2 Complementarities

The extent to which unprecedented policies such as those described in Chapter 5 and the first section of this chapter might have accelerated the economic recovery and inflation normalization remains a subject of active discussion and controversy among researchers and policymakers. Not surprisingly, given the innovative features of many of these policies and the limited stretch of time over which researchers have been able to observe their effects, empirical results on their efficacy span a broad spectrum from considerable impacts (Swanson (2020), Eberly et al. (2020), Sims and Wu (2020), and, on the euro area, Szczerbowicz (2015), Boeckx et al. (2017), Gambetti and Musso (2017), Podlich et al. (2017), Mouabbi and Sahuc (2019), Gibson et al. (2016), Neri and Siviero (2019)), to heterogeneous impacts (Burriel and Galesi (2018), Deutsche Bundesbank (2016)), to rather moderate impacts (Pattipeilohy et al. (2013), Greenlaw et al. (2018), Belke and Gros (2019)).

Within the new toolkit that central banks have assembled and deployed in trying to contain the crisis, probably no instrument has attracted a more vigorous debate than the NIRP. While Brunnermeier and Koby (2018) have defined a (negative) reversal rate above which the NIRP is expansionary, and below which the NIRP becomes contractionary, others have been more radical in disqualifying the NIRP as a valid instrument to ease policy. For example, Jackson (2015), Bech and Malkhozov (2016) and Eggertsson et al. (2019) put emphasis on the limited pass-through of negative rates to deposit rates and see this fact as evidence that the NIRP doesn't reduce the cost of bank funding, which in turn translates in higher lending rates. Heider et al. (2019) find that banks with a higher share of deposits in total funding display lower lending growth.

Motivated by the dispersion of expert opinions about the efficacy of unconventional policies in general, and the negative results on the NIRP in particular, we seek to contribute to the debate in two ways. First, in this section, we collect and systematize the available body of facts that we have commented on in various places of our chronicle regarding the channels though which each of the four ECB instruments appears to propagate in isolation and in concert with the other three instruments. While the perspective and style in this section is qualitative, we think that our taxonomy of interactions among the four instruments might be useful nonetheless. We believe that many of the favourable cross-externalities among tools that we have detected through the recent history of the ECB's policies are largely ignored in available analyses, but are in fact what has made them so powerful and probably indispensable within the ECB's multidimensional easing strategy. The second way in which we hope to contribute to the debate is by documenting the results of some fresh quantitative impact analysis. We refer readers to the next section for an exposition of the novel methodology by which we have generated our results, the degree to which we believe our methodology has succeeded in identifying the marginal contribution of each measure and evaluating the multiple interactions among measures, and the scope we see for further study.

Our taxonomy is described in the 4-by-4 matrix that we report in Table 6.1. The cells along the diagonal highlight the benefits of each of the four instruments as standalones. Off-diagonal cells describe the contribution—in terms of stance-easing potential—that each of the instruments listed in the left-most column can offer to the empowerment of the instruments listed along the top row.

6.2.1 The NIRP

Starting with the NIRP, cell 1.1 states that bringing the policy rate to (more) negative levels, at a minimum, simply extends the scope for conventional rate cuts, and thus sets in motion pretty much the same channels that conventional policy easing does when the starting point is at a far distance from the lower bound. These are two: the shaping of short-term rate expectations, given the inertia with which central banks tend to adjust policy rates—what Gürkaynak et al. (2005) refer to as the 'future path of policy' factor; and the influence that a rate change typically has on real term premia, even those paid over the far-out segment of the yield curve—because, as

Table 6.1 Complementarities between instruments

		TO			
		NIRP	**FG**	**APP**	**TLTRO**
FROM	**NIRP**	1.1 Empowered rate cut effect on rate expectations (removes their typical upward skew) and term premium (Gesell tax effect)	1.2 Signals a potential future rate cut, which generates curve inversion and downside pressure on lending rates	1.3 Reinforces impact of APP on term premium through the Gesell tax effect	1.4 Reinforces incentive scheme: stronger loan origination entitles banks to negative borrowing rate
	FG	2.1 Contains potential term premium volatility created by larger future rate uncertainty (open possibility to increase or cut rates in future)	2.2 Controls the front-end of the forward curve by pricing out expected rate paths inconsistent with the central bank's language	2.3 Anchors the short-end of the curve to ensure it doesn't back up prematurely as APP stimulates the economy	2.4 Together with NIRP, keeps the intermediate segments of the risk free curve used by banks to price loans at low levels, thus stimulating loan demand
	APP	3.1 Extra liquidity contributes to keeping overnight rate at the DFR. Contains potential term premium volatility created by larger future rate uncertainty (open possibility to increase or cut rates in future).	3.2 Extra liquidity makes the overnight rate indirectly controllable even if FG applies to DFR. Strengthens signal of accommodative stance for a long period of time	3.3 Extracts duration risk and compresses term premium directly through vast array of assets	3.4 Favours a decrease in the banks' return on bond holdings relative to the return on loan creation. Generates capital gains for banks and frees up balance sheet capacity that banks can redeploy to commercial loans under TLTRO
	TLTRO	4.1 Exempts borrowed funds from NIRP tax on reserves	4.2 Strengthens signal of low rates for longer through a fixed borrowing rate	4.3 Favours increase in banks' return on loan creation relative to bond holdings	4.4 Squeezes intermediation wedge by compressing funding costs while preserving lending margins

Hanson and Stein (2015)[9] have emphasized, a group of yield-oriented investors react to the easing of policy by searching for yield and climbing up the maturity scale (see also Gertler and Karadi 2015 for a similar result). This creates buying pressure that raises the price of the long-term bonds, and hence lowers expected excess returns and term premia across maturities. The NIRP, at the very least, keeps these two conventional channels of monetary policy alive, and—as we contend below—probably empowers them if the NIRP is deployed in conjunction with FG and the APP.

Indeed, the NIRP is also a generous contributor to what FG, the APP and TLTROs can deliver. Cells 1.2 and 1.3 argue that the NIRP gives an extra kick to both the Gürkaynak et al. expectations channel (1.2) and the Hanson and Stein term premium channel (1.3) of monetary policy. As we documented in Chapter 5, the NIRP is part of a double-dividend strategy in a liquidity trap situation. On the one hand, the NIRP is a demonstration that monetary policy is not constrained by a ZLB. This can remove the non-negativity restriction on future expected short rates and thus alleviate the substantial upward asymmetry in the distribution of future expected short rates which one observes in episodes where conventional monetary policy is constrained by the limitation of a zero (or positive) lower bound. Box 6.1 explains the mechanism using a simple two-period model populated by investors motivated by mean-variance preferences. In addition, if used in conjunction with an FG formulation that explicitly allows for the contingency of a future rate cut to even more negative levels[10] (cell 1.2), the NIRP produces an inversion of the yield curve in its short- to medium-maturity segments that can directly influence lending rates, as those segments of the curve that are subject to inversion provide the pricing kernel for loan rate fixation in the euro area. On the other hand, and this is the 'second dividend' from the NIRP, to enforce negative rates, central banks charge a fee on the reserve holdings of commercial banks. That fee operates as a Gesell tax on banks' excess liquidity holdings and, as such, it promotes tax avoidance practices among banks. Prominent among these are strategies to shed liquidity and seek longer-dated investments in an attempt to escape the charge. To push the analogy with a tax further, one can say that a Gesell tax[11] is in effect a Pigovian tax which, when applied on

---

[9] According to the theory expounded in Hanson and Stein (2015), an easing of monetary policy affects long-term real rates not via the usual expectations channel, but rather via what might be termed a 'recruitment' channel—by causing an outward shift in the demand curve of yield-oriented investors, thereby inducing these investors to take on more interest rate risk and to push down term premiums.

[10] See, e.g., Wu and Xia (2020) stressing the forward guidance element accompanying the third and fourth rate cut of the DFR below zero.

[11] In Box 2.2 we study a Gesell economy in which the central bank can effectively remove the lower bound altogether and implement a payments system based on bonds rather than zero-return currency. Keynes, an admirer of Silvio Gesell, so describes the contribution of the German-Argentinian economist in chapter 23 of his General Theory: '[Gesell] argues that the growth of real capital is held back by the money-rate of interest, and that if this brake were removed the growth of real capital would be, in the modern world, so rapid that a zero money-rate of interest would probably be justified, not indeed forthwith, but within a comparatively short period of time. Thus the prime necessity is to reduce the money-rate of interest, and this, he pointed out, can be effected by causing money to incur carrying-costs just like other stocks of barren goods. This led him to the famous prescription of "stamped" money, with which his name is chiefly associated and which has received the blessing of Professor Irving Fisher. According to

polluting activities, forces agents to internalize the incidental uncharged disservice that they impose on the rest of the system when pursuing their own best interest. In the case at hand, the disservice is created when banks decide to accumulate and sit on excess liquidity instead of lending it on, which may be the most attractive course of action from their individual cost-minimization perspective, but leads to an inefficient collective outcome. A Pigovian, or Gesell, tax on free reserves adds extra downward pressure on long-term rates through term premium compression by incentivizing a shift of portfolios from short-dated to long-dated securities. To the extent that the APP engages in a similar active compression of the term premium, the NIRP reinforces the APP (cell 1.3).

We have extensively discussed the amplification of banks' incentives to originate extra credit under TLTRO-II afforded by the NIRP: the prize for banks beating their lending performance threshold is the possibility to borrow at a rate as low as the DFR. Bottero et al. (2019) find significant effects of the NIRP on loan origination in abstraction from TLTROs. Their loan-level analysis shows that the NIRP works through a portfolio rebalancing channel, inducing banks to rebalance their portfolios from liquid assets to credit, with the NIRP-affected banks boosting credit supply especially to ex-ante riskier and smaller firms, but without ex-post increasing in non-performing loans.

To conclude on the NIRP: although central banks so far have been able to finesse the zero lower bound rather than eliminate it altogether, it is fair to assume that central banks that have deliberately eschewed the NIRP while trying to forestall the propagation of the crisis might in fact have foregone the extra leverage that reductions of the policy rate to even moderate negative levels can afford over financial conditions. A simple comparison between the level and shape of the forward—and futures—curves in the euro area and in the United States, respectively, over the period of unconventional policy is revealing (see Panel A and B of Figure 6.14). For much of the period marked by the grey zone, the yield curve in the euro area (Panel A) developed the characteristic inversion that was instrumental in driving the rate fixation benchmark—and the whole pyramid of market rates in synch—down (see Praet, 2017b). Overall, the shift in the forward curve most relevant for the pricing of loans—the 2-year OIS forward—was extremely pronounced too (compare the black dashed line with the red dashed line in Figure 5.15). As we mentioned already while commenting on the yield curve response to the surprise rate cut of September 2014, the term structure impacts of a reduction in the policy rate from a positive level to a negative level—or from a negative to a more negative level—is very atypical. Panel C and D of Figure 6.14 contrast the 'footprint' that a NIRP cut leaves on the term

this proposal currency notes (though it would clearly need to apply as well to some forms at least of bank-money) would only retain their value by being stamped each month, like an insurance card, with stamps purchased at a post office. The cost of the stamps could, of course, be fixed at any appropriate figure. According to my theory it should be roughly equal to the excess of the money-rate of interest (apart from the stamps) over the marginal efficiency of capital corresponding to a rate of new investment compatible with full employment.'

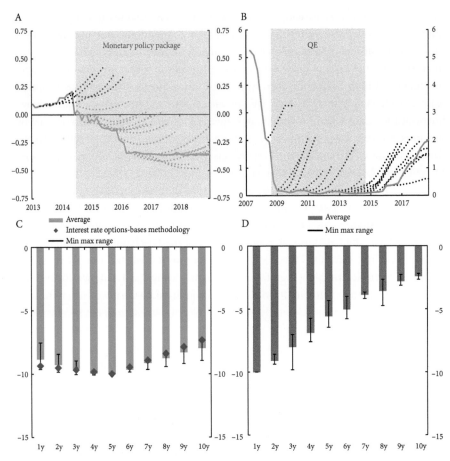

Figure 6.14 Expectations of future short-term rate throughout periods of non-standard measures (percentages per annum and basis points)

A. Euro area OIS forward curve

B. US Federal Funds Rate futures curves

C. Impact of a DFR cut in negative territory on the euro area term structure

D. Impact of a standard policy rate cut in positive territory on the euro area term structure

Sources: Bloomberg and ECB calculations.

Notes: Panel A: evolution of the OIS forward curve from pre-NIRP (black dotted lines) to post-NIRP (red dotted lines) period. Panel B: Evolution of federal funds rate futures curves. Panel C and D show the normalized footprint of policy rate cuts on the yield curve based on a range of approaches, including model-based and event-study approaches. Specifically, Panel C displays the footprint of a DFR cut in negative territory; the methodology based on Interest Rate Options refers to the methodology developed in this book, and described in Section 6.3. Panel D displays the footprint of a standard policy rate cut in positive territory. The changes are normalized to a 10 bps decline of the OIS rate at the maturity where the measure exerts the maximum impact, namely 1y for the standard rate cut, 5y for the DFR cut.

structure of interest rates with that associated with an equally-sized 'conventional' rate reduction in positive territory. Whereas the conventional rate cut exerts maximal impact at a one-year maturity and quickly fades monotonically over longer maturities (Panel D), the NIRP effects peak around the 5-year segment but extends throughout the maturity spectrum (Panel C). The pattern of transmission that we show in Panel C is a consistent finding that emerges from disparate models and identification strategies, including our own rate-options based analysis that we document below. By contrast, in the United States (Panel B), despite two rounds of large-scale asset purchases by the Fed, the front end of the yield curve has been steeply upward-sloping for the most part of the QE era, and probably more so than desired, until the FOMC moved to the date-based version of its FG in August 2011. If certain investors, such as money market funds or foreign central banks, are willing to pay a substantial premium for the shortest-maturity safe claims—which offer many of the same convenience and safety services as traditional money (see Greenwood and Vayanos 2014)—that are priced over that segment of the curve, then one might legitimately argue that anchoring the yield curve at zero or positive, rather than negative, rates amounts to subsidizing these investors.

6.2.2 Forward Guidance

As we could find out when we explored the June 2018 'instrument rotation' episode, even when deployed single-handedly, FG can be a potent instrument to ease financial conditions. In asset markets, it is often the beliefs of the most optimistic or pessimistic investors—rather than those of the moderates—that drive prices, as they are the ones most willing to take large positions based on their beliefs. In this setting, even a piece of news that delivers the median market expectation but truncates off some of the more extreme possibilities can have powerful effects on the 'average' view. With this in mind, imagine a scenario in which the overnight forward curve doesn't price in a rate hike before four quarters from now, and a central bank which—building on that evidence—unexpectedly makes a pledge to not raise interest rates for precisely the next four quarters. The central bank might think the statement would be neutral and simply 'cement' what agents already expect anyway. In fact, as the June 2018 experiment demonstrates, the announcement would carry information for a whole group of market participants, those who—departing from the mainstream market conviction—had been betting on quicker paths of rate normalization. They would likely respond to the news by shutting down those comparatively hawkish trades. And, by doing so, they would determine a downward shift in the entire distribution of future rates, including a drop and flattening of its mean, the forward curve. Cell 2.2 in our matrix refers to this magnetic effect of FG as a solo: like a magnetic field lining up the polarity of molecules, FG can change the orientation of all investors, including the median or average investor.

When married to the NIRP and the APP, FG also provides key safeguards to contain the rate volatility side effects that both those instruments may otherwise bring about. At the zero lower bound, in a no-NIRP world where expectations of a rate cut are entirely priced out and the central bank inspires expectations of a zero-rate path for long, the volatility of future rates hits a minimum. To the extent that the term premium compensates investors in long-dated securities for short-rate volatility, the reduced rate volatility in a no-NIRP/ZLB scenario suppresses the term premium too. But, as the NIRP re-establishes the possibility for a two-way variation in short-term interest rates, it has the potential for increasing rate volatility and the term premium as a result. FG (and APP) can mitigate this effect (cell 2.1). FG can also help anchor the rate expectations in conditions in which they may be destabilized to the upside while the central bank purchases bonds under an APP. If the bond purchases have the desired effect of accelerating economic recovery and reflation, investors may react to the brightening outlook by bringing forward the date by which they expect the central bank to raise its policy rates. Failing to push back on those expectations through a better anchoring of the front end of the forward curve may inadvertently produce a tightening in financial conditions while bond purchases are meant to ease them. FG, again, is an effective complement to the APP in this respect (cell 2.3).

The interaction with TLTROs is more mediated. In Chapter 5, we measured and visualized the cost of loan origination faced by banks, inclusive of a margin, in terms of an 'intermediation wedge', sandwiched between the benchmark rate used by banks as base to price loans on the downside, and the lending rate offered by banks to the commercial clients on the upside. Together with the NIRP, FG has generated an inversion in the risk-free curve over maturity portions that provide the benchmark for loan rate fixation. This has pulled down the whole pricing structure and the final lending rate, thus stimulating the demand for loans that banks could serve by funding themselves under TLTROs.

6.2.3 The APP

As we have argued consistently, the duration extraction cum portfolio rebalancing view of the APP has provided the main rationale for rolling out asset purchases and has dominated the ECB's doctrine concerning their transmission. Cell 3.3 summarizes a long stack of assumptions and empirical observations. The duration channel is the principal mechanism at play.[12] By purchasing long-dated assets, a central bank reduces the amount of duration risk—or interest rate risk—that is borne in aggregate, while simultaneously increasing the amount of short-term risk-free bank reserves in the system. This bids up the price of the purchased securities and,

---

[12] Empirical evidence, especially from the anticipation period of the APP, suggests indeed that the signalling channel of the (expected) purchase programme played only a limited role and portfolio rebalancing as induced by duration extraction was the main channel of the yield compressing effect, see, e.g. Lemke and Werner (2020) and the references given therein. Geiger and Schupp (2018), by contrast, find a more distinct role for additional signalling effects.

simultaneously, suppresses their expected return relative to a strategy of rolling over short-term investments paying the risk-free rate, or engaging in riskier strategies.[13] The latter strategy lies at the core of the portfolio rebalancing channel of APP, whereby yields and returns are lowered across a wide range of financial assets. But the APP is at the centre of a web of interlocking influences that spread widely across all the other instruments. First, the APP saturates the money market with the surplus of liquidity that is necessary to keep the overnight rate close to and controllable by the DFR. This is a pre-condition for arbitrage to ensure that the negative return to

---

[13] See, e.g., Cochrane and Piazzesi (2009) for a formal explanation and decomposition of the term premium in terms of current and future expected excess returns. Most of the arbitrage-free models of the term structure of interest rates that have become common in the fixed-income finance literature since Vasicek (1977) or Cox, Ingersoll, and Ross (1985) do not generally allow for effects of bond supply on premia and interest rates. In those models, the pure expectations hypothesis may not exactly hold, because investors in long-term bonds demand excess returns for bearing interest rate risk. This 'term premium' is priced according to a uniform stochastic discount factor across all maturities, but this stochastic discount factor is independent of supply or demand conditions in any market: it is induced only by economic fundamentals. In analyzing the portfolio balance channel, researchers have emphasized market segmentation between securities of different maturities, as in the formal preferred-habitat model, or between different fixed income securities with similar risk characteristics. For example, market segmentation between the government bond markets and other fixed income markets could reflect the specific needs of pension funds, other institutional investors, and foreign central banks to hold safe government bonds, and arbitrageurs that are institutionally constrained or simply too small in comparison to such huge demand flows. Along these lines, a more recent strand of research, starting with Vayanos and Vila (2021) and Greenwood and Vayanos (2014), combines the arbitrage-pricing perspective with a segmented market structure. In these models, investors with preferred-habitat preferences, e.g. portfolio managers who are rather insensitive to changes in the expected returns offered by assets with specific characteristics interact with arbitrageurs with limited balance sheet power. Essentially, in a Vayanos-Vila model, arbitrageurs do two things: first, they bridge the disconnect between long-term yields (that would be determined by clientele effects in an isolated manner otherwise) and the time-varying short rate, incorporating information about expected short rates into bond prices. (Suppose, for example, that the short rate increases, becoming attractive relative to investing in bonds. Investors do not take advantage of this opportunity because they prefer the safety of the bond that matures at the time when they need to consume. But arbitrageurs do take advantage by shorting bonds and investing at the short rate. Through this reverse-carry trade, bond prices decrease, thus responding to the high short rate.) And, second, arbitrageurs bring yields in line with each other, smoothing local demand and supply pressures. (Suppose, for example, that supply is high at a particular maturity segment. Absent arbitrageurs, the markets for different maturities are segmented, and yields are determined by local demand and supply. So, in the absence of arbitrageurs, the yield for that segment would be high but other segments would be unaffected. Arbitrageurs exploit the difference in yields, buying that segment and shorting other segments to hedge their risk exposure. This brings yields in line with each other, spreading the local effect of supply over the entire term structure.) While these arbitrageurs engage in relative-value trades, buying undervalued securities and selling overvalued securities short, they are unable to arbitrage away completely changes in relative returns—between a buy-and-hold strategy and a strategy of rolling over at a very short-term rate—because of balance sheet restrictions. The simultaneous presence of investors that prefer a specific amount of duration risk along with a lack of maturity-indifferent arbitrageurs with sufficiently deep pockets ensures that changes in the bond supply affect the aggregate amount of duration available in the market and the pricing of the associated interest rate risk term premia. In this context, central bank purchases of even a few specific bonds can affect the risk pricing and term premia for a wide range of securities, insofar as they extract duration from the market. King (2018) provides a more encompassing examination of the properties of the stochastic discount factor that allow for a duration channel to occur in (macro-finance) term structure models. Gagnon et al. (2011) provides indirect support for the duration channel—over the 'expectations channel'—by showing that the announcements of LSAPs lowered ten-year yields, arguably incorporating more term premium, by substantially more than two-year yields, incorporating less term premium. D'Amico et al. (2012), D'Amico and King (2013) point to the importance of preferred habitat or local supply mechanisms by finding that the announcements of asset purchases had the greatest impact on the specific securities being purchased relative to others with similar maturity that were not being purchased. See Li and Wei (2013) and Eser et al. (2019) for empirical studies evidencing the economic significance of the duration channel being at work for the US and euro area asset purchase programmes.

reserves under the NIRP translates into negative returns to other short-term liquid assets (cell 3.1). And it is a necessary condition for FG on the future path of the DFR to be able to influence expectations of the future path of the market overnight rate (cell 3.2). Second, along with FG, but over a more extended spectrum of maturities than rate FG alone can influence, it contains the potential term premium volatility associated with the larger future rate uncertainty created by the NIRP (cell 1.3). Box 6.1 shows how this mechanism works in the simplified two-period model environment with mean-variance investors used to study the NIRP.

6.2.4 TLTROs

The chief assignment of TLTROs was to help reduce the cost of loan origination. Cell 4.4 incorporates the former intermediate objective, while cell 4.1 describes the way in which a negative borrowing rate under TLTROs could help banks exempt part of their reserves from the negative rate charge. Mirroring the effect of the APP on the attractiveness of bonds versus loans as a profitable asset in the banks' business strategies (cell 3.4), TLTROs determined an increase in the risk-adjusted return on loans to the real economy over bonds (cell 4.3).

Box 6.1 Breaking through the zero lower bound—inspecting the mechanism in a two-period model

---

This box deploys a stylized two-period term structure model to illustrate the impact of a (zero) lower bound on short-term interest rates, expected future rates and long-term rates, and it discusses the effect of negative-rate policy on the term structure. The lower bound renders the predictive density of future short-term rates asymmetric as desired future policy rates (implied by some feedback rule) that fall below the lower bound are not feasible. This induces a positive wedge between expected actual short-term rates and expected desired policy rates. Hence, in addition to current rates being constrained by the lower bound, this bias in rate expectations constitutes another impediment to providing accommodation at and already near the lower bound. Deploying negative interest rate policy (NIRP) can shift the whole term structure to negative levels and—depending on the perception of the lower bound prevailing in the future—remove the bias in rate expectations. Forward guidance policy by contrast can only flatten the curve, but cannot decrease its overall level. QE policies can decrease the long end of the curve by compressing the term premium, but QE would be less effective than negative rate policy at the short end of the curve. As removing the lower bound may increase future rate uncertainty and hence the term premium, a combination of NIRP (bringing down the short end of the curve, but with uncertain implication on the term premium) and QE (controlling the term premium) may be a powerful combination in the model.

While the box serves to pinpoint certain features of monetary policy transmission through the term structure near, at and below the lower bound, the highly stylized nature of the model warrants caution of overly extrapolating its result. Its main benefit will hence be to structure and inform an understanding of the empirical findings presented in the main text. In particular, the box abstracts from discussing the macroeconomic impact of NIRP and especially the role of banks. The discussion and literature references in the main text provide further guidance on those channels as well as an overall (preliminary) assessment of the effectiveness and possible side effects of NIRP policies.

A Simple Two-Period Model of the Term Structure with a Lower Bound

The model is a two-period economy, in which a one-period and a two-period zero-coupon bond are traded.[14] Bond prices at time t are given as P_t^1 and P_t^2, respectively. Corresponding (continuously compounded) n-period bond yields are given by $R_t^n = -\frac{1}{n}\ln P_t^n$. The one-period bond pays off one unit of account at the end of period t, the two-period bond matures with the same payoff at the end of period $t+1$. At the beginning of time $t+1$, the two-period bond has one period left to maturity and trades at price P_{t+1}^1.

The one-period rate R_t^1 is determined by the central bank. It sets its desired or target interest rate S_t according to some feedback rule of the form

$$S_t = c + \alpha\, S_{t-1} + \beta(\pi_t - \bar{\pi}) + e_t^s, \tag{B.6.1.1}$$

where β governs the reaction of the policy rate to deviation of the inflation rate π from its objective, the parameter α governs interest rate smoothing, and e_t^s is a monetary policy shock.

We do not model explicitly the inflation process, take inflation as given at time t and assume its predictive density for time $t+1$ to be normal, which would be compatible with a variety of linear Gaussian models of the economy. The monetary policy shock e_t^s appearing in eq. (B.6.1.1) is likewise assumed to be normal.

The central bank is constrained by a lower-bound LB so that given its desired rate in eq. (B.6.1.1) the actual short-term rate that it can set is given by

$$R_t^1 = max(S_t, LB).$$

(Continued)

---

[14] The two-period model follows Doh (2010), which in turn incorporates elements of Vayanos and Vila (2021). As one of the first papers discussing from a monetary policy perspective the nonlinear relation between the short and long end of the yield curve at and near the lower bound see Ruge-Murcia (2006).

Box 6.1 Continued

Henceforth, we will refer to R_t^1 as the 'actual' short-term or policy rate, and to S_t interchangeably as the 'desired', 'target' or 'shadow' short-term or policy rate.

A representative investor equipped with zero net-wealth at time t borrows at the short-term rate and invests the receipts in long-term debt. He chooses bond hold-ings in order to maximize a linear-quadratic objective of expected wealth W over the first period[15]:

$$\max E\left(W_{t+1}\right) - 0.5\ \gamma\ Var\left(W_{t+1}\right)$$

The parameter γ can be interpreted as the investor's risk aversion. The model is closed by assuming that at time t, the two-year bond is in fixed supply of Q units. Using the evolution of wealth, the investor's first order conditions and setting his two-year bond demand equal to supply, the two-year rate at time t is given as

$$R_t^2 = 0.5\left[R_t^1 + E\left(R_{t+1}^1\right)\right] + 0.5\ \gamma\ Q\ Var\left(R_{t+1}^1\right). \qquad (B.6.1.2)$$

The small model describes the pair (R_t^1, R_t^2), namely the term structure of interest rate at time t. The long end of the term structure, R_t^2, is the sum of the expected average future short-term rate and a term premium component incorporating risk aversion, bond supply and future short rate uncertainty. Given the functional form of the central bank's reaction function and investor preferences, the model allows for conducting comparative statics exercises to infer the impact of a change in bond supply, risk aversion, the current short-term rate, the lower bound or the outlook for inflation on the level and slope of the yield curve.

The Relevance of the (Zero) Lower Bound for the Term Structure

The presence of the lower bound imposes a constraint on the rate setting of monet-ary policy. While the central bank likes to set the desired policy rate S_t according to its feedback rule (B.6.1.1), it is feasible to implement that policy only if S_t is above the lower bound.

The conditional predictive density of the desired policy rate S_{t+1} for time $t+1$ is normal, see the dashed line in Figure B.6.1.1, LHS. Its conditional mean $\mu_s \equiv E(S_{t+1})$ is a linear function of the current target rate S_t and expected inflation $E(\pi_t)$, and its conditional variance $\sigma_s^2 \equiv Var(S_{t+1})$ depends on the variance of inflation and monet-ary policy shocks. However, the associated predictive density of the actual rate R_{t+1}^1 is a *censored* normal, where desired rates *below* the lower bound are mapped into realizations *at* the lower bound.

---

[15] All expectations are conditional on time t information without explicating that.

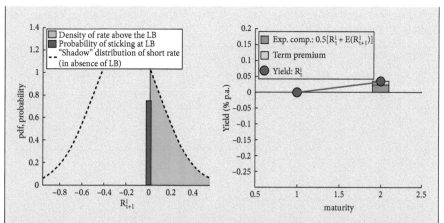

Figure B.6.1.1 Distribution of future shadow and actual short rate (LHS) and term structure of interest rates (RHS) under zero lower bound

This distribution is a combination of a probability point mass at the lower bound (see dark blue bar in Figure B.6.1.1, LHS) and a density piece to the right of the lower bound truncation point (see light blue area in the Figure). This skewed distribution implies a mean and variance of the future short-term interest rate given by[16]

$$E(R^1_{t+1}) = LB + \sigma_S \cdot z \cdot \Phi(z) + \sigma_S \cdot \phi(z) \tag{B.6.1.3}$$

and

$$Var(R^1_{t+1}) = \sigma^2_S \cdot \Phi(z) \cdot \left[(1-\delta) + (z+\lambda)^2 \cdot (1-\Phi(z)) \right] \tag{B.6.1.4}$$

where

$$z = \frac{\mu_s - LB}{\sigma_S}, \qquad \lambda = \frac{\phi(z)}{\Phi(z)}, \qquad \delta = \lambda^2 + \lambda z$$

respectively, and where ϕ and Φ denote the probability density and distribution function, respectively, of a standard normal.

The mean equation (B.6.1.3) implies that $E(R^1_{t+1}) > E(S_{t+1})$, namely there is a wedge between the expected actual rate and the expected shadow rate. Figure B.6.1.2, LHS, plots $E(R^1_{t+1})$ against $E(S_{t+1})$ for the example of a zero lower bound, $LB = 0$. In the absence of the lower bound, trivially $E(R^1_{t+1}) = E(S_{t+1})$, the red 45 degree line. With the lower bound in place, but the expected desired policy rate way above it, $E(S_{t+1}) \gg LB$, the expected target policy rate is essentially equal to the expected actual rate, $E(R^1_{t+1}) \approx E(S_{t+1})$, a situation as in the absence of the lower bound. For the

(*Continued*)

---

[16] See, e.g., Greene (1997).

Box 6.1 Continued

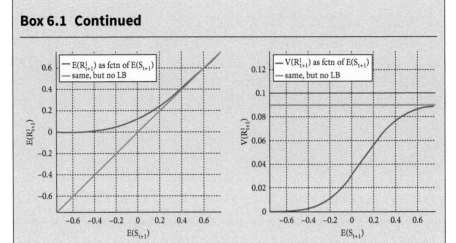

Figure B.6.1.2 Expected actual short rate (LHS) and variance (RHS) as function of expected shadow rate under ZLB

other extreme with the expected target rate sizeably negative, $E(S_{t+1}) \ll LB$, the actual rate is expected to be essentially *at* the bound, $E(R^1_{t+1}) \approx LB$. An interesting feature is that even if the lower bound is not expected to bind, namely $E(S_{t+1}) > LB$, there is still a wedge between the expected target rate and the expected actual rate, $E(R^1_{t+1}) > E(S_{t+1})$. This is reflected by the distance between the blue and red line in Figure B.6.1.2, LHS, at the lower bound of zero and in a local neighbourhood to the right of it.

That is, even if investors (understanding the central bank's reaction function and sharing its inflation outlook) expect the central bank's desired interest rate in the future to be at or somewhat above the lower bound, the expectation of the actual rate is biased upwards, namely above the expected desired policy rate. This is induced by the asymmetry of the distribution of the future short rate. Upside deviations from the expected shadow rate (e.g. if inflation turns out higher than expected) will map one-for-one into higher realized rates. However, in case a large negative shock hits the economy and the central bank would unexpectedly like to set rates below the lower bound, the lower-bound constraint maps *desired* rates *below* the lower bound into *actual* rates that would be *at* the lower bound instead of below, biasing the expectation of the actual rate upwards.[17]

In addition, the existence of the lower bound also diminishes the impact of a current rate cut on future expected rates. To see this, imagine the current policy rate is above the lower bound, $R^1_t = S_t > LB$. Then equation (B.6.1.3) implies how the expected future short rate reacts to a change in the current rate as follows:

---

[17] A simple discrete-space example for a lower bound of zero: let the future desired policy rate S_{t+1} have possible outcomes −1, 0, 1 with probabilities 0.25, 0.5 and 0.25, respectively, thus $E(S_{t+1}) = 0$. The

$$\frac{\partial E(R^1_{t+1})}{\partial R^1_t} = \alpha \cdot \Phi\left(\frac{\mu_s - LB}{\sigma_s}\right) \tag{B.6.1.5}$$

As under the absence of a lower bound this derivative is equal to α (the persistence of the short-term rate in the policy rule) and $\Phi(\cdot)<1$, it implies that current rate changes are transmitted less strongly to future rates in the presence of a lower bound.

So far we have seen that the presence of the lower bound drives a wedge between expected desired monetary policy rate levels and expected actual rate levels, and that it weakens the nexus between current rate decreases and expected future rate decreases. Overall, the presence of the lower bound thus constrains the degree of accommodation that can be exerted through the expectations component of long rates, see eq. (B.6.1.2).

At the same time, the presence of the lower bound also has an impact on the variance of expected future rates. From eq. (B.6.1.4), it is evident that the conditional variance of the future short rate is the lower the closer the expected shadow rate is to the lower bound. For $E(S_{t+1}) \gg LB$, the variance would be close to a level prevailing in the absence of a lower bound. The closer $E(S_{t+1})$ gets to the lower bound the variance decreases and essentially vanishes if $E(S_{t+1})$ is sufficiently below the lower bound. Figure B.6.1.2, RHS, summarizes this pattern by plotting the conditional variance as a function of $E(S_{t+1})$ for a lower bound of zero.[18]

In the stylized model considered here, a lower conditional volatility induced by greater proximity to the lower bound translates into a lower term premium. A polar case of that result would be a situation where conditional rate volatility would go down to zero (which, under a zero lower bound, would be induced by sufficiently negative expectations of the shadow rate), so that the term premium would converge to zero as well. This nexus of zero rate uncertainty implying zero term premium would also apply in richer models of the term structure and the macroeconomy. However, apart from this extreme case, the feature of lower rate volatility leading to a lower term premium prevailing in our stylized model needs to be read with caution. First, the possible compression of the term premium due to lower rate volatility might rather apply to short- or medium-term maturities, but does not necessarily carry over to longer maturities. Second, and especially for medium- to longer-term maturities, the presence of the lower bound and the associated constraints on monetary policy may render macroeconomic volatility to be higher, so that on net the term premium may increase rather than decline.

(Continued)

---

desired rate in the worst state would fall below the lower bound, so the corresponding realizations of the actual rates are 0, 0, 1, with an expected rate of $E(R^1_{t+1})=0.25 > E(S^1_{t+1})=0$.

[18] Applying a shadow rate model to the euro area, Lemke and Vladu (2017) find that indeed the short rate approaching the lower bound accounts for the trend decline in observed rate volatility.

Box 6.1 Continued

As a starting point (baseline case) for the following stylized policy exercises, Figure B.6.1.1, RHS, plots the term structure (R_t^1, R_t^2) corresponding to the expected rate constellation depicted in Figure B.6.1.1, LHS. In the example, the current desired policy rate S_t is at −20 bps, the lower bound is at zero, so that the current actual rate R_t^1 is at zero as well. The expected desired policy rate $E(S_{t+1})$ is likewise at −20 bps, hence below the lower bound. As explained above, this does *not* translate into an expected actual rate of zero (in line with the lower bound) but—due to the skewed distribution inducing a bias in rate expectations—rather to an expected actual rate $E(R_{t+1}^1)$ of about 5 bps, which enters the expectations component of the long rate (see green bar in Figure B.6.1.1, LHS). The positive conditional variance of future rates together with positive bond supply Q and risk aversion γ generates a positive term premium (yellow bar) on top so that the yield curve is upward-sloping.

Below the (Zero) Lower Bound: Negative Interest Rate Policy

In the stylized model, when being at or near the lower bound, the central bank would have essentially three options to decrease the term structure and provide more stimulus to the economy: first, to utter forward guidance on the future short rate thereby affecting $E(R_{t+1}^1)$ and $Var(R_{t+1}^1)$; second, to conduct quantitative easing (QE) by reducing Q and hence the term premium; or, third, to overcome the (zero) lower bound and conduct negative interest rate policy (NIRP). We will focus on the last policy option, but compare with the other two options in the end.

The starting point is the situation described at the end of the previous section, in which the central bank is initially constrained by the zero lower bound, but then it decides to decrease rates to the desired negative level. While the central bank clearly 'breaks through' the lower bound for the current rate (moving R_t^1 from 0 to −20 bps) this move may give rise to different expectations regarding the future location of the lower bound. We will consider two versions. In the first case ('NIRP-new-LB'), market participants perceive the new (negative) rate level as the new lower bound to prevail also in the future. In the second case ('NIRP-no-LB'), the move to negative rates is perceived as monetary policy being essentially unconstrained for the future, namely the lower bound is lifted completely.

In the first variant ('NIRP-new-LB'), the predictive density of the future short rate is again a censored distribution where feasible realizations are now cut off at a new lower bound, compare Figures B.6.1.3, LHS, and B.6.1.1, LHS. This policy implies a decrease and slight steepening of the term structure see Figure B.6.1.3, RHS.

The current policy rate decreases by 20 bps, simply due to the release of the lower bound. The expected actual rate $E(R_{t+1}^1)$ decreases as well. Note that now we have $E(S_{t+1}) = LB$ (while before we had $E(S_{t+1}) < LB$), but still the censored distribution implies that $E(R_{t+1}^1) > E(S_{t+1}) = LB$. In other words, even if the expected desired policy rate is now *at* the lower bound (namely in expectations unconstrained) the expected actual rate is *above* the lower bound due to the censoring of rate cuts below the new

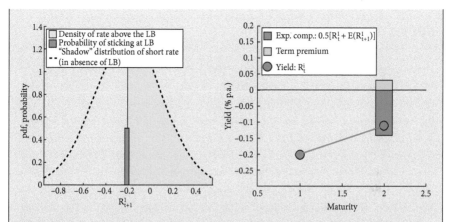

Figure B.6.1.3 Distribution of future shadow and actual short rate (LHS) and term structure of interest rates (RHS) under negative lower bound

lower bound. The term premium is a bit higher than before as the variance of the predictive distribution rises somewhat, but overall the long-term rate is decreased.

In the second variant ('NIRP-no-LB'), the predictive density of the future short-term rate is now normal, see Figure B.6.1.4, LHS, in comparison to Figure B.6.1.1, LHS. The wedge disappears, namely the expected negative intended policy rate $E(S_{t+1})$ now equals the expected short-term rate $E(R^1_{t+1})$. This implies that the expectations component decreases by more than 20 bps (release of the lower bound plus disappearance of the wedge). However, at the same time the conditional variance of the expected short-term rate is higher, which translates into a higher term premium. Again, overall, the term structure declines and steepens (compared to the ZLB scenario), see Figure B.6.1.4, RHS.

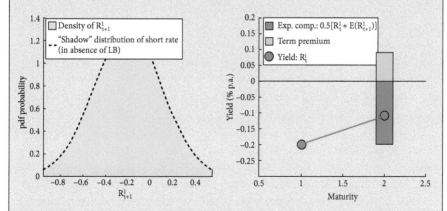

Figure B.6.1.4 Distribution of future shadow and actual short rate (LHS) and term structure of interest rates (RHS) without lower bound

(Continued)

Box 6.1 Continued

How Does the Impact of NIRP on the Term Structure Compare to the Effects of Other Policy Measures?

Under ('Odyssean') forward guidance policy, the central bank would commit to keeping the rate at its current level also in the next period. Due to that (credible) commitment, other potential trajectories of future rates are immediately priced out, the expected rate equals the committed rate, the conditional variance vanishes and the term premium becomes zero. Overall, though, compared to forward guidance, NIRP provides more accommodation, simply because negative rates are now feasible. Moreover, in a richer model, the effect of forward guidance on the term premium may not be as clear-cut and forward guidance may even have an increasing effect on the term premium, especially as regards longer maturities.[19] Finally, under NIRP the central bank sticks to its policy rule, while it does not under forward guidance.

Turning to QE policy, the central bank could withdraw supply available to the representative investor thereby decreasing the term premium—see again eq. (B.6.1.2)—and bringing the long rate down. However, by that compression of the term premium, QE would be incapable of bringing down the short end of the curve, see Figure B.6.1.5, which can be achieved by NIRP. But such a decrease of shorter-term maturities may be needed in case the economy would be reactive also—or especially—to lower short-term rates (e.g. via decreasing loan rates linked to shorter-term rates).

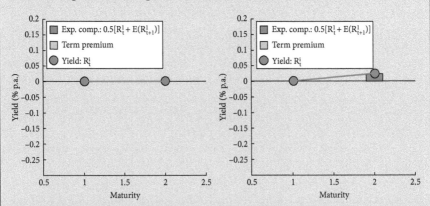

Figure B.6.1.5 Term structure of interest rate under forward guidance (LHS) and under QE policy (RHS) with zero lower bound

Combining negative rates with QE may hence be a sensible option in this stylized model: NIRP could enable negative rates, but it would maintain or even increase (depending on the version of NIRP) conditional rate volatility, which may positively impact the term premium; QE could then become handy as a complementary tool bringing down the term premium.

---

[19] See, e.g., Kliem and Meyer-Gohde (2019).

6.3 Impact Analysis

This book contributes to the debate on the achievements of unconventional policy with the novel quantitative results that are the subject of this section. Notoriously, efforts to measure the effects of monetary instruments, particularly when they are combined in complex packages, are bedevilled by identification issues. In the case at hand, such issues are magnified by those interlocking cross-influences among the ECB's four instruments that we described in the previous section. One strategy for identifying and quantifying these influences could have involved using a structural model to simulate worlds in which the central bank would have contemplated or avoided NIRP, FG, APP or TLTROs. An evaluative method based on a structural model has many advantages, including discipline and coherence with theory. But it has two non-trivial drawbacks. First, it requires making very strong propositions about the impact of policy pronouncements on agents' expectations regarding not only the future path of policy, but also the future state of the world (their own income and consumption possibilities) more in general. Second, in order for us to be able to quantify precisely the contribution of the cross-externalities mentioned in even only a few of the cells in Table 6.1 to a given observed change in credit conditions, we would have to simulate a quite complex structural model comprising multiple sectors and channels. To name only a few of them, the model would have to incorporate forms of money illusion and/or heterogeneous investors—à la Hanson-Stein—to generate the Gesell-tax effects that we mention in cell 1.3. But, in order to support any direct effect of central bank bond purchases on term premia (cell 3.3), the Hanson-Stein market segmentation hypothesis would need to co-exist with another type of investor heterogeneity: the presence of risk-neutral arbitrageurs with limited balance sheet capacity alongside buy-and-hold investors with a preferred habitat. Liquidity provision—a collateral implication of central bank asset purchases that is often ignored in structural modelling of QE—would have to be explicitly allowed for to yield the effects mentioned in cells 3.1 and 3.2 a chance. And, again, the pervasive, but nuanced signalling channels that we categorize in a variety of cells (1.2, 2.1, 2.2, etc.) would require hard-wiring various behavioural assumptions about agents' expectations formation process.

Therefore, in the interest of tractability, we had to make hard choices and cut through many corners. First, we confined our analysis to only few dimensions: essentially, the 'diagonals' in Table 6.1—cells 1.1, 2.2, 3.3 and 4.4, which we consider the first-order effects of the four instruments, respectively—with very selective inroads into 'off-diagonals'. Among the latter, we believe our quantitative analysis can reasonably evaluate 1.2 and 2.1. Box 6.1 also explains the simple intuition of why APP is a good complement of NIRP (cell 3.1) in a very parsimonious two-period model, but does not quantify the extent of the complementarity. Second, we adopt a general identification scheme which assigns sets of instruments to observed adjustments in the yield curve that financial intermediaries use as the basis to price credit, and in credit spreads, respectively. In line with the general taxonomy of Table 6.1, the NIRP, the PSPP (the sovereign bond component of the APP) and FG are seen as influencing primarily the yield curve, while TLTROs and the private bond components of the APP are important determinants of the 'intermediation wedge', the difference between the final cost of loans for households and firms, and the risk-free interest rate that banks and other intermediaries take as reference for rate fixation in pricing those loans. Our main contribution is in trying to tease apart the effects on financial conditions, growth and inflation of the NIRP, FG and the PSPP, in particular. Here, again, the general identification assumption is that the NIRP and FG enhance the central bank's traction on the short- to medium-maturity segment of the overnight forward curve, while the PSPP operates principally on the long end of the sovereign curve. Throughout this section, we present our identification and estimation approaches in a largely non-technical manner: while we explain the general ideas underlying the adopted techniques, we refer to our working paper[20] for further technical and implementation details.

6.3.1   The NIRP, FG, and the Yield Curve

The third methodological choice we make is to avoid imposing too many priors on the data generating process, for both the term structure of interest rates and the economy. We first seek to disentangle the relative impacts of the NIRP and FG focusing on the front end of the money market forward curve. Here, we generate counterfactual worlds without NIRP—a *no*-NIRP scenario—*with* and *without* FG which, when contrasted with the history of yield curve adjustments, deliver an estimate of the yield effects that one can trace to the NIRP and FG, respectively. To isolate the impacts of the NIRP and FG, jointly and separately, we use a methodology that requires minimal priors on the underlying macroeconomic structure and on the power of central bank pronouncements. We proceed in four steps.

First step. For each trading date between June 2014—when the ECB brought the rate on its deposit facility to −0.1%—and December 2018, we construct a fan chart around the EONIA forward curve, see left panel of Figure 6.15. Each fan chart is a sequence of interpolated risk-neutral densities of future three-month OIS rates. These risk-neutral densities are in turn derived from options on three-month EURIBOR futures.[21] The fan chart shown in the figure merits two observations. First, the quantiles of that distribution, corresponding to the last trading day in our sample (28 December), can be thought of as embedding the probability-weighted rate paths that investors expected to observe over the next 18 months looking out from the vantage point of end-December 2018. There is one such distribution per each trading day in

---

[20]   See Rostagno et al. (2019).

[21]   Risk-neutral densities are derived according to the methodology described in de Vincent-Humphreys and Puigvert Gutiérrez (2012) in turn deploying the results of Breeden and Litzenberger (1978). For translating Euribor densities into densities of the corresponding three-month OIS rates we correct for the EURIBOR-OIS spread.

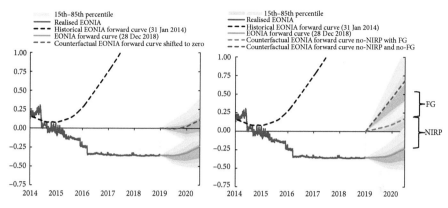

Figure 6.15 Expectations of future short-term rates: observed and counterfactual (percentages per annum)

Sources: ECB and ECB calculations.

Notes: LHS: The risk-neutral option-implied densities for future EONIA (obtained from the density for 3M Euribor by subtracting the EURIBOR-EONIA spread) are given by the blue fan chart around the red solid line. As the first step in constructing our counterfactual scenario, they are shifted parallelly upwards such that EONIA is at zero, leading to the higher blue fan chart around the dashed-blue line, which is parallel to its red counterpart. This in-between constellation does not obey the ZLB yet. RHS: Starting from the LHS density around the dashed blue line, the probability mass at or below zero is re-apportioned to zero ('point mass'), hence obeying the ZLB, giving rise to the green density. Its mean—the counterfactual forward curve under that scenario—is the dashed green line. This is the no NIRP, with FG counterfactual. Lifting the percentiles of the green densities using the forward guidance impact factors from Figure 6.17 leads to the blue density. This is the no NIRP, no FG counterfactual.

our sample. Second, the red thick line, the central tendency of the distribution, coincides with the overnight forward curve that one could derive from the overnight-indexed swap market on that date, a key ingredient in central banks' and analysts' monitoring of the representative rate expectations in the money market.

Second step. Having constructed predictive densities for rate paths, the next steps in our methodology entails manipulating the historic densities—such as the left-bottom object shown in Figure 6.15—to make them minimally consistent with the alternative policy scenarios that we want to simulate: a world without the NIRP, *with* and *without* FG. By 'minimally consistent' we mean that we alter those paths to the extent, and only to the extent, that they might embody expectations that would patently be inconsistent with the counterfactual policy regime that we hypothesize.

In other words, a *no*-NIRP world should be one in which no rate path in the bundle that makes up each predictive density should contemplate a rate cut once the overnight rate has been brought to its zero lower bound. So, in the second stage of our procedure, we parallel-shift all the daily predictive probability density functions observed between September 2014 and December 2018 and re-anchor them to a level of zero, reflecting the notion that, in a *no*-NIRP world, those distributions would not have been anchored at a negative overnight rate. The top distribution in the left-hand panel of Figure 6.15 visualizes this second stage of our procedure. It is simply a vertical displacement of the bottom historical density. While the latter is anchored at the 28 December 2018 overnight rate fixing of around −0.35%, the former is anchored at a counterfactual overnight rate level of zero.

Third step. The previous step brings us closer to a '*no*-NIRP *with* FG' world, but not quite there. Why? Because, by assumption, in such a zero-lower-bound world we assume that the ECB would have expressed the intention to keep the path of the overnight rate flat at zero for as long as it did pledge to keep the policy rates at the 'current or lower level' in history (see Section 6.1). Reflecting this assumption (while excluding the 'or lower' part of that statement in line with the assumption of a *zero-lower* bound under that scenario), therefore, we re-apportion the probability mass assigned to rate paths dipping below zero in each one of these shifted historical densities to zero. Each one of these displaced and truncated counterfactual densities,[22] in turn, entails a counterfactual forward curve. We show the outcome of the second stage of our procedure as the green fan chart in the right-hand panel of Figure 6.15. The green dashed curve is the counterfactual EONIA forward curve in a '*no*-NIRP *with* FG' world corresponding to 28 December 2018. Intuitively, stacking the below-zero portion of the displaced density mass toward zero produces a counterfactual series of daily forward curves that are invariably steeper than those observed.[23] We cross-checked the outcome of this density-based counterfactual scenario with an exercise based on a shadow-rate term structure model, which gave similar results.[24]

To be sure, the density-based method for deriving the '*no*-NIRP *with* FG' counterfactual is based on a couple of assumptions and subject to model uncertainty. For example, the original historical densities and the '*no*-NIRP *with* FG' counterfactuals, by assumption, assign the same probability mass to future rate trajectories that range above the rate level (negative or zero, respectively) at which they happen to be anchored. We justify this assumption on FG credibility considerations, namely on the idea that whatever degree of credibility the FG pledge made by the ECB in history would have been preserved in the counterfactual world. However, one could conceive of an alternative, equally reasonable assumption, namely that the central bank's FG language would have been even more explicit and self-committing than in history and this sharper communication would have led to tighter densities in the counterfactual world. In this sense our counterfactuals would provide an upper bound of the NIRP effect (measured as the distance between the actual and counterfactual forward curve). At the same time, we believe it would be unrealistic to assume the other extreme that the densities would have collapsed to a point distribution at zero as—empirically—under any regime of FG, some probability of increasing rates (and

---

[22] For each horizon, the counterfactual risk-neutral rate distribution is strictly speaking not a density, but a mixture of i) the original density (truncated at zero) and ii) a discrete probability ('point mass') corresponding to the cumulative probability that was assigned to negative realizations before the truncation took place.

[23] A simple example with discrete state space supports the intuition. Fix a horizon and assume that the corresponding predictive rate distribution centred at zero supports rate realizations of r = −1, 0, 1 with risk-neutral probabilities 0.25, 0.5 and 0.25, respectively, so that the forward rate E(r)=0. The censoring of sub-zero outcomes and re-apportioning them to zero generates a new distribution with rate outcomes r = 0,1 with probabilities 0.75 and 0.25, respectively, so that the forward rate is now 0.25.

[24] See Box B.11 in Rostagno et al. (2019).

hence some steepness of the forward curve) has always been observed. If anything, pictures like Panel B of Figure 6.15, tend to support the view at the opposite side of the spectrum: despite generous recourse to FG, central banks eschewing the NIRP found it hard to flatten the forward curve by as much as they likely saw desirable, a sign that the rate path distribution might tend to display even more extreme upward skewness in those circumstances than we presume when running our '*no*-NIRP *with FG*' simulations.

What is the horizon for constant rates that the ECB would have communicated in a '*no*-NIRP *with FG*' world? We consult market- and survey-based expectations to test whether, in history, investors expected the ECB's FG on rates to apply for at least an 18-month horizon looking into the future from any point in time. As mentioned above, 18 months is the maximum horizon for which the data on option-implied risk-neutral densities are available.

Figure 6.16 displays the historical evolution of time to lift-off, in the form of number of months to an expected 10 basis point DFR increase.[25] Indeed, since mid-2017, evidence based on both surveys and the EONIA forward curve consistently point to

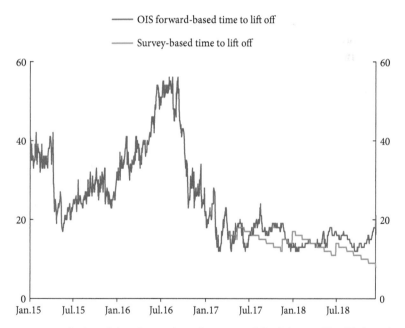

Figure 6.16 Evolution of time interval to a future rate hike ('time to lift off'), based on OIS forward curve and surveys of market participants (number of months)
Sources: Refinitiv and ECB.
Latest observation: 31 December 2018.

[25] The survey-based time series is visible only starting from mid-2017: before that date, market participants did not foresee an increase in the DFR above levels prevailing at the time over the forecast horizon covered by the survey. The survey refers to the median across Reuters survey's respondents.

a time to lift-off fluctuating close to a horizon of 18 months. Before mid-2017, the time to lift-off priced in by financial markets has been persistently above 20 months, reaching the peak of just below 60 months in the aftermath of the Brexit referendum. Overall, considering the above evidence, we conclude that it is reasonable to use our 'no-NIRP, *with* FG' counterfactual in the subsequent impact analysis (i.e. when conducting the BVAR-based assessment of the impact on GDP and inflation, see Section 6.3.4, for a horizon of up to 18 months.

Fourth step. In this final stage of our procedure, we derive a '*no*-NIRP/*no*-FG' counterfactual. In order to do so, we make use of a 'FG factor' that allows us to measure forward guidance shocks over time. Following the methodology adopted in Altavilla and Giannone (2017), we construct a time series for FG innovations using Google Trends data.[26] We take the number of Google queries as an indication of the general interest in forward guidance stemming from media discussions, economic releases, and official communications. More specifically, we extract a normalized index of Internet search queries from the largest euro area countries for the term 'forward guidance' and restrict the search category to 'finance'. We then combine these country-based indices into one index for the euro area as a whole, and employ the obtained time series in a regression analysis to tell apart NIRP and FG.[27]

The 'FG factor' (FG) derived from our Internet-based measure is used to estimate the effects on the probability density functions that we derive in step three.[28] Specifically, the factor is regressed on the quantiles of the densities as follows:

$$\Delta f_{t,h}^{(q)} = \alpha_h^{(q)} + \beta_h^{(q)} FG_t + \Phi_{t,h}^{(q)}$$

Where $\Delta f_{t,h}^{(q)}$ is the one-day change in the percentile q of the risk-neutral predictive density of future EONIA at horizon h. This regression is estimated over a sample that spans June 2013 to September 2019. Panel A and B of Figure 6.17 display the impact of the FG factor (i.e. the cumulated fit of the above regression) on selected quantiles of forward rates at horizon 12 and 18 months, starting from the beginning of 2013.

Finally, in order to generate counterfactual densities reflecting a 'no-NIRP/*no*-FG' world, the estimated impact of the FG factor is combined with the 'no-NIRP *with*

---

[26] Google Trend data aggregates billions of queries that individuals type each day into the Google search box. Although each search is driven by diverse objectives that might be uncorrelated to the researcher's questions at hand, aggregating up these billions of queries might give important insights on the expectations or concerns related to a particular topic. A Google Trends count of Internet search queries has been recently used in academic researches on identifying seasonal trends, studying revealed preferences, and forecasting macroeconomic aggregates.

[27] We have data on Germany, France and Italy; for Spain there is no sufficient data traffic. Box B.11 in Rostagno et al. (2019) provides robustness analysis. It documents how the pattern of transmission of this measure of FG across the yield curve is similar to that generated by an alternative measure based on high-frequency changes in OIS yields over a narrow window of time (10 minutes) before and after each ECB press conference, as proposed in Altavilla et al. (2019).

[28] See Hattori, Schrimpf, and Sushko (2016) for a similar exercise inspecting how unconventional US monetary policy affects the tail properties of option-implied densities of the stock market and interest rates.

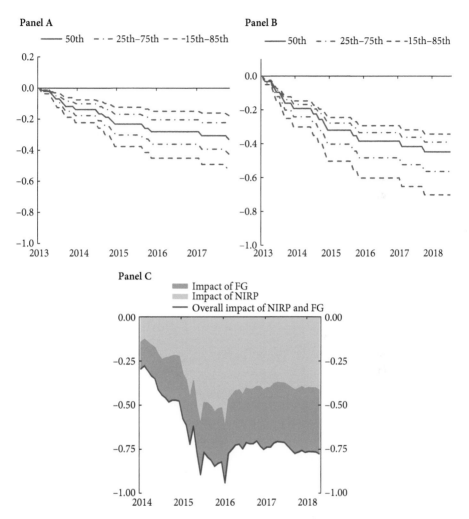

Figure 6.17 Impact of forward guidance and NIRP on forward rates and forward rates quantiles

Panel A: Impact of forward guidance on forward rates quantiles: 12 month horizon (pp)

Panel B: Impact of forward guidance on forward rates quantiles: 18 month horizon (pp)

Panel C: Overall impact of NIRP and forward guidance on 12 months forward rate (pp)

Sources: ECB, Google Trends and ECB calculations.

Notes: Panels A and B: Evolution of the impact of forward guidance on selected quantiles of the 3-month in 12- and 18-month OIS forward rate distribution starting from June 2013. The impact is derived via regressing the quantiles on a forward guidance factor. The latter is extracted from Google Trends data. Panel C: Overall impact of forward guidance and NIRP on the 12 months OIS forward rate displayed starting from September 2014.

Latest observation: December 2018.

FG' counterfactual: at each point in time, for a selected group of percentiles, the estimated negative FG impact is added back the 'no-NIRP *with* FG' distribution, which leads to a new sequence of no-NIRP/*no*-FG' counterfactual distributions. These distributions are invariably more upward skewed than those observed in history and under a 'no-NIRP *with* FG' scenario. The upper fan chart on the right-hand side of Figure 6.15 is the 'no-NIRP *no*-FG' distribution corresponding to the last trading day of December 2018.[29] The distance between the green and blue dashed lines represents the contribution of FG to the decline in the forward curve (central tendency) at the different horizons covered by our methodology, while the distance between the green and red lines represents the contribution of the NIRP. Panel C of Figure 6.17 displays the contributions of the NIRP and FG separately, referring to the central tendency of the counterfactual densities at a 12-month horizon.

6.3.2 APP and the Yield Curve

As for the quantification of the pure APP effect, we concentrate on its duration channel (cell 3.3 in Table 6.1). We estimate the term premium effect of the APP utilizing an arbitrage-free affine model of the term structure with a quantity factor (see Eser et al., 2019). The quantity factor is proxied by the fraction of overall bond supply in the hands of price-sensitive investors (what we refer to as 'free-float').[30] The model maps paths of anticipated purchases of a GDP- and maturity-weighted portfolio of bonds issued by the governments of the four largest jurisdictions (Germany, France, Italy, and Spain)—which translate into lower expected future free-float volumes to be held by price-sensitive investors—into changes in term premia.[31] We show the portfolio as a fraction of the universe of purchasable bonds in Panel B of Figure 6.10. The term premium impacts of different vintages of APP recalibrations are reported in Panel C of Figure 6.10.

Figure 6.18 shows the time series of in-sample impacts of the APP on sovereign yields across 2-, 5- and 10-year maturities estimated with the Eser et al. (2019) model. The narrow perspective we take by concentrating on the duration channel might in fact understate the efficacy of the APP for two reasons. First, to the extent that the purchases are a concrete demonstration of a desire to provide additional stimulus, they may reinforce the signal—released primarily by FG—about the likely trajectory of future policy rates (cell 3.2 in Table 6.1).

---

[29] Quite often, no data is available for the 6-months horizon, so that this scenario is built upon information at the 12- and 18-month horizon only. All shorter horizons are then computed by interpolation between the zero and 12-month horizon.

[30] Price-insensitive investors are defined as hold-to maturity investors (e.g. insurance companies and pension funds) as well as the (euro area and foreign) official sector, namely comprising market participants that are less likely to respond to changes in prices or the supply and maturity structure of the bond universe. The remaining group of bond holders are classified as price-sensitive.

[31] The model has as similar structure as Li and Wei (2013), which is used by the Federal Reserve to estimate the yield impact of large-scale sovereign bond purchases. The impact estimates as far as the announcement period is concerned are broadly in line with Altavilla et al. (2015).

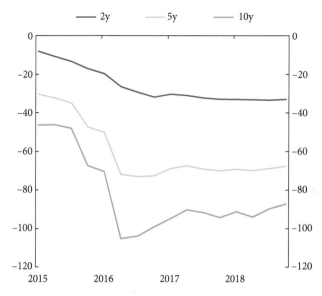

Figure 6.18 APP impact on euro area sovereign term premia (basis points)

Notes: Evolution of the impact of the APP on euro area sovereign term premia at selected maturities. The impact is derived on the basis of an arbitrage-free affine model of the term structure with a quantity factor (see Eser et al., 2019). The model results are derived using GDP-weighted averages of the yields of the big-four sovereign issuers (DE, FR, IT, ES).

This extra signal makes the trajectory lower and shallower than it would have been in the absence of the APP. So, the APP may have influenced the short-rate expectations component of long-term yields, as well as their term premium component.

Second, the purchases effectively raised banks' capital ratios by increasing the value of the existing assets on their balance sheets. So, asset purchases may have stimulated spending by increasing loan supply beyond levels that could have been attained solely by deploying TLTROs (cell 3.4 in Table 6.1).

6.3.3 TLTROs and Lending Rates

As for the quantification of the pure TLTRO effect, we concentrate on its impact on the intermediation wedge by compressing funding costs for banks (cell 4.4 in Table 6.1). We compute the funding cost relief for banks by considering both direct and indirect channels. The direct channel arises for banks participating in the TLTROs. It is computed as the funding cost relief per unit of borrowing combined with the TLTRO uptake by banks.

Figure 6.19 displays the evolution over time of TLTRO borrowing by euro area banks. The funding cost relief per unit of borrowing is given by the difference

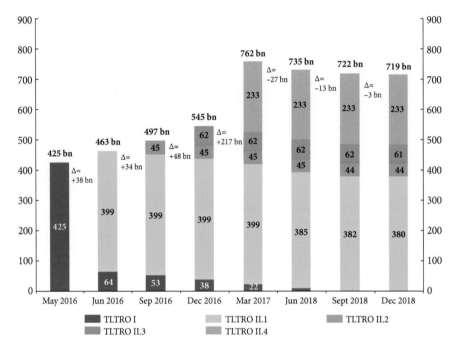

Figure 6.19 Evolution of TLTRO borrowing by euro area banks (EUR billion)

Source: ECB.

Notes: TLTRO gross uptakes by euro area banks under TLTRO-I and through the various operations under TLTRO-II. Numbers may not add up due to rounding.

Latest observation: 2018Q4.

between the funding cost of more expensive sources of funding, which we proxy with bank bonds, with affordable long-term borrowing from the ECB. The analysis is performed at the country level in order to account for an unequal distribution of TLTRO take-up and significant differences in banks funding costs across euro area countries. The indirect effect arises from the reduction in bank bond yields that benefit all banks and is generated by scarcity effects of lower bank bond issuance by TLTRO-participating banks.

We assume that this scarcity effect operates in a qualitatively and quantitatively similar manner to a reduction of free-float amounts of bonds in the hand of the private sector due to the ECB's asset purchases. Having quantified the funding cost relief for banks via direct and indirect channels, we map this into the impact on lending rates charged by banks for NFC loans using a standard pass-through model.[32] The resulting impact on lending rate to loans to non-financial corporations is shown in Figure 6.20.

---

[32] The mapping from changes in banks' funding costs into lending rates is carried out using a time-series model with rich bank's balance-sheet information.

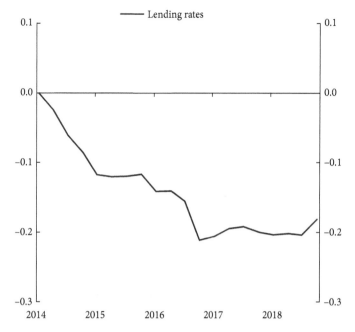

Figure 6.20 TLTROs impact on lending rates to loans to non-financial corporations (percentage points)

Sources: ECB and ECB calculations.
Notes: The impact is derived by mapping the funding cost relief provided by TLTROs to euro area banks into a lending rate impact. The decline in funding costs is calibrated off model, on the basis of the funding structure of euro area banks, as well as their participation to TLTROs operations. The impact on lending rates is then computed using a pass-through model.
Latest observation: December 2018.

6.3.4 NIRP-FG-APP-TLTROs and the Macroeconomy

To complete the analysis of impacts, we quantify the transmission of the ECB policy measures via macromodel simulations. Given the variety of the measures and the challenge in modelling their transmission channels in a fully-fledged microfounded macromodel, we opt for a rather agnostic approach based on a large BVAR.[33] In particular, we feed the counterfactual history of forward curves—the 'no-NIRP/no-FG' and the 'no-NIRP *with* FG' yield curve configurations—and the counterfactual history of lending rates generated by the TLTROs—into a large BVAR where we can

---

[33] Whereas some DSGE models have been recently enriched by including a detailed modelling of unconventional measures, they have tended to focus on one specific type of measure at the time, see for instance Gertler and Karadi (2015) on QE. In addition, even in such cases, to limit complexity the modelling of QE has abstracted completely from 'term' premia, which is central to our narrative, and focused on what is more akin to credit premia. Facing these challenges, we regard that a more agnostic approach based on a large BVAR with minimal identifying restriction may represent a more robust avenue. In any case, in this chapter we extensively compare the results based on our BVAR with the ones derived from alternative modelling approaches available in the literature.

interact them with a wide spectrum of financial prices and with the macroeconomic state. This last stage of our procedure produces the counterfactual histories for output growth and inflation that one would have observed in absent the ECB policy measures taken since 2014 or subsets of them. The model includes 14 variables: real GDP, HICP inflation, loans to non-financial corporations, loans to households, the EONIA, the 3-month EONIA forward in 12 and 18 months, the 2- 5- and 10-year euro area sovereign yields, the lending rate on loans to non-financial corporations and households, and the interest rates applied to deposits of non-financial corporations and households. For the estimation of the VAR, we address the curse of dimensionality problem by using Bayesian shrinkage, as suggested in De Mol, Giannone, and Reichlin (2008).[34] The sample period spans the first quarter of 1999 through the last quarter of 2018.

For simulation purposes, we partition the set of endogenous variables into three subsets; the slow moving macroeconomic variables (y_{1t}), the policy-related variables (Z_t), and the fast-moving variables that do not enter into the policy-specific conditioning path (y_{2t}). More precisely, GDP, inflation and lending volumes belong to y_{1t}. The set of variables included into the vector z_t, instead, changes according to the policy considered in the simulation. For the APP, z_t contains the 2-, 5-, and 10-year sovereign bond yields, and we impose that the impact of the APP on those variable is the one shown in Figure 6.18;[35] for NIRP/FG, it contains the EONIA spot rate as well as the 3-month EONIA forward in 12 and 18 months, and we impose that the impact of NIRP/FG on those variables is the outcome of the methodology we present above; for TLTRO, z_t includes only the lending rate to firms, and we impose that the impact of TLTROs on the lending rate is the one shown in Figure 6.20. All variables not included in y_{1t} and z_t are included into y_{2t}.

The impact of policy measures on GDP and inflation is carried out with a counterfactual analysis. This is done by comparing a no-policy scenario with a policy scenario. The no-policy scenario is simply given by the unconditional forecast of the VAR model.[36] In the policy scenario, we construct the conditioning path for the policy-related variables (z_t) by applying to their unconditional forecast the policy impact we have described above. The remaining fast-moving endogenous variables are allowed to respond contemporaneously. The set of slow-moving macroeconomic

[34] In more detail, we use Normal-Inverse Wishart prior distributions: we impose the so-called Minnesota prior, according to which each variable follows a random walk process, possibly with a drift (Litterman, 1979). Moreover, we impose two sets of prior distributions on the sum of the coefficients of the VAR model: the 'sum-of-coefficients' prior, originally proposed by Doan, Litterman and Sims (1984), and an additional prior that was introduced by Sims (1993), known as the 'dummy-initial-observation' prior. The hyper-parameters controlling for the informativeness of the prior distributions are treated as random variables (following Giannone, Lenza, and Primiceri, 2015) and are drawn from their posterior distribution, so that we also account for the uncertainty surrounding the prior set-up in our evaluation.

[35] The APP-induced decline in the term premia for sovereign bonds with maturities of 2-, 5-, and 10-year that we have shown in Figure 6.18 is added to the observed yields and the model is simulated conditional on the counterfactual yields and the historic short-term rates.

[36] Notice that, given that results are computed in terms of deviations from the no-policy scenarios in a linear VAR model, this assessment is independent of the path assumed for the no-policy scenario.

variables, and notably including real GDP, inflation, and lending volumes, do not react to the policy on impact, but only over time. These restrictions are an important feature of our methodology because they help to tell apart the monetary policy impulse from other demand shocks. These restrictions amount to a timing restriction of the sort used in the literature on the impact of monetary policy shocks identified using a recursive scheme, in which macroeconomic variables such as economic activity and inflation are not allowed to move on impact.[37]

More formally the impact of the measures is derived as follows:

$$u_{t+h} = E(y_{1,t+h} \mid \Omega_t, z^*_{t+h}) - E(y_{1,t+h} \mid \Omega_t, z_{t+h})$$

where Ω_t is the state of the economy at time t, $y_{1,t+h}$ is the path of slow moving variables up to horizon h, z^*_{t+h} are the policy-induced conditioning paths, and z_{t+h} the unconditional paths for the relevant policy-specific variables. u_{t+h} measures the response of GDP and inflation to non-standard policies (see Canova, 2007; Altavilla, Giannone, and Lenza, 2016; and Altavilla, Canova, and Ciccarelli, 2019).

Figure 6.21 documents the difference between the sovereign bond yields that would have prevailed in absence of the ECB policy measures and the actual history of the sovereign bond yields. It shows that NIRP has exerted a very strong impact also at intermediate maturities of the yield curve, with approximatively a parallel shift of the curve up to 5-year maturities and exerting a strong impact also on the 10-year maturity. As we already pointed out above commenting on Panel C and D of Figure 6.14, this is different from the impact of a standard policy shock in normal times, which is typically found to affect mainly the short end of the yield curve, with monotonically declining impact along the maturity structure and about no impact on the 10-year maturity (see also Altavilla et al., 2019). Figure 6.21 shows that also the impact of FG on the yield curve is very persistent along the maturity structure. It should be noted that in the NIRP and FG counterfactuals we condition only on the short-end of the curve, so the behaviour of medium and long maturities is an outcome and not an assumption. Finally, as already discussed when we commented on Figure 6.18, the impact of the APP on the yield curve is stronger the longer the

---

[37] Without imposing some identification restrictions of the type we use, conditional forecasts in VARs may not be well suited to compute the response to monetary policy shocks because (i) the conditioning path on interest rates would be fulfilled by using a combination of shocks weighted by their relative variance in sample, and (ii) in a typical sample, the contribution of monetary policy shocks may be small and therefore the conditional forecast would pick up mainly non-monetary policy shocks. However, our restrictions help to tilt the balance towards monetary policy shocks. In addition, over the last several years monetary policy interventions have been very large, making it easier for our methodology to correctly infer monetary policy. To the extent that our results may still confound accommodative policy shocks (bringing down interest rates) with negative demand shocks (bringing down interest rates), our quantification of the impact of the policy measures would be an underestimation in that the boost in inflation and economic activity would be even larger than the one we find and documented in Figure 6.22 because negative demand shocks would bring interest rates down but at the same time also inflation and activity would decline.

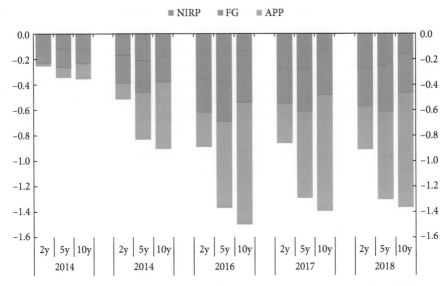

Figure 6.21 Impact of ECB's non-standard measures on euro area sovereign yields
(percentage points)

Source: ECB calculations.
Notes: Evolution of the downward pressures that ECB's non-standard measures have exerted on euro
area sovereign yields at selected maturities. The figure illustrates the contributions of individual
measures. The results are based on a BVAR. The impact of NIRP and FG on sovereign yields works via
the EONIA rate and the OIS forward curve illustrated in Figure 6.15 and the impact of the APP works
via the term premia illustrated in Figure 6.18.

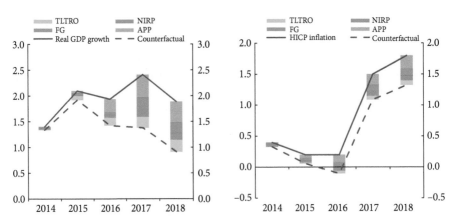

Figure 6.22 Actual real GDP growth and HICP inflation, and counterfactual paths in
absence of ECB's non-standard measures

Real GDP growth (average annual % change)

HICP inflation (average annual % change)

Source: ECB calculations.
Notes: The distance between the actual data (solid line) and the counterfactual path in absence of ECB's
policy measures is the estimated impact of those measures (dashed line). The impact is disaggregated
into the contribution of the individual measures (coloured bars). The results are based on a BVAR.

maturity. As shown in Figure 6.22, we find that, in the absence of the package, GDP would have been roughly 2.7% lower by end-2018, and annual inflation one third of a percentage point weaker on average over 2015–2018.[38] Around a fifth of the overall impact on the 2017 (i.e. the peak-year) growth rate is attributable to the NIRP as a standalone instrument, a surprisingly elevated contribution given the contained size of the cumulated rate adjustments in negative territory (a spread of only 40 bps over an interval of two years). Our estimates show that the APP explains the lion's share of the overall effect on output growth in 2017. TLTROs lead to an enduring support to the economy, accounting for a fifth of the overall impact on output growth in 2017.[39]

Comparing these estimates with the range of estimates produced by a coordinated Eurosystem-staff assessment group at the time of the adoption of the policy measures in 2015 and 2016, our results lie in the upper part of the range for real GDP growth and in the lower part of the range for inflation: over the period 2015–2018 the median across the Eurosystem-staff range of estimates was 2.2 percentage points for real GDP growth and 1.9 percentage points for inflation over the same period. The Eurosystem-staff estimates used a large suite of models including DSGE models, which tend to produce estimates at the higher end for inflation. In contrast, in time-series models such as BVARs the impact on inflation was found to be more back-loaded.[40]

6.4 Efficiency

The impact analysis whose findings we document in the previous section demonstrates that there is a predictable relationship between adjustments to the monetary policy instruments included in the ECB's unconventional tool box and intended changes in the economic variables that the ECB seeks to influence over a medium-term horizon. As we saw in Section 5.10, such a demonstrable, predictable, if delayed connection between instruments and goals is a *condicio sine qua non* for the monetary policy strategy enacted since 2014 in the euro area to pass the first of the triad of criteria laid out by the ECJ in its December 2018 ruling to assess the legality of PSPP: suitability. Yes, the decision to ease policy through a time-varying combination of tools such as those deployed since 2014 was indeed *suitable* or, in a jargon more familiar to monetary economists, *efficacious* in the ECB's legitimate battle against

---

[38] The overall uncertainty surrounding the estimates would need to consider also the uncertainty arising from the first stage in which the path of the conditioning financial variables is derived.

[39] Note that in 2017 the worldwide acceleration in activity and trade had a positive impact on growth, while sclerotic domestic demand exerted a negative impact. The discussed policy measures contributed to keeping growth stable in 2017 as opposed to letting it slide below 2016 levels.

[40] A coordinated Eurosystem-staff assessment group at the time of the adoption of the policy measures in 2015 and 2016 carried out analysis to estimate the impact of asset purchases on the basis of a large suite of models spanning different modelling approaches (DSGE models, time-series models, large semi-structural models). From our perspective, the BVAR approach we use here has the advantage of being flexible and adaptable, making it suitable for the assessment of a variety of policy measures. For a recent survey by Eurosystem staff on the impact of non-standard measures, see Neri and Siviero (2019).

pernicious disinflation. But, was PSPP, in the specifics, *necessary* as well? In other words, could the ECB have made recourse to alternative means or combination of means with potentially less unintended effects than those allegedly associated with PSPP? This question pertains to the second of the three criteria that the ECJ has articulated in its legality test on PSPP: *necessity*.

In this section, we recast the necessity test in terms that are tractable by economic analysis and seek to contribute to this test with quantitative results. We reformulate the question as follows: was PSPP an *efficient* instrument of monetary policy? Or, equivalently, could the ECB have secured the same outcomes that it attained in history by abstaining from large-scale purchases of bonds and compensating the identified contribution of PSPP to the observed macroeconomic developments by more generous application of other tools? Building on the analysis expounded in Section 6.2, we consider the NIRP as the instrument most proximate to PSPP, in terms of propagation through the yield curve and transmission chain. So, we specialize the exercise into a thought experiment—a counterfactual—that seeks to work out the implications for NIRP usage, had the ECB never activated PSPP but still aimed at the same ultimate impacts on inflation that, in Section 6.3, we find can be ascribed to PSPP. In calibrating the exercise, we assume that the other policy instruments, including the level and the forward guidance on the expected future path of the MRO rate, and the timing, size and cost of the TLTROs, would have been the same as those observed in history.

The results of this assessment suggest that the additional DFR cuts necessary to generate the same path for inflation as observed in history in the absence of the PSPP would have required reducing the DFR to unprecedented and possibly unviable low levels from 2015 onward. Figure 6.23 plots the actual evolution of the DFR (red line) against the counterfactual path (blue line). While the exact alternative path is subject to some model and estimation uncertainty,[41] the requisite fall in the DFR that could have made up for the lack of action in the form of sovereign bond purchases would have brought its level well into a range of values at which the ability of the rate reduction to provide extra easing impulse to the economy would have been crippled and possibly entirely neutralized by countervailing actions taken by banks and depositors, as they sought to escape the high negative-rate charge on their liquid balances. While wholesale conversion of banks' electronic reserves and savers' deposits into physical cash is deterred by hoarding cost considerations when the negative-rate charge is moderate, such a strategy is likely to become attractive when the short term interest rate hovers around −2%, the level to which DFR would have dropped in 2019, according to our computations.

---

[41] One particular issue is that there is in principle not one but a multiplicity of DFR paths that can deliver the same impact on inflation at a certain horizon. To address this issue, we rely on the BVAR used for the impact analysis in Section 6.3, and allow the model to pin down the DFR counterfactual path based on past regularities so as to match the estimated PSPP impact on inflation in each of the years between 2015 and 2019 (rather than in cumulated terms). This helps recover the DFR counterfactual path, thereby proving a selection criterion.

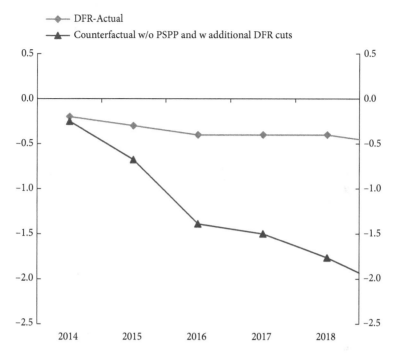

Figure 6.23 DFR: actual, and counterfactual in the absence of the PSPP (percentages per annum)

Sources: ECB and ECB calculations.
Notes: The assessment is based on the BVAR model underlying the impact analysis presented in Section 6.3. The counterfactual without PSPP refers to a scenario in which the DFR path is adjusted so that the additional DFR cuts deliver the same impact on inflation as PSPP.

The implications of the counterfactual policy path on important economic variables other than inflation would have been more pronounced than those actually observed. For instance, Figure 6.27 shows that the alternative DFR path would have resulted in a more pronounced decline in bank deposit rates—a proxy for the remuneration of household savings—as the aggressive reduction in the DFR would have pulled the overnight interest rate deeper into the sub-zero area, and deeply negative overnight rate would have exerted a large impact on the shorter end of market interest rates, particularly bank deposit rates, but also short- to medium-term maturity sovereign yields (Figures 6.24, 6.25, and 6.26).

6.5 The Cost Side of the Equation

Overhanging all discussions of the 2014–2015 policy package was the notion that the costs of allowing inflation to deviate from its medium-term norm, and economic activity to drift away from its potential for an extended period of time, were likely to be unacceptably large compared to any future economic benefits that might accrue

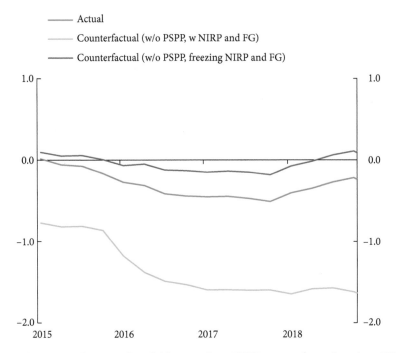

─── Actual
─── Counterfactual (w/o PSPP, w NIRP and FG)
─── Counterfactual (w/o PSPP, freezing NIRP and FG)

Figure 6.24   2-year EA sovereign yields: actual, no-PSPP counterfactual, and no-PSPP counterfactual with additional DFR cuts (percentages per annum)

from using monetary policy to lean against the financial imbalances that the package potentially could introduce. Indeed, the taxonomy that we illustrate in Section 6.2 is premised on the assumption that, when inflation drifts down in lockstep with an economic slump, more accommodation is more appropriate than less accommodation. So, any combination of instruments that is more powerful in keeping the yield curve—and the spectrum of credit spreads faced by private borrowers—low and shallow is preferable to other combinations of instruments that lack that traction. At the same time, history suggests that extraordinary doses of monetary support administered for a sufficiently long time can come with their own side effects that might either create the conditions for endogenous instability down the line, or place the economy on a weaker footing in the event of an adverse exogenous shock. Adverse shocks in the presence of system vulnerabilities can degrade financial stability, and stall the economic recovery. Much debated among those side effects are the implications of low—and negative—interest rates for the earning capacity and balance sheet position of banks and other financial intermediaries. The feared possibility, in this respect, is that financial intermediaries might be decapitalized and thus debilitated to the point, where they disengage from financial intermediation and become a hindrance, rather than key propagators, of the central bank's stimulus. Another concern is that low interest rates for a sustained period might drain a

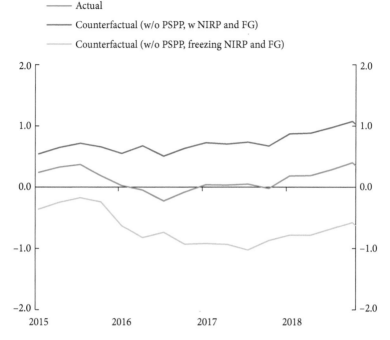

Figure 6.25 5-year EA sovereign yields: actual, no-PSPP counterfactual, and no-PSPP counterfactual with additional DFR cuts (percentages per annum)

Sources: Bloomberg, ECB and ECB calculations.
Notes: Figure 6.24 and Figure 6.25 refer to the GDP-weighted average of the four largest euro area economies. The counterfactual without PSPP and unchanged DFR refers to a scenario in which the PSPP easing impact on yields and the macro is shut down, and the DFR path is kept unchanged as observed in history. The counterfactual without PSPP and with additional DFR cuts refers to a scenario in which the DFR path is adjusted so that the additional DFR cut delivers the same impact on inflation as PSPP.
Latest observation: December 2018 for realized data.

meaningful source of consumers' purchasing power, interest income, and thus curb, rather than foster, aggregate spending.

The 'cost side of the equation', of course, attracted sharp reflections and scrutiny—as we document in Section 5.10—when the ECJ deliberated on the legality of PSPP. So, keeping accurate track of the evolving balance between the benefits and costs of the ECB's policies—not only PSPP—since 2014 assumes relevance from more than one standpoint. The list of undesired effects that one can attribute to aggressive stimulus applied over an extended period of time is rather long, ranging from financial buoyancy and adverse income effects to banks' and other financial intermediaries' capacity to originate income organically. We leave an evaluation of the impact of the ECB's policies on real estate markets, on the valuations of different financial asset classes, on the sustainability of the business model of insurance companies and other non-bank intermediaries for future analysis. Instead, we concentrate this section on two areas of cost valuation: the banking sector and the income/loss accounting of

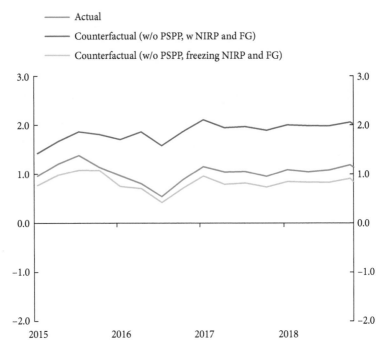

Figure 6.26 10-year EA sovereign yields: actual, no-PSPP counterfactual, and no-PSPP counterfactual with additional DFR cuts (percentages per annum)

private savers. On the former front, the questions we want to answer here are essentially two: did the package propel the demand for borrowing to levels that are stronger than empirical regularities would consider physiological, considering the cyclical position of the economy? And: to what extent has the ECB's package contributed to the low profitability of the euro area banking sector? As a sore spot for the critics of a low-for-long rate environment has been the role of the NIRP in causing the severest hardships for depository institutions, we devote particular attention to the effects of the NIRP for the banks' bottom lines, but we also analyse the role of PSPP in changing the business environment of the banks. On the latter front—who gained and who lost out most as a result of the ECB's unconventional policies—we extend existing research that traces the impact of monetary policy to the net-wealth position of households. Based on a map of positive and negative *net savers* in each constituent country, we then derive an economy-wide cost/benefit assessment that applies to the euro area economy as a whole.

6.5.1 NIRP, PSPP, and the Banks

We start with the banks. Figure 5.21 utilizes the 'credit gap' construct to detect signs that exuberance in credit creation might be a source of overheating for the economy.

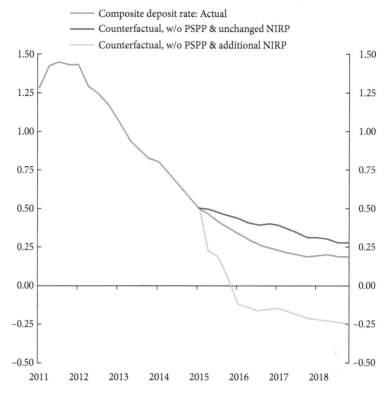

Figure 6.27   Euro area composite deposit rate: actual, no-PSPP counterfactual, and no-PSPP counterfactual with additional DFR cuts (percentages per annum)

Sources: Bloomberg, ECB and ECB calculations.

Notes: Figure 6.26 refers to the GDP-weighted average of the four largest euro area economies. Figure 6.27 is based on a BVAR model that uses individual balance sheet data from the IBSI dataset matched with Supervisory and SNL data. The counterfactual without PSPP and unchanged DFR refers to a scenario in which the PSPP easing impact on yields and the macro is shut down, and the DFR path is kept unchanged as observed in history. The counterfactual without PSPP and with additional DFR cuts refers to a scenario in which the DFR path is adjusted so that the additional DFR cut delivers the same impact on inflation as PSPP.

Latest observation: December 2018 for realized data.

The figure shows the contribution of the 'credit gap' to output gap. More specifically, the 'credit gap' is measured by computing the difference between the actual and the counterfactual path of the outstanding amount of loans to non-financial corporations. The latter is retrieved by employing the multi-country BVAR of Altavilla et al. (2016) and the counterfactual path is obtained by measuring the stock of loans consistent with pre-crisis business cycle regularities. The results indicate that at the end of the sample (in 2018) the model does not detect any sign of credit exuberance in Italy and Spain. On the contrary, in Germany and France the developments in credit origination in the last observation appear to be slightly above the past regularities thereby signalling potential exuberance in bank loans.

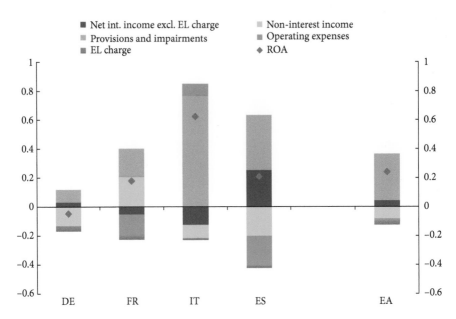

Figure 6.28 Change in Return on Assets and its components over the period 2014–2018 (contribution to ROA in percentage points)

Sources: ECB, ECB Supervisory Reporting and ECB calculations.
Notes: Operating expenses and provisions and impairments are inverted so that positive numbers represent a positive contribution to ROA. Data on a consolidated basis for a balanced sample (195 institutions) adjusted for the largest M&As. EL Charge is cost of holding excess liquidity due to negative deposit facility rate. Net int. income stands for Net interest income; Non-interest income includes Net fee and commission income.

In trying to cast some light on the connection between low profitability among euro area banks and the low interest environment brought on by the accommodative measures, we first look at unfiltered data. Figure 6.28 breaks down the change in the return on euro area banks' assets between 2014 and 2018 into its main components. Few aspects of the figure are worth noticing. First, the return on assets has increased in the euro area aggregate, and in most member states, rather than declined over this period. Second, the change in interest income, net of the negative-rate charge on banks' free reserves deposited with the Eurosystem, has been positive in aggregate and in most countries, except in France and Italy. Third, a strong drop in provisions, owing to the recovery, has been universal, including in core countries, where bad loans had a limited incidence over banks' assets to start with. As we remarked before, the quantity effects of the measures—an expanded and better-quality business activity for lenders—have more than compensated their price effects—a decline in unit margins (see the decomposition of price versus quantity effects in Figure 6.29).

This evidence is in line with the finding of Altavilla et al. (2018) who find that accommodative monetary policy have on average not compressed euro area bank profits. More specifically, the authors show that the compression in net interest income was largely offset by broader ('general equilibrium') effects that a more

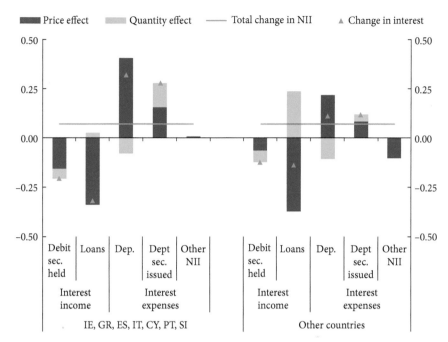

Figure 6.29 Contribution to the change in net interest income between 2014 and 2018 (percentage of assets)

Sources: ECB Supervisory Reporting and ECB calculations.

Notes: Based on data for a balanced panel of institutions under the supervision of the ECB that report accounting data on a consolidated basis (82 significant institutions and 108 less significant institutions). One large outlier is excluded from the sample. Interest expenses are inverted, so that a decrease in costs is shown as a positive contribution to net interest income. Income and expenses are calculated by summing up the amounts from the last four quarters and scaling by the average total assets over the same period. Debt sec. stands for debt securities, dep. stands for deposits, and NII stands for net interest income.

accommodative policy have on loan quality and loan loss provisions. Fourth, as a vast literature has emphasized recently, a low-rate environment, with the NIRP front and centre as a factor contributing, indeed diminishes banks' deposit-creating franchise to some extent. However, up until the end of 2018, rate cuts and the impact on falling asset yields have been met by corresponding, and oftentimes larger, declines in banks' funding costs, a reflection of the same rate environment, and of the NIRP especially. Figure 6.30 plots the distribution of bank deposit rates in the periphery and core countries. While the picture confirms that the density of rate observations across banks has a tendency to stack up at zero in the peripheral countries, the frequency of negative deposit rates in the core economies is not negligible, particularly in Germany. Obviously, the ZLB doesn't apply to nearly the same extent that much of the recent literature has implied, even if one looks narrowly at the pricing of bank deposits. This has permitted a limited degree of pass-through from negative reserve remuneration to deposit remuneration, which has made the NIRP a less taxing scheme for banks than is often presumed.

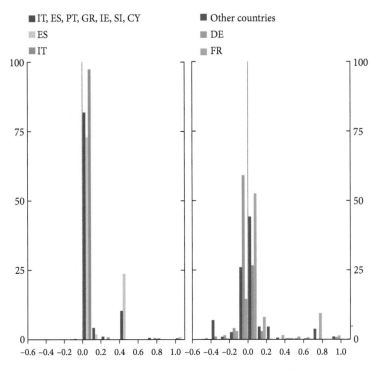

Figure 6.30 Distributions of deposit rates to NFCs across individual MFIs in December 2018 (x-axis: deposit rates in percentages per annum; y-axis: frequencies in percentages, weighted by volumes)

Figure 6.31 takes a different perspective. For ease of reference, the picture reports the same time varying profile of the bank margin statistic that we commented upon with reference to Figure 5.15. The picture presents evidence on the evolution of two definitions of banks' margins: the narrow loan-to-*deposit* margin—to measure the putative loss of deposit-creating franchise among euro area banks—and the more encompassing loan-to-*funding-cost* margin—a more relevant metric to quantify the direct effects of the low-rate environment on banks' mark-ups. By end-2018, both measures had shown no tendency to contract, either in countries where bank loans bear a fixed rate, or in countries where rates are indexed to money market benchmarks. This evidence supports the conclusion that much of the literature that has emphasized the costs of a low (and negative) rate environment for banks has likely under-estimated the space left open for banks to offset the rate pressure on their asset side with substantial cuts in a wide spectrum of funding costs, including deposits, on their liability side. In other words, as we have remarked before, banks are *payers* as much as they are *receivers* of low (and negative) rates. Figure 6.31 shows that this rate-resetting mechanism has shielded euro area banks' bottom lines at least until the end of 2018. If, as we do in our analysis of Figure 5.15, we were to account for the sharp fall in the capital cost of loan creation—in terms of supervisory capital

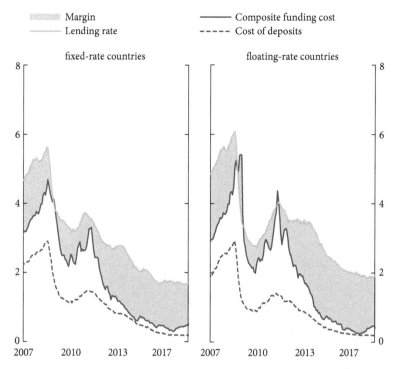

Figure 6.31 Deposit rates and banks' margins over composite funding costs (percentages per annum)

Sources: ECB and ECB calculations.

Notes: LHS: Deposit rates on outstanding amounts as reported by individual banks for each of the available product categories, weighted by outstanding amounts in December 2018. RHS: Margins are calculated as difference between new business lending rates to NFPS (weighted by their corresponding outstanding amount volumes) and composite funding rates. Composite funding rates are the weighted cost of deposits and market debt funding (only investment-grade bank bonds are considered). 'Fixed-rate countries' are Belgium, Germany, France and the Netherlands. 'Floating-rate countries' are the remaining countries forming the 12 euro area bloc, with the exception of Greece, which is excluded due to limited data availability. from Jan 2020. The latter is computed using the projections for the eligible lending growth (Dec 2018 BMPE with update). Deposit rates are computed as a weighted average of overnight deposits, deposits with agreed maturity and deposits redeemable at notice, with their corresponding outstanding amount business volumes.
Latest observation: December 2018.

charges and to account for expected losses—this benign effect of the low-rate environment on banks' mark-ups would be amplified.

Building on this suggestive, yet circumstantial evidence, we seek confirmation that indeed monetary policy was not *in and of itself* a decisively negative factor sapping banks' net earnings and inhibiting their business operations by using a model counterfactual. The question that helps define the counterfactual is: have the NIRP and/or the PSPP eroded banks' profits in-sample since 2014, or are they expected to eat away at banks' profits looking into the foreseeable future from the vantage point of December 2018 (the last month of our sample), conditional on the yield curve observed at the time and the macroeconomic outlook implicit in the ECB staff

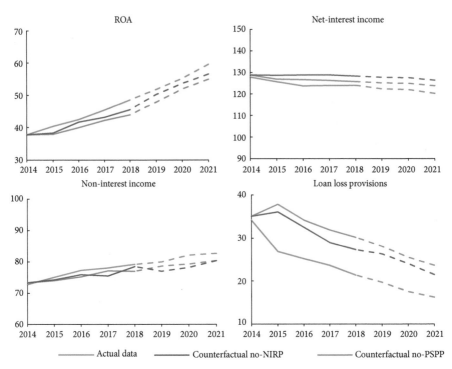

Figure 6.32 Return on assets and its main components under different scenarios (basis points of total assets)

Sources: ECB, ECB Supervisory Reporting, S&P Market Intelligence (SNL Financial) and ECB calculations.

Notes: The figures report observed (red line) and counterfactual (blue line) return on assets (ROA), net interest income, non-interest income and loan loss provisions over the period 2014–2018 obtained with a dynamic VAR model similar to Altavilla, Boucinha, Peydró (2018) that uses individual balance sheet data from the IBSI dataset matched with Supervisory and SNL data. The variables included in the model are: ROA, net-interest income, non-interest income, provisions, lending rates, deposit rates, loan volumes, real GDP growth, inflation rate, Eonia, and interest rates with a remaining maturity of 2-, 5-, and 10-years. The no-NIRP scenario is given by the forecast of the BVAR model conditional on the assumption that the ZLB would be enforced at all times, therefore preventing the term structure to assume negative values across all maturities. The no-PSPP scenario is given by the forecast of the BVAR model conditional on the assumption that the flattening impact of PSPP on the yield curve quantified in Figure 6.21 would have not been materialized.

projections of December 2018? Figure 6.32 plots the euro area aggregate return on assets (ROA) and its main components (net interest income, non-interest income and loan loss provisions) between 2014 and 2018. The red line corresponds to the data and—for the dashed part—the baseline projections for ROA from the standpoint of December 2018; the blue line represents the BVAR-based 'no-NIRP/no-FG' scenario described in Section 6.3; the green line corresponds to a world with zero bond purchases. The no-PSPP scenario is derived as a BVAR conditional forecast by removing the impact of PSPP quantified in Figure 6.21 from the yield curve. The dashed portion of the the blue and green lines represents the BVAR-based projected paths in the no-NIRP and no-PSPP scenarios, respectively, conditional on the yield curve observed in December 2018 and on the December 2018 ECB staff macroeconomic projections.

To start, it is interesting to note that, despite a decline in the net interest income between 2015 and 2016, and a levelling off thereafter, the euro area banks' ROA has been *growing* in the four years covered by the picture (red line), a trend which in December 2018 was expected to continue at least through 2021. This upward trend is due, both in-sample and out-of-sample, to a steep decline in loan-loss provisions and a sustained increase in the 'other income' component. But, the most interesting insight offered by the exercise, and the answer to our question, comes from a comparison between the red line, on one side, and the blue and the green lines, on the other. In a no-NIRP or no-PSPP world, the euro area banks' net interest income would indeed have been higher and would have continued to outpace its projected evolution in the December 2018 baseline macroeconomic scenario (see the right Panel in the top row). However, the *overall* ROA would have been weaker than it turned out to be in actuality (the red line is above both the blue and the green lines), as the negative contribution to the banks' earnings from other income sources—in a world in which the yield curve would have been higher and steeper—would have more than offset the positive impact of higher rates on the interest margin. Finally, if one contrasts the two counterfactual scenarios, without NIRP and without PSPP (the red and the green lines), respectively, PSPP—on the scale enforced by the ECB between 2014 and 2018—appears to have been a stronger supporting factor for banks' overall ROA and less of a drain on banks' interest income than NIRP. In synthesis, the general equilibrium effects of the NIRP and the PSPP, and the capital gains collected on banks' bond holdings in the early phase of the ECB's policy easing strategy which saw the steepest decline in market yields, have boosted banks' capacity to generate returns since 2014, even as the exceptionally low term interest rates have weighed on the coupons received by banks over the latter phase.

6.5.2 The NIRP and the 'Reversal Rate'

Finally, we come to the important question about the '*reversal rate*'. The concept has been defined and popularized by Markus Brunnermeier and Yann Koby in an important contribution (Brunnermeier and Koby, 2018). In their own words, 'the reversal interest rate is the rate at which accommodative monetary policy reverses and becomes contractionary for lending'. Why should monetary accommodation encourage banks to disengage from credit creation and even tighten their loan policies? Because, the authors contend, if banks' business model is particularly reliant on retail deposits and on maturity transformation, low levels of interest rates extending throughout the yield curve squeeze term spreads and thus reduce banks' net interest income. If low profitability interacts with stringent regulatory capital requirements, the bank has an incentive to retrench from intermediation if interest rates fall below a threshold. That threshold is the 'reversal rate'.

As we remarked above (see, for example, Panel A of Figure 6.22), the ECB's combined policies since 2014 have been particularly effective in lowering and flattening the term structure of interest rates. At least since early 2016, when the 'calamitous misadventure' narrative—referred to the NIRP—started to spread and gain credence, the extraordinary compression and flatness of the yield curve have often been taken as a sign that interest rates might be close to an inflection point, where the monetary stimulus turns into restriction because banks become uncooperative. So, the interest rates relevant to the broad economy do not go down in line with the policy rates, and there is no follow-through in wider monetary expansion, but rather the reverse.

In the remainder of this section, we take up the 'reversal rate' hypothesis and seek to locate that threshold in our BVAR-economy framework. The question is usually formulated around the level of the very short-term interest rate, and how far that rate can sink in the sub-zero area without spurring perverse effects for bank intermediation. So, we specialize our exercise to the NIRP only. The question the exercise seeks to answer is simple: is it possible to define a level for the DFR and the overnight interest rate so deeply negative that would induce banks to cut down on their loans to NFCs, taking into account the transmission of the NIRP across the yield curve and to the macro-economy that we document in Section 6.3? Said differently: how low is the 'reversal rate' in the euro area?

We project three hypothetical scenarios for the out-of-sample years 2019, 2020, and 2021. We imagine that, at the start of 2019, the ECB lowers the DFR from the −0.4% level enforced at the time to −0.5%, −0.75% or −1%, respectively, in the three scenarios in one single move, and keeps it constant at those levels over the following three years. We then construct yield curves corresponding to each of those three policy scenarios, assuming the term structure of the NIRP impacts across the yield curve that we document above; likewise, we construct macroeconomic scenarios that, according to our transmission analysis, would correspond to those rate adjustments; and, finally, we use our BVAR to project the banks' balance sheet positions and loan evolution for 2019, 2020, and 2021 in the three policy and macroeconomic scenarios, conditional on the counterfactual term structures and macroeconomic outlooks. Critically, in projecting the banks' balance sheet and credit behaviour, we impose two non-linearities: we deactivate any pass-through from the DFR to the banks' customer deposit rate, essentially imposing a lower bound on the cost of deposit funding equal to the level reached by the deposit rate at end-2018; and, similarly, we stabilize the loan-loss provisions as a fraction of banks' assets at their end-2018 value, on the assumption that the quality of banks' loan book would not improve further, even as the macroeconomic outlook—because of the additional monetary stimulus—might evolve in a more favourable direction.[42] We show the

---

[42] To note, we do not impose a third type of non-linearity which might well come to bind in practice: capital constraints. We assume this further potential constraint away because we conduct 'local' exercises around levels of the policy rate that would not materially differ from those observed in the sample. So, the scope for capital erosion is limited within the range of scenarios that we explore, and insufficient to drive the banking system as a whole close to hitting minimum regulatory requirements. Indeed, as Figure 6.33 shows, even a radical reduction of the DFR to −1% would not be sufficient to undermine the banks' capacity to generate income organically.

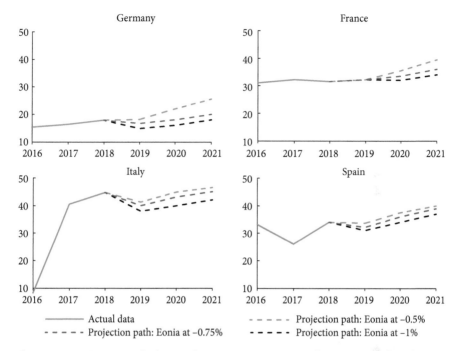

Figure 6.33 ROA across the largest four euro area countries (basis points of total assets)

Sources: ECB, ECB Supervisory Reporting, S&P Market Intelligence (SNL Financial) and ECB calculations.

Notes: The figure reports the observed (median) return on assets (ROA) for the largest four euro area countries (red solid lines), as well as projections for ROA under alternative scenarios. These scenarios assume that the overnight rates decrease to −0.5% (red dashed line), −0.75% (dashed blue line) and −1% (black solid line), and that the deposit rate and the loan loss provision are kept constant at the level observed in December 2018. The model used in the simulation is a dynamic VAR model that uses individual balance sheet data from the IBSI dataset matched with Supervisory and SNL data. The variables included in the model are: ROA, net-interest income, non-interest income, provisions, lending rates, deposit rates, loan volumes, real GDP growth, inflation rate, Eonia, and interest rates with a remaining maturity of 2-, 5-, and 10-years.

results of our exercise in Figures 6.33 and 6.34. The dashed lines in Figure 6.33 correspond to the simulated evolution of banks' ROA beyond 2018 in the four largest euro area countries under the three policy scenarios. The dashed lines in the four panels of Figure 6.34 represent the range of values for banks' NFC loan growth in the three scenarios. We note two features of our results and end this section with an important caveat. First, the pattern of transmission of the rate reductions appears heterogeneous across economies, with more aggressive rate cuts being felt comparatively more, in terms of bank ROA, in core economies rather than in the periphery. Second, notwithstanding the erosion of banks' income, the capacity of banks to create credit appears largely unperturbed in all scenarios. In fact, lower overnight (and longer-term) interest rates are associated with stronger loan growth. This seemingly counterintuitive finding is explained by two countervailing forces. On one hand, lower intermediation margins curb banks' incentive to lend. On the other hand,

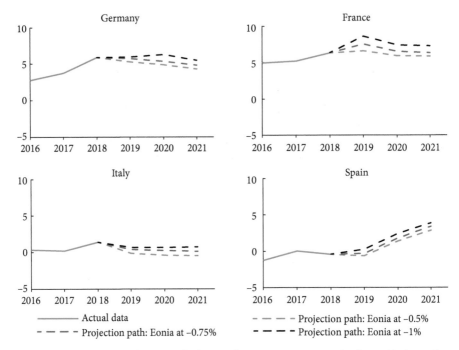

Figure 6.34 Loan growth across the largest four euro area countries (y-o-y % change)

Sources: ECB, ECB Supervisory Reporting, S&P Market Intelligence (SNL Financial) and ECB calculations.
Notes: The figure reports the observed NFC loan growth for the largest four euro area countries (red solid lines), as well as projections for lending under alternative scenarios. These scenarios are described in the notes to Figure 6.33.

absent binding capital constraints—which indeed are assumed not to bind in our experiment—more negative rates encourage risk taking and loan origination. Our time-series model has observed in-sample a systematic negative association between policy rates and loan growth and, accordingly, it tends to project the same correlation forward.

On the face of it, these results seem reassuring: the 'reversal rate' might not be in sight in the euro area for still quite a while, at least over the range of levels for the overnight interest rate that we have considered in our simulations. At the same time, a lot of caution is in order in interpreting our figures. First and foremost, we warn that under all scenarios we abstract from the occurrence of negative shocks that could autonomously undermine the strength of the underlying economy. Our simulations are predicated on a pure monetary policy experiment, whereby the central bank's easing comes as a surprise in an otherwise unchanged macroeconomic environment. But, in fact, it is hard to believe that a central bank would consider bringing its policy rates to such low levels in the absence of negative shocks having downgraded the prospects for the economy and inflation, relative to their expected constant-policy baseline evolutions. In our understanding, the 'reversal rate' is a state-contingent construct—being higher if macroeconomic prospects deteriorate and banks' lending becomes riskier. In other words, the 'reversal rate' is not independent of the 'neutral rate', namely the rate that keeps the economy on a balanced growth path and inflation at the central bank's target. In fact, our results tend to support the notion that for banks—as much as for any other agent in the economy—the relevant margin remains the latter rather than the former. At least over a range of plausible levels of negative rates, the 'reversal rate' does not seem to impose an additional restriction or non-linearity on the law of motion of the economy compared to the 'neutral rate'. Over that range, it is only by assuming a plunge in the 'neutral rate' to even lower levels than those enforced by the central bank that would be likely to see both the ROA and loan growth lines in Figures 6.33 and 6.34 to bend materially downward compared to the levels we show.[43]

6.5.3 Low Interest Rates and Households

Perverse income effects may stand in the way of a stimulative policy based on enforcing low interest rates. Low interest rates make current consumption more attractive than future consumption, and thus can induce households to frontload spending by borrowing purchasing capacity from the future. But, to the extent that coupon income is an important contributor to consumers' purchasing capacity, a policy that erodes that source of income by driving market interest rates lower could be detrimental to consumers' wealth accumulation and their intertemporal spending possibilities. Can a negative income effect eclipse the positive intertemporal substitution effect and thwart the central bank's plans to reflate the economy? The first and key step toward answering this question is to chart out a map of 'winners' and 'losers' among households, from a purely cash-flow accounting perspective. While this step is inconclusive on whether, say, a certain identified decline in interest cash flows is sizeable enough to over-compensate the household's incentive to frontload consumption and run down saving in response to a drop in yields, forming a good understanding of how large such declines might be and what sign they carry for different households is already very informative.

Here, we extend the analysis presented in Dossche et al. (2020) to cast some light on the extent to which the ECB's policies since 2014 have modified households' interest cash-flows in the euro area. Integrating information from the sectoral accounts with the Household Finance and Consumption Survey (HFCS),[44] we estimate the

---

[43] The positive impact of NIRP on macroeconomic conditions is in line with the finding by Altavilla et al. (2019) who show that the negative interest rate policy provides stimulus to the economy through firms' asset rebalancing: firms with high current assets linked to banks offering negative rates appear to increase their investment in tangible and intangible assets to avoid the costs associated with negative rates.

[44] The ECB's Household Finance and Consumption Survey collects information on the assets, liabilities, income and consumption of households, based on 84,000 interviews conducted in 18 euro area countries. The first wave of the HFCS was conducted mainly in 2010 and was published in 2013. The

effect of the ECB's policies on market interest rates and thus, indirectly, on the net interest income accruing to the households observed in the survey. Box 6.2 provides details on the exercise and Figure B.6.2.1 illustrates the findings. We suggest a few takeaways. First, the positive cash flows to net savers, which have declined since 2014 due to the fall in interest rates, would have declined even in the absence of NIRP and PSPP, albeit to a lesser extent. The fall in market interest rates has an underlying trend component that transcends monetary policy action, and the switch-off of no single instrument could have reversed that trend: compare the blue bar with the green and yellow bars in Figure B.6.2.1. In addition, the net interest payments of net borrowers, which have become less onerous since 2014, would have remained broadly unchanged in the absence of NIRP and PSPP combined. This suggests an important role of monetary policy measures in supporting spending by easing the financial burden of indebted households. Second, if the ECB had compensated the lack of stimulus from the PSPP by making more aggressive recourse to policy rate reductions (to more negative levels) to the extent documented in Figure 6.23, the income benefits to the net borrowers and the income losses to the net savers would have been twice as large as those observed since 2014.

The map of financial 'losers' and 'winners' can be made more granular, a necessary step toward drawing meaningful and precise inference about the population's consumption possibilities. The analysis does so by making a distinction between the wealthy who have no financial constraint and thus can substitute consumption intertemporally as desired ('no-hand-to-mouth' households, roughly 50% of population), the wealthy who are indebted (paying a property mortgage) and thus cannot freely substitute consumption intertemporally but must consume off current income ('wealthy hand-to-mouth' households, 12%), and finally the poor who have near-zero wealth and are forced to consume out of current income ('poor hand-to-mouth' households, 37% of population). This extension of the interest-income accounting analysis shows that financially constrained 'hand-to-mouth' households, both wealthy and poor, on net benefit more from the low interest rate environment, as they tend to have a higher propensity to consume. Conversely, 'non-hand-to-mouth' households suffer in a low-interest-rate environment.

Our grand conclusion here is that, all else equal, and to the extent that the ECB's policies since 2014 have been a major—but not unique—contributing force pulling down the whole spectrum of interest rates, those policies have shored up aggregate household spending through a robust consumption channel. By and large, this channel has worked via redistribution to the benefit of those income/wealth household groups that have a substantially higher marginal propensity to consume (Jappelli and Pistaferri, 2014; Kaplan et al., 2014).

HFCS questionnaire consists of two main parts: (i) questions relating to the household as a whole, including questions on real assets and their financing, other liabilities and credit constraints, private businesses, financial assets, intergenerational transfers and gifts, and consumption and saving; and (ii) questions relating to individual household members, covering demographics, employment, pension entitlements and income.

Box 6.2   The impact of the PSPP and negative interest rate policy on savers and borrowers

To understand the heterogeneous effects of monetary policy across households, Dossche et al. (2020) estimate the size and composition of households' balance sheets using the ECB's Household Finance and Consumption Survey (HFCS).[45] By this approach, the paper assesses the extent to which different types of households in the euro area have been affected by the drop in interest rates since 2007. Below this framework is extended, with three counterfactual exercises, to assess the contribution of the NIRP and PSPP, respectively, to the redistribution of households' interest income since the end of 2014.[46] This estimate is based on the second round of the HFCS, which was conducted between 2013 and the first half of 2015 (Household Finance and Consumption Network, 2016). As this survey is only conducted every three years it cannot be used to derive direct information on the changes in net interest income at the individual household-level over the full period considered in the analysis. To overcome this problem we make use of the information on interest income and payments at the aggregate sectoral level reported in the quarterly financial accounts and apply the implicit interest rates—which are derived as a ratio between interest income and payments on assets and liabilities—computed at the aggregate household-sector level to the individual exposures reported in the HFCS. Given that changes in the cross-sectional wealth distribution of households are slow-moving, it is reasonable to assume that the individual balance sheets evolve broadly in line with the overall stock measured at the aggregate household sector level.

In order to produce a meaningful map of the income gains and losses within the household sector, one has to first distinguish between net savers and net borrowers. Net savers (borrowers) are defined as households with a positive (negative) net financial wealth position. The proportion of net savers (borrowers) in the euro area is around 70% (30%) of total households.

While net interest income of net savers has decreased since the end of 2014, the net interest income of net borrowers has improved significantly. The average euro area net saver has suffered a reduction of around EUR 200 per year since 2014 (see blue bar in LHS panel of Figure B.6.2.1), on account of lower interest earnings. Conversely, the average euro area net borrower has gained close to EUR 300 per year, on account of lower interest payments, a gain that represents around 1% of her total gross income.

What is the contribution of the NIRP and PSPP to these shifts in the net income position of savers and borrowers? What would have happened if the ECB had replaced action on the bond-buying front with more intense usage of NIRP action?

(Continued)

---

[45] This Box was authored by Maarten Dossche, Jacob Hartwig, and Beatrice Pierluigi.
[46] The counterfactual exercises are obtained by estimating the pass-through from a wide range of interest rates to household-level net interest income.

Box 6.2 Continued

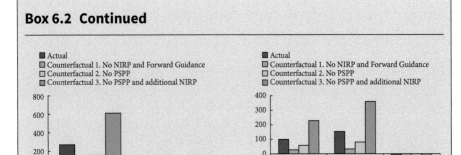

Figure B.6.2.1   Change in annual net interest income: 2014–2018 (EUR/household)

Source: Dossche et al. (2020).
Notes: Net borrowers are defined as households with a negative net financial wealth position; net savers are defined as households with a positive net financial wealth position. Poor Hand-to-Mouth (HtM) = credit constrained households with a high propensity to consume; rich HtM = wealthy households that are consuming their current income, are indebted and with few liquid assets; not HtM = households without credit constraint. Percentages on the x-axis of the figure indicate the share of the respective groups in total households. Vertical axis: euros per household (change in annual earnings, 2014–2018).

To answer these questions, we compare the actual changes in net interest income observed in the period 2014-2018 for different types of households with those that would have arisen under three counterfactual scenarios. The scenarios are defined as follows: (1) *no*-NIRP/*no*-FG, but unchanged PSPP; (2) *no*-PSPP, but unchanged NIRP/FG; and (3) the replacement of PSPP with additional DFR cuts to achieve the same inflation path as historically observed. To build these counterfactuals, we use the identified impacts on market interest rates of the NIRP and the PSPP policies documented in Section 6.3, and the extra reductions in the DFR that the ECB would have needed to implement in order to achieve the historical path of inflation if it had decided to abstain from the PSPP (as documented in Section 6.4 and shown in Figure 6.23). This allows computing how the counterfactual market yields resulting from the three scenarios would have altered the net interest income of euro area households in our sample. The computation is done in three steps. First an estimate of the pass-through from the observed market rates to the implicit interest rates that apply to households' assets and liabilities is computed. As these implicit rates are derived from the quarterly sectoral accounts they also reflect the underlying portfolio composition of households. Second the estimated pass-through elasticities are used to compute counterfactual interest income flows between 2014 and 2018 making use of our identified effects of individual measures on the yield curve. Third, we take the difference between the end and the beginning of the period for each derived net interest income path and use this as the main metric to gauge the impact of the monetary policy measures on the income positions of net borrowers and net savers.

The results of the counterfactual exercises are documented in Figure B.6.2.1 (LHS panel). First, the *no*-NIRP/*no*-FG counterfactual exercise shows that even without NIRP—and rate forward guidance—the positive cash flows to net savers would have nevertheless declined (by around 130 EUR/year per household compared to the realized decline of 200 EUR/year) and the net interest payments of net borrowers would have also declined (with a net income gain of around 70 EUR/year per household compared to the realized 270 EUR/year). Second, without the PSPP but with unchanged NIRP, the net interest payments for net borrowers would have been about 100 EUR/year higher than observed and, correspondingly, the loss of income for net savers would have been slightly lower. Last, if the ECB had compensated the lack of stimulus from the PSPP by making more aggressive recourse to policy rate reductions (to more negative levels) to the extent documented in Figure 6.23, the income benefits for the net borrowers and the income losses for the net savers would have been twice as large as those observed since 2014. To a large extent this result is due to the fact that the remuneration of households' assets, which are mostly composed of deposits, is predominantly affected by movements in markets' short term interest rates.

Across countries similar patterns apply. However, the redistributive impact of both the PSPP and NIRP is somewhat smaller (for both savers and borrowers) in Germany and France than in Italy and Spain, on account of a weaker estimated impact of the PSPP and NIRP on deposit rates and lending rates in the first two countries.

How would these differential patterns in interest cash flows have altered the households' incentives to consume? In history, the observed decline in market interest rates has promoted a redistribution of net interest income from households with a low propensity to consume to households with a higher propensity to consume (both groups account for about 50% of all households). The HFCS allows to distinguish among three types of households: (i) a non-hand-to-mouth group, namely households that have no credit constraints and are therefore able to save out of current income, (ii) wealthy hand-to-mouth households, namely those with substantial illiquid assets (mostly housing) but few liquid assets who as a result tend to consume their current income but are indebted, and (iii) poor hand-to-mouth households, namely low-wealth households with few liquid and illiquid

(Continued)

Box 6.2 Continued

assets (Figure B.6.2.1, RHS panel) who by and large spend their earning and do not save.[47]

Hand-to-mouth households have been gaining from the low interest rate environment, while non-hand-to-mouth households have lost out. This pattern correlates strongly with the distribution of gains and losses across the age distribution, the home owner status of households (mortgagors vs. outright owners and renters), and the wealth distribution. The losses are typically concentrated among old, rich households without any outstanding debt. Conversely, the gains are typically concentrated among young, middle-class households with mortgage debt. Again here both NIRP and PSPP have contributed to this redistribution since 2014. The counterfactual exercises show that policy measures have entailed some redistribution from non-hand-to-mouth consumers to hand-to-mouth consumers, in the form of lower interest income for the former and reduced interest payments for the latter. And again, replacing the PSPP with more negative policy rates would have entailed much larger redistribution effects from non-hand-to-mouth to hand-to-mouth than were actually observed.

6.6 The Policy Mix

Demand support from monetary policy was strong by all accounts. But what about the support provided by other policies?

Fiscal policy loosened sharply in reaction to the Lehman debacle. But already by 2010, with signs that the economy had bottomed out, its focus shifted toward exit. Budget targets embodied the objective of halving deficits by 2012 and achieving a primary balance by 2015 consistent with the G-20's Toronto Summit Declaration in the summer of 2010. While these objectives were not fully met, a significant fiscal contraction was set in train. By 2012, the cyclically adjusted government balance, net of government assistance to the financial sector, as a ratio to GDP had tightened by almost 1.5%, nearly completely reversing the earlier stimulus (see Figure 6.35).

---

[47] The definition of 'hand-to-mouth' households follows HFCS (2016); hand-to-mouth households are defined as those having less than two months of gross income worth in liquid assets. The categorizations along the 'net savers/net borrowers' and 'hand-to-mouth' (HtM) divide are not nested. The net 'savers/net borrowers' categorization is about net financial wealth and whether a household is net payer or net receiver of interest income. The HtM category is about the level of liquid assets and is meant to be informative about borrowing and liquidity constraints. The 'non-HtM' group, in practice, is comprised mostly of net savers. The wealthy and poor HtM households are in part net savers and in part net borrowers. Wealthy HtM households are characterized by limited liquid assets and substantial illiquid assets. They may qualify as net borrowers (e.g. households having significant real assets, i.e. a house, but with larger debt, i.e. a mortgage), or net savers, if their illiquid financial assets exceed their liabilities. Similarly, poor HtM households are simply defined by their very low holdings of liquid assets relative to their income level. As such, they can be both net savers and net borrowers.

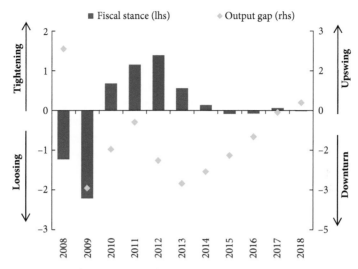

Figure 6.35 Euro area fiscal stance and output gap (percentage points and percentage)
Source: ECB.
Notes: Fiscal stance is approximated by a change in the ratio to GDP of the cyclically adjusted primary government balance, net of government assistance to the financial sector.
Latest observation: 2018.

In Chapter 1, and in the two twin Boxes 1.2 and 2.2, we went to some lengths to describe the strong interpretative influence that the NKM paradigm exerted on much of the conceptualization of policy-making and institution-building that occurred in the fifteen years following the beginning of the new millennium. Intrinsically, the paradigm entailed a hyper-cautionary tale about the ability of any central bank to control the economy *alone*. As it happened, the multidimensional message encapsulated in the fragility of inflation targeting (IT) and the centrality of the prevailing fiscal regime—two key tenets of NKM, as we showed before—was received only very selectively. Rather than that twofold deep lesson, what mainstream macroeconomics distilled out of the dominant model was a certain degree of hubris in the power of central banks and solid monetary regimes to achieve even the most ambitious objectives.

For example, there was a sense that panics and 'scares' would be ruled out—or at least made transitory phenomena with revertible consequences for the economy—if only longer-term inflation expectations could be anchored tightly to the central bank's objective. Shocks of all kinds could cause drawn-out oscillations away from the desired equilibrium. But they would not fundamentally undermine economic stability if the inflation objective could act as a potent attractor. And the target implicit in IT would do just that: tie expectations—and the economy at large—at the mast of the central bank's objective.

In this intellectual climate, the role of fiscal policy was partly recognized and partly ignored in the EU's institution building and policy discourse. It was acknowledged that, in order to avoid high inflation, the fiscal authority had to behave conservatively, accepting to bring debt sustainability considerations to bear on its everyday fiscal decisions. It became part of the core of consensus that, in normal times, macroeconomic stability hinged on an act of abstention and delegation by the fiscal agent. In fact, delegation by society to the central bank of the task to determine inflation in the system wasn't even viable unless the fiscal agent abstained from systematically destabilizing its own debt, and in fact actively offset any effect that the interest rate policy of the central bank might exert on the debt so as to keep it on a sustainable trajectory in all states of the world.

But the role of fiscal policy in deflationary scenarios, either as the subject of an independent policy lever or in support of central bank unconventional policies, was not part of consensus. More generally, the policy consensus that formed around IT failed to internalize one key insight that NKM had produced: monetary policy is an intimate part of public demand management. This notion applies *not only* when extraordinary circumstances force the central bank to move away from conventional instruments and deploy balance sheet operations (QE-type policies), which ostensibly blur the confines between the central bank's and the state's balance sheet, or unconventional and uninituitive configurations of policy interest rates (NIRP): it applies *always*, at *all* times. And this was no trivial omission.

In this light, it doesn't appear as an unconceivable paradox that fiscal policy could remain contractionary over the couple of years following 2010, even as the economy was slumping amidst looming risks of deflation, and could turn neutral only in 2015. What is remarkable is that the cross-currents that such a pro-cyclical conduct of fiscal policy created for monetary policy did not impede the robust expansion that started in late 2016 and reached a climax in 2017. With reference to the phase diagram that we show in Box 1.2, one could conclude that, while fiscal policy was a force pulling the economy away from the 'virtuous equilibrium', monetary policy was successful in keeping the economy anchored around it. We view this fact as testimony to the potency of monetary policy instruments, when a central bank is determined to deploy them with the necessary conviction and vigour.

However, building on the model analysis expounded in Box 1.2, one cannot rule out more extreme scenarios than those faced by the ECB in the years following the financial crisis, in which the economy sinks into an even deeper and more lasting contraction, and ingrained disinflation takes hold. When the economy, for any reason, veers in those undesired directions, macroeconomic stability, once more, can't be attained and preserved unless fiscal policy cooperates. And cooperation here might mean a twofold switch in regime along the lines laid out in B.2 and B.4: a switch that involves both devolution to, and deliberate partnership with, the central bank, and direct fiscal initiative. On the side of devolution, our two boxes posit that the central bank—when things precipitate—should turn off IT and switch to a constant-money-growth rule with fiscal backing, or should reset from IT to a constant-negative-interest-rate pledge, with the fiscal authority assisting in the background with a coordinated switch of regime on its side. Both switches are designed to eliminate the prospect that declines in nominal interest rates, if they occur along with the rise in expected future surpluses, might postpone, rather than rule out, the deflationary pressure. If short-term interest rates are pushed into negative territory and/or long-term yields are compressed by bond purchases, and the resources thus extracted from the banking system and savers are allowed to feed through the budget into reduced nominal deficits, the expansionary monetary policy winds up simply nurturing deflation, rather than inflationary tendencies.

On the side of partnership, we suspect that, should the economy ever find itself in such a predicament, a more policy-enabling environment—including a comprehensive set of non-monetary policies and growth-enhancing fiscal interventions—would be helpful for monetary instruments to exert the favourable effects that we document in this book. What form should growth-enhancing fiscal interventions take? Here, the evidence for large cross-border spillovers of national fiscal policies within the euro area is weak.[48] The reason is straightforward. Excessive deficit in country A will raise spending and suck in more imports from country B, stimulating the economy and stoking inflation in the latter country. At the same time, however, deficits in A will drive up interest rates both at home and abroad; those higher interest rates will tend to moderate spending and inflation in B. Since these two offsetting effects on B work in opposite directions, their net effects on area-wide and single-country growth and inflation might be vanishingly small.

When cross-country spillovers are small, and country preferences for a fiscal boost are aligned, the best approach is to elevate responsibility for counter-cyclical fiscal action to the European level. For fiscal policy, then, the appropriate reform is more Europe, not less.

---

[48] The empirical findings from the literature on fiscal spillovers suggest that cross-border spillovers of public spending tend to be positive but generally small, while spillovers from fiscal revenues tend to be much lower than for government expenditures. Beetsma et al. (2006) estimate that a spending-based fiscal expansion of 1% of GDP in Germany would lead to an average increase in the output of other European economies by 0.15% after two years. Similarly, IMF (2017) finds that on average for advanced economies a 1% of GDP increase in public spending has a spillover effect of 0.15% of GDP within the first year, in line with the findings from Auerbach and Gorodnichenko (2013). Fiscal spillovers are estimated to be heterogeneous and to depend on the intensity of trade links, the state of the economy and the reaction of monetary policy (Blagrave et al., 2017). In the euro area, model-based assessments generally show that the interest rate channel plays a crucial role: when interest rates respond to the fiscal shock, the estimated magnitude of cross-border fiscal spillovers is much lower. See for example Alloza et al. (2019) and In't Veld (2016). For a review of cross-country fiscal spillovers in the euro area during the fiscal consolidation of 2010–2013, see Attinasi et al. (2017).

References

Acharya, V.V., Eisert, T., Eufinger. C., and Hirsch, C. (2018), 'Real Effects of the Sovereign Debt Crisis in Europe: Evidence from Syndicated Loans', *The Review of Financial Studies*, 31, 8, 2855–96.

Acharya, V.V., Eisert, T., Eufinger. C., and Hirsch, C. (2019), 'Whatever it Takes: The Real Effects of Unconventional Monetary Policy', *The Review of Financial Studies*, 32, 9, 3366–411.

Acharya, V.V., Pierret, D., and Steffen, S. (2018), 'Lender of Last Resort versus Buyer of Last Resort–Evidence from the European Sovereign Debt Crisis', *Swiss Finance Institute Research Paper Series*, 18–35, Swiss Finance Institute.

Adam, K. and Weber, H. (2019), 'Optimal Trend Inflation', *American Economic Review*, 109, 2, 702–37.

Adrian, T., Laxton, M.D., and Obstfeld, M.M. (2018), 'An Overview of Inflation-Forecast Targeting', Advancing the Frontiers of Monetary Policy, International Monetary Fund, Washington D.C., pp. 3–14.

Aiyagari, S.R. and Gertler, M. (1985), 'The Backing of Government Bonds and Monetarism', *Journal of Monetary Economics*, 16, 1, 19–44.

Albanesi, S. (2007), 'Inflation and Inequality', *Journal of Monetary Economics*, 54, 4, 1088–114.

Albertazzi, U., Notarpietro, A., and Siviero, S. (2016), 'An Inquiry into the Determinants of the Profitability of Italian Banks', Questioni di Economia e Finanza Occasional Papers, No 364, Banca d'Italia, Rome.

Alesina, A., Blanchard, O., Galí, J., Giavazzi, F., and Uhlig, H. (2001), 'Defining a Macroeconomic Framework for the Euro Area', *Monitoring the European Central Bank*, 3, Centre for Economic Policy Research.

Alesina, A. and Tabellini, G. (2007), 'Bureaucrats or Politicians? Part I: A Single Policy Task', *American Economic Review*, 97, 1, 169–79.

Alloza, M., Cozmanca, B., Ferdinandusse, M., and Jacquinot, P. (2019), 'Fiscal Spillovers in a Monetary Union', ECB Economic Bulletin, Issue 1/2019.

Altavilla, C. and Giannone, D. (2017), 'The Effectiveness of Non-Standard Monetary Policy Measures: Evidence From Survey Data', *Journal of Applied Econometrics*, 32, 952–64.

Altavilla, C., Boucinha, M., and Peydró, J.-L. (2018), 'Monetary Policy and Bank Profitability in a Low Interest Rate Environment', *Economic Policy*, 33, 96, 531–86.

Altavilla, C., Brugnolini, L., Gürkaynak, R. S., Motto, R., and Ragusa, G. (2019), 'Measuring Euro Area Monetary Policy', *Journal of Monetary Economics*, 108, December 2019, Pages 162–79.

Altavilla C., Burlon, L., Giannetti, M., and Holton, S. (2019), 'Is There a Zero Lower Bound? The Real Effects of Negative Interest Rates', Working Paper Series, No 2289, ECB, Frankfurt am Main.

Altavilla, C., Canova, F., and Ciccarelli, M. (2020), 'Mending the Broken Link: Heterogeneous Bank Lending and Monetary Policy Pass-Through', *Journal of Monetary Economics*, 110, April 2020, Pages 81–98.

Altavilla, C., Carboni, G., and Motto, R. (2015), 'Asset Purchase Programmes and Financial Markets: Evidence from the Euro Area', Working Paper Series, No 1864, ECB, Frankfurt am Main.

Altavilla, C., Giannone, D., and Lenza, M. (2016), 'The Financial and Macroeconomic Effects of the OMT Announcements', *International Journal of Central Banking*, 12, 3, 29–57.

Altavilla, C., Pagano, M., and Simonelli, S. (2017), 'Bank Exposures and Sovereign Stress Transmission', *Review of Finance*, 21, 6, 2103–39.

Altonji, J.G. and Devereux, P. J. (2000), 'The Extent and Consequences of Downward Nominal Wage Rigidities', *Research in Labor Economics*, pp. 383–431, Emerald Group Publishing Limited.

Anderson, B.D.O. and Moore, J.B. (1979), *Optimal Filtering*. Englewood Cliffs, NJ: Prentice Hall.

Andrade, P., Breckenfelder, J., De Fiore, F., Karadi, P., and Tristani, O. (2016), 'The ECB's Asset Purchase Programme: An Early Assessment', Working Paper Series, No 1956, ECB, Frankfurt am Main.

Andrade, P., Cahn C., Fraisse, H., and Mésonnier, J.-S. (2018), 'Can the Provision of Long-Term Liquidity Help to Avoid a Credit Crunch? Evidence from the Eurosystem's LTRO', *Journal of the European Economic Association*, 17, 4, 1070–106.

Andrés, J., López-Salido, J.D., and Nelson, E. (2009), 'Money and the Natural Rate Of Interest: Structural Estimates for the United States and the Euro Area', *Journal of Economic Dynamics and Control*, 33, 3, 758–76.

Angelini, P., Bofondi, M., and Zingales, L. (2017), 'The Origins of Italian NPLs', *mimeo*, June.

Arrata, W. and Nguyen, B. (2017), 'Price Impact of Bond Supply Shocks: Evidence from the Eurosystem's Asset Purchase Program', Banque de France Working Paper, No 623.

Association for Financial Markets in Europe (2012), *The Economic Benefits of High Quality Securitization to the EU Economy*, London.

Attinasi, M.G., Lalik, M., and Vetlov, I. (2017), 'Fiscal Spillovers in the Euro Area: A Model-Based Analysis', Working Paper Series, No 2040, European Central Bank.

Auerbach, A.J. and Gorodnichenko, Y. (2013), 'Output Spillovers from Fiscal Policy', *American Economic Review*, 103, 3, 141–6.

Bagehot, W. (1873), *Lombard Street: A Description of the Money Market*. London: HS King.

Baldwin, R. and Giavazzi, F. (eds.) (2015), *The Eurozone Crisis: A Consensus View of the Causes and a Few Possible Solutions*, VoxEU.org Book.

Ball, L. (1992), 'Why Does High Inflation Raise Inflation Uncertainty?', *Journal of Monetary Economics*, 29, 3, 371–88.

Ball, L., Mankiw, N.G., and Romer, D. (1988), 'The New Keynesian Economics and the Output-Inflation Trade-off', *Brookings Papers on Economic Activity*, 1, 1–65.

Bańbura, M., Giannone, D., and Lenza, M. (2015), 'Conditional Forecasts and Scenario Analysis with Vector Autoregressions for Large Cross-Sections', *International Journal of Forecasting*, 31, 3, 739–56.

Barbagallo, C. (2017), 'I crediti deteriorati delle banche italiane: problematiche e tendenze recenti', remarks given at Primo Congresso Nazionale FIRST CISL 'La fiducia tra banche e Paese: NPL, un terreno da cui far ripartire il dialogo', Rome, 6 June.

Barro, R.J. and Gordon, D.B. (1983), 'Rules, Discretion and Reputation in a Model of Monetary Policy', *Journal of Monetary Economics*, 12, 1, 101–21.

Bean, C.R. (2010), 'The Great Moderation, the Great Panic and the Great Contraction', Special Max Weber Lecture, Villa la Fonte, 20 January.

Bean, C.R., Paustian, M., Penalver, A., and Taylor, T. (2010), 'Monetary Policy after the Fall', paper presented at the Federal Reserve Bank of Kansas City Annual Conference, Jackson Hole, Wyoming, 28 August.

Bech, M.L. and Malkhozov, A. (2016), 'How Have Central Banks Implemented Negative Policy Rates?', BIS Quarterly Review, March.

Beetsma, R., Giuliodori, M., and Klaassen, F. (2006), 'Trade Spill-Overs of Fiscal Policy in the European Union: A Panel Analysis', *Economic Policy*, 21, 48, 640–87.

Begg, D.K., Canova, F., Fatas, A., De Grauwe, P., and Lane, P.R. (2002), 'Surviving the Slowdown', *Monitoring the European Central Bank*, 3, Centre for Economic Policy Research.

Begg, D.K., De Grauwe, P., Giavazzi, F., Uhlig, H., and Wyplosz, C. (1998), 'The ECB: Safe at Any Speed?', *Monitoring the European Central Bank*, 1, Centre for Economic Policy Research.

Belke, A. and Gros, D. (2019), 'QE in the Euro Area: Has the PSPP Benefited Peripheral Bonds?', Ruhr Economic Papers, No 803.

Bénassy-Quéré, A., Brunnermeier, M., Enderlein, H., Farhi, E., Fratzscher, M., Fuest, C., et al. (2018), 'Reconciling Risk Sharing with Market Discipline: A Constructive Approach to Euro Area Reform', CEPR Policy Insight No. 91, January.

Benhabib, J., Schmitt-Grohé, S., and Uribe, M. (2001), 'The Perils of Taylor rules', *Journal of Economic Theory*, 96, 1–2, 40–69.

Bernanke, B.S. and Boivin, J. (2003), 'Monetary Policy in a Data-Rich Environment', *Journal of Monetary Economics*, 50, 3, 525–46.

Bernanke, B.S. and Gertler, M. (2000), 'Monetary Policy and Asset Price Volatility', NBER Working Paper, No 7559.

Bernanke, B.S. and Mihov, I. (1997), 'What Does the Bundesbank Target?', *European Economic Review*, 41, 6, 1025–53.

Bernhard, W. and Leblang, D. (2002), 'Political Parties and Monetary Commitments', *International Organization*, 56, 4, 803–30.

Bini Smaghi, L. (2011a), 'The Challenges Facing Monetary Policy', speech at Prometeia, Bologna, 27 January.

Bini Smaghi, L. (2011b), 'Private Sector Involvement: From (Good) Theory to (Bad) Practice', speech at the Reinventing Bretton Woods Committee, Berlin, 6 June.

Bini Smaghi, L. (2011c), 'The European Debt Crisis', speech delivered at Atlantik-Brücke, Meeting of Regional Group Frankfurt/Hesse, Frankfurt am Main 17 October.

Bindseil, U., Corsi, M., Sahel, B., and Visser, A. (2017), 'The Eurosystem collateral framework explained', Occasional Paper Series, ECB, No 189.

Bindseil, U. and König, P. (2012), 'TARGET2 and the European sovereign debt crisis', *Kredit und Kapital*, 45, 2, 135–74.

Blagrave, P., Ho, G., Koloskova, K., and Vesperoni, E. (2017), 'Fiscal Spillovers : The Importance of Macroeconomic and Policy Conditions in Transmission', Spillover Notes, No 11, International Monetary Fund.

Blinder, A.S. (1998), *Central Banking in Theory and Practice*. Cambridge: MIT Press.

Blinder, A.S., Ehrmann, M., De Haan, J., and Jansen, D.-J. (2017), 'Necessity as the Mother of Invention: Monetary Policy after the Crisis', *Economic Policy*, 32, 92, 707–55.

Bloomberg (2008), 'Another Black Monday for Wall Street', article published on 30 September.

Boeckx, J., Dossche, M., and Peersman, G. (2017), 'Effectiveness and Transmission of the ECB's Balance Sheet Policies', *International Journal of Central Banking*, 13, 1, 297–333.

Bofinger, P. (1999), 'The Monetary Policy of the ECB under Treaty Article 105', Economic Affairs Series, ECON-112.

Borio, C. and Lowe, P. (2004), 'Securing Sustainable Price Stability: Should Credit Come Back from the Wilderness?', BIS Working Papers, No 157.

Bottero, M., Minoiu, C., Peydro, J.-L., Polo, A., Presbitero, A.F., and Sette, E. (2019), 'Negative Monetary Policy Rates and Portfolio Rebalancing: Evidence from Credit Register Data', Working Paper, International Monetary Fund.

Brainard, W. C. (1967), 'Uncertainty and the Effectiveness of Policy', *American Economic Review*, 57, 2, 411–25.

Brand, C. and Cassola, N. (2004), 'A Money Demand System for Euro Area M3', *Applied Economics*, 36, 8, 817–38.

Brand, C. and Mazelis, F. (2019), 'Taylor-rule Consistent Estimates of the Natural Rate of Interest', Working Paper Series, No 2257, ECB, Frankfurt am Main.

Brand, C., Reimers, H.E., and Seitz, F. (2003), 'Forecasting real GDP: What Role for Narrow Money?', Working Paper Series, No 254, ECB, Frankfurt am Main, September.

Breeden, D. and Litzenberger, R. (1978), 'Prices of State-Contingent Claims Implicit in Option Prices', *Journal of Business*, 51, 4, 621–51.

Bruggeman, A., Donati, P., and Warne, A. (2003), 'Is the Demand for Euro Area M3 Stable?', Working Paper Series, No 255, ECB, Frankfurt am Main, September.

Brunnermeier, M.K., James, H., and Landau, J.P. (2016), *The Euro and the Battle of Ideas*. Princeton, NJ: Princeton University Press.

Brunnermeier, M.K. and Koby, Y. (2018), 'The Reversal Interest Rate', NBER Working Paper, No 25406.

Burriel, P. and Galesi, A. (2018), 'Uncovering the Heterogeneous Effects of ECB Unconventional Monetary Policies across Euro Area Countries', *European Economic Review*, 101, 210–29.

Buti, M. and Giudice, G. (2002), 'Maastricht's Fiscal Rules at Ten: An Assessment', *JCMS: Journal of Common Market Studies*, 40, 5, 823–48.

Buti, M., Deroose, S., Gaspar, V., and Nogueira Martins, J. (2010), *The Euro: The First Decade*. Cambridge: Cambridge University Press.

Calvo, G.A. (1983), 'Staggered Prices in a Utility-Maximizing Framework', *Journal of Monetary Economics*, 12, 3, 383–98.

Calza, M.A., Gerdesmeier, M.D., and Levy, M.J.V.F. (2001), 'Euro Area Money Demand: Measuring the Opportunity Costs Appropriately', IMF Working Paper, No 1/179, International Monetary Fund.

Camba-Mendez, G. (2003), 'The Definition of Price Stability: Choosing a Price Measure', in Issing, O. (ed.), *Background Studies for the ECB's Evaluation of its Monetary Policy Strategy*, pp. 31–42. Frankfurt am Main: ECB.

Camba-Mendez, G., Gaspar, V., and Wynne, M. A. (2002), *Measurement Issues in European Consumer Price Indices and the Conceptual Framework of the HICP*. Frankfurt am Main: ECB.

Camba-Mendez, G. and Werner, T. (2017), 'The Inflation Risk Premium in the Post-Lehman Period', Working Paper Series, No 2033, ECB, Frankfurt am Main, March.

Campbell, J.R., Evans, C.L., Fisher, J.D., and Justiniano, A. (2012), 'Macroeconomic Effects of Federal Reserve Forward Guidance', *Brookings Papers on Economic Activity*, 44, 1, 1–80.

Campbell, J. Y., Sunderam, A., and Viceira, L. M. (2009), 'Inflation Bets or Deflation Hedges? The Changing Risks of Nominal Bonds', *Critical Finance Review*, 6(2), 263–30.

Canova, F. (2007), *Methods for Applied Macroeconomic Research*. Princeton, NJ: Princeton University Press.

Card, D. and Hyslop, D. (1997), 'Does Inflation "Grease the Wheels" of the Labor Market?', *Reducing Inflation: Motivation and Strategy*, pp. 71–122. Chicago, IL: University of Chicago Press.

Carpinelli, L. and Crosignani, M. (2018), 'The Design and Transmission of Central Bank Liquidity Provisions', Working Paper.

Carstensen, K. (2004), 'Is European Money Demand Still Stable?', Kiel Working Paper, No 1179, Kiel Institute for the World Economy.

Caruana, J. (2013), 'The Changing Nature of Central Bank Independence', panel remarks at the Bank of Mexico's international conference on 'Central bank independence—Progress and challenges', Mexico City, 14–15 October.

Cecchetti, S., Natoli, F., and Sigalotti L. (2015), 'Tail Co-Movement in Option-Implied Inflation Expectations as an Indicator of Anchoring', Temi di Discussione, No. 1025, July, Banca d'Italia.

Cecchetti, S.G., Genberg, H., Lipsky, J., and Wadhwani, S. (2000), Asset Prices and Central Bank Policy. *Geneva Reports on the World Economy*, No 2, International Centre for Monetary and Banking Studies and Centre for Economic Policy Research.

Cecchetti, S.G. and Wynne, M.A. (2003), 'Defining Price Stability', *Economic Policy*, 38, 37, 395–434.

Centre for European Policy Studies (CEPS) (2000), 'Quo Vadis Euro?', Second Report of the CEPS Macroeconomic Policy Group.

Cette, G., Fernald, J.G., and Mojon, B. (2016), 'The Pre-Great Recession Slowdown in Productivity', *European Economic Review*, 88, 3–20.

Chari, V.V., Kehoe, P.J., and McGrattan, E.R. (2007), 'Business Cycle Accounting', *Econometrica*, 75, 3, 781–836.

Chen, A.Y., Engstrom, E., and Grishchenko, O. (2016), 'Has the Inflation Risk Premium Fallen? Is It Now Negative?', FEDS Notes, Board of Governors of the Federal Reserve System (US).

Christiano, L.J., Ilut, C., Motto, R., and Rostagno, M. (2010), 'Monetary Policy And Stock Market Booms', Economic Policy Symposium Proceedings, Federal Reserve Bank of Kansas City.

Christiano, L.J., Motto, R., and Rostagno, M. (2003), 'The Great Depression and the Friedman-Schwartz Hypothesis', *Journal of Money, Credit and Banking*, 35, 6, Part 2, 1119–97.

Christiano, L.J., Motto, R., and Rostagno, M. (2007), 'Financial Factors in Business Cycles', 2008 Meeting Papers, No 52, Society for Economic Dynamics.

Christiano, L.J., Motto, R., and Rostagno, M. (2008), 'Shocks, Structures or Policies? The Euro Area and the US after 2001', *Journal of Economic Dynamics and Control*, 32, 8, 2476–506.

Christiano, L.J., Motto, R., and Rostagno, M. (2014), 'Risk Shocks', *American Economic Review*, 104, 1, 27–65.

Christiano, L.J. and Rostagno, M. (2001), 'Money Growth Monitoring and the Taylor Rule', NBER Working Paper, No 8539, October.

Christoffel, K., Coenen, G., and Warne, A. (2008), 'The New Area-Wide Model of the Euro Area: A Micro-Founded Open-Economy Model for Forecasting and Policy Analysis', Working Paper Series, No 944, ECB, Frankfurt am Main, October.

Chung, H., Laforte, J.P., Reifschneider, D., and Williams, J.C. (2012), 'Have We Underestimated the Likelihood and Severity of Zero Lower Bound Events?', *Journal of Money, Credit and Banking*, 44, 47–82.

Clarida, R.H. and Gertler, M. (1997), 'How the Bundesbank Conducts Monetary Policy', in *Reducing Inflation: Motivation and Strategy*, pp. 363–412. Chicago, IL: University of Chicago Press.

Clarida, R.H., Galí, J., and Gertler, M. (1998), 'Monetary Policy Rules in Practice: Some International Evidence', *European Economic Review*, 42, 6, 1033–67.

Clarida, R.H., Galí, J., and Gertler, M. (1999), 'The Science of Monetary Policy: A New Keynesian Perspective', *Journal of Economic Literature*, 37, 4, 1661–707.

Cochrane, J.H. (2019), *The Fiscal Theory of the Price Level*, book manuscript.

Cochrane, J.H. (2011), 'Determinacy and Identification with Taylor Rules', *Journal of Political Economy*, 119, 3, 565–615.

Cochrane, J.H. and Piazzesi, M. (2009), 'Decomposing the Yield Curve', AFA 2010 Atlanta Meetings Paper, January.

Coenen, G. (2003), 'Downward Nominal Wage Rigidity and the Long-Run Phillips Curve: Simulation-Based Evidence for the Euro Area', in Issing, O. (ed.), *Background Studies for the ECB's Evaluation of its Monetary Policy Strategy*, pp. 127–36. Frankfurt am Main: ECB.

Coenen, G. and Warne, A. (2014), 'Risks to Price Stability, the Zero Lower Bound, and Forward Guidance: A Real-Time Assessment', *International Journal of Central Banking*, 10, 2.

Coenen, G. and Wieland, V. (2005), 'A Small Estimated Euro Area Model with rational Expectations and Nominal Rigidities', *European Economic Review*, 49, 5, 1081–104.

Coenen, G. and Vega, J.L. (2001), 'The Demand for M3 in the Euro Area', *Journal of Applied Econometrics*, 16, 6, 727–48.

Coeuré, B. (2013), 'Outright Monetary Transactions, One Year On', speech given at the conference 'The ECB and its OMT programme', organised by the Centre for Economic Policy Research, German Institute for Economic Research and KfW Bankengruppe Berlin, 2 September.

Coeuré, B. (2015), 'Embarking on Public Sector Asset Purchases', speech delivered at the Second International Conference on Sovereign Bond Markets, Frankfurt am Main, 10 March.

Coeuré, B. (2017), 'The Transmission of the ECB's Monetary Policy in Standard and Non-Standard Times', speech given at the workshop 'Monetary policy in non-standard times', Frankfurt am Main, 11 September.

Coeuré, B. (2019a), 'The Rise of Services and the Transmission of Monetary Policy', speech delivered at the 21st Geneva Conference on the World Economy, 16 May.

Coeuré, B. (2019b), 'The Effects of APP Reinvestments on Euro Area Bond Markets', speech delivered at the ECB's Bond Market Contact Group meeting, 12 June.

Coeuré, B. (2019c), 'Inflation Expectations and the Conduct of Monetary Policy', speech given at an event organised by the SAFE Policy Center, Frankfurt am Main, 11 July 2019.

Coibion, O. and Gorodnichenko, Y. (2015), 'Is the Phillips Curve Alive and Well after All? Inflation Expectations and the Missing Disinflation', *American Economic Journal: Macroeconomics*, 7, 1, 197–232.

Coibion, O., Gorodnichenko, Y., and Kumar, S. (2018), 'How Do Firms Form Their Expectations? New Survey Evidence', *American Economic Review*, 108, 9, 2671–713.

Constâncio, V. (2011), 'Contagion and the European Debt Crisis', lecture delivered at the Bocconi University/Intesa Sanpaolo Conference on 'Bank Competitiveness in the Post-crisis World', Milan 10 October.

Constâncio, V. (2015), 'Understanding Inflation Dynamics and Monetary Policy', panel remarks delivered at the Jackson Hole Economic Policy Symposium, Federal Reserve Bank of Kansas City, 29 August.

Constâncio, V. (2018), 'Completing the Odyssean journey of the European Monetary Union', remarks delivered at the ECB Colloquium on 'The Future of Central Banking', Frankfurt am Main 16–17 May.

Conti, A., Neri, S., and Nobili, A. (2017), 'Low Inflation and Monetary Policy in the Euro Area', ECB Working Paper No. 2005.

Cox, J.C., Ingersoll Jr, J.E., and Ross, S.A. (1985), 'A Theory of the Term Structure of Interest Rates', *Econometrica*, 53, pp. 385–407.

Cristadoro, R., Forni, M., Reichlin, L., and Veronese, G. (2005), 'A Core Inflation Indicator for the Euro Area', *Journal of Money, Credit and Banking*, 37, 539–60.

Crosignani, M., Faria-e-Castro, M., and Fonseca, L. (2020), 'The (Unintended?) Consequences of the Largest Liquidity Injection Ever', *Journal of Monetary Economics*, 112, June 2020, 97–112.

Crowe, C. (2008), 'Goal Independent Central Banks: Why Politicians Decide to Delegate', *European Journal of Political Economy*, 24, 4, 748–62.

Cukierman, A. (2008), 'Central Bank Independence and Monetary Policymaking Institutions – Past, Present and Future', *European Journal of Political Economy*, 24, 722–36.

D'Amico, S., English, W., López-Salido, D., and Nelson, E. (2012), 'The Federal Reserve's Large-scale Asset Purchase Programmes: Rationale and Effects', Economic Journal, *Royal Economic Society*, 122, 564, 415–46.

D'Amico, S. and King, T.B. (2013), 'Flow and Stock Effects of Large-Scale Treasury Purchases: Evidence on the Importance of Local Supply', *Journal of Financial Economics*, 108, 2, 425–48.

Darracq Pariès, M., Sørensen, C.K., and Rodríguez Palenzuela, D. (2011), 'Macroeconomic Propagation under Different Regulatory Regimes: Evidence from an Estimated DSGE Model for the Euro Area', *International Journal of Central Banking*, 7, 4, 49–113.

De Grauwe, P. (2002), *Economics of Monetary Union*, Oxford.

De La Dehesa, G. (2008), 'Is the Present Upward Inflation Shift Going to Last?', Briefing Paper for the Monetary Dialogue of the European Parliament.

De Marco, F. (2019), 'Bank Lending and the European Sovereign Debt Crisis', *Journal of Financial and Quantitative Analysis*, 54, 1, 155–82.

De Mol, C., Giannone, D., and Reichlin, L. (2008), 'Forecasting Using a Large Number of Predictors: Is Bayesian Shrinkage a Valid Alternative to Principal Components?', *Journal of Econometrics*, 146, 2, 318–28.

De Pooter, M., Martin, R.F., and Pruitt, S. (2018), 'The Liquidity Effects of Official Bond Market Intervention', *Journal of Financial and Quantitative Analysis*, 53, 1, 243–68.

De Santis, R.A. (2019), 'Redenomination Risk', *Journal of Money, Credit and Banking*, 51, 8, 2173–2206.

De Santis, R. and Holm-Hadulla, F. (2020), 'Flow Effects of Central Bank Asset Purchases on Sovereign Bond Prices: Evidence from a Natural Experiment', *Journal of Money, Credit and Banking*, 52, 6, 1467–1491.

De Vincent-Humphreys, R. and Puigvert Gutiérrez, J.M. (2012), 'A Quantitative Mirror on the Euribor Market Using Implied Probability Density Functions', *Eurasian Economic Review*, 2, 1, 1–31.

Debelle, G. and Fischer, S. (1994), 'How Independent Should a Central Bank Be?', Working Papers in Applied Economic Theory, No 94–05, Federal Reserve Bank of Boston.

Demiralp S., Eisenschmidt, J., and Vlassopoulos, T. (2019), 'Negative Interest Rates, Excess Liquidity and Retail Deposits: Banks' Reaction to Unconventional Monetary Policy in the Euro Area', Working Paper Series, No 2283, ECB, Frankfurt am Main, May.

Detken, C. and Smets, F. (2004), 'Asset Price Booms and Monetary Policy', Working Paper Series, No 364, ECB, Frankfurt am Main, May.

Deutsche Bundesbank (2016), 'The Macroeconomic Impact of Quantitative Easing in the Euro Area', monthly report, Vol. 6.

Deutsche Bundesbank (2018), 'Lower Bound, Inflation Target and the Anchoring of Inflation Expectations', Deutsche Bundesbank Monthly Report, June, pp. 31–55.

Dmitriev, M. and Kersting, E.K. (2016), 'Inflation Level and Inflation Volatility: A Seigniorage Argument', *Economics Letters*, 147, 112–15.

Doan, T., Litterman, R., and Sims, C.A. (1984), 'Forecasting and Conditional Projection Using Realistic Prior Distributions', *Econometric Reviews*, 3, 1–100.

Doh, T. (2010), 'The Efficacy of Large-Scale Asset Purchases at the Zero Lower Bound', Economic Review, Federal Reserve Bank of Kansas City, Second Quarter.

Dokko, J., Doyle, B.M., Kiley, M.T., Kim, J., Sherlund, S., Sim, J., et al. (2009), 'Monetary Policy and the Housing Bubble', Finance and Economics Discussion Series: Divisions of Research & Statistics and Monetary Affairs Federal Reserve Board, No 2009-49, Washington D.C.

Dossche, M., Hartwig, J., and Pierluigi, B. (2020), 'The Redistribution of Interest Income in the Euro Area, 2007–2019', mimeo.

Draghi, M. (2012a), 'Verbatim of the remarks made by Mario Draghi', speech by Mario Draghi at the Global Investment Conference in London, 26 July.

Draghi, M. (2012b), 'Introductory statement with Q&A', transcript, ECB, Frankfurt am Main, 2 August.

Draghi, M. (2012c), 'Introductory statement with Q&A', transcript, ECB, Frankfurt am Main, 6 September.

Draghi, M. (2013), 'Introductory statement to the press conference (with Q&A)', transcript, ECB, Frankfurt am Main, 4 July.

Draghi, M. (2014a), 'Monetary policy communication in turbulent times', speech at the Conference De Nederlandsche Bank 200 years: Central banking in the next two decades, Amsterdam, 24 April.

Draghi, M. (2014b), 'Introductory statement to the press conference (with Q&A)', transcript, Brussels, 8 May.

Draghi, M. (2014c), 'Introductory statement to the press conference (with Q&A)', transcript, ECB, Frankfurt am Main, 5 June.

Draghi, M. (2014d), 'Introductory statement to the press conference (with Q&A)', transcript, ECB, Frankfurt am Main, 3 July.

Draghi, M. (2014e), 'Unemployment in the euro area', speech at the annual central bank symposium, Jackson Hole, 22 August.

Draghi, M. (2014f), 'Introductory statement to the press conference (with Q&A)', transcript, ECB, Frankfurt am Main, 4 September.

Draghi, M. (2014g), 'Introductory remarks at the EP's Economic and Monetary Affairs Committee', speech at the EU Parliament, Brussels, 22 September.

Draghi, M. (2014h), 'Introductory statement to the press conference (with Q&A)', transcript, Naples, 2 October.

Draghi, M. (2015a), 'Introductory statement to the press conference (with Q&A)', transcript, ECB, Frankfurt am Main, 22 January.

Draghi, M. (2015b), 'Introductory statement to the press conference (with Q&A)', transcript, ECB, Frankfurt am Main, 4 March.

Draghi, M. (2015c), 'Hearing at the European Parliament's Economic and Monetary Affairs Committee (introductory remarks and Q&A)', EU Parliament, Brussels, 23 March.

Draghi, M. (2015d), 'Introductory statement to the press conference (with Q&A)', transcript, ECB, Frankfurt am Main, 3 September.

Draghi, M. (2015e), 'Monetary policy: past, present, and future', speech at the Frankfurt European Banking Congress, 20 November.

Draghi, M. (2015f), 'Introductory statement to the press conference (with Q&A)', transcript, ECB, Frankfurt am Main, 2 December.

Draghi, M. (2016a), 'Introductory statement to the press conference (with Q&A)', transcript, ECB, Frankfurt am Main, 21 January.

Draghi, M. (2016b), 'How central banks meet the challenge of low inflation', Marjolin lecture at the SUERF conference organised by the Deutsche Bundesbank, Frankfurt am Main, 4 February.

Draghi, M. (2016c), 'Introductory statement to the press conference (with Q&A)', transcript, ECB, Frankfurt am Main, 10 March.

Draghi, M. (2016d), 'Introductory statement to the press conference (with Q&A)', transcript, ECB, Frankfurt am Main, 8 December.

Draghi, M. (2017a), 'Monetary policy and the economic recovery in the euro area', speech at The ECB and Its Watchers XVIII Conference, 6 April.

Draghi, M. (2017b), 'Introductory statement to the press conference (with Q&A)', transcript, ECB, Frankfurt am Main, 8 June.

Draghi, M. (2017c), 'Introductory statement to the press conference (with Q&A)', transcript, ECB, Frankfurt am Main, 26 October.

Draghi, M. (2018a), 'Introductory statement to the press conference (with Q&A)', transcript, ECB, Frankfurt am Main, 14 June.

Draghi, M. (2018b), 'Monetary policy in the euro area', speech by Mario Draghi at the ECB Forum on Central Banking, Sintra, 19 June.

Draghi, M. (2018c), 'Central bank independence', First Lamfalussy Lecture at the Banque Nationale de Belgique, Brussels, 26 October.

Duisenberg, W. (1998a), 'The stability-oriented monetary policy strategy of the European System of Central Banks and the international role of the euro', speech at the Economic Club of New York, New York, 12 November.

Duisenberg, W. (1998b), 'Introductory statement', transcript, ECB, Frankfurt am Main, 13 October.

Duisenberg, W. (1999), 'Introductory statement with Q&A', transcript, ECB, Frankfurt am Main, 8 April.

Duisenberg, W. (2000), 'Testimony before the Committee on Economic and Monetary Affairs of the European Parliament with the President of the European Central Bank, in accordance with Article 113(3) of the Treaty on European Union', transcript, Brussels, 23 November.

Duisenberg, W. (2001a), 'Introductory statement', transcript, ECB, Frankfurt am Main, 10 May.

Duisenberg, W. (2001b), 'Testimony before the Committee on Economic and Monetary Affairs of the European Parliament with the President of the European Central Bank, in accordance with Article 113(3) of the Treaty on European Union', transcript, Brussels, 28 May.

Duisenberg, W. (2001c), 'The ECB's quantitative definition of price stability and its comparison with such definitions or inflation targets applied in other large economic areas', letter of Dr. W. F. Duisenberg, President of the ECB to the Chairperson of the Committee on Economic and Monetary Affairs, 16 October.

Duisenberg, W. (2001d), 'The ECB's monetary policy strategy and the quantitative definition of price stability', letter to the Chairperson of the Committee on Economic and Monetary Affairs, 13 December.

Duisenberg, W. (2001e), 'Testimony before the Committee on Economic and Monetary Affairs of the European Parliament with the President of the European Central Bank, in accordance with Article 113(3) of the Treaty on European Union', transcript, Brussels, 18 December.

Eberly, J.C., Stock, J.H., and Wright, J.H. (2020), 'The Federal Reserve's Current Framework for Monetary Policy: A Review and Assessment', *International Journal of Central Banking*.

ECB (1998), 'A stability-oriented monetary policy strategy for the ESCB', press release, 13 October

ECB (1999), 'The stability-oriented monetary policy strategy of the Eurosystem', Monthly Bulletin, January, pp. 39–50.

ECB (2000), 'The two pillars of the ECB's monetary policy strategy', Monthly Bulletin, November, pp. 37–48.

ECB (2003a), 'Estimating the size of portfolio shifts from equity to money', Monthly Bulletin, May, pp. 11–14.

ECB (2003b), 'The ECB's monetary policy strategy', press release, 8 May.

ECB (2005a), 'Approaches to identifying and estimating portfolio shifts into and out of M3', Monthly Bulletin, January, pp. 13–16.

ECB (2005b), 'Asset price bubbles and monetary policy', Monthly Bulletin, April, pp. 47–60.

ECB (2005c), 'The impact on M3 of portfolio shifts arising from heightened uncertainty', Monthly Bulletin, October, p. 59.

ECB (2009), 'Tracking extraordinary portfolio shifts into money during the period of financial turmoil', Monthly Bulletin, January, pp. 17–20.

ECB (2010), 'ECB decides on measures to address severe tensions in financial markets', press release 10 May.

ECB (2011), 'The information content of option prices during the financial crisis', ECB Monthly Bulletin, February 2011, pp. 87–99.

ECB (2014), 'Euro area risk-free interest rates: measurement issues, recent developments and relevance to monetary policy', Monthly Bulletin, July, pp. 63–77.

ECB (2015), 'ECB announces expanded asset purchase programme', press release, 22 January.

ECB (2017), 'Low inflation in the euro area: causes and consequences', Occasional Paper Series, ECB, No 181, January.

Eccles, M. (1935), 'Banking Act of 1935', US Congress, House Committee on Banking and Currency, Hearings, 18 March, p. 377.

Eggertsson, G.B. and Le Borgne, E. (2010), 'A Political Agency Theory of Central Bank Independence', *Journal of Money, Credit and Banking*, 42, 4, 647–77.

Eggertsson, G.B., Juelsrud, R.E., Summers, L.H., and Wold, E.G. (2019), 'Negative Nominal Interest Rates and the Bank Lending Channel', NBER Working Paper, No 25416.

Eisenschmidt, J., Kedan, D., Schmitz, M., Adalid, R., and Papsdorf, P. (2017), 'The Eurosystem's Asset Purchase Programme and TARGET Balances', Occasional Paper Series, ECB, No 196.

Eser, F., Lemke, W., Nyholm, K., Radde, S., and Vladu, A. (2019), 'Tracing the Impact of the ECB's Asset Purchase Programme on the Yield Curve', Working Paper Series, No 2293, ECB, Frankfurt am Main, July.

Eser, F. and Schwaab, B. (2016), 'Evaluating the Impact of Unconventional Monetary Policy Measures: Empirical Evidence from the ECB's Securities Markets Programme', *Journal of Financial Economics*, 119, 1, 147–67.

European Monetary Institute (EMI) (1997), 'The single monetary policy in stage three: elements of the monetary policy strategy of the ESCB', European Monetary Institute, Frankfurt.

Eurostat (2001), 'Compendium of HICP reference documents', European Commission Working Documents, (2/2001/B/5).

Fahr, S., Motto, R., Rostagno, M., Smets, F., and Tristani, O. (2013), 'A Monetary Policy Strategy in Good and Bad Times: Lessons from the Recent Past', *Economic Policy*, 28, 74, 243–88.

Falagiarda, M. and Reitz, S. (2015), 'Announcements of ECB Unconventional Programs: Implications for the Sovereign Spreads of Stressed Euro Area Countries', *Journal of International Money and Finance*, 53, 276–95.

Fischer, S. (2015), 'Central Bank Independence', speech at the 2015 Herbert Stein Memorial Lecture National Economists Club, Washington D.C., 4 November.

Fitoussi, J.-P. and Creel, J. (2002), 'How to Reform the European Central Bank', Centre for European Reform, London.

Fratianni, M., Hagen, J.V., and Waller, C. (1997), 'Central Banking as a Political Principal-Agent Problem', *Economic Inquiry*, 35, 2, 378–93.

Friedman, M. (1970), 'A Theoretical Framework for Monetary Analysis', *Journal of Political Economy*, 78, 2, 193–238.

Gagnon J.E., Raskin, M., Remache, J., and Sack, B.P. (2011), 'Large-Scale Asset Purchases by the Federal Reserve: Did They Work?', Economic Policy Review, Federal Reserve Bank of New York, May, pp. 41–59.

Galí, J., Gerlach, S., Rotemberg, J., Uhlig, H., and Woodford, M. (2004), 'The Monetary Policy Strategy of the ECB Reconsidered', *Monitoring the European Central Bank*, 5, Centre for Economic Policy Research.

Gambetti, L. and Musso, A. (2017), 'The Macroeconomic Impact of the ECB's Expanded Asset Purchase Programme (APP)', Working Paper Series, No 2075, ECB, Frankfurt am Main, June.

García-Herrero, A., Gaspar, V., Hoogduin, L., Morgan, J., and Winkler, B. (eds.) (2001), First ECB Central Banking Conference: Why Price Stability?, European Central Bank, Frankfurt am Main.

Garcia-Posada, M. and Marchetti, M. (2016), 'The Bank Lending Channel of Unconventional Monetary Policy: The Impact of the VLTROs on Credit Supply in Spain', *Economic Modelling*, 58, 427–41.

Geiger, F. and Schupp, F. (2018), 'With a little help from my friends: Survey-based derivation of euro area short rate expectations at the effective lower bound', Deutsche Bundesbank Discussion Paper, No 27.

Geithner, T. F. (2015), *Stress Test: Reflections on Financial Crises*, Broadway Books.

Geraats, P., Giavazzi, F., and Wyplosz, C. (2008), 'Transparency and Governance', *Monitoring the European Central Bank*, 6, Centre for Economic Policy Research.

Gerberding, C., Seitz, F., and Worms, A. (2005), 'How the Bundesbank Really Conducted Monetary Policy', *The North American Journal of Economics and Finance*, 16, 3, 277–92.

Gertler, M. and Karadi, P. (2015), 'Monetary Policy Surprises, Credit Costs, and Economic Activity', *American Economic Journal: Macroeconomics*, 7, 1, 44–76.

Ghysels, E., Idier, J., Manganelli, S., and Vergote, O. (2016), 'A High-Frequency Assessment of the ECB Securities Markets Programme', *Journal of the European Economic Association*, 15, 1, 218–43.

Giannone, D., Lenza, M., and Primiceri, G.E. (2015), 'Prior Selection for Vector Autoregressions', *The Review of Economics and Statistics*, MIT Press, 97, 2, 436–51.

Giannone, D., Lenza, M., and Reichlin, L. (2010), 'Business cycles in the Euro Area' in Alesina, A. and Giavazzi, F. (eds.) Europe and the Euro, NBER.

Giannone, D. and Reichlin, L. (2004), 'Euro Area and US Recessions: 1970–2003', in Reichlin, L. (ed.), The Euro Area Business Cycle: Stylised Facts and Measurement Issues, Centre for Economic Policy Research.

Giannone, D. and Reichlin, L. (2006), 'Trends and Cycles in the Euro Area: How Much Heterogeneity and Should We Worry About It?', Working Paper Series, No 595, ECB, Frankfurt am Main, March.

Gibson, H.D., Hall, S.G., and Tavlas, G.S. (2016), 'The Effectiveness of the ECB's Asset Purchase Programs of 2009 to 2012', *Journal of Macroeconomics*, 47, 45–57.

González-Páramo, J.M. (2007), 'The Role of Information and Communication in Central Bank Policy: The Experience of the Recent Financial Turmoil', keynote address at SUERF Conference on 'Tracking Financial Behavior: Where do Macro and Micro Meet?', Milan.

González-Páramo, J.M. (2011a), 'The Sovereign Debt Crisis and the Future of European Integration', speech delivered at the Oxford University European Affairs Society, London 24 November.

González-Páramo, J.M. (2011b), 'Sovereign Contagion in Europe', speech delivered at the Distinguished Speaker Seminar of the European Economics and Financial Centre, London 25 November.

Goodfriend, M. and King, R.G. (1997), 'The New Neoclassical Synthesis and the Role of Monetary Policy', *NBER Macroeconomics Annual*, 12, 231–83.

Goodhart, C. and Lastra, R. (2018a), 'Potential Threats to Central Bank Independence', VOX CEPR Policy Portal, 11 March.

Goodhart, C. and Lastra, R. (2018b), 'Populism and Central Bank Independence', *Open Economies Review*, 29, 1, 49–68.

Greene, W.H. (1997), *Econometric Analysis*. Englewood Cliffs, NJ: Prentice Hall.

Greenlaw, D., Hamilton, J.D., Harris, E., and West, K.D. (2018), 'A Skeptical View of the Impact of the Fed's Balance Sheet', NBER Working Paper, No 24687.

Greenspan, A. (2001), 'Transparency in Monetary Policy', remarks at the Federal Reserve Bank of St. Louis Economic Policy Conference.

Greenspan, A. (2005), 'Testimony of Chairman Alan Greenspan', Federal Reserve Board's semiannual Monetary Policy Report to the Congress, Before the Committee on Banking, Housing, and Urban Affairs, U.S. Senate, 16 February.

Greenwood, R. and Vayanos, D. (2014), 'Bond Supply and Excess Bond Returns', *The Review of Financial Studies*, 27, 3, 663–713.

Gropp, R., Hakenes, H., and Schnabel, I. (2010), 'Competition, Risk-shifting, and Public Bail-out Policies', *The Review of Financial Studies*, 24, 6, 2084–120, June.

Gürkaynak, R.S., Sack, B., and Swanson, E. (2005), 'Do actions speak louder than words? The response of asset prices to monetary policy actions and statements', *International Journal of Central Banking*, 1, 1, 55–93.

Gürkaynak, R.S., Levin, A., and Swanson, E. (2010), 'Does inflation targeting anchor long-run inflation expectations? Evidence from the US, UK, and Sweden', *Journal of the European Economic Association*, 8, 6, 1208–42.

Haldane, A.G. (2015), 'How Low Can You Go?', speech given at the Portadown Chamber of Commerce, Northern Ireland, 18 September.

Hancock, D. and Passmore, W. (2011), 'Did the Federal Reserve's MBS purchase program lower mortgage rates?', *Journal of Monetary Economics*, 58, 5, 498–514.

Hansen, L.P. and Sargent, T.J. (2013), *Recursive Models of Dynamic Linear Economies*, Princeton University Press, Princeton.

Hanson, S.G. and Stein, J.C. (2015), 'Monetary Policy and Long-Term Real Rates', *Journal of Financial Economics*, 115, 3, 429–48.

Hartmann, P. and Smets, F. (2018), 'The First Twenty Years of the European Central Bank: Monetary Policy', Working Paper Series, No 2219, ECB, Frankfurt am Main, December.

Hattori, M., Schrimpf, A., and Sushko, V. (2016), 'The Response Of Tail Risk Perceptions to Unconventional Monetary Policy', *American Economic Journal: Macroeconomics*, 8, 2, 111–36.

Heider, F., Saidi, F., and Schepens, G. (2019), 'Life Below Zero: Bank Lending under Negative Policy Rates', *Review of Financial Studies*, 32, 10, 3728–3761.

Hellwig, M. and Schnabel, I. (2019), "Verursachen Target-Salden Risiken für die Steuerzahler?' *Wirtschaftsdienst, Springer; German National Library of Economics*, 99(8), 553–61, August.

Hoffman, J. (1998), 'Problems of Inflation Measurement in Germany', Discussion Paper, No 1/98, Economic Research Group of the Deutsche Bundesbank.

Holston, K., Laubach, T., and Williams, J. C. (2017), 'Measuring the Natural Rate Of Interest: International Trends and Determinants', *Journal of International Economics*, 108, 59–75.

Honohan, P. (2018), 'Real and Imagined Constraints on Euro Area Monetary Policy', Peterson Institute for International Economics Working Paper, No 18–8.

International Monetary Fund (2017), 'Cross-border Impacts of Fiscal Policy: Still Relevant?', World Economic Outlook.

In 't Veld, J. (2016), 'Public Investment Stimulus in Surplus Countries and their Euro Area Spillovers', *Economic Briefs*, 16, Economic and Financial Affairs, European Commission.

Issing, O. (1996), 'Europe: Political Union through Common Money?', IEA Occasional Paper, No 98.

Issing, O. (1998), 'The European Central Bank on the eve of EMU', speech delivered to the LSE European Society London School of Economics, London, 26 November.

Issing, O. (1999), 'The ECB and Its Watchers', speech delivered at the ECB Watchers Conference, Frankfurt am Main, 17 June.

Issing, O. (2000), 'The Monetary Policy of the European Central Bank: Strategy and Implementation; the European Monetary Union', CESifo Forum, 1, 2, 3–9.

Issing, O., Gaspar, V., Angeloni, I., and Tristani, O. (2001), *Monetary Policy in the Euro Area: Strategy and Decision-making at the European Central Bank*. Cambridge: Cambridge University Press.

Issing, O. (2002a), 'Monetary Policy and the Role of the Price Stability Definition', panel speech at the ECB Watchers conference, Milan, 10 June.

Issing, O. (2002b), 'Monetary Policy in a Changing Economic', speech at the symposium 'Rethinking Stabilisation Policy', Jackson Hole, 30 August.

Issing, O. (2002c), 'Monetary Policy in a World of Uncertainty', *Économie Internationale*, 4, 165–79.

Issing, O. (ed.) (2003), *Background Studies for the ECB's Evaluation of its Monetary Policy Strategy*. Frankfurt am Main: ECB.

Issing, O. (2008), *The Birth of the Euro*. Cambridge: Cambridge University Press.

Jackson, H. (2015), 'The International Experience with Negative Policy Rates', Bank of Canada Staff Discussion Paper, No 13, November.

James, H. (2012), *Making the European Monetary Union*. Cambridge, MA: Harvard University Press.

Jäger, J. and Grigoriadis, T. (2017), 'The Effectiveness of the ECB's Unconventional Monetary Policy: Comparative Evidence from Crisis and Non-crisis Euro-area Countries', *Journal of International Money and Finance*, 78, 21–43.

Jappelli, T. and Pistaferri, L. (2014), 'Fiscal Policy and MPC Heterogeneity', *American Economic Journal: Macroeconomics, American Economic Association*, 6(4), 107–36.

Jonung, L. and Drea, E. (2009), 'The Euro: It Can't Happen. It's a Bad Idea. It Won't Last. US Economists on the EMU, 1989–2002', European Economy—Economic Papers, No. 395, December.

Joslin, S., Singleton, K.J., and Zhu, H. (2011), 'A New Perspective on Gaussian Dynamic Term Structure Models', *The Review of Financial Studies*, 24, 3, 926–70.

Kaplan, G., Violante, G.L., and Weidner, J. (2014), 'The Wealthy Hand-to-Mouth', *Brookings Papers on Economic Activity*, 45(1), 77–153.

Keynes, J.M. (1936), *The General Theory of Employment, Interest and Money*. Basingstoke: Palgrave Macmillan.

Khan, A., King, R.G., and Wolman, A.L. (2003), 'Optimal Monetary Policy', *The Review of Economic Studies*, 70, 4, 825–60.

Kimball, M.S. (1995), 'The Quantitative Analytics of the Basic Neomonetarist Model', *Journal of Money, Credit and Banking*, 27, 4, 1241–77.

King, M. (2002), 'No Money, No Inflation—The Role of Money in the Economy', Bank of England Quarterly Bulletin, summer, pp. 162–77.

King, M. (2016), *The End of Alchemy: Money, Banking, and the Future of the Global Economy*. New York: W.W. Norton & Co.

King, R.G. and Wolman, A.L. (1996), 'Inflation Targeting in a St Louis Model of the 21st Century', National Bureau of Economic Research, No. 5507.

King, T.B. (2018), 'Duration Effects in Macro-Finance Models of the Term Structure', mimeo.

Klaeffling, M. and López Pérez, V. (2003), 'Inflation Targets and the Liquidity Trap', Working Paper Series, No 272, ECB, Frankfurt am Main, September.

Kliem, M. and Meyer-Gohde, A. (2019), '(Un)expected Monetary Policy Shocks and Term Premia', Goethe University Frankfurt, Institute for Monetary and Financial Stability (IMFS), Working Paper No. 137.

Kohn, D. (1994), discussion of paper 'Monetary Aggregates Targeting in a Low-inflation Economy', by William Poole for a conference held at North Falmouth, Massachusetts, June.

Kontolemis, Z. (2002), 'Money Demand in the Euro Area: Where Do We Stand (Today)?', IMF Working Paper, No 2/185, International Monetary Fund.

Krishnamurthy, A., Nagel, S., and Vissing-Jorgensen, A. (2017), 'ECB Policies Involving Government Bond Purchases: Impact and Channels', *Review of Finance*, 22, 1, 1–44.

Krishnamurthy, A. and Vissing-Jorgensen, A. (2011), 'The Effects of Quantitative Easing on Interest Rates: Channels and Implications for Policy', Brookings Papers on Economic Activity, pp. 215–87.

Krishnamurthy, A. and Vissing-Jorgensen, A. (2013), 'The Ins and Outs of LSAPs', Economic Policy Symposium Proceedings, Federal Reserve Bank of Kansas City.

Krugman, P. (1991), 'Increasing Returns and Economic Geography', *Journal of Political Economy*, 99, 3, 483–99.

Kydland, F.E. and Prescott, E.C. (1977), 'Rules Rather than Discretion: The Inconsistency of Optimal Plans', *Journal of Political Economy*, 85, 3, 473–91.

Lane, P. (2012), 'The European Sovereign Debt Crisis', *Journal of Economic Perspectives*, 26, 3, Summer.

Lane, P. (2013), 'Capital Flows in the Eurozone', European Economy Economic Papers, No. 497, April.

Lane, P. (2015a), 'The Funding of the Domestic Irish Banking System During The Boom', CEPR Discussion Paper, No. 10777, August.

Lane, P. (2015b), 'International Financial Flows and the Eurozone Crisis', in Baldwin, R. and Giavazzi, F. (eds.), *The Eurozone Crisis: A Consensus View of the Causes and a Few Possible Solutions*, VoxEU.org Book.

Lane, P. and Milesi-Ferretti, G.M. (2012), 'External Adjustment and the Global Crisis', *Journal of International Economics*, 88, 2, 252–65.

Lane, P. and Milesi-Ferretti, G.M. (2015), 'Global Imbalances and External Adjustment after the Crisis', in Raddatz, C., Saravia, D., and Ventura, J. (eds.), *Global Liquidity, Spillovers to Emerging Markets and Policy Responses*, Central Bank of Chile, pp. 105–39.

Laubach, T. and Williams, J.C. (2003), 'Measuring the Natural Rate of Interest', *The Review of Economics and Statistics*, 85, 4, 1063–70.

Leeper, E.M. (1991), 'Equilibria under 'Active' and 'Passive' Monetary and Fiscal Policies', *Journal of Monetary Economics*, 27, 1, 129–47.

Leiner-Killinger, N. and Nerlich, C. (2019), 'Fiscal Rules in the Euro Area and Lessons from Other Monetary Unions', Economic Bulletin Articles, Issue 3, ECB, Frankfurt am Main.

Lemke, W. and Vladu, A. (2017), 'Below the Zero Lower Bound: A Shadow-Rate Term Structure Model for the Euro Area', Working Paper Series, No 1991, ECB, Frankfurt am Main, January.

Lemke, W. and Werner, T. (2020), 'Dissecting Long-term Bund Yields in the Run-up to the ECB's Public Sector Purchase Programme', *Journal of Banking and Finance*, 111, 105682.

Li, C. and Wei, M. (2013), 'Term Structure Modeling with Supply Factors and the Federal Reserve's Large-Scale Asset Purchase Programs', *International Journal of Central Banking*, 9, 1, 3–39.

Litterman, R. (1979), 'Techniques of Forecasting Using Vector Autoregressions', Federal Reserve of Minneapolis Working Paper, No 115.

Lucas Jr, R.E. (1980), 'Two Illustrations of the Quantity Theory of Money', *American Economic Review*, 70, 5, 1005–14.

Lucas Jr, R.E. and Stokey, N.L. (1983), 'Optimal Fiscal and Monetary Policy in an Economy Without Capital', *Journal of Monetary Economics*, 12, 1, 55–93.

Lucas Jr, R.E. and Stokey, N.L. (1987), 'Money and Interest in a Cash-in-advance Economy', *Econometrica*, 55, 3, 491–517.

Mankiw, N.G., Reis, R., and Wolfers, J. (2003), 'Disagreement About Inflation Expectations', *NBER Macroeconomics Annual*, 18, 209–70.

Masuch, K., Nicoletti-Altimari, S., Rostagno, M., and Pill, H. (2003), 'The Role of Money in Monetary Policymaking', BIS Papers, No 19, pp. 158–91.

McCallum, B.T. (1995), 'Two Fallacies Concerning Central-Bank Independence', *The American Economic Review*, 85, 2, 207–11.

McCallum, B.T. (1997), 'Crucial Issues Concerning Central Bank Independence', *Journal of Monetary Economics*, 39, 1, 99–112.

McCallum, B.T. (2001), 'Should Monetary Policy Respond Strongly to Output Gaps?', *American Economic Review*, 91, 2, 258–62.

Mertens, T.M. and Williams, J.C. (2019), 'Tying Down the Anchor: Monetary Policy Rules and the Lower Bound on Interest Rates', Federal Reserve Bank of San Francisco Working Paper, No. 14.

Merkel, A. and Sarkozy, N. (2010), 'Statement for the France-Germany-Russia Summit', Franco-German Declaration, Deauville, 19 October.

Mésonnier, J.-S., O'Donnell, C., and Toutain, O. (2017), 'The Interest of Being Eligible', Banque de France Working Paper, No. 636, August.

Micossi, S. (2015), 'The Monetary Policy of the European Central Bank (2002–2015)', CEPS Special Report, No. 109.

Modigliani, F. and Miller, M.H. (1958), 'The Cost of Capital, Corporation Finance and the Theory of Investment', *American Economic Review*, 48, 3, 291–7.

Mody, A. (2018), *EuroTragedy: A Drama in Nine Acts*. Oxford: Oxford University Press.

Mooslechner, P. (2019), '20 years of EMU, 10 Years in Crisis Mode: What Might the Future 'New Normal' of Monetary Policy Look Like?', in European Economic and Monetary Union: The first and the next 20 years, proceedings of the 46th Economics Conference 2019 of the OeNB in cooperation with SUERF.

Mouabbi, S. and Sahuc, J.-G. (2019), 'Evaluating the Macroeconomic Effects of the ECB's Unconventional Monetary Policies', *Journal of Money, Credit and Banking*, 51, 4, 831–58.

Natoli, F. and Sigalotti, L. (2018), 'Tail Co-movement in Inflation Expectations as an Indicator of Anchoring', *International Journal of Central Banking*, 14, 1, 35–71.

Nelson, E. (2002), 'Direct Effects of Base Money on Aggregate Demand: Theory and Evidence', *Journal of Monetary Economics*, 49, 4, 687–708.

Neri, S. and Siviero, S. (2019), 'The Non-standard Monetary Policy Measures of the ECB: Motivations, Effectiveness and Risks', Banca d'Italia Occasional Papers (Questioni di economia e finanza), No. 486.

Neuenkirch, M. and Tillmann, P. (2014), 'Inflation Targeting, Credibility, and Non-Linear Taylor Rules', *Journal of International Money and Finance*, 41, 30–45.

Nicoletti-Altimari, S. (2001), 'Does Money Lead Inflation in the Euro Area?', Working Paper Series, No 63, ECB, Frankfurt am Main, May.

Nickell, S. and Quintini, G. (2003), 'Nominal Wage Rigidity and the Rate of Inflation', *The Economic Journal*, 113, 490, 762–81.

OECD (1999), 'EMU Facts, Challenges and Policies', OECD Publishing, March.

Padoa-Schioppa, T. (2004), *The Euro and Its Central Bank: Getting United After Union*. Cambridge, MA: MIT Press.

Paloviita, M., Haavio, M., Jalasjoki, P., and Kilponen, J. (2019), 'What Does "Below, But Close to, Two Percent" Mean? Assessing the ECB's Reaction Function with Real Time Data', Bank of Finland Research Discussion Paper, Vol. 29.

Papademos, L. and Stark, J. (eds.) (2010), *Enhancing Monetary Analysis*. Frankfurt am Main: ECB.

Papadia, F. and Välimäki, T. (2018), *Central Banking in Turbulent Times*. Oxford: Oxford University Press.

Pattipeilohy, C., Van Den End, J.W., Tabbae, M., Frost, J., and De Haan, J. (2013), 'Unconventional Monetary Policy of the ECB During The Financial Crisis: An Assessment and New Evidence', DNB Working Paper, No 381.

Persson, T. and Tabellini, G. (1993), 'Designing Institutions for Monetary Stability', *Carnegie-Rochester Conference Series on Public Policy*, 39, 53–84.

Pisani-Ferry, J. (2014), *The Euro Crisis and Its Aftermath*. Oxford: Oxford University Press.

Poole, W. (1994), 'Monetary Aggregates Targeting in a Low-inflation Economy', Conference Series [Proceedings], Vol. 38, Federal Reserve Bank of Boston, pp. 87–135.

Popov, A. and Van Horen, N. (2014), 'Exporting Sovereign Stress: Evidence from Syndicated Bank Lending During the Euro Area Sovereign Debt Crisis', *Review of Finance*, 19, 5, 1825–66.

Posen, A.S. (1993), 'Why Central Bank Independence Does Not Cause Low Inflation: There Is No Institutional Fix for Politics', *Finance and the International Economy*, 7, 40–65.

Posen, A.S. (1995), 'Declarations Are Not Enough: Financial Sector Sources of Central Bank Independence', *NBER Macroeconomics Annual*, 10, 253–74.

Podlich, N., Schnabel, I., and Tischer, J. (2017), 'Banks' Trading after the Lehman Crisis: The Role of Unconventional Monetary Policy', Deutsche Bundesbank Discussion Paper, No 19.

Praet, P. (2017a), 'Calibrating Unconventional Monetary Policy', speech at The ECB and Its Watchers XVIII Conference, 6 April.

Praet, P. (2017b), 'Unconventional Monetary Policy and Fixed Income Markets', remarks at the Fixed Income Market Colloquium, Rome, 4 July.

Praet, P. (2017c), 'Communicating the Complexity of Unconventional Monetary Policy in EMU', speech delivered at the ECB Central Bank Communications Conference 'Communications challenges for policy effectiveness, accountability and reputation', Frankfurt am Main, 15 November 2017.

Praet, P. (2018a), 'Maintaining Price Stability with Unconventional Monetary Policy', speech at the Council of the European Union, Brussels, 29 January.

Praet, P. (2018b), 'Assessment of Quantitative Easing and Challenges of Policy Normalisation', remarks at The ECB and Its Watchers XIX Conference, Frankfurt am Main, 14 March.

Praet, P. (2019), 'Providing Monetary Policy Stimulus after the Normalisation of Instruments', remarks at The ECB and Its Watchers XX Conference, Frankfurt am Main, 27 March.

Praet, P., Saint-Guilhem, A., and Vidal, J.-P. (2019), 'The Single Monetary Policy: 20 Years of Experience', in 20 Years of European Economic and Monetary Union, ECB, Frankfurt am Main.

Rodríguez Palenzuela, D., Camba-Mendez, G., and García, J.-A. (2003), 'Relevant Economic Issues Concerning the Optimal Rate of Inflation', in Issing, O. (ed.), Background Studies for the ECB's Evaluation of its Monetary Policy Strategy, ECB, Frankfurt am Main, pp. 91–125.

Rogoff, K. (1985), 'The Optimal Degree of Commitment to an Intermediate Monetary Target', *The Quarterly Journal of Economics*, 100, 4, 1169–89.

Rostagno, M., Altavilla, C., Carboni, G., Lemke, W., Motto, R., Saint Guilhem, et al. (2019), 'A Tale of Two Decades: The ECB's Monetary Policy at 20', Working Paper Series, No 2346, ECB, Frankfurt am Main, December.

Rotemberg, J.J. (1982), 'Monopolistic Price Adjustment and Aggregate Output', *The Review of Economic Studies*, 49, 4, 517–31.

Ruge-Murcia, F.-J. (2006), 'The Expectations Hypothesis of the Term Structure when Interest Rates Are Close to Zero', *Journal of Monetary Economics*, 53, 1409–24.

Sachverständigenrat zur Begutachtung der gesamtwirtschaftlichen Entwicklung (2002), 'Zwanzig Punkte für Beschäftigung und Wachstum', Jahresgutachten 2002/03, Metzler-Poeschel, Stuttgart.

Sandbu, M. (2015), *Europe's Orphan: The Future of the Euro and the Politics of Debt*. Princeton, NJ: Princeton University Press.

Sargent, T.J. and Wallace, N. (1981), 'Some Unpleasant Monetarist Arithmetic', *Federal Reserve Bank of Minneapolis Quarterly Review*, 5, 3, 1–17.

Sahuc, J.G. and Smets, F. (2008), 'Differences in Interest Rate Policy at the ECB and the Fed: An Investigation with a Medium-Scale DSGE Model', *Journal of Money, Credit and Banking*, 40(2–3), 505–21.

Scheller, H.K. (2006), *The European Central Bank: History, Role and Functions*, European Central Bank.

Schlepper, K., Ryordan, R., Hofer, H., and Schrimpf, A. (2017), 'Scarcity Effects of QE: A Transaction-level Analysis in the Bund market', Deutsche Bundesbank Discussion Paper, No 06.

Schmitt-Grohé, S. and Uribe, M. (2004a), 'Optimal Fiscal and Monetary Policy under Sticky Prices', *Journal of Economic Theory*, 114, 2, 198–230.

Schmitt-Grohé, S. and Uribe, M. (2004b), 'Optimal Fiscal and Monetary Policy under Imperfect Competition', *Journal of Macroeconomics*, 26, 2, 183–209.

Sims, C.A. (1988), 'Projecting Policy Effects with Statistical Models', *Revista de Analisis Economico*, 3, 3.

Sims, C.A. (1993), 'A Nine-Variable Probabilistic Macroeconomic Forecasting Model', in Stock, J.H. and Watson, M.W. (eds.), *Business Cycles, Indicators and Forecasting*, pp. 179–212.

Sims, C.A. (2016), 'Fiscal Policy, Monetary Policy and Central Bank Independence', paper presented at the Federal Reserve Bank of Kansas City Annual Conference, Jackson Hole, Wyoming, 23 August.

Sims, E.R. and Wu, J.C. (2020), 'Evaluating Central Banks' Tool Kit: Past, Present, and Future', *Journal of Monetary Economics*, in press.

Smets, F. and Wouters, R. (2003), 'An Estimated Dynamic Stochastic General Equilibrium Model of the Euro Area', *Journal of the European Economic Association*, 1, 5, 1123–75.

Smets, F. and Wouters, R. (2007), 'Shocks and Frictions in US Business Cycles: A Bayesian DSGE Approach', *American Economic Review*, 97, 3, 586–606.

Smets, F., Christoffel, K., Coenen, G., Motto, R., and Rostagno, M. (2010), 'DSGE Models and their Use at the ECB', *Journal of the Spanish Economic Association*, 1, 51–65.

Söderström, U. (2002), 'Monetary Policy with Uncertain Parameters', *Scandinavian Journal of Economics*, 104, 125–45.

Stark, J. (2010), 'The New Normal', intervention at the 13th Euro Finance Week, Frankfurt, 16 November.

Stiglitz, J. (2016), *The Euro: How a Common Currency Threatens the Future of Europe*. New York: W.W. Norton & Co.

Stock, J.H. and Watson, M.W. (1999), 'Forecasting Inflation', *Journal of Monetary Economics*, 44, 2, 293–335.

Stock, J.H. and Watson, M.W. (2002), 'Macroeconomic Forecasting Using Diffusion Indexes', *Journal of Business and Economic Statistics*, 20, 2, 147–62.

Svensson, L.E.O. (1997), 'Inflation Forecast Targeting: Implementing and Monitoring Inflation Targets', *European Economic Review*, 41, 6, 1111–46.

Svensson, L.E.O. (1999), 'Monetary Policy Issues for the Eurosystem', *Carnegie-Rochester Conferences Series on Public Policy*, 51, 1, 79–136.

Svensson, L.E.O. (2000), 'Monetary Policy and the Current Economic and Monetary Situation', briefing paper for the Committee on Economic and Monetary Affairs (ECON) of the European Parliament for the quarterly dialogue with the President of the European Central Bank.

Svensson, L.E.O. (2001a), comment on Wyplosz, C. (2001), 'Do We Know How Low Inflation Should Be?', in: García-Herrero, A., Gaspar, V., Hoogduin, L., Morgan, J. and Winkler, B. (eds.) (2001), 'First ECB Central Banking Conference: Why Price Stability?'. Frankfurt am Main: European Central Bank.

Svensson, L.E.O. (2001b), 'The Fed Does Not Provide the Solution to the Eurosystem's Problems', briefing paper for the Committee on Economic and Monetary Affairs (ECON) of the European Parliament for the quarterly dialogue with the President of the European Central Bank.

Svensson, L.E.O. (2002), 'A Reform of the Eurosystem's Monetary-policy Strategy is Increasingly Urgent', briefing paper for the Committee on Economic and Monetary Affairs (ECON) of the European Parliament for the quarterly dialogue with the President of the European Central Bank.

Svensson, L.E.O. (2020), 'Monetary Policy Strategies for the Federal Reserve', NBER Working Paper, No w26657.

Swanson, E.T. (2020), 'Measuring the Effects of Federal Reserve Forward Guidance and Asset Purchases on Financial Markets', *Journal of Monetary Economics*, in press.

Szczerbowicz, U. (2015), 'The ECB Unconventional Monetary Policies: Have They Lowered Market Borrowing Costs for Banks and Governments?', *International Journal of Central Banking*, 11, 4, 91–127.

Taylor, J.B. (1993), 'Discretion versus Policy Rules in Practice', *Carnegie-Rochester Conference Series on Public Policy*, 39, 195–214.

Taylor, J.B. (1994), 'The Inflation/Output Trade-Off Revisited', Goals, Guidelines and Constraints Facing Monetary Policymakers, Federal Reserve Bank of Boston, pp. 21–38.

Taylor, J.B. (1999), 'A historical analysis of monetary policy rules', *Monetary Policy Rules*, pp. 319–48. Chicago, IL: University of Chicago Press.

The European Council (2010), 'Statement by the Heads of State and Government of the Euro Area', Statement, 25 March.

Thomson, C. (2014), 'Weak ECB Loans Take-Up Paves the Way for QE', *Financial Times*, 19 September.

Trebesch, C. and Zettelmeyer, J. (2018), 'ECB Interventions in Distressed Sovereign Debt Markets: The Case of Greek Bonds', *IMF Economic Review*, 66, 2, 287–332.

Trichet, J.-C. (2003a), 'Some Reflections on the Development of Credit Derivatives', keynote address at the 22nd Annual General Meeting of the International Swaps and Derivatives Association (ISDA).

Trichet, J.-C. (2003b), 'The ECB's Monetary Policy Strategy after the Evaluation and Clarification of May 2003', speech at the Frankfurter Finanzgespräch organised by the Konrad Adenauer Stiftung.

Trichet, J.-C. (2007), 'Introductory statement with Q&A', transcript, ECB, Frankfurt am Main, 6 September.

Trichet, J.-C. (2008a), 'Risk and the Macro-economy', keynote address at the conference 'The ECB and its Watchers X', Frankfurt am Main, 5 September.

Trichet, J.-C. (2008b), 'Introductory statement with Q&A', transcript, ECB, Frankfurt am Main, 5 June.

Trichet, J.-C. (2008c), 'Introductory statement with Q&A', transcript, ECB, Frankfurt am Main, 3 July.

Trichet, J.-C. (2009a), 'Ten years of the Euro: Successes and Challenges', speech in Osnabrück, 12 February.

Trichet, J.-C. (2009b), 'Introductory statement with Q&A', transcript, ECB, Frankfurt am Main, 7 May.

Trichet, J.-C. (2009c), 'Macro-prudential Supervision in Europe', speech at the Economist's 2nd City Lecture, London, 11 December.

Trichet, J.-C. (2010a), 'Introductory statement with Q&A', transcript, ECB, Frankfurt am Main, 14 January.

Trichet, J.-C. (2010b), 'Introductory statement with Q&A', transcript, ECB, Frankfurt am Main, 4 March.

Trichet, J.-C. (2010c), 'Introductory statement with Q&A' transcript, ECB, Frankfurt am Main, 8 April.

Trichet, J.-C. (2010d), 'Introductory statement with Q&A', transcript, ECB, Frankfurt am Main, 10 June.

Trichet, J.-C. (2011a), 'Introductory statement with Q&A', transcript, ECB, Frankfurt am Main, 7 April.

Trichet, J.-C. (2011b), 'Introductory statement with Q&A', transcript, ECB, Frankfurt am Main, 7 July.

Trichet, J.-C. (2011c), 'Statement by the President of the ECB', press release, ECB, Frankfurt am Main, 7 August.

Tucker, P. (2018), *Unelected Power: The Quest for Legitimacy in Central Banking and the Regulatory State*. Princeton, NJ: Princeton University Press.

Vasicek, O. (1977), 'An Equilibrium Characterization of the Term Structure', *Journal of Financial Economics*, 5, 2, 177–88.

Vayanos, D. and Vila, J.L. (2021), 'A Preferred-habitat Model of the Term Structure of Interest Rates', *Econometrica*, 89, 1, 77–112.

Véron, N. (2015), 'Europe's Radical Banking Union', Bruegel Essay and Lecture Series, 5.

Vickers, J. (1998), 'Inflation Targeting in Practice: The UK Experience', *Bank of England Quarterly Bulletin*, 38, 4, 368–75.

Visco, I. (2014), 'The Challenges for Central Banks', Central Banking, August.

Visco, I. (2018), 'Banks and Finance after the Crisis: Lessons and Challenges', *PSL Quarterly Review*, 71, 286, 255–77.

Walsh, C.E. (1995), 'Optimal Contracts for Central Bankers', *American Economic Review*, 85, 1, 150–67.

Walsh, C.E. (2017), *Monetary Theory and Policy*, Fourth Edition. Cambridge, MA: MIT Press.

Watson, M.W. (2003), 'Macroeconomic Forecasting Using Many Predictors', *Econometric Society Monographs*, 37, 87–114.

Williams, J. C. (2014), 'Monetary Policy at the Zero Lower Bound: putting Theory into Practice', Hutchins Center on Fiscal and Monetary Policy Working Papers, January.

Wilson, J.Q. (1989), *Bureaucracy: What Government Agencies Do and Why They Do It*. New York: Basic Books.

Woodford, M. (1996), 'Control of the Public Debt: A Requirement for Price Stability?', NBER Working Paper, No. 5684, July.

Woodford, M. (2003), *Interest and Prices: Foundations of a Theory of Monetary Policy*. Princeton, NJ: Princeton University Press.

Wu, C. and Xia, D. (2020), 'Negative Interest Rate Policy and the Yield Curve', *Journal of Applied Econometrics*, 35, 6, 653–672.

Wynne, M.A. (2005), 'An Estimate of the Measurement Bias in the HICP', Working Paper, No 509, Federal Reserve Bank of Dallas.

Wynne, M.A. and Rodríguez-Palenzuela, D. (2004), 'Measurement Bias in the HICP: What Do We Know and What Do We Need to Know?', *Journal of Economic Surveys*, 18, 1, 79–112.

Wyplosz, C. (2001a), 'The ECB Communication Strategy', briefing paper for the Committee on Economic and Monetary Affairs (ECON) of the European Parliament for the quarterly dialogue with the President of the European Central Bank.

Wyplosz, C. (2001b), 'Do We Know How Low Inflation Should Be?', in García-Herrero, A., Gaspar, V., Hoogduin, L., Morgan, J. and Winkler, B. (eds.) (2001), *First ECB Central Banking Conference: Why Price Stability?* Frankfurt am Main: ECB.

Yates, T. (1998), 'Downward Nominal Rigidity and Monetary Policy', Bank of England Working Paper, No. 82.

Yun, T. (1996), 'Nominal Price Rigidity, Money Supply Endogeneity, and Business Cycles', *Journal of Monetary Economics*, 37, 2, 345–70.

Index